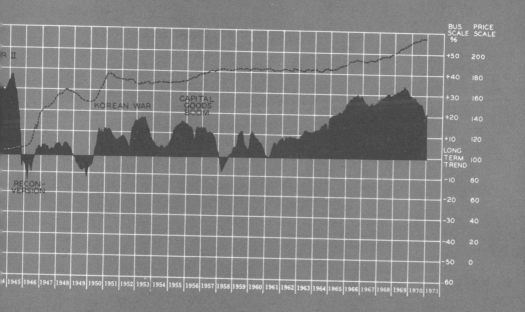

This chart from 1914 through 1970 shows fluctuations above and below the long-term trend for wholesale commodity prices and industrial production. The dashed line represents the changes in wholesale commodity prices with 1926 having been selected as the base year of 100. The solid portion of the chart indicates the index of industrial production with percentage changes from the trend reduced to a per capita basis.

Source: The Cleveland Trust Company, Cleveland, Ohio.

An introduction to the
American business enterprise

revised edition

An introduction to the American business enterprise

JERRY B. POE

Director, Breech School of Business Administration
Professor of Business Administration and Economics
Drury College

 1972

Richard D. Irwin, Inc. *Homewood, Illinois 60430*
IRWIN-DORSEY LIMITED *Georgetown, Ontario*

LEARNING SYSTEMS COMPANY—
a division of Richard D. Irwin, Inc.—has developed a
PROGRAMMED LEARNING AID
to accompany texts in this subject area.
Copies can be purchased through your bookstore
or by writing PLAIDS,
1818 Ridge Road, Homewood, Illinois   60430.

Revised Edition

The previous edition was published as
The American Business Enterprise.

First Printing, January, 1972
Second Printing, August, 1972

Library of Congress Catalog Card No. 79–180499
Printed in the United States of America

Preface

This revised edition of *The American Business Enterprise* provides students in a first course in business with a text which emphasizes the vital role of business in our society through a discussion of both the external environment of business and the internal management of the business enterprise.

There is an increased emphasis in this edition on marketing, with a close examination of the role of the consumer. A new chapter has been added on the problems and challenges faced by business in the fight against environmental pollution. Also, there is a new chapter which explores the problems faced by America's minorities in participating more fully in the private enterprise system either as employees or as owners. The chapter on business-government relationships has been expanded to reflect the extensive role of government in the American business system. The management chapter has been revised to include an introduction to the systems approach to business. Throughout the book, concepts have been clarified and updated, and the most recent statistics available from authoritative sources have been used.

This edition is designed to provide students with a balanced approach to business through expanded text coverage and end-of-chapter materials which meet a variety of needs. The book is organized so that Section One covers much of the external environment of business by setting the economic, political, and governmental framework within which business functions. Section Two discusses the internal management and control of the business enterprise after a chapter on the important role of profits in the American business system. Section Three covers the vital human elements of business including human relations, personnel management, and labor relations. Section Four discusses the key areas of marketing and production of goods and services. Section Five consists of chapters on accounting and finance and also provides background information on the functioning of the variety of financial institutions which affect both business and consumers. Section Six concludes the book with the dynamic areas of computers, international business, and the importance of business in its relation to the total society with a discussion of the challenges of the future. Throughout the book, an integrated approach to the total functioning of the business enterprise is emphasized with references to interrelationships among the different functional areas of business and with the various elements in its external environment.

Each chapter opens with an introductory statement of the general nature of the material covered along with questions to guide the student's reading. A system of major and minor subheadings provides a means of outlining each chapter. A brief end-of-chapter summary brings together the major topics raised.

A variety of learning devices are provided at the end of each chapter and at the end of the book. The end-of-chapter terms for review provide the student with a check on some of the key concepts and terminology. Because of the importance in any introductory course of the acquisition and understanding of vocabulary, an extensive glossary containing over 550 words and terms used in the book is included. Although new words and terms usually are defined when they are first used in the text, the glossary can be used to refresh the student's memory when a term is repeated later or when it is not defined in the body of a chapter. All end-of-chapter terms for review are contained in the glossary. The student is encouraged to make use of the glossary in deepening his understanding of the language of business.

The end-of-chapter questions can be used either for self-study and review or prepared for class discussion. Some questions draw on an understanding of specific concepts discussed in the chapter, while others require outside research or original thinking on the part of the student based on his newly acquired background information from the chapter.

The business briefs at the end of each chapter are all new in this edition. They provide a basis for understanding the dynamic nature of today's business world. Each business brief has been taken from public news reports of current interest. However, the basic issues in the business briefs reflect future problem areas for business as well as matters of topical interest.

The cases in this revised edition have been selected to provide discussion material which will help students develop their capabilities of problem identification, analysis of alternatives, and recommendations for management action. The cases also provide the student with specific applications of his understanding of the concepts raised in the chapters. Questions are provided at the end of each business brief and case to assist the student in his analysis. A short appendix discussing the analysis of cases is provided at the end of the book.

In this edition the increased amount of text material and the variety of end-of-chapter learning devices provide the student and the instructor with a maximum of flexibility in the application of this book to the specific course situation. An effective course can be developed to meet the needs and interests of the students through a selective approach to the end-of-chapter materials.

Acknowledgments to a number of groups and individuals are appropriate for this revised edition. Students and faculty at the Breech School of Business Administration, Drury College, and at Florida Technological University were helpful in their reactions to the new material which went into this edition. Their positive responses encouraged me to make these additions and to revise some of the material from the first edition.

At the Breech School, Dr. Wilber C. Bothwell permitted me to use certain of his labor arbitration files for case materials and to draw on his writing on the motivations of workers in joining labor unions. Dr. Albert A. Evans was a helpful reviewer of the manuscript as well as a collaborator with Professor James A. Carson of City College of San Francisco on the Work Book and Study Guide to accompany this text. Mr. Thomas R. Lloyd, formerly of the Breech School faculty, provided three cases which were used in the areas of business and society, and marketing.

My sincere thanks go to the numerous faculty members across the country who made helpful suggestions after having used the first edition of this book. Their constructive criticisms and encouragement have been most useful. Reviews of the entire revised manuscript were made by Professors Richard Brunell, Santa Ana College; Norm Woodin, Kalamazoo Valley Community College; Edward Burda, Cabrillo College; and Dr. McKee Fisk.

I also appreciate the cooperation of those businessmen who provided case materials and examples for this edition.

Although every attempt has been made to avoid errors, any which remain are the responsibility of the author.

As in the first edition, I would like to give special recognition and thanks to my wife, Carol, for her assistance and support. It is to our daughters, Cheryl and Jenny B., that this revised edition is dedicated.

December, 1971   JERRY B. POE

Contents

section two   Management of the business enterprise

section three   *Human elements of administration*

Seniority and ability. Employee transfer. Down-grading and layoffs. Discipline of employees. Relationship between personnel management and labor relations. The personnel department: *Personnel manager. Employee services. Housekeeping duties. Advisory role.* Summary.

Business brief
Turnover of college graduates, 246
Cases
Artwein Manufacturing Company, 247
A case of fighting, 250

Legislation affecting labor relations: *The Wagner Act. The Taft-Hartley Act. The Landrum-Griffin Act.* Growth in union membership. Why workers join unions: *Economic motives for union membership. Noneconomic motives for union membership. Union membership required for employment.* The structure and organization of the labor union: *Craft and industrial unions. Local unions. Regional and national union organization.* The union contract: *The bargaining unit. Union security. Grievance procedure and arbitration. Wages and hours. Pay or work guarantees. Holidays and vacations. Employee benefits. Discipline and discharge. Management and union rights. Seniority provisons. Strikes and lockouts. Working conditions and safety.* The grievance process and arbitration: *The grievance process. Arbitration, conciliation, and mediation.* Summary.

Business briefs
The four-day week, 281
Welfare benefits for strikers, 281
Cases
Forty minutes of overtime, 282
Grievance over disciplinary action, 284

Who are the minorities? *Definition of minority groups. The nature of discrimination.* The economic status of Negroes: *Black employment. Black unemployment.* Educational levels of minority races. Government actions in minority employment: *Legislation. Executive orders. The courts. Human resource development programs.* Spanish-speaking Americans: *Mexican Americans. Puerto Ricans. Cuban Americans. Other Spanish-speaking Americans. Government programs to aid Spanish-speaking Americans.* American Indians: *Government actions to aid the American Indians.* Developing minority enterprises: *Ghettos in the past and today. Obstacles to minority enterprise. Steps in expansion of minority-owned enterprises. Government programs to aid minority businessmen. Private actions to aid minority businessmen. MESBICs.* Jobs and ownership. Summary.

Business briefs
Cheetah Charter Bus Service Co., 316

section four   *The provision of goods and services*

11   **The marketing concept and the consumer** **321**
The importance of marketing. The marketing concept of business.
Translating consumer needs to wants. The consumer: *Ultimate consumers. Individual consumer behavior.* The consumer of the 1970s:
*Higher consumer income. Factors contributing to higher family
income. More discretionary income. Demographic changes.* Consumerism and consumer protection legislation: *Consumerism. Criticism of
FTC. Other consumer groups.* Consumer protection legislation and
administrative actions: *Recent legislation. Administrative actions to
aid consumers.* Summary.

Business briefs
Pricing airline fares, 340
Truth in auto advertising, 341
Advertising Profile bread, 342
CORFAM®—A substitute for leather? 342

12   **The marketing mix** **345**
The marketing mix. Product: *Product defined. Importance of new
products. Developing the product. Classification of consumer products.*
Promotion: *Personal selling. Advertising. Cost of advertising. Spending
on advertising. Advertising media. Sales promotion. Total promotion
mix.* Pricing: *Practical pricing considerations. Consumer demand.
Importance of nonprice competition. Costs. Stage of the product life
cycle. Government controls.* Place: *Channels of distribution. Institutions of distribution—wholesalers. Institutions of distribution—retailers. Functions performed in channels. Physical distribution.* Organization of the marketing department. Summary.

Business briefs
"Avon calling," 375
Baskin-Robbins ice cream, 376
Cases
The Sure-Cover Company, 377
Mansfield National Bank, 380

13   **Production** **387**
The location of production facilities: *The importance of factory
location.* The production system: *Research and product design. Process
design.* Production control and scheduling: *Orders and authorization
of production. Production scheduling.* Purchasing industrial goods:
Steps in the purchasing process. Price and quality considerations.
Selecting sources of supply. Make or buy decision. Inventory control.

Purchase of major equipment. Other elements of the production system: *Motion and time analysis. Quality control. Maintenance.* Automation. Organization of the production department: *Manufacuring management. The factory foreman.* Summary.

section five   *Accounting and finance*

The use of accounting data: *Management uses of accounting. Outsiders' use of accounting information.* The basic accounting statements: *The balance sheet. The income statement.* The financial analysis of accounting statements: *Measures of liquidity. Measures of profitability. Measures of solvency.* The basis of accounting data. Summary.

Our system of financial institutions. Role of the U.S. Treasury. The Federal Reserve System. Types of financial markets: *Markets: Users of funds. Markets: Length of debt maturities. Markets: Primary or secondary.* Specific financial institutions: *Commercial banks. Life insurance companies. Savings and loan associations. Mutual savings banks.* Other financial institutions: *Finance companies. Credit unions. Personal trust departments. Pension funds. Fire and casualty insurance companies. Investment companies.* Functions of the investment banker: *Underwriting. Private placements. Best-efforts offering. Brokerage function.* The stock market: *Organization of stock markets. Buying and selling stock through an organized exchange. Over-the-counter markets.* Investing in securities: *Investment objectives. Selection of common stocks.* Summary.

section six   *Business in a changing world*

Business briefs
Campbell Soup Company, 594
Social benefits—social costs, 595
Cases
The image scrimmage, 596
Personal decisions in business, 599

The external environment of business

Courtesy Evergreen Plaza Merchants Council

*Enclosed shopping malls
are being designed
to provide greater
comfort and convenience
for consumers.*

I

The economic, political, and social basis of business

American business in the 1970s is in a position to be where the action is. Many of the challenges facing society today have roots in the economic questions of what goods will be produced and how these goods will be distributed. The political and social issues both within the United States and in international relations have elements relating to business and economic activity.

Business is one of the most important and dynamic institutions in American society. The functioning of business enterprises significantly influences the life of every American. The majority of Americans spend their adult lives as part of the business system producing goods and services. All of us are consumers of the products of business enterprises.

This chapter analyzes the economic, political, and social environment of business. The following issues are discussed.

What is the nature of economic activity?

How are societies organized to answer the three basic economic questions?

What are the major characteristics of the private enterprise system?

How does the systems concept apply to business?

The nature of economic activity

Economics defined

The word "economics" has its derivation in Latin and Greek. The Greek word, *oikonomia,* represented a combination of *oikos,* house, and

3

nomos, a derivation of "to manage." Hence, economics referred to the management of a family household and was gradually extended to include not only management of households but the management of businesses, communities, and governments. Therefore, economics could be defined as the study of how man manages the human and material resources which are available in society. There are several elements in the management of the business enterprise which are discussed in later chapters. However, the distinguishing feature of management is that it involves decision making. Managers are required to make intelligent choices from among alternative courses of action to further the effective operation of the business enterprise.

The economic problem of scarcity

Economics may also be defined as the study of how scarce resources are allocated in a society of unlimited wants. Every society has an economic system which provides food, clothing, shelter, and other material goods and services for man's basic and acquired needs. Because these goods and services are available in limited quantities, with many people wanting them, they have value. Scarcity is a basic fact which underlies all economic activity. If there were a complete abundance of goods and services then man would not have to concern himself with the issue of allocating scarce resources.

It is easy to recognize the limitations which are imposed upon man by nature and economic circumstances. There is just so much land to be tilled. Timber and mineral resources are definitely limited. We have only a given number of factories equipped with a limited amount of machinery at any one time. There are only so many workers to produce the goods and services which we consume. Our knowledge about how to produce more goods, although constantly expanding, is finite. In short, we live in a world where material goods are limited.

Although the resources of our world are limited, the wants of people are not. Indeed, one of the important assumptions of economics is that total human wants are insatiable. No matter how much we have, we seem to want more. As people's incomes increase so does their desire for more and better goods and services. How many times have you said, "If I could just have this particular item I would be completely satisfied." But when you obtained the good, perhaps an automobile, did it satisfy your material wants? It did not, if you are a typical person. When some material wants are satisfied others take their place. This means that the economic system can never produce enough to satisfy everyone completely. Thus arises the need for a system of efficient allocation of the scarce goods of society among peoples who have unlimited wants.

The economic resources

Scarce economic resources consist of all the natural, man-made, and human factors that go into the production of goods and services. These resources can be classified broadly as property resources and human resources.

Property resources consist of land and capital. *Land* refers to all natural resources which are used in the production process including timber, oil and mineral deposits, and water, as well as land itself. *Capital* refers to all machinery, tools, equipment, and buildings required to produce goods and distribute them to consumers. The use of capital goods enables workers to produce more with the same amount of physical effort. Consider the relative productivity of a service station attendant hand-polishing automobile finishes all day compared with another worker doing the same job with an electric buffing machine. The addition of a piece of capital equipment greatly improves the worker's productivity.

Human resources consist of labor and entrepreneurial ability. *Labor* refers to all physical and mental talents that individuals expend in producing goods and services with the exception of entrepreneurial talent, which is classified separately. Labor includes the manual labor of the trash hauler and the knowledge and skill of the brain surgeon. *Entrepreneur* was originally a French word which means enterpriser. The entrepreneur provides the managerial ability to bring together land, capital, and labor to produce goods and services. The entrepreneur in his managerial capacity assumes the risks associated with the organization and operation of a business enterprise and in turn hopes to make a profit from his activities. In traditional economic theory the return which accrues to land is called rent; the return to capital resources is interest income; and labor is paid wages. The entrepreneur gets his return from the profits of his business operations, although at times profits may be replaced by losses if the enterprise is not well managed.

Another important economic resource which might be classified as a human resource is technology. *Technology* refers to the accumulated fund of knowledge which is helpful in efficient organization for the production of goods and services. Economic efficiency depends in large measure on the technical state of knowledge of production and distribution processes. A given state of technology in a particular area of economic activity represents the heritage of man's practical application of science, which has been accumulated from previous generations to the present.

The U.S. Department of Commerce in analyzing the different economic indicators does so through a system of national income accounting. *National income* is defined as the aggregate earnings of labor and property which arise in the current production of goods and services by the nation's economy. National income is the sum of compensation

TABLE 1–1

Components of national income, 1966 and 1970

	Billions of dollars		Percent change
	1966	*1970*	
National income	621	800	+29
Compensation of employees	436	600	+38
Proprietors' income	61	67	+10
Rental income	20	23	+15
Corporate profits	83	77	− 7
Net interest	21	33	+57

Source: Council of Economic Advisers, *Economic Indicators*, April, 1971.

of employees, proprietors' income, rental income, net interest, and corporate profits. The components of national income for 1966 and 1970 are shown in Table 1–1, along with the percentages of change over this period.

Utilities possessed by goods

From the point of view of consumers, the end result of business activity is the goods that they consume. *Goods* are things that are useful in satisfying a human want. Goods may be either tangible, such as automobiles and stereo sets; or they may be intangible, such as legal advice or school teaching. Intangible goods are usually called *services*. Goods also may be classified as consumer or producer goods. *Consumer goods* satisfy individual needs directly and include nondurable items such as food and clothing and durable items such as automobiles, furniture, and appliances. *Producer goods* are the tools, machines, and equipment used to make consumer goods, and thus they satisfy individual needs indirectly.

Utility is the power to satisfy human wants. For something to be a tangible good it must have four different types of utility:

1. *Form utility.* Goods must possess the proper physical characteristics. A motorist does not want steel, rubber, glass, and paint; he wants an automobile.
2. *Place utility.* Goods must be where the consumer has access to them. The new automobile in Detroit is of no use to the prospective purchaser until it has been transported to his local dealer.
3. *Time utility.* Goods must be available when they are wanted. When a person purchases a new car he wants delivery as soon as possible.
4. *Possession utility.* Goods must be owned or controlled by the people who consume them. Through credit arrangements consumers are able to obtain possession of automobiles and other goods even though they do not have sufficient money to pay for them immediately.

Types of economic systems

Whenever a society faces choices between alternative uses of scarce resources an economic system must be organized. All economic systems must provide means of answering three basic questions:

1. What goods will be produced from the scarce resources that are available?
2. How will these goods be produced?
3. How will these goods be distributed; that is, who will consume the goods?

How these questions are answered depends upon the nature of the economic system prevailing in the society being studied. There are two theoretical ways by which economic systems in industrialized countries may be organized—capitalism and socialism. Under *capitalism* the means of production and distribution of goods are privately owned and controlled. Under the economic system of *socialism* the means of production and distribution are owned and controlled by the government.

In practice the economic systems functioning in the world today have elements of both private and governmental ownership and control. However, there is a significant degree of difference among the economic systems of major industrial nations ranging from the United States at one end of the spectrum to the Soviet Union at the other end. In between are the mixed economies of countries such as Great Britain.

In describing the economic systems existing today it is also important to consider the political environment within which the economic activity takes place. Political systems may be organized on a democratic or totalitarian basis. Essential to the functioning of a *democracy* is the choice of governmental leaders by the people through free elections with freedom of speech, the press, and assembly. A *totalitarian* governmental system is one in which one party or group has absolute control. The people are not free to change their leadership through elections since candidates for office are chosen by the one party that is in power. Freedom of speech, the press, and assembly are restricted.

The following examples illustrate some of the basic differences in the organization of existing political-economic systems.

Great Britain

In Great Britain the political-economic system might be characterized as democratic socialism. Although there is still a considerable amount of private business ownership, basic industries, including gas, electric power, communications, transportation, steel, mining, and central banking, are owned and operated by the government. There is some degree of central planning. In the nationalized industries private profit is not a goal or a measure of the efficiency to which the economy's needs are met.

In a democratic-socialist country the people have free elections to choose political leaders who will legislate and govern their country. Strong opposition parties which compete for the votes and confidence of the electorate exist.

The Soviet Union

In the Union of Soviet Socialist Republics the political-economic system might be characterized as totalitarian socialism. The means of production and distribution are owned and controlled by the state. The concept of private profit is lacking in economic planning and motivation. There is a high degree of central planning for the economy. Generally the economic objectives which are set by state planning agencies emphasize heavy industry and the production of industrial and military goods rather than consumer goods.

For practical purposes a dictatorship exists. There is no freedom to organize opposing political parties. Dissent from the established order is discouraged both in politics and economics.

Capitalism and the private enterprise system

In the United States the political-economic system might be characterized as democratic capitalism. In general the means of production and distribution are owned and controlled privately. Private profit represents an incentive to businessmen to enter the marketplace with goods and services which are desired by individual, industrial, and governmental customers.

In this political system individuals are free to organize political parties to advance constitutional change. Differences of viewpoint often are very much in the open. As the result of the political process the government responds to the views of the majority since elected officials tend to reflect the public's thinking.

The form that capitalism has taken in the United States is sometimes called the *private enterprise system*. There are four important characteristics of American capitalism:

1. Private property.
2. The profit motive.
3. The market system and competition.
4. The nature of the relationship between business and government.

Private property

Private property is a fundamental element in a capitalistic society because without it there could be no private ownership and use of capital. The essence of private property is the right of individuals to own things of value and control their use. Of particular importance is the freedom of individuals to acquire, utilize, and dispose of the factors of production. An extension of this right is the legal contract which specifies the conditions under which anything that is owned may be used by others.

Private property serves two important functions in capitalism. First, it places in the hands of individuals power over the utilization of productive resources. Economic activity cannot occur unless someone makes decisions about which goods are to be produced and when and how they are to be produced. The more complex the method of production the more crucial is the decision-making process. The owners of resources may delegate part of their powers to others, but for there to be capitalism the ultimate determination of resource use must reside with them. Second, private property serves as an incentive for the accumulation of wealth. This incentive is indispensable if the stock of capital in the economy is to grow. The right of property owners to benefit from the use of their property in the productive process stimulates them to save and invest in capital goods.

In the United States the capital owned by individuals is used by them to make a profit through investing in the production process. In the Soviet Union individuals are permitted to own property for their own use but with few exceptions are not permitted to own property for the production or distribution of goods and services. One exception in the U.S.S.R. is the small truck farming plots where the individual family has about one-half acre of its own to cultivate, with the produce being sold in markets operated by the collective farm.

The profit motive

The profit motive is a basic characteristic of capitalism. *Profit* is defined as the money difference between what it costs to produce and sell a product and the revenue from its sale. The term *profit motive* refers to the desire to engage in economic activity in order to earn profit.

In every economic system someone must decide how to combine the scarce resources of capital and labor to produce goods. In the American economy private enterprise management determines the most efficient balance between the factors of production, depending on their availability, quality, and price. The profit motive acts as the central controlling mechanism. The businessman is motivated by profits to expand the output of goods for which consumer demand is great and to cut back the production of less sought-after goods. Without the lure of profit the owners of business enterprises would not be willing to bear the risks inherent in the production process. To the extent that businessmen activate the entire economic system and that their decisions are based on profit calculations, the profit motive is the key institution of the capitalistic economy.

In the U.S.S.R., except for the concept of planned profit used by government officials in setting industry goals, profit does not play an important role in the production process. Government planners can choose to subsidize industries in which the sales of goods do not cover the cost of labor and materials if it is to the state's advantage to do so. For example, in international trade it may be politically desirable to sell goods below cost. In a totalitarian planned economy the whole concept of "costs" is different from that in a free market economy. In the planned economy the various kinds of costs are arbitrarily allocated by government to meet its objectives, rather than allowing the costs of labor and materials to be determined in the marketplace.

The market system and competition

In the private enterprise system the economy is organized as a system of markets in which buyers and sellers come together and exchange money for goods and services. The market price which results from these exchanges reflects the behavior of the buyers and sellers. The market functions to match the supply and demand for each type of product. Consumers strongly influence what will be produced by exerting economic power in purchasing a product or passing it over for a competing product. Producers attempt to influence consumers through the introduction of new products, through improving existing products, and through various types of promotional activities aimed at selling consumers on their particular products.

The essential characteristic of the marketplace in the American economy is that it is not formally regulated as to type, quantity, and price of goods that are produced and sold. It is the rivalry of buyer against buyer and seller against seller—called by the 18th century Scottish economist Adam Smith "the invisible hand of competition"—that is responsible for the orderly operation of markets. There are many ways to determine prices, but free and open market pricing is the one most consistent with the private enterprise system. It is the market which is responsible for the creation and preservation of fair prices and economic efficiency. The degree to which the market system is permitted to function without excessive controls is a measure of the extent of democratic capitalism in the economy.

In socialistic economies there is an absence of competition and the free marketplace. In totalitarian socialism what will be produced and in what quantity is based on production quotas set by government planning bureaus. Prices are set to control consumption of different types of products based on "costs" that have been set by government.

The relationship between business and government

Capitalism, particularly democratic capitalism, has always stressed the importance of individual freedom in economic affairs. In the 18th and 19th centuries the economic doctrine of laissez faire was associated with capitalism. Laissez faire is a French term meaning "leave us alone." This was the cry of businessmen in those days against the regulation by the state of their private economic activities. In its most extreme form laissez faire capitalism limited the government's participation in economic activity merely to the provision of such vital public services as police and fire protection.

Today it is generally accepted that the role of government in our complex industrial society is different than it was in the days of the laissez faire capitalists. As a result of the prolonged depression of the 1930s, the American people placed responsibility in the hands of government to manage its fiscal and monetary affairs (i.e., government taxation and spending and control over the money supply) in such a way as to encourage the full employment of labor and other resources in the economy. A number of governmental agencies, such as the Federal Trade Commission, the Securities and Exchange Commission, and the Food and Drug Administration, show that society has recognized the need to be protected from harmful or deceptive business practices.

Despite the increased role which government has assumed in economic affairs in the United States over the past 40 years, our economic system remains predominantly capitalistic. We still depend upon individual consumers and business enterprises to make the vast proportion of economic decisions. Nearly 80 percent of all the goods and services produced in the economy are purchased by individuals and private business enterprises with the remainder being purchased by various levels of government.

Advantages of the private enterprise system for Americans

Based on the values of most Americans, the private enterprise system has a number of advantages for the individual. Our economic system has developed in a pragmatic fashion unlike the more doctrinaire economic systems in some European countries. Americans have been willing to experiment to solve economic problems, and the result has been an economic system which, although predominantly capitalistic, has a positive role for government. Because of this willingness to use various means to achieve economic ends, our system is called a "mixed economic system" with emphasis upon private ownership and the profit motive but with government also having a role in many aspects of the economy.

Freedom of choice by consumers

One of the strengths of our form of democratic capitalism is the fact that consumers have considerable freedom of choice in determining what goods and services they will buy and have a great abundance of products to choose from. The freedom in the American economic system tends to encourage innovation and change, both for new products and improved methods of producing and distributing them. Generally goods are distributed among consumers on the basis of their ability and willingness to pay the going market price. Since we cannot consume all the goods and services we want, the existing stock of goods is allocated on the basis of the purchasing power of the many consumers.

In totalitarian economies one of the major criticisms by the people is the lack of quantity and quality of consumer goods since government planners have emphasized production of industrial and military goods at the expense of consumer goods. Although in these countries people are relatively free to spend their incomes, the lack of consumer goods or the poor quality of these goods limits that freedom.

In the U.S.S.R. housing has been of poor quality. Clothing is often of limited choice and poorly made. Consumers are showing their disapproval by refusing to buy poor quality goods. Instead they are choosing to save their money or to purchase goods on the black market or from the limited private enterprises which exist.

The marketing system of the Soviet Union is inefficient by American standards. Frequently people have to stand in one line to determine whether a product is available, then move to another line to pay for merchandise, and finally stand in a third line to receive their goods. Moscow planners are beginning to give more attention to consumers, but the emphasis in the Soviet Union's economy continues to be on industrial products.

Decentralized decision making

The freedom of choice in the American economy provides for a high degree of decentralization of decision making. This freedom occurs within the market system where the incentives of profit, income, and job satisfaction, and the consumption of desired goods and services all help to determine what will be produced and consumed.

Government planning in the United States. There is some central government planning in the American economy to channel our resources in certain directions, but it is of a more generalized character and less dominant than in socialist economies. Our federal government does plan taxation and expenditure programs to promote the general growth of the economy. In some cases, through tax incentives and expenditures, government stimulates specific programs ranging from highway and hospital construction to pollution control and education. Through the Federal Reserve System, our central monetary and banking authority, the supply of money and the availability of credit is influenced to encourage orderly economic development.

It is possible for government to encourage business and individuals to utilize economic resources in certain ways. Frequently this is done not by forcing compliance but by making it profitable for business enterprises and individuals to conform to government direction. For example, by the use of tax reduction incentives, the government is able to encourage business to spend money for factories and equipment in certain industries. By placing special taxes on certain products, individuals are discouraged from their consumption.

Government planning in socialist economies. Advocates of socialism have suggested that one of its strengths is its centralized planning and control. Government draws up production plans (such as the five-year plans in the Soviet Union) and directs the resources of the economy to fulfill those plans. However, central planning has not always been able to achieve its goals. When they are achieved it is at the expense of the freedom of the individuals in the society to determine for themselves what is best in an economic sense.

There is a serious question as to whether it is possible in the multi-billion dollar economy for centralized planning to be efficient in decision making, even with the use of computers, regarding the utilization of resources for the production and distribution of goods and services. With rising levels of expectations for consumer goods, many economists believe that the open marketplace with its emphasis upon decentralization of decision making not only provides more freedom but is more efficient in the allocation of scarce economic resources than centralized socialist planning.

High productivity

For Americans, an important advantage of our economic system is its great ability to produce goods and services. As a result Americans enjoy an increasingly higher standard of living. As Table 1–2 indicates

TABLE 1–2
Median family income in the
United States
(*in constant dollars—1970 base*)

Family money income
1970	$9,867
1960	7,376
Increase	$2,491

Source: U.S. Bureau of the Census, *Current Population Reports*, Series P-60, No. 78, May, 1971.

there was an increase of 34 percent in median family income[1] over the recent ten-year period. These dollar amounts are shown in constant 1970 dollars, which means that they have been adjusted to account for inflation and are stated in terms of 1970 buying power. Even in the most prosperous industrialized countries, family incomes average far less than in the United States.

On the average, total production has doubled every 20 years. Today industrial production is more than four times what it was in 1940. Figure 1–1 shows the rise in industrial production in the United States over the past 50 years.

Types of business enterprises

Business enterprises may be classified according to the four types of activities performed which provide goods with utility.

---

[1] The term *median income* means that half of the family units had incomes higher than the stated figure and half had incomes lower. Thus the *median* represents the midway point in a series of data which divides the number of units in half.

FIGURE 1-1
Industrial production since 1918

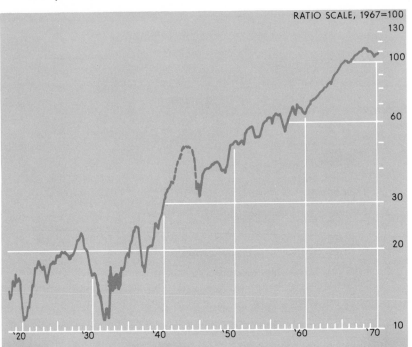

Source: Federal Reserve System, *Federal Reserve Bulletin*, July, 1971.

1. *Processing enterprises* transform the natural resources that come from the mines, forests, farms, and oceans into the raw materials used to manufacture goods.
2. *Manufacturing enterprises* fabricate consumer and producer goods out of raw materials.
3. *Marketing enterprises* distribute the finished goods to ultimate consumers.
4. *Facilitating enterprises* perform indispensable auxiliary functions in such fields as finance, insurance, transportation, construction, and services.

Those business enterprises which engage in the same type of economic activity constitute an *industry*. For example, the manufacturers of passenger cars make up the automobile industry. However, this is a somewhat vague concept because many business enterprises

FIGURE 1–2
Percentage of 1970 national income generated by different industries

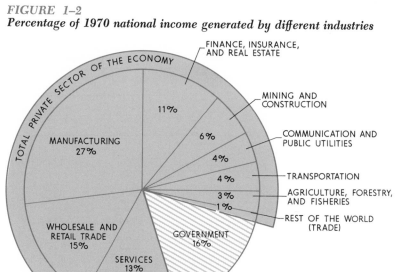

Source: U.S. Department of Commerce, *Survey of Current Business*, May, 1971.

produce more than one type of good or service and really are a part of the much broader industry sector called manufacturing. Figure 1–2 indicates the broad industrial sectors which make up the economy and shows the percentage of national income which each sector supplied in 1970.

Figure 1–2 reveals the key role which is held by manufacturing enterprises in our economy. This sector of business enterprise not only accounts for more than one fourth of national income, but also greatly influences economic activity in such fields as transportation, trade, and finance.

Legal forms of business organization

The three most important legal forms of business organization in the United States are the proprietorship, the partnership, and the corporation. Table 1–3 shows a summary of the more than 11 million business

TABLE 1-3
Number of enterprises operating in principal industries in the United States, period ending June 30, 1969

Industry	Number of firms (in thousands)		
	Proprietorships	Active partnerships	Active corporations
Agriculture, forestry, and fisheries	3,206	121	31
Mining	43	13	13
Construction	663	50	127
Manufacturing	172	33	192
Transportation, communication, and public utilities	286	15	66
Trade	1,910	209	474
Wholesale	268	32	153
Retail	1,623	175	316
Finance, insurance, and real estate	516	299	408
Service	2,390	176	230
All industries	9,212	918	1,547

Note: Because of multiple industry listings, totals are less than the sum of individual items.
Source: Department of the Treasury, Internal Revenue Service, *Preliminary Statistics of Income 1968, Business Income Tax Returns* and *Preliminary Statistics of Income 1968, Corporation Income Tax Returns,* October, 1970.

enterprises in the United States according to their legal form of organization and the major type of economic activity performed.

The single proprietorship

The single proprietorship is the most simple legal form of business organization. The proprietor is the sole owner of the business enterprise and is able to exercise complete control over its operation. The owner is personally liable for the debts and other legal obligations of the enterprise. The profits of the proprietorship are considered as part of the owner's income. Therefore, there is no separate federal income tax on the business's profits, but the owner does have to report the enterprise's profits as part of his personal income for tax purposes.

The proprietorship is by far the most numerous legal form of business in the United States as Table 1-3 indicates. Proprietorships are most common in farming and fishing and the retail trades. Generally they are small enterprises. Frequently proprietorships are not very profitable because of their size, problems of obtaining efficient management, and intensive competition. However, this form of legal organization continues to be popular because of the number of persons who want to have their own business and because of the ease in starting a proprietorship.

The partnership

A partnership is formed when two or more persons agree to start a business enterprise as coowners. Each partner customarily contributes some economic assets to the business enterprise in the form of money, property, skill, or labor. Partners share in the profits or losses of the business according to an agreed upon ratio. However, each partner is liable for legal obligations, such as losses or court judgments against the partnership, to the full extent of his personal fortune. This tends to limit the size of partnerships. Another limiting factor is that customarily when one of the partners dies a new partnership must be formed.

The control and management of the partnership is vested in the hands of the partners equally. Any one of the partners is able to commit the enterprise by his decisions. Therefore, a serious mistake by one partner can affect all the partners.

The partnership is relatively easy to form. Although a written partnership agreement is desirable, there need not be a written statement between the partners for them to join together in business activity. However, if a disagreement occurs and there is no written partnership agreement it may be necessary for the courts to determine if a partnership was really formed.

The profits of the partnership are considered to be part of the owners' incomes. Therefore, there is no separate federal income tax on the partnership's profits, but the partners do have to report their portion of the enterprise's profits as part of their respective personal incomes for tax purposes.

The corporation

A corporation is a legal entity, separate and distinct from the persons who are its owners. It comes into being when a charter is obtained from the state where the corporation is being formed. The corporation has only those powers which are given by the state and expressed or implied in its charter. The owners contribute money or other assets and receive shares of stock for their monetary interest in the corporation.

There is a legal distinction between the corporation and its stockholders. This permits the corporation to buy, own, and sell property; enter into contracts; sue and be sued; and carry out business activities as a legal entity separate from its owners. This separate entity concept also means that the income of the corporation is taxed by government, and any cash dividends which are paid to the stockholders are taxed as personal income of the individual stockholders.

The stockholders of the corporation elect a board of directors to exercise control of the corporation. Usually each share of stock is entitled to one vote. Shareholders either vote in person at stockholders' meetings or by *proxy,* which is a written authorization for someone else to cast the stockholders' votes. Customarily the board of directors solicits proxies from stockholders which are then voted to support the incumbent board of directors. If a group of stockholders becomes dissatisfied with the board of directors they may solicit proxies in an attempt to gain control of the corporation. Such proxy fights are relatively rare and may be expensive to conduct when there are thousands of stockholders.

The board of directors is responsible for seeing that the corporation functions in the best long-run interests of the stockholders. Specific duties of the board of directors include the election of the officers to manage the corporation (including the president), the determination of major policies, approval of important operating decisions, and the exercise of overall control. Directors are normally elected annually by the stockholders. Thus, in the corporation form of legal organization there is a separation of roles. The stockholders are the owners. The elected directors exercise control of the corporation. The officers and other executives manage the business enterprise.

There are considerably fewer corporations than proprietorships as Table 1–3 indicates. However, Table 1–4 shows that the corporation has by far the greatest economic impact upon society in terms of business receipts (sales) and net profits.

There are a number of advantages to the corporation form of legal organization over the proprietorship and the partnership:

1. The liability of the owners of the corporation for the corporation's obligations is limited to the amount of their investment in the corporation. Therefore, stockholders' entire personal fortunes are not

TABLE 1-4

Business receipts and net profits of U.S. enterprises in principal industries, period ending June 30, 1969
(in millions of dollars)

Industry	Business receipts			Net profit (less loss)		
	Sole proprietorships	Active partnerships	Active corporations	Sole proprietorships	Active partnerships	Active corporations
Agriculture, forestry, and fisheries	$ 37,362	$ 5,581	$ 9,490	$ 3,545	$ 654	$ 149
Mining	1,220	1,036	14,452	74*	73	707
Construction	19,334	7,522	72,173	2,887	802	979
Manufacturing	6,673	5,598	640,695	757	545	23,071
Transportation, communication, and public utilities	6,175	1,254	111,878	925	151	5,469
Trade	106,886	34,784	449,429	7,644	2,279	5,888
Wholesale	20,432	11,080	206,602	1,796	556	2,501
Retail	85,490	23,199	239,780	5,778	1,688	3,346
Finance, insurance, and real estate	7,760	10,668	146,986	2,501	1,067	11,062
Services	36,548	16,460	49,951	13,645	5,824	1,027
All industries	$222,105	$82,940	$1,495,174	$31,871	$11,405	$48,349

* Net loss exceeds net profit.

Note: Because of multiple industry listings, totals are less than the sum of individual items.

Source: Department of the Treasury, Internal Revenue Service, *Preliminary Statistics of Income 1968, Business Income Tax Returns* and *Preliminary Statistics of Income 1968, Corporation Income Tax Returns,* October, 1970.

placed in possible jeopardy as with the proprietorship and the partnership.

2. Depending upon the terms of its charter, the corporation may have perpetual life. Its existence does not depend upon any particular group of owners.

3. There is relative ease of transfer of ownership of the corporation. A stockholder can simply sell his shares of stock to someone else without directly affecting the functioning of the corporation or the other stockholders.

4. Because of the advantages of the corporate form, it is generally easier to attract the large amounts of capital necessary for many types of business operations than with other legal forms of organization.

5. Because of the relative ease of assembling large amounts of economic resources, the corporation frequently is able to obtain managerial talent and specialized skills easier than when other legal forms of organization are used.

The owners of the small corporation may not always be able to realize all the advantages listed above. For example, a bank may require the principal owners to personally endorse a loan which the bank makes to a small corporation. Such an endorsement negates the advantage of limited liability for those stockholders since if the corporation is unable to repay the loan the bank has a legal claim against the personal assets of the endorsers of the loan. However, such an arrangement is not usual with the large corporation which has numerous stockholders.

The systems approach to business

The systems approach to business has received much attention in recent years because of the breadth and complexity of the issues facing management. These issues include the changes brought on by exploding technological advances, vastly improved communications throughout the world, and a questioning of the traditional priorities and values of society. The relationship between business and other institutions and the impact of economic, political, and social problems has made it necessary for managers to reexamine their approach to the functioning of the business enterprise.

The emphasis of the systems approach is upon the wholeness of the functioning of the business enterprise in society with an examination of business's relationship to its total environment and to its component parts. The systems approach to business is useful because it emphasizes an understanding of the comprehensive nature of business activities and the structure and process through which these activities are carried out.

A *system* is defined as a set of elements which have a relationship to each other. The elements within a system are referred to as *subsystems*. Thus each system is composed of subsystems which in combination have a meaningful unity or wholeness. The elements within the system are interrelated and interdependent and constitute the internal environment of the system. If the economy as a whole is considered as a system, then individual enterprises would be viewed as subsystems. If, for purposes of study, a single business enterprise is considered as a system, then the various departments and functions performed are the subsystems which interact with each other.

Business functions as an open system which is continually influenced by factors in the external environment. As a result of information received, which is called *feedback,* business is constantly changing both to adapt to its environment and to influence the external systems with which it comes into contact.

When business is studied in the framework of the whole economic system, the total flow of economic activity by business and consumers is examined. This is referred to as *macroeconomic* analysis. The "macro" approach to business deals with the institution of business in its relationship with other systems in society.

Figure 1–3 shows the functioning of a simple model of the economic system which is influenced by a number of other systems in its external environment. This broad macroeconomic approach to business illustrates how business functions in the economic system and how it is influenced by other systems. Throughout this book several topics are discussed which relate the whole institution of business to its external environment. These topics are covered in such chapters as those dealing with environmental pollution, government relationships, consumers, labor unions, and financial institutions.

Notice in Figure 1–3 how business enterprises use the inputs of labor, capital, land, and management in order to produce the outputs of goods and services which are demanded by individual and institutional consumers. This activity takes place within the internal environment of the economic system.

The economic system is affected by other institutions in society and in turn influences them. The legal system is important to business be-

FIGURE 1–3
The economic system in American society

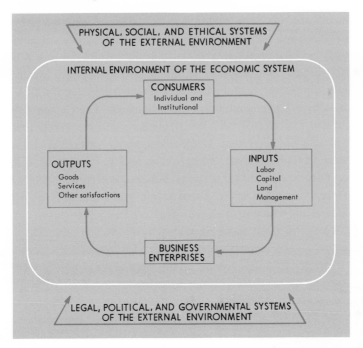

cause our economic system is based upon the concept of private property rights. Business operations depend upon contractual agreements which may be enforced through the courts of law. Business is involved in the political system because of the effect of political decisions on business operations and because of business influence on the governing process.

Since people are important in the functioning of the economic system there is a system of social relationships which influences business. Business is influenced by cultural and religious institutions because of the interrelated nature of people's values and business activities.

Another way to study business is from the point of view of the functioning of the individual business enterprise. This approach is called *microeconomic* analysis. "Micro" analysis is concerned with the internal functioning of the subsystems of the enterprise and with the total management of the firm as it relates to its environment. Several chapters, including those on management, control, marketing, personnel, production, and finance, are devoted essentially to the study of the functioning of the individual business enterprise.

Summary

Economics is the management of the human and material resources of society. Economics can also be defined as the allocation of scarce resources in a society of unlimited wants.

Economic resources consist of all the natural, man-made, and human factors that go into the production of goods and services. Property resources are land and capital. Human resources are labor and entrepreneurial ability.

Goods, which may be either tangible or intangible, are useful in satisfying human wants. Intangible goods are called services. Goods may also be classified as consumer goods or producer goods.

In order for goods to have economic value they must have some type of utility. Utility is the power to satisfy human wants. Tangible goods have form, place, time, and possession utility.

The three basic economic questions which must be answered in every economic system are:

1. What goods will be produced?
2. How will these goods be produced?
3. Who will consume (or control) these goods?

Economic systems functioning today have elements of capitalism and socialism. The U.S. economic system is a modified form of capitalism called the private enterprise system. Private property, the profit motive, the market system, and a particular relationship between business and government are important characteristics of the private enterprise system. The American people enjoy many advantages under our economic system.

The three most commonly used legal forms of business organization are proprietorships, partnerships, and corporations. Corporations are the dominant legal form of organization in terms of impact on the economy.

The systems approach to business helps management understand the relation of business as an institution to other elements in the social system and the individual business enterprise as it relates to its component parts. Systems analysis focuses on the comprehensive nature of business activities with emphasis upon wholeness and interrelationships. Business may be studied from either a macroeconomic or a microeconomic point of view.

Terms for review

economics
economic resources
national income
consumer goods
producer goods
utility
capitalism

socialism
private enterprise system
proprietorship
partnership
corporation
system

Questions

1. Why is scarcity a fundamental part of the economic system?
2. *a)* What changes have occurred in the components of national income from 1966 to 1970?
   b) Determine what recent changes have occurred in national income by checking the *Survey of Current Business, Economic Indicators,* or other government publications in the library.
3. *a)* What are the three basic economic questions which must be answered in every society?
   b) How are these questions answered in the United States today?
4. What kinds of economic utility are there? Give an example of each.
5. In what ways does the functioning of the U.S. economy differ from that of the Soviet Union? In what ways are they similar?
6. *a)* Should some governmental body have the power to control prices and wages?
   b) What would be possible positive and negative consequences of such controls?
   c) Examine publications such as *Business Week, Fortune,* and the *AFL-CIO American Federationist* for current views on the subject.
7. Under what circumstances would it be most advisable to organize a business enterprise as:
   a) a proprietorship?
   b) a partnership?
   c) a corporation?
8. Using Tables 1–3 and 1–4, analyze the relative importance of proprietorships, partnerships, and corporations in the various broad industrial categories. How do you account for these relationships?
9. What is the macroeconomic approach to the study of business? Why should students have an understanding of the whole economic system?
10. What are some of the other institutions in society which affect the economic system? How is this influence felt by business? In what ways does business influence these other institutions?

A new generation enters business

College graduates going into business management in the 1970s are quite different from those who entered business in the 1950s and 1960s. In the 1950s the young manager was typified as being an organization man who was willing to accept management's goals and values. In the 1960s the junior executive was more skilled at problem solving; he was pragmatic and confident of his role, without too much questioning of corporate goals. In the 1950s and 1960s junior executives had a strong commitment to the established business system.

According to *Fortune* magazine, today's young people are going into business as junior managers "not as comfortable successors to power but as rebels and reformers who will carry out important changes in both the substance and the style of managing corporations."[1]

These young persons are interested in the improvement of society and its environment and feel that business enterprises should actively pursue these goals. The current generation has been characterized as being competent and self-confident with an interest in human values, change, and individuality. They are impatient because they feel there has been an inadequate response by the business community to what they define as relevant problems and inequities in the economic system. Many are anxious to help others, idealistic, and willing to work hard for the objectives they consider worthwhile. These young executives are interested in personal projects which they consider socially important, such as advising minority owners of small businesses, doing ecological research, and organizing cleanup campaigns.

Many young managers are critical of their bosses for being overly concerned about profits. While most do not criticize the concept of profit or its necessity, many young managers do question the way in which profit is utilized.

This new breed of junior managers wants the responsibility for making important decisions and is eager for rapid advancement. Although materialism is not a stated objective, beginning pay levels between

---

[1] Judson Gooding, "The Accelerated Generation Moves into Management," *Fortune* (March, 1971), p. 101.

$10,000 and $15,000 are expected as a matter of fact, but the junior managers do not emphasize fringe benefits.

1. Summarize the values held by young people going into business management positions today.
2. What problems do older management personnel face with this new type of junior manager?
3. What values are important to you as a person going into business?

CASE

Purchasing power of U.S.S.R. workers

A study reported in the May, 1971, *Monthly Labor Review* published by the U.S. Department of Labor indicates that the purchasing power of workers in the Soviet Union has increased steadily since World War II, but that this purchasing power is still far behind U.S. workers' ability to buy goods and services. Also, continued shortages of consumer goods and services limit the U.S.S.R. workers' ability to exercise their increased buying power.

In the Soviet Union the average annual increase in wages was reported to be about 5 percent during the 1965–70 period compared with an annual rate of increase of only 2.5 percent during 1959–64. Monthly earnings of selected occupations in the U.S.S.R. are shown in Table A.

TABLE A
Monthly earnings of selected occupational groups in U.S.S.R., 1970

Occupation	Monthly earnings (in rubles[1])
Scientist (academician)	800 to 1,500
Opera star	500 to 2,000
Professor (medicine)	400 to 600
Manager of enterprise	100 to 1,000
Engineer	90 to 200
Physician, staff	90 to 170
Teacher, high school	80 to 137
Worker, skilled	100 to 250
Worker, semiskilled	70 to 90
Worker, unskilled	60 to 70

[1] The official tourist rate of exchange fixed by the Soviet government is 1 ruble = $1.11 U.S.
Source: U.S. Department of Labor, *Monthly Labor Review* (May, 1971), p. 41.

The prices of selected consumer durable goods in the Soviet Union are shown in Table B.

TABLE B
Prices of selected consumer durable goods in U.S.S.R., 1970

Durable good	Price (in rubles)
Automobile, Fiat	5,500
Automobile, "Moskvich-412"	4,936
Motorcycle, "M-105"	350
Refrigerator	250
Bicycle, man's	50
Tape recorder, "Orbita-2"	210
Radio set, "Mikron," lowest-priced	26
Electric razor, "Kharkov"	23

Source: U.S. Department of Labor, *Monthly Labor Review* (May, 1971), p. 42.

TABLE C
Approximate work time required to buy selected commodities at state-fixed prices in Moscow and at retail stores in New York City, 1970

Commodity	Approximate work time	
	Moscow	New York City
Food		
Beef, rib roast, per pound	63.0 minutes	19.0 minutes
Sugar, per pound	40.0 minutes	2.5 minutes
Butter, salted, per pound	140.0 minutes	16.0 minutes
Milk, fresh, per quart	24.0 minutes	5.6 minutes
Potatoes, per pound	3.9 minutes	2.1 minutes
White bread, per pound	17.0 minutes	5.4 minutes
Eggs, per dozen	93.0 minutes	12.0 minutes
Clothing, men's		
Cotton shirt	11.4 hours	1.7 hours
Leather oxford shoes, pair	35.0 hours	6.0 hours
Wool suit, single-breasted, middle price range	157.0 hours	26.3 hours
Clothing, women's		
Dress, man-made fibers	42.0 hours	5.6 hours
Shoes, leather oxfords, middle price range	33.0 hours	5.3 hours
Stockings, nylon, per pair	2.9 hours	17.5 minutes
Other commodities		
Soap, toilet (3½ ounces)	16.0 minutes	2.0 minutes
Cigarettes, nonfilter, regular size	15.0 minutes	8.5 minutes
Vodka, fifth	6.6 hours	1.6 hours

Source: U.S. Department of Labor, *Monthly Labor Review* (May, 1971), p. 43.

Table C shows the approximate work time required by the average Moscow worker to buy a variety of nondurable commodities compared with the work time required for the average New York City worker to buy similar items.

1. In those occupations for which statistics are available in the U.S. Department of Commerce's *Statistical Abstract of the United States,* compare the salaries of U.S. occupational groups with those shown in Table A.
2. *a)* Compare the prices of selected consumer goods from Table B with current prices for similar items in the United States.
   b) How can officials in the Soviet Union influence consumer behavior even with the increases in earning power of U.S.S.R. workers in recent years?
3. By studying Table C along with other information provided in this case, compare the standard of living of your family with what it might be if you lived in the Soviet Union with a similar occupational status.

President Nixon conferring with his economic advisers at Camp David before his August 15, 1971 announcement freezing prices and wages. From left to right are Arthur Burns, John Connally, President Nixon, George Shultz, and Dr. Paul McCracken. Standing behind is Dr. Herbert Stein.

2

Business and government

Government has an impact on business just as it does on the life of every citizen. Some businessmen complain about the amount of government regulation and taxes. However, business looks to government to maintain a social and legal climate within which economic institutions can function.

This chapter is designed to give the student a basic understanding of the many ways in which business is affected by government. Background information is provided on a number of issues, including taxation, government spending, business regulation, and the power of the presidency. Succeeding chapters discuss the government's role in relation to business in such areas as environmental pollution, labor relations, and consumer protection.

The following questions relating to business and government are discussed in this chapter.

What taxes does business pay to support the operation of government?

Which services are provided to business by government?

How are business enterprises regulated by government?

What is the role of government as a customer of business?

In what ways does government subsidize business?

What enterprises are government owned and operated in the United States?

Taxation of business

The functions of government are paid for either with tax revenues, receipts from users of government goods and services, or borrowed monies. When governmental units borrow money to finance operations, interest is paid for the use of these funds and ultimately the borrowings must be repaid through the collection of taxes or by additional borrowing.

In addition to raising revenue, taxes may be used for the regulation of business. An example of this is the taxation of narcotics under the Federal Narcotics Act which restricts dealing in narcotics to scientific and medical purposes. The taxes on these narcotics are relatively low and little revenue is produced. However, the regulations require record keeping which emphasizes the criminal nature of unauthorized traffic in drugs. Therefore, the primary purpose of the tax on narcotics is not to raise revenue but to regulate the flow of drugs.

The principal revenue-producing taxes levied by the federal government include individual and corporation income taxes, social insurance taxes, and excise taxes on specified manufacturers and retailers sales transactions. State and local governments' main tax sources include sales taxes, individual and corporation income taxes, property taxes, and various types of license fees. Figure 2–1 illustrates the relative importance

FIGURE 2–1

Sources of federal, state, and local government tax dollars, 1970

WHERE THE FEDERAL TAX DOLLAR COMES FROM....

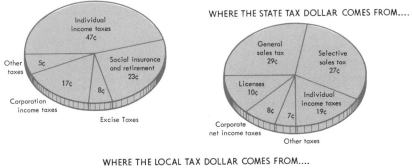

WHERE THE STATE TAX DOLLAR COMES FROM....

WHERE THE LOCAL TAX DOLLAR COMES FROM....

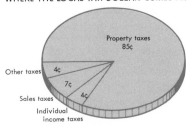

Source: U.S. Department of Commerce, Bureau of the Census.

of these various types of tax revenues to federal, state, and local governments.

Types of taxes

Income taxes. Income taxes are levied upon both personal and corporation income by the federal government and by many state and local governments. Corporate income is taxed after the deduction of business expenses. The income of business enterprises organized as proprietorships and partnerships is taxed after deduction of business expenses as part of the personal incomes of the owners of these enterprises.

The income tax is viewed by many authorities on taxation as a desirable type of tax since it is relatively easy to collect, falls upon those who have the ability to pay, and produces substantial revenue. Critics claim that high income tax rates reduce profits, which lessens the incentive of individuals and business enterprises to take risks by investing funds. However, to some extent business may be able to pass on the effect of income taxes to its customers through higher prices. Despite complaints about the income tax, it continues to be a very important source of governmental revenue. Approximately 60 percent of the total tax revenues collected in the United States are from the individual and corporate income taxes levied by federal, state, and local governments.

In 1971 corporate profits were taxed by the federal government at a rate of 22 percent on the first $25,000 of taxable income plus a surtax of 26 percent on income above $25,000. This results in a tax rate of approximately 48 percent for large, profitable corporations. In addition, many states have corporate income taxes though these rates are considerably lower than the federal income tax rate.

Sales taxes. Sales taxes are levied on the sale of goods to consumers and sometimes on consumer services. Sales taxes provide the largest single source of tax revenue for state governments. Sales taxes may be *general* if they apply to all, or nearly all, retail sales, or they may be *selective* in applying to some specific product such as cigarettes, liquor, or gasoline.

Selective sales taxes are used in all states for liquor and gasoline and in a number of states on other products as well. General sales taxes are used by most states. The business enterprises collect the sales taxes when retail sales are made and turn the funds over to state revenue departments.

Property taxes. Property taxes are levied on the assessed value of real estate, tangible and intangible property. For the business enterprise this means that taxes are levied on the assessed value of its land and buildings, equipment, and inventories. Property taxes are determined on annual rates based on the appraised value of property. Property taxes are vital sources of revenue for local government, making up 85 percent of local tax collections. They are insignificant to state governments and not used by the federal government.

Other taxes. A tax paid by business but passed on to the consumer is the excise tax which is either a *manufacturers excise tax* or a *retailers excise tax* depending upon which type of enterprise collects the tax. Manufacturers federal excise taxes are levied on such items as tires, liquor, tobacco, motor fuel, firearms, fishing equipment, and sugar. These taxes take the form of added costs which the consumer pays usually without knowing that they have been collected by the manufacturer of the goods. Retailers excise taxes have been levied in the past on jewelry, silverware, and other luxury items. Most retailers federal excise taxes have been repealed although these taxes are still collected on motor fuels, liquor, and tobacco products. Federal excise taxes are collected on such services as air transportation and telephone service.

Employment taxes are paid by employers and employees who come under the Federal Insurance Contributions Act. These taxes provide for old-age, survivors', and disability insurance benefits and for government health insurance. Self-employed individuals are also subject to this tax. In 1971 business and employees were each taxed 5.2 percent on the first $7,800 of the employee's annual wages.

Business also pays *unemployment insurance taxes* and *workmen's compensation taxes* under a national system administered by the states. States use unemployment insurance taxes to finance payments for a stipulated number of weeks to workers who are out of work and searching for employment. Workmen's compensation insurance covers employee payments for job-related injuries. Some states have state coverage, and some states permit employers to purchase private insurance protection against accidents. Costs depend upon the employer's accident record and the type of work in which his employees are engaged.

Customs duties are taxes collected on goods imported into the United States from other countries. These serve both as a revenue measure and to protect American producers from competing lower priced imports.

A variety of other taxes are levied upon business at different levels of government including licenses, incorporation taxes, and utilities taxes. The importance of these taxes to business depends upon the nature of the enterprise's operations and the particular location of the business enterprise.

Impact of taxes on business decisions

Taxes influence business decisions in a number of ways. Three examples are mentioned below.

Interest paid on borrowed money is a tax deductible expense. This reduces the amount of income taxes paid by the enterprise and therefore has the effect of lowering the cost of borrowing.

Spending for new factories and equipment is influenced by the changes in government tax policy on depreciation. Depreciation charges are allocations over a number of years of the cost of durable goods such as factories and equipment. The depreciation charges are tax deductible expenses, but government tax regulations determine the length of time over which the cost of these investments can be charged against business income.

At the state and local level of government, the location of new manufacturing or distribution facilities may depend upon the nature of state and local taxes in relation to the availability of governmental services.

Provision of public services

In return for the taxes paid by business enterprises and individuals, a wide variety of services are provided by government ranging from national defense to police and fire protection and numerous social services. Because of the importance of the services provided by government at all levels, most businessmen and other citizens are willing to pay their fair share of taxes but expect that government be reasonably efficient in the spending of tax dollars. In order to encourage the efficient functioning of government a number of organizations composed of businessmen and other interested citizens have been formed to study government and its operations. An example of these nonpartisan organizations at the national level is the Tax Institute of America, which sponsors symposiums and other educational activities in the field of public finance. At the state level organizations such as the Missouri Public Expenditures Survey make studies and review governmental functions to encourage better use of the taxpayers' money.

FIGURE 2–2
Federal, state, and local government expenditures, 1940–1970

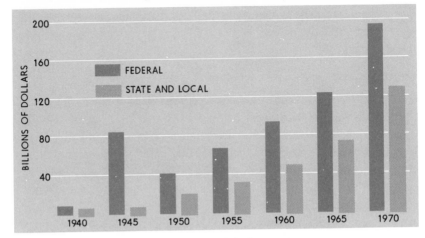

Source: U.S. Department of Commerce, Bureau of the Census.

The total expenditures of federal, state, and local governments have increased substantially in the past 30 years. Figure 2–2 illustrates this rise in government spending.

Federal government services

The wide variety of federal programs is illustrated by the federal government's budget expenditures for 1970. Figure 2–3 shows the major categories of these expenditures.

FIGURE 2–3
Federal government spending programs, 1970

WHERE YOUR FEDERAL TAX DOLLAR GOES....

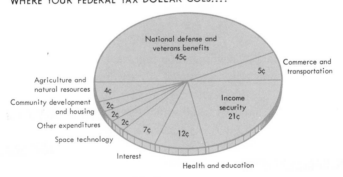

Source: U.S. Department of the Treasury.

National defense and veterans' benefits accounted for about 45 cents of each dollar spent. Federal monies were also spent on programs for space research and technology, agriculture and natural resources, highway construction and other transportation programs, community development and housing, health and education, and income security. In addition, 7 percent of the federal government's expenditures, or over $14 billion, was paid in interest on money borrowed to finance past governmental operations. A number of the federal government's programs were carried out in cooperation with state and local governmental units.

State and local government services

Many of the functions of government which directly affect the business enterprise and individual citizens are performed by state and local governments. Figure 2–4 shows the spending of state and local governments based on the nature of the service provided.

FIGURE 2–4
State and local government general expenditures by function

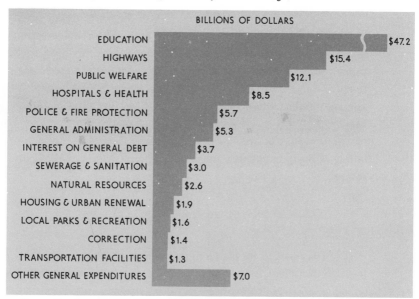

Source: U.S. Bureau of the Census, *Governmental Finances in 1968–69*, September, 1970.

Government's impact on the economy

The relationship between tax receipts and governmental expenditures has an effect on the overall economy. When government's spending exceeds its tax receipts the effect is expansionary on the economy. This deficit spending is accomplished by government borrowing through the sale of debt obligations. When the economy is functioning with less than full employment of people and productive facilities the general effect of government deficit spending is to stimulate economic activity and increase the flow of goods and services. When the economy is already operating at or near capacity the result of deficit spending is a further stimulation of the economy which contributes to inflationary price increases.

When government collects more taxes than it spends a budgetary surplus occurs. The general effect is to reduce the level of economic activity (an opposite effect of deficit spending).

The role of the U.S. Treasury and the Federal Reserve System in managing the federal government debt and influencing the money supply is discussed in Chapter 15.

Regulation of business

The major purpose of regulation of business by government is to promote the public welfare and to benefit the economy as a whole. At times special interest groups may take advantage of government regulation for their own gain. However, the general philosophical thread in the legislation, administration, and adjudication of economic matters in this country has been protection of the public interest and promotion of employment, production, and purchasing power. The means of regulation of business include legislation, administrative control, and judicial review.

Legislation affecting business

The laws passed by the Congress which affect business are wide-ranging and complex. In addition, each of the states and municipalities in which a business enterprise operates has laws regulating the conduct of business. Much of the significant national legislation and the role of a number of important governmental agencies are discussed in other chapters which are closely related to those topics. In Chapter 9 the labor-management laws and the National Labor Relations Board are discussed. Legislation relating to environmental pollution is discussed in Chapter 3. Government protection of the consumer is discussed in Chapter 11. This chapter's discussion covers the impact of government's influence on business through the antitrust laws, including those on competition and monopoly, price discrimination, and resale price maintenance.

The background of antitrust legislation

The economic development of the United States during the period following the Civil War was characterized by the construction of a network of railroads which extended to the West Coast, the settlement of the West, and the industrialization of America with the corporation becoming the dominant form of business organization. The corporation facilitated the growth of enterprises and fostered increasing concentration in many industries. The economic fluctuations of the quarter century following the Civil War caused business to seek relief from cutthroat competition by combining operations, dividing markets, controlling industry practices through trusts, and by other actions which were characteristic of monopolies. A monopoly results when one producer or distributor has such control over the supply of a product that he can determine price independently. By the 1880s, such major industries as petroleum, cottonseed oil, linseed oil, whiskey, sugar, and lead were essentially monopolies in the United States.

These monopolies functioned through a form of organization called a *trust,* which was created when the owners of the controlling shares of stock in competing corporations transferred control of their shares to a group of trustees. In exchange for their controlling shares, the former corporate shareholders received trust certificates and were entitled to a share in the profits of the combined corporations. The trustees voted the stock certificates in all the participating corporations thereby electing corporate directors and controlling corporation policies; the result was that several corporations were run as a single business enterprise.

The trust was first used by the promoters of the Standard Oil Company in 1879. A trust agreement was formed with about 40 companies which gave a group of nine trustees control of 90 to 95 percent of the oil refining capacity in the country. During the following decade the trust was used in numerous industries with a resulting increase of industrial concentration in America. The subsequent laws dealing with these trusts came to be known as antitrust laws and this phrase is now broadly applied to any legislation which deals with restrictions on trade and business organization.

With the development of the trusts in the latter part of the 19th century many different groups in the community were adversely affected. Farmers, laborers, producers of raw materials, and small businessmen were all forced to conform to the policies laid down by these industry giants. Farmers experienced a decline in farm prices combined with high costs of materials, credit, and freight rates. Laborers were faced with increased competition for jobs, severe working conditions, and poor living conditions in the cities. Raw materials producers were forced to sell to a single manufacturer in many industries and therefore had no alternative for disposition of their produce, and small businessmen were driven out of business in many instances when they refused to be absorbed or to cooperate with the trusts.

The powerful economic action of the trusts resulted in a political reaction from those groups which felt oppressed. This political reaction centered on a strong movement against monopolies. Political parties based on farmers' organizations and drawing support from labor and independent businessmen ran candidates during the 1880s, many of whom were successful in gaining office in state governments and in the Congress. Concerned about the widespread support of antitrust sentiment, the two major national political parties adopted platforms opposed to monopoly. Out of this background in 1889 a number of states passed antitrust laws and the way was opened for national legislation in 1890.

Antitrust laws

The important antitrust legislation passed by the U.S. Congress started with the Sherman Act and includes the Clayton Act, the Federal Trade Commission Act, the Robinson-Patman Act, and the Wheeler-Lea Amendment.

The Sherman Act (1890). The Sherman Act passed in 1890 contained two major provisions:

Section 1. Every contract, combination in the form of a trust or otherwise, or conspiracy, in restraint of trade or commerce among the several states, or with foreign nations, is hereby declared to be illegal. Every person who shall make any such contract or engage in any such combination or conspiracy, shall be deemed guilty of a misdemeanor . . . .

Section 2. Every person who shall monopolize, or attempt to monopolize, or combine or conspire with any other person or persons, to monopolize any part of the trade or commerce among the several states, or with foreign nations, shall be deemed guilty of a misdemeanor . . . .

The first section applies only to agreements involving two or more persons, while the second section is broader and applies also to individual efforts to monopolize. This legislation actually contained nothing that was not already a part of the common law, but it did explicitly make restraint of trade and monopolization federal offenses with administration of the law under the Justice Department. U.S. district attorneys under the Attorney General could institute both civil and criminal proceedings against those who allegedly violated the law. Parties guilty under criminal suits were punishable by fines up to $5,000, imprisonment up to one year, or both. Those persons who were injured by illegal restraint of trade or monopolies were entitled to sue for triple damages.

Administration of the Sherman Act, 1890–1912. The Sherman Act was the only significant antitrust legislation to be enacted for nearly a quarter century. Its enforcement was quite variable from one presidential administration to another.

Shortly after the turn of the century there were several spectacular prosecutions during Theodore Roosevelt's administration, including one in which officials and employees of the American Sugar Refining Company were found guilty of tampering with their scales in order to avoid duties on sugar imports. The federal government recovered more than $4 million from this action in addition to the $30,000 fine levied on the guilty corporation. Under Roosevelt, proceedings were begun to dissolve the American Tobacco and Standard Oil trusts. However, Roosevelt felt that not all trusts were bad and that those which had come about as a result of natural business growth should not be bothered as long as they operated within the law. Regulation, not destruction, increasingly became Theodore Roosevelt's answer to the trust problem. He stated, "We do not wish to destroy corporations, but we do wish to make them subserve the public good."

In 1912 Democrat Woodrow Wilson was elected president. The Democratic platform had been based on the assumption that a greater role must be played by the federal government in order to meet the changing social and economic conditions. Wilson had hoped that many of the progressive actions could be achieved through state governments with minimal federal government intervention in business. Wilson felt that the answer was to restore competition and, unlike Roosevelt, contended that excessive size of corporations was in itself bad. He wanted the antitrust laws strengthened, tariff reduction, and a reform of the national banking system in order that the farmers and small business-men could be freed from the money trust.

The Clayton and Federal Trade Commission Acts (*1914*). In 1913, with Wilson as president, the new Congress passed legislation establishing the Federal Reserve System, reducing tariffs, and instituting the federal income tax. Then in 1914 the problem of monopoly received detailed congressional attention. Extensive hearings and debate preceded the passage of the Clayton Act, which outlawed price discrimination, exclusive and tying contracts, intercorporate stockholdings, and interlocking directorates. A special administrative agency was established to strengthen the observance and enforcement of the antitrust laws in the Federal Trade Commission Act.

The principal provisions of the Clayton Act included:

Section 2, which forbade sellers to discriminate in price between different purchasers of commodities unless there were differences in the grade, quality, or quantity of the commodity sold, where the lower prices made only due allowance for differences in the cost of selling or transportation and where they were offered in good faith to meet competition.

Section 3, which prohibited sellers from leasing or making a sale or contract for the sale of commodities on the condition that the lessee or purchaser shall not deal in the commodity of a competitor.

Section 7, which prohibited any corporation engaged in commerce from acquiring the shares of a competing corporation or from purchasing the stocks of two or more corporations that were competitors.

Section 8 prohibited interlocking boards of directors between business corporations where one of them had capital accounts of more than $1 million and where the elimination of competition between them would constitute a violation of any of the provisions of the antitrust laws.

Provisions of Sections 2, 3, and 7 were not absolute prohibitions and were forbidden only where their effect would be to substantially lessen competition or tend to create a monopoly.

In the Federal Trade Commission Act unfair methods of competition in commerce were declared unlawful, and a federal agency called the Federal Trade Commission was set up to police the antitrust laws. This act also provided that the federal government might initiate suits against those possibly engaged in illegal monopoly practices without waiting for suits from private individuals or business enterprises. The general provisions of the Sherman Act were made more explicit by the Clayton Act, and the Federal Trade Commission was created to deal with prevention as well as punishment for practices which reduced competition.

The National Industrial Recovery Act (*1933*). In the depression years of the 1930s one of the measures which President Franklin D. Roosevelt hoped would stop some of the extreme business competition was a means of industrial self-government. Some of the techniques of minimizing cutthroat competition included stabilization of production, pricing, and marketing practices. However, since the antitrust laws would not permit this, a special procedure had to be worked out. This took the form of the National Industrial Recovery Act, passed in 1933, which provided that "codes of fair competition" could be drawn up by industrial groups and then submitted to the presidential administration to insure that the proposed codes were "not designed to promote monopolies or to eliminate enterprises." After the president decided a particular code was fair, he would formally approve it, and then all enterprises in that industry had to follow the code or be liable for violations whether or not they had helped draw up the code. This was to be tried for two years during which time activities of approved codes were to be exempted from antitrust laws. With the advent of the NIRA, trustbusting was no longer the national policy. Instead, it was hoped there would be enlightened cooperation between government and business.

Just as the time for the two-year National Industrial Recovery Act experiment was ending in 1935 and controversy was raging over whether Congress should extend the act, the Supreme Court in the landmark case of *A.L.A. Schechter Poultry Corporation v. United States* unanimously overturned the lower court's decision in which the Schechter Corporation had been convicted because of violating certain provisions of the live-poultry code. The Supreme Court held that the NIRA was unconstitutional because it gave too much legislative power to the president and permitted the federal government to regulate wages and hours in businesses which were engaged only in intrastate commerce, such as the Schechter Corporation.

The Robinson-Patman Act (1936). With the National Industrial Recovery Act declared unconstitutional, smaller business enterprises demanded increased protective legislation as they charged that chain stores and other mass merchandisers were obtaining price concessions which were greater than the saving in costs allowed under the Clayton Act. In 1936 the Robinson-Patman Act revised Section 2 of the Clayton Act which dealt with price discrimination. The original Section 2 had been designed to prevent large manufacturers from forcing their smaller competitors out of business by temporarily cutting prices on particular products or in certain markets while at the same time maintaining prices elsewhere. The 1936 legislation sought to give increased protection to smaller retailers including grocers and druggists against unfair competition from their large competitors because of their tremendous purchasing power. The Robinson-Patman Act outlawed:

1. Discounts on volume purchases which cannot be justified by the lower cost of selling and delivery of large quantities.
2. Payments of a broker's commission (in effect a reduction in price) when an independent broker is not employed.
3. Allowances for advertising and promotion on purchases made by volume buyers which were not available on proportionally equal terms to smaller competing buyers.
4. Discounts which varied for the same quality of merchandise in the same quantities to different purchasers.
5. Sale of goods at unreasonably low prices where the practice was for the purpose of destroying competition or eliminating a competitor.

The Miller-Tydings Act (1937). Small businessmen had also been active in securing protective legislation at the state level. By 1937 most of the states, following California's lead, had passed fair trade legislation. This permitted manufacturers or distributors of branded merchandise to establish the minimum retail price for which the product would be sold to the consumer. However, these laws passed by states on fair trade practices were applicable only in intrastate commerce. In interstate commerce, where manufacturers and retailers or wholesalers were in different states, the resale price maintenance contracts violated the antitrust laws. Because the majority of branded goods moved across state borders the effectiveness of state laws was limited. The Miller-Tydings Act, despite President Roosevelt's opposition, was passed by Congress in 1937 as an amendment to the Sherman Act and exempted resale price maintenance contracts from antitrust laws provided they were permitted by state laws. By 1941, only Missouri, Texas, Vermont, and the District of Columbia did not have state fair trade laws.

Following court tests of the Miller-Tydings Act the Congress passed the McGuire Act in 1952 which permitted states to include nonsigner clauses in their resale price maintenance laws. The nonsigner clause states that all retailers in a state are bound by resale price agreements as long as one retailer in the state signs such an agreement.

Needless to say, fair trade prices have not been popular with consumers. Today a number of states have repealed their retail price maintenance laws, and a number of large manufacturers have abandoned their policy of fair trade pricing. A relatively small proportion of goods is now sold with fair trade prices. However, certain products, such as drugs, are still subject to resale price maintenance laws in a number of states.

The Antimerger Act (1950). The Congress passed the Antimerger Act of 1950, which strengthened the Clayton Act. This legislation provided that not only was the purchase of stock of a competing corporation a violation of the antitrust laws, but it was now illegal to acquire the assets of a competing firm. Thus all types of mergers were prohibited provided the Federal Trade Commission could demonstrate that the result might be a substantial lessening of competition. This would include horizontal, vertical, and conglomerate mergers.

A horizontal merger occurs when two or more companies which manufacture or distribute the same product join together. In a vertical merger, enterprises involved in successive stages of production of a product are joined together. For example, in the automobile industry the acquisition of a glass manufacturer or a steel producer by an automobile maker would be a vertical merger. A conglomerate merger exists when enterprises producing different product lines are merged. This has been the case with Litton Industries, which has product lines ranging from book publishing to missile guidance systems.

General impact of the courts upon business

The judicial system in the United States has an impact upon the conduct of business just as do the laws passed by state and national legislative bodies. The courts function to adjudicate disputes which arise between business enterprises or between business and its customers. The courts provide a mechanism for the interpretation and enforcement of contracts. The legal system constitutes a framework for the orderly transfer of property among parties, and along with the body of legislation the system provides a set of ground rules for the basic conduct of business. The courts also act to interpret those questions brought before them regarding legislation and actions taken by other governmental agencies. In this sense, the interpretation process of the U.S. courts is that of remaking or clarifying legislation passed by Congress. The Supreme Court acts as the interpreter of the U.S. Constitution in economic matters as well as in social and political areas.

The interpretations of the courts are not completely rigid. They show a degree of flexibility which varies over a period of time as constitutional interpretations reflect in part the needs of the economy in a given era. With changes in the nature and structure of the economy there have been changed legal interpretations. The same interpretations and laws which were relevant for the relatively rural economy of the past century often hinder the solution of the complex problems of the urban, manufacturing economy of this decade. Within the past 30 years interpretations of how business activities are affected by the public interest and interstate commerce have changed drastically from views prevailing at the turn of the century. Such legislation as the National Labor Relations Act of 1935 and the Civil Rights Act of 1964 would have probably been viewed quite differently by the courts in an earlier era of American economic development.

Influence upon business by the executive branch of government and administrative agencies

Along with the various legislative bodies of government and the courts system, the executive branch of government and administrative agencies have an influence on the conduct of business.

Influence of the president on business

The president of the United States exercises his influence over business in a number of ways. The president may recommend legislation to the Congress to deal with economic problems either of a national character or those which may arise in a given industry or region of the country. Although the Congress is not necessarily obliged to follow the president's recommendations, his influence with the legislative branch of government is substantial.

The president appoints top officials of various administrative agencies which directly influence and in some instances control the conduct of business. These appointments range from the president's cabinet to the commissioners of various administrative agencies. The president has direct control over his cabinet officers. However, he has only indirect control over the administrative agencies since once commissioners in these agencies are appointed customarily they are independent of the president's direct control during their term of office.

The president is able to influence public opinion toward business and other groups in society through speeches broadcast over nationwide television and radio and in press conferences. The influence of the president may be felt in bringing industry and union leaders together to press for a solution to labor disputes which threaten the nation's economy.

The president may appeal personally to business leaders to influence business decisions. Such personal appeals can be effective because businessmen are reluctant to refuse a request from such a high public official, and they also are aware of the considerable powers which he has at his command. These powers include administrative leeway under laws passed by Congress in such matters affecting business as accelerated depreciation rates and other allowable deductions for federal income taxes. In addition, the government's important purchasing agencies in the Department of Defense and the General Services Administration have a profound influence upon business in their negotiations for goods and services. The Office of the President has stand-by powers in import and export controls, stockpiling of strategic materials, and credit controls. The threat of investigations from governmental agencies concerning alleged antitrust activities, tax return irregularities, or other violations of the law constitutes another power of government over business. These investigations, whether or not the businessman is ultimately found guilty, are difficult because of the executive time and expense required in answering the government's charges.

The president may publicly put pressure on a company or an industry to take some particular action. An example of this was President Kennedy's public denunciation in 1962 of some major steel producers who attempted to raise prices. In view of the economic situation, the president said that the higher steel prices would be inflationary and therefore contrary to the public interest. At the same time the Department of Defense indicated it would buy industrial products made of steel only from those producers who did not raise prices, and the Justice Department talked of initiating antitrust studies of the steel industry. Following these actions by the Office of the President the increases in steel prices were revoked.

A dramatic example of presidential action was President Nixon's "New Economic Policy" announced on August 15, 1971, which froze wages and prices in the United States and suspended redemption of dollars held by foreigners for gold at $35 an ounce. The president's 90-day program also included a 10 percent surtax on most imported goods and requests for Congress to pass legislation eliminating the

7 percent automobile excise tax along with tax reductions for business and individuals. This three-month period was followed by a second phase of the president's economic program which had the objective of stabilizing prices, reducing unemployment, and improving the United States' international balance of payments. During this period of time government controls over the economy were increased substantially to meet what the president termed an economic emergency.

The Council of Economic Advisors

The president is assisted in economic matters by a Council of Economic Advisors which consists of three members appointed by him and approved by the Senate. These three council members are professional economists who analyze and interpret economic developments and recommend national economic policy to the president for our private enterprise system. The council was created by the Congress with the passage of the Employment Act of 1946. The purpose of the Employment Act was to state as a matter of national policy the responsibility of the federal government in assisting the private sector of the American economy to promote maximum employment, production, and purchasing power. The Employment Act also requires that early in each regular session the president must give to Congress an economic report which discusses the state of employment, production, and purchasing power in the United States along with current trends in the economy. In this report the president also reviews federal government programs and may recommend legislative action which he feels necessary to improve the state of the national economy. The act also established a Joint Committee on the Economic Report composed of members of the House of Representatives and the Senate to guide legislative thinking on economic matters.

The functioning of administrative agencies

The administrative agencies for which the president appoints policy-making officials represent an important aspect of government control over business. While there is no single type of administrative agency, usually a commission consisting of a given number of officials is determined by law and selected by the president with the consent of the legislative branch of government. The administrative agency has in various instances quasi-legislative, quasi-judicial, and quasi-executive functions. In this respect, the legislature gives up some of its policy formulating powers to the agency; the court system releases a portion of its authority in determining right and wrong; and the executive branch of government turns over a portion of its enforcement authority. These quasi-executive, quasi-legislative, and quasi-judicial agencies are becoming increasingly important in the complex pattern of business-government, labor-government, and individual-government relationships.

Examples of these administrative agencies discussed in other chapters include the National Labor Relations Board, which deals with labor-management disputes; the Securities and Exchange Commission, which deals with financial markets and protection of investors; the Board of Governors of the Federal Reserve System, which deals with national monetary and banking policy; and the Federal Trade Commission, which polices the antitrust laws. Other federal agencies include the Federal Deposit Insurance Corporation, which insures the deposits of all federal banks and state banks which want to participate up to a maximum of $20,000 for each account; the Export-Import Bank, which aids in financing trade between the United States and other nations; the Civil Aeronautics Board; the Atomic Energy Commission; the Federal Power Commission; the Small Business Administration, which handles the problems of small business at the national level; and the Interstate Commerce Commission, which regulates carriers engaged in interstate commerce. This list is by no means exhaustive of the administrative agencies functioning at the national level of government. However, it does illustrate the scope and importance of these bodies.

There has been some criticism directed toward administrative agencies because it is charged that the administrative agency exercises judicial power over its own interpretations of the law. Critics have pointed out that such agencies as the Federal Trade Commission and the Interstate Commerce Commission as well as the National Labor Relations Board act as investigators, prosecutors, and judges at the same time. These judicial functions may be exercised in disputes between the government and business enterprises or between private parties. Federal administrative agencies customarily follow basic court procedure in their judicial duties. However, generally these procedures are modified in the interest of time, simplicity, and the objective of a fair hearing to both points of view. After the testimony is taken by both sides in the dispute, investigations are carried out and final decisions are rendered. Either party to the decision may appeal the administrative agency's decision through the federal court system.

The legislative functions of such agencies customarily are to carry out the procedures and interpretations of the specific laws passed by the legislative branch of government. However, it is not unusual as new conditions become apparent for the administrative agencies to issue new orders which will extend or modify the basic legislation. This removes the necessity for continuous changes in the law by the Congress.

The investigative function of these federal agencies is important. Without the ability to do fact finding, the efficiency and purpose for which these agencies were created would be severely hampered. Therefore, sufficient staffs and budgets are required if administrative agencies are to be effective. Indeed, one of the prime means of control which the Congress has over most federal administrative agencies is through the budgetary appropriations, which are made on an annual basis.

Government as a consumer

Even though the private sector of the economy consumes the vast majority of goods and services produced in America, government constitutes an important consumer too. The magnitude of government's importance as a purchaser of goods and services over the years is illustrated in Table 2–1, which shows government expenditures for goods and services in relation to the Gross National Product, the total value of goods and services produced in the nation.

Table 2–1 is shown in constant 1958 dollars, which means that dollar amounts for each year are stated in terms of the 1958 price level. This

TABLE 2–1
Government purchases of goods and services in relation to
Gross National Product in constant dollars
(billions of 1958 dollars)

| Year | GNP | Government purchases of goods and services | | |
		Total	Federal	State and local
1940.......	$227.2	$ 36.4	$ 15.0	$21.4
1945.......	355.2	156.4	139.7	16.7
1950.......	355.3	52.8	25.3	27.5
1955.......	438.0	85.2	50.7	34.4
1960.......	487.7	94.9	51.4	43.5
1965.......	617.8	114.7	57.9	56.8
1970.......	724.3	141.8	67.7	74.1

Source: U.S. Department of Commerce, *Business Statistics, 1969,* and *Survey of Current Business,* February, 1971.

adjustment of GNP and government expenditures for price changes makes the dollar amounts from one year to another comparable in terms of real goods and services.

Government purchases of goods and services amounted to 22.6 percent of GNP in 1970. This does not include $74 billion in government transfer payments to individuals since the recipients of transfer payments rather than the government make the decisions on how these funds will be spent. *Transfer payments* consist of income received by persons for which no services are currently rendered and include payments under social security, state unemployment insurance, veterans benefits, and direct relief.

As was indicated earlier the largest portion of federal spending is for national defense. In areas such as armaments and the aerospace industry the federal government is virtually the sole purchaser of goods produced by private business enterprises. Such large corporations as McDonnell-Douglas Corporation, General Dynamics, and North American Aviation are greatly dependent upon government contracts. Corporations such as General Electric, RCA, and General Motors supply significant amounts of goods to governmental agencies. Medium-size and small business enterprises share in government spending directly and as subcontractors to prime contractors. The Apollo program, involved in putting American astronauts on the moon, used some 20,000 different business enterprises employing an estimated 300,000 workers in nearly every state in the nation.

The fact that government accounts directly for only 22.6 percent of GNP expenditures does not diminish the importance of government as a consumer. This represents a huge amount spent by a single class of consumer and is very influential in the overall functioning of the economy.

Subsidies to business

Government has acted to promote business through subsidies beginning with protective tariffs against imported goods in the early 1800s. As indicated by Table 2–2 business has received substantial direct subsidies in recent years along with government assistance to other groups in the economy.

The economic growth of this country was facilitated by the assistance of government in the development of transportation systems. This

TABLE 2–2
Subsidy programs of the federal government
(millions of dollars)

	1960	1965	1970
Business	$1,358	$1,618	$2,052
Labor	324	465	767
Agriculture	3,900	4,223	5,831
Community development	111	278	1,223
Other	114	207	400

Source: U.S. Bureau of the Census, *Statistical Abstract of the United States, 1971* (92nd ed.), Washington, D.C., 1971.

assistance included early government programs to encourage the building of roads and canals and the development of rivers and harbors. Later, in the middle part of the 19th century, the government provided substantial subsidies to the railroads to encourage the development of the rail system. These subsidies consisted of large land grants, guaranteed loans, and other forms of assistance.

Subsidies have been authorized to the ocean shipping industry for the difference in the higher cost of construction of ships in American shipyards over the cost in foreign shipyards. Certain preferences for government-financed cargoes in U.S. flagships, mail payments, and tariff benefits have all aided the ocean shipping industry.

In recent years the U.S. airline industry has benefited by subsidization beginning with mail subsidies in the 1920s, which have continued to the present. Airlines also receive government help in the form of aids to navigation and aeronautical research and development expenditures.

The trucking industry along with the general public has received the benefit of the highway system which has been built with state and federal funds.

Another form of subsidy to business has been the lower postal rates given to mail other than first-class mail. Newspapers and magazine publishers have benefited from these lower rates as well as those businesses which send their merchandise or advertising through the mails. In general the cost of carrying other than first-class mail has not been fully covered by the postal charges on second-, third-, and fourth-class mail.

Several general government aids and subsidies to business exist, including the monopoly protection given to invention and written creativity under the patent and copyright laws. The federal government is also important in the financing of research and development by industry.

As mentioned earlier, the Small Business Administration has a program for assisting small business enterprises in obtaining loans and other assistance.

Reductions in federal income taxes are available to business through accelerated depreciation allowances on new factories and equipment. The tax laws also provide for special depletion allowances which benefit the oil and mining industries. These allowances have the effect of reducing the amount of income taxes paid by companies in these industries.

Over the years the federal government has stockpiled strategic materials, including mineral products, which has provided price supports for these products.

A number of subsidy and assistance programs are available to agriculture in the United States including commodity price support programs, programs to remove surplus production from the marketplace, programs to restrict production of farm goods, and programs to assist in conservation, farm credit, technical assistance, and research.

Government ownership of business

While it has been the general practice of government in the United States to purchase goods and services from private industry, in a number of instances government owns and operates businesses. This is true at the federal, state, and local levels.

Federal business operations

The ownership of businesses by the federal government ranges from the production and sale of electric power to retail enterprises located on military reservations. In service areas such as finance and insurance the government has active agencies which directly serve private business and individual consumers.

The federal government is deeply involved in the production and sale of electric power. The Tennessee Valley Authority came into being in the 1930s and is one of the largest government hydroelectric power operations in the world. Its purpose is overall promotion of the economic and social welfare of the Tennessee River basin. In addition to the production and distribution of electricity, TVA controls floods and shipping, creates recreational areas, and encourages industrial expansion of the area. Other important hydroelectric power facilities owned and operated by the federal government include the Hoover Dam and other projects on the Colorado, Columbia, St. Lawrence, and Missouri rivers. Some of these projects are carried out in cooperation with private utility companies and local governments.

The Department of Defense operates a variety of business activities on military bases which are directly or indirectly in competition with private business. These include retail operations such as restaurants and bakeries, laundries, motion picture houses, and merchandise sold in military post exchanges and commissaries. The military not only manufactures products which either help make the military establishment self-sufficient and independent of civilian sources of supply but also manufactures products which are not produced in sufficient quantity by the private sector of the economy. However, where it is feasible the Department of Defense has generally chosen to purchase goods and services from private commercial producers.

The financial and insurance agencies of the federal government include the Social Security System, the Federal Deposit Insurance Corporation, and the Federal Savings and Loan Insurance Corporation. The Federal Home Loan banks and other agencies act to encourage the construction of residential housing, while the Rural Electrification Administration and other agencies assist in improving the economic condition of the farmer.

There are other important government-sponsored business operations. The U.S. Government Printing Office is the largest publishing house in the world. In 1971 the National Railroad Passenger Corporation (Amtrak) began the operation of railway passenger service in the United States. Also in 1971 the U.S. Postal Service, organized as an independent government agency, took over the mail service formerly provided by the Post Office Department.

State and local government business operations

Business operations are not limited to the federal government. State and local governments also own a variety of businesses, sometimes in competition with private business.

Municipalities frequently operate their own electric, water, and gas utility distribution systems. City ownership and operation of airports, harbors, and local transportation facilities are common in the United States.

A number of states operate liquor stores for the purpose of controlling the liquor traffic and for the substantial source of revenue which they contribute to state treasuries. In some areas where state liquor stores exist, private businesses may be licensed to sell beer and wine and to sell liquor by the drink but package sales of hard liquor are a state-owned monopoly.

Summary

Government has an impact on business through taxation, provision of public services, regulation, subsidization, and as a consumer of goods and services produced by business.

Income taxes are the greatest source of revenue for the federal government. Sales taxes provide the most tax dollars for the states, and property taxes provide the vast majority of tax revenues for local governmental bodies.

Important antitrust laws which affect business include the Sherman Act, the Clayton Act, the Federal Trade Commission Act, the Robinson-Patman Act, and the Wheeler-Lea Amendment. The Justice Department and the courts have been influential in determining how the antitrust laws are administered and interpreted.

The president of the United States exercises influence over business by his public statements and personal prestige, the legislation which he recommends to the Congress, and the appointments which he makes to his cabinet and the administrative agencies.

The Employment Act of 1946 placed responsibility upon the federal government to assist the private sector of the economy to promote maximum employment, production, and purchasing power. The act created the Council of Economic Advisors to assist the president in economic matters.

The various administrative agencies of government exercise quasi-executive, quasi-legislative, and quasi-judicial powers. These agencies are important in the complex pattern of business-government, labor-government, and individual-government relationships.

Government has acted to promote business through subsidies to transportation, agriculture, publishing, mining and petroleum, and other industries.

Government is an important purchaser of goods and services from private business enterprises. Federal, state, and local governments generally have chosen to purchase goods from private business rather than set up their own production facilities. In some instances, such as in electric power production and military retailing operations, the government has gone into the production of goods or services which directly or indirectly compete with private business.

Terms for review

income tax	trust
sales tax	antitrust laws
property tax	Council of Economic Advisors
deficit spending	Employment Act of 1946
monopoly	Gross National Product

Questions

1. *a*) What types of taxes are most important at the federal, state, and local levels of government?
   b) How does this tax structure help to explain the problems of financing state and local government needs?

2. *a*) What types of taxes are paid by business enterprises?
   b) Which taxes does a business enterprise have to pay whether or not it makes a profit?

3. *a*) List the services that government performs based on:
   (*1*) government expenditures for services that mainly contribute to furthering the general needs of society.
   (*2*) government expenditures for services which directly aid business.
   b) Give several examples of business enterprises which would receive direct benefits from government spending even though for most enterprises these spending programs would provide only general benefits as part of society.

4. *a*) Why is business regulated?
   b) Why were the Sherman, Clayton, and Federal Trade Commission acts passed?

5. *a*) What is the difference between horizontal, vertical, and conglomerate mergers?
   b) In what ways might these different types of mergers be contrary to the public interest?
   c) How might these different types of mergers serve the public interest in a positive way?

6. Using the *Reader's Guide to Periodical Literature* or the *Business Periodicals Index,* write a paper on the impact of President Nixon's historic economic address delivered on Sunday, August 15, 1971. The following points might be covered:

   a) List President Nixon's major economic proposals in the speech.

   b) Which of these actions could be carried out by executive order and which required action by Congress?

   c) What reactions were there to the speech by:

   (*1*) American businessmen

   (*2*) American labor leaders

   (*3*) the American public

   (*4*) professional economists

   (*5*) countries such as Canada, Japan, and those of Western Europe with which the U.S. does much trade

   (*6*) the stock market in the United States

   (*7*) the Tokyo stock market

   d) What conclusions do you draw about the power of the President of the United States in economic matters?

7. *a)* What advantages might there be for a business enterprise if a substantial proportion of its sales were made to a unit of government?

   b) What problems might be created for such a business enterprise?

8. *a)* To what extent should government promote business through subsidies or other forms of assistance, for example, guarantees for loans to individual enterprises such as Lockheed Aircraft Corporation?

   b) What guidelines would you suggest to government policy makers for such assistance to business?

9. How can the ownership of business operations by government be justified in the United States? What advantages and disadvantages come with government ownership?

BUSINESS BRIEFS

When is a corporation too big?

In August, 1971, the Justice Department required the conglomerate International Telephone & Telegraph Corporation to divest itself of acquisitions that would eliminate $1 billion of sales revenue in order to retain its new acquisition, the Hartford Fire Insurance Company with its $1 billion annual premium revenues. This government action pointed up the continuing problem for businessmen as to how antitrust laws are interpreted in determining what is "too big" in American industry.

Some businessmen want more definite government guidelines on what will be permitted in corporate mergers. One congressman has proposed a new government agency that would review every proposed merger in any field. Strict guidelines would apply to the size of enterprises involved in mergers. Opponents claim that such action would not be flexible enough to handle antitrust questions fairly. A U.S. senator indicated that the basic antitrust laws ought not be changed as long as the Justice Department can stop the mergers it feels should be prohibited. And so the controversy continues—how should it be decided when a corporation is too big?

1. Do you think that the government should spell out more precisely what will be permitted in corporate mergers?
2. What would be the advantages and disadvantages of establishing such guidelines?
3. What would be the advantages and disadvantages of having a government agency rule on every proposed corporate merger before it could be consummated?
4. What criteria should be applied to the kind of mergers that are permitted between U.S. corporations?

How should competition be measured?

Vocal consumer advocates such as Ralph Nader have contended that the only way to insure competition and thereby protect the consumer from the actions of big business is to have many small business enterprises competing in the market. Some business critics maintain that no company should have more than one eighth of a particular market and argue that the country's largest corporations should be broken up to insure more competition.

On the other hand, managements of such corporate giants as General Motors have claimed that competition now exists even in the auto industry where a few large corporations dominate the market. GM executives contend that there is much competition year after year among the auto makers to woo consumers. Each year between one third and two thirds of auto buyers change brands, which the auto industry maintains is an indication of competition.

Conglomerates pose more difficult problems when attempting to measure the degree of competition that exists. As multiproduct companies the conglomerates generally do not dominate individual markets. However, the Justice Department has been concerned that the sheer size of some conglomerates, such as International Telephone and Telegraph (IT&T) with its $1.7 billion in assets, would tend to scare away would-be competitors.

However, the managements of conglomerates such as IT&T have contended that their subsidiaries have actually stimulated competition rather than lessened it. For example, Avis auto rental, which is known for its famous "We're No. 2, We Try Harder" campaign, was acquired by IT&T in 1965. Some of the improvements at Avis, such as the use of a new device for quickly checking cars for safety and cleanliness, were developed with the aid of the optical and aerospace division of IT&T. Avis management indicated that an important factor in their race to overtake Hertz in the auto rental field was that Avis was required by IT&T to develop a sophisticated system of budgeting and planning. However, in August, 1971, IT&T agreed to give up Avis along with five other companies it had acquired in order to be allowed by the Justice Department to keep Hartford Fire Insurance Company.

Canteen was another company IT&T agreed to dispose of even though a federal district court ruled that IT&T could keep Canteen since they had actually increased competition in the food industry by applying time-and-motion studies to vending machine repairs and using computers to plan menus for Canteen.

The Justice Department's actions in 1971 against IT&T indicate to some authorities that Washington wants to keep the major conglomerates from acquiring a subsidiary that would be a leading firm in an oligopolistic industry (an industry where a few enterprises dominate the market). The legal order accepted by IT&T defined an oligopolistic industry as one where 50 percent or more of the total business is done by the top four companies in the industry. This would include most American manufacturing industries. A "leading firm" was defined as one having at least $25 million in sales volume and at least 15 percent of any market with total annual sales of $100 million or more.

1. Are more smaller producers in a given industry likely to serve the consumer better than fewer larger producers? If so, in what ways? If not, why not?
2. List possible advantages and disadvantages for the consumer in the Justice Department's attempt to prevent conglomerates from acquiring companies in oligopolistic industries.

Courtesy U.S. Steel Corporation

*New methods for reducing
environmental pollution
are of interest to
businessmen.*

3

Pollution and business

In his State of the Union message in January, 1970, President Nixon said:

The great question of the seventies is: Shall we surrender to our surroundings or shall we make our peace with nature and begin to make reparations for the damage we have done to our air, to our land and to our water?

This question voiced the concern felt by many Americans about the quality of our environment both now and for the future. With increasing population and affluence the problems of pollution are more acute than ever before. Some scientists predict that mankind has less than 40 years before disaster results from misuse of resources and overpopulation unless massive efforts are made to turn back the tide of pollution. Business is both affected by this challenge and in a position to make positive contributions to meaningful environmental improvements.

The following issues are discussed regarding environmental pollution and business.

What elements of the environment are being polluted?
What actions are being taken to control pollution?
What are the problems business faces in reducing environmental pollution?
Who will pay for pollution control?

Definition of pollution

The National Academy of Science has suggested the following definition which is relevant for our consideration:

Pollution is the undesirable change in the physical, chemical, or biological characteristics of our air, land, and water that may or will harmfully affect human life or that of other desirable species, our industrial process, living conditions, cultural assets; or that may or will waste or deteriorate our raw material resources.

A definition by the Congressional Subcommittee on Science, Research, and Development seems appropriate when considering business in relation to pollution: "Pollution is regarded as waste management gone wrong."

Increasing public awareness of pollution

One of the earlier public concerns over pollution came about in the 1940s. Citizens' indignation over the smoke blanketing their communities resulted in large cities such as St. Louis and Pittsburg leading the way in adopting antismoke ordinances. With the burning of coal with lower sulphur content, increased use of natural gas for heating, and the change from coal-burning to diesel locomotives, the smoke nuisance was substantially reduced in many urban areas.

In the 1950s the public was made aware of a new type of air pollution. This was radioactive fallout from explosions in the atmospheric testing of nuclear devices. The fallout was absorbed by plants which were eaten by cows and then showed up as strontium 90 in the teeth of children who drank the cows' milk. Such evidence contributed to the signing of the 1963 nuclear test-ban treaty on atmospheric detonations.

In the 1960s it was brought to the public's attention that water pollution resulted not only from sewage and industrial waste dumpings, but also from detergents and runoff containing fertilizers and chemical pesticides. In addition to pollution of water caused by such wastes, the ecological balance in bodies of water was found to be affected by changes in water temperature. Such thermal pollution stems from industries which use water for cooling.

The third dimension of environmental pollution is that caused by the disposal of solid wastes. As the population increased and concentrated in cities, the problems of trash collection and disposal mounted. With the increasing number of automobiles following World War II, Americans became more and more conscious of the trash which litters streets and highways. The disposal of old and wrecked automobiles became a major problem as some seven million cars are junked every year.

American public awareness of the air, water, and waste pollution of our environment reached a peak as we entered the 1970s. With the recognition that these hazards to the environment are a real threat, the federal government began programs to deal with these problems. The issues are being more clearly defined and antipollution standards established. The action phase to combat pollution, which will require substantial amounts of public and private funds, is beginning to take shape.

Systems approach to flow of matter

In dealing with the problems of pollution it is essential to recognize that when goods and services are consumed waste products are inevitable. Nothing is really destroyed but is merely changed in form. Thus, while we talk about the consumption of goods by individuals and industrial users, actually utilities are extracted from goods in the consumption process and waste materials are given off. In industry a great amount of air, water, and solid waste pollutants result from the extracting and manufacturing processes. As individual consumers we extract utilities from goods and discard the remainder whether this is an empty beer can, an old pair of shoes, or waste products from gasoline burned in our automobiles.

The production and utilization of material goods along with the wastes given off can be depicted by the system illustrated in Figure 3–1. This flow of goods illustrates how the inputs of fossil fuels, agricultural products, and minerals are processed into materials or energized before becoming outputs to final consumption or to increase industrial or consumer inventories. As goods are utilized at different stages there are outputs of pollutants which lack usefulness in their present form. However, except for items such as art objects and precious gems, all goods are ultimately cycled back into the production process or into the environment as wastes.

This flow chart suggests that the problems of pollution cannot be eliminated from our society but can be controlled better than is presently the case. This reduction in the negative dimensions of pollution can be accomplished by (1) recycling more wastes, (2) changing the form of wastes or being more creative in their disposal, and (3) producing fewer goods or different kinds of goods.

FIGURE 3–1
Systems approach to flow of matter

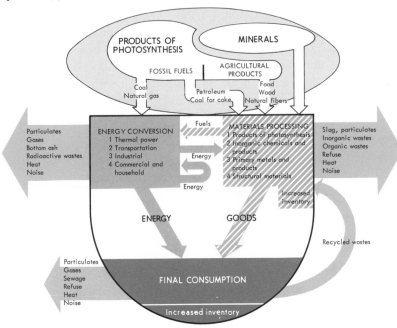

You can't get rid of matter, according to a well-known law of physics. All you can do is transform it. Modern economies, like that of the U.S., are good at taking the concentrated and transforming it into the diffuse; they are not so good at doing the opposite. It is easy to turn coal into pollutants such as fly ash, gases, and soot, but difficult—economically, if not technologically—to turn the fly ash back into, say, cinderblocks. But we have to find ways to slim down those thick pollution arrows and fatten up that skinny recycled-wastes arrow. This diagram of material flows in the economy is adapted from a concept worked out by economist Allen V. Kneese and physicist Robert U. Ayres. Intermediate goods that are neither discarded nor used go into material-processing inventory, distinct from final-consumption inventory. The "final consumption" category embraces all goods that do not require further processing or assembly, regardless of who does the consuming.

Source: Tom Cardamone Associates, Inc. for Fortune Magazine, *Fortune*, February, 1970, p. 121.

Types of pollution

Air pollution

The U.S. Council on Environmental Quality, created as part of the National Environmental Policy Act in 1969, has estimated that over

215 million tons of the five most noxious air pollutants are released into the atmosphere over the United States each year. These five pollutants are carbon monoxide, sulphur oxides, hydrocarbons, dust (particulates), and nitrogen oxides. Figure 3–2 shows the composition of the total air pollution problem and the source of the pollutants.

FIGURE 3–2
Air pollution in the United States

TYPE OF POLLUTANT

SOURCES OF AIR POLLUTANTS
PERCENT BY WEIGHT

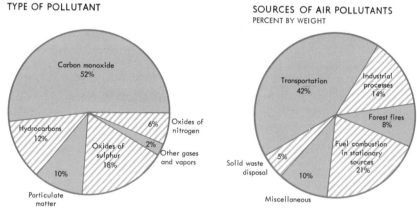

Source: National Academy of Sciences and National Air Pollution Control Administration.

Automobiles, trucks, and buses, which are powered by internal combustion engines, are the major emitters of carbon monoxide, hydrocarbons, and nitrogen oxides. Most of the sulphur oxide is produced by the generation of electric power as the result of burning the fossil fuels of coal and oil. Industrial operations cause the most dust and miscellaneous pollutants. It is evident from Figure 3–2 that motor vehicles in total represent the single largest source of air pollution. Industry and power generators together are the second largest source of air pollution. The major industries polluting the air are iron and steel, petroleum, nonferrous metals, chemicals, and pulp and paper.

Water pollution

Rivers and lakes have the natural ability to purify themselves provided they are not overloaded with wastes and provided the oxygen level needed to support beneficial bacteria which consume some pollutants is not reduced too much. Today the load placed upon our waterways from dumping of wastes by cities, industry, and governmental units such as the military has strained many waterways past the breaking point.

The composition of water pollution is very complex. At least six types of contaminants may be found in bodies of water today:

1. Phosphorus from detergents and fertilizers
2. Pesticides and herbicides used by agriculture and home gardeners
3. Bacteria and viruses contained in improperly treated sewage and other waste water
4. Trace amounts of metals from industrial waste and other sources
5. Acid from mine drainage
6. Other organic and inorganic chemicals from a variety of sources.

The degree of pollution of some inland bodies of water was dramatically illustrated in the summer of 1969 when the Cuyahoga River in the vicinity of Cleveland burst into flames, threatening two bridges. It was reported at the time that this river was so badly polluted with municipal and industrial wastes that little, if any, marine life could survive. This is not an isolated example of the degree of fresh water pollution which existed in the late 1960s and early 1970s. Scientists, for example, spoke of the "death of Lake Erie," due in part from the phosphate-based detergents which had been discharged into the lake over a long period of time.

In addition to contamination of fresh water rivers and lakes, the volume of pollutants being dumped into the oceans has caused some scientists to worry about the ability of the ocean to absorb these wastes. Evidence has been obtained that already there are areas of the Pacific Ocean off the California coast where marine life has been eliminated by pollution caused by man.

Authorities overseas are also concerned about the effects of oceanic pollution as well as pollution in their own countries. Committees within the United Nations are considering undertaking an international survey to measure the extent and degree of marine pollution. International scientists are recommending the establishment of a worldwide pollution monitoring system using such means as ships, aerial photography, and satellite observations to spot pollution sources.

As mentioned earlier, industries using large amounts of water for cooling have raised temperatures in some bodies of water to levels where life balance can be upset. In the United States electric power companies account for about 80 percent of this heat discharge. Nuclear power plants are becoming more common and do not pollute the air as fossil-fuel burning power plants do. However, nuclear power plants are a major potential thermal polluter since they use 50 percent more water for cooling than do conventional power plants.

Solid waste pollution

Overall about 4⅓ billion tons of solid wastes are disposed of in the United States annually. As Figure 3–3 indicates, almost four billion tons or over 91 percent of this volume comes from mining and agricultural operations.

FIGURE 3–3
**Sources of solid waste
(millions of tons)**

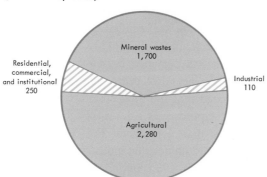

Source: Department of Health, Education and Welfare and Department of Interior.

The manner of disposition of these wastes is important. However, even more important for the individual citizen is the disposal of the 250 million tons of trash from residences, commercial enterprises, and institutional sources each year along with 110 million tons of industrial wastes, only about half of which is recycled.

Noise pollution

Although it is difficult to measure, many persons will attest to the presence of noise pollution in our society. In 1970 the amendments to the Clean Air Act included an authorization for research into noise pollution. The noise created by jet aircraft and other forms of transportation as well as industrial noise is not only disturbing but there is evidence that noise can cause fatigue and over a long period of time exposure to loud noise can damage the ability to hear.

Damages from pollution and costs of its control

It is virtually impossible to determine with any degree of precision the costs of various types of pollution in the United States. However, the nature of damages to society can be categorized as:

1. Harmful effects of pollution on humans, animals, and plants
2. Deterioration of materials in buildings and equipment
3. Extra maintenance and cleaning of objects exposed to pollution
4. Extra costs to ward off the effects of excessive pollution.

It is also difficult to estimate the cost for pollution cleanup and abatement in the United States. The actual amount will depend upon how much the results of past pollution are rectified and how strict a standard is set to reduce future contaminants.

The federal government has provided estimates of expenditures for pollution abatement over the next five years. The Council on Environmental Quality has estimated that the total cost to control industrial air pollution would be about 1 percent of sales although the cost would be higher for some industries than for others. For municipalities in 100 metropolitan areas the CEQ estimates that industries and cities will spend some $2.6 billion in the 1970–1975 period to combat air pollution.

President Nixon stated that it would take $12 billion to improve municipal sewage treatment plants through 1974. Private industry in this five-year period must spend some $3.3 billion for equipment to treat water. This figure does not include the operating and maintenance costs which will run in the millions of dollars each year. To reduce thermal pollution the Council on Environmental Quality says the cost would approximate $2 billion over the next five years. It would probably take $6 billion to control sediment and acid mine drainage. Whether or not municipalities and industries will spend as much as these estimates, it is evident that the cost will be counted in billions of dollars annually.

Actions to control pollution

A number of trends in American society suggest that environmental pollution will continue to be a major problem for action. These trends, all of which aggravate our present pollution problem, include the increasing population, more concentration of the population in urban centers, increasing industrialization, and further technological developments. Also there will be continuing increases in demand for water as well as for fossil fuels for heat and power sources. Given these trends and the magnitude of our present pollution problems, actions are being taken by government, business, and the public to control environmental contamination.

Governmental actions

Most of the early federal government studies and programs of the Department of Agriculture and the Department of the Interior were in the area of conservation of natural resources. Some research studies of environmental pollution were conducted in the 1950s and a modest program of technical and financial assistance was made available to state and local governments for such projects as municipal sewage treatment plants. However, relatively little was done by the federal government regarding environmental pollution control until the 1960s. Since pollution problems occur without respect to state and municipal boundaries, federal legislation was necessary to assure that problems of environmental quality would be dealt with and to encourage regional cooperation in solving these problems. A summary of important federal legislation in environmental improvement follows.

Rivers and Harbors Act of 1899. Although relatively little pollution control was undertaken by the federal government prior to the 1960s, Section 13 of the 1899 Rivers and Harbors Act specifically prohibited the discharge from "any ship, barge, or other floating craft of any kind, or from the shore, wharf, manufacturing establishment, or mill of any kind, any refuse matter of any kind or description whatever other than that flowing from streets and sewers and passing therefrom in a liquid state. . ." into any U.S. navigable waters or their tributaries. The legislation stated that refuse could be deposited in navigable waterways provided application was made to the federal government and that such dumping was within defined limits and under certain conditions. This early legislation has been the basis of some of the modern day attempts to control water pollution.

Clean Air Act of 1963. Federal legislation in the Clean Air Act of 1963 broadened the scope of action by government. This act authorized federal grants to state and local air pollution control agencies to establish or improve their programs. It also gave the federal government power to take action in interstate air pollution cases. Research and technical activities were expanded in programs on motor vehicle and sulphur oxide pollution. The U.S. Public Health Service was directed to study the effect of pollution on human health and property.

In 1965 and 1966 amendments were passed to the Clean Air Act which authorized the Secretary of Health, Education and Welfare to establish emission standards on new automobiles and enlarged the grants-in-aid program to other governmental units. Annual federal spending on air pollution control rose from $2 million in 1955 to $35 million in 1966. This spending increased to over $100 million in 1971.

Water Quality Act of 1965 and Clean Water Restoration Act of 1966. The Water Quality Act of 1965 and the Clean Water Restoration Act of 1966 provided for the establishment of water-quality standards and plans for their implementation. The federal government is working with state governments in such programs as improved treatment for municipal and industrial sewage. Also, local officials are being assisted in dealing with water pollution problems, especially those of an acute nature such as might occur if an oil tanker broke up near land.

Air Quality Act of 1967. The Air Quality Act of 1967 was a broad piece of legislation calling on the Department of Health, Education and Welfare to define geographic air-quality control regions and to develop criteria for air-quality standards for various pollutants in these areas. State governments were to work with federal agencies in developing and administering their own air-quality control standards. Federal funding was provided for many of these state programs along with air-quality monitoring programs undertaken in cooperation with the states. In critical situations where health is immediately and substantially endangered the government can seek a court injunction to halt the practice causing the pollution. The act also expanded the amount of money being spent on air pollution research and development programs.

National Environmental Policy Act of 1969. The National Environmental Policy Act, passed by the Congress in 1969, has been characterized as a major statement of national environmental policy in the same way that the Employment Act of 1946 was a landmark statement of national economic policy. The legislation declares it to be the continuing policy of Congress "to use all practicable means . . . to create and maintain conditions under which man and nature can exist in productive harmony and fulfill the social, economic, and other requirements of present and future generations of Americans."

Federal agencies are directed to consider the environmental effects of existing and proposed programs and to cooperate with the Council on Environmental Quality which was established by the act. The CEQ, consisting of three members reporting to the president, is responsible for studies, policy recommendations, and assistance in preparing an annual Environmental Quality Report.

In 1970 the president issued an executive order making the Council on Environmental Quality an agency with considerable powers over environmental matters instead of merely having report-study responsibilities. Power was centralized in the council to exercise authority over proposals, programs, and policies dealing with environmental problems.

To carry out the policies of the Council the Environmental Protection Agency was established. The Environmental Protection Agency has combined the programs from other federal agencies concerned with air and water pollution, pesticide usage, radiation control, and ecological research.

Water Quality Improvement Act of 1970. The Water Quality Improvement Act of 1970 provided that the operators or owners of a vessel or facility could be held liable for the cleanup costs of an oil spill unless it could be proved that it was not their fault. While there are dollar limits of several million dollars set on the liability, if the owners are found guilty of willful negligence or misconduct there is no limit to the liability charges. Provisions of this act also cover nuclear power plants, mine acid drainage, and ships and pleasure craft.

Resource Recovery Act of 1970. The Resource Recovery Act of 1970 provided a three-year authorization of several hundred million dollars annually for research programs and grants to encourage the development of innovative solid waste disposal systems. Unlike earlier federal programs the legislation emphasized the recycling and recovery of materials and energy from solid waste rather than merely disposal of the wastes.

Clean Air Amendments of 1970. The 1970 amendments to the Clean Air Act had several key provisions which were quite specific in their intent to reduce air pollution.

Standards were set for auto emissions. Model year 1975 cars must have 90 percent less carbon monoxide and hydrocarbons emissions than the 1970 models had. Also, in 1976 models the level of nitrogen oxides must be reduced by 90 percent compared with 1971 models. The legislation provided that one-year extensions may be granted to the auto industry by the administrator of the Environmental Protection Agency if the above reductions cannot be met on schedule.

This law also established controls on emissions by new stationary sources of pollution and provided new antipollution regulations for automobile fuels, aircraft engines, and aircraft fuels. The administrator of the Environmental Protection Agency was instructed to devise national air-quality standards relating to public health and welfare.

Recent government actions. From the amount of legislation put on the books in the past few years it is apparent that the government has greatly expanded its antipollution efforts. It is too early to say whether the present legislation is written so as to achieve its intent or whether its funding and administration will be adequate.

However, in 1971 a number of actions were taken by the federal government which indicate the increasing importance of environmental considerations in national policy. The Environmental Protection Agency set water temperature standards for Lake Michigan which could cost electric power utilities hundreds of millions of dollars to meet. The EPA also acted in cooperation with state and local agencies to urge compliance of business enterprises with antipollution recommendations. Government agencies delayed the development of the Alaska oil pipeline pending further studies of possible environmental damage. The president halted work on a barge canal across Florida that had drawn criticism from conservationists. And Congress denied further funding for the supersonic transport airplane partly because of its potential for pollution, especially of the upper atmosphere.

State and local laws and programs vary widely at present in their effectiveness. While some municipalities are making significant improvements in dealing with pollution problems other cities are lagging far behind. For example, in 1971 a major new sewage treatment system was put into operation in St. Louis which has reduced considerably this source of pollution of the Mississippi River. However, further downstream some cities were still dumping raw sewage into this important waterway.

Actions by business

American business because of its technology and control over economic resources has the capacity to make significant contributions to the reduction of environmental pollution. There are a number of areas relating to control of pollution at its source which are subject to research and development on the part of business. Once pollutants have been released into the environment it is difficult if not impossible to correct the situation. Therefore, air pollution must be controlled by reducing or eliminating the contaminants which are released into the atmosphere.

Auto industry technology. Automobile manufacturers such as the Ford Motor Company are working with petroleum producers to develop better methods for reducing auto exhaust emissions. Automobiles produced beginning in the late 1960s were equipped to emit fewer pollutants than earlier models. Conversion kits are on the market which enable individuals to have their older model cars adapted to produce lower levels of harmful emissions. Improvements have been made progressively through the 1972 models with further reductions in harmful exhausts planned through the 1970s. Although some analysts have suggested abandonment of the internal combustion engine in favor of electric or battery-powered cars, the present state of technology does not make this a reasonable alternative in the immediate future. Instead, most experts believe that an internal combustion engine can be designed by the 1980s which will result in a massive reduction of auto-generated pollution.

Other antipollution technology. Technological improvements are being developed in other industries. Systems are available and in use in many plants for collection of particles from air and gas in industrial processing. The four main techniques used in collecting industrial air pollution before it is thrust into the atmosphere are fabric cloth collectors, electrostatic precipitation systems, scrubbers or wet collectors, and mechanical systems.

Fabric cloth collection systems use natural or synthetic fibers such as cotton or glass fibers which are made into tubes that act as filtering devices for dust particles. This system works on the same general principle of pollution collection as the household vacuum cleaner.

Electrostatic precipitation systems operate on the principle that opposites attract. Particles in the stream of polluted air are charged negatively with electricity and are attracted to surfaces charged positively which then hold the particulate matter.

Scrubbers or wet collectors are systems which spray liquid, frequently water, through gas streams containing particulates. The spray hits the particulate solids and washes them from the gas thereby cleansing the exhaust.

Mechanical systems employ various means including centrifugal force to separate dust particles from gas and air streams.

The recognized need for better handling of environmental pollution has provided the stimulus for a whole new industry. There is a multi-billion dollar opportunity in pollution abatement which will provide jobs and investment and profit potential to an extent not anticipated fully even in the late 1960s. Enterprises presently engaged in the design and production of pollution control systems will be able to expand. Other companies will create new divisions in this field, and new enterprises will be established to meet this need.

Industry begins to clean up. Many industries are involved in the battle against pollution and are faced with the prospect of increased spending to reduce the contaminants resulting from their production processes and from their products. The electric utilities, cement, chemical, metal processing, nonferrous metals, paper and allied products, petroleum, and steel industries all have major responsibilities in the cleanup of the environment.

In 1970 according to a McGraw-Hill Survey, U.S. industries spent $1.6 billion in pollution control. Examples of what some well-known corporations are doing give an indication of the steps being taken by American industry to deal with environmental problems. DuPont, the world's largest chemical producer, spent $20 million in 1970 for antipollution equipment plus $45 million to operate and maintain it. More than 1,500 persons were involved in pollution control work. Estimated expenditures in these areas by DuPont will more than triple in the early 1970s.

In 1971 Gulf Oil Corporation spent an estimated $45 million to reduce pollution. This represented an increase of over 50 percent in antipollution expenditures over previous years.

From 1965 to 1970 General Electric spent over $20 million for air, water, solid waste, and noise pollution control. Company sources indicate that many GE plants already are able to meet the new, more rigid environmental standards. General Electric plans to spend nearly $50 million in the period from 1971 to 1975 on environmental improvement programs.

Although it will be costly for industries and for business enterprises to meet government antipollution standards, compliance also provides an opportunity for the modernization of plants which can incorporate greater productive efficiency as well as better pollution control. In some instances older factories and processing facilities will be closed down because of the cost of meeting new standards. Some of these closings in favor of new facilities will be accomplished according to plans which were already part of the enterprises' long-range expectations although the timetable may be stepped up to comply with government regulations. The financial impact of investment in control equipment will be moderated in most enterprises by the ability to charge off as depreciation the cost of this equipment as a tax-deductible expense over a period of years. Nevertheless, investments in antipollution will generally add to the costs of doing business.

Problems for business

There are a number of problems for business managers which are immediate and pressing in dealing with pollution abatement. These include the problems associated with the setting and enforcing of uniform environmental standards, the limitations of present pollution abatement technology, and the problems of recycling waste products.

Problems in setting standards. Some enterprises are reluctant to proceed too rapidly with expensive pollution control systems because government standards either are not yet sufficiently developed or are conflicting from one level of government to another. Thus, many managers are unwilling to volunteer to commit resources to corrective action unless guidelines and regulations are clear or unless the need is acute and obvious.

There has been a definite lack of uniformly applied pollution control standards both within industries and in various parts of the country. This tends to place those enterprises which have spent millions of dollars on pollution control at a disadvantage in the marketplace when competing with those firms in the same industry which have lagged on this kind of socially responsible action. Enterprises which have spent large sums for handling pollutants must either increase prices or absorb these costs in lower profit margins since pollution controls generally do not increase the efficiency of production or improve the quality of the product. Therefore, since pollution abatement equipment adds to costs but not to profits it is frequently viewed without much enthusiasm by managers who are judged largely on the calculated profitability of their operations.

The two factors discussed above indicate the need for uniform federal standards, applied on an equitable basis, so that enterprises can act in a socially responsible manner and still maintain their respective positions in the marketplace. Without a degree of uniformity across the country, the temptation exists for industry to relocate where regulations are more lenient or where they are not enforced by state or local governmental agencies.

However, there are problems in establishing quality standards relating to the environment. Because of the difficulty of defining an absolute standard, many goals for pollution reduction are of the trend type. Thus, objectives are expressed in terms of percentage reductions from present levels of pollution. For example, improvement in auto waste emissions for the 1975 models are stated as percentage reductions from the level of pollutants from 1970 models. Final standards of quality are hard to establish because of insufficient research on reliable cause-and-effect relationships between specified amounts of pollutants and the health of people under specified conditions.

Problems in developing antipollution systems.   There is no easy or simple method to correct many of the dimensions of environmental pollution present in society today. In some instances a control mechanism or solution will have wide applicability in easing the harmful effects of pollution. Thus, in some areas, such as auto emissions control, a technical development can be widely utilized. However, in dealing with pollution abatement in most factories and other industrial situations, each solution has to be somewhat unique to meet the specific circumstances and problems of the case. Because of variables such as the topography, climate, size and type of industrial equipment, population density, and causes of pollution, it is necessary in many instances that solutions be custom tailored. This makes pollution control expensive in terms of money, time, and technical resources. Furthermore, although control equipment is being improved, it is still inadequate for many situations. Scientific knowledge on pollution reduction is generally more advanced than the engineering technology either to prevent the formation of pollution or to deal with pollutants once they are in the environment.

Problems in synthetics and recycling.   Although technology can aid in abating pollution, sometimes it furthers it. Research expenditures by both government and business tend to contribute to the introduction of new materials, many of which release contaminants into the environment which have unknown effects. Modern technology has spawned the development of thousands of synthetic substances and products. In many cases it has been found that these synthetics are resistant to the natural process of decay which recycles waste products back into a form which is compatible with the environment. Industry has produced aluminum beverage cans that do not rust, radioactive wastes that continue to be toxic for centuries, and inorganic plastic products which will not decompose.

Even with increased emphasis on recycling some of these wastes back into the production process, in many instances the original products are not in a form which can be readily or economically recycled. Thus, there are metal cans that contain alloys making them uneconomic to recycle. Nonreturnable glass bottles often have a metal ring around the top which was originally part of the cap. When these bottles are salvaged the cost of removing the metal from the glass makes recycling difficult to justify economically.

Action by the public

The public collectively and individually has generally favored the concept of a national commitment to improve the environment. This is evidenced by the support of legislation at the federal, state, and local levels of government toward these ends. Conservation groups are experiencing a substantial increase in membership and public financial support. Educational programs from grade school through college are putting renewed emphasis on problems of the environment and ecological balance. Earth Day and Earth Week activities have received wide attention, particularly on the part of young people.

Lists of suggestions have been published indicating what individuals can do to improve the environment. These suggestions include numerous specific daily actions such as substituting walking for auto driving, reduced consumption of scarce natural resources, and refusal to purchase products which are ready sources of environmental contamination. Other suggestions include political and educational actions which individuals can take to fight pollution.

The public is also showing support for business enterprises whose products produce the least pollution, such as biologically degradable laundry products and returnable beverage containers. With public approval a number of municipalities and county governments in 1971 passed bills outlawing the sale of laundry products containing phosphorus, which is a prime source of water contamination.

Contrary public actions. However, Americans are not always consistent in their actions regarding environmental pollution. For years citizens of communities having industrial plants which polluted the atmosphere or waterways ignored the pollution or excused it on the basis that the factory provided jobs. When faced with the dilemma of pollution or possible closing of a factory or substantial employee layoffs, many individuals and communities have chosen pollution.

When given a free choice individuals have frequently elected not to purchase goods which would reduce environmental contamination, particularly when the immediate cost of those goods was more than competing products. For example, in 1971 the petroleum industry reported a generally poor reception to lead-free antipollution gasolines that usually were priced one or two cents a gallon above regular leaded gasoline. Automobile manufacturers indicate that although conversion kits were available to reduce air contaminants from older cars, the public is not buying these conversion kits.

Despite the general attitude favoring a clean environment, the amount of trash littering streets, beaches, and public areas indicates a lack of complete commitment on the part of citizens toward reducing this type of pollution. Strong negative reaction from individuals has greeted municipal ordinances prohibiting burning of leaves and trash to conform with state laws in order to receive financial and technical assistance in dealing with local pollution problems.

Who will pay for pollution control?

In his 1970 State of the Union Message to Congress, President Nixon devoted considerable attention to problems of pollution. In part, the president said:

We can no longer afford to consider air and water common property, free to be abused by anyone without regard to the consequences. Instead, we should now begin to treat them as scarce resources, which we are no more free to contaminate than we are free to throw garbage in our neighbor's yard. It also requires that, to the extent possible, the price of goods should be made to include the costs of producing and disposing of them without damage to the environment.

The cost to society of the environmental pollution caused in the manufacturing and ultimate disposal of goods usually has not been considered in the pricing of products. Manufacturers and processors have generally considered the waste disposal capacity of a body of water or the availability of open air to dissipate pollutants as free goods. Thus, the polluters who do not have to pay for the costs of their pollution are able to sell their goods cheaper than if they were forced to bear the extra costs of manufacturing without polluting the environment. On the other hand, a plant down the river from a major polluter may face extra costs before using needed water. This tends to raise unfairly the costs of the second manufacturer's goods.

For example, a pulp and paper mill which is free to dump its wastes into a river may have its costs understated while down river a chemical plant which incurs extra costs in purification of the polluted water tends to have the costs of its products overstated. The net result of this example would be that users of chemicals are unknowingly subsidizing the users of pulp and paper products.

Methods of encouraging pollution reduction. There are different methods for stimulating business to include the full costs of producing and disposing of their products without damage to the environment. These methods range from public pressure brought by irate citizens to tough federal enforcement of antipollution standards which may even halt production until the production process is cleaned up.

One way to discourage pollution by industrial enterprises would be to make the penalty cost of pollution more than the cost of cleaning up production processes or installing better waste disposal systems. One plan to do this proposes a system of "effluent charges" which would require industry to pay by the pound for pollutants they discharge. Such effluent charges could generate several billion dollars a year in revenue which would provide the government with more funds to combat pollution. If it were less expensive for industry to avoid pollution than to pay the effluent charges, industry would be stimulated to install antipollution systems.

To encourage the development and use of containers that would either be biologically degradable or easily and economically recycled, a container tax could be imposed based on the difficulty of recycling.

A system of incentives could also be worked out where special tax credits would be given to encourage pollution abatement. Such a solution would tend to have the public as a whole bear the cost of pollution abatement rather than the manufacturers or consumers of the particular product.

An interesting law to discourage one form of pollution was proposed in Sweden recently. This law would place a "junk tax" of up to $40 on all new automobiles. The tax would be returned to the final owner if he brought the car to a scrapping authority. The purpose of this law would be to discourage the abandonment of old cars, which is a problem in Sweden as it is in the United States.

Ultimate cost of pollution. Although business profits will be reduced in some instances, over the long run the cost of improving the environment will be borne in large measure by consumers and individual taxpayers.

Consumers will pay for reductions in industrial pollution through higher prices for goods and services. For example, because of a cost increase of one cent a gallon for unleaded gasoline, American drivers would pay approximately $700 million more for gasoline each year to reduce this source of air pollution from autos. To reduce thermal pollution of Lake Michigan has been variously estimated to cost the consumer somewhere between 3 percent and 25 percent more in his monthly electric bill.

Taxpayers will pay the cost for government programs at municipal, state, and federal levels. Most analysts indicate that even though the total spending needed for these improvements will be high, the price tag for the individual consumer will be low when compared to the benefits both now and in the future.

Summary

Many responsible persons believe that environmental pollution has reached a critical point in the United States and requires the attention of all elements of society.

The systems approach to the flow of matter suggests that pollution cannot be eliminated from society but can be controlled better than is presently the case.

Emissions from motor vehicles, power-generating sources, and industrial processes account for more than three quarters of the air pollution in the United States.

Water pollution is caused by an overburdening of the waterways beyond their capacities for self-purification. Agriculture, industry, cities and other governmental units all contribute to conditions which cause water pollution.

Although mining and agricultural operations account for most of the solid wastes produced annually, the disposition of the trash from residences, businesses, and institutions is a significant problem.

The damages caused by pollution and its costs are difficult to measure accurately. However, estimates indicate that improved control of pollution will require substantial amounts of money for years in the future.

Government legislation to control pollution includes the Clean Air Act, Water Quality Act, Air Quality Act, and the National Environmental Policy Act.

Because of its technology and economic resources, business actions to control pollution can be significant. Generally control of pollutants has to occur by reducing or eliminating contaminants before they are released into the air or water. Numerous companies are improving their products and production processes to reduce sources of industrial pollution although business faces many problems in accomplishing these objectives.

The public can help reduce environmental pollution through group programs and as responsible individual citizens.

Pollution control will be costly in terms of total dollars required. Ultimately the consumer will pay for pollution control either in higher costs of goods and services or through higher taxes. However, many persons feel that the price will be worth the benefits to society.

Terms for review

air pollution
water pollution
thermal pollution
solid waste pollution
Council on Environmental
    Quality

National Environmental Policy
    Act of 1969
Environmental Protection
    Agency
effluent charges

Questions

1. Why has environmental pollution become an important public issue?
2. What kinds of pollution constitute major problems today?
3. What solutions are there to combating environmental pollution in our society? What would be the result of effecting the solutions you suggest?
4. By examining local publications, talking to local government officials and businessmen, and by personal observation try to determine the nature of environmental pollution in your area. What actions are being taken to reduce this pollution?
5. *a)* What can business do to reduce environmental pollution?
   b) What can individuals do to reduce pollution?
   c) What responsibilities does government have in reducing pollution?
6. What are the major provisions of recent legislation to improve the quality of the environment?
7. What difficulties are there for business in trying to reduce environmental pollution immediately?

8. What *negative* immediate results might occur for individuals and communities as the result of government actions to reduce environmental pollution?

9. *a)* Who will pay for pollution control?

   b) Can we afford pollution control? Can the society afford not to have better pollution control? Explain your answers.

BUSINESS BRIEFS

Oil refinery rejected

The plans of a fuel company to build a $150 million oil refinery on the coast of Maine were rejected in the summer of 1971 by the state's Environmental Improvement Commission.

Conservationists had maintained that the refinery would threaten the state's coastline with the danger of oil spills. On the other hand, the project had been advocated by the state's Department of Economic Development because it would provide needed jobs and stimulate the area's stagnant economy. According to the supporters of the project, the refinery would have provided employment for as many as 450 people.

In rejecting the project the environmental commission indicated that the action doesn't "in any way limit future consideration of similar oil-related development in Maine." The location of the proposed refinery would have been near some of the area's most scenic coastline.

The president of the fuel corporation indicated that the decision might be appealed to the Maine Supreme Court.

1. What dilemma did the Maine Environmental Improvement Commission face in deciding the issue of whether to permit construction of the oil refinery?

2. How is it that one state agency supported this project while another state agency vetoed the project?

Weyerhaeuser company

At a time when many companies in the pulp and paper industry are being criticized for their disregard of the environment, Weyerhaeuser

Company emerges as a corporation which exemplifies ecological foresight. At the turn of the century, when many paper companies were stripping their forest holdings and selling the land for a quick profit, Weyerhaeuser showed concern in its harvesting techniques and retained most of its land. Now they have a large stock of low-cost timber which makes it possible for the company to absorb the costs of protecting the environment and still remain competitive. Weyerhaeuser is now the most profitable paper and pulp company in the industry. Over the past 25 years Weyerhaeuser has spent over $145 million on environmental improvement. In 1970 some $20 million was spent in this way. Sales in 1970 were $1.2 billion.

Years before it was required to do so Weyerhaeuser began to devise ways to minimize the pollution from its manufacturing process. Research and recycling were emphasized. Where possible, techniques to protect the environment were coupled with production savings. For example, as far back as 1939 Weyerhaeuser developed a process to recover chemicals which reduced water pollution and also produced valuable chemical by-products from pulp.

As the result of this long-range approach, when other companies in the industry are facing high costs to reduce pollution in response to public and government pressure, Weyerhaeuser has already taken many of the necessary steps. Nine of the company's ten paper mills already have a significant amount of equipment installed to reduce water pollution. In 1971 this was the best record among the large paper producers.

The company has not solved all of its pollution problems. However, it has earned a reputation as a far-sighted enterprise that seeks to act in a responsible manner.

1. What have been the benefits from Weyerhaeuser's early antipollution actions?
2. Should Weyerhaeuser be expected to do even more in environmental protection? Why or why not?
3. What can other managements learn from the example of Weyerhaeuser?

Tax the pollutants?

One of the proposed ways to deal with pollution has been to levy a use tax on those products which contribute to pollution. In July, 1971, New York City became the first to levy such a tax—two cents on plastic containers. The use tax was opposed by the plastics industry, which pointed out:

a) Plastics represent only about 3 percent of typical municipal refuse.

b) There is no tax levied on bottles or metal containers which make up a larger percent of solid wastes than do plastics.

c) There has been an overrating of the hazards of the hydrochloric acid which results from burning the polyvinyl chloride plastics (the industry's second biggest seller).

d) Although the plastics industry predicts its business will triple by the 1980s, work is progressing on techniques which will make it economically feasible to recycle plastics. This should solve the problem without the necessity of a use tax.

1. What is your opinion of the use tax as a means of controlling pollution? Explain your answer.

2. Study current magazines and newspapers to determine what is being done to control pollution, such as using effluent charges or use taxes.

CASES

Southwest Rendering Company, Inc.

On June 9, 1970, the Southwest Rendering Company submitted a report to the State Air Conservation Commission on its attempts to comply with the commission's regulations on air pollution. The rendering plant's facilities are located just outside the city limits of Springfield, Missouri, a community of 120,000. The plant has been in its present location for more than 30 years.

The rendering process basically consists of dehydrating and separating grease and protein elements in animal matter. Rendering companies convert waste products of the meat-packing and poultry-processing industries, dead animals, and restaurant greases into products which are used in both industrial and consumer markets. Tallow and grease extracted in the rendering process are used in many products, including soap, animal feeds, lubricants, cosmetics, and plastics. Protein products, including meat and bone meal and dried blood, are important nutritive additives in all types of livestock feed and pet food.

The raw materials from which grease and protein elements are extracted consist of waste fat, bones, and meat scraps from meat-packing plants, poultry-processing plants, restaurants, and food stores. These materials are picked up by the renderer's trucks on a regular route basis—generally once daily. In addition the rendering company picks up dead livestock on farms and cooperates with public officials in removing large animals which may be littering highways.

These waste products are dumped into two large hoppers (each of which has a capacity of 30,000 pounds), crushed, and ground to $\frac{1}{8}$-inch particles. These particles are continuously fed from the grinder to cooker tanks, each having a capacity of 2,000 pounds of material per hour. Here the raw materials are cooked for at least 30 minutes under steam pressure of approximately 240° F.

During the cooking process the greases are constantly drained off into settling tanks. The protein materials are pressed through a system of expellers which reduces it to a mashlike substance that is then dried and transferred to bins for storage and blending into animal and poultry feed.

Prior to 1958 the Southwest Rendering Company had been relatively isolated from the city since it was located to the north of the city limits with little other economic or residential development in the immediate vicinity. When a new high school was located nearby and a subsequent residential area was developed, the management of the plant began to get complaints about odors coming from the plant.

Until 1964 the management of Southwest Rendering adopted various means of odor control devices similar to those used throughout the industry. A deep well was used to provide cold water to run jet condensors. A hot well was added along with an afterburner to take care of gases which could not have their odors reduced without heat. Despite these attempts to reduce odors, complaints from the neighbors continued. The management then adopted an in-plant spray system using chemicals to mask the odors created in the rendering process. Although this reduced the number of complaints, citizen criticism of the rendering plant's operations continued.

In 1964, following studies made by outside engineers, the management decided to incorporate a stack dilution process with a new type continuous dry rendering system. An equipment manufacturing company was requested to design equipment utilizing the latest known technology to make the plant as odor-free as possible. During 1966 this new equipment was installed at a cost of $20,000 after delays because of problems in securing the necessary building permits.

Just before the new stack facility was started up in 1966 the rendering company's management appeared before a county grand jury for possible indictment as a public nuisance. As the result of the grand jury's investigations the company was not indicted.

Despite the installation of the new processing equipment and the stack dilution system, the company continued to receive complaints about odors. One problem was that the plant was located in a valley some 90 feet below the surrounding terrain. The gases from the rendering plant were of relatively low temperature. Thus, the plume of gases coming from the 150-foot stack did not have sufficient bouyancy to carry it high enough to dilute the odors adequately before they reached ground level.

By the spring of 1967 the company had received enough complaints to be reasonably sure that the stack was not sufficient. Therefore, in 1967 a chemical air-scrubbing system was added which treated the gases before they were blown up the stack into the open air.

In February, 1968, Southwest Rendering was approached by a burner and incinerator manufacturer who wanted to build an incinerator for the plant on an experimental basis.

By the end of May, 1969, the company's total investment in air pollution control equipment was $68,000 with an annual operating cost of $32,000 or $5 additional cost per ton of produced material. Company records indicated that 18 percent of the original equipment cost was for air pollution control equipment and 15 percent of plant operating costs were for the control of odors.

In November and December, 1969, a number of repairs and alterations were made to the plant to improve the air and odor control process. Plant officials considered the most important of these to be covers placed at strategic places over equipment to isolate gases and odors at their source to bring these fumes directly into the incinerator to destroy the odors. The cost of these changes was about $4,000.

From November, 1969, until May, 1970, management received a few odor complaints. The cause of these complaints apparently was equipment which was not functioning properly. From time to time the incinerator pilot light went out and controls did not work properly. In early May new pilot light equipment was installed and existing controls were recalibrated to operate at higher temperatures.

In the community other events were taking place. In early October, 1969, an attorney representing the local school board met with the county prosecuting attorney requesting an investigation to determine whether the rendering plant was in violation of any law. As the result of this request the prosecutor contacted the state health department requesting an investigation into the possibility of a health menace created by the plant.

In November, 1969, a report was made by a health officer of the state division of health. In summary the report indicated that the overall sanitation in and around the plant appeared to be satisfactory. There was no offensive odor at the time of the inspection. In view of his inability to uncover any diagnosed illness as the result of the odors, the health officer was unable to certify that the plant constituted a public health hazard.

Upon receiving this report the county prosecutor went to the state capitol to visit with the licensing and inspecting authority in the state veterinarian's office. Upon his return to Springfield the prosecutor quoted the state veterinarian as saying that in his opinion the plant was one of the most modern rendering plants in the United States; that the firm was not a public nuisance; and that there would be a public nuisance if the plant were closed because there was no other firm in the area to dispose of dead animal carcasses. Based on his investigation the prosecutor concluded that he had no legal basis for court action unless new evidence was uncovered.

During 1969 the Southwest Rendering Company collected over 30 million pounds of decay-prone waste for processing. Over $160,000 was paid to grocery stores, restaurants, meat packers, and poultry processing plants for the raw materials collected. Some 5,500 tons of high-energy protein and animal feed were produced by the company and sold to area feed companies to mix into livestock, poultry, and pet food. The company's sales in 1969 were approximately $2,000,000, and 46 employees were paid over $250,000 in wages.

In a letter sent with his report to the Missouri Air Conservation Commission in June, 1970, the president of Southwest Rendering Company said:

. . . [ours] is a perfect case history of what can happen to a firm when it moves ahead too rapidly in the almost nonexistent methods of controlling air pollution. We moved entirely too fast in acquiring suggested, but unproved, equipment, the expense of which placed us in a position of having costs in excess of our competition, resulting in a net operating loss. . . . [now] there is no question that we have a unique economic disadvantage in our industry. We cannot add the cost of air pollution control to the selling price of our finished product (because of competition). We must compete on an open market governed by the economic law of efficiency, or by lowering our raw product costs. In any event, we must be prepared to control our odors within the limits of what is economically possible to do.

1. What factors have increased the problem of pollution for the Southwest Rendering Company beginning in the late 1950s?

2. How responsive was the management of Southwest Rendering in dealing with these problems in the 1960s.

3. Discuss the dilemma faced by the management of the Southwest Rendering Company in operating this business in the public interest.

Union Carbide

In 1971 Union Carbide, the second largest U.S. chemical company, received much bad publicity from what was acknowledged to be a mishandling of its pollution problems. Three of its factories in Ohio and West Virginia had long been recognized as bad polluters of the air with sooty smoke and sulphur dioxide.

The 37-year-old Union Carbide factory in Alloy, West Virginia, emitted some 70,000 tons of particulates a year—more than all the particulate matter dumped on New York City by all of its industries combined. The Department of Health, Education and Welfare said that the air pollution in Alloy from the Union Carbide factory was more than four times the level that causes respiratory diseases in children and five times the level that can cause an increase in mortality in the aged and middle-aged.

After confrontations with state and federal pollution authorities Union Carbide in 1971 began moving dramatically to cut back its air pollution. In the Alloy, West Virginia plant virtually all pollution should be eliminated by 1974 at an estimated cost of $32 million. No employees are scheduled to be laid off as the result of these improvements. Another pollution control program is underway at the company's Anmoore, West Virginia plant which also will not require employee layoffs.

However, in the Marietta, Ohio plant, which has been characterized as a major polluter in the Ohio—West Virginia bi-state area, management has claimed that to meet the 1972 deadline of a 70 percent reduction in sulphur dioxide imposed by Health, Education and Welfare it would have to curtail production and lay off 500 workers of the 1,500 work force. When the Marietta plant was started 20 years ago Union Carbide was proud of some of the pollution controls it installed—particularly those to trap the fly ash. However, the plant still emitted a large amount of sulphur dioxide, primarily from the one million tons a year of high sulphur coal that Union Carbide strip mined nearby and burned to hold down costs.

About half of the Marietta, Ohio plant workers live across the river in West Virginia, a state that in 1970 had an unemployment rate above the national average and ranked fifth from the bottom in per capita income. Many of the West Virginia workers had called the black factory smoke "gold dust" because of the importance of the factory jobs and payroll. Union officials were divided over whether or not the government should give the Marietta plant an extension of time to solve the pollution problem in a way that would not require laying off workers.

Environmentalists claimed that Union Carbide could use more low-sulphur coal at Marietta and meet the government's requirements to cut sulphur dioxide pollution by 70 percent in 1972 without employee layoffs. Union Carbide claimed that low-sulphur coal was not available and even if available would greatly increase their coal costs and therefore raise overall production costs. The company had been spending some $4.5 million annually for high-sulphur coal, which amounted to 20 percent of production costs at the Marietta plant.

During this controversy much ill will was created between the company, government officials, and the local populace. Union Carbide did not have a public relations program which effectively explained what had been done to control fly ash pollution along with the high costs and technological problems in controlling the sulphur-dioxide air pollution. Instead of trying to cooperate with local people and government officials in dealing with the pollution problem, company officials had refused to give complete data on their emissions of pollutants and at one time barred federal inspectors from coming into the plant. Even though legally within their rights, Union Carbide engendered ill will by their lack of cooperation. In 1971 there was sufficient legislation on the books to enable the Department of Health, Education and Welfare to recommend and to enforce air pollution standards for companies such as Union Carbide.

Union Carbide has now made some changes in its management personnel and the management hopes to improve the situation. However, in 1971 the management still indicated that 500 workers would have to be laid off if the 1972 deadline for pollution control was not changed.

1. Should the government make exceptions to pollution control deadlines if meeting an antipollution standard means closing down a factory or laying off workers? Explain your answer.

2. What could other companies with pollution problems learn from the experience of Union Carbide?

Management of the business enterprise

*Expansion of industry is
encouraged by the
expectation of profit.*

4

The role of profits

One of the essential characteristics of the private enterprise system in the United States is the profit motive. The profit motive has been attacked by some groups in recent years as being something that is not quite legitimate in today's modern and complex society. In fact, some businessmen are apologetic about the profit motive and turn discussions on profits to other aspects of business such as the provision of goods and services for the community, providing jobs for the population, or emphasizing the community betterment programs which their firms may be supporting. Many of the attacks on the profit motive and the apologies for profits may be traced to a lack of understanding of the role of profits in our economic system.

In this chapter the following questions which deal with profit and the profit motive are discussed.

What is the profit motive?
How are profits defined?
How do risks relate to profits?
What are the functions of the profit motive?
How profitable are American corporations?

Definition of the profit motive

Both words in the phrase "profit motive" are important. *Profit* means the residual which is left after all appropriate costs have been deducted from business revenues. A *motive* is a drive, impulse, or desire that moves one to action. Thus the *profit motive* refers to the financial difference between revenues and costs as an incentive to action. The profit motive is in operation when individuals, business partnerships, or corporations are moved to some kind of economic activity because of the prospects of receipts which are greater than the expenses necessary to generate those receipts. An important implication of this definition of the profit motive is that persons are motivated to take economic action because of the prospects of *future* profits. This means that the business manager will be influenced by past profits (or losses) only as the events of the past may provide information about probable happenings in the future.

Two ways of defining profit

Businessmen and economists view profit somewhat differently. The distinction which is made between economic profits and business profits turns on a definition of the costs which are considered in the calculation of each. It is important for the student of business administration to understand both these ways of defining profit, since business profits are customarily computed by an enterprise's accounting system, while an understanding of the economist's view of profits may provide a basis for better business decisions.

Business profit is calculated by subtracting from the total receipts for the sale of a product the appropriate portion of fixed and variable costs. Fixed costs include expenses—such as rent, executive salaries, minimum utilities, property taxes, and interest on borrowed money— which continue whether or not the enterprise is producing goods. Variable costs include materials and wages for production workers, which are directly influenced by the number of units produced. In general the costs, which are deducted from sales revenues to determine business profits, cover allocations made to provide for returns to all factors of production except the owners of the business enterprise. What is left after the deduction of all "outsiders" costs represents *business profit* and accrues to the owners of the enterprise, whether it is a corporation, partnership, or sole proprietorship. As is discussed in Chapter 14 on accounting, the business profit figure is the bottom line on the accounting report called the Income Statement and is labeled as net income, net profit, or profit after taxes if the figure is positive. If the total of fixed and variable costs exceeds income, the figure is negative and represents a business loss.

Economists accept the businessman's cost calculations for economic factors provided by outsiders, but take an additional important cost element into consideration, that of opportunity cost. *Opportunity cost* is an important economic concept and represents the cost assumed when a person or business enterprise forgoes the alternative of making some other use of his economic assets. There are various ways in which economic assets may be employed. When a person elects to invest his money in a particular business enterprise he gives up the opportunity of investing these funds in any other business, at least for the time being. The opportunity cost for these funds would be considered to be what they could earn employed in some other manner, perhaps by putting the money into a savings account in a bank. This opportunity cost, say 5 percent per year, would be one of the elements to be subtracted from business profits to obtain an economic profit figure.

Consider another type of opportunity cost. Suppose a person works in his store, organized as a proprietorship, and calculates a business profit of $15,000 for a particular year. In the proprietorship form of legal organization the owner's work efforts are not considered a business cost, and net profit does not include any deduction for the owner's labor. The opportunity cost of the owner's labor should be deducted from business profits to determine economic profit. If the owner could be employed in another business enterprise for an annual salary of $10,000, this amount should be subtracted from his profit figures if the concept of economic profit is being employed. If the owner had $25,000 of his own money invested in the business enterprise we might assume an alternative cost of 5 percent (in line with the savings account example mentioned above) or $1,250 per year. This would result in a calculation of economic profit as follows:

Profit from accounting system (business profit)		$15,000
Less opportunity costs:		
Alternative salary cost	$10,000	
Imputed interest cost	1,250	11,250
Economic profit		$ 3,750

Consideration of the concept of economic profit may be valuable to the businessman in the selection of projects for the investment of funds. This means that a businessman should carefully appraise the full range of investment alternatives open to him before committing money to a particular project. The question "Is this the best opportunity available to me for the investment of money and effort?" can be a valuable check before projects are undertaken to determine whether profit prospects are consistent with the amount of risk the businessman is willing to assume.

Also, for the businessman who is operating at relatively low levels of business profit over a considerable period of time, the consideration of the concept of economic profit may reveal an economic loss in operations after deductions are made for his efforts and the imputed return to the funds he has invested in the business. This is an especially relevant point for the small business operated as a proprietorship or for the farmer who may be making a very small return on his investment not counting any cost for the many hours of labor he puts into running the farm. To be sure, there are noneconomic incentives which cause individuals to continue in business operations which yield little or no economic profit over a period of time. However, such a businessman should at least be aware of the cost which he is paying for continuing his small business or the particular type of farming operation. If he wished to make an economic profit and still remain in basically the same kind of enterprise, he might consider some alternatives like a different line of merchandise, or another type of small business operation, or switching from dairy farming to beef cattle farming or hog raising. Such alternatives might preserve the business operation and put it on a sounder economic basis.

A logical question at this point would be "Why is the concept of business profits so widespread, and why shouldn't all enterprises switch to some sort of calculation of economic profit?" Although consideration of the concept of economic profit may be helpful to the businessman in analyzing his operations, there are persuasive reasons for retaining the concept of business profits too. In the first place, there are significant conceptual problems involved in the application of economic profits to a single business enterprise. On what basis would the individual determine how much his labors were worth in another business enterprise? He might have a firm offer of employment in another enterprise, but this would be the situation only in a very limited number of cases. To change his place of employment might mean severe personal adjustments which would not be worth the economic benefits that might be gained. In most cases there would be no reliable basis for determining an alternative price to place upon his work efforts. The same problem arises when the concept of alternative or opportunity costs is applied to the money a proprietor has invested in his business enterprise. Should the alternative calculation be in a type of investment in the same risk class as his present business operation; or should the calculation be made on the basis of an investment in government bonds or an insured savings account, both of which may yield less than his present investment but would also have much less risk?

The practical problem of comparability of the accounting statements of one business enterprise with another would be greatly magnified if business profits were abandoned in favor of economic profit. Our entire system of financial analysis, tax reporting and collection, investment analysis, and industry comparison is based on conventional accounting systems.

From the preceding discussion it is apparent that there is a substantial difference between the businessman's concept of profits as expressed in the conventional accounting statements and the economist's view of profits. This does not mean that one view of profits is right and the other is wrong. What it demonstrates is that different groups may come to substantially different conclusions regarding business because of the different frame of reference they use in defining terms which may have the same name. Students should be aware of the different ways that business phenomena are viewed and be able to determine which definition is appropriate to the circumstances under discussion and which analysis should be used. Henceforth in this book whenever the term "profit" is used it will be applied as the concept of business profit. When the concept of economic profit is involved in the discussion it will be labeled as such.

While the profit motive implies that people are stimulated to undertake economic activity because of the expectation of profit, in a private enterprise society generally there is no guarantee that profits will result from a given enterprise activity. When a private business enterprise undertakes operations that result in greater costs than revenues, the company operates at a loss. Although an enterprise may be able to operate at a loss for some time before being forced out of business, over the long run the private business enterprise must generate some profits in order to survive. Thus, while the profit motive may stimulate economic activity by business, the possibility of loss also exists. Because of this risk of loss which the businessman must bear, the private enterprise system is often referred to as a *profit and loss system.*

Business risks

The profit motive causes businessmen to assume the risks inherent in the production and distribution of goods and services in a private enterprise economy. Among the many risks involved in the operation of a business enterprise are the six illustrated in Figure 4–1.

FIGURE 4–1
Types of risks faced by business enterprises

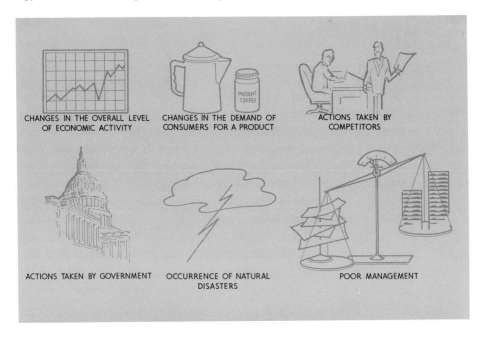

Risk due to changes in overall economic activity

In our country there are fluctuations in the level of economic activity which are characteristic of industrialized economies. The fluctuations in business activity affect both individuals and organizations in our economy and are of concern to government because of their impact on orderly economic growth. The business manager is interested in business fluctuations because of the way in which his operations are influenced and because of their impact on profitability.

Economists have identified three types of fluctuations in economic activity. These are the trend, seasonal changes, and business cycles.

The trend. The *trend* is the underlying long-run tendency which persists despite shorter term changes. In the United States the trend in overall economic activity has been upward at a rate of about 3 percent per year in real growth of goods and services. This upward trend is due to many factors, including the development of a new continent, natural resources, increases in population, increases in the stock of capital goods, improved productivity of labor, better management, and continuing technological development.

Seasonal changes. *Seasonal changes* are due to the changing seasons of the year or to holidays or the calendar. Certain agricultural products are available for processing only at particular times of the year. Both manufacturing and retailing enterprises are profoundly affected by sales demand arising out of the Christmas holiday period and the Easter season. Extra shopping days falling in a month due to variations in our calendar and the timing of paydays by business enterprises also contribute to seasonal changes in economic activity.

Business cycles. The effect of the trend and seasonal fluctuations in economic activity is overshadowed in the short run by the recurring expansion and contraction of the level of business activity. These recurring variations are called *business cycles.* Starting from a low in cyclical business activity called a *trough* in the business cycle, the generation of demand for goods and services from a relatively low level causes business to expand production. Although numerous factors may account for expansion of production, increased government expenditures either on domestic programs or in defense activity have sometimes proved to be the stimulus to increase demand for goods and services.

As production expands, earning power improves, and the economy moves into a period of "recovery" or "expansion." As some industries show improved business conditions this spreads to other industries, and the expansion continues until a *peak* in business activity is reached. The peak is followed by a decline in business activity called a "recession" or "contraction." The factors which contribute to a peaking of economic activity and the subsequent decline include reduced spending by business for capital equipment because of the belief that profit prospects are poor, excessive inventories built up during the expansion phase of the business cycle which when cut back reduce demand for production, and changing patterns of consumption. Recessions have also occurred in the adjustment of the economy following some of the wars in which the United States fought. Should a recession become pronounced and prolonged it is called a depression. Figure 4–2 illustrates the overall growth of the Gross National Product, which is the sum total of goods

FIGURE 4–2

Gross National Product in constant dollars and average growth rate

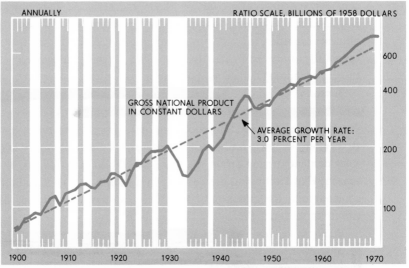

Source: Federal Reserve System, *Historical Chart Book.*

and services produced in the economy. The trend line shows a 3.0 per-cent growth rate. Periods of recession in business activity are indicated in white on the chart.

Business cycles have been the subject of extensive study. A number of explanations have been advanced as to the cause of business cycles. Theories as to causative factors include such widely ranging ideas as the cost and amount of credit available; changes in consumption, saving, and investment patterns; whether there are innovations, such as the invention of the automobile or the discovery of plastic which create opportunities for further investment; and the prevailing psychological climate—whether business or consumers tend to be generally optimistic or pessimistic about the future. Many economists think that business cycles are caused by a number of these factors interacting, with no single explanation being sufficient for the complex nature of the problem.

The National Bureau of Economic Research, a private nonprofit research organization, has identified several economic indicators which normally tend to either lead, lag, or coincide with the general level of economic activity. Examples of the leading series are:

Average hours worked per week by employees in manufacturing.

New orders for durable goods industries.

New building permits for private housing.
Corporate profits after taxes.
Changes in business inventories.

Examples of the economic indicators which tend to coincide with the business cycle are:

Employment in nonagricultural enterprises.
Index of industrial production.
Level of Gross National Product.
Sales of retail stores.

Examples of the economic indicators which tend to lag or follow the business cycle are:

Business expenditures for new plants and equipment.
Wage and salary cost per unit of output in manufacturing.
Bank interest rates on short-term business loans.

Despite the complexity of business cycles and forecasting their fluctuation, businessmen should attempt to anticipate fluctuations in the overall level of economic activity and make applications to their own industries and enterprises. Considerable help is available from private sources such as trade associations and from federal government agencies which employ a large staff of economists to measure the current state of the economy and attempt to forecast its direction of movement.

Risk due to changes in consumer demand

The businessman must also concern himself with the market demand for his individual product. Even though his product is as good or better than his competitors, there is no guarantee that he will make a profit. There may be a shift in consumer demand away from the entire industry. Look what the development of the automobile did to the sale of buggy whips!

Actions taken by competitors

The businessman must be aware of what his competitors are doing, as well as having close knowledge of his own operations. Profits are threatened whenever new products are brought onto the market by competitors or whenever they take any of a variety of actions ranging from lowering the price of their goods to lengthening the credit terms extended to customers.

Actions taken by government

Actions taken by governmental bodies may substantially affect the profit of business enterprise. Such governmental activities range from the restriction by a city council on a manufacturer's dumping of waste products into a steam, to a U.S. Justice Department move to block a merger between two firms which threatens to reduce competition in a particular industry.

Natural disasters

The impact on enterprise profits of some natural disasters, such as fire, hail, and wind damage, can be minimized by taking out insurance, but it is not possible to eliminate all such risks. The business enterprise which has its main plants located along a large river that periodically floods will likely find that the cost of flood protection through insurance will be extremely expensive if it is available at all. Also, it is almost impossible to measure the impact on business profits of a natural disaster in terms of the opportunity to operate normally had the event not occurred.

Poor management

Last, but not least in importance of the risks faced by business, is the possibility of financial loss because of poor management of the business enterprise. While big business is not immune to poor management, the small business enterprise is especially vulnerable to this risk. Problems of morale, organization, and communication are often found in the small business. One of the most common problems of small businesses is that frequently they are too small to obtain the kind of management skills which they need. The top jobs in small and medium-size business enterprises may require as much competence and greater versatility than corresponding positions in big business. The small business enterprise is faced with a lack of financial resources to hire competent management, and generally there are fewer managers available in the small firm for specialized decisions in the different types of business problems. Sometimes the business is family-owned and the best jobs go to family members regardless of their qualifications. This tends to discourage good men from accepting employment in the small-scale business enterprise. Too often the small business manager is not willing to subject his decisions to the outside advice and counsel which is usual for the top management of large-scale business enterprise.

Willingness of businessmen to bear risks

With this long list of risks that could result in losses, one may doubt that people are willing to invest any money in business enterprises. However, Americans show a surprising willingness to bear risk. The degree of risk investors are willing to bear depends on profit expectations. Normally, additional risks will be assumed only if there is a fair chance to earn very high profits. Some industries are quite stable and subject to very little risk, while others are speculative in nature. An example of a stable industry is that of public utilities. Although there has been an upward trend in profits for utilities, because of the nature of demand for their services and the controls exercised by governmental regulatory bodies there is relatively little risk involved. On the other hand, the "wildcat" oil drilling operator is subject to great risk and wide variations in his profit potential. The possibilities of his operations range from the dry hole which means a complete loss of money invested in the drilling operation to the gusher which will return substantial profits.

Why does one man invest in utility stocks whereas another invests his last dollar in a drilling company which may bring fame and fortune or bitter disappointment? The difference is in the subjective values which each of these men places upon risk bearing. The former wants security, and the latter's slogan is "nothing ventured, nothing gained." Neither investor is right or wrong about his willingness to accept risk. They merely express different preferences, and both are needed to provide the wide variety of investments required in our complex private enterprise system.

Business failures

Although profit is an important goal and motivating force behind business activities, not all enterprises succeed in making a profit. If a business does not earn a profit over a protracted period of time it is likely to go bankrupt. How long it will take for an enterprise to fail when it does not operate profitably depends upon a number of factors including the financial strength of the enterprise, the amount of loss each year, the availability of credit, and the expectations for improved conditions.

The rate of business failures for each 10,000 concerns in operation is shown in Figure 4–3. Failure declined from a high in 1939 of 70 per year for each 10,000 enterprises to a low in 1945 of 4. Following this extremely low point at the end of World War II, the failure rate has shown an irregular increase to a 1961 high of 64, with 44 failures per 10,000 enterprises in 1970.

FIGURE 4–3
Business failure rates, 1939–1970

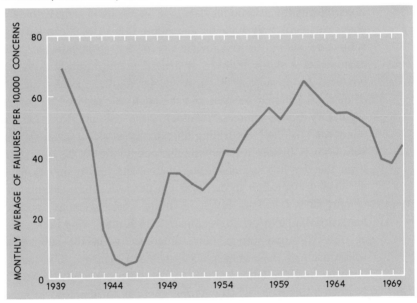

Source: U.S. Department of Commerce, *Business Statistics,* 1969 ed., and *Survey of Current Business,* April, 1971.

Characteristics of failing enterprises. Of the business enterprises that fail typically more than 75 percent owe less than $100,000 at the time of failure. This indicates that a high proportion of the enterprises that fail are small businesses. Many of these failures are new companies since the majority of failures occur in enterprises which are no more than five years old. Dun & Bradstreet, an enterprise specializing in the analysis and rating of business credit standing, has reported that failure rates in small-scale type retailing stores are generally above average.

In recent years failures in women's ready-to-wear, furniture and furnishings, gift shops, books and stationery, and cameras and photographic supplies have been above the national average.[1]

The chief cause of business failure could be summarized as inept management. The Dun & Bradstreet study just cited indicates that nearly 90 percent of the causes of business failure could be classified under the general heading of poor management. These included inadequate sales, heavy operating expenses, and competitive weakness. This evidence emphasizes the importance of effective management of the business enterprise, especially in its early years.

Use of economic resources. In the private enterprise system it is important that businesses have the freedom to make a profit, but it is also necessary that inefficient enterprises fail. The business enterprise that fails does so because it is not as efficient in meeting the needs of consumers as someone else is. The economic resources which previously were used by enterprises that fail flow to the successful enterprises in the economy to be employed in such a manner as to make a profit. The profit motive gives an incentive to produce goods and services at a competitive price and quality. Thus the profit motive results in an efficient utilization of resources to provide those goods and services which consumers desire to purchase.

Functions of the profit motive

There are three important functions which the profit motive fulfills in the private enterprise system. These are the allocation of economic resources to those goods and services which are most desired by consumers, stimulation of the economy to greater levels of production and consumption, and the provision of an important criterion for choosing among various investment opportunities.

The profit motive and allocation of resources

In any society the supply of goods and services is limited over the short run. This means that not all material wants can be satisfied. At any given time there is just so much capacity for producing steel, assembling automobiles, processing food, or generating electric power.

---

[1] *The Failure Record through 1969* (New York: Dun & Bradstreet, Inc., 1970), p. 5.

How are resources allocated among various alternative uses in the economy? How do businessmen determine whether to produce automobiles, or tractors, or motorcycles? In the private enterprise system in the United States the allocation of the economy's resources is accomplished in large measure by the expectations of profits on the part of those who control productive goods. A manufacturer produces rear-engine automobiles with bucket seats and automatic transmissions because he believes they can be sold at a profit. If the manufacturer correctly assesses the wants of the consuming public, there will be a demand for this type of product which can then be satisfied by the particular automobile being produced. Basically, goods and services are provided by enterprises in response to consumer demand, though sometimes consumer demand can be influenced or stimulated through sales promotion programs.

The result of each producer attempting to market goods and services with the expectation of profit will theoretically be the allocation of resources to those lines of goods which are most desired by the society. The general proposition that the profit motive results in allocation of goods throughout the economy on the basis of most desired needs is based on several assumptions: that producers are able to move freely into and out of markets, that a state of competition exists among sellers, and that buyers have full knowledge of competing products. However, in the reality of today's complex society these conditions are seldom, if ever, met. Because of large investment and the need for skilled workers and technological know-how, it is not possible to enter or leave many business operations with ease. The steel mill with its large investment in plant and equipment, skilled work force, and research laboratories dealing with highly technical problems is a good example of a type of business enterprise which cannot be established quickly even though the stimulant of profit prospects exists. Likewise, once an entrepreneur, along with many others, has committed himself to an investment in a steel mill it is difficult to quit the steel business, liquidate the assets of the firm, and move the capital to some other type of enterprise.

There are still some enterprises, such as the dry-cleaning business, which offer greater ease of entry and exit. Unlike the steel mill, dry cleaning does not require as much capital, as many skilled workers, or such a diversity of technological know-how. Furthermore, entry is facilitated since manufacturers of dry-cleaning equipment are generally willing to finance the necessary machinery, provide managerial assistance in setting up the business, and aid in determining a good shop location. If the business does not develop into a profitable operation, a market exists for the used equipment, and the entrepreneur is often able to withdraw from the dry-cleaning business with a minimum loss of his capital. Generally the larger and more complex the business enterprise, the greater the difficulty of entry and exit. The service enterprise and small retailing establishment provide for greater ease of entry into and exit from the marketplace.

There are other limitations to the proposition that the profit motive results in the allocation of economic resources as desired by consumers. A business enterprise may gain control of the production of some product. This control over the supply side of the market by one producer is called a *monopoly*. With monopoly control the producer may set prices higher than might otherwise be the case when there are many suppliers competing to meet the demand for a particular product. Under these circumstances the higher profit which results from this control is called *monopoly profit*. As was pointed out in Chapter 2, in order to protect the public against excessive monopoly power on the part of business the Congress has enacted legislation to control the growth and actions of monopolists. The general intent of Congress has been to prohibit restraint of trade, unregulated monopolies, unjustified price competition, unfair competition, and generally to protect the public's interest in the marketplace.

In addition to the possibility of monopoly influence, there are other factors which influence the allocation of resources in the economy. These include government controls, especially in time of national emergency; geographic limitations on both producers and consumers; traditional preferences and attitudes toward goods, such as consumer allegiance to brand names; and such artificial barriers as state fair trade laws which require the sale of certain goods at retail prices set by the manufacturer.

Despite these factors which complicate the assumption that the profit motive results in the allocation of economic resources to goods and services most desired by consumers, when profits occur this is still a good sign that the society wants a particular industry to expand. When an industry or a firm within an industry does not make a profit and suffers losses, this is often a signal that consumers are not anxious to have more resources devoted to this purpose. The absence of profits for a year or so is not necessarily proof that the resources of that enterprise should be changed to some other type of operation since profits or losses are dependent on many factors. However, when a business enterprise suffers losses, this is a sign for the management to investigate the cause of the loss with an eye to the possibility of allocating future capital expenditures to other fields where the expectation of profits is greater.

The profit motive and increased production of goods and services

Because of the expectation of profits, the entrepreneur is stimulated to invest resources in business enterprises. The mobilization of resources on the part of the entrepreneur sets off a chain reaction throughout the economy whereby demands for other goods and services are stimulated by utilizing the human and material resources of the economy more fully. As the goods or services which are produced by the business enterprise are purchased by consumers, consumption needs are being met. The production of these goods provides employment for more workers and a higher level of personal income. As the result of increased income, individuals are able to consume more goods and services which in turn stimulates the demand for additional production. Buildings are purchased or rented and the proceeds from these rents can be spent by landlords. Machinery is purchased from other manufacturers who employ workers and capital resources. All of this activity stemming from the enterprise's investment based on the expectation of profits tends to stimulate the economy.

Profits may accrue as the result of the entrepreneur providing some new product or significant improvement or greater variety of an old product. Under these circumstances profit is a reward for venturing out and providing a new good or service or improvement in existing goods and services. The entrepreneur's ventures do not succeed in every case. Frequently a new business enterprise will lose money instead of making a profit, but the profit motive encourages men to go ahead with other innovations to meet the consumer's basic and ever-changing acquired needs.

The profit motive and choice of investment alternatives

The profit motive provides a criterion for the businessman in determining which investment projects he will select from the variety of alternatives facing him. The rate of profit expected on a project in relation to risk may be the key factor in deciding which piece of machinery to purchase, whether to build a new factory, or how to market a new product. Since it is unlikely that enough funds will be available for all investment possibilities, some screening device must be adopted to establish project priorities. The rate of expected profit on each project is an excellent criterion for investment suitability.

The simplest way of measuring profitability is to calculate the percent of profit in relation to the asset value of the investment. Thus if profits on a piece of machinery were anticipated at a level of $3,000 annually and the machine cost $15,000 including installation, the expected return on this investment would be 20 percent.

Profitability of American corporations

Critics of the American private enterprise system often say that profits earned by corporations are too high. Let us examine some of the data which are available to determine the magnitude of corporate profits.

Table 4–1 shows the ratio of profits to sales for all manufacturing corporations in the United States and for selected industries for 1966 and 1970. Profits in 1966 were at a historical high in absolute dollars

TABLE 4–1
Manufacturing corporations profits as a percentage of sales, 1966 and 1970, before and after federal income taxes

	1966		1970	
	Before taxes (percent)	After taxes (percent)	Before taxes (percent)	After taxes (percent)
All manufacturing corporations	9.3	5.6	6.8	4.0
Petroleum refining	13.1	11.2	11.1	9.3
Drugs	19.7	10.8	17.2	9.4
Instruments	17.3	9.5	13.7	7.3
Basic chemicals	13.6	8.0	8.5	5.0
Motor vehicles and equipment	10.7	6.2	3.5	2.4
Tobacco manufactures	11.1	5.9	11.1	5.8
Iron and steel	9.8	5.8	3.5	2.5
Electrical machinery	9.0	4.8	6.1	3.3
Furniture and fixtures	6.8	3.9	4.9	2.5
Leather and leather products	5.4	3.0	4.8	2.5
Aircraft and parts	5.5	3.0	3.5	2.0
Food and kindred products	4.8	2.7	4.8	2.5
Apparel and related products	4.1	2.4	3.7	1.9

Source: Federal Trade Commission and Securities and Exchange Commission.

and the highest as a percentage of sales since 1950. The year 1970 was a year of recession with a lower level of profits.

Table 4–1 indicates that the profit percentage on sales for all manufacturing corporations in 1966 was 5.6 percent after taxes and 4.0 percent after taxes in 1970. The highest return on sales was in the petroleum refining, drugs, and instruments industries. Several industries earned 3 percent or less on sales after taxes in both years.

Another way of measuring profits is the ratio of profits to the owners' equity. This is the measure of profitability on the invested capital of corporation stockholders. Table 4–2 shows the ratio of profits to owners' equity for all manufacturing corporations in the United States and for selected industries in 1966 and 1970.

TABLE 4–2
Manufacturing corporations profits as a percentage of owners' equity, 1966 and 1970, before and after federal income taxes

	1966		1970	
	Before taxes (percent)	After taxes (percent)	Before taxes (percent)	After taxes (percent)
All manufacturing corporations	22.5	13.4	15.7	9.3
Instruments	38.1	20.9	26.6	14.2
Drugs	37.0	20.3	32.4	17.6
Motor vehicles and equipment	28.9	15.9	9.2	6.1
Electrical machinery	27.4	14.8	16.6	9.1
Aircraft and parts	26.4	14.4	12.0	6.8
Furniture and fixtures	25.1	14.2	15.8	7.9
Tobacco manufacturers	26.3	14.1	30.3	15.7
Basic chemicals	23.7	14.0	14.6	8.5
Apparel and related products	22.8	13.3	18.0	9.3
Leather and leather products	22.8	12.9	17.9	9.4
Petroleum refining	14.5	12.4	13.0	11.0
Food and kindred products	19.9	11.2	20.4	10.8
Iron and steel	17.4	10.2	6.2	4.3

Source: Federal Trade Commission and Securities and Exchange Commission.

In periods of recession, business profits are reduced as Tables 4–1 and 4–2 indicate. Pressure from competing business enterprises, labor unions, and government tax policies also tend to reduce unusually high profits. Historically, business profits have been unstable although trending upward. This is illustrated by Figure 4–4, which shows corporate

FIGURE 4–4
Corporate profits, income taxes, and dividends, 1929–1970

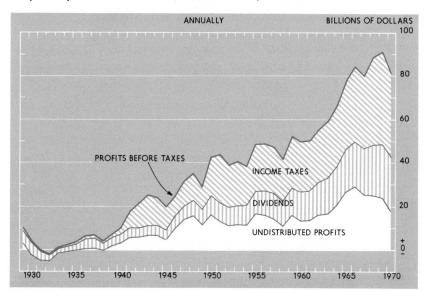

ANNUALLY   BILLIONS OF DOLLARS

PROFITS BEFORE TAXES

INCOME TAXES

DIVIDENDS

UNDISTRIBUTED PROFITS

Source: Federal Reserve System, *Historical Chart Book.*

profits before taxes, income taxes, dividends (profits paid to stock-holders), and undistributed profits (profits retained by the business enterprise) from 1929 through 1970.

Any statement about the level of profits being good or bad represents a value judgment on the part of the person making the statement. How many of you would be willing to go into business, assume the risks of investing your own money and managing the enterprise, and then have a return on your investment of much less than those shown? It may be that the critics of the profit (and loss) system are focusing on individual cases of excesses or abuses and not on the overall level of profits.

What about profit maximization?

Business enterprises seldom attempt to maximize profits at the expense of all other elements of business management. Producing a product of shoddy quality to be sold at a premium quality price may succeed for a period of time until consumers become aware of the inconsistency. However, this enterprise's share of the market is likely to be damaged when the product's shortcomings are discovered, and this will result in lower sales and perhaps substantial losses to the manufacturer. The best managed enterprises take a long-run view of profit potential.

There is not only the question as to whether a realistic objective of today's business enterprise is to *maximize* profits, especially over a short period of time, but there is the further question of whether the business manager is able to determine at just what point profits are being maximized. Although economists can describe the theoretical conditions under which profits will be maximized, it is very difficult for the businessman to determine this in his own business operations.

Even though businessmen may not be able to determine the point at which their operations return maximum profits, and few would probably choose to do so over the short run if they could, this has not reduced the importance of the profit motive to business. Critics of profits and the profit motive point to the increasing number of statements from top business executives of large corporations about the importance of business's social responsibility to the community and cite the increased financial support by business to charitable, educational, and welfare institutions. However, such support comes from business enterprises which are operating profitably and where the rate of return on the owner's investment is satisfactory considering the degree of risk involved. A satisfactory level of profits may be defined as profits which are high enough to attract capital investment in sufficient quantity to provide the level of goods and services desired by the consuming public.

Profit is an essential element of the private enterprise system where capital is privately owned and controlled. Just as individuals do not always act only as economic beings, so are business enterprises which are managed by humans not always operated strictly on a dollar profit basis. However, the expectation of profit represents the carrot of incentive to stimulate individuals and enterprises to invest money in projects that will produce goods and services desired by consumers.

Summary

One of the essential characteristics of the private enterprise system is the profit motive which moves individuals and business enterprises to undertake economic activity because of the prospects of receipts which are greater than the expenses necessary to generate the receipts. Business profits are calculated by subtracting appropriate fixed and variable costs from the total sales receipts of an enterprise. The difference between the revenues and attendant costs is the profit.

Economic profit is the concept of profit which deducts opportunity costs from business profit to take account of alternative uses of material or human resources used in a business.

Although the businessman seeks a profit from enterprise operations, there are a variety of risks which may result in losses. Business risks include changes in the overall level of economic activity, changes in consumer demand, actions taken by competitors, actions taken by government, natural disasters, and poor management.

A business enterprise can be expected to fail if it does not earn a profit over a long period of time. When an enterprise fails, the capital resources which were used by it flow to enterprises which appear to have better prospects for profitable utilization.

Thus, the profit motive serves to allocate economic resources to those goods and services which are most desired by consumers. It stimulates the economy to greater levels of production and consumption and provides an important criterion for choosing among various investment opportunities.

Two ways of calculating profits are to determine the ratio of profit after taxes to sales and the ratio of profit after taxes to owners' equity.

Most enterprises do not attempt to maximize profits in the short run because it is difficult to determine the operational point at which profit is being maximized and because businesses may have other goals which tend to negate the pursuit solely of profit. Most owners and managers do seek a satisfactory level of profits, which may be defined as profits high enough to attract capital investment in sufficient quantity to provide the level of goods and services desired by the consuming public.

Terms for review

profit
profit motive
business profit
opportunity cost
economic profit
trend

seasonal changes
business cycle
economic indicators
monopoly profit
ratio of profits to sales
ratio of profits to owners' equity

Questions

1. What is business profit? How is it determined?

2. How does the concept of economic profit differ from business profit?

3. Are all types of business enterprises equally subject to the various kinds of business risks? Give specific examples to explain your answer.

4. By checking publications such as *Business Conditions Digest* (published by the Commerce Department), *Survey of Current Business,* or the *Federal Reserve Bulletin,* determine the status of the economic indicators outlined in this chapter and the present state of the business cycle.

5. *a)* Why do business enterprises fail?

   b) Do you agree with the statement "It is necessary that inefficient enterprises fail"? State the reasons for your answer.

6. How may the profit motive serve the public interest?

7. *a)* What explanations might there be for the wide variation in profit percentages among different manufacturing industries (see Tables 4–1 and 4–2)?

   b) Explain the variation in profit percentages in the same industry from one year to another.

BUSINESS BRIEFS

L & M and the Surgeon General's report

In 1964 the U.S. Surgeon General's report linking smoking to lung cancer was published. In 1965 Liggett & Myers' profits dropped on a 5 percent sales decline to less than $22 million from over $26 million in 1964.

However, beginning in 1966 profits rose each year to a level of $32 million in 1970. In 1970 the Congress banned all cigarette advertising on television and radio after January 1, 1971. At the time Liggett & Myers was the sixth largest cigarette producer with L & M, Lark, Chesterfield, and Eve brands on the market. In 1970 it was estimated that the cigarette industry in the United States spent $220 million on television and radio advertising.

Liggett & Myers' promotional emphasis switched in 1971 to magazine and newspaper advertising, outdoor advertising, point-of-purchase displays, cigarette giveaways, and sports promotion. These are generally considered less expensive forms of promotion than TV and radio advertising.

In 1971 nontobacco products amounted to about 50 percent of Liggett & Myers' sales and profits compared to tobacco's making up 100 percent of sales in 1964. In 1971 nontobacco lines included J & B Scotch whisky, Alpo canned dog food, Wild Turkey bourbon, watchbands, imported wines, and household cleaning products.

Financial analysts estimated that Liggett & Myers' profits after taxes would reach $36 million in 1971.

1. What do you think caused the drop in profits in 1965 for L & M?
2. How has this enterprise managed to recover from this profits decline?
3. Compare profits in the tobacco industry with other major manufacturing corporations. See Tables 4–1 and 4–2 in text.
4. Assuming you had analyzed the company, would you purchase the common stock of Liggett & Myers for an investment? Explain your answer.

Defense contract profits

Are companies which receive defense contracts making excessive profits? The federal government's General Accounting Office did a two-phase study at the direction of Congress in 1970–71 on the profit levels of negotiated defense contracts. In such contracts there is no competitive bidding. Instead the federal government negotiates directly with a particular business enterprise to arrive at a contract in which both the price and profit are set.

In the first phase of its study the GAO examined 146 contracts for military hardware completed by 30 companies totaling over $4.3 billion. This study revealed that when profit was measured as a percentage of sales it averaged 6.5 percent. However, when measured as a return on owners' equity, the profit percentage rose to 56 percent.

The federal government often furnishes defense contractors with tooling and sometimes plant facilities. In addition, the government provides periodic progress payments of up to 85 percent of costs incurred. This means that many defense contractors do not have to make a very large investment in equipment or working capital. Critics contend that under this system contractors have no incentive to invest in better equipment to reduce costs and increase efficiency.

In the second phase of its study the GAO circulated a questionnaire to approximately 150 contractors requesting information on profits for both defense and commercial sales from 1966 through 1969. The following range of profit percentages on defense and nongovernmental work were reported by contractors (which were spot-checked by the GAO).

	Defense contracts	Commercial work
Profits as percent of sales	3.9% to 5.4%	7.9% to 11.6%
Profits as percent of owners' equity	19.8% to 28.4%	17.2% to 28.6%

These profit percentages are lower than the results of the first phase of the GAO's study. These results tend to support the defense contractors' contention that they earn less profit on defense contracts than on commercial work regardless of what measure of profit is used. In the GAO's draft report no explanation was given for the variation in profit percentages between the two phases of the study.

1. Do you think that the return on equity investment should be considered in addition to the rate of return on sales in negotiating the profits on defense contracts? Explain your answer.

2. What characteristics should be taken into account in determining a "fair profit" for defense contractors?

CASE

Jack Anderson

Jack Anderson graduated nine years ago from a large school of business administration located near his home town in the Midwest. While in college Jack had studied management under Professor Montgomery, who had taken a personal interest in him and had followed his career since graduation. When he was visiting in his home town, Jack would drive over to the university to chat with Professor Montgomery about his work and economic conditions in general. The following conversation took place during Jack's most recent visit.

"Dr. Montgomery, I'm facing a real crossroads in my life," said Jack

Anderson. "As you know, after I graduated I joined a large New York department store in their merchandising training program. While the starting salary wasn't as good as some of the other job offers I had, the opportunities developed very nicely for me. I was made an assistant buyer and then promoted to the job of buyer of women's coats. Two years ago I joined a New York firm which provides smaller merchandisers across the country with assistance and buying power in the major clothing markets. I have been pleased with this move since it has broadened my experience and I have made many contacts in the industry.

"Last year I had an offer to take a buying job with a major chain store organization which would have meant a move to Chicago. After my wife and I talked it over we decided against the change since it would have narrowed my contacts in the industry and the money wasn't that much more than I was already making.

"Now we're faced with another major decision. Two weeks ago I was contacted by the owner of a clothing store in Orlando, Florida, who wants to sell out and retire because of a heart condition which his doctor has just diagnosed. He contacted me as I had helped him on a number of sales promotions which gave us the chance to become acquainted over the past two years.

"The business apparently is considered to be one of the better clothing stores in the community. While the store does most of its business in men's clothing, there is a women's clothing department which has been remodeled and has shown a good increase in sales recently. This department specializes in women's sportswear.

"My wife and I would have to invest essentially all of our savings in the down payment for this store. The present owner would be willing to finance the rest of the purchase price by a loan which would have to be paid over the next ten years. There is a bank in the community which has been providing short-term loans to finance the purchase of merchandise for the principal selling seasons, and I suppose they would continue these credit arrangements if I were to purchase the business.

"We've enjoyed living in New York City these past years, and I guess it would take some adjustment to a smaller city although both of us grew up in medium-sized communities in the Midwest. Of course my wife is concerned about schools right now since our boy will be five years old his next birthday.

"I doubt that I would be able to draw as large a salary out of the business as I'm presently making in New York. But, if the area looks like a good prospect for retail sales growth, I should be able to do very well after a year or two.

"I don't feel like I absolutely have to make a move at this time. I'm doing well where I am. Also, I think there will be other opportunities in the future if I want to get out of the 'rat race' in New York. However, the idea of owning my own business is one I've toyed around with for some time. This is an attractive situation and the price would probably work out to be a fair one.

"I suppose the reason I came by today, Dr. Montgomery, is that I want you to react to these ramblings of mine. What do you think of this situation?"

1. Assume that this conversation occurred in the context of the present economic conditions. How would you respond to Jack Anderson's conversation if you were in the professor's position?

2. What factors should Anderson take into account in arriving at a decision?

3. How could Jack Anderson obtain answers to the questions which would be raised in Question 2?

4. If you were in Jack Anderson's position what would you do next? Why?

*Management trainees spend
some of their time
meeting with
first-line supervisors.*

5

Management

Business management has been called the oldest of the arts and the youngest of the professions. From the time that men began to specialize their labors, problems of coordination have arisen which have required managerial attention. Earlier studies of management have come from schools of public administration where techniques for the administration of governmental bodies were developed. Today the practice of management has benefited from the findings of the behavioral sciences of psychology, anthropology, and sociology along with the systems concept adapted from the natural sciences and mathematical techniques applied to model building through the use of electronic computers. Many of the generalizations regarding management are applicable to any institution or group which has common objectives. However, this discussion will center on the business enterprise as the focal point of managerial activities.

The following issues are discussed regarding management of the business enterprise.

What is the nature of management?

How does the systems approach relate to management of the business enterprise?

Why is planning a requisite for successful operations?

What factors are considered in developing the organizational structure of the business system?

How do authority-responsibility relationships apply to management?

What is the relationship between line and staff functions in the business system?

The nature of management

Management may be defined as achieving results by coordinating the activities of other people. This means that the manager provides leadership which results in the achievement of the objectives of an organization of which he is a part. There are many dimensions to managerial activity. The foreman in a factory acts as a manager when he schedules production runs and makes work assignments to the employees for whom he is responsible. The vice president for marketing acts as a manager when he is in conference with his district sales supervisors working out the marketing program for the coming season. In turn the district sales supervisors act as managers when they organize and direct their salesmen to contact customers and merchandise the enterprise's products. In all these examples the function of the manager is to provide an environment within which others can perform the actual work involved in the production and distribution of the enterprise's products.

An individual in the business enterprise who is designated as a member of management may on occasion also do some specific work in producing or selling the enterprise's product. Sometimes the president himself will act as a salesman in entertaining important customers or in working out an important contract. However, when a person has the label of "manager" this implies that the individual's main responsibility lies in indirect achievement rather than in the actual production of goods or services.

Management has also been called the art of decision making. It is true that managers are required to make decisions in the process of problem solving. Indeed, the hallmark of some of the outstanding managers in this country has been their ability under difficult conditions to make decisions which have been proven to be sound by the events that followed. The types of managerial decisions vary from those made by the board of directors and president of an enterprise as to whether to engage in a new type of business operation to the foreman's responsibility for which worker will be assigned a particular job.

A systems approach to management of the business enterprise

In Chapter 1 the systems approach to business was introduced. The systems concept can be applied to the management functions of an individual business enterprise. Although the external environment is important, in this chapter the internal system of the individual enterprise is emphasized in order to focus attention on the internal functions of management. The basic system of the enterprise is illustrated in Figure 5–1.

FIGURE 5–1
General model of the system of a business enterprise

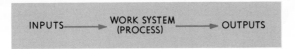

Figure 5–1 shows how the inputs flow into the work system where they are processed and become outputs. The inputs consist of material and human resources. The outputs are goods and services and other forms of satisfactions of human needs.

As a business enterprise increases in size and complexity, further division of labor is required for efficient functioning of the work system. Specialized workers and capital equipment are employed to make the work system more productive. To achieve an orderly flow of work in an increasingly specialized organization, coordination and direction by management is necessary. The work system may be thought of as being composed of technical, organizational, and human subsystems. The addition of these subsystems to the model of the business enterprise is illustrated in Figure 5–2.

FIGURE 5–2
Model of a business enterprise depicting the
technical-organizational-human subsystems

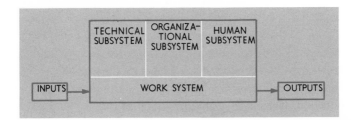

The *technical subsystem* consists of the equipment, layout, and technology required to produce and distribute a particular product. The nature of the technical subsystem depends upon the requirements of the product and varies widely from one industry to another. For example, a research laboratory of a pharmaceutical manufacturer requires a technical subsystem which is quite different from that of a magazine publisher. The nature of the requirements for a technical subsystem relate closely to the qualities and quantities of the human and material inputs needed to make the subsystem function effectively. Chapter 13 on production deals extensively with the functioning of the technical subsystem of the business enterprise.

The *human subsystem* exists in all business enterprises and consists of the values, motivations, and interactions of the persons in the enterprise. This subsystem involves the management in the practice of human relations. Because of the importance of developing a good human relations climate in the business enterprise, Chapter 7 is devoted to a discussion of this subject.

The *organizational subsystem* consists of the way in which the technical and human subsystems are organized, directed, coordinated, and controlled by management to achieve the enterprise's objectives. In the traditional view of management this involves such issues as planning, departmentalization, staffing, and authority relationships. The organizational subsystem could be considered as the formal means by which the technical and human subsystems are related to each other. There are also informal relationships between the technical and human subsystems which do not follow the formal structure of the organization. However, the formal structure is important in facilitating the effective coordination of the technical and human subsystems in the business enterprise.

There are numerous interactions among the technical, organizational, and human subsystems. Changes occurring in the technical subsystem can profoundly affect the human subsystem and may necessitate changes in the organizational subsystem. For example, the development of new technology which increases the use of automated production equipment may reduce the need for some production employees or require workers with different skills than those presently on the job. Such a change will have an impact on the morale of the work force and will create a problem requiring the attention of management. Such a technical change also may require a structural change in the departmental arrangements of the production system. In a different type of change, the development of a new product will cause changes in the human and organizational subsystems as new production facilities are constructed and the marketing program for the new product expands the requirements for personnel and an organization to direct their activities.

In any business system the various subsystems are constantly in a state of adjustment to changes caused by internal and external forces. The job of management is to deal with these change agents in such a manner that the total system of the enterprise will function efficiently in producing outputs desired by society.

The activities of management can be incorporated into the model of the business enterprise. The traditional management functions of planning, organizing, directing, and control are systematized in Figure 5–3.

FIGURE 5–3
The functions of management

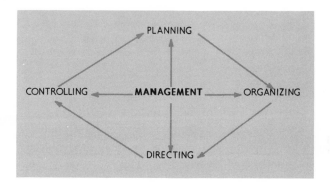

The relative importance of each of these management activities at a particular time depends upon the stage of the enterprise's development, its growth rate, competition, and other factors in the environment. Planning, organizing, and other considerations important to management such as authority-responsibility relationships and line and staff roles are discussed in this chapter. Directing is discussed in Chapter 7, dealing with human relations, and control is discussed in the next chapter.

Planning—requisite for successful operations

Planning is a primary function of management. In the new enterprise planning precedes the other functions of management. In the established enterprise system planning is an integral part of the total management process. Without adequate planning the manager's decisions are frequently made to deal only with immediate problems without a meaningful relationship to future expected needs. The management that does not plan ahead functions on a random, day-to-day basis. The executives in such an enterprise never seem to have time to anticipate the problems which may arise tomorrow and thereby create conditions within the enterprise's system to reduce future emergencies. Thus, *planning* may be called the process of rational decision making done sufficiently far in advance to promote the more effective functioning of the enterprise's total system. This means that one of the important planning functions of top management is systems design which will provide guidance throughout the enterprise's subsystems for decision making and planning at all levels. This involves the formulation of objectives, policies, and procedures, and the determination of an organizational structure which will provide a framework for the achievement of the enterprise's broad objectives.

Objectives

The planning process may be divided into three parts consisting of formulating objectives, policies, and procedures. *Objectives* embody the broad goals toward which the group activity of the business enterprise is directed. The following statement is the published objective of the Ideal Cement Company of Denver, Colorado:

> To manufacture and sell cement of the types and qualities, in such quantities, at such times and places, and to do such things in connection therewith, as will result in increasing the returns to the Company to the greatest extent with due regard for the rights and proper interest of customers, stockholders, employees, and all others affected by the activities of the Company.

This type of statement is an overall enterprise objective which to be effective should be supplemented with objectives of a more specific nature throughout the subsystems of the organization. While this broad goal of the enterprise would serve for top management, it should be translated into tangible, meaningful subgoals for each division and department of the enterprise. A subgoal of one of the manufacturing departments might be to produce the necessary quantity of cement of a particular specification at the lowest possible cost, or the traffic division might have a subgoal of maintaining shipping dates.

For enterprise objectives to be most effective they must have real meaning to the executives and involve their personal commitment. One means of improving individual loyalty to enterprise objectives is to let the individuals participate in drawing up the objectives, especially for the particular departments or divisions where they have responsibility. Since basic objectives are infrequently changed, a periodic review of them by departments is often helpful in developing employee loyalty. This review should seek to determine whether the stated objectives are still meaningful and well stated for the changing markets and circumstances of which the enterprise is a part. Since objectives set up the framework for all company planning, a meaningful formulation of enterprise objectives is a necessary first step in the planning process.

Policies

A *policy* is a framework for decision making that is consistent with the objectives of the enterprise. A good policy statement provides supervisors with guidelines for dealing in a consistent manner with issues which arise. Without policies each situation might have to be completely rethought by management before action could be taken.

Policies may be broadly stated so as to give considerable discretion to executives in their decisions or they may be quite specific as to how the policy is to be carried out. The amount of discretion allowed by a policy statement is usually greater the higher up in management one goes. At the top management level, consisting of the board of directors and the chief operating officer, policy statements provide for considerable freedom of thought and action. At the foreman's level, the first line of management in the technical subsystem, policies are usually more specific and are less flexible. As one moves down the hierarchy from top management of the business system, interpretations and policy decisions by higher executives tend to limit the freedom of policy determination at the subsystem levels. This is a logical arrangement of policy freedom since the degree of variance for thought and action is usually less necessary the further down the line of authority one goes. A fairly specific statement regarding enterprise policy on absenteeism is most helpful to the foreman who has many men to supervise and where production schedules are dependent on certain specified manning levels and skills. At the top management level work schedules are less rigid and responsibilities much broader, hence a less specific policy about hours of work and presence in the factory or office is appropriate. Figure 5–4 illustrates the concept of freedom of policy interpretation discussed above.

Despite less latitude for policy interpretation by first-line managers, some flexibility of policy interpretation is important here too. Since it is almost impossible to write a statement which will be applicable in

FIGURE 5–4

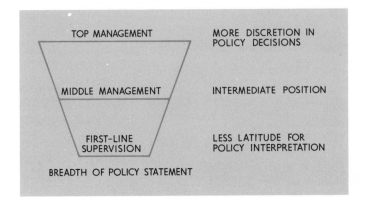

every set of circumstances, a certain amount of policy flexibility is usually desirable at subsystem levels in order to provide for varying circumstances at the point where action must be taken or results must be shown. Policies will be better accepted by first-line supervisors if they have some discretion in their application. The result of lower echelon discretion in policy administration is the delegation of decision-making power throughout the enterprise. This tends to have a positive effect on supervisors' morale and results in widespread participation in policy making and application.

Although flexibility in policy administration is desirable, it does come into conflict with the concept of consistency of policy application. Policy flexibility tends to lead to variations in application by individual supervisors. Management should be aware of this variation and strive to maintain as nearly consistent policy application as possible throughout the enterprise. Policies which are consistently applied can be a means for providing cohesion between the various subsystems of the business enterprise.

Consistent application is especially important where decisions directly affect employees. Even though a particular policy does not meet with the complete approval of employees, it is generally accepted if it is consistently applied. Wide inconsistencies in a particular policy's application will result in lower levels of employee morale and resulting problems for management in maintaining efficient operations. Management should be aware of the conflict between inflexibility and consistency of policy application and should seek to achieve a balance between these two important elements of sound policy administration.

As a part of policy administration, executives should understand that there is often a difference between the formal stated policy on a particular issue and what the actual policy application may be in the enterprise. Where circumstances have made the formal policy obsolete and resulted in informal policy changes, management should be prompt to update written policies, having the departments concerned with the problem participate in the review and revision. Significant problems have arisen for those managements which have openly tolerated vast differences between stated policies and actual policy administration in areas of employee safety, welfare, operational efficiency, and customer relations.

For policies to be most effective they should be well understood throughout the business system and should be clearly stated and written so that all employees will understand the basic framework within which decisions will be made. The old joke, "There's no good reason, it's company policy," has no place in today's business enterprise.

Procedures

Procedures constitute the third part of the planning process. A *procedure* is a series of steps carried out in a particular sequence to implement a given policy. Procedures provide little or no discretion on the part of the individual and may be instituted to carry out certain policies where a chronological sequence of events or uniform applications are important. For example, procedures may relate to such matters as to how information shall be released to the public about the enterprise's profit picture or what steps must be taken to insure safe operation of machinery.

In setting up procedures for implementing company policies and in establishing the guidelines for employee conduct, management should make clear whether a particular statement is a rule or a guide. *Rules* are statements which must be obeyed, while *guides* represent recommendations for action which are not necessarily mandatory. A rule usually is stated in a negative manner such as "No Smoking in this Area" or "No Admittance Without Safety Glasses." Even if the rules are stated in a more positive manner such as "Safety Glasses Must Be Worn Here," the negative connotation is still present. Rules should be applied only when necessary to govern employee conduct, and there should be a reason for the rule if it is to be understood and well accepted.

The planning process culminates with the development of programs for each subsystem and the relations between subsystems. These programs represent a mixture of policies and procedures to achieve the carefully outlined subsystem objectives. These programs include not only the guidelines for management thinking and action, but they are also complete with the necessary financial budgets to support the projects.

Good planning is essential

Planning is a continuous process to meet changing conditions and new needs of the business system. Once the new enterprise is established, planning becomes integrated with the rest of the functions of management. Planning reduces unproductive work and provides a necessary basis for controlling operations by setting a standard against which results may be measured. Good planning requires a realistic appraisal of the business system's assets and liabilities and should be done in the light of realistic goals.

In today's dynamic environment the process of planning can be utilized to accomplish changes in the system of the enterprise. Planning can be used throughout the enterprise to improve awareness of the total system and to promote creative change. Without planning the changes which come can be more detrimental to the human and technical subsystems than might otherwise be the case.

No business enterprise should spend more money on planning than the value of the anticipated benefits, and the measurement of dollar benefits of planning are difficult. The amount of money that could be spent on evaluation of alternative courses of action, forecasting of probable results, and alternative actions by competitors could be unlimited. Each management must determine how much it wishes to spend to get the information necessary for good planning. Time and executive talent available are also limiting factors in the planning process. However, good planning reduces the chances that executives will be forced to make snap decisions without adequate information on critical issues which may determine the future of their enterprise. Careful planning provides a sound basis for the further managerial functions of organizing, directing, and controlling.

Organizing the business enterprise

Organization of the business enterprise becomes necessary whenever it is more than a very simple one-man operation. The various activities that are necessary to carry out the purpose of the enterprise must be systematically arranged and assigned for efficient use of time and energy. There are a number of factors which should be considered in developing the organizational structure of any business system. These factors include departmentalization, staffing, authority-responsibility relationships, and line and staff relationships.

Departmentalization

The many different activities of the business enterprise must be compartmentalized and assigned so that the persons who are employed in the enterprise will clearly understand who is responsible for which activity. Can you imagine going into a large store that sells many different kinds of merchandise and does not have any departments? Suppose that each morning all the employees were assigned to their work places for that day on a random basis without any relationship to what they had done the day before, and that supervisors could do whatever they wanted without any division of the work load. The result of this unorganized situation would be chaos. It would be only through chance and a good deal of luck if the store were able to provide goods and services to the public and operate profitably.

Departmentalization provides the basis for organizing the work to be done in the business enterprise. When the business enterprise is thought of as a system, then each department can be viewed as a subsystem which has its own structure and functions relating to the other subsystems and to the business system as a whole. The value of considering the departments of the enterprise as subsystems is that this emphasizes the interrelatedness of each department in achieving both its own objectives and those of the enterprise. Such an approach stimulates individuals in the various departmental subsystems to expand their view beyond a single narrow functional activity. When management analyzes the system and subsystem relationships in its own enterprise it identifies the tasks to be accomplished along with the materials and time required. Such an analysis helps management evaluate the effectiveness of its organization and the performance of the subsystems as well as total system performance.

The division of the business enterprise into departments is a conventional basis for organizing the business system. More managements are beginning to view these departments as subsystems of the total enterprise. A detailed study of a particular enterprise would involve identifying the elements of the technical, organizational, and human subsystems in each department, which in effect are subsystems within subsystems. The nature of subsystem interrelationships would also be explored. Such a consideration of organization would be useful to a particular management in analyzing its own business system. However, for the purpose of providing an introduction to the way businesses are organized, it is not necessary to go into this much detail. The usual ways of organizing an enterprise into departmental subsystems are by function, by product line, or by geography. Other methods for departmentalization include subsystems based on the type of customer served or by individual project.

Functional departmentalization. When an enterprise is departmentalized on a functional basis the activities of a similar nature are grouped together. Thus, the activities of production and marketing are placed in separate departments and function as different subsystems. Other functional departments customarily include personnel, finance, and accounting. These subsystems are further organized to promote smooth operation both within the department and in relation to other departmental units of the enterprise. Only when all subsystems integrate their operations smoothly with others in the enterprise can the most efficient operations be conducted. Figure 5–5 illustrates the typical man-

FIGURE 5–5
Simplified organization chart of a typical manufacturing corporation on a functional basis

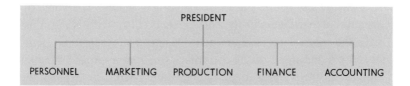

ufacturing enterprise's top management structure when it is departmentalized by function.

Each of the departments shown in Figure 5–5 has its own departmental subsystem, which will not necessarily be the same for each department. However, this functional type of departmentalization, which is frequently used at the top management level, may also be carried on throughout the organization. For example, the marketing department might be organized under a vice president in charge of marketing, with a further functional breakdown into subsystem managers for the various marketing functions of advertising, sales, promotion, and product development. Although the work of each of these subsystems should be closely coordinated, there is a meaningful difference in each of these functions so as to justify having separate divisions within the marketing subsystem. The five major departments illustrated in Figure 5–5 perform such an important role in the operation of the business enterprise that separate chapters are devoted to an analysis of the functions of each of these subsystems.

Product line departmentalization. A business enterprise may be organized according to the various types of products which it manufactures and sells. This is *product line departmentalization* and results in each product being handled almost as a separate system. An example of an industry where product line departmentalization is used is the automobile industry. The major automobile manufacturers have separate divisions for the production and distribution of each line to concentrate management attention on the problems peculiar to each segment of the market. Departmentalization by product line may be used in conjunction with functional departmentalization, with functional organization at the top management levels and some degree of functional integration at lower levels of the enterprise along with product departmentalization. For example, sometimes marketing departments are organized on a product line basis with advertising, sales, and promotion activities being carried on in one department for a particular product. This type of departmentalization can be especially helpful in coordinating the many details involved in the introduction of a new product to the public. (See Figure 5–6.)

Departmentalization by geography. Geographical departmentalization is logical when activities are carried on over a wide territorial range. Geography provides a good means for organizing subsystems when different markets and conditions exist across the country. Selling of the product is frequently departmentalized on a geographical basis because of the importance of having sales activities locally controlled to keep in touch with changes in market conditions.

Other means of departmentalization. Sometimes an enterprise may find it profitable to departmentalize on the basis of the *type of customer served.* This is done many times by enterprises producing both civilian and governmental products. Those enterprises which provide products for the armed forces through the Department of Defense have found that a separate division for defense contracts is helpful to maintain close control on standards and keep up to date on the complex requirements

FIGURE 5–6

Partial organization chart of a multiline manufacturing corporation on a product line basis

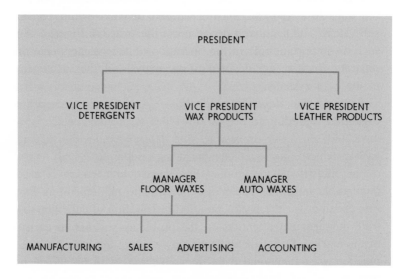

for dealing with the federal govenment. These same enterprises may use separate departments to produce and sell products for civilian use. Sometimes commercial banks and other financial institutions organize departments on a type-of-customer-served basis, such as departments for loans to retail stores, to customers, or to farmers.

In engineering and construction industries the *single-project type* of departmentalization is useful where large one-time projects are undertaken which will extend over a period of months or years. Highway construction contracts serve as a logical basis for single-project departments. Sometimes these subsystems are referred to as task forces where men and materials are marshalled for one special effort. Once the project is completed the personnel and equipment are reassigned to other activities.

There is no single best way to departmentalize a business enterprise. A careful analysis of the circumstances of the particular business enterprise should be undertaken before deciding upon the departmental structure.

Staffing and management succession

Once the organization structure has been planned and the subsystems identified, the next step is providing managerial personnel to fill the decision-making positions in the business enterprise. *Staffing* is the provision of qualified managerial personnel for the enterprise and is contrasted with employee hiring which consists of bringing nonmanagerial personnel into the enterprise. Many of the steps in hiring of personnel are the same for managers and nonmanagerial employees. The elements of a hiring and placement program are discussed in Chapter 8 dealing with personnel management. A key element in a good staffing program is to be sure that an adequate plan of management succession is developed and put into practice. No matter how competent a particular manager or team of executives is, these persons will not always be a part of the enterprise's organization. Therefore, sound management requires that a training program to provide qualified managerial personnel as replacements be a continuous top management responsibility.

Providing for management succession is critical for the small and medium-sized enterprise since most likely there will be proportionately fewer competent managers in smaller firms than in the large enterprise. In the enterprise where one executive acts as the principal decision maker and where no program to train future managers is undertaken, the existence of the enterprise depends upon the health and capacity of a single person.

Sources of executive talent. There are two sources of executives for staffing the organization. The first is to promote from within employees either in lower management echelons or nonmanagerial personnel. The second is to bring in executive personnel from the outside. Generally executive morale is higher if promotion comes from within the company ranks. However, if inside promotion is practiced this means that executive training programs should be in operation to assure that personnel will be prepared when vacancies occur. Also, there is a danger that inbreeding in executive ranks will result from exclusive promotion from within. This may tend to stifle new ideas and different points of view which are important to most enterprises to meet changing conditions and new problems.

When promotion from within is the policy for filling vacancies in managerial ranks, a good companion policy is that every manager consider it his obligation to train at least one man sufficiently to assume his position in the organization. The fear that some managers might have that their subordinates would replace them will be greatly reduced, if not eliminated, if higher management takes care to provide training so that middle management personnel can expect to have a chance at positions higher in the organization too. Not every first-line supervisor has the capacities for top management, and many would not want to assume such a position. However, morale among supervisors will be raised if managerial promotions are based on merit with the opportunity available for qualified personnel to move into higher positions.

Hiring executives from outside the enterprise can also have merit. Besides bringing new ideas into an organization, hiring an outside executive generally means that he is immediately ready to assume the responsibility for a given position. The lead time required for training of personnel may be cut down by hiring experienced men from other business enterprises. This is a good practice especially where no training programs have been undertaken and no capable managers have been brought along within an organization.

Management training. When management is faced with a shortage of trained personnel within an enterprise this may reflect a weakness in the management training program. There are four ways that personnel can acquire managerial training to qualify them for promotion. These are through job rotation, special assignments, formal training programs, and by staff assignments.

Job rotation involves the transfer of the individual through a series of different types of positions to acquaint him with the different elements of the enterprise's operations. This is especially helpful with the young man who is new to the enterprise and serves to provide a basis for a more permanent type of responsibility assignment later on.

Special assignments may be given somewhat more experienced personnel where they will have responsibility for a project that will show what abilities they have for organizing and carrying out a program. Special assignments provide one measure of a person's ability to deal with new and varied situations and act as a means for integrating his knowledge of several fields.

Formal training programs can be conducted within the enterprise and include lectures, special training courses, and discussions, or may provide for the executive going to some institution of higher learning for professional management training. Such programs tend to broaden the scope of the executive's knowledge, which previously had been limited to understanding in depth a particular functional area such as marketing or accounting.

By placing an individual in a *staff position,* such as an assistant to a member of top management, a real insight into the operation of the enterprise from the top down is provided. The assistant's role may be varied, but when used as a training device it should include work throughout the various levels in the organization. As this type of staff official, the individual acts to provide assistance or information but does not have to bear the final responsibility for decision making. Such assignments may give young managers a better understanding of the complexities of the decisions made by top executives and improve their grasp of the total managerial job.

Executive development and management succession is an area that should not be the sole responsibility of the personnel administrator or lower echelon managers. This is a responsibility of top management just as is a concern for the manufacture and sale of the enterprise's products. Without an adequate program of managerial training the long-run success of the enterprise is endangered.

Authority-responsibility relationships

The nature of authority

Authority as applied to the business enterprise is the delegated power to make decisions. Sometimes authority is defined as the right to direct the actions of others. This definition appears to de-emphasize greatly the importance of human relationships in the business enterprise and the social responsibilities of business. In its most extreme position, this latter view makes authority a divine right of business owners to exercise complete domination over employees. To counter this "right to direct" concept of authority, the concept has been developed that authority flows upward from the subordinate to the superior and that no authority can be exercised in the business enterprise without the permission of the employee. This "permissive" view of authority places great emphasis on the human relations aspect of enterprise management.

For the businessman faced with the many problems of running his firm, both points of view may provide helpful insights into better management of the business enterprise. The authority to manage an enterprise does stem from its owners, who bring together the assets to begin operations. The concept of private property is a basic value in our society. In this respect, the "right to direct" or more traditional view of authority is relevant. On the other hand, in a free society an employer is neither able to command enthusiastic cooperation of employees nor is he able to make them obey commands which they do not understand nor undertake activities which they are not able to accomplish. Therefore, a recognition of the importance of good communications, respect for the individual worker, and reasonable work standards is critical in the exercise of authority in the modern industrial enterprise. Thus, the definition of authority as the delegated power to make decisions seems to be a logical middle ground which encompasses elements of both the traditional and permissive views of authority.

Responsibility

Those with decision-making power are held accountable for their decisions. The concept of responsibility is closely tied to accountability. Supervisors at all levels of business are well aware of the nature of responsibility. They know that responsibility rests on their shoulders for the results of the men and materials put under their direction. However, one of the most frequently voiced complaints by supervisory personnel is that they do not have authority in decision making which is commensurate with their responsibility. A concept of good management is that with every responsibility should go sufficient authority to carry out the assigned mission. Responsibility for results should never be separated from the power to make the decisions necessary to achieve those results. This means that authority should be placed at the subsystem level where needed so that decisions can be made as close as possible to where the activities are being undertaken.

Delegation of authority

Another aspect of authority-responsibility relationships is the importance of proper delegation of authority to subordinates. A particular responsibility, as such, cannot be delegated to a subordinate, but one can delegate authority to make decisions to a subordinate and then create a new responsibility relationship from the subordinate to the superior. This does not relieve the superior of his responsibility to his boss, but such a delegation does make possible the disposition of work assignments to achieve the overall objectives of the business system.

Consider the example of the office manager who has responsibility for the work efforts of many clerks and other office employees. His responsibility for the smooth functioning of this subsystem is not removed when he divides the total work efforts into four sections (subsubsystems) and appoints a supervisor for each section who is responsible to him for the work of a particular section. In the creation of this new responsibility relationship and the delegation of authority to do the job, the office manager does not abdicate his responsibility for the results of the sections. However, now he is able to obtain valuable supervisory assistance through the new subsubsystems created to partition the work of the office.

In this example, each section supervisor should be well aware of the responsibilities he has to the office manager and what authority he has to meet these responsibilities. Without this clear understanding of the limits of his authority, and willingness to accept both the responsibility and authority, morale among office employees will deteriorate when they are unable to get answers to their questions from the section supervisor. Failure of this supervisor to meet his responsibilities to his boss, the office manager, and to his subordinates will result in employees going around the supervisor to the office manager. This not only creates misunderstanding and hard feelings in the office, but negates the purpose for which the position of section supervisor was created: that of relieving the office manager of many of the smaller administrative details of the office's functioning, which should enable him to concentrate his attention on more important questions relating to the effective management of the office.

Executives should be sure that subordinates have the qualifications to assume authority and responsibility and that these personnel have a clear understanding of what is expected of them when changes in the organization are made. Of equal importance is the communication to all employees who will be affected of the nature of the changes and the reasons for their adoption.

Degree of decentralization of decision making

In recent years many large enterprises such as General Electric Company have become much interested in the concept of decentralization of decision making in their organizations. As a matter of fact, the concept of complete centralization of decision making is not appropriate to the large business operation, and the really relevant question is not whether there is to be decentralization but to what extent shall decision making be decentralized. Even in medium-size and small-size business enterprises, where problems of great geographic distances and multiplant operations are not present, subsystems are being more effectively utilized through some decentralization of decision making.

In view of the interest in decentralization, the answers provided by management to each of the following five questions will give some guidelines for the extent of decentralization in a particular business enterprise.

1. What is the significance of the decision? In those instances where the decision is relatively minor it ought to be made by operating personnel on the spot. The cost of having the problem passed up through the organization may exceed the value of the decision itself. Where the decision that is made is critical to the overall success of enterprise operations then it probably should be made by more senior executives.

2. Who in the organization has the information necessary to make an informed decision? Most decisions should be made at the level in the organization where the needed information is readily available. With more complex decisions the necessity of drawing together information from several areas of the enterprise means that clear channels of communications will be required.

3. At what level in the organization do personnel have the capacity to make the decisions? Authority should normally be delegated as far down in the organization as employees have the experience and knowledge necessary to render a sound decision. There are times when personnel operating at the subsystem levels of management are better equipped to make a decision than higher management at the system level because their close association with the problem gives them a good understanding of the ramifications of whatever decision is made.

4. How rapidly must the decision be made? Some authority must be placed on the point of impact of the decision making. There is no sense in requiring permission from the plant manager before taking out a fire extinguisher and putting out a trash fire which may have started in a wastebasket. To delay the decision to act could be extremely costly as well as stupid. On the other hand, a major decision relating to expansion of plant capacity or extension of marketing areas probably can wait for a period of time until sufficient evidence is gathered to insure a more sound decision being made.

5. What will be the effect of employee morale of the degree of decentralization that is promoted in the enterprise? Generally decentralization improves initiative and creates good morale among employees. People like to feel that they can influence the events that occur in the enterprises where they are employed. This is particularly true in industries where rapid change and strong competition exist. However, this is by no means a uniform characteristic of all business systems. In those or-

ganizations where changes come more gradually and promotion of employees is slower, too much decentralization of decision-making power will tend to create discontent and result in lower echelon executives pushing top managers without seeing any results from their efforts or being constantly rebuffed for their suggestions and decisions. In these situations the level of employee morale might actually be lowered by too much decentralization.

Only after an analysis of these five questions, a careful study of its own operation, and an understanding of the philosophy of management of its own top executives can an enterprise's policy makers deal with the question of what degree of decentralization to undertake.

Span of control

A concept closely related to the issue of decentralization of authority is that of executive span of control. *Span of control* refers to the number of subordinates which a manager can effectively supervise. There are three main factors that tend to limit the number of employees any single manager can supervise. These are the executive's time and energy available, his mental capabilities and personal abilities for dealing with individuals, and the nature of the supervisory problems that will be encountered on the job.

The more face-to-face contacts that are necessary each day in the conduct of a department's affairs, the more time-consuming and demanding is the supervisor's role. Generally, the more complex the supervisory situation and the greater the variety of activities a person directs, the more limited will be the number of individuals he can supervise and consequently the more narrow the span of control. Some authorities indicate that at higher levels in the enterprise fewer persons can be effectively supervised, which leads to a more narrow span of control than at lower levels in the organization where problems are not of such great magnitude. However, in those enterprises where considerable decentralization of authority exists, a wider span of control at top management level can be very effective. In such cases the shorter lines of communication from the bottom to the top of the organization and the fewer levels of management personnel can improve the morale and effectiveness of subordinates. Figure 5–7 illustrates the difference in organization structure between a wide and narrow span of control.

Notice in Figure 5–7 that the number of production workers in each company is the same. However, the two organization structures are

FIGURE 5–7
Comparison of organization structures with wide and narrow spans of control

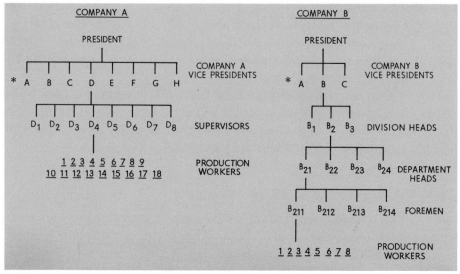

Summary:

Company A	Company B
1 President	1 President
8 Vice presidents	3 Vice presidents
64 Supervisors	9 Division heads
1152 Production workers	36 Department heads
1225 Total employees	144 Foremen
	1152 Production workers
	1345 Total employees

* Each level below the departmental level has a similar structure of supervisors and production workers as does Department D in Company A and Department B in Company B.

quite different. There are 18 production workers in each supervisory work unit in Company A and only 8 in Company B. In Company A there are only two levels of management between production workers and the president, while in Company B four levels separate workers and the president's office. While it is rather unrealistic to assume that workers will have much direct contact with the president, communication is more direct when fewer levels of supervision exist. The dangers that communication will be impaired are greater where the span of control is narrow and many levels of supervision occur. The span of control is much wider in Company A with more authority and responsibility being placed with individual supervisors than in Company B where authority is likely to be more divided among the various levels of supervisors.

There are 120 more supervisory personnel in Company B than there are in Company A. While this does not mean that all executives in Company B are not performing satisfactorily, the question can be raised as to the added expense of these additional salaries. Top management should always attempt to determine whether additional levels of supervision with more executives can be economically justified. Although some supervisory personnel in Company A may be more highly paid in view of their greater responsibilities than may be the case in Company B, the total executive wage bill probably will be higher in Company B.

Despite the issues which have been raised concerning the organization structure of Company B, it would be wrong to assume that a very wide span of control is always best. The optimum span of control or supervision for each level in the enterprise should be determined on the basis of the variety and importance of the activities being supervised, the stability of enterprise operations, the abilities of the executive and his total duties, the ability of subordinates, and the importance of executive salaries as an expense item in the enterprise. There are no pat, easy answers to questions relating to organization structure. Earlier concepts generalizing about the specific number of subordinates which can be directed effectively are giving way to a situational analysis of the enterprise's system and its subsystem relationships and the nature of the problems which are faced by a particular management.

Chain of command

The chain of command concept involves an understanding on the part of all employees as to whom they are directly responsible. Persons throughout the business system should also understand the nature of the authority which they have and how it is to be exercised. The chain of command runs through the system to the subsystems and subsubsystems.

Line and staff relationships

The problems that arise in organizations because of misunderstanding of line and staff functions are important enough to warrant a discussion of the essential nature of line and staff roles and the relationships between them.

Definitions of line and staff

The *line function* in the business enterprise consists of those activities that specifically and directly result in the achievement of the goals of the business enterprise. Thus, line activities in a manufacturing enterprise would be those relating to producing and selling the product. The *staff function* would include all other activities which assist the line in fulfilling the enterprise's objectives. Activities such as finance, personnel administration, and accounting would be considered as elements of the staff function. This means that the line and staff functions may be defined in terms of the kinds of activities accomplished. Those which are part of the main stream of enterprise endeavor are line functions, and those which support line activities are staff functions. These are illustrated by Figure 5–8.

FIGURE 5–8
Partial organization chart for manufacturing corporation showing line and staff functions

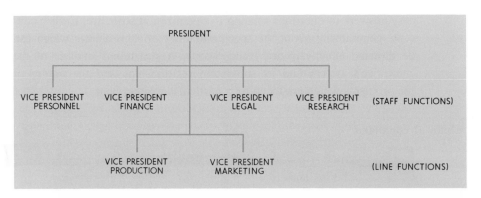

Line and staff functions may also be defined with regard to authority relationships. The concept of chain of command implies a direct line of authority running throughout the enterprise's system. In this sense, the line executive is one who has direct authority over another employee. Line authority consists of the power to make decisions and follow through to see that a mission is accomplished. The role of the staff executive is that of advice and consultation, not of final decision making. In terms of authority relationships the staff function is not decision making or direction but provision of assistance to improve decisions made by persons with line authority.

Students of business administration should be aware that the concept of line and staff may be defined either according to the kind of activity accomplished or in terms of authority relationships. A particular executive may be considered to perform both line and staff functions. For example, the vice president for personnel or the personnel administrator is head of his department and is the top of the chain of command of this area. He exercises authority over employees in his department and sees that their work is satisfactory. In this sense, the personnel administrator exercises a line function with respect to his department. However, personnel administration in the business enterprise is generally considered to be a staff function in that it provides advice and assistance to other departments in achieving the objectives of the enterprise of profitably providing goods and services for society. In an operational view such as might appear on an organizational chart, direct authority relationships would be recognized and personnel would be shown as a staff function, though the personnel department itself might be broken down to show the line function performed by the personnel administrator within his department.

Dimensions of the staff function

Although the staff function may be defined as representing all the activities necessary to support the line, there are different dimensions to the staff function. Staff personnel include technical advisors, personal assistants, housekeeping staff, and specialized staff.

Technical advisors are personnel such as legal counselors, public relations men, and engineers who provide information of a highly specialized nature. The advice given by technical staff members is tantamount to a directive. The line manager may ignore the advice, but it is unlikely that he will be in a position to make a different decision which will be technically sounder in view of the expertise of the advisor.

Personal assistants are persons who provide busy executives with information or recommendations or who handle details that the manager may not have time to take care of but does not wish to delegate to a lower level in the organization. This type of staff person is often titled as "Assistant to . . ." and the exact nature of his responsibilities will be determined by the executive for whom he works.

Housekeeping staff means just what the name implies. This includes the large number of personnel who perform custodial and maintenance duties, record keeping, health services, such as giving physical examinations and providing first aid, and routine personnel functions, such as interviewing prospective employees and providing testing services.

Specialized staff includes a variety of staff personnel whose common denominator is understanding in a particular field of knowledge that can be of vital assistance to the line executive. The accounting function in the business enterprise is generally considered as a specialized staff role as are elements of finance, purchasing, and engineering. Frequently specialized staff personnel will engage in long-run planning and provide the research information necessary for the successful continuation of the business enterprise.

What constitutes a staff function in one business enterprise may be a line function in another. Purchasing for many manufacturers is considered a staff function, but in a large retailing enterprise the buying or purchasing function is a vital responsibility of the line coupled with successful selling or marketing. Whatever represents the main thrust of an enterprise's economic function may properly be called the line, and those elements that support and assist may be called the staff.

Summary

Management consists of achieving results by coordinating the activities of other people.

The systems approach to management of a business enterprise focuses on the coordination of inputs of material and human resources into the work system where they are processed and become outputs of goods and services and other satisfactions of human needs. The work system is composed of technical, organizational, and human subsystems.

Planning is the process of rational decision making done sufficiently far in advance to promote the more effective functioning of the enterprise's total system. Planning consists of the formulation of objectives, policies, and procedures and determination of the organizational structure of the enterprise.

Departmentalization can be carried out functionally, on a product line basis, geographically, or as single-project-type organization.

Staffing the organization structure and providing for management succession are also management's responsibilities.

Authority is the delegated power to make decisions. When decision-making power is delegated an authority-responsibility relationship is created. Decentralization of decision making is an important trend in the management of today's business systems.

The line function in the business system consists of those activities which directly result in the achievement of the goals of the enterprise. The staff function includes all other activities which assist the line in fulfilling enterprise objectives.

Terms for review

management	authority
work system	responsibility
planning	span of control
policy	chain of command
procedure	line function
departmentalization	staff function
staffing	

Questions

1. How is the management of organizations such as government and educational institutions similar to the management of business enterprises? How does the management of business enterprises differ from other institutions?

2. Discuss the relationship between the technical, organizational, and human subsystems in a business enterprise. Give a specific example of how changes in one subsystem affect the other two subsystems.

3. An owner of a small business recently commented, "I can't afford to take the time to plan because of all the immediate problems I have to solve." What comments would you make to this businessman about the importance of planning and its benefits?

4. Why is consistency of policy administration important in managing the enterprise? Does consistency mean that there should never be variations in policy administration? Explain your answer.

5. Determine the nature of departmentalization in a business enterprise with which you are familiar or obtain a copy of a corporation's annual report from a stock brokerage firm or by writing to the secretary of the corporation. Draw up an organization chart of the enterprise showing its present form of organization. What other methods of organization could the enterprise have utilized? What possible advantages could be gained from a different form of organization?

6. a) When vacancies occur in key management positions in the business enterprise what are the advantages of filling these positions with persons presently employed by the enterprise?
   b) What are the advantages of filling key management vacancies with persons from outside the firm?

7. a) Contrast the traditional "right to direct" concept of authority with the "permissive," or human relations, concept of authority.

b) What types of authority have you seen exercised in organizations of which you have been a part? Was the exercise of authority in these organizations effective? Explain your answer.

8. What are the advantages of decentralization of authority in organizations?

9. How can staff personnel be effective in getting along with line supervisors?

BUSINESS BRIEF

A different approach to management training

Management training programs developed by universities, consulting firms, and business enterprises have been used for a number of years. Such conventional programs utilize case discussions, business simulation using computers, and lectures to improve management skills or to provide understanding of new developments in marketing, finance, control, or some other area of business.

A completely different approach to management development is being used by Outward Bound, Inc., which has programs in Colorado and North Carolina designed to motivate and improve managers through emphasis on physical challenge in the out-of-doors.

The Outward Bound program puts together a group of ten men from various business enterprises plus two instructors. This group travels to an isolated area such as Baja California in Mexico or the Far West. Participants are prohibited from bringing tobacco, liquor, watches, or billfolds. For a period of either 10 days or 21 days the men are on an expedition where together they plan a course through rugged terrain—climbing mountains, scaling cliffs, and running river rapids. All activities require teamwork along with individual effort. In the final three days of the course each man lives alone on his own resources.

The objective of such a program is to provide each participant with renewed self-confidence and new insights into the manner in which he works with other people. The expeditions require cooperation and coordination of efforts among participants.

The Outward Bound program is also used for other groups, including training of the hard-core unemployed under the sponsorship of the National Alliance of Businessmen.

1. How could a program like Outward Bound be effective in management development when business management is not the focus of activities?

2. How could a corporation's management justify paying the cost of $500 to $800 for each employee participating in the Outward Bound program plus the manager's salary and transportation expenses to the site of the expedition?

3. What benefits might managerial personnel gain from such a program?

CASES

United Insurance Company

Tom Findlay, office manager of the Aton district office of United Insurance Company, was faced with the question of what to do about the absenteeism of one of the most efficient typists in the office.

Tom prided himself that he had been consistent in applying personnel policies since he had been promoted to office manager eight months ago. Under his supervision were five analysts, four typists, three filing clerks, and a mailroom clerk. Typing and clerical work was sent into the office from other departments of the Aton district. The analysts worked on specific policy problems which were reported by the agents and referred by the district sales manager for detailed study.

The written personnel policies issued by the company's home office were quite explicit regarding absenteeism, indicating that employees were expected to be at work on time and that absenteeism was viewed as a serious matter except for genuine cases of personal hardship. District managers, who were in charge of all operations within their geographic areas, were directed to draw up specific procedures to be followed in dealing with absenteeism in their districts. The Aton district had written personnel policies which stated that the procedure to be followed for unexcused absenteeism was:

First unexcused absence—oral warning by the supervisor.
Second unexcused absence—written warning by the supervisor.
Third unexcused absence—two days' suspension without pay.
Fourth unexcused absence—discharge of the employee.

Whether the absence was excused or not was left up to the supervisor, although the district manager indicated that absences due to personal illness, family illness, or death of a relative would be considered excused, provided the supervisor was notified at the time. Other reasons by employees for being absent would have to be evaluated by the immediate supervisor as to whether they justified being excused. The United Insurance Company had a companywide policy allowing up to seven working days annually for such "excused" absences.

Shortly after he was named office manager, Tom Findlay had fired one of the clerks for excessive absenteeism. The young woman had failed to come to work for reasons which Tom had not considered "excused." She had been warned according to the established procedure, and after the fourth absence Tom Findlay dismissed her after briefly outlining the case to the district manager.

Now a similar situation had arisen with one of the best typists in the office. Jayne Jones had been absent three times in the past four months without what Tom Findlay considered to be a satisfactory explanation. Following the third absence Tom sent Jayne home for two days without pay. At the time she indicated that she had been having problems with her parents and really needed her job to enable her to pay some debts and then to move into an apartment which she had been looking for. She had been hired about six months ago and had proved to be an excellent worker except for the recent absences.

On Monday morning, two weeks following her third absence, Jayne called in sick. Late that afternoon an agent for the company returned to the office and remarked to Tom Findlay as he passed his desk, "Say, I saw Jayne Jones this afternoon at the Crestview shopping center. I thought she worked in this office."

The agent's remark disturbed Tom Findlay. He knew that Jayne had a number of friends among the other girls in the office force and that the typing section functioned more smoothly when she was there. He was aware that some of the managers in the insurance company were more liberal than he in the interpretation of unexcused absences. On the other hand, he wanted to avoid potential future morale problems in the office which could occur if he "let Jayne get away with something." Tom felt certain that his future promotion depended upon how well he managed the office and whether the work was accomplished efficiently. He wondered what he should do about Jayne.

1. What should Tom Findlay do at this point? Discuss both the immediate and long-range actions to be taken.

2. Discuss the merits and limitations of consistency in policy administration.

Hedgepath Early American Furniture Company

The Hedgepath Early American Furniture Company is a family-owned and family-managed enterprise started some 30 years ago by Ronald A. Hedgepath, Sr., who had developed the business into a successful furniture manufacturing operation employing some 250 production workers.

In 1970, Hedgepath's only son, Ronald Junior, was home for the summer from the state university where he was majoring in business administration. Ronald had worked in the factory in previous years and during the summer of 1970 was employed in the main office doing general office work. Because of some of the personnel practices he observed, and in view of what appeared to him to be a high rate of employee turnover, Ronald persuaded his father that what the company needed was a director of personnel administration.

The elder Hedgepath had built up his business by depending heavily on his plant foremen to do the hiring, training, and firing of employees. The ten foremen had been personally picked by him, and in the small southern town where the plant was located they had considerable prestige because of their positions with the company. Several of the foremen had been with the Hedgepath Company since its founding.

When the word got around that at young Ronald's insistence a new man was being brought in as "personnel director" and that all hiring and firing would now be centralized, there was considerable grumbling among the foremen. Particularly the old-timers declared that they understood Hedgepath personnel needs better than any outsider ever could.

Jim Curtis, age 29, was employed as the new personnel director. He had a bachelor's degree in business administration and had worked five years for a large automotive parts manufacturer as assistant personnel manager in a city approximately 200 miles from the Hedgepath Company's plant.

Mr. Curtis soon found that he had his hands full in trying to work out some uniform personnel policies for the Hedgepath plant. There was no union at the plant. For years each foreman had made his own "personnel policies," with considerable individual variation from foreman to foreman. The workers who had been employed for any length of time soon learned what to expect from their particular foreman. Hiring of friends and relatives was a common practice. When orders slowed down, there was no companywide policy for laying off workers.

Each foreman determined who was to be laid off. Although seniority was sometimes given consideration in laying off workers, more generally foremen attempted to retain those employees who were the most productive, or who were relatives, or with whom they had special friendships. When Mr. Curtis questioned one of the foremen why a particular worker with a marginal attendance record was being retained the foreman replied, "I have known Bob Jones for 18 years and I am not about to let him go." From the tone of his remark it was obvious to Mr. Curtis that the foreman did not wish to be pressed further on the matter.

As part of his investigation of the labor turnover situation, Mr. Curtis began conducting exit conferences with employees who were leaving the company. These conferences revealed that these employees were disgruntled not only with such things as special friendships and nepotism in hiring and laying off workers, but also with what they considered to be unfair treatment in such matters as allocation of overtime, promotions, transfers from one department to another, and discipline.

As Curtis began to develop standardized personnel procedures, some of the foremen cooperated, but he met resistance from a number of them. There was also a varied reaction from the workers. Some of the plant employees were glad to see the personnel director's actions since they thought they would get a "fairer shake." However, other employees resented the new personnel director, as they had things pretty well worked out with their foreman and didn't want this relationship threatened in any way.

Some of the employees who had complaints about the actions of their foreman began coming to Curtis to air these grievances. At the same time, several of the foremen began going to the plant superintendent whenever the new personnel director did anything which they felt threatened one of their prerogatives. Whenever a personnel decision made by Curtis failed to work out in their departments, they were quick to blame the personnel director. Curtis, in turn, claimed that these foremen were not cooperating with his attempts to work out sound personnel policies that all departments could live with.

As a result of this situation, the plant superintendent found that much of his time was occupied in settling arguments between his foremen and the new personnel director. After several weeks of this he went to the senior Mr. Hedgepath with the statement, "You're going to have to do something with that personnel man if we're going to get any work done around here!"

A chart of the Hedgepath Company is given in Exhibit 1 showing the major management positions in the company after the establishment of the personnel department in 1970.

EXHIBIT 1
Partial organization chart of the Hedgepath Early American Furniture Company

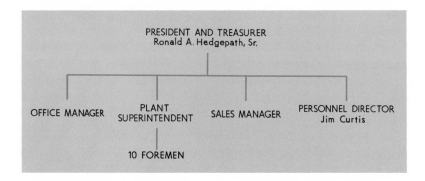

1. What are the problems involved in instituting a personnel department in the Hedgepath Company where none previously existed?

2. What should be the nature of the authority of the personnel manager?

3. In what ways could the foremen participate in improving personnel policies and practices?

4. What should Mr. Hedgepath do in response to the statement by the plant superintendent?

Courtesy U.S. Steel Corporation

*Control of production is
exercised through
such techniques as
closed-circuit television
in this steelworks.*

6

Control

Control is sometimes thought of as the last step in the management process of planning, organizing, directing, and controlling. However, a good system of control will be built into the management of the business system from its beginning.

The control system provides a means of informing management whether the other systems are functioning according to plan and also provides a basis for changes to correct problems which have already occurred.

The following issues regarding control are discussed.

How does the process of control relate to management?

What are the elements of a control system?

What are the requisites for effective control systems?

Why is the budgeting process a key management device?

The process of control

Without a good system of control the technical, organizational, and human subsystems of the business enterprise may be ineffective. The control system provides a means for measuring the progress of the business system toward its objectives. Control systems function in relation to the framework of planning which is done throughout the business enterprise. At the same time, feedback from the control process points out the need for adjustments in plans or for the need for new planning. The overall objective of the control process is to facilitate the functioning of the business enterprise's system and subsystems.

Control enables management to coordinate the many diverse subsystem activities by measuring actual output against expected performance. Control systems usually focus on a limited number of measurements and frequently are limited to a single criterion. This means that management should concentrate on the design of control systems for those dimensions of enterprise activity which are both controllable and important. In the established enterprise system the standards which are set should relate to past performance as well as to absolute standards desired by management.

Today's business enterprises are complex systems requiring the varied services and expertise of many persons. If the enterprise is to achieve its goals these diverse elements must work together for the common good. Management's system design, including control systems, should recognize the need for cooperation and a certain amount of conformity on the part of employees. Control systems help maintain individualistic behavior within limits which are tolerable for the efficient functioning of the business enterprise's system. However, the need for a certain amount of conformity to attain common goals should not result in the stifling of creativity and individuality. Therefore, the control system must also be geared to accommodate creative changes, especially those which enable the business enterprise to serve society better.

The elements of a control system

No matter what is being controlled in the business system, whether it is control of production, product quality, personnel performance, or cash, there are three essential elements in a control system. These are the establishment of standards, the measurement of performance, and the analysis and correction of deviations from planned standards. Figure 6–1 illustrates the basic elements in a control system.

FIGURE 6–1
Elements of a control system

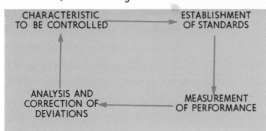

Establishing standards

Standards represent the goals which the business enterprise strives to attain. There are different types of standards which may be used as guidelines for control. These include monetary standards, physical standards, and intangible standards.

Monetary standards generally relate to the cost of operation, such as materials or labor cost per unit produced or the ratio of net profits to assets of the enterprise. Sometimes monetary standards will be in terms of revenues, such as the average sales per salesman in a particular marketing area. Monetary standards are widely used in the business system as a means for control in those circumstances where quantitative measurement is possible.

Physical standards, like monetary standards, are frequently quantitative in nature, but they may also be qualitative. Physical standards are quantitative when used to measure such things as number of units produced per man-hour, ton-miles of freight carried, or amount of energy expended per unit of production. The qualitative aspect of physical standards would include such things as the closeness of tolerances, the consistency in a color, or the tensile strength of metals or fabrics.

Intangible standards cannot be stated precisely in either monetary or physical terms and therefore tend to be frustrating to determine. How does one go about judging the effectiveness of the enterprise's public relations program? Or setting standards for the performance of executive personnel? Or establishing loyalty standards for the president's secretary who will have access to confidential data? There are problems in establishing intangible standards in these areas, but just because intangible standards are difficult to define and somewhat vague does not diminish their importance. Management must attempt to the best of its ability to establish good intangible standards.

In setting up any standards the broad objectives of the business system must always be kept in mind. It is sometimes easy for management to become overly impressed at the subsystem level with specific quantitative standards which can be easily measured, but at the same time management may miss the significance of broader issues which in the long run will have greater impact on operating results. For example, an auditor or department head may keep logs in which he carefully checks the number of telephone calls in an attempt to eliminate unnecessary long-distance calls and thereby reduce telephone expenses to a given ratio of sales. However, a telephone expense account may be over-controlled to the extent that additional sales and significantly higher profits are being missed because of too strict a control on long-distance calls. A supervisor needs to take a broader view and check to see whether a greater use of the telephone as a sales device might not increase sales that would more than make up for the additional expense of long-distance calls. Similar examples can be found in many other areas of control in the total management of the business enterprise.

Measuring performance

Provided that a standard has been properly set the measurement of performance should be a relatively simple matter. Does or does not the activity reach the standard which has been established? With routine production work where past experience and motion and time analysis has established a fair and easily measured standard of production, this may be a rather straightforward question. On the other hand, the question of measuring performance against a standard is not quite so easy in the shop where all work is for custom orders and each order requires a different combination of patterns, materials, and skills. In such a job-lot shop the careful analyst may be able to work out standards which can be applied, although perhaps with somewhat more allowance for variation than in the routine production line.

One of the most difficult areas for measuring performance is in the evaluation of individual managerial efforts. The role of management consists of directing the work efforts of others. Although an overall evaluation can be made of a production manager by the performance of his production department or a sales manager in terms of units sold, these are not always the fairest measurements. The criteria for the performance of a staff executive such as the personnel manager or the market research director are even less well defined. Personnel executives may be measured by the number of grievances of employees, by an index of labor turnover, by the number of strikes or absence of strikes, or by some other statistic collected by personnel to indicate the status of worker morale. However, these measures are frequently vague, and the more basic question is whether or not a personnel director necessarily should bear the major responsibility for worker dissatisfactions. The point of view taken generally throughout our study of management is that the line manager ultimately bears the responsibility for the performance of the enterprise. Having a skilled and effective personnel department may be of great assistance in warding off human relations and labor problems but it is certainly no guarantee that they will not arise.

The personnel director as a staff employee may give excellent assistance and advice but line management may choose to ignore it.

Analysis and correction of deviations

A good control process includes as part of its system an analysis of the deviations from standards and suggests the nature of the correction to bring performance back within acceptable limits. Sometimes correction of deviations requires examining all the steps in the management process to determine the best way of applying corrective action.

The analysis of deviations illustrates how controls should be built into the total management of the enterprise and not be something which comes after all plans are made, resources marshaled, and action initiated. Management should have in mind the range of expected results at any particular time in the cycle of the product's development and should devise means for making corrections before the enterprise encounters serious problems.

One feature of most control systems is that they tend to emphasize the negative factors of performance. Management becomes much concerned when productivity in a particular department fails to reach expectations or when sales of a product do not meet quotas. In these cases the control system seeks an explanation for the unexpected deviations and prods production or sales personnel to meet enterprise expectations. Not often enough does management become excited when something happens which is correctly done or when an objective is exceeded by good performance. Although management has a rigorous responsibility to see that the enterprise functions well with profitable operations, mobilizing all employees to do their best is likely to be done most effectively when recognition is not limited to calling out an individual or a department for below-standard performance.

Requisites for effective control

The kind of controls needed in an enterprise will vary depending upon such factors as size, nature of work performed, and the degree of accuracy and detail required. However, there are some characteristics which apply to any good control system. Controls should be diagnostic, therapeutic, accurate, timely, understandable, and economical.

Controls should be diagnostic

Controls ought to apply to significant processes or problems with which management should be concerned. These controls ought to ferret out errors, mistakes, deviations, and differences and hold them up for management attention. Controls should be sensitive enough that deviations are reported before a complete breakdown in some part of the system occurs. The best control system is one where operations are not permitted to sink into deep difficulty before any intelligent action is taken to remedy the situation.

Controls should be therapeutic

The excellent control system will not only call attention to deviations but also will suggest a means of curing the difficulty. Today's completely automated processes have built-in corrections for specific types of variations from standards, and these problems will be corrected automatically. Even in less automated situations the controls should present evidence to management in a form such that the solution to the problem is suggested. A skilled manager may be required to interpret the signals, and at times causes of deviations will be difficult to ascertain, but a control system should at least point the direction of the needed improvement.

Controls should be accurate and timely

It may appear quite obvious to point out that controls should be accurate and also that they should be timely or prompt in reporting deviations. However, when one desires both accuracy and timeliness in a control system a conflict situation may arise. In striving for a high degree of accuracy more time may be required to seek additional data to increase the certainty of one's conclusions.

An example of conflict between accuracy and timeliness can be seen in a typical problem of the market research director. If the market research director wanted to determine the success of a new product he might require a carefully selected sample of salesmen's reports, customers' reactions, and reorders from retailers. After receiving this information and processing it to remove some of the sampling errors, the marketing executive would be prepared to report to higher management how nearly the demand for the new product is in line with expectations.

However, consider the time and expense required for such a lengthy analysis. Often management cannot wait this long before setting production schedules and putting sales promotion programs into effect. More rapid analysis for control purposes, based on less elaborate data, with more generalized conclusions may be necessary for immediate control purposes with the more detailed analysis coming along later to be used in a follow-up report on total campaign effectiveness.

When time and accuracy come into conflict in controlling operations then management must decide which is more critical. The answer will depend upon the magnitude of the decision, the time pressure under which management is operating, and how much value the additional information is likely to be in making better decisions.

Controls should be understandable

The most sophisticated control systems are likely to be worthless if they are not understood by those personnel in the business enterprise who must use them or who make use of the information which they provide. Technical and staff personnel have a particular responsibility for seeing that control systems are thoroughly explained to line personnel at the subsystem level because the performance of line personnel will be judged by these controls. Line management must be made aware of the ways in which these controls may increase managerial effectiveness and improve profitability. The line manager should then take the responsibility to see that his subordinates understand the controls appropriate to their areas.

Frequently, the most significant problems in initiating new control systems are not those of a technical nature but are those which involve human relations and communications. A new report form, thrust into the hands of a foreman, perhaps already overburdened with paperwork, without an adequate explanation of its purpose and how the data may improve the functioning of his department, may not be filled out properly. No one should be too surprised if the form, for which the foreman understands no clear purpose, ends up at the bottom of a stack of papers on his desk.

Controls should be economical

The cost of controls should be justified in terms of the profit objectives of the business system. Controls should not be so elaborate and restrictive that they become an end in themselves. The amount of money spent on controls will depend upon the relative importance of the process being controlled, the loss which might be incurred without controls, and the size of the enterprise's operations. The elaborate control systems complete with sophisticated computerized applications used by McDonnell-Douglas Corporation and the National Aeronautics and Space Agency to track space explorations are obviously ridiculous for the small shop selling children's clothing. However, economy is a relative concept. Effective controls for a small enterprise are just as necessary for good management and profitable continuation of the business as are the extensive control systems which are appropriately utilized in a giant industrial firm today. Under any circumstances, management should not spend more money collecting and analyzing data than may be saved by the improvements that stem from the additional information.

The budget—a key management device

The budget is a key device for management in planning, coordination, and control of system operations. The *budget* itself is a document which outlines in quantitative terms the planned operations of the enterprise for a specified period of time. The budgeting process begins with broad planning by top management of the kind of needs the enterprise hopes to satisfy. Appropriate data are gathered from subsystems such as marketing and production and are translated into budgets which will culminate in a financial plan of monetary expenditures and expected receipts along with an estimate of the profitable return on the enterprise's investment in economic resources. Thus, budgeting provides a means of translating the goals of the enterprise into quantitative terms and also of setting a basis for control. The budget is valuable for coordination by management since it provides a guideline for informing different departments or subsystems of their part in the overall plans of the enterprise. Such communication of financial information aids in balancing different departmental plans and assists top management which bears the ultimate responsibility for overall subsystem coordination.

Though budgeting practice is quite varied among business enterprises as well as for governmental and nonprofit institutions, there are three types of budgets that are frequently used in business which in combination make up a sound budgeting system. These three types are operations budgets, cash budgets, and capital budgets.

The operations budget

The *operations budget,* sometimes called the revenue and expense budget, consists of a forecast of expected sales along with an estimate of the costs necessary to achieve the sales goal. Usually this budget will be made up in detail for the year ahead, though sometimes estimates for as long as three to five years are also made. However, the most important part of the operations budget is the estimate of revenues and expenses for the immediate upcoming period.

The revenues portion of the operations budget comes from a forecast of sales for the coming year. Since the sale of goods and services constitutes the chief source of operating revenues for most business enterprises, the sales forecast is a key variable in operations budgeting. The information for developing the sales forecast comes from both the external and internal environments.

External sources of sales estimates come from the general and more specific economic data developed by public and private agencies. The federal government is the most important source of national economic data. The U.S. Department of Commerce issues the monthly *Survey of Current Business* which contains information which is useful for all business enterprises. Both the *Federal Reserve Bulletin* published monthly by the Board of Governors in Washington, D.C., and the *Economic Indicators* issued by the staff of the Joint Congressional Committee on the Economic Report contain pertinent surveys and indices of economic activity. The Board of Governors also plays an important role in that it acts as the nation's central monetary authority affecting the supply of money and credit. The U.S. Bureau of the Census can provide useful information to the businessman on both a national and regional basis.

Private sources of business news include the daily editions of *The Wall Street Journal,* weekly *Business Week* and a number of monthly news magazines, such as *Fortune* and *Dun's Review.* These publications provide information on general business trends and an analysis of economic developments, while a wide variety of trade publications are available which serve the needs of particular industries and areas. These trade journals not only interpret the broad economic view but through the cooperation of member firms are able to collect and present data relevant to their own particular industries.

General economic data obtained externally must be analyzed by the particular enterprise and integrated with material the business gathers on its own. Sampling techniques are available whereby the enterprise can conduct its own surveys to obtain information about consumer attitudes or reactions to its products. This market research is valuable when the sample is properly prepared and the survey is well done. The use of mathematical techniques makes the design and the evaluation of the relatively small statistical sample within the reach of many firms in terms of cost and feasibility.

The enterprise must also use internal data in preparing the sales forecast. These data come from reports of sales personnel, marketing managers, top executives of the enterprise, and from mathematical analysis of the enterprise's past sales experience. Despite the increased availability of mathematical models and statistical analysis, the art of sales forecasting still requires the considered judgment of managerial personnel both in its formulation and application.

After the sales forecast has been made, a sales budget which contains the plans necessary to accomplish the goals set forth in the forecast is drawn up. This sales budget translates the plans into quantitative terms not only for anticipated revenues but also for the expenditures necessary to generate those revenues. This means that budgets for product development, advertising, and sales promotion should be related to the operations budget along with other spending plans necessary to achieve the sales objective for the upcoming period.

In order to check on how closely actual results are conforming to the budget it is necessary that the sales budget be broken down by products and months. Without this detailed breakdown a comparison of actual results with expectations would be relatively useless for good direction and control. Ultimately each salesman should have his own budget so that he can check his own performance as well as being subject to management's evaluation.

Budget review and flexibility. A means of review and revision is necessary if the operations budget is to be useful as a control device. The prompt reporting of actual sales results and comparison of these results with those anticipated by the budget provides the basis for control. There is no point in setting up a budget and then blindly pursuing it without regard to subsequent developments. Marketing executives should be able to make immediate adjustments to new opportunities or difficulties. Variations in sales will occur which even the best forecasting cannot take into account. When this happens management should appraise these changed conditions to see what effect this will have on the budget.

This does not mean that the basic operations budget is changed every time actual results vary from projected sales activity or every time expected circumstances change somewhat. The basic budget should serve as a frame of reference with a reasonable explanation being made for those variations which are bound to occur. This should not prevent supplementary or partial revisions during the year as circumstances dictate to make the budget more meaningful for coordination of the different activities of the enterprise.

The decision by management to make a major revision in the operations budget is a difficult one. The danger of losing the meaningfulness of the budget always exists when it is changed capriciously. Only when the variations from expected results become so large and widespread that the original budget has relatively little meaning should the entire document be completely revised. Since most operations budgets are drawn for the period of the year ahead, a thorough revision is always less than a year away, and management should use variations from expectations as a learning device to improve the forecasting and total budgeting process in future periods.

Sometimes two operations budgets representing the extremes of business optimism and pessimism will be drawn up for a year. One will be based on the assumption of excellent economic conditions and system success with the highest level of sales projected. This will be compared with a budget projecting the lowest level of operations assuming less buoyant economic circumstances and less effective results from management programs. Then, the most likely forecast, which normally comes somewhere between the extremes, will be outlined. This most probable expectation is adopted as the budget for the coming period with spending programs and expected results being based on this. However, supplementary budgets are prepared to be put into effect if results improve beyond expectations or if they do not measure up to budgeted figures. In planning the budget management must take into consideration that some expenses will vary depending upon the level of system activity. These variable costs include wages for production personnel, materials cost for additional units manufactured, along with certain selling and administrative costs. Taking these variable costs into account in the budgeting process provides management with a basis for control at whatever level of operations the enterprise achieves during the budget period.

Simplified example of an operations budget

Figure 6–2 is an example of an operations budget for a small retail enterprise showing operating results for 1970 and the operations budget for 1971. The management is projecting an increase in sales of 20 percent based on its analysis that 1970 was not a good year for retail sales in the area because of a drought affecting local farm income. Also, the owner plans to increase advertising spending by 50 percent in 1971 which should stimulate sales. This budget was prepared during the latter part of 1970 and finalized as the 1971 budget period was beginning.

FIGURE 6–2
Tot-Teen Shop operations budget—1971

		Actual 1970		Budget 1971
Sales		$70,000		$84,000
Cost of merchandise sold		42,000		50,000
Gross profit on sales		$28,000		$34,000
Operating expenses				
Selling expenses				
Sales salaries	$10,200		$10,400	
Advertising	2,400		3,600	
Miscellaneous selling expenses	400		500	
Total selling expenses	$13,000		$14,500	
General expenses				
General salaries	$ 4,800		$ 5,200	
Rent	2,400		2,400	
Utilities	900		1,000	
Miscellaneous taxes	700		900	
Insurance	300		300	
Miscellaneous general expenses	1,200		1,600	
Total general expenses	$10,300		$11,400	
Total operating expenses		23,300		25,900
Profit from operations		$ 4,700		$ 8,100
Income taxes		1,200		2,100
Net profit		$ 3,500		$ 6,000

The operations budget provides a means of systematic planning for the future and is a basis for control. Actual results can be compared with budgeted plans to determine whether operations are conforming to expectations. In actual practice the owner of the Tot-Teen Shop would prepare more detailed budgets for each department or for major items in the budget. This would facilitate taking remedial action if results were below expectations. Also, the budget period would customarily be broken down into shorter time periods within the year, such as quarterly or monthly budgets to improve the timeliness and useful-ness of this management tool.

Cash budgets

The cash budget is an estimate of the business enterprise's cash re-ceipts and cash disbursements over a specified period of time. This bud-get is used to forecast requirements for cash during future periods and is a helpful means of justifying a request for a short-term loan from a bank to finance a seasonal increase in business operations.

The cash budget usually extends over the year ahead with cash re-ceipts and disbursements being estimated on a monthly basis. Sometimes when cash balances are very large and closer control is justified the in-flows and outflows of cash will be estimated on a semimonthly, weekly, or daily basis. There is no reason why the cash budget cannot be adapted to any time period which will provide management with a better means of estimating cash needs, controlling cash balances, planning for short-term loans, or investing surplus cash.

Example of a cash budget

Figure 6–3 illustrates a cash budget prepared for the Tot-Teen Shop, a small retail enterprise, over a 9-month period having a sales peak in the spring and again in the late summer.

An analysis of the cash budget for Tot-Teen Shop reveals that addi-tional sources of cash will be required for the months of February, March, and August because of a cumulative cash shortage caused by more cash being paid out than was taken in. With this information the management can request a short-term loan from its banker. In March it is estimated that $1,350 could be repaid on the loan from March's cash surplus so that necessary bank credit at the end of March is pro-jected at only $4,500. In April the monthly net cash inflow from opera-tions is forecast at $6,300, which will be enough to repay completely the $4,500 bank loan and leave a cash surplus of $1,800 by the end of April. No further bank credit for operations will be necessary until the month of August when payment for large purchases, probably for the Christmas selling season, necessitates borrowing an estimated $2,250, which can be repaid during the month of September plus leav-ing a cash surplus of $400 if cash flow projections are reasonably accurate.

The preparation of a cash budget requires the management to con-

FIGURE 6–3

Tot-Teen Shop

(cash budget forecast for January through September, 1971)

	Jan.	Feb.	Mar.	April	May	June	July	Aug.	Sept.
Cash receipts:									
Cash sales	$3,000	$ 2,000	$4,000	$ 6,000	$3,000	$2,000	$2,000	$3,000	$5,000
Credit collections	6,000	4,000	2,000	4,000	6,000	3,000	2,000	2,000	4,000
Total monthly receipts	$9,000	$ 6,000	$6,000	$10,000	$9,000	$5,000	$4,000	$5,000	$9,000
Disbursements:									
Purchases	$7,000	$11,000	$2,000	$ 2,000	$7,000	$4,000	$2,500	$7,000	$4,000
Wages	800	800	1,000	1,000	800	800	800	800	1,000
Rent	200	200	200	200	200	200	200	200	200
Utilities and miscellaneous	150	150	150	100	100	100	150	150	150
Advertising	350	200	100	400	300	200	150	200	400
Taxes			1,200			1,200			600
Total disbursements	$8,500	$12,350	$4,650	$ 3,700	$8,400	$6,500	$3,800	$8,350	$6,350
Monthly cash change, inflow or outflow	+$ 500	–$ 6,350	+$1,350	+$ 6,300	+$ 600	–$1,500	+$ 200	–$3,350	+$2,650
Cumulative inflow or outflow of cash	+$ 500	–$ 5,850	–$4,500	+$ 1,800	+$2,400	+$ 900	+$1,100	–$2,250	+$ 400
Beginning cash	$1,500								
Minimum cash desired	$1,500								
Excess cash or cash shortage at the end of month	+$ 500	–$ 5,850	–$4,500	+$ 1,800	+$2,400	+$ 900	+$1,100	–$2,250	+$ 400
Monthly needs— Bank borrowings		$ 5,850	$4,500					$2,250	

sider carefully the nature of future operations by planning cash disbursements and estimating sales. The Tot-Teen Shop is a relatively simple business with the most significant variations in disbursements being in purchases which normally are paid for about three months ahead of the retail selling season. Advertising and sales promotion expenses also vary depending upon seasonal factors since this management has found that in certain off-season months additional funds spent on advertising bring in very little additional business.

Credit collections normally will come in the month following credit sales since the Tot-Teen Shop derives about half of its sales from 30-day credit accounts. Management watches its credit accounts carefully and screens requests for credit so that there is a very small proportion of overdue accounts which may ultimately become bad debts.

An important assumption of the illustrative cash budget in Figure 6–3 is that cash receipts and disbursements are made fairly regularly throughout the month. This is especially important since if significantly large disbursements had to be made by a specified time during the month, for example the tenth, then cash budgeting for the first ten days of the month would be very important and the cash budget should be divided into two periods per month instead of one. The complexity of the cash budget will depend upon the needs of the enterprise, the nature of cash inflows and outflows, and the degree of their predictability.

As can be seen from this illustration the cash budget can be useful as a planning tool since it requires management to think through its entire operation for coming months. Besides taking normal cash receipts and disbursements for operations into account, the cash budget can be used to plan for future capital expenditures such as equipment and building improvements.

By extending the cash budget ahead for future periods on a continuous basis, management has a control device which can be used as a check against actual cash receipts and disbursements. By using the cash budget as a standard for control purposes it is possible to improve the quality of cash forecasting and to enable management to anticipate cash shortages and make arrangements for proper financing in advance. Should the enterprise have such an abundance of cash that cash shortages normally do not occur, the cash budget can be used to show the magnitude of cash on hand above the amount necessary for operations. Then this excess cash can be invested by management in assets which will be more profitable than large idle cash balances in the enterprise's bank account.

Capital budgets

The capital budget consists of investment plans for assets which will last longer than a year. Such capital budgeting items include machinery, buildings, land, improvements to facilities, and a variety of other assets which will not be used up during the accounting period in which they are acquired. As with the operations budget, the capital budget is usually prepared for the year immediately ahead. However, additional capital budgets are also prepared for a longer period in the future in order to program large-scale investments and to coordinate finance, production, and marketing subsystem activities associated with major long-term expenditures.

The capital budget is made up of a list of proposed investment projects and normally includes a justification for each item on the list. One important criterion for justification of a capital investment proposal is the anticipated rate of return which the project is expected to yield. However, not all projects requiring capital investment can be evaluated on the basis of their profit returns since not all generate profits or savings over older investments. Such capital expenditures as money spent on an employees' cafeteria, or on paving the parking lot, or on renovating the home office building cannot be measured by the percentage of return on the required investment. Instead, this type of expenditure must be justified by virtue of improved morale, convenience, appearance, safety, or some other less quantitative measure.

Approval of the capital budget normally is done by the board of directors after budget committees have analyzed the capital budgets of the various departments or subsystems of the business enterprise. In the multiproduct company, with divisions functioning almost as independent systems, an overall framework is worked out by the board within which each division must develop its own capital budget before it is submitted to top management for approval. Once a major capital expenditure has been approved in principle, then the managers who will have direct responsibility for the project complete detailed plans and present these plans for final approval for authorization of actual cash expenditures.

The level of management which actually authorizes specific capital expenditures depends upon the amount of money involved and the policies adopted in each enterprise. An example of the type of authority required for capital expenditures might be something like this:

Departmental superintendents may authorize capital spending up to $500.

The factory manager may approve capital investments from $500 to $2,500.

Finance committee of the board of directors may approve projects from $2,500 to $20,000.

Full board of directors approval is required on all capital investment projects of over $20,000.

Once approval has been granted for the capital investment project, control should be a continuing part of the procedure. Reports should be prepared to show how nearly actual expenditures are in line with planned spending. This check continues through the construction and installation phases. After the project begins operation, the anticipated rate of return on the investment or the expected savings are compared with the amounts projected when the proposal was approved. Postcompletion audits of capital budgeting projects are essential to check on profit progress and to improve future budget planning procedures. In this way operating managers may be held responsible for their estimates of anticipated return on proposed capital investments as well as for the profitable use of funds already committed to their departments or subsystems.

Cost accounting for control

The record-keeping system in the business enterprise provides a means for control. Cost accounting generates data which can be used to establish centers of managerial responsibility for judging performance. Responsibility centers can be established for a division, a department, or at the foreman's level whenever costs can be controlled by managers in that particular subsystem. Cost accounting provides a basis for analyzing the controllable costs in a responsibility center.

Whenever a responsibility center's activities generate measurable revenues for the overall system it is possible to move one step further by designating the subsystem as a profit center where not only costs but also profits are analyzed. It is not feasible to designate all responsibility centers as profit centers since profits cannot be economically measured in all areas and not all subsystems have operations which directly produce revenues. A manufacturing department can usually be sectioned off into different profit centers, but the stockroom or the engineering department which provides staff services may not be judged on the basis of its profit contributions but on how well it assists other departments or subsystems.

Another important aspect of cost accounting is the determination of the proper amount of costs to assign each unit of production for the determination of product costs, pricing decisions, or profits. Cost accounting may also be used in providing information which will suggest the expected costs of taking various courses of action in the future. In these ways cost accounting is a valuable planning and decision-making tool as well as being useful for control purposes.

The accounting system discussed in Chapter 14 provides information which is the basis for other financial controls.

Summary

Control is an integral part of the management process. Control provides a means for measuring the progress which an enterprise is making toward its objectives. The three elements of control are the establishment of standards, measurement of performance, and analysis and correction of deviations from expectations.

Control systems will vary with the nature of the enterprise. However, any good control system should be diagnostic, therapeutic, accurate, timely, understandable, and economical.

The budget is a key control device. Budgets outline in quantitative terms the planned operations of the business system for a specified period of time. A variety of budgets are used, including operations budgets, sales budgets, cash budgets, and capital budgets.

Cost accounting generates data which can be used to establish centers of managerial responsibility for judging performance. A responsibility center, when it generates measurable revenues for the enterprise, can also be designated as a profit center, where not only costs but also profits are analyzed. Cost accounting can be used to assign costs for each unit of production for the determination of product costs, pricing decisions, or profit planning.

Appendix—break-even analysis

The technique of break-even analysis can be a useful management planning and control device for understanding the relationship between costs and revenues at different levels of operations. The break-even chart, sometimes called the profitgraph, assumes a particular pattern of variable and fixed costs and provides management with an estimate of profits or losses that would occur at various levels of sales. In constructing a break-even chart, first the cost functions are analyzed and then the sales revenue function is added.

In the first stage, Figure 6–4 shows how variable and fixed costs when added together equal the total costs of operations at different levels of volume. Variable costs for this particular product have been estimated

FIGURE 6–4
Estimated cost structure

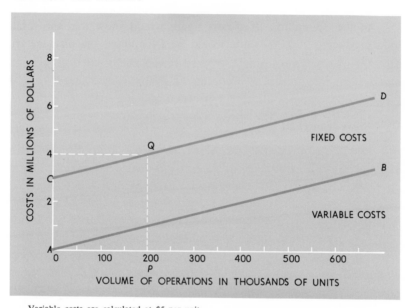

Variable costs are calculated at $5 per unit.
Fixed costs are at a level of $3 million for range of operations from 0 to 600,000 units annually.

at $5 per unit. Therefore, the total variable costs line, *AB,* increases at a rate of $5 for each additional unit produced to reflect the added costs of materials and labor for the extra units. Thus at the zero level of production there are no variable costs, while at the level of 200,000 units of production the total variable costs equal $1 million.

Fixed costs of $3 million remain constant regardless of the level of output for this particular business enterprise. Fixed costs are shown on

Figure 6–4 as the vertical distance between the *AB* and *CD* lines on the chart. At a level of zero units of production the fixed costs of $3 million are shown by the distance between points *A* and *C*. That fixed costs are constant at any level of output is illustrated by measuring the vertical distance between *AB* and *CD* at any level of production. Note the distance between *AB* and *CD* remains a constant $3 million.

Total costs of operations for the enterprise are represented by the *CD* line which includes both the total variable costs and fixed costs at any particular volume level. Total costs can be verified for any level of production by multiplying the units produced by the $5 variable costs per unit and adding the $3 million fixed costs. For example, if the 200,000 units of production are multiplied by the $5 per unit variable cost, this equals $1 million. The $1 million variable cost figure added to the $3 million fixed cost figure would show that the total cost of producing 200,000 units would be $4 million, the distance from *P* to *Q*.

FIGURE 6–5
Break-even chart

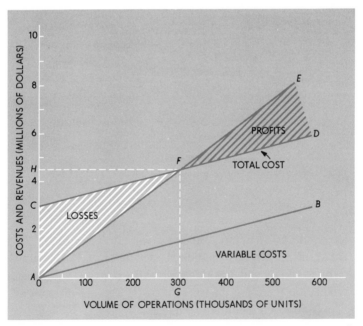

Variable costs calculated at $5 per unit. Fixed costs calculated at $3 million total.
Sales revenue calculated at $15 per unit.

In the second stage, Figure 6–5 is the complete break-even chart. It has the same cost structure as Figure 6–4. However, now a sales revenue line, designated as *AE*, has been added to complete the revenue and cost relationship. Sales revenue increases at a rate of $15 per unit, the assumed price for which each unit of the enterprise's product could be sold. The rate of sales revenue increase is constant, which implies that each unit is sold at the same price regardless of the number of units sold.

Notice that the total revenue line, *AE*, crosses the total costs line, *CD*, at point *F*. Point *F* is called the break-even point and is where revenues equal costs. In this example this is at a level of sales of 300,000 units, marked by point *G*, and at a cost of $4,500,000, marked by point *H*. At the break-even point the enterprise is neither earning a profit nor incurring a loss. At sales levels higher than *G* the enterprise generates a profit from operations. Below the break-even point sales revenue is insufficient to cover total costs and the enterprise suffers a loss.

Since the break-even point is where sales revenue is equal to total costs of operation, the break-even point may be determined more precisely by using the following formula than by looking at the graph:

$$\text{Sales revenue} = \text{Total costs}$$

or

$$\begin{bmatrix} \text{No. of} \\ \text{units sold} \end{bmatrix} \begin{bmatrix} \text{Price per} \\ \text{unit} \end{bmatrix} = \begin{bmatrix} \text{Total fixed} \\ \text{cost} \end{bmatrix} + \begin{bmatrix} \text{No. of} \\ \text{units sold} \end{bmatrix} \begin{bmatrix} \text{Variable costs} \\ \text{per unit} \end{bmatrix}$$

To calculate the break-even point by formula from the information given in the example for Figure 6–3: Let *X* equal number of units sold at break-even point.

$$(X)\ (\$15) = \$3,000,000 + (X)\ (\$5)$$
$$10X = 3,000,000$$
$$X = 300,000 \text{ units}$$
$$15X = \text{Total sales revenue at break-even}$$
$$= \$4,500,000$$

These figures may also be read at points *G* and *H* on the break-even chart in Figure 6–5 as was shown, although graphic presentations are more difficult to read with accuracy to the last digits.

The break-even chart is useful in demonstrating the factors which affect profits and the way in which profits may be controlled. A study of the break-even chart shows that profits will vary for each level of volume of operations. Observe on Figure 6–5 that the level of profits increases as sales increase past the break-even point. There are four ways in which the profit of a business can be increased, each of which can be analyzed through break-even analysis:

Variable costs per unit can be decreased.
Fixed costs can be decreased.
Selling price per unit can be increased.
More units can be sold.

Note what effect varying any of the above could have on the profits as shown in the break-even chart Figure 6–5. It would be useful for the student to work out a numerical example to demonstrate his understanding. Each factor should be worked through assuming the other three remain constant, even though in actual practice changes in one factor will likely have an influence on others. For example, an increase in the sales price per unit may well result in a lower volume of units sold.

In order to see the limitations in the use of break-even analysis one should keep in mind the assumptions on which the chart is based. It is assumed that variable costs increase at a constant rate; that is, materials and direct labor costs are the same for each additional unit of production. Fixed costs are the same throughout the given range of operations assuming no changes in the level of capital invested or changes in overhead which would alter these fixed costs. It is assumed there will be no changes in the market which may affect selling prices. The break-even chart assumes that production and sales move together with no significant change in inventories which might affect cost relationships. By depicting cost and revenue relationships simply as straight lines the estimates of losses at the low end of the scale and profits at the upper end of the scale may be of only limited value. However, normally the enterprise is not faced with a question of eliminating sales or cutting them back to a very small fraction of previous levels. Also, it is rare when management can increase sales as much as three times or more without significant additional capital investment. Therefore, the break-even chart can be used best by management in the analysis and control of business operations over a limited period of time and range of volume.

Terms for review

control
standards
budget
operations budget (revenue and
    expense budget)

sales budget
cash budget
capital budget
cost accounting

Questions

1. What is the purpose of control in the business enterprise?

2. What recommendations would you make to the owner of a new manufacturing enterprise for the development of a control system? What different types of controls would be needed?

3. Explain the characteristics of an effective control system.

4. What is a budget? Why are budgets important?

5. Outline a step-by-step procedure for developing an operations budget for a manufacturer which supplies replacement auto parts to wholesale supply distributors on the West Coast. How would you develop the sales forecast for such an enterprise?

6. Assume the cash disbursements for purchases shown in Figure 6–3 for the Tot-Teen Shop were made during the first ten days of each month instead of throughout the month. Restate the cash budget for the Tot-Teen Shop assuming that all other disbursements are made regularly throughout the month and that cash receipts are received in an even flow throughout the month.

7. What is the relationship of the capital budget to the operations budget and the cash budget?

8. In what ways is cost accounting useful to management?

CASES

Jim Rader, proprietor

After a period of several years as foreman and chief estimator for McGill Cabinet Shop in Nashburg, Jim Rader quit his job to begin his own woodworking shop. Two of the best craftsmen at McGill quit to join Jim's operation; some custom orders were received; and an initial order was obtained from a local lumber yard for preassembled door frames and windows which would keep the men occupied for a reasonable period of time.

Despite this good start for his new enterprise, Jim Rader was concerned as he recalled the nature of the control system used by his former employer. Jim felt that if his business were to prosper he would need controls on costs and the quality of his products. However, he was thoroughly dissatisfied with the control system under which he had been forced to work in the McGill Shop.

Jim called his friend, Larry Thomas, who was a certified public accountant and a partner in a local accounting firm, asking him for an appointment to discuss the new business and the kinds of controls which he would need. On the day of the appointment Jim arrived at the accounting firm's suite of offices.

"Larry," began Jim, "I want to approach you for some help with my new business. We have been successful initially in generating business, and I am pleased with the quality of our work force. However, with my experience at McGill I never did get a clear understanding of their control system. If what they had represents good controls I don't want any part of it. What I would like for you to do, Larry, is to analyze my business at this point and indicate what you think I need in the way of controls."

"I believe we are prepared to do a control analysis for you," responded the consultant. "Most of my time is spent now in providing management consulting services to our clients rather than the more traditional public accounting work. Many changes have occurred in our profession in recent years, and I am proud to say that while our partnership is small by big city standards, we have kept up with these changes.

"Why don't you start off by telling me something about the kinds of controls you didn't like at your former situation and then what your present operations are like. After this I can proceed with a preliminary written report for you and we can get together and talk it over before any elaborate system is designed. Among other things, you will need to control such items as the cost of consultants, and I think this approach will be best for both of us in the long run."

"To begin with," Jim said, "it seemed like McGill's management was penny-wise and pound-foolish. One of the things that really bugged me was telephone usage in the shop. Part of my job consisted of contacting customers as a kind of technical advisor. It would have been a lot easier to call out-of-town customers than to write letters, but Bill McGill, the company president, put his foot down on the use of long-distance telephone calls and said that I would have to plan my work so that such calls would be held to an absolute minimum. Also, every time I made a long-distance call I had to fill out a chit for the bookkeeper so when the phone bill came in it could be checked to see that none of us were making long-distance personal calls which were billed to the company.

"Another thing that I didn't like was the way the bookkeeper kept pestering the foremen to get in their time sheets and materials-in-process reports. You would have thought that everything revolved around the bookkeeper's office in that shop. I guess Mr. McGill thought so too since he always was complaining to the office force about not having reports completed on time.

"We never knew how we stood with the company although I'll say that the Christmas bonuses paid out by the McGills were sure nice to have at that time of the year. However, very little was ever said on how things were going in the shop unless McGill came down to complain about something going wrong.

"I guess you wonder, Larry," continued Jim Rader, "why I stuck it out as long as I did at McGill's. Sometimes I wonder myself. The old-timers said that Mr. McGill had been like that ever since his son was killed in Vietnam in 1967, and they just put up with it. Also, the firm does have a good reputation for quality work. I learned a lot there and the money was good. When I quit, Mr. McGill seemed surprised and said that he had me picked to be promoted to general manager of the shop when Sam Jones retired in a few years, but that was sure news to me and by then I already had made up my mind. However, this doesn't have anything to do with control systems.

"There was one good thing done in McGill's shop and that was the care which all the foremen were forced to use in keeping the jobs separate. As you may know, most of their business is big custom deals and every stick of wood that went into a job was accounted for. They sure knew which jobs they came out on and which lost money, and there weren't many jobs that they had any losses on.

"As I outlined over the telephone the other day, my business is a small one at present. We have two men working in the shop and there is a student I employ part time to handle miscellaneous jobs ranging from answering the telephone while I'm gone to cleaning up the shop and handling some paper work. However, most of the office work is done by my wife who comes in when she can, and I do all the selling as well as ordering the raw materials. We think we have the beginning of something which could work out very nicely, but I don't want to foul it up by too many controls or not enough."

1. Appraise the control system in the McGill Cabinet Shop as described by Jim Rader. Discuss positive and negative elements of the system as it is understood by Rader.

2. What steps could the management of McGill Cabinet Shop have taken to improve the effectiveness of its control system?

3. Outline a preliminary report from the accountant's office suggesting the basic nature of controls needed by Jim Rader at this time. Does Jim Rader need to be concerned with a control system with such a small business? Why or why not?

Tot-Teen Shop

The Tot-Teen Shop was established early in 1969 by Mr. and Mrs. Lloyd Bethany in a town of 20,000 in upstate New York. Mrs. Bethany acted as general manager of the shop and did the buying. Mr. Bethany who was a manufacturer's representative for several builders' supply manufacturers had little active part in the business except for general advice and assistance as it seemed desirable for him to provide. The shop was stocked with a quality price line of merchandise for children from birth up to age 13. Although there were other stores in town which sold children's clothing, the Tot-Teen Shop lines were of higher quality than the competition in the community.

Tot-Teen quickly became known for the quality of its merchandise and personal service, and business was brisk. In addition to Mrs. Bethany who put in full time at the shop, one full-time woman sales-clerk was employed and part-time sales personnel were used during seasonal sales periods or when Mrs. Bethany was required to be out of town on buying trips or on vacation. A part-time bookkeeper handled the paper work of the business.

In December, 1971, Mrs. Bethany was planning her sales program for next Easter, which was April 2, 1972. In past peak seasons the Tot-Teen Shop had borrowed funds from the First National Bank to cover inventory buildups. These seasonal borrowings had been promptly reduced after the selling season had ended. Mrs. Bethany assumed that funds would be available again from the bank.

To prepare her request for short-term credit Mrs. Bethany put down the information necessary to prepare a cash budget of cash receipts and disbursements for the first six months of 1972. Based on past years' results and her expectations for the current year ahead Mrs. Bethany estimated sales as given in Exhibit 1.

EXHIBIT 1
Sales estimates for first 6 months of 1972

January	$ 8,000
February	5,000
March	13,000
April	9,000
May	8,000
June	6,000

Approximately one half of the shop's sales are cash sales with the remainder being made on 30-day charge accounts. The Bethanys screen requests for credit carefully and for planning purposes it may be assumed that charged sales will be collected in the month following sale of merchandise. Customers' accounts receivable on December 31, 1971, will be $7,000 according to estimates.

In late December, 1971, the Tot-Teen Shop had a cash balance of approximately $1,500. The Bethanys considered this to be a satisfactory minimum level of cash so that funds would be available to take care of unforeseen needs which might arise.

The customary terms under which the Bethanys purchased merchandise for the shop provided for cash discounts for prompt payment. It had been the practice of the Tot-Teen Shop to take all cash discounts, which means that merchandise will be paid for in the month following its shipment. The cash discounts have already been deducted from the purchase figures in Exhibit 2. Therefore these amounts would be paid the month following purchase.

EXHIBIT 2
Estimated purchases of merchandise

December, 1971	$ 8,000
January, 1972	10,000
February	5,000
March	2,000
April	3,000
May	5,000
June	5,000

For planning purposes in this case, it may be assumed that the payments for merchandise would be made on a regular basis throughout the month in which they were due, not falling in large volume on any specific date.

The preceding schedule (Exhibit 2) was prepared by the Bethanys for their purchases for December, 1971, and estimated purchases the first six months of 1972. The amounts shown are for estimated invoice dates although actual order placement would occur in some cases before the time indicated.

Wages to be paid during the first six months of the year were estimated at $1,000 per month, except during March and April when an additional part-time salesperson would be employed which would result in approximately $200 per month being added to wages expense. The $1,000 included Mrs. Bethany's drawings as proprietor of the shop.

Rent and utilities payments had averaged $300 per month for the past year and there was no indication that this could not be expected in 1972, since two years remained on the Bethanys' lease on the shop building. Advertising was paid for in the month following its use. The advertising schedule was as follows:

December, 1971	$500
January, 1972	200
February	100
March	300
April	200
May	100
June	100

In addition, Mrs. Bethany estimated tax payments of approximately $1,200 in each of the months of March and June. Although the estimates were rough, it was likely that $200 monthly would be spent on miscellaneous items ranging from charitable contributions to minor repairs and expenses associated with buying trips.

After collecting this information, Mrs. Bethany sat down to put together a cash budget forecast to present to the loan officer with her request for credit to the First National Bank.

1. Prepare in good order the cash budget forecast from the information assembled by Mrs. Bethany.
2. What is the maximum amount of bank credit required assuming that any cash shortage will have to come from bank loans since there is no excess cash presently in the enterprise's bank account?
3. When will the maximum amount of the funds' need arise?
4. When, if at all during the six-month period, will Tot-Teen Shop be able to get out of debt to the bank?

5. If you were a bank loan officer what information would you want in addition to the cash forecast prepared for this case? Would you extend credit to this enterprise?

A problem in profit analysis

The ABC Manufacturing Corporation had one main product line for which management believed rather accurate costs had been calculated. Between production levels of 20,000 and 150,000 units it was estimated that variable costs were $10 per unit. At these levels of production the fixed costs were about $600,000. The current sales price of the product was $25 per unit in the quantities purchased by most customers.

Required:

1. Construct a break-even chart showing cost and revenue functions over the range of production indicated.

(a) At what point is the break-even sales volume in units and dollars?

(b) What is the amount of profit or loss at 20,000 units of production and sales? At 100,000 units? At 150,000 units?

2. In what ways could this analysis be helpful to the management of ABC Manufacturing Corporation?

3. What limitations are there to this analysis?

Human elements of administration

*Effective communication
is an important dimension
of human relations.*

7

Human relations

An understanding of human relations is essential for the effective manager in organizing the activities of people to promote the objectives of the enterprise. This chapter provides an introduction into the human relations aspect of management centering around the following questions:

What is the nature of the individual needs of employees?
What is the importance of direction in the management process?
Why must both the formal and informal organization be considered in developing effective human relations?
How do status and status symbols relate to the business enterprise?
How can managers develop a healthy work climate?

The individual and the business enterprise

Sometimes managers, particularly those at the head of a business enterprise, assume that because they are completely devoted to their company's endeavors that all employees will be similarly motivated. However, many managers recognize that there is likely to be a vast difference between the values which they hold regarding business and those of lower echelon employees. The good manager will understand the difference between individuals' goals and enterprise goals, what motivates individual employees, and the importance of human relations as an element in modern management.

Individual needs versus enterprise goals

The principal goal of the business enterprise is the provision of goods and services to consumers at a profit so as to assure continuation of the enterprise. To a certain extent all persons employed by business enterprises share this goal, since without business enterprise their immediate means of livelihood would be cut off. However, individuals are also concerned about their own personal needs and objectives, which are distinctly separate from the principal goals of the organizations where they are employed. Human relations consists of providing a climate in the business enterprise which will both foster the employee's individual satisfactions and result in achievement of the broad economic objectives of the enterprise.

Individuals have physical and material needs which are met largely through wages and fringe benefits in payment for their work efforts as employees. In today's expanding economy what will satisfy our material needs in the United States has changed greatly over the last 50 years. What was considered a luxury item only a few years ago may be considered a necessity today by a large number of the population. One of management's problems in dealing with employees is to devise wage payment systems which will fairly provide funds to meet the material needs of individuals. The level and system of wage payments is one factor affecting the morale of the work force. This topic is discussed in the next chapter on personnel administration.

However, human relations involves considerably more than merely providing for the physical and material needs of employees. A recognition of the nonpecuniary needs of employees is a key element in developing a good human relations climate in the business enterprise. These nonpecuniary needs are both psychological and social. Psychological needs pertain to the individual's own self-image and include love, self-respect, and a feeling of accomplishment. Social needs include all the needs which arise from man's relation to other individuals and groups and include recognition, acceptance, and group activity.

Some of these psychological and social needs are met by the family and other groups, and management should not assume that the business enterprise can fulfill all the individual's psychological and social needs. However, a large proportion of an individual's waking hours are spent on the job, and it is of critical importance that management recognize the nonpecuniary needs of its employees. An individual cannot shut off his social and psychological needs when he steps into the factory or office. He cannot be expected to react without emotions and feelings to the machines and situations which he encounters in the workplace. Particularly, the worker cannot be expected to put aside his feelings in his relationships with other individuals with whom he comes in contact at the business enterprise. Higher levels of employee morale can result from the enterprise recognizing and meeting the employee's psychological and social needs insofar as it is feasible.

Motivation of the individual

How does management deal with its employees so as to motivate them to perform well in the work situation? Early in Chapter 4 a motive was defined as a drive, impulse, or desire that moves one to action. Motivation begins with management recognition of the material, social, and psychological needs that individuals bring to the work situation. Workers are moved to action in order to satisfy their needs.

Individuals are motivated to work satisfactorily because of their desire for more goods and services. Once material needs are moderately well provided for, then other needs take on a greater importance. Psychologists suggest that in the United States social and psychological needs may be of ever-increasing importance because of our already high material standard of living.

The fact that material needs may be considered less important than social and psychological needs is highlighted by the results of a study of nearly 1,000 managers who changed jobs. It was found that money ranked fifth among the reasons why executives stated they quit. The four leading factors which ranked above money were: dissatisfaction with the present job; poor chance for advancement; conflicts at work, particularly with the boss; and altered duties or status because of corporate reorganization.

What seems to be the case for managerial personnel is also relevant for production employees. Workers bring to the job a variety of needs which motivate them, and an understanding of the wide range of these needs is important for management. When management has a clear understanding of employee needs, it has a firm basis for directing the activities of the enterprise along the lines of good human relations. Members of the management team should be aware of the types of skills which they will need to develop if they are to be effective in directing the work efforts of others. Only then will they be able to better understand the behavior of employees both in individual and in group situations. An understanding of the needs of employees can help develop a healthy work climate which is indispensable to a successful enterprise.

Direction—dealing with people at work

Direction is the process of aiding an enterprise's employees in carrying out their work activities. Direction is at the heart of management. Coordinating the activities of the many different people needed by the enterprise requires the major part of most managers' time. The process of direction occurs within the work situation at all levels. This means that managers throughout the enterprise should be concerned with good direction of subordinates. To understand the direction function of management one needs to know about the kinds of skills required of the manager, the different types of leadership possible, and the importance of good communications.

Skills required of the manager

In today's business enterprise the manager's job is complex. Different types of skills are required depending upon the manager's level in the organization. These skills may be classified as technical, human, and conceptual.[1] The mix among these three skills is illustrated in Figure 7–1.

Technical skill consists of a manager's ability in and knowledge of a particular process or technique. Technical skill basically requires knowledge of things rather than people. Examples of technical skill are to be found in the operating activities of typists, accountants, and engineers. Technical skill is especially important at the first level of supervision where a close understanding of techniques is frequently necessary. The higher in the management hierarchy one moves, the less important technical skill becomes, as managers rely more upon others for technical information and become increasingly involved in human and conceptual problems. By the time a person reaches top management little or no time is devoted to the exercise of technical skills. This may be one reason why top executives with well-developed human and conceptual skills can move with considerable ease from one industry to another in positions of high responsibility.

---

[1] Robert L. Katz, "Skills of an Effective Administrator," *Harvard Business Review*, January–February, 1955, pp. 33–42.

FIGURE 7–1
Skills required of the effective manager

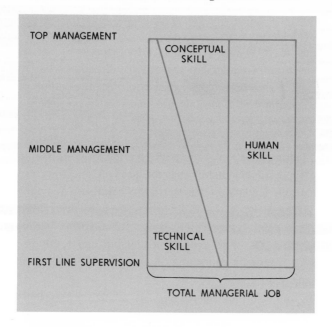

Human skill is the ability to work with people and to build effective work teams. Throughout the organization managers are required to work with people to further the enterprise's objectives. An awareness of the importance of human skill should be part of the new manager's orientation and should be developed throughout his career.

Conceptual skill is the ability to diagnose the different facets of a problem in relation to its total environment and to activate creative solutions. It is the ability to visualize the entire picture and use original thinking in solving identified problems. Conceptual skill is very important for top management in formulating long-range plans, making broad policy decisions, and relating the business enterprise to its industry and the economy. Conceptual skill deals primarily with ideas, human skill with persons, and technical skill with things.

Different types of leadership

Leadership is the element of direction which causes subordinates to follow, and it results in accomplishment of the goals of the enterprise. Leadership can be classified as authoritarian, free-rein, or participative.

With *authoritarian leadership* there is centralized authority and autocratic decision making. Subordinates are given little or no discretion in carrying out work assignments; they merely follow orders. *Free-rein leadership* depends upon the work group itself to define goals and provide solutions to problems. The leadership emerges from within the group. In this type of leadership there is no direction from a superior executive. *Participative leadership* consists of decentralization of authority among subordinates. Decisions are made by those where action is required. Suggestions from subordinates are encouraged. With this type of leadership an emphasis is placed upon communication from the leader to all members of the group and from the group to the leader.

All three types of leadership may be used at one time or another, although free-rein leadership has serious weaknesses for the business enterprise. Free-rein leadership fails to make use of the manager's abilities and places great responsibility on group members without giving them central direction. This type of leadership can result in different departments of the organization operating without proper coordination and with inadequate goals.

Although authoritarian leadership is sometimes criticized, the competent manager who directs in an autocratic manner may be able to accomplish quite well the work of the enterprise, especially in the short run. Less time is required than with either free-rein or participative leadership. Employees do not have to exercise much independent judgment; hence, personnel who have fewer capabilities may be hired. Despite some advantages for authoritarian leadership, in the long run the failure to use the capabilities of all employees and the dependence upon one person weakens this type of leadership for the business enterprise.

Participative leadership is widely regarded as having the most long-run advantages for the successful business enterprise. Management training programs tend to emphasize direction by this method because employee satisfactions and enterprise productivity tend to be maximized. Participative leadership recognizes the dignity of each employee and attempts to draw upon not only managers but all employees for the smooth functioning of the enterprise.

Although participative leadership is generally desirable, it is not to be undertaken unless the manager is genuinely concerned about the views of his subordinates. Neither this type of leadership nor human relations in general should be approached as a mask which the manager can don or remove as he sees fit. Though participative management does represent a philosophy of directing subordinates that can be useful to the enterprise, employees will quickly perceive when it is merely a facade and its usefulness will be severely limited. Under such circumstances the manager might be better advised to use authoritarian leadership openly so employees will clearly understand what is expected from them.

Also, not all individuals want to share the authority and assume the responsibility that goes along with participative management. When employees have been managed autocratically by a previous manager, a new supervisor may encounter difficulties when he attempts to use participative methods. Under such circumstances a gradual dispersion of authority throughout the enterprise or department concerned is advisable. Abrupt changes in leadership methods may result in severe disruption of the enterprise's organizational stability with resulting uncertainty and lower morale for the work force.

When a manager comes into a new supervisory situation, he is well advised to ascertain what has been the mode of operation prior to his arrival. Only after a thorough understanding of the existing situation should he institute changes in the operation of the organization unit unless circumstances are such that the enterprise's existence may be threatened or employee welfare endangered by temporary continuation of existing operations.

The exercise of good leadership by the manager can result in increased efficiency among his employees. With mediocre leadership subordinates will likely carry out their assigned tasks in an adequate manner to avoid reprimand or dismissal, but good leadership can result in employees putting out extra effort above the minimum required. Good leadership direction can increase the long-run effectiveness of the organization and result in a qualitative improvement in operations even though it may not be easily measured over the short run.

The importance of good communication

Definition of communication. Good communication is an essential element in the process of direction. Without communication the most brilliant plans conceived by management cannot be carried out, and management cannot be informed by subordinates of the severe operating problems which arise from time to time in all enterprises. Just what is communication? *Communication* is the transmission of understanding. This requires both a sender and a receiver, each in tune with the other.

Regardless of the form which the communication takes, unless both the communicator and the receiver are using the same frame of reference the transmission's meaning is likely to be garbled and may lead to misunderstanding, fear, frustration, and unacceptable results. A supervisor who, preoccupied by a problem at home, comes into the shop or office one morning and fails to speak to the employees as he usually does may set the entire department to wondering what is wrong and may actually reduce production for the day. His failure to greet the employees may be misinterpreted by them as displeasure with something they have done. The boss's comment to an employee, "Chuck, you're doing a hell of a job," may have either positive or negative interpretations depending upon the circumstances. Unless the frame of reference of the boss's remark is crystal clear to the employee, a compliment may be turned into a criticism in the mind of the subordinate when it was not so intended by the boss.

Communication throughout the organization structure. There are three dimensions of communications within the organization structure of the business enterprise. Information can be transmitted down through the organization from superior to subordinates, frequently following the chain of command. Communication may occur as information being sent up from lower echelons to higher levels in the organization, and there can be horizontal communication such as between departments or among employees at about the same level in the organization. Figure 7–2 symbolizes these dimensions of communication.

FIGURE 7–2
Diagram of vertical and horizontal communication

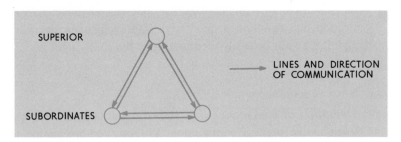

Too often management personnel assume that the only communication going on is the orders and information they send down to subordinates. Nothing could be further from correct. Valuable communications may be received by management from throughout the organization if managers are but aware of it. The number of employee grievances and their source, attitudes reflected in absenteeism or high scrappage rates, constructive suggestions by subordinates, all may be useful upward communication for management.

Horizontal communication in the organization structure provides for essential coordination and information transmission between departments and individuals. While lines of authority generally should be followed when a formal report or order is moving from one department to another, there is no reason why horizontal lines of communication should not be effectively utilized by individuals on the same level of the organization but in different departments. Organization charts showing authority-responsibility relationships should never be meant to limit communication only to those channels.

Written and spoken communications. Both written and spoken communications have important places in the business enterprise. Written communications are widely used for policy statements, procedures, rules, job descriptions, advertising, press releases, office memos, organization charts, letters to persons outside the enterprise, and many types of legal documents. From this wide, but by no means inclusive, list it is apparent that there is great variation in written communications. However, regardless of its nature, the written communication should be stated clearly and concisely with the reader in mind. Putting communications in writing has the advantage that they may be retained for future reference and may be more understandable than an oral communication. When a person writes down his thoughts for someone else the chances are good that the communication will be better stated than if it is spoken. Many persons give greater consideration to the written word than the spoken word since they can be more easily held accountable for it.

Written communication is not without two disadvantages which should be mentioned. First, the present volume of paper work in both business and government is reaching staggering proportions. Many reports, contracts, memoranda, and other paper work are saved long past their usefulness. Duplicated files are kept by departments and individuals to justify decisions or recommendations to higher management should any questions ever be raised. These files frequently far outlive their necessity with the result that valuable space and more clerical help are required for their maintenance.

Second, the fact that information to be communicated is written does not guarantee that it will be carefully thought out or clearly stated.

Furthermore, the written word may be costly by the time it is reproduced and disseminated to those for whom it is intended.

Spoken communication has advantages of speed and possible amplification. Face-to-face communication provides for the transmission of real meaning through tone and facial expression as well as in discussion of the intent of the communicator. The telephone industry has grown to mammoth proportions because of the advantages of instant oral communication over great distances.

As with written communication, clarity and conciseness are virtues in spoken communication. A conference or meeting involving the valuable time of many persons can be quite expensive for the enterprise and verbiage should be avoided by all concerned. A previously circulated written agenda, conscientiously followed by the chairman, will be a great help in making meetings worthwhile for all participants. The principal weakness in spoken communication is that in itself there is no means for future specific reference. The listener may not be sure afterward just what has been said unless some type of recording is made of the conversation.

The importance of listening. No discussion of communication should be undertaken without considering the importance of listening. For good communication to occur there must be a communicator who clearly transmits information, but equally important is the person to whom the datum is directed. Unless the recipient of the information understands the meaning of what is being said, communication cannot take place. Effective listening is as important to good communication as is clear speaking.

The two elements to consider in effective listening are what is heard by the listener and what the speaker means. When the listener hears the meaning intended by the speaker then true oral communication has occurred. A significant barrier to effective listening is the failure of the listener to perceive the frame of reference of the speaker. We do not really understand what is being said to us because we are busy evaluating the speaker's words from our own frame of reference. The question running through our minds when someone is speaking to us, especially when it is the boss, frequently is, "How is this going to affect me?" A more appropriate question would be, "What is this person trying to say?" There will be time later to evaluate the remarks from our own frame of reference. First, we should attempt to understand the speaker's meaning. The next time someone comes to you with a problem or question listen quietly to what he has to say without making any judgments on his statements. Listen with a view to perceiving the problem through the eyes of the speaker. By doing this you will have made an important step in improving the communication.

When a person listens more effectively he will discover that many miscommunications occur because of the failure of speaker and listener to perceive the same problem. One of the most important elements of communication, when persons attempt to discuss a situation which at least one of them views as a problem, is to establish the dimensions of the problem from the frame of reference of all parties. After this is done then discussion can proceed on the merits of various solutions from the different points of view. Sometimes just a careful definition of the issue will result in a conclusion that the originally stated problem does not really exist, but what had occurred was a serious lack of communication. Then action can be initiated to deal with this situation.

Organizational aspects of human relations

Although human relations is usually thought of in terms of interpersonal relationships, there are also organizational aspects to human relations in the business enterprise. The formal and informal organization of the business enterprise, the importance of status in organizations, and the labor union are three important organizational elements of human relations. The first two of these elements are discussed here while the role of unions is analyzed in detail in Chapter 9, which deals with labor relations.

The formal organization

The formal organization of the business enterprise has been discussed in some detail in Chapter 5. Recall that every business enterprise of any size is organized into departments each of which must develop workable authority-responsibility relationships, select line and staff personnel, delegate decision making, and establish the width of the management span of control. A strong thread of human relations runs through all aspects of the formal organization because of the involvement of persons.

In the formal organization each person occupies a particular position or *status* which may be diagrammed on an organization chart similar to Figure 7–3. Each status position carries with it an expected behavior pattern which may be referred to as the *role*. Thus in the functioning of the profit-making enterprise individuals perform the activities of the roles associated with the statuses they occupy. These statuses and roles are formally organized into a smoothly functioning unit designed to promote the enterprise's objectives. The duties and responsibilities involved in these roles continue regardless of who performs them. This means that if the vice president for marketing retires, the status of head of the marketing department does not disappear. Someone else must be selected to fulfill this important position in the business enterprise.

Figure 7–3 depicts part of a simple organization chart showing how the different status positions relate to each other in a hypothetical business enterprise engaged in manufacturing and selling a single product.

FIGURE 7–3
Smith Brothers Corporation
(partial organization chart)

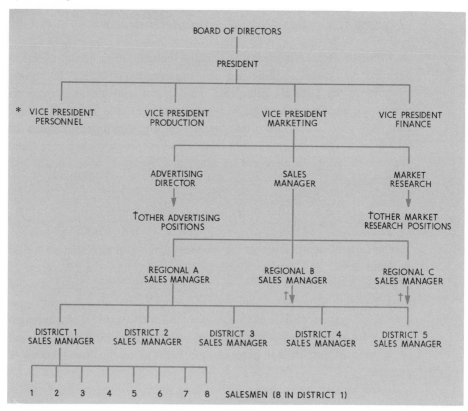

* There is an organization structure under each vice president which is not shown here except for the marketing department.
† Not detailed here for lack of space.

There are no persons named on this organization chart; only the statuses to be filled are given. A job description outlining the duties of each position would accompany this chart. Notice how in the formal organization of the enterprise the lines of authority and responsibility from the board of directors and the president run throughout the organization. This represents the formal and more traditional concept of the authority exercised in the enterprise. It is important for subordinate managers and workers to understand top management roles, as well as their own, since all employees must realize the authority associated with a particular status position if this authority is to be effectively exercised.

The informal organization

The formal organization that facilitates profit-making activities in the business enterprise makes little allowance for the natural desire of the individual to associate with other persons. In every enterprise informal organizations develop spontaneously to meet this social need of people. An *informal organization* is a self-grouping of employees in the work situation that is not detailed on the formal organization chart. The informal organization depends upon the personalities of individuals for its being rather than upon abstract statuses and roles which exist in the formal organization regardless of those who fill these positions.

Functions of the informal organization. The informal organization provides for the social needs and control of its members and facilitates communication among employees. In providing an outlet for the social needs of employees the informal organization may benefit management. On the assembly lines and in the large offices which characterize modern industry a single production worker or filing clerk may not have much recognition in the formal status hierarchy of the enterprise. However, as a member of an informal work group he is recognized, participates in banter or jokes, and has a circle of acquaintances with whom he can relate. This can be an important positive contribution to the work situation.

However, sometimes informal groups become a negative factor. They may exert significant and substantial pressure on individual employees to conform and withhold social recognition if this conformity is not forthcoming. The social control exercised by informal groups has frequently included setting of production standards by production personnel that fit the group's concept of a "fair day's work." These work standards will not necessarily conform either with management's assessment of a reasonable day's productivity or with that of the labor union if one is present in the plant. A fair assumption is that the informal organization's production standard would be set lower than the enterprise's industrial engineering department would recommend. Various means are available to the informal work group in enforcing its standards including refusing to communicate with an individual who refuses to accept their values. Property damage or physical injury might be included in the more extreme sanctions taken by informal group members against those who would not conform.

Informal communication—the grapevine. The second function of the informal organization—communication—is customarily known as the *grapevine.* Managements have found the grapevine to be both a help and a hindrance in operating the business enterprise.

The grapevine can be an effective means of rapidly disseminating information. Management may also get informal reactions to proposed actions before they are formally announced by placing information judiciously with informal group leaders in the business enterprise. This provides management with a trial balloon to test out ideas on employees. Sometimes information may be gained through this means which will cause changes in management's plans. Although members of the management team should promote good communication through the formal organization, the grapevine can also be a useful means of communication both up and down the formal chain of command. Since it is certain to exist in all enterprises, management should take advantage of the information it can provide.

The grapevine can be a hindrance to management when rumors are passed along its channels. In the business enterprise a *rumor* is characterized as incomplete, unconfirmed information which is frequently either incorrect or malicious in its intent. To avoid negative consequences of rumor, management should act to see that correct information is a part of the grapevine. This may include explaining or denying informally circulated information which is incomplete or incorrect along with an accurate explanation of the situation. Rumors will be less of a problem in the enterprise where workers understand that management views them as an important part of the company team. When workers feel secure in their positions and know that management seeks to inform them on matters of importance, the grapevine can be a useful, healthy avenue of communication rather than a disrupting rumor mill. A constant flow of information to employees on what is happening in the enterprise will reduce the negative impact of rumors on employee morale.

Nature of the informal work group. There are three factors that determine the nature of the informal work groups that develop in a business enterprise:

1. *The type of work performed.* There is a tendency for people whose occupation is the same to group together. Thus informal work groups may be composed either of factory workers or office workers. Only rarely would both types of workers be members of the same informal group. The difference in occupation leads to physical separation of the workplace as well as to different informal contacts based in part on the way different types of workers view their status and role and that of others.

2. *Physical location of the workplace.* Generally people become members of the informal group that is located in their own work area. People naturally form associations with those individuals with whom they have frequent contact. The more frequent the contact between people the greater the likelihood that they will become members of the same informal work group.

3. *The values held by the individuals.* The values of members of an informal work group must be compatible if the group is to hold together. For this reason an informal group is not likely to include union and nonunion workers or production workers and supervisors.

Structure of an informal work group. The structure of an informal work group is depicted in Figure 7–4. Notice that there are three classes of individuals who make up the group: those in the inner circle, those in the fringe area, and those who are not members of the group (the out group). The inner group is the heart of the informal work group. It is composed of a closely knit group of people who perform the same general kind of work in the same location and hold the same values. The inner group sets the tone of the informal work group and determines the membership. Smith, Jones, Roper, Day, and Forbes make up the membership of the inner group. The dotted lines indicate relations between the members in frequent contact. Notice that Randolph and Mason are in the outer circle as fringe members of the informal group. They have not been fully accepted by the members of the inner group, or they are not yet willing to give full allegiance to the values of the informal social system. Eventually they will either move into the inner circle of membership or to the out-group status.

Brown and Harris are not members of the informal work group. They may work in the same department or have a formal status relationship

FIGURE 7–4
Structure of an informal work group

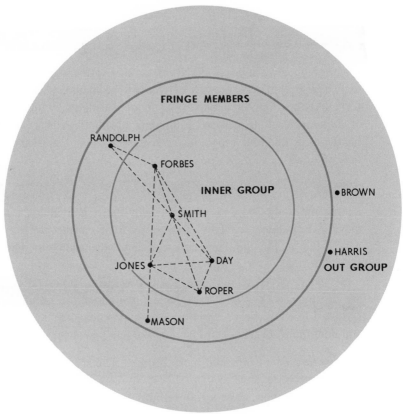

with the informal group members. However, they have neither close informal ties with the group members nor with each other. In a word, they are "loners." Usually such individuals are members of the out group by choice because they do not want to surrender their independence to the group or because their values are different in some significant way from those of the members of the group.

A group leader will emerge in the informal group situation. In Figure 7–4 Smith is the leader. He has frequent contact with five of the other six persons who, in addition to himself, compose the inner circle and the fringe membership in the system. Smith was not formally elected leader, but he came to occupy a leadership position because of his ability to recognize and meet the needs of the others for informal association. They listen to his opinions, generally follow his suggestions, and come to him with their problems and ideas. In short, Smith commands the respect of the members of the informal work group, and they voluntarily follow his lead. In contrast, a supervisor is obeyed because of the authority that he has by virtue of his status in the formal organization of the business enterprise.

The importance of status

Status has been defined as a relative position in the business organization. A good deal of popular comment has been heard in recent years about status in the business enterprise and its importance to employees. Articles, books, and comic strips have all contributed to the public's interest in business status. While many persons laugh about others' concern over status and the symbols attached to it, these same individuals may become quite agitated when some event occurs that seems to diminish their status in a business organization. Status is something which the business practitioner must understand to be effective in human relations.

Kinds of status

When an individual works to fulfill the requirements for a particular position and attains it, this is known as *achieved status*. Being a college graduate is achieved status since a person must earn his degree. Occupational status is achieved status since a person is not born as a business manager, a banker, a physician, or a bricklayer.

However, there are some status positions which are not achieved but instead are *ascribed*—that is, a person is assigned a status on the basis of some inherited characteristic such as sex, race, or the family into which he is born. Ascribed status can alter an individual's chance to achieve a position in a business enterprise commensurate with his abilities. Although family background in business seems to be less important today than in recent decades, status may accrue to a person in business because of his family ties. Higher status generally is afforded in industry to men than women despite recent legislation which outlaws employment discrimination by business on the basis of the sex and race of individuals.

The status of a racial or ethnic group of individuals in a work situation is influenced not only by achieved status positions they hold but also by the ascribed status of that particular group as viewed by the external community. In large metropolitan areas where ethnic and racial minorities live in relative isolation from the dominant society, patterns of status arise which the business manager should understand in developing a productive work force. Employees bring to the workplace their views of ascribed status which may not be wholly consistent with the formal status achieved by members of the minority in the enterprise. Despite management's interest in avoiding status based on race, cultural background, or sex, the informal organization in the enterprise is likely to take account of these factors for some time to come. For management this means a continuing program of promoting understanding among its workers as to the basis on which formal status, promotions, and job assignments are made along with management's recognition that problems may arise from time to time because of ascribed status.

Prestige and esteem

Associated with each status position is a certain amount of prestige. *Prestige* is the recognition and regard resulting from a person's status. Thus prestige accrues to an individual because of the status position he occupies. A person with more formal education generally has a higher status and therefore more prestige than one with less education or training. Employees using mental skills usually have higher status and more prestige than those doing manual labor.

How a person performs the role associated with his status determines the amount of *esteem* in which he is held. An employee such as a custodian has a position of relatively low status and prestige in the organization. However, if he fulfills his role well by doing a good job of keeping the office clean, he should be held in high esteem. A person of high status and prestige, such as vice president for sales, could be held in low esteem because of poor role behavior. This low esteem might result from lack of attention to his job, poor moral conduct, or general inefficiency in performance of his role. Nevertheless he would still occupy a status with much prestige. If over a period of time the people who occupy a certain prestigious status do not perform their role well, the status itself may come to have less prestige.

Two people can occupy similar status positions with one being held in low esteem and the other in high esteem. The difference in esteem may be traced to the personal qualities of leadership and resourcefulness which one individual exhibits as compared with the other who tends to do a poor job. These individual differences which do not show up on the formal organization of the business enterprise are of great importance to management in the operation of the business. Estimates of esteem are critical in the informal organization patterns.

Factors determining the prestige of a status. Among the business factors determining the prestige of a status are the level in the organization structure the position occupies, the nature of the work, salary, and the industry of which the business enterprise is a part.

The formal organization structure determines an individual's prestige level in the enterprise. A vice president has higher status and more prestige than a department head, who in turn has higher status and more prestige than a production worker. Likewise, the production worker has higher status than the production trainee. Interestingly enough, prestige may be generalized to include those who work closely with persons at the top of the organization structure. This means that the secretary to the president of the enterprise has higher status and more prestige than a vice president's secretary.

The type of work performed and the working conditions also determine the prestige of the status in the business enterprise. Clerical work has a greater prestige and higher status than production work. The distinction between white-collar workers in offices and blue-collar workers in factories is well understood by those employed in business.

Pay is also a determinant of the amount of prestige of a status. The level of wages is one recognition by higher management of the importance of the individual's contribution to the operation of the enterprise and of the status position he occupies. Changes in the pay for certain executive positions can result in more than a difference in the monthly checks of the persons involved. Significant pay changes may alter the entire status-ranking system of the management hierarchy. The higher the pay, the higher the prestige of the status in the organization when other factors are approximately equal.

Status symbols

With all the various determinants of status for the occupational positions and individuals who are involved in business, the matter of status is complex indeed! These determinants sometimes conflict with one another, and the result is a complicated pattern of status hierarchies for every business enterprise. Status in business is recognized by permitting certain symbols to be a part of the work environment. These status symbols are visible evidence of a person's rank in the business enterprise.

Examples of status symbols are wide-ranging, varying from desk pen sets and telephones in offices to rugs and paintings in executive suites. A cardinal rule of status symbols is that the symbol has meaning only if it is relatively scarce or at least is limited to those persons having about the same status level in the organization. Status symbols lose their significance when they become widespread. In one organization the vice presidents' offices had carpeted floors and this was considered a status symbol until the enterprise moved into a new building where not only executive offices were carpeted but so were those of department heads. When this occurred the carpeted floors ceased to be as significant a status symbol, and organizational rank switched to the floor on which the office was located. Since the building was served by automatic elevators those offices on the highest floors were occupied by executives of higher level in the organization and connoted higher status. Also, these offices were closest to the president's office and the board of directors' meeting room which were located on the top floor.

The danger always exists that management will place too much emphasis upon status symbols and will create a climate in the business enterprise that results in a ceaseless shuffling from one status crisis to another. An overemphasis by an individual or a group of employees on status symbols may indicate a basic insecurity as to their position and function in the enterprise. This may result from an unclear definition of responsibilities or inadequate authority being vested in an individual or group. Extreme sensitivity about status symbols may result from a lack of understanding of the goals and basic policies of the enterprise or from any of a number of factors external to the enterprise including a feeling of personal inadequacy by the individual himself. Management should constantly be alert for an overemphasis of status and status symbols in the enterprise and should be aware of the problems of which this condition may be a symptom.

Despite the dangers arising from status symbols and the problems which may be highlighted by them, status is an important concept in the business enterprise; and status symbols are an important element of stability in organizations. An essential prerequisite for an effective business enterprise functioning in a smoothly operating economy is a degree of order. In the enterprise status provides a system of order, and status symbols are easily recognized tangible evidence of that order. The security that comes when individuals understand their place in the social system of the enterprise, as well as of other dimensions of their lives, has a beneficial effect on reducing anxiety for individuals and permits them to concentrate on their assigned duties. Status and its symbols exist wherever people come together in organizations. For management to ignore its presence or to pretend it does not exist is unrealistic and may result in failure to understand more clearly the functioning of individuals in the work environment.

Developing a healthy work climate

A healthy work climate is developed in the business enterprise as the result of conscious effort on the part of management. Building high morale among employees requires day-to-day actions by supervisors which are consistent with sound human relations concepts. Little of lasting value will be achieved by crash programs to raise the level of morale and productivity if they are not accompanied by individual acts that demonstrate a genuine concern for employees. One of the most important aspects in improving human relations practices by managers is for them to develop an awareness of the implications of their attitudes and actions when dealing with persons in the daily conduct of business. To improve the manager's awareness of human relations the following suggestions should be helpful.

1. *The superior sets the tone in the enterprise.* The principal responsibility for determining the work climate rests with the superior, and subordinates will tend to follow his lead. This responsibility for promoting good human relations ranges from the president of the business enterprise down the management hierarchy to the first level of supervision. Each person who directs the activities of others should remember that his subordinates will be watching him to see what kind of an example he sets. This includes all manner of things which taken individually may appear to be of minor importance but when put together determine the substance of human relations in the shop or office.

Examples of ways in which a manager sets the tone for his subordinates include the friendliness he exhibits toward employees and how it is expressed, his manner of dress, the degree of professionalism in his associations with others, his commitment to the enterprise as measured by the energy and time devoted to the job, the attitudes he expresses toward the enterprise, and the prejudices which he may exhibit. The fact that the superior has primary responsibility for determining the work climate does not relieve subordinates of their responsibilities to behave in a manner that will be a positive contribution to the enterprise. However, when a poor example is set for employees by management there is little incentive for subordinates to do better.

2. *Make deserved praise public; reprimand in private.* The advice of "Praise publicly and reprove privately" is generally sound advice for the business manager. However, there are some important conditions that should be associated with this generalization. Most people like to have deserved recognition made public despite modest protestations by the individual that "it really doesn't make any difference" to him whether he receives public recognition. There are times though when the most effective praise will be a quiet word of commendation by the individual's superior for a job well done. The sincere few words of confidence expressed privately by the manager to a subordinate may be better than a public ceremony. Furthermore, public praise can easily be overdone, especially if it violates the informal group norms of the employee's work associates. For management to single out one employee for special recognition, particularly when several others may have also contributed to the success of a project, may alienate that individual from his colleagues and be detrimental to his group relationships. A private reprimand enables the individual employee to save face and may be more effective in changing his behavior patterns than publicly criticizing his actions or attitudes.

3. *Remember the importance of listening in good communications.* Avoid making judgments until the other person has told his story and you believe you fully understand the situation. Try to perceive the other person's view of the situation. It is very difficult to really listen if you are busy thinking of what your response will be. When giving directions to others be sure that you make clear your intentions and what you expect from others. Do not expect persons to respond effectively if they are not properly prepared to carry out your instructions.

4. *Preserve the dignity of the individual.* It is important for each person to preserve his own good self-image. Management should avoid placing the individual employee in a position where he has no opportunity to save face. When this does occur the supervisor should expect a defensive, perhaps violent, reaction that is not likely to be constructive in arriving at a satisfactory solution to the issue at hand.

5. *Management's view is not always the same as the employees' view.* A study made by the National Retail Merchants Association

revealed that the rankings of eight morale factors by both managers and employees were quite different. How would you rank the following morale factors: good physical working conditions, promotion on merit, fair pay, job security, credit and recognition, interesting work, counsel on personal problems, and understanding and appreciation? In order of importance, management ranked the factors as follows:

Morale item	Management ranking
Fair pay	1
Job security	2
Interesting work	3
Promotion on merit	4
Understanding and appreciation	5
Good physical working conditions	6
Credit and recognition	7
Counsel on personal problems	8

The employees of these business enterprises placed quite a different ranking on the same items:

Morale item	Employee ranking
Credit and recognition	1
Interesting work	2
Fair pay	3
Understanding and appreciation	4
Counsel on personal problems	5
Promotion on merit	6
Good physical working conditions	7
Job security	8

There was a substantial divergence of opinion between management and employees as to the relative importance of credit and recognition, and job security, with significant difference on the importance of counsel on personal problems, fair pay, and promotion on merit. These differences are not surprising considering the different frames of reference of managers and nonmanagerial employees.

The results of such surveys will vary with a particular enterprise, or with an industry, or with economic conditions. In time of a general recession it would be anticipated that job security would be of great importance, while in prosperity it would be relatively less important as many jobs are available. Sometimes workers will list as important those items they feel they don't have rather than the factors of greatest absolute importance. Even so, the significance of this survey is that it illustrates the difference of management and employee feelings on a given set of morale factors and shows what other studies have revealed—that there are many factors other than wages which are considered important by employees.

6. *How a change is made may be more important than the change itself.* While change is one of the characteristics of today's business scene, management should recognize that change tends to disrupt the lives and work habits of people. Most individuals prefer not to have patterns of behavior interrupted. Consider your own habits. Try dressing in a different order tomorrow morning; or in coming to class take a different route. If you are typical, you will resist such changes. In the work environment the same thing is true of individuals' habits. We resent changes that require us to establish new ways of doing things. This natural resistance to change causes one of management's greatest challenges: to effect the changes necessary to improve enterprise operations with a minimum of disruption of good work habits.

In making changes it is important that management communicate to workers the reasons for the change. A more participative type of managerial leadership would include having suggestions for changes emerge from the work group as the members felt changes to be necessary. Obviously this approach is not practical with many management decisions since all workers do not have access to information which shows the need for changes. Also, a great deal of time may be consumed by waiting for the group to push for a change. However, management should recognize that changes in organization structure, location of offices and shops, product lines, and personnel have definite human relations implications. The more information management is able to pass along to employees regarding anticipated changes the less disruptive the change is likely to be.

Furthermore, to promote good morale management should undertake actions to lessen the personal impact of changes on employees. This would include such actions as helping employees to find new homes if the enterprise's location were to be moved to a different city or working closely with industry and government employment agencies to provide new jobs for workers who were displaced by a change in the product lines or technological requirements of the enterprise. What may seem to be a relatively minor, insignificant change to top management may be a major disruption somewhere in the organization unless managers down the line are sensitive to the importance of the way in which the change is carried out. The proposed change which appears to be quite logical from a technical point of view may be quite difficult to effect if consideration is not given to the human relations aspects of its implementation.

Summary

Human relations consists of providing a work climate which will both foster the employees' individual satisfactions and result in the achievement of the broad economic objectives of the business enterprise. People have physical and material needs which are met largely through wages and fringe benefits. However, employees also have nonpecuniary needs both psychological and social which management should recognize.

Direction is the process of aiding an enterprise's employees in carrying out their work activities. To be effective in exercising direction, managers need technical, human, and conceptual skills. Generally, technical skill is required to a greater degree in first-line supervision, conceptual skill at the top management level, and human skills at all levels of management.

Leadership is the element of direction which causes subordinates to further the accomplishment of enterprise goals. Leadership can be exercised in three ways—authoritarian, free-rein, or participative.

Communication, the transmission of understanding, is essential in the process of direction. Two-way communication should occur vertically as well as horizontally in the business enterprise. Both written and spoken communications are used in business, and each method has its advantages and disadvantages. For there to be good communication, there must be both effective transmission and receipt of information, with the listener or reader understanding the frame of reference of the speaker or writer.

In the formal organization structure, each person occupies a particular status and is expected to fulfill the role associated with that status. These positions can be shown in a formal organization chart.

The informal organization is a self-grouping of employees in the work environment which depends upon the personalities of the individuals for its being. Informal work groups usually are made up of workers who perform the same general type of work in the same area and who hold similar values.

Status is a relative position in an organization. Status is achieved when a person earns it and ascribed when he receives his position because of some inherited characteristic. Prestige is an abstract concept which refers to the recognition and regard that go with a particular status. Esteem refers to how well a person performs the role associated with his status position. Status symbols are visible evidence of a person's rank in the business enterprise.

There are a number of considerations for management to remember in developing a healthy work climate:

The superior sets the tone in the enterprise.

Generally, it is good to praise in public and reprimand in private.

Listening is important for good communications.

Act so as to preserve the dignity of individuals.

Recognize that management and employees do not always view issues or circumstances from the same frame of reference.

When a change is made, it is important *how* the change is made.

Terms for review

human relations	free-rein leadership
psychological needs	participative leadership
social needs	achieved status
technical skill	ascribed status
human skill	prestige
conceptual skill	esteem
authoritarian leadership	

Questions

1. What differences are there in enterprise goals and individual needs?
2. *a)* What examples of good human relations have you observed practiced in the organizations with which you have been associated?
   b) What incidents have you observed that indicated a lack of sensitivity to the importance of human relations?
3. What is most important to you in considering a job opportunity? What difference, if any, would it make if you were considering a summer position before returning to college instead of a permanent position?

4. What explanation can you give for the changing balance of skills required of a manager depending upon his level in the organization?

5. Comment on the following statement by the owner of a medium-size department store: "I would like to have more participation by my supervisors and other employees, but I can't afford the time that is required for them to make a decision. Also, I feel that I know more about my business than anyone else."

6. Prepare three statements that could be given opposite interpretations depending upon the frame of reference of the speaker and the listener. How could these statements be rephrased so the transmitted message would be what was intended?

7. "Since informal organizations are bound to arise within any business enterprise, a formal organization is really of secondary importance." Comment on this statement.

8. What kinds of status symbols have you observed in the organizations of which you have been a part? Are people serious about the importance of status symbols? Why or why not?

9. Why may the way in which a change is made be as important as the substance of the change itself? Give an example to illustrate such a situation.

BUSINESS BRIEFS

Levi Strauss

Levi Strauss, the manufacturer of jeans, is a family-controlled enterprise which was founded in 1850 and still projects a family image. Its shares of common stock were sold to the public for the first time in 1971. One of its junior executives, in his twenties, stated that what he really likes about the company is that it is very people-oriented. This young man was impressed that on chance meetings with the president, the top executive would speak to him by his first name. Furthermore, the junior manager feels that management is open to suggestions. People are encouraged to cross departmental lines to discuss ideas. Pride is felt that Levi Strauss has been a leader in such projects as employment of minorities.

1. What insights into the human relations climate at Levi Strauss can be gained from this brief?

Blue-collar blues

A U.S. Department of Labor official has stated, "The alienation of blue-collar workers is one of the most important issues of the day."

Evidence of the blue-collar workers' discontent is shown by the Ford Motor Company, which reported that absenteeism more than doubled in the past ten years. In 1970 absenteeism averaged 5.3 percent at Ford with an even higher rate before and after weekends. In addition, union officials as well as managements of many manufacturing enterprises have expressed concern about the turnover of workers, especially young employees who simply walk off a job when they get tired of working in a particular factory.

Worker reaction to numerous production jobs includes such comments as boring, no pride in the work, dead-end job, dirty, and noisy.

Product quality has declined in a number of instances and in a limited number of cases some products have been sabotaged on the assembly line by disgruntled workers.

Union officials have also expressed concern about the attitudes of younger workers, not only toward the company and their jobs but toward the union as well. One long-time union member stated, "These young kids don't appreciate what they have now. They're too impatient." At the same time the attitude of many younger workers is that the union is pretty much part of the establishment.

According to the Bureau of Labor Statistics, in June, 1971, average weekly earnings were $185 for production workers in transportation equipment manufacturing.

1. How can a management determine the extent to which the above problems apply to its business enterprise?
2. What implications for human relations does this brief raise?
3. What can management do about the problems outlined above?

CASES

Merkley Company

The Merkley Company is an electronics manufacturing plant employing approximately 2,300 employees. Of this group, approximately 2,000 are production employees and about 300 are office employees composed of both clerical and administrative personnel.

Within this plant the company provides a modern, well-equipped cafeteria. Although the Merkley Company owns the facilities, an outside catering firm is contracted to prepare and serve the food. All menus are planned by the catering firm with the services of an industrial dietitian and approved by the Merkley Company plant personnel department.

Menus had always included a choice of two hot plate lunches and "ready-made" sandwiches, prepared earlier in the day and wrapped in cellophane. In addition, employees had the regular choice of beverages, desserts, and small dishes of salad which were also prepared earlier in the day. Both production and office employees made their food selection from the same menu—there was no executive dining room or special menu for executives.

The cafeteria can serve 500 employees at a time. Thirty-minute lunch breaks, starting at 11:15 a.m., are staggered over about two hours to accommodate the 2,300 employees. All employees eating in the plant are required to eat in the cafeteria, even though they may have brought their lunch from home. Since the lunch breaks have to be staggered, the production employees eat during the earlier lunch periods, and the office employees eat during the last lunch periods.

The plant had been in operation about one year when the personnel department began receiving complaints from the office personnel regarding the food in the cafeteria. The complaints didn't seem to come from the production employees, only from the office employees. Within a few days, more and more office personnel were complaining about the food and menus, and finally, a marked difference was noticed in the number of office personnel purchasing the lunches in the cafeteria. Although there were only 30 minutes allowed for lunch, more and more clerical people were leaving the plant to go out for lunch.

Conversations with various office employees seemed to indicate the complaint was not so much the quality of the food, but rather the menu itself. The personnel manager began to think that office personnel tended to have different eating habits than production personnel. He felt that since the production employees were exerting greater physical energy in the performance of their duties, they needed a heavier lunch, e.g., meat, potatoes, and beans; and the office employees desired lighter lunches, e.g., sandwiches and large salad plates.

It had been the practice of the Merkley Company general plant manager to hold monthly office employee meetings to discuss general plant operations and to keep them up to date on such items as the latest developments of new products. One of these meetings was held at the time the personnel department was getting the most cafeteria complaints. During this meeting, the subject of the cafeteria menus was raised by several office girls. They all agreed that the lunches offered were too heavy and that they would much prefer to have sandwiches or maybe a salad plate. It was pointed out to them that ready-made sandwiches were already available as were salads. The office employees argued that the salads were too small to make a complete lunch and since they had to eat last, after all the production employees, there were no salads left and the sandwiches were usually stale.

Some employees suggested that the company put in a sandwich bar offering such items as "made-to-order" cold sandwiches, hamburgers, and malted milks, and also providing large salad plate lunches. Later that day, the general plant manager and industrial relations manager discussed the suggested new sandwich bar. However, they both hesitated installing the extra kitchen equipment necessary for such a bar, believing the expense would be too great unless more than just the office employees were interested. To determine this interest, they decided to conduct a survey to determine just how much interest there was in the plant for such a salad and sandwich bar.

The industrial relations manager asked the cafeteria manager to have his employees conduct a survey among the production employees to determine their interest in a light lunch menu. The light lunch would be offered in addition to the heavier hot lunch. The surveys were conducted the following Monday as the production employees filed past the serving counter collecting their noon lunch. They were shown a sample menu for the proposed sandwich bar including the prices and asked whether or not they would be interested in patronizing such an eating facility.

Of this group, 91 percent of the production employees surveyed indicated that they were not interested and that they preferred a hot plate lunch. Early the next day, the general manager called the industrial relations manager into his office to discuss the results of the survey. Although there was apparently little interest on the part of the production employees, they decided to go ahead and set up a short-order sandwich and salad bar anyway, but on a much less elaborate basis than would be necessary to serve the entire plant.

Since the vast majority of the production employees said that they were not interested in short orders, the new menu would be available only to the office personnel. Since it would take an additional person to operate the bar, it did not seem economically feasible to have it open for the production employees, especially since so few indicated an interest in patronizing it.

After the arrangements had been made the additional limited cafeteria equipment was installed, and the new facility was opened one week later. On the opening day as the first few groups of production employees began coming in to the cafeteria at 11:15, only the hot plate line was set up. But at 11:45 as other groups came into the cafeteria, the cafeteria employees were beginning to set up the sandwich bar in preparation for the office personnel who would be coming in at 12:10 and 12:20 p.m. As the last 30 to 40 production employees filed past the new sandwich bar, a few attempted to order a sandwich of their choice. Each was informed that this food was for office employees only. A few of these production employees expressed mild displeasure, but management heard very little about it during the rest of the day. The office employees we're very well pleased with the new arrangements and voiced much appreciation.

The next day, 92 percent of all production employees boycotted the cafeteria. Each brought his own lunch from home. Although they all ate their home-prepared lunch in the cafeteria, they refused to buy food from the regular hot food serving line. As a result of this boycott much of the prepared hot food had to be destroyed at a cost of nearly $800. Later during the lunch period, employees began to explain to cafeteria personnel that they were protesting because they couldn't buy the sandwiches they wanted.

1. Why do you think the production workers boycotted the cafeteria after the survey had indicated their lack of interest in the sandwich bar?

2. What alternatives are open to management at this time? What would be the likely consequences of each of these alternatives?

3. What would you recommend?

"Lessons Learned"

Tom Jones eyed the correspondence and memos on his desk. The nearby calendar told him that ten months had passed since he had come to Falls City to help open a new plant (see Exhibit 1) for Acme Products Company, a nationwide packaging concern. Tom paused to

EXHIBIT 1
Acme Products Company
(Falls City plant organization chart)

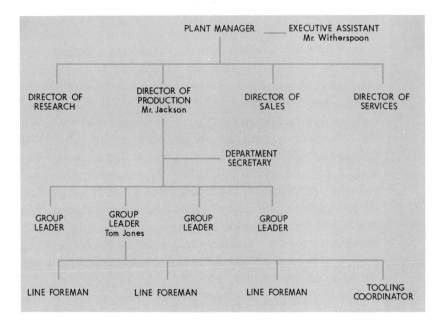

reflect on how busy these past months had been. As a group leader, he had been confronted with a wide variety of problems and had been constantly on the go in an effort to help get the plant into production on schedule. Only in the past month had things slacked up a little.

The ringing telephone summoned Tom from his thoughts and into the office of Mr. Jackson, his department head. Handing Tom a memo, Mr. Jackson said, "We have a request here from our general manager in Chicago. He'd like to have us submit to him some of the "Lessons Learned" by us during our new plant startup and shakedown. They'd be of benefit in planning future expansions. Can you put together some ideas?"

Tom replied that several of the group leaders had already discussed the need for more detailed installation drawings. He then asked, "Should this be strictly technical or should it include other problems?"

"List anything serious that's confronted you fellows," was Mr. Jackson's answer.

During the next week, Tom sought out the other group leaders individually and acquainted them with his assignment. He solicited their thoughts and asked for recommendations. Upon condensing and editing all of the ideas, he found that they fell into three categories:

1. Facility installations and drawings.
2. Tooling tolerances and finishes.
3. Unclear personnel assignments and absence of an organization chart.

All three of these items had been subjects of discussions on numerous occasions in almost all the departments of the new plant.

Upon receiving the drafts back from typing, Tom reviewed them with the other group leaders and then sent them for Mr. Jackson's consideration. On the following day, his draft copies were returned with Mr. Jackson's note, "Well Done."

The next day Mr. Jackson left for a conference in Dallas. Tom had not had an opportunity to discuss the final report on "Lessons Learned" with his boss before the departure. While Tom was on the telephone, the executive assistant to the plant manager, Mr. Witherspoon, stormed into the department office, slammed down a handful of papers and lashed out at the nearest secretary, "This rubbish is obviously incorrect. These conditions don't exist." The assistant continued, "This was written by a misguided, ignorant individual and is in poor taste without thought or fact." As Witherspoon departed he haughtily advised that the papers should be destroyed. As the secretary returned the papers to Mr. Jackson's mailbox, Tom saw the heading "Lessons Learned."

After completing his telephone call, Tom turned his thoughts on the executive assistant's reaction to the "Lessons Learned" report. Some of the following thoughts ran through Tom's mind: Should I speak to the executive assistant in an attempt to explain the report? Would it be better to go over the 'old-paper-shuffler's' head and deliver the report directly to the plant manager? Had Mr. Jackson really studied the report or had he merely rubber-stamped it? Since the general manager in Chicago had requested the report he must have considered it important.

As Tom went to the water cooler for a drink he wondered what action, if any, he should take.

1. Discuss the central problems involved in this case.
2. *a)* What courses of action are open to Tom Jones?
   b) What do you recommend to Tom Jones? Why?

*Videotape recording can
be a useful technique in
management training and
development.*

8

Personnel management

As American business enterprises became larger and more complex, personnel departments were a logical development to aid management in processing and maintaining the records required for a work force of many employees. Also, managers became aware of the importance of the human factors in operating an enterprise and began to depend upon personnel departments for assistance. This chapter analyzes the personnel function as it may be used effectively to assist with the difficult and complicated problems of today's business enterprise:

> *What is the personnel management function?*
> *What are the responsibilities of the personnel department for the profitable management of the enterprise?*
> *What is the relationship between personnel management and labor relations?*
> *How is the personnel department organized?*

The personnel management function

The personnel function encompasses the roles of recruitment, selection, induction, and training of employees for the various departments of the business enterprise with the goal of a well-motivated and effective total work force. Good personnel management places an emphasis upon personal development of employees. Good personnel management seeks to provide a climate whereby individuals may more fully utilize their capacities and obtain satisfaction from the work group of which they are a part. The degree of success in integrating the individual objectives of employees with the objectives of the business enterprise to achieve an efficient work situation is dependent in large measure on the effectiveness of the personnel department's programs and the extent to which it can assist management in other departments.

The personnel department is in an excellent position to advise top management on the state of morale of the work force and to suggest methods of strengthening employee-management relations. In those business enterprises where employees are organized into labor unions, the personnel department also provides assistance in dealing with the union representatives and in the conduct of negotiations for the labor contract.

To carry out the personnel management function there are three groups which have important responsibilities. The overall responsibility for personnel management should be assumed by top management. The president of the business enterprise sets the work climate in the organization. He is responsible to the board of directors for the establishment of the broad objectives and policies of personnel management. He appoints the director of the personnel department and other key executives who are concerned with the successful functioning of the enterprise. The president should see that the personnel efforts of subordinates are properly coordinated and executed. He has to evaluate the effectiveness with which the desired objectives have been achieved so that future personnel plans may be improved.

Without the support and efforts of the other executives active in the management of the enterprise, all the president's personnel activities can be wasted. This second group, the supervisors throughout the enterprise, are the individuals who come into direct contact with those employees in the shops, factories, and offices where the goods and services are produced. These supervisors must be aware of the personnel policies which have been established by top management and must actively support these policies with actions at the operating level that are consistent with the personnel point of view in the enterprise. The foremen, department heads, district managers, group leaders, and other first-line supervisors are the people who actually put into practice the procurement, training, development, and use of the work force. Good personnel practices for this group of executives are essential if the enterprise is to achieve its objectives in the area of personnel management.

The third group having essential responsibilities for personnel management is the personnel department. This department is generally established as a "staff" department, which means that its purpose is providing service to other departments but without authority of its own to force those departments to accept its services or advice. Therefore, the personnel department hires employees, may train them, provides such services as record keeping and testing, suggests safety and recreation programs, and may participate in negotiations with labor unions. However, ultimately the decisions must be approved by supervisors in the departments which are concerned with the particular problems at hand.

Responsibilities of the personnel department

Hiring and placement of employees

There is much more to satisfactory hiring and placement of employees than merely filling vacancies as they occur in the business enterprise with any person who may be available. To achieve most satisfactorily the objectives of the enterprise and the interests of employees there are several policy decisions which have to be understood by management.

First, to provide for efficient and uniform hiring practices, all employment activities should be centered in the personnel department. Here all employment records can be kept up to date, interviews and testing can be efficiently carried out, and specialists can be used to determine which persons may best qualify for positions which are available. Sometimes foremen and other supervisors object to the centralization of hiring since they feel it takes away from their authority to operate their departments. Properly administered centralized hiring should complement, not replace, the supervisor's responsibilities. The supervisor in the department where the prospective employee will work should still retain the right to accept or reject the applicant who is recommended to him by the personnel department. The personnel department can relieve the supervisor of many of the details and records associated with hiring and placement of personnel and thus contribute to a more efficient office or production department.

Job specifications. The first step in hiring of workers comes when the supervisor turns in a request for personnel to fill certain job specifications. These job specifications should be drawn up to describe accurately the requirements of the position to be filled. The specifications should be realistic so as not to call for a superman or to disregard important aspects of the job which require special abilities in the new employee.

FIGURE 8–1
Steps in hiring and placement

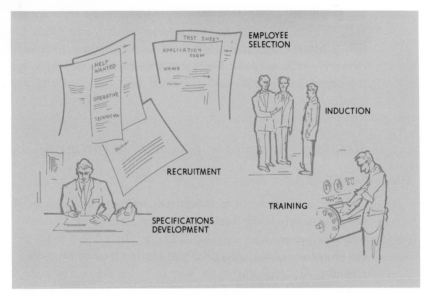

Recruitment. After the request for personnel has been turned in, the personnel department undertakes the recruitment phase. Except when labor is in very short supply, the personnel department should have a list of potential candidates for employment to fill vacancies as they arise. This list is made up from a variety of sources and includes former employees who are qualified but who have been laid off or who have voluntarily left the enterprise. Other important sources of labor include the suggestions of present employees who are pleased with the business enterprise as a place to work, along with advertising and contacts with such local groups as schools, trade unions, private employment agencies, clubs, law enforcement and correctional authorities. These groups all are interested in knowing when an enterprise of repute in the community has job openings for permanent positions. The local office of the public employment service is also an extremely helpful source of employment information and is probably best qualified to act as a clearinghouse for information about local labor-market conditions. Depending upon the needs for workers and the scope of the enterprise's activities, recruitment may extend over a wide geographic area and draw workers from a considerable distance.

Employee selection. The selection of those individuals who will be offered employment is a six-step process consisting of a screening interview, application form, employment tests, physical examination, reference check, and comprehensive interview. The *screening interview* may be conducted by an assistant in the personnel department and provides an opportunity to make a preliminary decision about the applicant's suitability for employment. An applicant may be turned down for employment to a specific job at this stage not only because he is deficient in some respect, but because his education or intelligence are too high for the job which is currently vacant. If the applicant appears to be a good candidate, then the screening interview may be used to explain the rest of the employment process. In those cases where the screening interview comes before the application blank is filled out, this is an opportunity to explain the blank itself.

The *application blank* provides information about the candidate in writing, acts as a simple test of the ability of the candidate to express himself in writing, and should contain items which the business enterprise has found to correlate with job success. This means that it is important for each company to develop its own application form.

The development of a *testing program* is a complex undertaking, and management should understand the limitations as well as the potential benefits from a thoughtfully devised program. If the tests which attempt to measure the enterprise's needs are used, if management recognizes the tests' limitations, and if supervisors are ready to accept tests to improve hiring procedures, then the program may be of great value. Benefits include the measurement of the applicant's abilities and weaknesses for a particular job including a measure of the degree of accident-proneness for a given job, checking on the applicant's reported previous experience, and the provision of an objective comparison between applicants.

The *physical examination* should be given to applicants who may be considered seriously for employment both as assistance to the enterprise and the individual. Employees should not be placed in jobs which might be harmful to themselves or where they might endanger other workers. The enterprise should be protected against the risk of claims for compensation from persons who are troubled with disabilities prior to employment.

The investigation into the *job references* provided by the applicant gives the enterprise a check on past work records. In addition to the confirmation of facts, the reference checks test the applicant's accuracy and honesty.

The main purpose of the *comprehensive employment interview* is to complete or to correct the picture of the applicant which has been provided by the previous steps. Individual qualities of the applicant may be drawn out by the skillful interviewer which in previous steps have not been covered. This is the opportunity to explain the requirements of the job fully and to seek to determine why the applicant wants this particular position (in addition to the paycheck which will go with the job).

If the applicant qualifies in all respects for employment he is accepted for employment, sometimes on a probationary period. The supervisor under whom he works may have met the employee before he is finally selected. The supervisor should have some authority in determining which workers come into his department. However, in large enterprises where a substantial number of employees are being hired fairly regularly, the supervisor's most important function in the hiring process is to provide a realistic list of requirements for the positions in his department to be filled. Then he should depend upon the personnel department to select the applicants who will meet those requirements. When a variety of selection methods are used by experts in personnel management, the applicant's skills and interests are more likely to be assessed fairly than if the foreman made this judgment on a spur-of-the-moment decision at the factory gate.

Employee induction

After an individual is hired as an employee and before he is placed into a specific job in the business enterprise, he should be introduced formally into the organization. A good induction into the organization provides the new employee with useful and accurate information about the enterprise, the policies which will affect him, and the services which may be provided for his benefit. The first impressions of the new employee are very important in determining his attitudes toward the enterprise for a long time to come. Starting the new employee off with a good induction program enables him to obtain the full benefit from the job training which he will be given later.

A good program of employee induction has these three elements:

1. The personnel department provides introductory information to employees either individually or in groups.
2. Additional information is provided by the new employee's supervisor about his department and the requirements of the job.

3. A short while after the employee's first days on the job, a follow-up interview is held either by the supervisor or the personnel department to check on the employee's progress, to answer additional questions, or to repeat some information which was provided earlier.

An initial tour of the entire factory is helpful to give an overall view of operations before the employee is placed into one particular department. This way the employee is better able to relate what he is doing to the entire operation of the enterprise. The entire induction program should be directed toward giving the new employee a feeling of belonging to the organization and that the management is concerned about his welfare and his success in his new job.

Employee training

Besides the induction program, the employee may be subject to specific training which will relate to the job which he is assuming. There are four types of employee training:

1. *Apprenticeship training* is used in jobs requiring long periods of training and a high degree of skill. The employee works under supervision of trained employees and is required to meet rigid performance standards. Employers may use apprenticeship programs in cooperation with trade unions to maintain skill standards and to provide greater job security for union members by limiting the number entering such training.

2. *Vestibule training* is essentially off-the-job training where workers are trained in an area of the plant physically separated from their ultimate workplace. Machinery and jobs similar to the conditions in the shop itself are duplicated as nearly as possible. This method of training provides a good opportunity for teaching the best methods of doing a particular job, and employees have an opportunity to become accustomed to the job before actually entering the department. However, vestibule training takes place in essentially an artificial setting and some adjustment is necessary when workers ultimately move to the shop where they will work.

3. *On-the-job training* places the worker in the shop at a machine or workplace where he will be trained by a supervisor, a special instructor, or an experienced employee. The effectiveness of this type of training depends upon the quality of instruction that is provided. Without

attention being given by management to the instructors who provide this training, the new employee is likely to find this type of instruction frustrating, or at best there will be little uniformity in the training of personnel.

4. *Vocational-school training* may be used where the employee takes courses outside the enterprise in such areas as welding, blueprint reading, or automobile mechanics. This training may precede employment, or outside training may supplement the training that is provided by the enterprise in its own plant.

Training represents a continuing responsibility for management. New methods, products, and individual abilities of workers dictate that the business enterprise is not finished with a worker's training after he is placed in a shop or office. The personnel department should stand ready to provide advice and assistance to management in setting up educational and training programs which are concerned with all employees, not merely those recently hired.

Job analysis

In order to maintain a satisfactory level of worker morale and employee efficiency, a means must be available within the business enterprise to assure that wages paid employees are adequate and fair. Good personnel policies include those which seek to establish a system of wage payments that will take account of differences in the jobs in an enterprise and also provide for individual differences in performance on the same job. The personnel administrator is also concerned with the general level of wages paid in relation to wages for similar types of work in the community. Finally, the personnel administrator should be able to advise other managers regarding the best methods of calculating wages, whether on the basis of time, productivity, or some combination of these methods.

Job description. The first step in the process of job analysis is to determine what jobs are performed in the enterprise. This is done by writing a *job description* that contains the essential elements of each specific job including such factors as physical effort, skill, responsibility, mental effort and working conditions.

Job evaluation. Once job descriptions have been written for all jobs in the enterprise, the process of job evaluation begins. This consists of measuring the value of each job in relation to the other jobs in the enterprise. Although precise judgments on the relative worth of different jobs are difficult, a carefully administered program of job evaluation will result in a logical scale of jobs which can be used as a basis for setting relative wage scales. It is important to remember that job evaluation rates *jobs,* not the *individuals* on the jobs. The evaluation of individuals is *employee rating* which is discussed later in this chapter.

The simplest method of job evaluation is to identify the factors to be singled out for the analysis and assign weights to each factor. For example, physical effort may be assigned a maximum of 40 points, while skills required may be assigned a maximum of 110 points. The determination of the maximum weights assigned each job depends upon the industry and the type of jobs which the enterprise has. Next, the personnel administrator selects several jobs in the plant which are used as bench marks against which all other jobs will be later measured. These bench-mark jobs are then evaluated according to the point scales established for each factor in the evaluation scheme. The bench-mark jobs should be those which employ a number of persons and which are widely known by all employees. The job of a machinist first class might be assigned the following point spread: physical effort 20, skill 100, responsibility 60, and working conditions 20 for a total of 200; whereas a job of custodian might carry points as follows: physical effort 30, skill 10, responsibility 20, and working conditions 30 for a total of 90 points. Once these bench-mark jobs are evaluated, they are ranked on the basis of the total points assigned to each. All other jobs in the enterprise are ranked in relation to these bench-mark jobs. A careful handling of the point assignments and relative rankings is necessary to maintain fairness and as accurate an evaluation as is possible considering that the evaluator generally is dealing with job qualities which are difficult to measure precisely.

Despite the fact that job evaluation does provide the enterprise's management with a more desirable basis for wage determination than a haphazard scheme of wage payments based on less thoughtful analysis, by no means is such a system without limitations. No job evaluation system is completely scientific in the sense that there is an unquestionable exactness and precision of the process. Evaluators must determine the maximum points to be assigned to each factor in the analysis and then must assign factor points to each job according to some system of evaluation.

Also, some jobs may be viewed by workers as of unequal attractiveness even though the point analysis makes them of equal value. This is true of jobs which seem to be stepping-stones to higher positions, while some jobs are viewed as dead-end assignments. In some cases exceptions to the job evaluation system may be necessary to attract workers to a particular job where skilled labor may be in short supply.

Wage determination. After the job evaluation is completed, management must fit the scale of jobs in the enterprise to the wage scale which the enterprise wants to put into effect. The level of wages paid and the wage scale for a particular enterprise will depend upon such factors as the level of wages in the community for similar jobs, the ability of the enterprise to pay higher wages, and the bargaining strength of the labor union if the company employees are unionized. The wages paid in other firms in the community and in the industry of which the particular enterprise is a part are important in setting the wage scale. This information may be obtained by a survey of these other enterprises and sometimes is available through trade associations and governmental agencies.

In putting into effect a job evaluation system where none has previously existed, the best psychology to use is to bring it in at the time of a general wage increase so that those jobs which have been paid at too high a rate can be brought into the scale without lowering those rates, merely raising other rates up to their relative level. Sometimes it may be necessary to leave individuals who are receiving higher wages than may be justified under the new system at their higher pay rates, but bring new employees in under the proper wage scale. Thus the implementation of a job evaluation plan may require a period of time before all jobs are "in line" with a fair scale.

Performance rating

Once a system of job evaluation and wage scales has been worked out, then individuals must be selected to fill the various jobs which are required to carry out the activities of the business enterprise. For each job classification there should be a range of pay which will provide latitude for supervisors to recognize individual differences in performance for the same job. Since an employee's performance on the job will determine how much he is paid for his work within the wage range for that particular job, the supervisor has the responsibility for keeping employees informed about their progress. This is accomplished through a performance rating system, sometimes called a merit rating system. (See Figure 8–2.)

The performance rating system is used to make merit increases in wage rates within job classifications and to guide management in selecting employees for promotion to better jobs in the enterprise. The formal performance rating of employees reduces the practice of giving raises on the basis of either quick judgment or favoritism which may be the case where only an informal rating of employees' performance is used by supervisors. When no formal performance rating of employees exists in the enterprise, management finds it difficult to select workers for promotion or pay increases within job classifications on a basis which can be defended when questions arise. Also, the lack of a performance rating makes it more difficult to assure that the best man is promoted or the deserving employee is given a raise.

The performance rating system provides managers with a means of rewarding effective employees and furthering operating efficiency of the enterprise. If these two objectives are to be achieved, any performance rating system must have the support of management. Supervisors should be trained in the process of rating employees, and ratings should be discussed with employees on a periodic basis. Whatever system is adopted and regardless of the factors selected for rating performance, the system should be clearly understood by both supervisors and employees. For this reason complicated plans should be discouraged. Systems which use class ratings such as A, B, C, D, and E have merit over systems which assign points to the various performance factors, since the point systems suggest a degree of precision that is generally not obtainable in the performance rating system. Discussions with employees about their ratings should take a positive direction wherever possible. Morale and productivity in the business enterprise are much easier to influence positively by pointing out good elements in the employee's performance than by emphasizing weaknesses.

Performance rating is only one source of evidence by which promotions or pay increases may be determined. Rating systems may supplement and provide valuable additions to information provided by production records of output, quality of work, attendance, and other records that are objective measures of the individual's contribution to the enterprise. The best-managed companies make use of all available sources of information relating to the employee and his work situation in determining changes in work assignments or wages.

FIGURE 8–2

PERFORMANCE RATING REVIEW

Name:_____ Job Title:_____ Dept.:_____ Date:_____

Instructions to Supervisor: Summarize the individual's performance by checking each of the 4 evaluation factors below. Your ratings should reflect your judgment based on your observation of the employee. Use N/E (not evaluated) if you have insufficient evidence on which to make a rating. However, normally all items should be evaluated. These ratings should indicate what the employee has actually accomplished, not what you believe him to be capable of or what you would like for him to achieve. Remember that personnel performance rating and development represents an important responsibility of management.

Rating System: A – Exceeds Departmental Expectations
B – Meets Departmental Expectations
C – Below Departmental Expectations

Evaluation Factors   Ratings

	A	B	C
Quality of Work	Consistently does high quality and accurate work; creative with high degree of ingenuity and practicality.	Usually can be depended upon for good work; few mistakes; practical; some creativity.	Work performed in a careless and slip-shod manner; frequent mistakes; lacks creativeness.
Quantity of Work	Consistently high output; works rapidly.	Satisfactory production level; works steadily.	Below average in output; slow; wastes time.
Knowledge of Job	Expert knowledge of job and related areas; rarely requires instruction.	Good knowledge of job and related work; requires only normal instructions.	Has limited knowledge of job; requires frequent instruction and guidance.
Cooperation and Attitude	Enthusiastic and cooperative team worker; inspires confidence; loyal to company; solicits suggestions for improvement.	Responsive and cooperative; interested in job and company; accepts constructive criticism.	Lack of cooperation; little job interest; resents suggestions and constructive criticism.

Instructions: Check the appropriate block for the qualities listed below:

Capacity for Advancement: Qualifications	Is qualified for higher position with no further training or experience.	May be qualified for higher position with additional training and/or experience.	Qualified for present job, but has only limited potential for advancement.
Capacity for Advancement: Leadership Ability	Has demonstrated many of the qualifications for leadership; excellent supervisory material.	Has demonstrated some of the qualifications for leadership; possible supervisory material.	Has demonstrated few, if any, of the qualifications for leadership; not considered supervisory material.

	Yes	No
Is attendance satisfactory?	___	___
Is the employee punctual?	___	___

Remarks and/or Recommendations:

Rater's Signature_____   Supervisor's Signature_____ Date_____
  Title_____   Title_____

After Supervisor's signature, forward orginal copy of Performance Rating Review to the Personnel Office. Retain copy in local files. This Review is to be discussed with the employee before it is filed.

Promotion

Promotion is the advancement of an employee to a better job with more responsibility, increased skill, or higher status in the organization. An additional important requisite of the promotion is that it results in an increased salary or rate of pay for the employee. Promotions may range all the way from moving an employee up to a more skilled job within the same basic job classification, such as from second-class machine operator to first-class machine operator, or to a major upward shift in jobs from a production worker to a foreman's job that requires supervision of other workers.

Seniority and ability

Regardless of the magnitude of the promotion, there are two basic factors which affect promotion—seniority and ability. The determination of the relative importance of seniority and ability in making promotions is most significant for management in drawing up a promotion policy. Frequently labor unions and the workers they represent take the attitude that seniority should be the basis upon which promotions are decided. On the other hand, management may feel that ability should be the most important single criterion in making promotions. A satisfactory resolution of this difference of views can come only after a careful definition of what circumstances are involved and in what way each factor may be important.

Since the supervisor in a department is responsible for the productivity of his personnel and what goes on in his department, he should be able to select those employees for promotion which have the greatest capabilities and the most likely chance for success in new positions. Promotion should be the reward for those employees who increase their skills and exhibit evidence of probable ability for better jobs. To limit a supervisor by promoting only on the basis of seniority is to place an unfair restriction on management in view of the responsibility for departmental results. The factor of seniority should be taken into account when making promotions, but only when the other qualifications and two candidates for a better job are substantially equal.

At the same time, the criticism of workers of the ability factor and the way management goes about making promotions is often justified. Supervisors cannot expect to win the confidence of workers in their promotion policies when promotion is based on favoritism, personal relationships, and is colored by recent events that do not take the full work record into account. Senior employees should be considered for promotions in light of their abilities, based upon good performance ratings, and objective production records along with personal interviews by supervisors. Even though management may place ability to do a job first in selection of personnel, the junior employee should be selected for the job only where it can be clearly shown that he is superior to his more senior fellow worker. The practical effect of this type of policy is that minor differences in ability will not affect promotions, but critical differences in areas of importance will. A further consideration is that if management establishes the proper kind of training program within the enterprise, seniority will have more meaning because more training will have been given employees over time rather than merely having the same kind of work experience year in and year out.

Whenever seniority is used as one of the criteria for promotion the question arises as to how seniority is to be computed in the particular business enterprise. Seniority may be determined by length of service in the enterprise, plant, department, or job classification. An employee's seniority can start from the time he is first hired into any of the above units. The basis of determining seniority is critical for employees because it will vary depending upon which unit is used. An employee who has been with the company for a long time but has moved from one department to another has relatively little seniority on a departmental basis, but considerable seniority as an enterprise employee. The question of handling seniority when an employee is transferred, laid off, or has been previously promoted is one with which management must deal. Whatever system of seniority is adopted, after negotiation with union representatives if the workers are unionized, the seniority lists showing each employee should be publicly posted so that all workers have knowledge of their relative standing and possible errors can be ironed out before the lists are put into effect.

Employee transfer

In contrast to promotion which is an upward change in jobs, *transfer* is the movement of an employee from one job to another at about the same wages and on the same level in the organization. Although the specific type of work done by the employee may change with a transfer, there is no significant change either up or down in the duties and responsibilities. Employees may be transferred within the enterprise for a number of reasons including shift transfers, production transfers, and remedial transfers.

Shift transfers are used when the plant operates on more than a normal eight-hour-day basis. The evening shift usually runs from about four o'clock in the afternoon to midnight and the night shift from midnight to eight o'clock in the morning. Most workers prefer to work the regular day shift to keep evenings free for family life or community activities. Workers on the night shift have their normal pattern of waking and sleeping hours reversed and many dislike this aspect of shift work. However, if production requirements necessitate multiple shift operations, some workers will have to be hired for these extra shifts; and from time to time transfers will be required from one shift to another. One positive aspect of shift work from the employee's point of view is that normally the unusual shifts carry a pay premium. Also, there are individuals who prefer the shift assignments for various personal reasons.

Production transfers are necessitated when there is a change in the job requirements from one department to another. Some jobs may be eliminated and perhaps other types of work require additional workers. In this case workers are transferred for production purposes to avoid laying off present employees and hiring new ones. The personnel department can be an effective clearinghouse for departmental supervisors to use in channeling excess workers and reporting job vacancies. Production transfers may also occur when replacements are needed because of retirements, dismissal, or promotion of other workers in the enterprise.

Remedial transfers are made because of some problem which has arisen with a particular person on a particular job. The worker may be getting too old to bear the physical burden of his job or changing health conditions may necessitate a transfer. A worker may become tired of a particular job and with a remedial transfer both he and the enterprise may be benefited. Furthermore, the initial placement of the worker in a particular job may have been at fault causing a change to be advisable; or the worker simply may not be getting along with his supervisor or the people in the department but may be useful in another job in another part of the plant.

Basic issues to be determined in arriving at a sound personnel policy on transfers include deciding the circumstances under which transfers will be made, the jobs to which employees may be transferred, which supervisors have responsibility for transfers, the rate of pay for transfers, and the basis for transfers such as the role of seniority or ability.

Downgrading and layoffs

Sometimes transfers, particularly production transfers, result in *downgrading* which means that employees are moved to jobs which require less skill than those previously performed. The alternative to this downgrading may be to lay off the worker involved because of a lack of work available for his higher skilled job. When this situation arises the question is whether it is better to downgrade the employee or to lay him off. Generally neither solution offers a perfect answer. Although downgrading may result in a loss of worker morale, if there is widespread unemployment in the community the employee may be thankful to have any type of work with the enterprise rather than being forced to seek out another employer. Under other economic circumstances when jobs are more plentiful, the employee facing downgrading may accept a layoff rather than being downgraded.

From time to time the business enterprise may be faced with a reduction in demand for its products which will require that the size of the work force be cut down. This means a layoff of workers, sometimes of substantial proportion. Although both downgrading and layoffs may be only temporary, sometimes relatively permanent changes in work force size and composition are required. When this happens there are major problems which management will have to consider. Personnel policies relating to downgrading and layoffs include the thorny question of whether the hours of work should be reduced before any employees are laid off. Many employers lay off probationary employees first when work force reductions are necessary and then make some reduction in hours of work before making wholesale layoffs of permanent employees. In good personnel practice any overtime work will be eliminated except where the specialized nature of the work cannot be done by other employees with whom the work might otherwise be spread. However, there are limitations on management in sharing work by reducing the number of hours for each employee. When workers are reduced to two or three days a week considerable dissatisfaction is expressed by all concerned, and it is probably better to lay off workers so as to provide at least four days of work a week for those who remain in the enterprise's employ.

An important consideration in event of layoffs is on what basis are workers to be retained. Normally seniority is a critical factor in determining which workers will be retained and which will be laid off. In unionized plants seniority is especially important. However, sometimes consideration is given to skill and ability of workers. For the long-time employee whose work is satisfactory, the knowledge that his seniority will keep him employed during a time of layoffs will maintain morale of the work force. Junior workers should clearly understand the enterprise's policy, whatever it is, regarding layoffs, and this is one of the many things which should be explained during the induction and training of new workers into the business enterprise. As is discussed in the earlier section on promotion, the determination of seniority is not a simple concept, and a clear definition of what seniority means under different conditions of employment is essential so that workers can be informed as to how they will stand should different circumstances arise.

The least that the personnel department can do for employees who are being laid off is to provide some assistance to place these individuals in other enterprises in the locality. Here the services of the public employment service can be used to good advantage, along with personal contacts from the personnel department to other employers in the community to provide information on qualifications of workers who are being released because of reductions in the work force.

Discipline of employees

A good discipline policy is one which provides for constructive, positive actions by supervisors carried out consistently under a clear set of regulations. Most employees are anxious to do what is expected of them, and the enterprise's discipline policy should be administered so as to foster self-discipline on the part of the employees. At the same time, provision should be made for prompt action against the relatively small number of employees who do not conform to reasonable rules for plant conduct. When morale is high in a plant, good teamwork may result in pressure from workers on one of their number who steps out of line on either conduct or workmanship. However, management should realistically realize that in every enterprise there are a few employees who will require correction administered by supervisors.

There are four factors which should be a part of every good disciplinary policy:

1. There should be a written list of clear and reasonable rules which employees are expected to abide by, along with the penalties which will be applied for infractions.
2. All employees should be informed of what is expected in terms of plant rules and standards of work.

3. A means of informing employees how well they are meeting standards of conduct and work should be established.
4. A careful investigation of incidents prior to disciplinary action should be carried out. If and when guilt has been established, this should be followed by prompt application of corrective action.

A partial listing of plant rules enumerating conduct which will not be condoned in the plant usually include:

Gambling on company property.
Fighting or attempting to injure others except in self-defense.
Deliberate destruction of company property.
Drinking liquor on company property or drunkenness on the job.
Violation of safety regulations.
Smoking in prohibited areas.
Failure to wear safety glasses in machine shops.
Unexcused absences for more than two consecutive days without notifying the company.
Refusal to accept a proper job assignment.

The above list indicates the wide range of rules used in industry. Usually the rules are drawn up in consultation with supervisors and employee representatives.

After an employee's guilt has been clearly established, the disciplinary action may include one or a combination of the following penalties which are ranked in order of severity:

1. Oral warning.
2. Written warning.
3. Suspension or disciplinary layoff for a specified period of time.
4. Demotion to less desirable job.
5. Discharge from the enterprise's employ.

The penalty to be applied to a particular infraction of discipline should depend upon the nature of the offense and whether there have been previous infractions of this kind by the employee. Ordinarily for first offenses a warning either verbal or written is sufficient unless the infraction is serious enough to demand immediate discharge. The use of demotions is questioned by some authorities on personnel administration unless the employee is failing to meet the established standards for the higher job. In this case the demotion to a job that the employee can perform satisfactorily may be a happy solution for both the enterprise and the worker.

Relationship between personnel management and labor relations

When the enterprise's employees are unionized the interaction between the union and management is called labor relations. The labor relations director customarily is part of the personnel department. In some cases the personnel manager also will be designated as the labor relations director. The labor relations director acts to represent and to advise top management in the negotiation of the labor contract which spells out the terms under which union members will work. Labor relations personnel are involved in handling grievances by union members over disputed matters relating to their work situation.

When an enterprise's nonmanagerial employees are unionized, the most significant change is in how personnel policy is formulated. When no union exists in a shop, personnel policy is usually determined unilaterally by management. Such personnel functions as hiring and placement of employees, setting wage rates, establishing seniority rules, determining work standards, and taking disciplinary action can be carried out without consultation or approval from members of the labor force. The fact that personnel policies may be unilaterally determined and administered by management in the nonunion work situation does not necessarily mean that poor personnel policies are being applied. There are excellent examples of enterprises having no unions where enlightened personnel policies are carefully administered to create a healthy work climate for employees. However, in the nonunion shop the employees usually have little or no chance to appeal the actions taken by management which may affect their welfare.

Where a union exists in an enterprise, personnel policies are bilaterally determined. Questions relating to employees' welfare are decided by management either after consultation with union representatives or are jointly decided by management and the union. Supervisors must be able to justify their applications of personnel policies if disputes arise, and decisions must be within the language and meaning of the labor contract signed by both management and the union. In this respect, labor unions place limitations upon the freedom of management to operate the business enterprise. In some cases the limitations are severe and tend to handicap management in exercising independent judgment regarding business operations.

However, the introduction of the union and the labor contract into the enterprise's picture can also have positive implications for management. There is a consistent pattern established for dealing with employee grievances. Management is forced to analyze its position on various issues which affect employee welfare and to weigh carefully in advance the possible implications of proposed changes. Through seniority lists and established layoff procedures, management is spared making individual decisions as to which workers will be released if reductions in the size of the work force become necessary. Where labor unions negotiate contracts with a number of employers for the same wage rates, this puts one enterprise on a par with others as far as wages expense is concerned if one assumes that labor is used with approximately equal effectiveness in the different enterprises.

Because of the importance of unions in many industries today, the next chapter is devoted to a discussion of labor relations.

The personnel department

The personnel department acts in a staff capacity to the other departments of the business enterprise. This means that the personnel department provides certain services along with advice and assistance, but is not responsible for giving orders to line supervisors in the production or marketing departments. (Note Figure 8–3.)

FIGURE 8–3
Partial organization chart of a personnel department

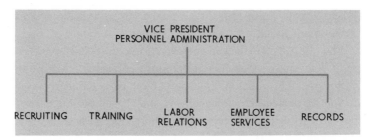

Personnel manager

The head of the department is the personnel manager, or the personnel administrator as he is sometimes called. The personnel manager normally reports either to the president of the enterprise or the executive vice president. The personnel function is so important to the operation of the enterprise that it is almost mandatory for the head of this department to have the ear of top management. Depending upon the size of the enterprise and the number of employees there are a variety of other individuals such as labor relations men, recruiters, interviewers, training supervisors, and clerical assistants who compose the personnel department.

Employee services

In addition to the substantial number of duties performed by the personnel department for line supervisors, most personnel departments administer a variety of employee services. These service programs include those relating to health, safety, insurance, and retirement. Also, the personnel department handles the mechanics of sponsoring company recreational activities, including athletic teams, picnics, and news bulletins with information of personal interest to employees. Such community activities relating to the enterprise and its employees may be handled in part by the personnel department, such as Community Chest drives for local charities. This involvement does not relieve line managers from their responsibilities as community citizens, but the personnel department is in an ideal position to provide this kind of service.

Housekeeping duties

As well as the numerous responsibilities already discussed, the personnel department also provides a number of housekeeping duties for the business enterprise. Records on each employee are maintained by the personnel department. These include data relating to recruitment, interviewing and initial employment, training, health records and other personal information, wage history, disciplinary actions, and promotions or transfers. These records provide a wealth of information for line supervisors in running their departments when historical background is needed on an employee. At the same time, the personnel department should be sure to respect the confidential nature of employee records, especially those which contain personal information, and the information outlined above should only be provided to authorized persons after safeguards have been established for its use.

Advisory role

The personnel department cooperates with other departments in the business enterprise in carrying out its many activities. It works with safety engineers to see that safety regulations are enforced throughout the plant and to improve safety features on machinery and in the production process. Personnel administrators can be valuable in assisting industrial engineers in conducting productivity studies to improve operating efficiency and to motivate employees to better efforts. Personnel officials may maintain contact with union officials as a means of facilitating communication with top management on matters of concern to employees.

Finally, in its capacity of advisor to top management, the personnel department is able to help management ascertain the level of morale and the degree of labor-management teamwork in the enterprise through collecting and interpreting such data as absentee rates, labor turnover, complaints and grievances, accidents, and production efficiency. Once these data are analyzed, the personnel department has the responsibility of making constructive suggestions to management throughout the organization for the improvement of the enterprise as a place in which to work.

Summary

The functions of the personnel department include providing staff assistance in the recruitment, selection, and training of employees for the business enterprise and acting as advisor to management in matters of employee morale and employee-management relations. Top management and supervisors throughout the enterprise, as well as the personnel department, have important roles to perform in personnel management.

The personnel department, functioning as the center for employment activities, performs five basic steps in the hiring and placement of employees:

Working with line management in determining job specifications.
Recruiting job applicants.
Carrying out the selection process.
Performing induction of new employees.
Coordinating a program of employee training.

The personnel department normally performs the function of job analysis to determine that wages are fair, based on the jobs which employees perform and the level of their performance. The first step in job analysis is to draw up a job description covering the essential elements of each specific job. Then job evaluation ranks each job in relation to other jobs in the enterprise. Following job evaluation, the wage scale is drawn up.

A performance rating system is used to evaluate the employee's performance in order to make individual merit increases in wages within job classifications and to guide management in selecting employees for promotion. Both seniority and ability are important considerations in promotion policy.

The personnel department should formulate policy on transfers of employees from one job to another, between departments, from one work shift to another, or for remedial reasons.

Downgrading and layoffs are important areas relating to workers under certain circumstances and should be covered by formulated personnel policies.

A discipline policy should provide a clear statement of what is expected of employees and should be fairly administered.

When workers are unionized, the personnel department can assist management in developing positive policies and attitudes toward organized labor and can aid supervisors in the administration of these policies.

The organizational structure of the personnel department which functions in a staff capacity includes a personnel manager and subordinate managers in the areas of recruiting, training, labor relations, employee services, and records. The head of the personnel function should report to the chief operating officer and be considered a member of top management.

Terms for review

personnel management	job description
job specifications	job evaluation
recruitment	performance rating
apprenticeship training	promotion
vestibule training	seniority
on-the-job training	employee transfer
vocational school training	discipline

Questions

1. Outline the steps that a personnel department might go through to add an additional shift of both skilled and nonskilled workers in a television manufacturing enterprise.
2. What types of training programs would be appropriate for the different kinds of workers hired as the result of the expansion outlined in Question 1?
3. Distinguish between job analysis and performance rating. What is the importance of each?
4. Why is a written disciplinary policy important for the business enterprise?
5. Assume the role of the owner of a small manufacturing enterprise and draw up a statement of your views of the relative importance of seniority and ability in making promotions or layoffs for production workers.
6. Assume the role of the labor union president in a small manufacturing enterprise and draw up a statement of your views of the relative importance of seniority and ability in making promotions and wage increases for production workers who are members of the union.
7. *a)* What changes occur in the development and administration of personnel policies when an enterprise's nonmanagerial employees become unionized?
   b) What positive and negative implications are there for management in such a development?

BUSINESS BRIEF

Turnover of college graduates

A personnel manager for a large midwestern manufacturing corporation recently voiced the following comment:

We are hiring college graduates in business administration and paying them $10,000 a year and up. Top management has indicated that we are to hire more of these young people. However, we haven't been able to keep many of them more than a year. After an orientation period of two weeks they are rotated from one department to another for three-month periods in one of our factory locations. At the end of a year we put them in a spot which may be open and where the trainee expresses an interest. Then the supervisor takes over their work assignments. One problem is that many of our supervisors are getting very little more in salary than these college graduates even though they have been with the company for a number of years.

1. What personnel problems are implied in this statement?
2. What suggestions would you make to the personnel manager for reducing turnover in college graduates and for maintaining supervisors' morale?

CASES

Artwein Manufacturing Company

Ed Walters was the personnel director of Artwein Manufacturing Company. One of his responsibilities was to provide notification to employees when new jobs opened up throughout the factory which made possible transfers and promotions for the work force. Notification was carried out by posting vacancies or new jobs on two bulletin boards convenient for the workers. When an employee saw a job posted that he wanted to try for, he would inform the management through a "bid" system. This bid system, which generally functioned smoothly, had been worked out with the union to which all production workers belonged.

The labor contract, which both management and the union had signed, was quite detailed regarding the selection of employees for a promotion when vacancies or new jobs developed. The agreement stated:

VI–3–B. Vacancies and openings will be filled on the following basis:
1. From the department in which the opening exists in order of departmental seniority, providing the ability of the applicants is relatively equal. The following factors will be considered in determining ability.
a) The quality and efficiency of the employee's performance in his or her current job.
b) Physical fitness (consistent with requirements of the vacancy).
c) Background of education and experience, including experience in similar or related work (consistent with requirements of the vacancy).
d) Record of unexcused absenteeism.
2. From other departments of the plant on the basis of plant seniority, provided the ability of the applicants, as defined in Paragraph VI–3–B—1 above, is relatively equal.

In November, 1970, Ed Walters posted a new job for bid in the shipping department. The new job was titled main sealer operator and maintenance man. It was placed in labor grade 7, that of semiskilled work, with a rate of $2.88 an hour. This job involved operating and maintaining a new carton-sealing machine through which ultimately 60 percent of the total production of the plant would go. Although initially the machine would be used only on the day shift, it was planned that eventually the machine would be in operation 24 hours a day. The employee first selected for this job would work the day shift, and it was expected that he would have the responsibility of instructing other employees who would be subsequently selected for the second and third shifts when the machine went into full production. The employee initially hired for the job would have to undergo training in the operation and maintenance of the equipment provided by factory representatives of the manufacturer.

The carton-sealing machine which the employee would be operating was a new type which cost approximately $50,000 including installation charges. On the advice of the manufacturer of the machine it was decided to use a combination operator and maintenance man for this piece of equipment. The manufacturer advised that the man selected for the job be an individual who was familiar with machinery and who had mechanical training and experience. There were many minor, but critical, adjustments to be made on the machine, and the equipment was more likely to break down and have failures if these adjustments were not properly made.

The personnel director prepared a list of all employees who had bid on the new job. There were 35 bids from throughout the plant including four men in the shipping department where the sealer machine would be used. The names on the list were arranged in order of departmental seniority. This was in line with the labor agreement which required that first consideration be given to employees in the department where the opening exists in order of departmental seniority. These four men from shipping were interviewed by the personnel director and the assistant plant manager in charge of production and shipping. The purpose of the interview was to get additional information about the applicants' education and experience other than what might be shown on company records. All men were physically fit for the job.

On the basis of the interviews and the company's personnel records the following summaries were made concerning the four applicants for the new job:

Ray Jones was the employee with the greatest departmental seniority. His seniority date in the shipping department was June 18, 1961. His job classification was inside truck driver. Some years ago he had taken on-the-job training in dairy farming conducted by the Veterans Administration. In this program he had some training in the maintenance and use of farm tools and machinery. He was considered to be a satisfactory employee by his supervisor, and personnel records showed no unexcused absenteeism.

The employee who stood second in departmental seniority among the applicants was John Robertson. His seniority date was April 4, 1962. He had two years of college compared to the other four applicants who had only high school diplomas. Although Robertson did not claim any mechanical background or training, he was considered a reliable worker by his supervisor in the shipping department. His attendance record was good.

Tod Smith was the third man on the seniority list. He had a seniority date in the shipping department of July 19, 1964. His job classification was inside truck driver. In the interviews Smith indicated that he had had experience with tractors and combines in his farming work. He also indicated that he had taken four years of on-the-job farm training under the Veterans Administration program. His attendance was satisfactory.

Richard Carlson was the fourth man on the list and had a seniority date of July 31, 1967. He was also classified as inside truck driver. His personnel record showed that while in the Air Force he had attended radar school and served as radar crew chief for about six months. Carlson's high school program included machine shop courses and work in shop mathematics, blueprint reading, and shop theory and practice. He had machine shop training during 1968–69 at an evening course at the local high school. His work and attendance records were satisfactory.

The personnel director and assistant plant manager looked over the records of the most senior employees outside the department who had bid on the job and decided that they would be able to select one of the four men interviewed from within the shipping department to fill the initial position of main sealer operator and maintenance man. The new job would be considered a promotion for any of the four men.

1. What are the issues relevant for management in this case?
2. As an assistant to the personnel director which employee would you recommend be selected for main sealer operator and maintenance man? Why?

A case of fighting

Walter Sloan and Tommy Burke were employed by the company as waste handlers on the graveyard shift to fill large bins with waste materials from the production areas of the plant and remove it to the rear of the factory building for further disposal. Both men were union members. The following events occurred in the early morning of October 13, 1970.

According to reports obtained by questioning the two men, about 2:30 a.m. Tommy Burke passed Walter Sloan on his way to the storage room to pick up an empty bin. Burke made an obscene remark and gesture to Sloan who returned a remark. This incident culminated in Burke grabbing the front of Sloan's coveralls and ripping them slightly. Before this could develop further, the supervisor, Mr. Kirby, appeared and ordered the men back to work. This broke up the incident with Sloan going on back to the department where he had been working and Burke picking up an empty waste bin from the storage room. At this point Mr. Kirby took no further action.

About an hour and a quarter later, at 3:45 a.m., Walter Sloan went to the storage room to get an empty bin which he needed. He found an empty bin and headed toward his department with it. However, as Sloan later told company officials, Tommy Burke came up to him and grabbed the bin, saying he was taking "that bin." Sloan allowed him to take the bin. Another employee, Jim Thompson, who was working in the area observed this incident and pointed out another bin which Sloan could use.

Sloan then went to get the one which had been pointed out but found that it was half full of waste. He then started for another bin which he thought was empty. Just as he was about to take this bin Burke ran up to Sloan, grabbed both his arms, and told Sloan he was not going to get that bin either. Sloan jerked his arms loose and shoved Burke back into the bin. Later Sloan said that he told Burke to leave him alone as he shoved him away.

Burke became angry and approached Sloan with his fists clenched, saying to Sloan that he was "going to knock the hell out of him." When Burke was close enough to him, Sloan struck Burke with his fists at least twice. The blows were sufficient to knock Burke down for a few seconds. Burke sustained two cuts, one on his lip and one over his eye.

Then Sloan left the storage room area and obtained a bandage to place over a cut which he sustained on his hand as the result of striking

Burke. Sloan was reluctant to inform management of the fight, and when he encountered the supervisor, Mr. Kirby, who had observed the previous incident, he said he had cut his hand on a piece of wire.

In the meantime, Mr. Kirby had found Burke and noticed his injuries. Kirby took Burke to the first-aid room and later Burke was taken to the hospital where his cuts were treated by a physician. Sloan was sent home for the remainder of the shift but was informed to return at 7:30 a.m. when statements concerning the affair would be taken.

Subsequent investigation revealed that the incident occurred substantially as had been reported.

1. What are the relevant issues which should concern management in this case?

2. If you were a member of management, how would you proceed in an investigation of an incident similar to this? What additional information would you find helpful in arriving at a decision in this case other than that which is given? How would you obtain this information?

3. As a member of the personnel department of the company, what recommendation would you make to management regarding disciplinary action, if any, for Sloan and Burke? Give the reasons for your position.

Courtesy United Steelworkers of America

*Contract negotiations are
an important dimension
of labor relations.*

9

Labor relations

The emphasis placed by managers upon the importance of good human relations and the role of personnel administration leads to a discussion of a third area directly involving members of the work force—that of labor unions. Customarily when management deals with the work force through union representatives this is referred to as labor relations. The subject of labor unions is one which produces strong emotional feelings on the part of many individuals. Much public interest is exhibited in management and union relations when a work stoppage by employees, called a strike, occurs or when some other dispute is widely publicized. The fact is that most of the day-to-day contacts between unions and managements take place in an atmosphere quite unlike that envisioned by the public as the result of the publicity given to these relatively infrequent but more spectacular events. Those interested in the study of the private enterprise system should approach labor relations with the goal of objectivity in appraising the effect of organized labor on the operation of the business enterprise. The following questions concerning labor relations are discussed in this chapter.

How has significant national legislation affected labor relations?
What has been the growth in union membership?
Why do workers join unions?
How are labor unions organized?
What provisions are normally included in the labor contract?
How does the grievance process contribute to a healthy work climate?

Legislation affecting labor relations

To understand the relationship between labor unions and today's business enterprises one should see how this relationship has evolved over the years and how management's dealings with unions have been influenced by national legislation. Many significant incidents, legislative acts, and court decisions could be considered important to the development of today's labor-management climate in this country. However, there are three modern pieces of national legislation which must be included in the discussion of today's relationship between business and organized labor. The first of these acts is the Wagner Act of 1935. It was followed by amending legislation in 1947 known as the Taft-Hartley Act and in 1959 by the Landrum-Griffin Act.

The Wagner Act

The Wagner Act, formally known as the National Labor Relations Act of 1935, represented a Magna Carta for organized labor in the United States. Prior to this legislation business had used any means at its disposal to suppress union activities and to discourage employees from joining unions. During the 1920s and earlier in the United States it was not unusual for an employee to be fired from his job merely because he had been suspected of union activity. Furthermore, a worker might find it impossible to be hired throughout the industry where he had worked because owners circulated *blacklists* to other employers with the names of former employees who had been discharged for union activities. Sometimes a worker was required to sign a *yellow-dog contract* in which he agreed not to join a union as a condition of employment.

Employers did not limit their antiunion activities to economic pressure but also used hired strikebreakers, labor spies, and armed guards in attempting to prevent unions from organizing their factories. There are numerous recorded incidents of all types of violence including clubbing, shooting, and dynamiting which occurred on the part of both business and workers in the battles over the laboring man's right to organize into unions and bargain collectively with the enterprise's management. During this period of American history the political and legal climate generally stressed property rights and favored management's attempts to avoid unionization.

It was with this background that the 1930s ushered in the worst economic depression this country has experienced. Jobs were scarce; unemployment was high; and many workers felt that they had been treated unfairly by management. Workers felt they should have some voice in the determination of their employment conditions, and unions were an important avenue for this representation. On the other hand, few employers were willing to recognize voluntarily the right of their employees to join a union and bargain collectively with management over wages and working conditions. With this refusal by industry to accept unions voluntarily, and as a part of a variety of legislation designed to help the country out of the Great Depression, in 1935 the Congress under the leadership of President Franklin D. Roosevelt passed the National Labor Relations Act.

The basic assumptions of the National Labor Relations Act, known as the Wagner Act, are that the refusal of employers to accept union organization and collective bargaining leads to industrial strife and interruption of the flow of commerce; that the inequality of bargaining power between individual employees and employers organized as corporations tends to aggravate depressions by keeping wage rates low and thus further reduces purchasing power; and that the legal protection of the right of employees to organize into unions would reduce industrial unrest. In recognition of these three factors the Wagner Act declared it the policy of the United States that employees "shall have the right to self-organization, to form, join, or assist labor organizations, to bargain collectively through representatives of their own choosing."

To protect workers against the earlier antiunion practices by employers, the Wagner Act declares as illegal any interference or restraint of employees as they engage in union activities. This general prohibition on actions by employees is backed up with a specific list of acts which are considered illegal. An employer cannot discharge an employee for union activity. No type of discriminatory action can be lawfully taken against an employee for joining a union. No company unions are permitted. These had been organized in the past by some managements in an attempt to dominate the union organization and avoid bargaining with an independent union by employees. Also considered to be an unfair labor practice is an employer's refusal to bargain with a union selected by his employees to represent them.

The administration of the Wagner Act is the job of the National Labor Relations Board originally composed of three men. The organization of the board includes field examiners who investigate complaints of unfair labor practices along with trial examiners who conduct formal hearings and pass their findings on to the board itself for affirmation. Decisions of the board can be appealed through the federal courts to the Supreme Court on legal grounds such as whether or not the board has jurisdiction in a particular instance or has overstepped its legal bounds.

Another important function of the National Labor Relations Board is the conduct of elections to determine whether groups of workers in a particular enterprise desire representation by a union. These elections are held upon proper application by a union which is able to certify interest by a number of employees in such representation. A union may also be certified by the board as representing the workers in a given plant provided the union can show that a majority of the workers are already members of that union.

The Wagner Act marked a turning point in the growth of unions in America. In 1935, there were less than four million union members in the United States. By 1947, when the Wagner Act was significantly amended, more than 15 million American workers belonged to unions. During this 12-year period there were numerous factors which caused the increase in union membership. However, the Wagner Act contributed greatly to this increase.

The Wagner Act minimized the industrial disputes stemming from whether employees shall be represented by a union. The NLRB election procedure is a better means for determining whether or not an enterprise is to be unionized than the strikes and violence which had marked earlier representation battles.

However, the Wagner Act was not particularly successful in reducing strikes in already organized industries. The combination of a flood of union activity between 1935 and 1941, World War II with its controls on wages and prices and wartime shortages, and the relatively new experience of many managements and union leaders in negotiating labor contracts led to almost 5,000 strikes in 1946. These strikes involved more than 4.5 million workers. The time lost through strikes in 1946 amounted to 116 million man-days idle time—three times higher than in the previous year or any other year. Excesses on the part of unions and some union leaders and the limitations of the Wagner Act and its administration started a movement to correct some labor abuses. The pendulum of public opinion and federal support for union activity, which had reached a high point with the passage of Wagner Act and in the years immediately following, began to swing the other way. The change in public opinion, combined with Republican Party control of the Congress in 1946, set the stage for significant revision of the Wagner Act.

The Taft-Hartley Act

The Labor Management Relations Act of 1947, commonly known as the Taft-Hartley Act, was actually an amendment to the Wagner Act. In an attempt to correct some abuses by organized labor, the Taft-Hartley Act adds some restrictions on the activities of labor organizations and gives employers some explicit rights not spelled out in the earlier legislation. The administration of the act remains with the National Labor Relations Board, which was increased from three to five members.

The 1947 act defines as unfair labor practices by an employer essentially the same ones that the Wagner Act had spelled out. However, the Taft-Hartley Act goes further by outlawing certain labor practices by unions. There is to be no restraint or coercion by employees in determining which union would represent them. The union cannot interfere in the right of an employee not to participate in union activity. Nor can the union force an employer to discriminate against an employee for nonunion membership unless the union shop is authorized. A *union shop* is an employment situation where the employer agrees that employees must join the union within a period of time after they are hired, but union membership is not a prerequisite for being hired. The Taft-Hartley Act makes it an unfair labor practice for a union which has a union-shop agreement to charge excessive initiation or membership fees.

A *closed shop* is an employment situation where workers must be members of the union before they may be hired by an employer. The closed shop is illegal under the Taft-Hartley Act. However, in certain industries where managements had already accepted hiring of union members as being to their interest as well as the union's, this provision of the law is being circumvented. The advantage to such employers is that the union is able to provide a source of skilled workers on demand, and problems of recruitment and training of employees are largely avoided by management. This arrangement gives obvious security and power to unions and their leaders and is well accepted by them.

Under the Taft-Hartley Act employers or self-employed persons cannot be forced to join a union. This provision prevents unions from forcing independent businessmen such as plumbers or deliverymen to join a union or employer's association even though their earnings and working conditions might affect the work standards of employees who work for hire in the same occupations.

Secondary boycotts by unions were also outlawed. A *secondary boycott* is where employees of Company A with a grievance against that employer attempt to picket Company B or persuade Company B employees to strike because Company B uses Company A's products. A *primary boycott* is one in which employees refuse to use the products of their employer with whom they have a dispute. This is permitted since it involves direct action against their own employer. Although easy to define in a simple example, in practice the secondary boycott is often difficult to distinguish from direct action against an employer.

The Taft-Hartley Act also prohibits unions from forcing employers to recognize or bargain with one union if another union has already been certified by the NLRB as the bargaining agent. The purpose of this clause is to avoid the disastrous effects on both employers and employees resulting from conflicts among different unions as to which represents employees in a particular enterprise. *Jurisdictional strikes* which grow out of controversies as to which craft has the right to perform particular jobs were outlawed. The building-trades unions were particularly affected by jurisdictional disputes because of overlapping of skills among their members. Another labor practice by unions defined as unfair is *featherbedding,* which requires an employer to pay for services which are not performed. However, the interpretation of this provision allows for payment for some time put in by employees even though they do little or no productive work. An example would be the use of "standby musicians" during recorded broadcasts or when outside bands play in local theatres.

The Taft-Hartley Act also requires that each union which makes use of the NLRB services must file affidavits executed by each officer of the union that he is not a member of the Communist Party and does not support any organization that advocates the overthrow of the U.S. government by force. This provision tended to weaken some of the left-wing unions and strengthened the hand of rival unions which gained members as the result of the breakup of some of these more extreme groups.

Protection for the public. The part of the Taft-Hartley Act that most affects the public are the provisions for protecting the community from strikes which would cut off the flow of essential goods and services. Whenever the president of the United States determines that a labor dispute threatens the national health or safety, he can order the attorney general to obtain an injunction from a federal court which has the effect of postponing any strike for a period of 80 days. During this time workers cannot strike nor can management lock workers out of the plant. Terms of work and pay are frozen for the time, and the parties are obliged to make every effort to settle their differences. The offices of the Conciliation Service of the U.S. Labor Department are available for assistance of both parties. Before the 80-day injunction period is over, if no settlement has been reached, the National Labor Relations Board is required to poll employees to see whether they would accept the last offer of management. If no settlement is reached through this procedure then the president submits a report to the Congress with or without his recommendations for action.

The right-to-work controversy. A controversial part of the Taft-Hartley Act is Section 14b which provides that individual states may outlaw union-shop contracts under which workers are required to join a union. In 1971, 19 states had these right-to-work laws on their statute books. In recent years nine other states have had right-to-work proposals defeated by referendum, and six states have had right-to-work laws repealed. Table 9–1 details these states.

TABLE 9–1
A review of right-to-work laws—1971

States with right-to-work laws in effect
  Alabama, Arizona, Arkansas, Florida, Georgia, Iowa, Kansas, Mississippi, Nebraska, Nevada, North Carolina, North Dakota, South Carolina, South Dakota, Tennessee, Texas, Utah, Virginia, Wyoming.

States where right-to-work proposals have been defeated by referendum
  California, Colorado, Idaho, Maine, Massachusetts, New Mexico, Ohio, Oklahoma, Washington.

States where right-to-work laws have been repealed
  Delaware, Hawaii, Indiana, Louisiana,* Maine, New Hampshire.

    * Louisiana still applies a right-to-work law to agricultural laborers and employees engaged in processing certain agricultural products.
    Source: The U.S. Department of Labor.

A state right-to-work law substantially weakens unions in organizing new workers. Unless employees can be forced as a condition of employment by the labor agreement to join a union after being hired, it is difficult to promote a solid union membership. Unions maintain that many of the gains for all workers come as the result of collective bargaining—the costs of which are incurred by union members. Union leaders and members reason that all workers in a unionized factory should bear their share of the cost of benefits secured by the union by joining the union, paying the dues, and supporting its activities.

The Taft-Hartley Act amending the Wagner Act by no means represented a perfect piece of legislation. Generally union leaders were critical of the restraints imposed on unions by the legislation, while business praised the act but felt it either did not go far enough or provide sufficient penalties for what some considered wrongdoing by unions. Some of these problem areas were dealt with in the next major piece of labor relations legislation which was passed in 1959.

The Landrum-Griffin Act

The Labor-Management Reporting and Disclosures Act of 1959, commonly known as the Landrum-Griffin Act, placed the federal government for the first time in the position of policing the internal affairs of labor unions. The need for new controls over labor organizations and their leaders came to light as the result of lengthy investigations of congressional committees which disclosed glaring irregularities and questionable practices in some unions and on the part of some managements in their relations with union officials.

Some of the principal provisions of the Landrum-Griffin Act are as follows:

1. All labor organizations are required to have a constitution and bylaws which spell out such matters as membership eligibility, fees and dues, handling of union funds, and procedures for collective bargaining and strike authorizations.

2. Regardless of the union's constitution, union members have certain inalienable rights regarding participation in the union's business; safeguards against improper discipline; protection against unreasonable dues and initiation fees; and democratic controls over union officials. Union members may have these rights enforced by appealing to the federal courts if necessary.

3. Unions and union officials, as well as managements and consultants, must file reports with the Secretary of Labor regarding their activities and finances. These reports are similar to those previously required of corporations and managements under the Federal Securities Act. This put on record many of the internal workings of unions which had previously not been subject to review by any outside agency.

4. Limitations were placed on unions with regard to organizing tactics and on employers for countermeasures to union activities. The purpose of these limitations was to restrict these activities on both sides

to peaceful persuasion of workers. The Taft-Hartley Act restriction against secondary boycotts was strengthened. Picketing by unions hopeful of persuading nonunion shop employees to vote for the union was limited.

The Landrum-Griffin Act was wide sweeping in its scope and detailed in its requirements. The chief limitations were imposed upon unions, as many of the provisions in the act of 1959 were framed to deal with specific union problems brought to light by the legislative investigations at the time.

Growth in union membership

The union movement has had its ups and downs in growth depending upon such factors as economic, political, and social circumstances along with the shifting tide of public opinion and legal decisions. Figures 9–1 and 9–2 show how the strength of union membership has varied from 1930 to 1968.

As Figure 9–1 indicates, there was a spectacular growth in union membership between 1936 and the end of World War II. The passage of the Wagner Act in 1935 plus a keen rivalry between the AFL and the CIO stimulated the organizing efforts of the unions. The number of union members increased during World War II as the result of higher employment levels and wider union recognition.

Following the end of World War II in 1945 a wave of industrial unrest and work stoppages began. In the year following V-J Day more than 10 million men and women were demobilized from the armed forces. Thousands of factories had to retool to make the change to a peacetime economy. Some factories shut down either temporarily or permanently. Hours of work were cut back and unions fought to keep take-home pay at wartime levels, which had often included substantial overtime pay at premium rates. Numerous strikes occurred and the prestige of unions was damaged. The Taft-Hartley Act was passed in 1947. This period was one of leveling off in union growth.

The Korean emergency in 1950 gave a new impetus to union growth. With the merger in 1955 of the AFL and CIO the groundwork was laid for achievement of union membership of 17.5 million workers in 1956. However, the merger did not solve all of organized labor's problems. In the late 1950s, the nature of the labor force was changing as

FIGURE 9–1
*Membership of national and international
unions, 1930–1968*

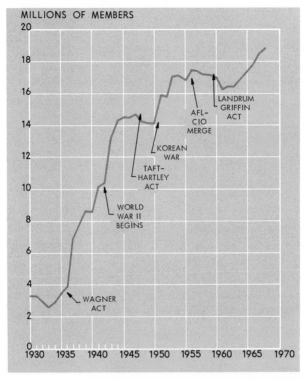

MILLIONS OF MEMBERS

Source: U.S. Department of Labor, *Directory of National and International Labor Unions in the United States.*

the number of blue-collar workers declined and the white-collar workers increased. Automation was of increasing importance, and rivalry continued between various AFL–CIO affiliated unions for membership and job jurisdiction. The Landrum-Griffin Act passed in 1959 put pressure on unions to "clean house."

By 1968, the number of unionized workers reached an all-time high of 18.9 million members. However, as Figure 9–2 illustrates, the proportion of union members in the labor force actually slipped from a 1956 high of 25 percent to 23 percent in 1968. Union membership as a percentage of the nonagricultural work force dropped from an all-time high in 1945 of 35 percent to 28 percent in 1968.

Other measures of union membership include those based on sex, geography, and industry. Figure 9–3 illustrates that nearly three out of

FIGURE 9–2
Union membership as a percent of the labor force, 1930–1968

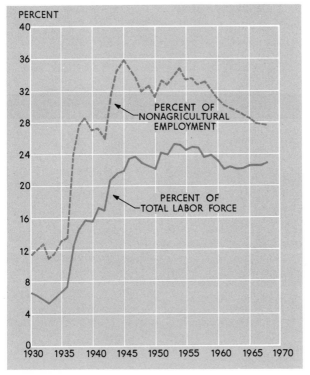

Source: U.S. Department of Labor, *Directory of National and International Labor Unions in the United States.*

every ten male workers belong to a labor union while only one out of seven female workers are unionized.

Some states have more union members than others. The states of New York, California, and Pennsylvania together account for about one out of three union members. When Illinois, Ohio, and Michigan are added to this group, the six states have more than half of all union members in the United States.

Table 9–2 shows the degree of unionization in different industries in the United States. The transportation and transportation equipment industries have the highest percentage of union membership, while various types of financial institutions have relatively little unionization. Agriculture and fishing traditionally have had little unionization.

There has been a substantial increase in unionization of professional

FIGURE 9–3

PROPORTION OF NATION'S MALE LABOR FORCE BELONGING TO UNIONS--1968

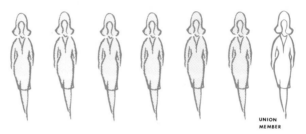

PROPORTION OF NATION'S FEMALE LABOR FORCE BELONGING TO UNIONS--1968

Source: U.S. Department of Labor.

TABLE 9–2
Industries ranked in order of the degree of union organization of employees

75 percent and over	Electric and gas utilities
Transportation	Rubber
Transportation equipment	Printing and publishing
Contract construction	Tobacco manufactures
Ordinance	
Paper	*25 percent to less than 50 percent*
Petroleum	Federal government
	Machinery
	Fabricated metals
50 percent to less than 75 percent	Leather
Electrical machinery	Furniture
Primary metals	
Food and kindred products	*Less than 25 percent*
Mining	Instruments
Apparel	Textile mill products
Chemicals	Service industries
Miscellaneous manufacturing	Wholesale and retail trade
Telephone and telegraph	State and local government
Lumber	Finance
Stone, clay, and glass products	Agriculture and fishing

Source: U.S. Department of Labor, *Directory of National and International Labor Unions in the United States.*

and technical, clerical, and sales employees in recent years. The white-collar worker has traditionally been less receptive to union organization than the factory worker or the tradesman. However, white-collar attitudes are changing because these workers feel that their wages have lagged behind the higher prices for goods and services and because groups such as teachers, policemen, and firemen have felt that the community was not supporting them as it should as they faced increased pressures in carrying out their responsibilities. In the ten-year period from 1958 to 1968 the number of white-collar union members increased from 2.2 million to 3.2 million, an increase of 45 percent.

Why workers join unions

Contrary to the belief of some managers, the reasons why workers join unions are much more complex than simply that they want more pay or are highly critical of the business enterprise. Usually a variety of factors will determine why workers join unions. These include both economic and noneconomic considerations.

Economic motives for union membership

The three main economic factors which motivate workers to join labor unions voluntarily are wages, fringe benefits, and security in employment and wage income.

Not only does the prospect of higher wages motivate workers to join a union, but fringe benefits such as health insurance, disability benefits, sick leave, life insurance, pensions, and paid vacations are becoming increasingly important. Workers also desire security in employment and wage income to protect them against losses from layoffs due to seasonal variations and declines in general business activity.

Noneconomic motives for union membership

Noneconomic motives influencing employees to favor establishment of unions or to join a union may be stronger than the economic motives. Eight noneconomic motives for union membership can be identified.

1. Employees desire protection against arbitrary action by supervisors in discipline and discharge. The union provides a procedure for

dealing with grievances to insure some measure of equity and fairness in the standards applied by management.

2. Workers desire a voice in making the decisions which affect them. Employees like to participate in such decisions as how overtime will be distributed, how workers shall be laid off in the event of a reduction of forces, and how increased compensation shall be divided between pay raises and various fringe benefits.

3. There is a need for establishing channels of communication between employees and top management which becomes increasingly important as the enterprise grows and the line between employees and management sharpens. The union organization with its grievance procedure provides one avenue of communication between workers and management.

4. The union offers an opportunity for increased individual satisfaction associated with the work experience. The employee who becomes active in the union organization frequently feels a sense of accomplishment and purpose in holding a union office or participating in union activities. The union provides an opportunity to satisfy the worker's psychological needs for self-realization. This is especially true when the work environment is routine and monotonous and the employee has more than average capabilities.

5. In today's complex industrial society most individuals feel a need for identification with some group. Group identification tends to reduce feelings of insecurity in the individual employee. Union membership can provide an important kind of group identification.

6. Individual workers are motivated to join a union by the social pressure of the informal work group. Employees with negative or indifferent attitudes may become union members in order to conform to the attitudes of the work group. The worker who refuses to join may encounter hostile attitudes from his fellow workers and not be accepted in the informal organization of the enterprise.

7. Union sometimes provide for the recreational, social, cultural, and educational needs of workers. Particularly in certain industries or in large urban areas, the labor organization plays a large part in meeting these needs of employees.

8. The employee may be motivated to union membership because of his family ties. Studies have shown that a worker with a family background of union membership is more likely to become a union member than a worker from a nonunion family.

Union membership required for employment

Where a union shop has been lawfully agreed to by an employer and an existing union, all members of the work force covered by the labor agreement will be required to join the union within a specified period of time after being hired. Under this arrangement an employee has no option of whether or not to join a union. It is a condition for continued employment.

The structure and organization of the labor union

Craft and industrial unions

Unions are customarily organized on the basis of craft or industry. *Craft unions* draw their members from a particular trade or occupation. An example of the craft union is the International Brotherhood of Electrical Workers, which includes electricians whether they are employed in factories, the building trades, or shipyards. The *industrial union,* typified by the United Automobile Workers, organizes the workers in a particular industry regardless of the kind of work they do. Sometimes the line between craft and industrial unions is blurred as each type reaches out beyond its original scope of skills or industry to organize workers in other categories.

Local unions

The hierarchy of union organization includes the local union, the regional, and the national union. The local union is the unit which deals most directly with individual union members. In some respects, the local union is analogous to municipal government. The local usually includes members from one enterprise or geographical area and has its own officers. These officers may devote full time or part time to union activities depending upon the size and strength of the local. Sometimes the local will have a business agent or secretary-treasurer who will take care of most of the affairs of the union and will be paid for his services from the local union treasury. Local unions may draw assistance from a business agent appointed by the national union who will serve more than one local in a particular area.

Important members of the local union organization are the shop stewards or committeemen. These individuals are usually elected by the union employees with whom they work. Although the shop stewards are full-time employees of the enterprise, they discuss grievances of union members with the foremen, carry out union activities in the enterprise, and generally represent union membership to first-level supervisors. In some instances stewards may collect dues for the union treasury. Just as the foremen have a great influence in determining the human relations climate, so the union stewards tend to set the tone for union activities in the enterprise.

Regional and national union organization

The local union is generally affiliated with a national or international union which may have a regional organization to coordinate the activities of local unions and act as an intermediary between local and national union organization. National and regional union organizations provide assistance to locals in bargaining with managements and have a part in the grievance procedure at higher levels. The degree of authority exercised by the national or international union over its locals varies.

The organization of the labor union is essentially political in character. Local union leaders must meet the demands and needs of individual workers who compose the local membership. If these local leaders are not able to "deliver" on issues of importance, they are likely to be replaced by new officers the next time union elections are held. The same political circumstances are true with the national labor organization. The national union has to meet the needs of its local affiliates if the national leaders are to retain their offices for any period of time. The national unions have paid representatives who, since they are usually appointed on a political basis, tend to promote the stature of the national union leaders. These union representatives act so as to gain support for the national leaders from local membership and to promote union solidarity. National representatives provide assistance for local unions in negotiations with management either for contract agreements or in grievances which have not been settled at lower levels. They also act as organizers to reach nonunion employees of enterprises within their jurisdictional areas. In this way the representatives seek to strengthen the national by increasing the size of the union and improving the bargaining power of local unions by reducing the number of nonunion workers.

Most national and international unions having locals in the United

States are affiliated with the AFL–CIO, the combined organization of the American Federation of Labor and Congress of Industrial Organizations. Today the AFL–CIO unions, which were united in 1955, represent the majority of American union members. However, there are significant unions which are not affiliated with the AFL–CIO. These independent unions include the Teamsters, the Automobile Workers, and the United Mine Workers.

As has been the case for some time, there is a heavy concentration of membership in a few unions. Table 9–3 lists the unions reporting membership in excess of 150,000. The teamsters', automobile workers', and steelworkers' unions each has over one million members. Together these three unions account for almost one fourth of union membership in the United States.

TABLE 9–3

National and international unions reporting 150,000 or more members, 1968 (in thousands)

Union	Members	Union	Members
Teamsters (Ind.)	1,755	Government (AFGE)	295
Automobile Workers (Ind.)	1,473	Musicians	283
Steelworkers	1,120	Railway clerks	280
Machinists	903	District 50, allied	
Electrical (IBEW)	897	and technical (Ind.)	232
Carpenters	793	Letter carriers	210
Laborers	553	Rubber	203
Retail clerks	552	Painters	200
Meat cutters	500	Textile workers	183
Hotel and restaurant	459	Pulp, sulphite	183
Garment, ladies'	455	Retail, wholesale	175
Service employees	389	Oil, chemical	173
Clothing workers	386	Ironworkers	168
State, county workers	364	Electrical (UE)(Ind.)	167
Communications workers	357	Postal clerks	166
Engineers, operating	350	Teachers	165
Electrical (IUE)	324	Bricklayers	160
Plumbers	297		

Source: U.S. Department of Labor, *Directory of National and International Labor Unions in the United States.*

The union contract

When the management of a business enterprise bargains collectively with its employees through union representatives over conditions of employment the result is a contract agreement between management and the union which customarily runs for two or three years. The contract may be relatively simple or it may encompass many pages of details by which both management and employees will be expected to abide. Despite the unique nature of each union contract, there are certain issues which are dealt with in most contracts. These issues, which are discussed in the following pages, form the framework within which labor relations are handled in the individual enterprise.

The bargaining unit

One of the first elements of the union contract is the *recognition clause* which spells out the fact that the management of a particular enterprise acknowledges a certain union as representing the bargaining interests of a designated group of employees. The *bargaining unit* defines the employer and the employees covered by the union contract. On the employer side, the bargaining unit may be one business enterprise or it may include a number of firms dealing with the same union in what is called *industrywide* bargaining. On the employee side, the bargaining unit may be defined to include employees in certain departments, in certain job classifications, or in a particular factory if the enterprise is a multiplant operation. When job classification is the basis for definition of the labor bargaining unit, management may have to bargain with more than one union with each representing different crafts such as electricians, pipefitters, and carpenters.

Union security

Customarily the contract will spell out the provisions for union security. In most instances this means that all employees covered by the contract will be required to join the union within a specified time after being employed and will be required to maintain their membership in the union. Frequently, a *checkoff* clause in the contract authorizes management to deduct union dues from the employee's pay and turn this sum directly over the union treasury.

Grievance procedure and arbitration

Virtually all labor contracts contain a rather detailed statement of procedures to be followed in dealing with complaints by union members against management. Grievance procedures spell out a succession of steps through which complaints may be processed from lower to higher echelons of management and union officials. In the event that the disputes cannot be settled by the parties themselves, an impartial third person called an *arbitrator* is called upon to settle the issue.

Because of the importance of the grievance process and arbitration to labor relations, this area is discussed in detail following the remaining major union contract provisions.

Wages and hours

Wage rates represent a subject of major importance in collective bargaining. General wage scales are outlined in the contract with detailed wage scales for various job classifications listed in appendices to the basic contract. Such elements as overtime premiums, bonuses, wage incentive systems, automatic wage adjustments, and wage reopening discussion clauses are usually a part of this section of the labor contract.

Hours of work and overtime provisions are also important to the contract. The most common schedule of daily and weekly working hours is the 8-hour day and the 40-hour week, although some labor contracts currently have short workweeks. Recently there has been considerable interest expressed in a four-day week consisting of ten hours per day providing workers with a three-day weekend. The objectives of such a workweek are to reduce absenteeism and to raise employees' morale.

Pay or work guarantees

The inclusion of a guarantee of pay represents a relatively new, but important, feature of the collective bargaining agreement. As recently as ten years ago *supplementary unemployment benefit* plans were virtually unknown. These SUB plans consist of payments made by employers to a fund that is used to pay employees who have been laid off. This money supplements unemployment benefits paid under state plans. Unions which have negotiated unemployment benefit plans include the United Auto Workers, the steelworkers, and the rubber workers.

In contrast to the relatively recent guaranteed pay plans, some guarantee of hours of work for employees over a given period has been in existence for years. Such work guarantees include the 36-hour-week guarantee in the meat-packing industry, weekly hours guarantee in various transportation enterprises, and a minimum number of hours-per-week guarantee in sugar refineries.

Holidays and vacations

Almost all labor contracts include a statement regarding holidays. On a paid holiday employees are paid for a workday even though they do not work. Those employees who may be required to work on designated holidays are then paid a premium, such as time and a half or double time. The number of days recognized as holidays has increased steadily over the years with the number of paid holidays commonly ranging from six to nine.

Paid vacations are a part of the labor contract with the length of the vacation keyed to the employee's years of service with the enterprise. Paid vacations usually run from one to four weeks with the tendency being to lengthen the vacation period for long-term employees.

Employee benefits

Employee benefits cover a broad range of insurance and pension provisions. The area of employee benefits represents an important aspect of the union contract which has increased considerably in recent years. Most contracts call for some or all of the following types of insurance for employees: life insurance, medical and hospitalization coverage, accidental death and disability insurance associated with the job, and nonoccupational sickness and accident insurance.

The majority of union contracts provide for pensions for employees retiring after long service with the enterprise. The tendency in recent years has been for the amount of pension benefits to increase and for the retirement age to be liberalized. An important feature of pensions is whether or not the employee has a *vested interest* in pension benefits. When benefits are vested the employee is entitled as a matter of right to the contribution after a specified period whether or not he is still in the employment of the enterprise at retirement age. The present tendency is to provide for vested pension rights. This increases the mobility of the individual employee since he need not remain with one employer in order to qualify for some retirement benefits in addition to his federal social security.

Discipline and discharge

Union contracts include mention of the measures of discipline which an employer may undertake for certain activities of employees. Contracts seldom contain detailed lists of graduated disciplinary measures short of discharge. Instead, broad reference to disciplinary measures is made in a general management rights clause. Discipline short of discharge includes oral and written warnings, suspension, transfer, demotion, or pay penalties. An important feature of disciplinary sections of the contract is that some form of notice to employee and union be given. Frequently, some sort of hearing is required before disciplinary action can be taken.

Discharge is the strongest form of disciplinary action the enterprise can take against an employee short of bringing court action in a civil suit or support of criminal prosecution. Almost all contracts detail the basis for discharge of employees, including the grounds for the dismissal, procedures for notification, action, and appeal. Reference should be made to Chapter 8 for a discussion of personnel policies dealing with discipline, plant rules, and employee conduct.

Management and union rights

It is not unusual to find a statement regarding management's rights or prerogatives in the labor relations contract. The general statements of managerial rights customarily contain provisions relating to the right to direct the working force and the right to conduct the business, including determining products and prices. Some statements discuss rights to control production methods. Frequently, a statement is made to the effect that the management retains all its rights except those which may be specifically detailed in the contract as subjects for collective bargaining.

Sometimes limitations will be placed on management's rights to contract work, including restrictions on subcontracting. A common provision regarding subcontracting is that this would be prohibited if it would result in a layoff of employees or if the enterprise already has employees in a layoff status. Other restrictions such as limitations on use of purchased products as opposed to company-manufactured products, changes in production methods, and type of work performed by supervisors can be found in union contracts.

Union rights may be spelled out in terms of access of union representatives to the plant, control of the union label such as in the apparel industry, and permission for union bulletin boards. Also, the contract may call for management to collect dues for the union automatically from employees' pay through the *checkoff system.*

Unions may be restricted by the contract in such matters as the number of union stewards in the plant, conduct of union activities on company time, and solicitation of union members during company time.

Seniority provisions

Nearly all union contracts cover seniority as it affects employees in matters of job retention or advancement as well as for other purposes. Ordinarily employees with greater length of service with the enterprise get preference over those with lesser seniority. As is discussed in Chapter 8, seniority may be computed on the basis of service with the enterprise, plant, department, or job classification. Generally the union's goal is to stress the role of seniority and compute it on the widest basis, but at the same time it is recognized that seniority does not entitle the employee to a job he cannot perform.

There are different degrees of emphasis on the role of seniority for purposes of promotion. The most weight is given to seniority when the clause "seniority shall prevail" is the basis for determining which employee shall be promoted. Another clause used regarding seniority indicates that seniority shall prevail with the promotion given to the most senior candidate "if qualified." The "if qualified" clause places relatively less weight on seniority since the most senior employee could be passed over if he were not qualified for the promotion. Management has the most latitude when seniority is a factor to be considered in promotions when the "if equal" clause is included. The "if equal" clause means that the most senior employee will be given the position if his ability and qualifications are equal to other competing candidates.

Although management usually prefers to have as much latitude as possible in selecting personnel for promotion, transfer, or in layoffs in the event they become necessary, seniority systems do provide for a measure of consistency in management actions. Although disputes sometimes arise as to the application of seniority provisions of the union contract, with a large work force and many jobs which do not require a high degree of skill or specialization some use of seniority for employee selection can be a genuine aid for management.

Strikes and lockouts

Nearly all union contracts provide for some form of no-strike clause. These no-strike clauses are either unconditional bans upon work stoppages and interference with production during the life of the contract or conditional bans on strikes such as a statement that strikes may take place only after the grievance procedure is not effective or a deadlock occurs during bargaining on a new contract and the old one has expired.

A *strike* represents action taken by workers to cease work and is usually followed by picketing by union members to prevent other personnel from entering the struck plant. An analogous action by management is called a *lockout,* where the workers are not permitted by management to enter the enterprise's facilities because of a dispute. Customarily management will give a no-lockout pledge in the labor agreement when the union accepts a no-strike clause.

Some contracts having no-strike clauses call for disciplinary penalties ranging up to discharge for individual participants in unauthorized strikes. In some instances the liability of the union organization is limited for violations of the no-strike clause. These limitations began to appear in contracts after the Taft-Hartley Act made it easier to press damage suits against unions for violations of the labor contract. Wildcat, or unauthorized, strikes do occasionally occur in industry today. Management should investigate carefully the causes for the work stoppage and try to correct the difficulty within the framework of the labor agreement.

As Table 9–4 indicates, strikes over wages accounted for the majority of work stoppages in 1970. Many of the strikes occurred while manage-

TABLE 9–4
Work stoppages by major reason, 1970

Major issues	Work stoppages	Workers involved (1000)	Man-days idle during year (1000)
General wage changes	2,848	1,843	36,159
Supplementary benefits	56	63	475
Wage adjustments	222	240	1,134
Hours of work	7	1	26
Other contractual matters	107	380	18,347
Union organizational security	587	106	6,107
Job security	170	51	376
Plant administration	921	401	1,714
Other working conditions	175	59	418
Interunion or intraunion matters	566	149	1,577
Not reported	58	12	81
Total	5,717	3,305	66,414

Source: U.S. Bureau of the Census, *Statistical Abstract of the United States,* 1971.

ment and union officials were bargaining over terms of a new labor agreement after the old contract had expired.

Working conditions and safety

Although many sections of the labor agreement refer directly or indirectly to working conditions, more specific mention is made in some contracts to working conditions and safety. A variety of guarantees are made against discrimination by either management or union toward individual employees on account of race, creed, sex, age, and/or some other ascribed status. Employee health and safety is referred to in the contract in such clauses as those dealing with union-management safety committees, safety equipment and who shall pay for it, first-aid provision, and physical examinations. Sometimes services and working conditions, such as company dining rooms, parking lots, rest rooms, locker and shower facilities, and statements regarding premium pay and protection for uncomfortable or potentially hazardous work, are included in this section of the contract.

From this lengthy discussion which has only outlined the principal and most frequently encountered provisions in the typical union contract, it should be apparent that a great deal of time and effort on the part of both management and organized labor go into the development of the contract and that it is an important part of the American industrial scene.

The grievance process and arbitration

The grievance process

The grievance process has been characterized as one of the major contributions of American unionism to industrial human relations. The grievance process is customarily a three- or four-step procedure capped by a provision for a decision by an impartial third party if management and labor cannot settle the grievance at an earlier stage. A typical grievance procedure would include the following four steps.

First, the employee or employees with a complaint would present the grievance in writing to the foreman where it would be discussed by the aggrieved, the union steward, or a member of the union grievance committee, and the foreman and/or general foreman. If the grievance is settled at this first step to the satisfaction of both management and labor the subsequent steps are unnecessary. If the grievance is not settled by the foreman, union steward, and the aggrieved, then the written complaint is signed and dated and sent on to the second step.

Second, the written grievance is discussed by union representatives of the grievance committee and the next higher level of management, perhaps the factory superintendent or his representative. At this stage a local staff member of the industrial relations department may advise or represent management in attempting to settle the grievance.

Most grievances should be settled in the first or second steps by the foreman or the next higher supervisor. If all grievances go to the third step where they are dealt with by the national union representative and top management further conflict and confusion develops. A substantial number of grievances should be settled on the floor by the foreman. If the foreman doesn't have the authority and doesn't understand policy well enough to settle grievances, his prestige with his subordinates is undermined. If grievances are to be settled effectively in the first and second steps it is necessary that personnel policies, disciplinary policies, and policies in interpreting the contract must be clearly formulated and communicated. Supervisory personnel down to the foreman should participate in the formulation of these policies. Better understanding and loyalty to the policies will result from such participation.

Third, if the grievance is not settled in the second step it is sent to a committee composed of a representative of the national union of which the local union is a part and the factory manager or some higher member of management. At this stage the local union has brought in outside assistance and the enterprise's industrial relations director is probably involved on the management side. Each side will likely conduct its own investigation of the complaint and attempt to establish a basis for settling the dispute.

Fourth, if top management and the national union representative are unable to agree on a solution to the grievance, the issue may be dropped if the aggrieved and the union wish, or it may be submitted to a third, impartial party for arbitration. The contract will provide that issues taken to arbitration are final and binding on both parties provided the issue is one which may be properly submitted to arbitration and that the arbitrator does not overstep the limits of the issue in handing down his decision. The arbitrator is selected with the mutual consent of both parties with each side bearing the expenses necessary to prepare and present its own case. Customarily the cost of the arbitrator is borne equally by the business enterprise and the union.

Arbitration, conciliation, and mediation

The role of the arbitrator is sometimes confused in the field of industrial relations. Arbitration, conciliation, and mediation all have different meanings. *Arbitration* is a judicial process with the arbitrator assuming the role of a judge. The parties are required to submit evidence and cross-examine the other's case. After the arbitrator has heard both sides and has had a period of study and deliberation he renders his decision. The backlog of previous decisions by arbitrators has resulted in the fast-growing field of industrial jurisprudence.

Conciliation is the action of a third party to bring together management and labor when a dispute exists between them. The conciliator's role is merely to get the parties to the bargaining table to talk over their dispute in the hope of reaching a settlement. On the other hand, *mediation* is the process whereby a third party brings the two sides together and *also* actively participates in the discussions. The mediator hopes by his actions to bring about a compromise which will be acceptable to both parties. This may involve talking first to one side and then to the other privately, or mediation may take place in a three-way discussion.

Although so far the discussion of the grievance process has been in the context of a unionized situation, management may establish a grievance procedure where no union exists, with the exception that in the final stage, arbitration will not be included. For the grievance process to be effective it must be used. In an unorganized enterprise management must definitely encourage employees to use it and develop a human relations atmosphere where employees will not fear reprisal when they bring a grievance to management's attention.

There are several functions that a good grievance process performs in the modern industrial enterprise. By raising a complaint on an issue which he considers to be important, the employee brings dissatisfactions to the surface where they may be evaluated and resolved. Even though the grievance is invalid under the labor contract or has no merit, the employee may voice the grievance. This gives the employee an emotional release for dissatisfactions and frustrations. The union may carry the grievance even though it does not believe it can be successfully prosecuted in order to satisfy the employee. Even though the grievance is ultimately lost the employee feels that he has done something about it and that the union has provided him some support.

If the employees are unionized, the grievance process provides an orderly procedure for resolving disputes in the application and interpretation of the labor agreement. Even if no union exists, the grievance actually provides a system of communication from employees to higher levels of management. If a grievance is not resolved in the first steps of the process the grievance automatically goes to higher management.

The nature of the grievance process enables higher management to locate poor first-line supervision. If an unusual number of grievances, especially grievances with little merit, originate among the employees of a particular supervisor there should be an investigation of the quality of management in that department. The existence of the grievance process is a check upon arbitrary and capricious actions by supervisors. If the supervisor's actions are subject to review he is likely to be more careful in his decisions because he may have to be able to justify them.

Finally, the adjustment of grievances tends to prevent future complaints. As management seeks to determine the underlying problems which caused the grievance it may discover corrective action that will lead to a better work climate. Management should always ask the question, "What can we learn from the fact that this grievance was filed?" A properly functioning grievance process is an important tool in developing a good labor relations climate and for improving the human relations understanding of supervisors throughout the organization structure.

Summary

Labor relations is part of the broad function of personnel management and is concerned with management's dealings with the labor union or unions which represent the enterprise's employees.

The National Labor Relations Act of 1935, commonly known as the Wagner Act, represented a Magna Carta for organized labor in the United States. The Wagner Act prohibits employers from interfering with employees engaging in union activities. The act is administered by the National Labor Relations Board, which hears complaints of unfair labor practices and conducts union representation elections.

The Labor Management Relations Act of 1947, commonly known as the Taft-Hartley Act, was an amendment to the Wagner Act and outlawed certain unfair labor practices by unions. The Taft-Hartley Act gave power to the president of the United States to effect a postponement in any strike threatening the national health or safety.

The Labor-Management Reporting and Disclosures Act of 1959, known as the Landrum-Griffin Act, gave the federal government the role of policing certain internal affairs of labor unions.

Total union membership reached a high in 1968, although as a proportion of the labor force it had slipped from the 1956 high.

Economic motives for joining a union include higher wages, fringe benefits, and security in employment and wage income. Noneconomic motives for union membership include protection against arbitrary action of supervisors, a voice in decision making, the need to identify with a group, and family ties which are prounion.

Unions are usually organized on either a craft or industry basis and may have local, regional, and national organizational structure.

The union contract normally includes a wide variety of provisions, such as statements on wages and hours, union security, grievance procedures, holidays and vacations, and working conditions and safety.

The grievance process provides a means whereby complaints of employees can be given a hearing by management in an orderly manner.

Terms for review

National Labor Relations Act of
1935 (Wagner Act)
Labor Management Relations
Act of 1947 (Taft-Hartley
Act)
union shop
closed shop
right-to-work laws
Labor-Management Reporting
and Disclosures Act of 1959
(Landrum-Griffin Act)

union or shop steward
union contract
strike
lockout
grievance procedure
arbitration
conciliation
mediation

Questions

1. Summarize the economic, political, and social conditions that preceded the passage of the National Labor Relations Act in 1935.
2. What economic, political, and social conditions preceded the passage of the Labor Management Relations Act of 1947?
3. What are the functions of the National Labor Relations Board?
4. How do you account for the recent increase in the unionization of professional, technical, clerical, and sales employees?

5. What conditions might influence an individual to join a labor union? Consider the relative importance of economic versus noneconomic motivations.

6. Why is the labor contract an important document for both management and the union?

7. Examine current publications reporting business and economic news for labor contracts which are in the process of negotiation. What issues seem to be most important to each side in arriving at a satisfactory agreement?

8. After a study of materials available in the library, write a 300-word summary either supporting or opposing the application of compulsory arbitration by the federal government of labor-management disputes which affect the public welfare.

BUSINESS BRIEFS

The four-day week

In 1971 several hundred business enterprises in the United States were experimenting with the four-day workweek. Although for some time labor union officials had advocated a four-day week based on 32 working hours, most four-day weeks instituted by companies consisted of four 10-hour days. This left three days a week of free time for employees.

Two large insurance companies extended the concept and placed their computer personnel on a 36-hour week based on three 12-hour days.

1. What advantages would a four-day workweek have for employees?
2. How might a four-day week be helpful to management in achieving a business enterprise's objectives?
3. What problems would be raised for business enterprises and employees by moving to a four-day week?

Welfare benefits for strikers

During the 10-week strike of the United Automobile Workers against General Motors in 1970 over a new labor contract, striking workers collected between $12 million and $14 million of federally financed food stamps in October and November. In Michigan some 75,000 of 200,000 striking GM employees were certified eligible for food stamps. Over 25,000 received welfare under either the aid-to-dependent-children or general-assistance programs. Dependent-children benefits paid to the strikers' families during the last quarter of 1970 totaled $4.3 million.

In the 101-day national General Electric strike in 1969–70 it has been estimated that union members received $30 million of publicly financed aid. This amount was ten times larger than the special strike fund collected by the AFL–CIO to support the GE strikers.

These two examples highlight the use of public funds to help strikers and their families during periods of labor-management difficulties. Public assistance programs have been available to workers during strikes for years. However, liberalization of welfare-eligibility rules and new programs, such as food stamps, have increased the utilization of welfare aid by union members during strikes.

1. What reasons can you give justifying the use of public assistance funds for workers who are on strike?
2. What reasons can you give opposing the use of public assistance funds for strikers?

CASES

Forty minutes of overtime

The management of Amalgamated Manufacturing Company became involved in a dispute with the union over an incident which occurred on May 18, 1971. An important customer of Amalgamated had given the company short notice that it wanted certain production units revised. The customer wanted shipment on May 18 on a given number of the modified units. There was a deadline of 6 p.m. that day for production of these units in order to meet the airline shipping schedule.

The changes on this model required special arrangement for tooling, gauging, and precise measurements along with some modifications in the methods of assembling the units. Amalgamated's management started on these changes early on the morning of May 18. Certain women employees were selected from other assembly lines to work on this particular assembly line and were instructed in the methods of assembling the units for the special rush order. Work was started on this assembly line at approximately 3 p.m. The work was not completed at the end of the shift at 4:30 p.m.

At this point management made a decision to go ahead with the same girls on the assembly line. These were the assemblers who had already been instructed on the changed methods. Had management brought on other employees to complete the work additional time would have been required to instruct the new employees, which might have prevented the order from being shipped on time. Ten employees worked overtime for 40 minutes on May 18 and completed the assembly work at approximately 5:10 p.m. The units were boxed and reached the airport in time for the 6 p.m. deadline.

The labor contract between Amalgamated and the union contained a provision regarding the equalization of overtime among employees. One paragraph of the contract states:

All overtime work shall be rotated equally among the employees on seniority in a classification. If extra employees are needed, the overtime shall then be offered on a seniority basis to employees who formerly worked in that classification.

In actual practice this provision had been applied so that every employee in a classification did not wind up with an equal number of overtime hours. Instead, overtime had been equalized on the basis of opportunities for overtime rather than on the basis of equalization of overtime hours actually worked. Rather than maintaining an overtime equalization roster where the employee who has the least amount of overtime is entitled to overtime work as it is available, each employee who had seniority in a classification was given the opportunity for overtime work on a rotation basis regardless of his accumulated period of overtime. If an employee turned down the offer for overtime work when it was her turn according to the seniority list, that employee was passed over and the next most senior employee was asked. The employees who worked 40 minutes overtime on the project of May 18 were not the employees who would have been entitled to work this overtime on such a rotation basis. However, for the reasons stated the management decided to go ahead and assign the overtime work to these ten employees.

In the past, in similar emergency situations, the rotation of overtime opportunities had also been departed from. One specific incident was on record when a shop steward had agreed that the overtime could be assigned on the basis of production requirements in an emergency situation.

The next day when union officials were informed of the company's action by some of the workers, the union filed a grievance on behalf of the ten employees who would normally have been granted the opportunity for overtime under the contract and according to company rotation practice. The union requested that the company pay each of these ten employees for the 40 minutes of overtime that they had been deprived of on the previous day. The union referred to the contract provision and alleged that the management had violated the labor agreement by assigning this overtime to the ten employees who were already working on the assembly line.

1. What action would you recommend for company officials in response to this grievance by the union? Why? Discuss both the possible immediate and long-run consequences of the action you suggest.

2. Would you suggest any changes in the manner in which the company has been handling overtime? If so, what changes and why?

Grievance over disciplinary action

On October 15, 1970, Walter Sloan and Tommy Burke were given 15-day suspensions from work without pay by the factory management as a disciplinary penalty for the fighting incident of October 13, described in "A Case of Fighting" (see Chapter 8, Cases). A statement of the disciplinary action taken, which included a detailed account of the incident and a warning, was placed in the personal history record of each employee. The statement indicated that both Sloan and Burke were informed that any future incident of fighting involving either man would result in his immediate and final dismissal from employment.

On October 19, Walter Sloan filed a grievance complaining that the disciplinary action was not fair to him and that he had acted only in self-defense. Sloan asked that the disciplinary suspension be lifted and that the warning letter be removed from his personal history record. The other employee involved, Tommy Burke, did not file a grievance.

The grievance was processed through the various steps according to the union's contract with the company. However, no settlement of the issue could be reached that was satisfactory to both the union and the management. Therefore, the case was submitted to an arbitrator for hearing and disposition. By the time of the hearing both men had served their suspensions and had returned to work.

In addition to the description of the incident given in the earlier case, the following information was brought out by testimony during the arbitration hearing. The account of the facts of the case came largely from the testimony of the grievant, Walter Sloan. The one witness to the incident beginning with the taking of the first bin from Sloan by Tommy Burke was Jim Thompson, who was operating a machine in a nearby area. Thompson was in a position to observe the events, although he could not hear all that was said. Thompson's testimony in the arbitration hearing agreed in all important points with that of Sloan's.

Burke had been interrogated regarding the incident by several supervisors and by the personnel director of the firm. Burke did not appear to testify at the arbitration hearing, but other witnesses testified that he was very vague in his account of what happened. Burke had stated the fight started over a bin, but that he didn't remember anything more until he was in the hospital. He did remember the obscene incident which occurred an hour before the fight. Burke indicated that he was only kidding with Sloan.

During the arbitration hearing Sloan testified that Burke had bothered him since the incident in question, once by shouldering him, and once by pulling a power dolly out in front of him. He said that he had brought this to the attention of the personnel director.

There were several union witnesses who testified at the hearing that Burke was known among the employees as a bully, that he was given to frequent horseplay, that he had had trouble with other employees, that he had been in two fights shortly before the incident in question, and that he had bothered women employees. Apparently, none of this had ever been reported by employees to supervisors, nor had it been witnessed by supervisors, or at least if observed by supervisors it had not been reported. Much of this testimony was based on hearsay.

The basis for the company's position that Sloan was due a penalty was summarized by the personnel director in his testimony at the hearing. The company's decision to penalize Sloan as well as Burke was based upon four reasons:

1. Sloan had not reported the fight to a supervisor.
2. Sloan had made no attempt to avoid engaging in fighting.
3. Sloan had concealed the true cause of injury to his hand.
4. Sloan's actions were responsible for the company becoming involved in costs of $88 under workmen's compensation.

After the hearing the arbitrator told both the company and the union that he would inform them in writing of his decision and the reasons for it.

1. Assume the role of the arbitrator who was asked to decide this industrial dispute. State how you would decide the case and give the reasons for your decision.

2. Assume the role of the personnel director and frame a policy statement for management's discussion and ultimate approval of disciplinary penalties for fighting.

Opportunities are increasing for minority-owned business enterprises.

10

Minority employment
and business ownership

Not all citizens have participated fully in the increasing abundance of the private enterprise system in recent years. Blacks, Spanish-speaking Americans, and American Indians are minorities who generally have substantially lower standards of living than white Americans. This chapter analyzes the economic status of these minorities and their relationship with business, especially in matters of employment and enterprise ownership.

Effective solutions to the economic and social problems of minorities are not simple. In the past it has been popular for politicians and others to take the approach of overpromise and underdelivery in dealing with minorities' problems. John Gardner, former Secretary of Health, Education and Welfare, has written about the flaw that is apparent in many discussions of social and political reform:

. . . reality is supremely boring to most social critics. They are extremely reluctant to think about the complex and technical processes by which the society functions. And, in the end, their unwillingness to grapple with those processes defeats them.

This chapter contains information which should enable the student to understand better the complex and technical processes involved in making it possible for minorities to participate more fully in the private enterprise system. Questions discussed in this chapter include the following.

What types of discrimination have been exercised against minorities in employment and ownership of enterprises?

How does the economic status of minorities compare with whites?
*In what ways has government acted to improve the employment of
minorities?*
*What different kinds of problems are faced by blacks, the Spanish-
speaking people, and American Indians in improving their economic status?*
*What obstacles must be overcome to increase the number of minority-
owned business enterprises?*

Who are the minorities?

Definition of minority groups

Minority groups in the United States have distinguishing characteristics based on race, nationality, language, or religion which make them
the object of prejudice and subject to various kinds of discrimination
on the part of the dominant society. This chapter discusses those minorities which because of prejudice and discrimination are not sharing proportionally in the wealth created by American business enterprises.
Today the largest minority group in American society is made up of
Negroes, who constituted 11 percent of the population in 1970. In addition to blacks, other minority groups discussed in this chapter are the
Spanish-speaking Americans and American Indians.

The nature of discrimination

Discrimination against minority groups can take many and varied
forms. The purpose of this chapter is to deal with minority relationships
with business, in particular the problems of job opportunities and business ownership. There are two types of discrimination relating to minorities. First, there is *overt discrimination,* such as where an individual
is not hired for a job because of his or her race or because of some
other characteristic relative to the person's minority status. This type
of open discrimination is becoming less prevalent today than in past
years, not only because it is illegal but because the dominant attitude
in American society is turning against such discrimination.

The second type of discrimination is somewhat more subtle in its
manifestation but exerts profound influence on the life chances of the
minority group. This is *institutional discrimination,* where the individual
is discriminated against because of the structural nature of the society

of which he is a part. For example, many minorities live in particular geographic areas which are adjacent to certain kinds of industries. Housing patterns bring minority persons together, mostly with others of their own racial or ethnic background. The movement of home offices and factories outside central city areas limits the access of minority groups to certain job opportunities because of the general inadequacy of public transportation to the suburbs. In the past, institutional discrimination has existed because of stereotyped images about the abilities or inabilities of certain minorities to perform certain jobs.

Overt and institutional discrimination have been major factors which have influenced the employment and economic status of minorities. Other factors, such as education, government actions, and attitudes and practices of labor unions and management, are also important determinants of the economic position of minority groups.

The economic status of Negroes

The general level of family income of nonwhites in the United States is considerably below that of white families. Table 10–1 shows median family income over a 20-year span for blacks and other races compared with whites.

TABLE 10–1
Median family income in the United States, selected years in 1970 constant dollars

	Nonwhite families	White families	Ratio of nonwhite/white family income
1970	$6,516	$10,236	64%
1960	4,236	7,664	55%
1950	3,014	5,601	54%

Source: U.S. Bureau of the Census, *Current Population Reports*, Series P-60, No. 78, May, 1971.

There has been considerable improvement in nonwhite family income since 1950 in terms of real purchasing power and in relation to white family income. However, income for black families is still far below that of white families, and the absolute difference in dollar income between blacks and whites has increased over this period.

In 1970, 34 percent of blacks compared with 10 percent of whites in the United States were below the poverty level as designated by the federal government. The subject of poverty in the United States is discussed in more detail in Chapter 19.

The economic position of each minority varies in the United States and even within a given minority group. For example, while the median family income for black families was about $6,500 in 1970 compared with $10,200 for whites, over 28 percent of the Negro families had incomes above $10,000.

Black employment

There has been improvement in the occupational status of blacks from the late 1950s to 1970. In 1958 only 3.3 percent of white-collar jobs were held by Negroes, whereas by 1970 this percentage had increased to 6.2. Also, in the blue-collar job categories 6.8 percent of craftsmen and foremen were black in 1970 compared to only 4.5 percent in these occupations in 1958. Figure 10–1 shows the relationship among the various occupations in 1958 and 1970 for blacks and whites who were employed.

As Figure 10–1 indicates, there were some dramatic percentage gains in a number of occupations for blacks by 1970. Twenty-eight percent of black workers were employed in white-collar jobs in 1970 compared with only 14 percent in 1958. The proportion of service workers, especially private household workers, declined among black employees over the 12-year period. There was a dramatic decline in the percentage of Negroes employed as farm workers from 12.5 percent in 1958 to 4 percent in 1970.

Despite the improvement in occupational status of blacks in recent years, in 1970 blacks were concentrated disproportionately in the service occupations and to a lesser extent in some blue-collar jobs. The fact that these jobs in the economy have relatively lower wage rates than many white-collar or skilled craft jobs helps to explain the lower level of median family income for minority racial groups.

Black unemployment

Lower median family income among blacks is also partially explained by higher unemployment rates than for white workers. Figure 10–2 compares unemployment rates in 1969 and 1970 for blacks and whites in various categories.

The economic recession of 1970 resulted in substantially higher unemployment rates for all workers regardless of race. On an overall

FIGURE 10–1
Employed persons by occupation and race, 1958 and 1970 (percent distribution)

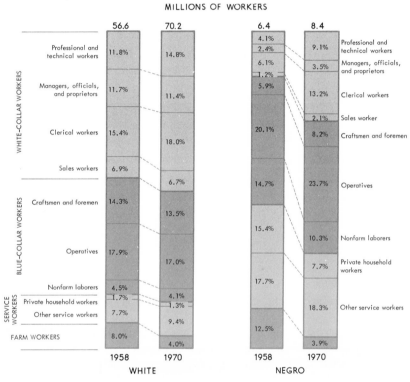

Note: Department of Labor statistics include Negro and other minority races here, although blacks account for more than 90 percent of the data. Because of rounding, sums of individual percentages may not equal 100.
Source: *1971 Manpower Report of the President*, p. 217.

basis the unemployment rate for blacks was about double the rate for white workers in 1969 and almost double in 1970. The overall unemployment rate of 8.2 percent for Negroes in 1970 was the highest since 1965.

Unemployment is not spread evenly throughout the various age sectors of the work force. In general, adult male workers had the lowest rate of unemployment, with unemployment running higher for women

Unemployment rates, Negroes and whites, 1969 and 1970

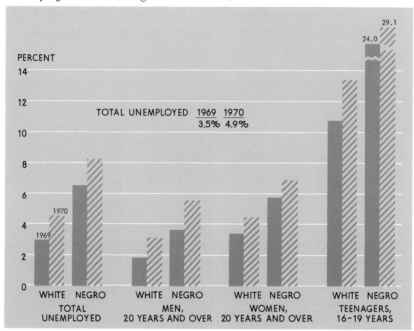

Source: *1971 Manpower Report of the President*, p. 16.

in the work force. However, unemployment among teenagers has been particularly high, and in the case of black teenagers the unemployment rate climbed to an alarming 29 percent in 1970. Also, actual unemployment among all elements of the work force is higher than the stated percentages since a worker is classified as part of the unemployed only as long as he or she is actively seeking work. Thus, both blacks and whites who have become discouraged and ceased looking for work are no longer included in unemployment statistics.

Even though the unemployment rate for blacks increased in 1970 there are some factors which tended to limit this increase. These factors include the following:

1. There has been a long-term rise in the educational level of blacks which has provided them with training to enter occupations where joblessness tends to be low.
2. Government manpower programs have enrolled a relatively high proportion of Negroes.

3. There has been a greater emphasis on the part of private employers on hiring and retaining Negro workers.
4. The service industries in which a relatively high proportion of blacks, especially women, are employed were less affected by the 1970 recession.

Educational levels of minority races

In addition to discrimination, type of occupation, and amount of unemployment, another factor affecting the income difference between whites and nonwhites is educational achievement levels. For adults in 1970 the median number of school years completed for Negro and other races in the United States was 11.7 compared with 12.4 for whites. However, the median educational gap between whites and nonwhites has been greatly reduced in recent years. For example, in 1952 the median school years completed for blacks and other races was 7.6 com-

FIGURE 10–3

Comparison of median annual earnings for blacks and whites with high school or college education

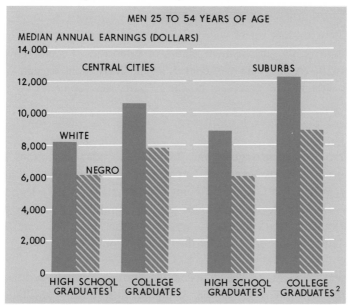

[1] Without college education.
[2] Negro sample less than 35,000.
Source: *1971 Manpower Report of the President,* p. 93.

pared with 11.4 for whites. This relative increase in educational achievement by minorities should provide a basis for further occupational and income improvement in the future, provided the barriers to job opportunities can continue to be reduced.

Despite the relative importance of education, a study reported by the Department of Labor indicated that increases in education have had a substantially lower payoff for blacks than for whites. The study indicated that the weekly wage of white high school graduates in the slums was nearly $25 higher than for whites who had not attended high school. However, Negro high school graduates earned only $8 more a week than Negroes who had not attended high school.

Problems of racial discrimination in income relative to amount of education are also evident from the data presented in Figure 10–3. The data indicate that the average income for Negro college graduates is about the same as that of white high school graduates in both central cities and the suburbs. In all four comparison categories the median annual earnings of blacks are significantly below that of whites with the same level of education.

Government actions in minority employment

There are four major ways in which the federal government has acted to improve the employment status of minorities. Federal government action in recent years has come through legislation, executive orders, the courts, and programs for human resource development.

Legislation

State and local legislation. Legislation outlawing various kinds of discrimination has been passed in over half the states and in many cities since World War II. Fair employment practices (FEP) legislation in many of the states has improved job opportunities for persons who frequently have been subject to employment discrimination. State and local legislation has generally established commissions which:

1. have powers to investigate complaints of discrimination
2. attempt to resolve the complaints through conciliation and persuasion
3. conduct public hearings

4. seek court orders to support the commissions' activities and findings
5. undertake and publish studies of discrimination.

The Civil Rights Act of 1964. At the federal level of government the Civil Rights Act of 1964 is the most important antidiscrimination legislation of modern times. The act has a number of titles, including those outlawing discrimination in voting; public accommodations, facilities, and schools; federal assistance programs; and employment. Title VII deals with employment.

Title VII of the Civil Rights Act bans discrimination in employment by employers, labor unions, employment services, and registered apprenticeship programs. Initially the law applied only to organizations with 100 or more employees or members, but the legislation was written so that by 1968 all enterprises and unions with 25 or more persons were included.

The act resulted in the establishment of the Equal Employment Opportunity Commission (EEOC) to deal with charges of discrimination. Under Title VII the hiring, promotion, and discharge of persons is to be done on the basis of ability and qualification without regard to race, color, religion, sex, or national origin. Charges relating to racial discrimination have accounted for the largest proportion of complaints with those relating to sex being second in number.

The EEOC's powers are limited to responding to specific complaints from persons who believe they are being discriminated against. This case-by-case investigation depends heavily on informal procedures such as conciliation to encourage compliance with the law. In the more than 30 states which have fair employment practice commissions the EEOC must wait 60 days until state or local authorities have shown an inability to resolve the complaint.

Title VII of the Civil Rights Act does provide the attorney general with authority to institute court proceedings at the request of the EEOC where voluntary compliance has not been secured. In some cases the attorney general may proceed on his own to assist private individuals in the courts in employment discrimination cases.

A number of individual cases of discrimination have been corrected as the result of this legislation. However, this case-by-case approach is not as efficient in correcting widespread inequities as would be legislation providing for industrywide or class action. Also, as is true with any legislation, the effectiveness of the law is no better than its enforcement by administrative bodies and the courts.

Executive orders

Another means of enforcing equal access to job opportunities is the executive orders issued by the president of the United States. A number of these directives have been issued since 1941 to prevent discriminatory employment practices.

One of the most important directives is Executive Order 11246, which covers all employers who have federal government contracts. Approximately one third of the labor force is employed by business enterprises having government contracts. This order forbids government contractors to discriminate on the basis of race, creed, color, sex, or national origin. Also, it requires that employers take "affirmative action" and guarantee equal access to all persons. These contractors are required to state in all job advertisements that they are equal employment opportunity employers. Subcontractors are included in the order's provisions, and labor unions in these enterprises are prohibited from discriminatory practices.

The Office of Federal Contract Compliance in the Department of Labor coordinates the administration of this executive order by each federal agency. The order has penalty and sanction provisions which include cancellation, termination, and suspension of contracts and blacklisting of those business enterprises which fail to cooperate. Although no contract has ever been canceled or terminated under the order, there have been delays in contract negotiations, and on occasion an employer has been blacklisted for future contract participation.

The courts

Minorities have turned to the courts to overcome discrimination by employers and unions. From 1965 through 1970 more than 400 Title VII cases have been litigated in the federal courts. Under court interpretations of the National Labor Relations Act and the Railway Labor Act, unions which acquire the privilege of exclusive bargaining rights have the duty to represent all members of the bargaining unit fairly. Minority groups have brought suit against labor unions for damages resulting from alleged violation of their legal rights.

Lawsuits require considerable time and expense on the part of aggrieved minority persons and groups. Also, the final outcome of the suits is uncertain while they are in process. However, the threat of such lawsuits has been a weapon available to minority persons to ward off employment discrimination by employers and unions.

Human resource development programs

A variety of federally assisted work and training programs exist to increase the employability of jobless and underemployed workers. Most of these efforts began with the Area Redevelopment Act of 1961 and the Manpower Development and Training Act of 1962 (MDTA). Since that time the number of persons enrolled in such programs has increased. For example, in 1964 less than 300,000 persons were enrolled in MDTA, vocational rehabilitation, and other programs. In 1970 the number of individuals enrolled in federally assisted work and training programs had increased to over 1,800,000, with a projected increase to 2,200,000 by 1972.

Examples of human resource development programs. The following examples of human resource development programs illustrate the scope of government efforts for better employment opportunities for Americans.

The Concentrated Employment Program (CEP) is designed to channel training and other services to people in urban slums and rural poverty areas. Over 110,000 persons were enrolled in CEP in 1971.

The Work Incentive (WIN) Program for welfare recipients is a relatively new program which has been expanded rapidly. By the end of 1971 about 125,000 persons were participating in the WIN Program. While enrollees are in training courses they continue to receive their welfare payments plus a $30 per month training incentive.

A federal program in cooperation with the National Alliance of Businessmen is the Job Opportunities in the Business Sector (JOBS) Program which provides work-training opportunities for the disadvantaged worker. Business receives federal financial assistance to cover the extra costs involved in hiring and training the disadvantaged. This and other on-the-job training programs enrolled over 200,000 persons in 1971.

Vocational rehabilitation programs involving federal-state cooperation first began in 1920. These programs aid individuals who have a physical or mental disability which constitutes a substantial handicap to employment but which will respond to rehabilitation services. Over 400,000 persons were enrolled in vocational rehabilitation in 1971.

The largest of the manpower programs sponsored by the Department of Labor in 1971 was the Neighborhood Youth Corps (NYC) which had over 470,000 first-time enrollments. About 90 percent of participants worked with in-school and summer programs. The in-school programs are designed to aid dropout-prone high school students by providing them with financial assistance, remedial education, counseling, and other supportive services. The summer NYC programs provide remedial education and supportive services as well as work projects that benefit the community. For example, during 1970 Operation Clean Waters used Neighborhood Youth Corps enrollees in many communities to assist in cleaning waterways and to work in water treatment and sewage plants.

The remaining 10 percent of NYC enrollees are in the out-of-school program for high school dropouts. Remedial education, skills training, and supportive services are provided. Enrollees are encouraged to return to school or to work on a general education development certificate, which is the equivalent of a high school diploma.

Studies of Neighborhood Youth Corps participants indicate that the major contribution of the program is orientation of the disadvantaged youth to a work environment. Research shows that most of the youth feel the program gives them a new appreciation of work. The major criticism of the NYC program is that it does not provide sufficient training and skill acquisition for the young people involved.

From these examples of human resource development programs sponsored by the government, it is apparent that there is a wide range of agencies and programs to assist Americans to improve their economic status. Millions of individuals have been helped by such programs. However, the proliferation of these agencies and programs raises serious questions as to whether minority access to the benefits of these programs would not be improved with consolidation, reorganization, or at least better coordination of these agencies and programs. In some instances additional legislation is needed to reduce discrimination further. In other cases the funding of these programs has been insufficient, or their administration has been less than effective.

Characteristics of manpower program enrollees. In the early 1970s government manpower programs continued to concentrate mainly on disadvantaged persons who were under 22 years or over 45 years of age. About one third of all enrollees were receiving public assistance at the time they entered the programs or, in the case of youth in the Neighborhood Youth Corps, were from families on public assistance.

The vast majority of participants were school dropouts. Not counting those NYC in-school and summer programs, two thirds of all enrollees had not obtained a high school diploma.

Blacks composed nearly half of all enrollees in 1970, and another 15 percent were Spanish Americans. In a number of the manpower programs in addition to a large proportion of Negroes, between 10 and 12 percent of the participants were American Indians, Eskimos, or Orientals.

Nearly half of the enrollees in all programs were women. In 1970 more than 70 percent of the participants in the expanding Work Incentive Program were women.

Spanish-speaking Americans

The second largest minority group in the United States is the Spanish-speaking population, which numbers over ten million. Their economic status has been adversely affected by language barriers and discrimination by the dominant American culture. To understand better the problems of the Spanish-speaking citizens a separate examination is made of the Mexican Americans, the Puerto Ricans, and the Cubans.

Mexican Americans

The largest group of Spanish-speaking peoples are Mexican Americans who number about seven million with over 80 percent of them living in Texas and California. Most of the others are concentrated in Arizona, Colorado, and New Mexico. Some of these Mexican Americans are descendents of early Spanish settlers of the Southwest who were there hundreds of years before this area was part of the United States. These Spanish-speaking people tended to retain their close ethnic ties—bound together by a common religion, close family interrelationships, and a common Spanish heritage. Generally they resisted assimilation into the culture of the English-speaking peoples who moved west. The English-speaking peoples tended to discriminate against the Spanish-speaking settlers who were already in the Southwest.

A major wave of immigration of Mexicans to the United States took place in the period from 1910 through the 1920s. This was stimulated by the Mexican Revolution of 1910–1920, which caused many middle-class Mexicans to flee the country. Also, during this period the United States was confronted with a labor shortage stemming from World War I (1917–1918). Mexicans were recruited by the trainload as cheap labor to work in the fields of Colorado, California, and Texas as well as in the copper mines of Arizona and for the railroads being built in the West.

World War II (1941–1945) caused another labor shortage. Again, the United States sought to attract Mexican labor primarily through a war emergency measure called the *bracero* program. The United States signed a formal agreement with Mexico which made certain guarantees for employment and working conditions for Mexican laborers for short periods of seasonal farm labor. This "emergency" bracero program, which tended to keep wages of agricultural workers low, did not end until December, 1964. During this period the wages of agricultural workers fell far behind those of manufacturing workers.

Although the bracero program ended, Mexicans illegally slipped across the border and continued to cause depressed wages for American agricultural workers. In 1968 alone it was estimated that 300,000 Mexican workers entered the country illegally.

Along the Mexican–United States border areas Mexican Americans also face labor competition from Mexican nationals who commute daily across the border to work in the United States though they live in Mexico where the cost of living is cheaper. This has forced some of the Mexican Americans into migrant labor streams as they attempt to find work outside the border states.

Migratory farm workers in the United States number about 250,000. Mexican Americans make up a substantial portion of these workers. Migrants travel from state to state following the crops. Living conditions are poor, and no money is paid them while they are in transit from one job to another. A recent study of the Mexican-American migratory farm workers whose home base was in the Rio Grande Valley of Texas showed the typical male head of the family to be over 40 years old with a family of six, all of whom were expected to work in the fields. The average yearly income of the male family head was $1,813, and when all the family's earnings were combined they totaled only $3,350.

Many Mexican Americans have moved to the cities of the Southwest. More than 80 percent are now located in urban areas where they have a lack of education and urban job skills, language problems, and are faced with discrimination. As a result they have high rates of unemployment and generally live in poverty. In years of schooling completed they are below both Anglo-white and black Americans.

A very small portion of Mexican Americans are in white-collar positions. In the urban Southwest only 5 percent are managers or proprietors compared with 15 percent for Anglos.

Americans of Mexican ancestry are sometimes referred to as *Chicanos*. This term is now being used especially by young people who have a sense of pride in their cultural identity and who are working to promote the economic development of their people.

Puerto Ricans

In the past several decades there has been a substantial migration of Puerto Ricans to the United States. Today there are about 1.5 million Puerto Ricans in the mainland United States. Most are concentrated in New York City, where their population continues to expand. Other cities with large Puerto Rican populations include Chicago with about 80,000; Philadelphia with 45,000; Detroit with 10,000; and Cleveland with 8,000.

As citizens of the United States, Puerto Ricans are able to come to the mainland freely. Most come from agricultural backgrounds. Their lack of urban job skills coupled with the language barrier and discrimination typically faced by immigrant groups has caused extremely high unemployment rates among Puerto Ricans.

Cuban Americans

Since the advent of the Castro regime in Cuba in 1959, over 500,000 Cubans have entered the United States. Many had been members of the Cuban middle and upper classes who left when Castro expropriated Cuban as well as foreign-owned properties. In contrast to their attitudes toward many other immigrant groups, Americans were generally friendly to Cuban immigrants since they sympathized with their flight from Communism. Most Cuban refugees have jobs, although often unskilled and low paying. Thousands of Cuban artisans and professionals who first assumed rather menial jobs in the United States in order to earn a living, after becoming proficient in English became involved in flourishing businesses in this country.

The heaviest concentration of Cubans is in the Miami, Florida, area where about one third of the population of the city is now Cuban. However, other U.S. cities also have significant numbers of Cuban Americans including Chicago, which has an estimated 80,000. Manpower experts hold the view that generally the Cuban immigrant has made an unusually successful adjustment to life in the United States.

Other Spanish-speaking Americans

The rest of the Spanish-speaking population in the United States numbers about 1.5 million. They are scattered throughout the country and have come from diverse areas of Central and South America. It is difficult to generalize about their experiences. These peoples run the gamut from those locked into poverty because of a lack of language and job skills to those who have adjusted quite well to life in the United States.

Government programs to aid Spanish-speaking Americans

To aid the Spanish-speaking minorities in the United States several steps are being taken. First, there is a more adequate recognition of the special kinds of problems faced by these peoples. In 1969 Congress created a Cabinet Committee on Opportunities for Spanish Speaking People to advise federal agencies on developing and implementing programs to aid the Spanish-speaking Americans. As a result of the committee's work the 1970 census included questions to provide more information about the size, nature, and problems of this large minority group. A strong emphasis is being placed on enrolling Spanish-speaking Americans in some of the many training and work-experience programs administered by the Department of Labor. In 1970 over 150,000 Spanish Americans participated in such programs.

Since one of the most difficult barriers is a lack of English skills, additional government attention is being focused on devising programs to improve English language capabilities by using new training techniques. In pilot programs such improvement made a significant contribution both to job retention and upgrading.

American Indians

The minority group that has fared the worst in the United States is the American Indian. There are about 775,000 Americans who are at least one-quarter Indian. Some 460,000 Indians live on or near a federal reservation. About 80 percent of the reservation Indians are below the poverty income level with average annual incomes of $1,500 per family. It is estimated that three fourths of the Indians who have moved to urban areas also live in poverty. The unemployment rate of the Indians is ten times that of the national average. Half of the able and available Indian work force is without jobs. On some reservations unemployment is as high as 80 percent.

The Indians suffer from poor diets, housing, and health services as well as a lack of English and job skills. However, there has been some improvement in educational achievement as Indian youths who are not yet 21 will on the average complete ten years of school. This compares with an average of only six years of schooling for the Indian population over 21.

The Indian population is increasing more rapidly than any other minority group in the United States. Over half of the Indians are now under the age of 21.

Since most of the Indians have remained on the reservations, their cultural values have been perpetuated. These values generally differ from those of the dominant American society. Indians have traditionally stressed communal instead of individual achievement. Land was to be enjoyed by all rather than carved into small individually owned tracts. Competitiveness and desire to accumulate personal wealth have not been important values.

Government actions to aid the American Indians

In the 1950s the federal government tried a program to force Indians to integrate into the dominant society. The plan involved selling tribal lands, over which the federal government exercises trusteeship, with the money going to tribal members. Indians were then encouraged to relocate in urban areas. The result of this program tended to be a loss of tribal identity. At the same time the social and economic conditions of the tribal members deteriorated. Without training or proper preparation, thousands of Indians were relocated in urban areas. Many wound up in urban slums or returned embittered to a reservation. In 1958 this policy of involuntary termination was discontinued.

There is disagreement among experts as to the best way to help the American Indians. Some suggest the reservations should be the focal point of attention. The federal Office of Economic Opportunity spent $17 million in 1970 on community projects to aid development of the reservations in 23 states. Programs have been undertaken to encourage industrial plants to locate on or near reservations to provide employment for the Indians. However, the relative isolation of many of the reservations makes it difficult and expensive to transport raw materials and manufactured goods. Some economists believe that it is not realistic to think that the reservations can be made into viable economic centers where goods and services can be produced at a price competitive with similar goods manufactured in an urban area.

Those who think that the ultimate solution to the poverty of the Indian is to integrate him into the mainstream of society point out that with proper help the Indian could make the adjustment to urban life. Several federal programs now in operation have this objective. For example, in 1970 a number of federal agencies were working together to support Indian centers in seven major cities where Indians who are making the transition from the reservation to the city can find help. There is an increased emphasis on enrolling Indians in manpower training programs. In 1970 nearly 24,000 Indians were enrolled in a variety of government training programs. This represented 2 percent of all the first-time enrollees even though the Indian population is less than 0.5 percent of the total American population. Other federal programs are in operation to aid the Indians. Some progress in improving the welfare of the Indian was made in the 1960s, and continued improvement should be evident in the 1970s.

Developing minority enterprises

Although blacks, Spanish-speaking Americans, and Indians make up about 16 percent of the U.S. population, less than 3 percent of the nation's business enterprises are owned by members of these minority groups. Minority-owned business enterprises are usually small and account for less than 0.5 percent of the economy's business receipts and assets.

A Small Business Administration study revealed the typical black-owned business to be a one-man personal service or retail shop in the central city with $20,000 or less in sales annually. About one third were family-operated stores, and only one out of ten black-operated business enterprises employed more than ten workers. Negroes have tended to own enterprises such as life insurance companies, funeral homes, beauty and barber shops, restaurants, cleaning shops, secondhand stores, grocery stores, garages, and shoe-repair shops which depend upon black clientele. Usually these are situated away from prime commercial locations and have insufficient financing.

One approach being taken by government and private enterprise to improve the economic status of minorities is to aid in the formation and management of minority-owned business enterprises. There are a number of problems to be overcome before significant progress can be made in expanding minority business ownership.

Ghettos in the past and today

Today's minority groups face different kinds of problems than did earlier minorities who were primarily European immigrants. The Europeans often brought with them a background of business tradition and worked hard to put these skills to use in their new homeland. To them America was a land of opportunity. Though discriminated against initially, they learned the English language and began to prosper economically, with most of them being assimilated into the dominant American culture. The European immigrants were not hampered by the racial prejudice that blacks face. The success story of the poor European immigrant who started as a pushcart peddler in the slums of New York City becoming the owner of a chain of stores has been repeated numerous times.

Blacks who are the dominant group in today's ghettos generally lack a tradition and background in business. Most came from rural areas or small towns. Since World War II blacks have moved to cities in large numbers. Instead of going into business those blacks who had upward mobility because of education, ability, or economic backing frequently went into law, government, or teaching.

The slums of the early 20th century also differed in numerous respects from today's ghettos. The slums which developed shortly after the turn of the century were teeming with activity—a way up and out for many. Today's ghettos are more likely to be enclaves of urban decay. Instead of offering hope for a better life, a mood of futility prevails in the ghettos partially caused by high unemployment and a lack of the capital and skills necessary to take advantage of economic opportunities. Many ghetto residents see no hope in the mainstream of the dominant society and turn to crime as a means of survival. Dead-end jobs pegged at the minimum wage with little or no chance for advancement generally are unattractive to youth in the ghetto, who see little possibility for any significant improvement in their overall standard of living by taking such jobs.

Obstacles to minority enterprise

Minority entrepreneurs who have started their own businesses have been confronted by many obstacles. Those business enterprises located in the ghettos are faced with a hostile environment subject to frequent crimes ranging from pilferage and robbery to vandalism. Some businessmen, both black and white, have given up and closed their shops after numerous holdups. When minority enterprises are located in high crime-rate areas the cost of insurance, if available, is more. If the enterprise is to be profitable such added costs mean higher prices for goods and services or lower quality merchandise if regular prices are charged. This problem results in frustration among ghetto residents who complain that they are being overcharged by businessmen in these neighborhoods.

Another major obstacle for the minority businessman has been difficulty in securing the capital funds necessary for his business. Any new business enterprise entails considerable risk. Over the years it has been estimated that 50 percent of new businesses change ownership or cease operations in their first 18 months. Commercial banks recognize this high risk for any new business and have either been reluctant to make loans to minority enterprises or would do so only at higher interest rates.

One result is that minority businessmen who were unable to get necessary loans elsewhere have turned to the loan sharks. This has meant that they have had to obtain short-term loans for long-term needs such as for the purchase of necessary equipment. Funds are often insufficient to permit the purchase of adequate inventories or for a store to grant credit to its customers. Loan sharks have been able to exact as much as 20 percent interest per month for the money they lend to hard-pressed black businessmen.

As American society has become more integrated, the ghetto businessman has often been hurt by new competition. Now blacks may eat in restaurants, stay in motels, or buy at stores that previously would not serve them. Where the black businessman could once depend upon black customers, today he must compete with white-owned businesses. These white enterprises have access to greater amounts of funds and frequently are able to offer black consumers a wider range of goods and services on credit at better prices than the minority-owned enterprise is able to do.

Steps in expansion of minority-owned enterprises

All these obstacles mean that if the number of successful minority-owned enterprises is to be expanded there are five steps which should be taken:

1. Potential minority entrepreneurs must be found. Individuals with energy and ability who are willing to work hard must be sought out and encouraged to enter business. The black community should help identify the potentially successful businessman and stimulate interest in

black enterprises. Organizations such as the National Urban League, NAACP, CORE, the Southern Christian Leadership Conference, and black business groups in large cities can provide leadership in identifying individuals who can be encouraged to go into business.

2. Since these persons may lack skills in key business functions, such as purchasing, personnel hiring and training, sales and promotion, and accounting and finance, these potential businessmen must receive training in these areas. Blacks are beginning to participate more in business school training programs. The greater number of blacks graduating from high school and the expansion of junior colleges in urban areas are providing more opportunities for formal business training for minority citizens Also; the federal government is providing more assistance to blacks and other minorities in how to take advantage of the many different types of government aid provided to small businessmen.

3. A market survey should be conducted to ascertain the needs of a particular area for a business enterprise. A location, whether in or out of the ghetto, must be found where there is a strong potential market for the goods or services to be offered.

4. An adequate source of capital is vital to the minority entrepreneur. Money is necessary to initiate business operations plus a reserve fund or line of credit to meet needs for continued operation, for seasonal increases in inventories, or simply to meet financial obligations through a lull in business.

5. Many of the owners of fledgling business enterprises will require continued management assistance in the areas of marketing, finance, and accounting if they are to operate profitably.

Government programs to aid minority businessmen

In 1969 President Nixon authorized the establishment of the Office of Minority Business Enterprise (OMBE) in the Department of Commerce in order that minorities might have better access to business opportunities. One of OMBE's roles is to coordinate the different federal assistance programs now available to encourage minority citizens to take advantage of these programs. An OMBE survey of 27 of the major federal programs that aid business by grants, loans, and loan guarantees revealed that in the 1970 fiscal year over $300 million was available to assist minority entrepreneurs. For these funds to be used effectively the different types of assistance and how it may be obtained must be communicated to potential and present minority businessmen.

The federal government also has been using some of its tremendous buying power to aid minority businesses. In 1970 the General Services Administration committed $10 million of government contracts to minority business enterprises. The Post Office committed $2.4 million to minority suppliers. Other government agencies and departments are being encouraged to follow these leads.

The Small Business Administration, which gives financial assistance to small businesses that have difficulty securing financing on reasonable terms, is relaxing some of its requirements to aid minority enterprises. In the first nine months of 1969 the number of SBA loans to minority-owned businesses more than doubled and the dollar volume nearly tripled over the same period in 1968.

The Office of Economic Development is working to promote community-based economic development in order that chronic unemployment and poverty might be combated at the local level. The Special Impact Program makes grants to development corporations that are formed to invest in programs that create jobs for the poverty area residents, help to develop managerial skills, and stimulate opportunities for poverty area residents to own businesses. These community corporations may provide loan guarantees, give technical assistance, and even provide equity funds for a new enterprise.

Private actions to aid minority businessmen

Though the federal government has an important role to play, existing private enterprise is also being encouraged to help minority-owned businesses get started. The Office of Minority Business Enterprise enlisted the help of private enterprise in stimulating the growth of minority businesses. Some of the ways in which private business is cooperating include the following:

1. In 1970, 122 insurance companies, which account for 90 percent of the life insurance business in the United States, pledged through their national organization, the Life Insurance Association of America, a second billion dollars for loans in the inner cities. The first billion was spent by this group primarily to construct, repair, or aid in the purchase of housing. The second billion is to be oriented toward loans that will create new businesses and jobs in the inner cities. This is being done initially by making deposits in minority-owned banks and savings and loan associations so that these institutions will have additional loan funds for inner city businesses and individuals.

2. Franchisors are being encouraged to sell franchises to members of minority groups. The Office of Minority Business Enterprise has initiated a program of inviting franchisors to Washington in groups of 25 to discuss the program of minority franchises. OMBE is seeking to get each franchisor to provide at least 25 franchise opportunities to minority persons in the next two years. This has become known as the $25 \times 25 \times 2$ program. There are over 1,000 national franchisors with about one fifth of them involved in this program.

Franchisors are being asked to modify their capital requirements and to take other steps to encourage minority ownership. The SBA is helping out with loan guarantees to franchisors in the program. As of 1970 more than 750 franchise opportunities were earmarked for qualified minority individuals. Most of these franchises were food oriented, with the second largest number in the automotive industry.

Franchising can be a valuable technique in developing new minority enterprises. The well-known name of a successful franchise will tend to attract customers who recognize that they will be getting a quality product or service. Also, the national franchisor provides much assistance in the form of management training, marketing techniques, and accounting and financial systems. All of these factors help reduce the risks of business failure for the new enterprise.

3. The four major U.S. automobile manufacturers have agreed to cooperate by increasing the opportunities for minority-owned auto dealerships. This would take place both through creation of new dealerships and through transfer of existing dealerships to minority businessmen when the opportunity arises. The first Negro auto dealership was established in 1967 in Chicago through General Motors.

4. After meeting with the Secretary of Commerce, 18 major oil companies agreed to expand substantially over the next five years the number of service stations owned by members of minority groups. In addition, the industry will provide opportunities for minority operators to obtain training, financing, and management assistance in operating their service stations.

MESBICs

There are many other programs where business and government are cooperating to aid minority business ventures. One program operates through private investment corporations that are set up to provide long-term capital as well as management assistance to minority businesses.

These corporations are known as Minority Enterprise Small Business Investment Companies (MESBICs). A MESBIC is formed when a sponsor (an organization or group of individuals or firms) puts up at least $150,000 in capital, incorporates as an investment company, and obtains a license to operate from the Small Business Administration. The MESBIC then becomes eligible to borrow double the amount of private capital from the SBA up to $10 million. In addition, the SBA can guarantee up to 90 percent of the loans made by commercial banks to the MESBIC. Thus, with a little seed money from a private sponsor, a great deal of venture capital can be generated for minority businessmen. Figure 10–4 illustrates how this financing arrangement could work to increase the use of private investment funds.

FIGURE 10–4
Potential capital to minority enterprises from one MESBIC

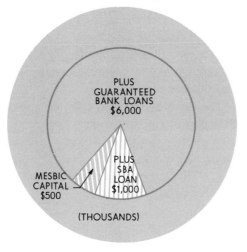

Original MESBIC capital	$ 500,000
SBA loan to MESBIC	1,000,000
"Seed capital" investments in minority enterprises	$1,500,000
SBA-guaranteed bank loans to minority enterprises	6,000,000
Total capital flowing to minority enterprises	$7,500,000

In addition to providing financing the MESBICs may also provide important management assistance. This could take the form of aiding the new business in planning, counseling management once the enterprise is in operation, and offering technical assistance in such areas as marketing, accounting, or inventory management. Management assistance can often mean the difference between success and failure for the new business enterprise.

A few of the numerous corporations that are now participating in the MESBIC program and the amount of venture capital they have committed to minority enterprises are shown in Figure 10–5.

FIGURE 10–5
Selected operating MESBICs

Name	License date	Paid-in capital	Primary area of operation
Ban Cap Corp. Sponsor: A group of New York City banks	5/71	$955,000	New York City
Baltimore Community Investment Company Sponsor: Baltimore Council on Equal Business Opportunity	5/70	$150,000	Maryland
Equal Opportunity Finance, Inc. Sponsor: Ashland Oil & Refining Company	9/70	$150,000	Kentucky
Motor Enterprises, Inc. Sponsor: General Motors Corp.	4/70	$500,000 ($1,000,000 commitment)	Nationwide (70 plant cities)
Prudential Minority Enterprise, Inc. Sponsor: Prudential Insurance Company of America	3/70	$150,000	Metropolitan Newark

Source: U.S. Department of Commerce, *MESBICs and Minority Enterprise,* May, 1971.

Jobs and ownership

Most knowledgeable students of American society feel that better opportunities for job training, employment, and promotion are vital to improve the economic status of minorities. However, the following quotation of the late Whitney M. Young, Jr., when he was executive director of the National Urban League, points up the importance of minority business ownership as well as job opportunities:

Important as jobs in the larger society are—and creation of such jobs must be the main thrust of economic efforts toward equality—there is a pride and dignity in ownership that must be satisfied within the black community, as it is within the white.

Summary

Minority groups in the United States have been subject to overt and institutional discrimination because of race, nationality, language, religion, or geographic location. This discrimination has had a negative effect on the economic status of minorities. Factors such as education, government actions, and attitudes of labor unions and managements are other determinants of the economic position of minority groups.

Generally the family income of Negroes, Spanish-speaking Americans, and American Indians is substantially below that of white Americans. Unemployment rates are considerably higher for these minorities than for whites. The average years of schooling completed by minority persons is below that of the total population.

A variety of government actions have been taken to improve the employment status of minorities. These include legislation, executive orders, the courts, and human resource development programs. In addition to the federal Civil Rights Act of 1964, many state and local governments have passed legislation which provides for fair employment practices of minority persons. Presidential executive orders also prohibit employment discrimination on the part of enterprises providing goods and services to the federal government.

The emphasis in most government human development programs is upon providing financial assistance, education, counseling, and other services to help the disadvantaged person improve his qualifications for employment. The majority of enrollees in these programs have been high school dropouts from minority groups.

In addition to more jobs for minority persons, there is a need for more ownership of business enterprises by minorities. Government agencies such as the Small Business Administration and the Office of Minority Business Enterprise are available to assist minority persons in overcoming the obstacles to business ownership. Private groups, such as business corporations, minority organizations, community corporations, and investment groups, have a role to play in encouraging the development of minority-owned businesses. The Minority Enterprise Small Business Investment Company (MESBIC) is a form of corporation which combines private capital with government funds and loan guarantees to make financial and management assistance available.

Despite the programs and progress in recent years to improve the economic status of America's minority groups, further improvement is necessary.

Terms for review

minority group
overt discrimination
institutional discrimination
Civil Rights Act of 1964

human resource development
    programs
Office of Minority Business
    Enterprise (OMBE)
MESBIC

Questions

1. How does discrimination affect the economic position of minority persons in the United States?

2. *a)* How has the economic status of blacks improved in the past 20 years?

   b) In what ways has the economic position of blacks either declined or improved only slightly over the past 20 years?

3. *a)* Comment on the merits of giving blacks and other minority persons preferential treatment in hiring, training, and promotion to improve their economic status.

   b) What problems would be faced by the management of a business enterprise which carried out such a policy of preferential treatment?

4. *a)* How have legislation, including Title VII of the Civil Rights Act of 1964, and executive orders of the president improved economic opportunities for minority persons?

   b) What further steps need to be taken if minority persons are to achieve greater economic opportunities?

5. Discuss the various government programs designed to improve employment opportunities for Americans.

6. Describe the different groups which make up the ten million Spanish-speaking Americans.

7. Contrast the merits and problems associated with the two different approaches to improving the economic status of American Indians.

8. *a)* What are the obstacles to establishing more minority-owned business enterprises?

   b) Discuss how these obstacles can be overcome.

BUSINESS BRIEFS

Cheetah Charter Bus Service Co.

Douglas Gray drove a bus for ten years in New York City. As a black, he was aware of the kind of charter bus service that minority groups were getting from established bus lines. He knew that the charter buses provided to minority groups often were not modern, without lavatories, and poorly maintained. Also, it was sometimes difficult to charter a bus for certain areas of Harlem. Gray knew that the demand for charter buses was growing and that this service had a good profit potential.

In the late 1960s Douglas Gray put together a plan to establish his own charter bus company to serve Harlem. After months of leg work, Gray obtained a commitment for a $65,000 loan from Morgan Guaranty Trust Company, fifth largest bank in the United States, along with a loan from the Ford Foundation of $70,000 plus a $90,000 line of credit for his second year of operation. He also managed to obtain $30,000 from an affiliate of the New York Urban Coalition. Even with all this financial backing, Gray was still short of the money to purchase five buses, which cost $65,000 each. This problem was overcome when General Motors Acceptance Corporation, the financing division of GM, offered an eight-year loan for $204,000 to cover the balance due on the purchase of GM buses.

The problems for the Cheetah Charter Bus Service were not limited to finances. Before the company could carry passengers it was necessary to obtain a license from the Interstate Commerce Commission. In Washington, Gray had to face the opposition of some 27 other bus companies which opposed the granting of the license. These bus companies claimed that Harlem residents were already being provided adequate bus services by existing operators. However, the ICC granted Gray's company the right to serve Harlem and much of the southeastern United States.

Actual charter operations began in February, 1971. Business that month was slow with only 12 charter groups being booked. However, the number of charter trips increased to 27 in March and 33 in April. Business during the summer of 1971 boomed. Customers included schools, fraternal organizations, unions, clubs, and church groups. In the latter part of 1971 Douglas Gray began planning to buy five more buses and to open his own depot in Harlem.

The company's emblem, which decorates its buses and office, is a bounding cheetah. When asked why the cheetah emblem adorns his buses, Gray told a *Business Week* reporter, "The cheetah is the fastest animal on land, is very surefooted, and is an African derivative." And then he added with a smile, "Some people say cheetahs eat greyhounds."

    1. *a)* What problems did Douglas Gray face in establishing a new business enterprise?
       b) How were these problems solved?
    2. How do you account for the early success of this enterprise?
    3. What could other persons interested in starting business learn from Gray's experience?

Proportional employment

As the result of recent court decisions the Equal Employment Opportunity Commission, which was created to enforce the 1964 Civil Rights Act, has been strengthened. In a recent case a federal court ordered one business enterprise to hire two black workers for each white hired in the next four years or until production and clerical employees "contain a ratio of blacks proportional to the nonwhite civilian work force between the ages of 18 and 44" in the county where the enterprise is located.

    1. What problems might the management of the business enterprise encounter in carrying out the above court order?
    2. *a)* Discuss the merits of a quota system for the employment of minority persons.
       b) What are the weaknesses of using a quota system?

Fairchild Camera and Instrument Corporation

Programs by business enterprises to hire minority employees have often ended in failure. However, with the leadership of a young plant manager Fairchild Camera and Instrument Corporation was able to overcome many problems in a factory for integrated circuits on a Navajo Indian reservation in Shiprock, New Mexico.

The program, begun in 1965, floundered as management had difficulty overcoming cultural and language barriers. In 1967, 36-year-old Paul W. Driscoll became plant manager and brought creativity to the job of dealing with the language and cultural differences. Driscoll had a genuine respect for the Indians who were employed at the factory. He capitalized on some of the positive Navajo traits. For example, their cultural background of weaving rugs with complicated designs provided a natural transfer to memorizing the complex patterns of integrated circuit design. The Navajo patience, pride in work, and respect for property were positive job assets. When the Navajo workers confronted problems on the job, Driscoll showed sensitivity and imagination in solving their problems. The productivity of the Shiprock factory improved until it ranks among the company's highest.

The plant employs 750 workers. All but 26 are Indian. The factory is located on a reservation where unemployment has often been as high as 50 percent. In 1971 Paul Driscoll received an award from *Business Week* magazine for his leadership in the Shiprock factory.

1. What factors do you think are important if an enterprise is to be successful in hiring and training minority workers?
2. What are the benefits to a business enterprise as the result of a successful program of minority worker employment?

The provision of goods and services

*Choices made by the
consumer in the
marketplace will influence
decisions as to which goods
will be produced.*

The marketing concept and the consumer

Marketing has been described as both the creation and delivery of America's standard of living. This imaginative definition does not tell us in specific terms what goes into the process of marketing in the business enterprise, but it does give the flavor of the exciting nature of marketing in today's affluent American economy. Marketing may also be defined as the activities that move goods and services from producers to consumers to satisfy needs. Chapter 1 indicated that goods have utility when they have the power to satisfy human wants. Marketing imparts place, time, and possession utility to goods. The production function, discussed in Chapter 13, directly imparts form utility to goods. However, even the nature of the form utility provided by production is influenced by what can be marketed to consumers.

The following issues are discussed regarding the marketing concept and the consumer.

What is the marketing concept of business?
What are the factors which influence consumer behavior?
How is the nature of the American consumer market changing?
Why has consumerism developed?
What is government doing to protect consumers?

The importance of marketing

Marketing is as vital in today's economy as is the production of goods and services. It has been estimated that about 50 percent of the consumer's dollar is spent for marketing—moving the product from its point of production to the consumer. Our market economy is directed by the spending decisions of all types of consumers ranging from the teenager spending money earned from a part-time job to the Department of Defense, which spends over $75 billion yearly for military purposes. Despite the presence of some poverty in the United States, today the vast majority of our family units are faced with decisions on how to spend incomes which have been steadily rising over the past several years. For most American families the question is no longer one of whether there is sufficient food on the table, but which luxury goods to purchase and how to adapt to an increased amount of leisure time.

The marketing concept of business

The increased emphasis on marketing in recent years has led to the development of the marketing concept of business. The essence of *the marketing concept of business* is finding or creating a consumer need, developing a product to satisfy this need, and in the process earning a profit for the business enterprise which solves this problem. This means that the thinking of managers throughout the enterprise must be oriented around the importance of the consumer. Such a point of view must have the support of top management and permeate executive thinking throughout the various levels of the organization structure. Marketing becomes everybody's job, not just the responsibility of a few marketing managers.

The General Electric Company provides an example of an enterprise oriented toward the marketing concept of business. In an annual report to its stockholders General Electric stated:

> Marketing, through its studies and research, will establish for the engineer, the designer, and the manufacturing man what the customer wants in a given product, what price he is willing to pay, and where and when it will be wanted. Marketing would have authority in product planning, production scheduling, and inventory control, as well as in the sales distribution and servicing of the product.

When the marketing approach permeates all areas of the enterprise, the actual act of selling a product is but the last step in a sales effort which starts when the product is first conceived. Consumer appeal is built into each product from the design stage on through to final markets, with the marketing manager being part of the cycle of activity from the very beginning.

The marketing concept of business emphasizes the importance of consumers. The objective is to produce consumer satisfactions. Goods and services have no value in or of themselves. It is only when they are desirable to consumers that they take on value.

The enterprise must have a market for the goods and services it hopes to produce. A market consists of consumers who are willing and able to buy the goods produced by a particular business enterprise. These markets must be created and stimulated by managers. In today's rapidly changing economy the creative management does not wait for customers to seek out their product. Management woos the customers and actively tries to draw them to their product lines in competition with other enterprises.

Translating consumer needs to wants

A basic objective of marketing is to translate consumer needs into wants. To need something is to depend upon it to carry out a way of life. People need all kinds of goods and services to carry on an established pattern of living. However, they are not always fully conscious of their needs. The challenge of creative marketing is to focus the consumer's attention on his needs and to suggest products that will meet these needs. Through the marketing process needs are translated into wants. To want a product is to recognize that it is available and that it can satisfy a need.

There is no shortage of needs in our world today even in the United States. People need more than they have in food, clothing, shelter, health and safety, education, and the many conveniences of life. In many instances, however, these needs are not clearly understood. Creative marketing can bring such general needs into sharper focus and can translate a dimly perceived need into a want for a specific good that will fulfill the need.

Marketing is sometimes criticized on the grounds that it results in the production of goods that the American people really do not need. This charge is not based on an understanding of the close relationship between needs and wants. Wants arise from needs. It is not possible to stimulate a person to want a product when he does not feel some need for it. At the same time it is clearly recognized that not all needs have the same priorities. The need to see television shows in color is not as basic to life as are certain essentials of food and shelter. However, even such gadgets as electric shoepolishers meet a need. They do serve a useful function. The fact that people could survive without a certain good or service does not mean that these products are not needed to achieve a certain standard of living.

Once a need has been turned into a specific want on the part of the consuming public the American standard of living is never the same again. Consider how much different and less productive would be the American business scene without air conditioning. At one time air conditioning was virtually unknown except by primitive methods available to a few. Protection from the summer's heat and humidity was a latent need which today has been translated into a want of most Americans. Not only in our places of work but in our homes we want to have air conditioning. Out of this want has grown a new industry which is increasingly important in the American economy today. New jobs have been created, new investment opportunities opened up, and new managerial challenges provided as the result of a translation of this consumer need into a clear-cut want.

The process of translating a need into a want is a job for marketing management. The consumer's attention must be called to the nature and the significance of the need and how often and deeply it is felt, whether consciously or unconsciously. Many needs have an emotional rather than a rational basis. A good marketer learns when to appeal to emotion, to reason, or a combination of the two. Sometimes when needs having an emotional basis are put into a more rational perspective the consumer becomes more receptive to the product of the marketer. The opposite can also be true.

It is possible for unconscious emotional factors to cause consumers to react negatively to a new product. This happened when instant coffee was first introduced. Although the use of instant coffee saves time and is more convenient than the preparation of regularly brewed coffee, some women were unwilling to use the instant product because they subconsciously felt it reflected on their self-image as good housewives, even though many of these same women also held full-time jobs outside the home. Through various advertising programs designed to demonstrate how instant coffee contributes to gracious living, which presumably is the goal of every housewife, the consumer's attention was focused on the need for a better way to prepare coffee given an increasing press of time on the wife's schedule. One television advertising series pictured an experienced household domestic servant showing an attractive young married woman how she could improve the quality of her meals by serving a particular brand of instant coffee which the husband proclaimed tasted "better than fresh perked" coffee.

The consumer

Ultimate consumers

With the marketing concept placing the emphasis upon the consumer, it is important that the consumer be defined and analyzed. *Ultimate consumers* are individuals or households who use goods or services for the satisfaction of personal needs. *Industrial users* who buy products for use in producing other goods or services are discussed in the next two chapters. When the term "consumer" or "consumers" is used in this book it applies to individual or ultimate consumers.

Individual consumer behavior

Consumers buy particular goods and services for a variety of reasons. We do not know exactly why an individual makes a buying decision at a given time. A consumer is influenced by a variety of stimuli out of which comes a response either to purchase or not to purchase some product or service. The factors affecting the consumer's behavior can be classified as economic, psychological, and social.

Economic factors. Economic considerations affecting consumer behavior center around the individual's rational use of his scarce resources to satisfy his needs. Thus, the consumer's income level, whether his income is rising or falling, his savings, and the availability of credit would be important as he enters the marketplace. The increase in America's consumer income is so important to the marketing concept that it is discussed in detail later in this chapter. Price of the good, its durability, and expense of operation and repair are all factors relating to economics which may influence the consumer. The price of competing goods or goods that could serve as substitutes is also an economic consideration that may influence the consumer's decision. However, important as they are, economic factors are not the sole determinants of consumer behavior. Psychological and social influences also affect consumer decision making.

Psychological factors. Psychologists are not in agreement as to what provides the best explanation of consumer behavior. What may explain one individual's motivations would not necessarily explain another's behavior. Also, the marketing manager is interested in actions of groups or classes of consumers since marketing programs usually must appeal to numerous individuals. However, the research and concepts of psychologists can be helpful in providing insights into buying motives.

One theory of motivation is provided in Maslow's hierarchy[1] of needs which arrays five needs in the order in which an individual tends to seek their satisfaction:

1. Physiological needs—for food, drink, sex, and shelter.
2. Safety needs—for security, order, protection, and family stability.
3. Belongingness and love needs—for affection, belonging to a group, and acceptance.
4. Esteem needs—for self-respect, reputation, prestige, and status.
5. Self-actualization needs—for self-fulfillment, doing what one is best fitted for.

In addition, Maslow suggested two additional classes of needs for those individuals who may have satisfied the first five needs:

1. The need to know and understand.
2. The need for aesthetic satisfaction—beauty.

Theoretically a person tends to try to fulfill all of his needs at one level before moving on to a higher level of needs. In actual practice most people attempt to fill needs on different levels at the same time, probably never completely satisfying the needs at any one level. However, people do have some priority of needs even if every individual does not have the same priority. For example, a college student who enjoys good music may habitually skip lunch (a physiological need) and spend his money to build an extensive record collection (an aesthetic need). Perhaps what is important for the businessman to recognize is that people have different levels of needs, and that for consumers to spend their income for his particular goods they must be convinced that some need will be satisfied. Also, people tend to feel those needs most strongly which have not yet been satisfied.

---

[1] A. H. Maslow, *Motivation and Personality* (New York: Harper & Row, Inc., 1954), pp. 80–97.

Social factors. Marketing managers have traditionally used income as a means of predicting buying behavior. Today about half of the American families have incomes of $10,000 and above. This group includes blue-collar workers as well as professional and white-collar employees. These families tend to vary in their spending patterns depending partly upon the social class with which they identify.

This is illustrated by Coleman's example[2] comparing three families from different social classes having the same relatively high income. An upper-middle-class family (perhaps a lawyer and his wife) would likely spend a relatively large share of its income on a home in a prestige neighborhood, expensive furniture, quality clothing, and club memberships or cultural entertainment. A lower-middle-class family (perhaps a salesman and his family) would probably spend the same income on as good or better house in a less fancy neighborhood, more on furniture and clothing but not from such expensive stores, and have a larger savings account. In comparison, the upper-lower-class family whose husband might be a welder has a smaller house in a less desirable neighborhood but the family may have a larger, newer automobile; newer television set; and the husband spends more on sports.

In addition to the social class with which he identifies, other groups in society influence the consumer's behavior. These include the clubs to which he may belong, schools he attends, and labor unions, athletic teams, or church groups in which he participates. The values of these formal groups along with informal groups in society influence their members. Young people tend to seek approval from their peers by dressing, behaving, and buying what others do. Businessmen generally act and spend in patterns which gain the approval of their associates. Even college professors are influenced by their colleagues in their buying decisions.

The marketing manager must be aware of the differences which exist in the consumer market based upon social groupings. When a product may have special appeal to a particular group in society the advertising and sales promotion program should take this into account. Beverage manufacturers, magazine publishers, and fashion designers have all found that their markets may be segmented, at least partly, depending upon various social classifications. Different forms of advertising will be necessary to reach these segments of the market. While the marketing

---

[2] Richard P. Coleman, "The Significance of Social Stratification in Selling," in *Marketing: A Maturing Discipline,* ed. Martin L. Bell (Chicago: American Marketing Association, 1961).

manager cannot depend upon a rigid application of social classes or groups in selling his product, the recognition that they exist is important.

The consumer of the 1970s

The 1970s mark a time of dramatic change for consumer markets in the United States. In economic terms the proportion of high-income families has increased significantly. Changes are occurring in the population in the age, education, and composition of the work force which also affect spending patterns. Some of these economic, demographic, and social factors which affect business are discussed below.

Higher consumer income

The U.S. consumer market is changing. In past decades we moved from a nation of predominantly low-income families to one of middle-income mass markets. Now the move is into an era of high-income mass markets with about one half of families having an income exceeding $10,000 per year. Figure 11–1 shows the changing nature of American

FIGURE 11–1
Number of families by family income in 1947 to 1969 (in constant 1969 dollars)

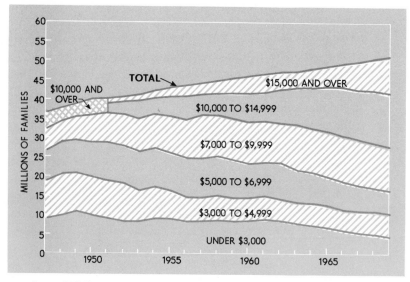

Source: U.S. Bureau of the Census, *Current Population Reports,* Series P-60, No. 75, December, 1970.

families' income over the past 22 years. Over the past 22 years median family income in real terms has increased 90 percent.

The distribution of families by income class has also changed dramatically over the past 23 years. Figure 11–2 illustrates the increase in the proportion of families having incomes of $10,000 and above and the substantial reduction in the number of families with incomes below $5,000 annually.

FIGURE 11–2
*The changing pyramid of family income
(total families each year = 100 percent; based on 1970 dollars)*

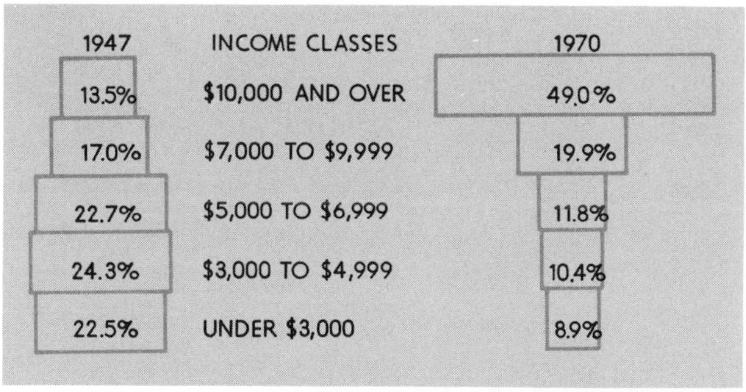

1947	INCOME CLASSES	1970
13.5%	$10,000 AND OVER	49.0%
17.0%	$7,000 TO $9,999	19.9%
22.7%	$5,000 TO $6,999	11.8%
24.3%	$3,000 TO $4,999	10.4%
22.5%	UNDER $3,000	8.9%

Source: U.S. Bureau of the Census, *Current Population Reports,* Series P-60, No. 78, May, 1971.

Factors contributing to higher family income

Educational achievement. Contributing to the rising income level of American families is the rising level of educational achievement. Figure 11–3 shows the increasing proportion of the adult population which has attended high school and college. Notice how the number of college graduates has increased and is projected to become even greater in the 1980s.

Generally the greater the level of educational achievement the higher the person's lifetime income. Figure 11–4 compares the estimated lifetime income for adult men depending upon whether their highest educational achievement was elementary school, high school, or college graduation.

Working wives. The increased number of households having two wage earners also has contributed to higher family incomes. From 1950 to 1970 the overall percentage of husband-wife families with the wife

FIGURE 11–3

Educational attainment of adults 25 years and over, 1950–1970, projected to 1985

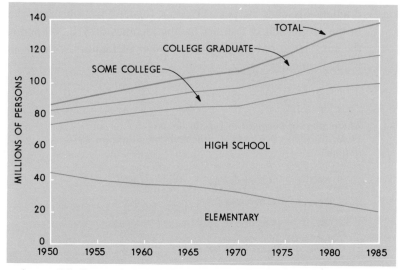

Source: U.S. Bureau of the Census, Current Population Reports, Series P-20 and unpublished data.

FIGURE 11–4

Estimated lifetime income in 1968 for men 18 years and over in the U.S., depending upon educational achievement

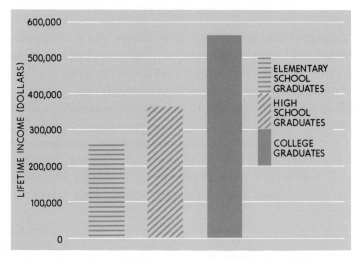

Source: U.S. Bureau of Census, *Current Population Reports*, Series P-60, No. 74, October, 1970.

in the paid labor force increased from 19 to 34 percent of all families. The increase was even more dramatic in the affluent $10,000-and-over family income bracket where the proportion increased from 24 to 47 percent. Thus, in 1970 in almost half of upper income families the wife earned income which helped raise the family's standard of living.

More discretionary income

Discretionary income is the income left over after covering the family's spending for necessities. Discretionary income may be spent for luxuries or saved and invested. The rising real income of Americans provides additional discretionary income. This increases the challenge for marketing managers as they seek to attract the consumer's discretionary spending dollars in competition with a wide variety of goods and services. For example, more consumers are now able to make large discretionary purchases and will choose between such items as a vacation home at a lake, a trip to Europe, or a third car for the family. Once basic transportation is provided, the auto manufacturer competes not only with other automobile manufacturers but with the vacation home industry, foreign travel agencies, art dealers, and other widely varied producers of goods and services.

The job of marketing is complicated further by the fact that what one family considers necessities may be considered luxuries by another family. Also, with higher standards of living the definition of what is considered a necessity will change. What were previously luxury goods will become necessities, opening up new areas for luxury spending. The consumer durable goods industries offer many examples of this concept. Twenty years ago television was considered a distinct luxury. Today most families think of television as a necessity.

In the early 1950s the color television industry was in its infancy but grew until it became the exotic consumer appliance of recent years. Figure 11–5 shows the degree of saturation of color television and other consumer durable goods owned by American households. These statistics do not include renters who have appliances such as refrigerators and ranges furnished by the landlord.

Figure 11–5 illustrates that while there are still opportunities for further sales both to expand the market for durables and to replace present models in use, industry is challenged to develop new products which will meet or expand consumers' needs. It remains to be seen whether mass markets will develop for such items as microwave ovens,

FIGURE 11–5
Percent of total U.S. households owning selected consumer durable goods, 1970

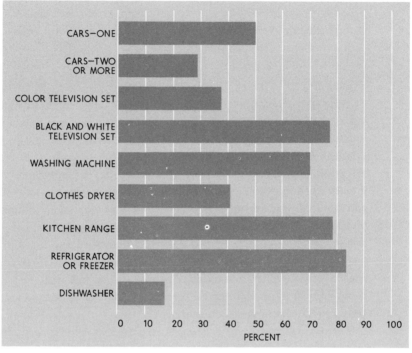

Source: U.S. Bureau of the Census, *Current Population Reports,* Series P-65, No. 33, October, 1970.

home trash disposers, instant home movies, or color video recorders to be used at home.

Demographic changes

In order to predict better the kinds of goods and services that consumers will need, alert marketing executives study changes in the size and composition of the population. Figure 11–6 shows the U.S. population and growth rate since 1945 and its projection to 1990. While the total population continued to increase, the growth rate began a steady decline in the early 1960s until 1970 when it is projected to increase slightly into the 1980s. The decreased growth rate may be attributed to a declining birth rate. The lower birth rates may be caused by a number of factors including the desire by couples for a higher standard of

FIGURE 11–6
U.S. population and growth rate, 1945–1990

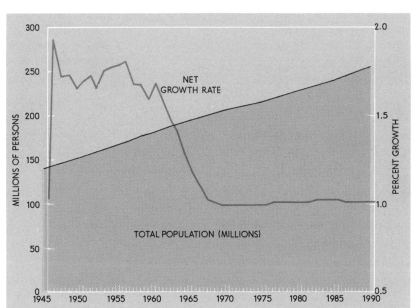

Source: U.S. Bureau of the Census, *Current Population Reports,* Series P-25, No. 442, March, 1970, and Series P-25, No. 448, August, 1970.

living which can result from postponing or having fewer children and having the wife work outside the home. The cost of rearing a child to college age has been estimated by the Institute of Life Insurance to be $23,000 for the average family. When another $12,000 per child is added for those who go on to college it is apparent that the reduction in family size from three or four to one or two children significantly reduces the economic cost of children to the family.

In addition to total size, the composition of the population will change during the 1970s, as is illustrated by Figure 11–7. There will be a substantial increase in the 25 to 34 age group of the population along with a significant increase in the 20 to 24 age bracket. This increase in these two age groups will mean a larger work force with increasing competition for jobs. Furthermore, these workers will not have as great an advantage in educational qualifications over older age groups as had been the case in earlier generations.

The changes in the size and composition of the population will have varied meanings to different manufacturers and service enterprises. For

FIGURE 11–7
Population growth by age groups

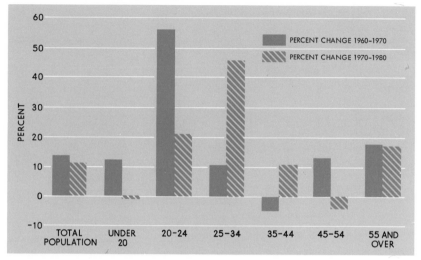

Source: U.S. Bureau of the Census, *Current Population Reports,* Series P-25, No. 448, August, 1970.

example, for manufacturers in such industries as toys, baby foods, appliances, and furniture, the new family formations resulting from the World War II baby boom will provide increasing sales opportunities. However, increasing competition for jobs in these populous age groups may mean that both husband and wife will seek jobs, that they will reduce the number or postpone having children, or feel less free to spend their income fully or go into debt. If these actions should become widespread then the impact of the post–World War II baby boom will not be as expansive for the economy as otherwise.

Consumerism and consumer protection legislation

Consumerism

Despite the importance of the consumer to American business and the fact that most business enterprises attempt to serve consumer needs well, complaints about business products and service have long been heard.

Considerable legislation has been enacted over the years for the protection of consumer interests. The Federal Trade Commission and the

Food and Drug Administration were both created prior to World War I and have responsibilities in the consumer protection field. Following protests by consumers the authority of both agencies in the consumer area was strengthened by legislation in 1938. The Federal Trade Commission has responsibility for policing advertising and marketing practices and for enforcing a variety of legislation including labeling acts for products of wool, fur, and textiles. These responsibilities are in addition to the FTC's duties in enforcing the antitrust laws discussed in Chapter 2. The Food and Drug Administration is charged with regulation in such areas as maintenance of drug standards and evaluation of new drugs, food purity, and cosmetic products.

In the 1960s protest by consumers against business practices and products which did not live up to their expectations became a force to be reckoned with both by business and politicians. This protest has been labeled *consumerism*. Today's consumers are making themselves heard to an extent previously unknown by American business. They express concerns about the poor quality of products, the lack of proper service, the use of food additives which may be harmful, products which are unsafe, and practices by business which contribute to pollution.

Consumerism as a movement gained focus with the publication in 1965 of Ralph Nader's *Unsafe at Any Speed*. This book, critical of the Corvair auto, became a best seller. Following the book's publication, sales of General Motors' Corvair dropped and in 1969 GM ceased production of this rear-engine car. Nader is also credited with significant influence in the passage of federal legislation benefiting consumers in such areas as auto safety and food processing and distribution.

Criticism of FTC

There have been several recent studies made which have suggested that the Federal Trade Commission should be more active in protecting consumers. In 1969 a number of law school students and professors under the direction of Ralph Nader published a report on the consumer protection activities of the FTC. One of the conclusions of those making the study was that the commission had not provided adequate protection for the consumer.

Also in 1969 President Nixon requested the American Bar Association to study the Federal Trade Commission. This report recommended a "new and vigorous approach" in protecting consumers against fraud along with other suggestions for changes in the FTC.

Notwithstanding the criticism which has been leveled at governmental agencies for a lack of vigilance in consumer protection, these bodies are playing a role in making business more conscious of its responsibilities to consumers. The Federal Trade Commission has moved against some deceptive advertising and merchandising practices, and the Food and Drug Administration has banned certain products which were potentially hazardous to consumers.

Other consumer groups

In addition to consumers who have organized to deal with particular types of problems, there are two nonprofit organizations which test and rate products for the benefit of consumers. They are Consumers' Research and Consumers Union, both of which issue monthly publications which report the results of their studies. Better Business Bureaus are sponsored in major metropolitan areas by businessmen to encourage responsible business practices and to provide information to consumers regarding complaints or to answer consumer inquiries about a particular enterprise.

The vigor of the current consumer movement in the United States indicates either that not enough business enterprises are sincerely committed to the marketing concept of business and the importance of the consumer or that this commitment is not evident to the public. If business is insensitive to the concerns and welfare of individual consumers it is reasonable to expect that additional legislation will be passed in an attempt to correct what many people feel are abuses by American business.

Consumer protection legislation and administrative actions

Recent legislation

The following legislation passed in recent years is of importance to consumers.

The *National Traffic and Motor Vehicle Safety Act of 1966* requires auto manufacturers to notify first purchasers of cars by certified mail of any safety defects discovered subsequent to manufacture and delivery. This law also provides for the issuance of safety standards for motor vehicles and for other programs to improve highway safety.

The *Wholesome Meat Act of 1967* updated and strengthened the standards for inspection for red meat animals. Two thousand of the 17,000 slaughter and packing houses in the country which produce 85 percent of the meat eaten in the United States had been subject to federal meat inspection since 1907. Now, in cooperation with the states, the remaining 15 percent of the meat produced by small or seasonal plants is subject to standards designed to improve the quality of meat products.

The *Truth in Lending Act of 1968* requires creditors to furnish individuals to whom credit is about to be extended a statement of the amount of financing charges and the percentage rate of interest charged annually. Before this law was passed, practice had varied considerably regarding the degree of disclosure to consumers of actual annual interest rates. This act is considered to be one of the most important consumer laws enacted by Congress since the 1930s.

Also in 1968 the *Wholesome Poultry Products Act* was signed into law by President Johnson. This act extended federal inspection standards to poultry sold intrastate.

Two 1970 pieces of legislation were directed primarily toward the protection of children. The *Poison Prevention Packaging Act* requires manufacturers to distribute dangerous substances in safety containers with caps which are difficult to remove except for one size container which is designed for the use of the handicapped and the elderly. The *Child Protection and Toy Safety Act* provided increased protection for children from toys which might have mechanical or electrical hazards.

Also in 1970 the 1965 *Cigarette Labeling and Advertising Act* was amended to strengthen the warning on cigarette packages to read "Warning: The Surgeon General Has Determined That Cigarette Smoking Is Dangerous To Your Health." The act also regulated cigarette advertising with television advertising of cigarettes ceasing after January 1, 1971.

Another piece of 1970 legislation was the *Fair Credit Reporting Act* which contained a number of provisions to protect consumers in credit matters. This act requires that all agencies reporting consumer credit rating data follow reasonable procedures to assure the accuracy of their information. Any user of credit information who rejects a consumer for credit, insurance, or employment must inform the individual of the source of the credit report. Also, consumers may use the courts to obtain identification of the sources of information behind the credit reports.

In 1971 considerable interest was expressed by consumer advocates for national legislation which would permit "class action" suits by a group of consumers against business. If such a law were passed it would permit lawsuits for damages against a business enterprise by any group of consumers allegedly injured for the same reason as the result of any violation affecting interstate commerce. Proponents of this legislation claim that such class action suits would provide a better chance for justice rather than if citizens as individuals were required to file separate suits against a large corporation.

Administrative actions to aid consumers

As the result of administrative action by President Kennedy and President Johnson the Consumer Advisory Council was created in 1963 to represent consumers' interests regarding matters of government policy. Both presidents sent messages to the Congress requesting various legislative programs benefiting consumers.

In 1971 President Nixon created an Office of Consumer Affairs to report to him. This office was assigned the responsibility of analyzing and coordinating all federal activities in the field of consumer protection. At the same time the president called on the Congress for new legislation under the broad heading of a "Buyer's Bill of Rights" which would create new programs in such areas as product safety and fraud prevention.

Summary

The marketing concept of business involves finding or creating a consumer need, developing a product to satisfy that need, and in the process earning a profit for the business enterprise. The marketing concept means that the thinking of managers throughout the business enterprise must be oriented around the importance of the consumer. A basic objective of marketing is to translate consumer needs into wants.

Customers of business may be either ultimate consumers or industrial users. Individual consumer behavior is influenced by economic, psychological, and social factors.

The consumer of the 1970s has a rising level of real income resulting in increased amounts of discretionary spending power. The income distribution pyramid has changed significantly since 1947 with median family income up by 90 percent in real terms. This higher family income is attributed to higher educational achievement and an increase in the number of families which have both husband and wife working. More discretionary income and changes in the size and composition of the population will present challenges for marketing managers in the future.

Consumerism is increasing in importance with both government and private groups becoming more insistent that business avoid deceptive practices and unreliable products. Legislation passed in recent years to protect the consumer includes the National Traffic and Motor Vehicle Safety Act, the Wholesome Meat Act, the Truth in Lending Act, and the Cigarette Labeling and Advertising Act.

Terms for review

marketing
marketing concept of business
market
want
need
ultimate consumer

industrial user
Maslow's hierarchy of needs
family income
discretionary income
demographic changes
consumerism

Questions

1. Is the application of the marketing concept of business more important today than at some other period in our economic history, such as in the depression of the 1930s or the period immediately following World War II? State the reasons for your answer.

2. Explain why consumers do not always act in a rational manner when buying goods and services.

3. Cite ten examples of products advertised in the mass media to illustrate where an appeal is made to one or more of the five basic needs in Maslow's hierarchy.

4. Give five examples of items that you feel are purchased by college students in which the motivation is more psychological or social than economic.

5. What are the implications for business in the changing nature of the income distribution pyramid illustrated in Figure 11–2?

6. What do the statistics in Figure 11–5 imply for the future product development and sales promotion by durable goods manufacturers?

7. What are the implications for business in the changing nature of the population as illustrated in Figures 11–6 and 11–7?

8. How do you account for the interest in consumerism at a time when the incomes of American families generally are at historically high levels?

9. Outline the important consumer legislation passed by the Congress in recent years.

10. From current periodicals examine statements by consumer groups that American business and governmental bodies are not living up to consumers' expectations. Also examine statements in defense of business's actions. Write a 300-word paper summarizing your conclusions from this study.

BUSINESS BRIEFS

Pricing airline fares

During the summer of 1971 a number of airlines drastically reduced the cost of flying from the United States to Europe for youths and students up to approximately 25 years old. These rates were cut to about $200 for round-trip air transportation between New York and various European cities. This was about one half the regular ticket price for summer travel to Europe.

Industry sources indicated that the price cutting was started by Belgian's government-controlled Sabena airlines at the order of their government. Sabena and other regularly scheduled transatlantic airlines belong to the International Air Transport Association which has rules prohibiting price changes in fares unless ordered to do so by a government. Once one carrier lowers fares then any airline that flies the same route may adopt the same fares in order to meet the competition. Pan American, which flies to Brussels, lowered its fare for students to meet Sabena's rate. The new fare structure for students was then swept up by Air France, Trans World Airlines, British Overseas Airways Corp., and Italy's Alitalia on their transatlantic flights.

These low youth fares cut into the nonscheduled charter airlines traffic which for some time had charged lower fares than the scheduled airlines for special group flights.

Following these fare reductions, Pan American World Airways was faced with a multimillion dollar suit in federal court by persons who alleged that Pan Am's actions in the sale of youth fare tickets were discriminatory and arbitrary against persons over the age of 25.

1. What factors should have been considered by the airlines in making the youth-student fare reductions in 1971?

2. Should students be able to fly to Europe for substantially less cost than any other person interested in travel? Explain your answer.

Truth in auto advertising

The Federal Trade Commission moved against the automobile industry in 1971 by requiring General Motors, Ford, Chrysler, American Motors, and foreign producers (Volkswagen, Toyota, and Datsun) to substantiate their advertising claims.

The FTC ordered the auto companies to produce evidence within 60 days to support some 60 claims made by advertisements used in the United States. For example, documentation was requested on Dodge's claim of 30 m.p.g. on its Colt; on Ford's statement that the LTD was 700 percent quieter; and on Chevrolet's Chevelle ad that there were 109 advantages to prevent aging. Volkswagen was ordered to show how the new Super Beetle had 89 ways to distinguish a new model from an old one.

FTC officials stated that the objective of the campaign was to "encourage advertisers to have adequate substantiation before claims are made" which will permit consumers to make a "rational choice among competing claims."

The commission spokesman indicated that the move on the auto industry was the first of an industry-by-industry drive to verify advertising claims for consumer products. The same official pointed out that it was expected that most of the ads would be verified.

1. What other industries would you suggest should be requested by the FTC to prove their advertising claims?

2. Cite examples of advertisements which provide some evidence to support their claims. Cite some examples which lack such evidence.

3. Should the FTC's consumer division be concerned with such issues as proof of advertising claims; i.e., do the American people take advertising very seriously anyway?

Advertising Profile bread

In mid-1971 Continental Baking Company reluctantly agreed to comply with the Federal Trade Commission's insistence that it run "corrective" advertising to clarify what the FTC charged had been misleading information on the weight-reducing claims that Continental had made for its Profile bread. For a period of one year Continental agreed to spend 25 percent of its advertising expenditures for Profile bread on FTC approved ads that will point out that the bread is not an effective weight reducer. This agreement by Continental to run "corrective" advertising was the first time the FTC's pressure for such action had been acceded to by a business enterprise.

1. Do you feel that the FTC requirement was too harsh? What steps short of requiring "corrective" advertising might the FTC have taken?
2. What specific actions would you take as the management of Continental Baking to conform to the above agreement?

CORFAM®—A subsititute for leather?

In its 1963 annual report the Du Pont Company, the world's largest producer of chemicals, announced the development of a substitute for leather which was given the trade name Corfam®. Some analysts anticipated that Corfam® would replace leather in the shoe industry as nylon had replaced silk in the women's hosiery field.

Corfam® had a number of advantages over leather, including water repellency, resistance to cracking, uniformity, and durability. Its finish provided shoes with considerably more ease of maintenance than when leather was used.

In the 1964 annual report the Du Pont management stated, "many of the major shoe manufacturers in the U.S. are either using or considering the use of Corfam® in their shoes. Plans are underway for worldwide marketing . . . ." In 1966 Du Pont reported that demand for Corfam® exceeded production capacity. Other chemical producers began to enter the synthetic leather field, frequently with cheaper leather substitutes to compete with premium-priced Corfam®.

In the late 1960s men's and women's shoe styles changed rapidly. For example, in quick succession women's shoes changed from rounded toes to pointed toes, then to squared toes. Heels changed from high, pointed ones to low, chunky styles. Less emphasis was placed by the consumer on durability and more on keeping up with the latest fads and fashions.

In 1971 an announcement was made by Du Pont's management that the production and sale of Corfam® would cease. Based on company reports, some financial analysts estimated that the total loss on Corfam® to Du Pont might approximate $100 million over its product life cycle.

1. What advantages did Corfam® have which initially made prospects for product success good?
2. What factors contributed to the demise of Corfam®?
3. What generalizations can be drawn from this experience of Du Pont?

*Fashion is an increasingly
important element in the
marketing of
consumer goods.*

The marketing mix

Once consumers' needs and wants have been determined, the management of a business enterprise must create a marketing program to satisfy the needs of the firm's target customers. The marketing program of a business enterprise can be thought of as being composed of four important variables which constitute the marketing mix. These variables can be abbreviated as Product, Promotion, Price, and Place.

The following issues are discussed regarding the marketing mix.

What factors are considered in determining the right product for the target customers of the business enterprise?

What means can be used in the promotion program to communicate effectively with the target customers?

At what price should the product be offered to target customers?

How shall the business enterprise place the goods where they can reach target customers?

The marketing mix

The four variables which comprise the marketing mix are symbolized in Figure 12–1 as they focus on the consumer. Each of the 4 *P*'s in the marketing mix is discussed in this chapter. The importance of the *C* was discussed in Chapter 11.

Product

Product defined

A simple definition of a product is a physical object with certain characteristics. A better definition from the marketing viewpoint is that a

FIGURE 12–1
The marketing mix

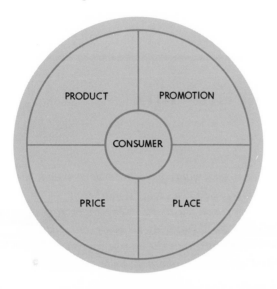

product is whatever satisfies customers whether it has tangible or intangible characteristics or some combination of both. This definition provides for the inclusion of both goods and services as products. Also, making consumer satisfaction an important criterion of a product enables us to distinguish between different types of physical goods depending upon such features as brand name, color, packaging, the manner of distribution, price, and the nature of service provided. Thus, a color television set sold by a department store which provides credit, delivery, servicing, and a large inventory is not an identical product with the same television model purchased on a cash-and-carry basis from a discount house which has a limited selection of models and no service department. The inclusion of services as products is also important since a large proportion of the labor force is engaged in this sector of the economy. Since World War II consumers have increased their spending on services more than for either durable or nondurable goods. The emphasis on customer satisfaction with goods or services is a key dimension of the marketing concept.

Importance of new products

New product development is a major element in the marketing program of the business enterprise. Business must continually give consumers new and improved products to hold old customers and to win new ones. In today's markets manufacturers cannot prosper without new products. It is not unusual for major corporations to have 50 percent of their sales in products which did not exist ten years ago. Marketing research experts have estimated that within the next three years approximately 75 percent of the economy's growth in sales volume can be expected to come from new products and new brands of merchandise. In such industries as electrical machinery, chemicals, and textiles, more than 50 percent of sales growth in recent years has come from newly

FIGURE 12–2
Product life cycle for sales and profit margin

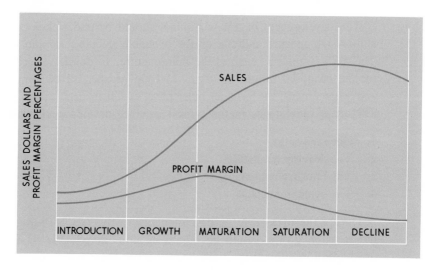

marketed products. Those enterprises which are preparing today with the research and development programs necessary for new products will be the companies which will experience the greatest growth in sales and profits in the future.

Products tend to have a life cycle pattern of sales and profit margins as shown in Figure 12–2. Both the sales and profit margin curves slope upward, reach a peak, and then decline. However, there is a significant difference in the timing of their peaks. The sales curve continues to rise for a period of time after the profit margin curve has already reached its peak. This can partially be explained by competition from other enterprises producing similar goods, forcing the price and therefore the profit margin down. This means that to insure continued high-profit margins on total sales the business enterprise must innovate and develop new products to take up the slack of declining profit on products which are still increasing in sales volume. This emphasis on profits rather than sales volume alone is an important aspect of good marketing management.

New product development is complicated by the actions taken by an enterprise's competitors. A business firm must be ahead of the competition in development and introduction of at least some of its products unless management is willing to operate with lower profit margins than those enterprises which emphasize research and development.

Developing the product

The development of a new product should be undertaken only after a thorough market analysis of the probable demand for the product. The market analysis enables the manufacturer to develop specifications for the proposed product in terms of what prospective customers want and what quality the product must have to sell in a given price range. There are four stages in the typical product development program:

1.   The idea stage.
2.   The development stage.
3.   The improvement stage.
4.   The evaluation stage.

During the idea stage of development creativity is encouraged, and the research group should be bound as little as possible by tradition or conventional thinking. While some people have more creative ability than others, this is a facility that can be developed through practice. Frequently, helpful results have come from placing a problem before new personnel who are able to face it without the "built-in" thinking that limits the range of imaginative new solutions.

Once the idea for a new product has been accepted, the product enters the development stage. This calls for designing the product and constructing a working model. At this stage it is important to see exactly what the product will look like, how it will operate, and to obtain some preliminary cost estimates. Management makes frequent appraisals during the development stage and can close out the project if problems are encountered which cannot be solved satisfactorily.

After the development phase, the product is tested in the field to determine whether it has any "bugs" in it. Generally design simplifications and other improvements which lead to a better product are uncovered during field tests. As the result of this improvement stage, modifications are made in the product, and the model that will be placed on the market takes shape.

In the evaluation stage the final tests and modifications are undertaken. Production drawings and final cost estimates are made up. The final production models are constructed and all production details are worked out before the production lines are set up. In practice, improvement never ends; modifications will take place even after commercial production begins. However, the use of a pilot production program and careful testing and evaluation in the final stage of product development reduces the number of such changes, which are more costly the further along they occur in the development of the product.

Not all new products are successful. As a matter of fact, failure is far more common than success in new product invention. For every five products developed to the point where they are ready for mass production, only one is ever actually produced and distributed. Of those new products which are placed on the market only about half are commercially successful.

Classification of consumer products

The distinction between products for ultimate consumers and industrial users was made in Chapter 11. Marketing of consumer goods is discussed in this chapter. Industrial goods and the process by which they are purchased is discussed in Chapter 13. Consumer goods may be classified according to the nature of consumer buying habits as convenience goods, shopping goods, and specialty goods.

Convenience goods. *Convenience goods* are products which consumers purchase with a minimum of effort at the nearest available location. Convenience goods are low-price items about which the consumer has considerable knowledge. Usually brand identification of the product is not so strong that the consumer will not accept a substitute brand if his first choice is unavailable.

Convenience goods may be classified further as staples, impulse goods, and emergency goods. *Staples* are goods which are bought and used frequently without much consideration being given to their purchase. Many food products in supermarkets and nonprescription drug items are staple goods. Although brand identification may have some weight in the buying decision, usually ready availability will be more important than what the brand is. Thus, items such as bread, milk, and aspirin are considered staples and ready availability to consumers is important in their distribution.

Impulse goods are items which customers buy on sight without having gone out specifically for their purchase. Their unit price is usually low, and the purchase of an impulse good satisfies a need which is strongly felt at the moment. Retail stores frequently place items near doors or at cash registers which will be bought by customers on an impulse. Candy bars, chewing gum, and cigarettes are frequently displayed in this way.

A good might be either a staple or an impulse item depending upon the purpose of the good's use and whether it was purchased as the result of an immediately felt need. Candy bars purchased to be put into lunch boxes as part of a weekly grocery shopping trip might be considered staple goods, while a candy bar out of the same carton might be an impulse item if it were purchased and eaten on the spot because the person just happened to see it.

Emergency goods are bought only when an urgent need is felt. In this situation price is not too important. The customer needs the goods at once. Tire chains purchased at a turnpike service station during a snow storm or ambulance service for a person with a sudden illness are examples of emergency products.

Shopping goods. *Shopping goods* are products which are compared with competing products for price, quality, style, or service by the customer before he buys. Frequently the customer lacks complete knowledge about the shopping goods before he arrives at the store. This presents an opportunity for personal selling on the part of the sales personnel. Shopping goods typically have a relatively high unit price and are bought less frequently than convenience goods. Examples of shopping goods include men's suits, women's apparel, jewelry, shoes, and furniture.

Since the customer likely will want to compare shopping goods with the competition, retail stores selling these goods find it desirable to be located close together. The manufacturer of shopping goods has fewer retail outlets than the producer of convenience goods. In many cases the name of the retail store is more important to the customer than the name of the manufacturer. This means that for shopping goods the retailer has a considerable responsibility and opportunity for promotion to increase sales.

Specialty goods. *Specialty goods* are products which are identified by customers as having strong brand identification or particular features which justify a special buying effort. The customer usually has knowledge of the product before he begins the buying trip and is willing to go out of his way to find a certain brand. Examples of specialty goods include photographic equipment, expensive men's clothing, electronic equipment for home use, and health foods. An automobile might be considered a specialty good by the customer who had a strong preference for a particular manufacturer's models.

Although specialty goods might have a high unit price, this is not a necessary characteristic. Even an inexpensive item might be considered a specialty good if the customer had a strong brand preference for the item. Thus, for many persons Kodak film and processing are specialty goods since they will use no other brand even though film and processing of other manufacturers may be priced lower.

Blurred classifications. The classification of consumer products can be useful to marketing managers. However, it is not an inflexible system nor do all products necessarily fit neatly into this classification scheme. Items may be considered in different categories by customers under varying circumstances. Customers' shopping habits may change over time. For example, people now buy many products in supermarkets which they formerly purchased in drugstores or variety stores. As incomes rise families may buy products which formerly were shopping goods as convenience goods. Changes in the buying habits of customers have implications for different marketing mixes on the part of enterprise managers.

Promotion

Promotion of the business enterprise's product to encourage the potential customer to buy is another important element of the marketing mix. Promotion constitutes the communications dimension of marketing, where target customers are informed and persuaded regarding the product or the enterprise itself. As the result of feedback from promotion the management becomes aware of the consumers' needs and reactions to the specific product offered. With the increasing amount of discretionary income available to consumers, the pressure is on the individual business enterprise as it competes with other enterprises to fulfill the expanded needs and wants of affluent consumers. Effective promotion programs can be instrumental in meeting this challenge. Three principal methods of promotional activities are discussed—personal selling, advertising, and sales promotion.

Personal selling

Personal selling is almost always an important method of promotion, and in many enterprises it is the sole form of sales activity. Selling involves some method of communication with the customer. The most direct and effective form of communication is a personal presentation which has the advantage of tailoring the sales effort to each particular customer but the disadvantage of a high cost per each personal communication.

Salesmanship. The heart of personal selling is salesmanship. This involves contact with prospective buyers and preparation of appeals to influence them to buy. Modern salesmanship emphasizes the importance of providing the buyer with information to aid him in making the best decision from the customer's standpoint rather than the use of high-pressure tactics. Most enterprises depend heavily upon repeat business for their sales volume, which means that it is important for the buyer to be satisfied with his purchase. Today's salesman is equipped with knowledge regarding his competitor's products as well as his own and is educated to provide prospective customers with product information and service. The orientation of today's most successful personal selling programs is vastly different from the old-timer who depended solely upon personal friendship for his sales success or the drummer who got out of town as rapidly as possible after making a sale.

Personal selling is important to the entire economy as well as to the individual business enterprise. According to the U.S. Bureau of the Census about 10 percent of the total labor force in the United Sates is engaged in sales work.

Special types of salesmen. To assist the salesman who takes orders and makes specific sales there are two types of special salesmen—the missionary salesman and the technical specialist. The *missionary salesman* works for a manufacturer to develop goodwill and generally stimulate demand on part of potential customers but normally does not take orders or make specific sales. He may assist with sales promotion programs or provide training assistance for a customer's sales force. The *detail man* who represents drug manufacturers and calls on physicians and others in the medical profession is one type of missionary salesman.

His responsibilities include promoting the company's reputation and the quality of its products along with providing information on new products and distributing professional samples.

The *technical specialist* usually has scientific or engineering training and knowledge of an enterprise's products so that he can talk with the customer's technical personnel. He may provide information or solutions to particular problems and suggest special applications of equipment or products which will be helpful to the customer. The technical specialist is usually called in by the regular salesman after a particular problem or condition has been discovered.

In order to develop an effective sales force, management must provide programs for selecting, training, compensating, and controlling its salesmen. Salesmen need to work closely with others in the marketing department to relate sales activities to the other promotional activities and the marketing mix of the enterprise.

Advertising

Enterprises serving wide markets must carry on at least some of their promotional activities on a broad basis if they are to achieve mass distribution. Therefore, advertising becomes an important selling tool. *Advertising* is the communication of a group message by an identified sponsor regarding a good, service, or idea. Through advertising it is possible to communicate ideas about a product to many persons simultaneously using media such as newspapers, television, direct mail, magazines, radio, or outdoor advertisements.

While advertising is less direct and less flexible than personal selling, it has the advantage of lower cost per customer contacted. Also, advertising may impart information to the potential customer which will cause him to seek out the product or to be in a more responsive mood when contacted personally by a salesman. Thus, advertising can provide support for the personal selling program of the enterprise.

Advertising reaches individuals who may be inaccessible to salesmen. Even though a salesman cannot get an appointment with an executive or consumer, the advertisement can reach the desk or home to convey its sales message.

Advertising by a manufacturer can strengthen the position of its dealers, attract new dealers, or enable the business enterprise to enter new geographic or customer markets.

The introduction of a new product usually includes advertising as part of the promotion campaign to inform and interest potential customers. Such campaigns may also be used to increase sales of a product through more frequent replacement, such as motor oil changes, or to lengthen the selling season, such as encouraging consumers to buy flowers at other times than holidays or special occasions.

Product and institutional advertising. Advertising may be classified as product or institutional. *Product advertising* has a message which has the objective of providing information and selling a specific good or service. *Institutional advertising* seeks to develop goodwill for the business enterprise or an industry rather than directly selling a particular product. Institutional advertising's objective is to improve the long-term relationships with the various publics with whom the enterprise has contact.

Product advertising may be aimed at developing a consumer demand for a general product rather than a specific brand, especially in the introduction phase of a product's life cycle. Thus, in the early stages of color television the appropriate theme for advertising campaigns by RCA, the pioneer of today's color television system, was upon the general idea of color television instead of black and white.

In the growth and maturity stages of the product life cycle the emphasis of product advertising normally turns to the promotion of a specific brand. In the growth stage of color television RCA, Zenith, Magnavox, and other manufacturers tended to stress the merits of their own brands. RCA emphasized its long experience in color television. Zenith emphasized handcrafting in its chassis. Magnavox stressed its hand-finished cabinet quality and design. And Motorola advertised its pull-out parts panel for ease and economy of repair in the consumer's home.

As the product life cycle matures and reaches its saturation or sales decline phase, the advertising may turn to reminder advertising which reinforces the product in the customer's mind. An enterprise with a dominant industry position may use this type of advertising to maintain its market position.

Institutional advertising may be used on a local level by businesses or institutions to develop the community's confidence in the enterprise. For example, banks and savings and loan associations often use institutional advertising to create an image of strength and integrity without promoting a specific service. Large worldwide corporations may use institutional advertising to emphasize the quality and research behind all their products. General Motors Corporation uses the GM "Mark of

Excellence" in much of its advertising, and the General Electric Company uses the phrase "Progress Is Our Most Important Product" as part of their institutional advertising. At times an advertising campaign may contain elements of both product and institutional advertising.

Institutional advertising can also be used to counteract negative publicity or consumer reaction to a particular event. For example, one oil company, wishing to counter negative public opinion of the oil industry stemming from oil discharges from tanker ships which polluted beaches, ran a series of television advertisements stressing the many positive things their company does which protect or enhance the environment.

Cost of advertising

The total advertising bill for a product can be very high. A single-page ad or a minute network television spot may cost thousands of dollars. However, the millions of people who may be influenced by the enterprise's message provide justification for large advertising expenditures. In most cases it would be prohibitively expensive to contact this number of individual prospects by company salesmen. When the cost of mass media advertising is calculated on the basis of the circulation of magazines or newspapers, or the number of viewers or listeners for television or radio, the cost of advertising becomes reasonable. Although it is difficult to measure its effectiveness, mass media advertising does represent an economical means of reaching those who purchase consumer goods to inform, persuade, and remind them of the advantages of the advertiser's product. Many professional advertising agencies, both independent and associated with the different media, are available to assist the marketing manager in devising ads which will be effective in reaching potential customers.

Spending on advertising

Figure 12–3 shows the amount of advertising expenditures as a percentage of sales for several major industry groups. Although in total dollars the expenditure for advertising is great, generally advertising spending is relatively small when compared to sales. For example, automobile manufacturers spent over $500 million for advertising in 1967, but this amounted to only about 1 percent of sales dollars. For all manufacturing industries in 1967 only about 1.4 percent of sales was spent

FIGURE 12–3
Expenditures for advertising in selected industries, 1967, expressed as percent of sales

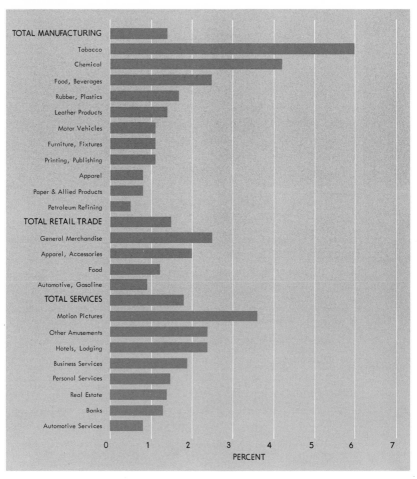

Source: U.S. Treasury Department.

for advertising. In contrast to a cost of from 1 to 3 percent of sales for advertising, many enterprises spend in excess of 10 percent of sales for personal selling.

The trend in total advertising expenditures over the years by medium is shown in Figure 12–4. Total spending on advertising over this period of time has increased from about $6 billion to almost $20 billion. During this 20-year period this has amounted to about 2.2 percent of Gross National Product annually.

FIGURE 12–4
Advertising expenditures by medium

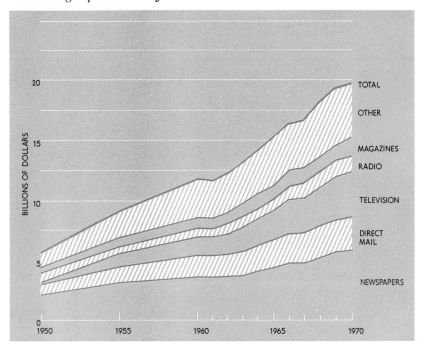

Source: *Marketing/Communications,* February, 1971 (prepared by McCann-Erickson).

Advertising media

The marketing manager can select from a variety of advertising media. The most widely used media include newspapers, television, direct mail, magazines, radio, and outdoor advertising.

Newspapers. Newspapers provide a flexible and timely medium which can be used to provide coverage in a specific city or trade territory. Newspaper advertising can be inserted on short notice and used for the length of time needed. It is adaptable to local conditions, and the costs per prospect are relatively low, based on the newspaper's circulation.

Television. Television is the newest and fastest growing of major advertising media. It appeals to both the eye and the ear of the potential consumer. Television can be geared to a geographic market or to a particular time during the day or evening when a desired segment of the target customers is most likely to be watching television. Its message can be put in a personal way, and elaborate production possibilities are limited only by the creative abilities of those producing the ad and the budget of the advertiser. Television advertising is relatively expensive unless large audiences who react favorably to its message are reached.

Direct mail. Direct mail can reach the exact market which an advertiser desires and therefore may be highly selective. Its copy and form of presentation are flexible. While direct mail is costly on the basis of prospects reached, it has the advantage of going into the hands of interested customers, provided the mailing list is current and focused on the proper target customers.

Magazines. Magazines can reach nationwide markets with a relatively low cost per prospect, or regional editions may be used for more limited geographic coverage. Specialized magazines and trade journals can reach audiences who represent clear-cut prospects for the advertiser's product. High-quality printing and color reproduction are possible in magazine advertisements. To the extent that a magazine may be reread or saved the advertisement has a longer life than is true of most other media.

Radio. Radio advertising has the advantage of saturation coverage for a limited geographic area or for wider coverage on the networks. Most stations have program formats which cater to audiences with specific characteristics. Although the radio ad's message and life are brief, it can be repeated a number of times during an advertising campaign at a relatively low cost.

Outdoor signs. Outdoor advertising when properly placed reaches a large number of people and therefore is generally used for products which have a wide market. The outdoor ad's message must be short. Details cannot be communicated effectively. A particular advertisement's cost may be relatively low per person contacted, but the cost of placing these ads over a wide geographic territory can be high. Outdoor advertising is often used effectively to attract consumers to tourist facilities and to give information to travelers.

Sales promotion

Sales promotion acts as a link between personal selling and advertising to make each more effective. Personal selling aims at specific customers, and advertising is directed at large numbers of potential consumers. The function of sales promotion is to fill the gap between these extremes by focusing selling efforts on selected small groups. Targets of sales promotion efforts are the enterprise's own salesmen, whole-salers, retailers, and consumers. Sales promotion includes preparing displays and other sales aids, developing material for training salesmen, and conducting contests and premium programs for customers. The key to good sales promotion is flexibility and ingenuity to meet new problems in improving the effectiveness of personal selling and advertising. In this respect, sales promotion may be carried on by either the sales force or the advertising department or may be handled by a separate group of individuals who act in a staff capacity to assist in better marketing programs.

Total promotion mix

Different combinations of personal selling, advertising, and sales promotion efforts may be effective in successfully marketing a particular product. One type of promotional activity may be increased or used to the reduction or exclusion of some other type of promotion. For example, consumers can be reached through both personal selling and advertising. If an enterprise uses little advertising probably it will have to rely heavily upon personal selling. The Fuller Brush Company spends very little for advertising, but each product in its line is sold personally by door-to-door salesmen who make use of sales promotion samples and small catalogs. On the other hand, the tobacco companies have large advertising budgets and make almost no use of personal selling in promoting their brands of cigarettes. Avon Products has introduced television advertising to support its door-to-door personal selling campaign for cosmetics. One of the key marketing problems for any enterprise is the determination of which combination of promotional efforts is best for its products.

Pricing

Pricing is one of the major elements in the marketing of an enterprise's product. Price directly affects both the sales volume of the enterprise and its profit picture. However, the degree of control exercised by a particular management over the prices charged for its products varies widely. At one extreme are sellers who exercise virtually no control over the price received for their goods. In these cases of pure competition the marketer accepts the going market price and is not able to influence price through any action which he may take. There are few examples in industry approximating this situation, but the American farmer who raises such standardized commodities as wheat can recognize his marketing position here.

At the other extreme is the seller who acts as a monopolist who can establish his own selling price since he is the only supplier of a particular good or service. Here, too, examples in American economic life are difficult to find since our national policy is to limit the monopolist. Where natural monopolies do exist, as in the case of public utilities, the prices charged customers are regulated by public commissions where the objective is to provide a fair return to the enterprise for providing the service and yet to protect consumers by keeping rates within reasonable limits.

Someplace between these extremes of pure competition and monopoly lies the pricing situation of most enterprises in American industry. Varying degrees of imperfect competition lead to a wide variety both of pricing practices and emphasis upon price and nonprice competition.

Practical pricing considerations

Economists have outlined important theoretical foundations underlying pricing in industry. With the acquisition of more knowledge about the American marketplace and the use of high-speed computers, marketing managers increasingly are improving their pricing decisions. However, in most instances the manager in the individual business enterprise still does not have the detailed knowledge of the market situation necessary to construct a sophisticated price structure model. Therefore, there are several practical pricing considerations which should be taken into account by marketers. These include consumer demand, importance of nonprice competition, costs, stage of the product's life cycle, and government controls.

Consumer demand

Ideally the marketing manager would know how important the price of his product is to the consumer in relation to other factors such as quality, service, reliability, and effective sales promotion. Sometimes price is an important determinant of consumer demand. When changes in the price of a good result in substantial changes in consumer demand the good is said to have a high degree of *elasticity of demand*. When price changes bring about little or no change in demand for a product the good has *inelasticity of demand*. An example of a good with a relatively high degree of demand elasticity would be beefsteak. When the price of steak goes up many people switch from the consumption of steak to other types of meats, including roasts and hamburger. As the price of steak declines these same consumers switch back to steak. The classic example of a product which has price inelasticity of demand is table salt. Most people would not use more salt even if the price were reduced substantially, neither would they decrease their consumption of salt if the price were doubled or tripled.

There are three tests which may be applied to determine the general nature of elasticity of demand for a product. Generally the demand elasticity is greater when numerous substitutes are available, when the product is considered to be a luxury good and can be dispensed with fairly easily, and when the good makes up a large part of the consumer's total expenditures, such as the purchase of a new home.

Importance of nonprice competition

As with other factors influencing the pricing decision in the business enterprise, estimates of consumer demand and reactions to price changes are only one consideration in the marketing process and have to be weighed along with other relevant factors. Where there is a tendency in an industry toward uniformity of price, market share is determined largely through sales promotion efforts, quality and service competition, and fashion. Such nonprice competition may reduce the importance of the pricing decision.

In the tobacco industry the chief emphasis for cigarette sales success is upon nonprice competition through advertising since prices of different brands of cigarettes are essentially the same. An attempt is made by each manufacturer to distinguish his product in the mind of the consumer from other competing tobacco products. This is done mainly by advertising which appeals to the emotions.

Although price is probably an important marketing consideration with such products as refrigerators, washers, and dryers, quality and service are also important nonprice sales considerations. Such brand names as Maytag, Cadillac, Texaco, Omega watches, and Hart Shaffner & Marx call forth an image of either quality or service which reduces the importance of price as a competitive marketing technique.

Fashion is the style of a particular product which happens to be popular at a given time. Improved methods of communication and better use of advertising media have contributed to an increased emphasis on fashion. Alert purchasing and selling efforts by retailers are necessary when fashion is an important factor in their merchandise lines since out-of-fashion goods may be difficult to dipose of unless large price markdowns are made with resulting reduced profit margins. Today's consumer is more fashion minded, and the recognition of this is an important aspect of consumer goods marketing. To the extent that an enterprise can emphasize the fashion aspect of its products the less important price becomes.

Costs

One of the most obvious considerations in pricing is the cost associated with producing and distributing the goods and services of the business enterprise. As a generalization over the long run the manager must cover all his costs of doing business if he is to avoid operating at a loss. In fact, in order to generate profits for the business enterprise it is necessary that all the businessman's costs be covered and that there be some revenue remaining for profit. The student is reminded of the discussion of the importance of profits in Chapter 4 and of the terminology developed there.

While it is easy to state that all costs should be covered over the long run in pricing decisions, the application of cost analysis to immediate or short-run pricing decisions is considerably more complicated. One difficulty in taking costs into account is that the total cost involved in producing and distributing a product includes a variety of different types of costs. Costs vary depending upon such factors as the quantity of goods produced, the nature of fixed and variable costs, expenditures for research and development, and the amount spent for sales promotion. The problems involved in the determination of costs for pricing decisions have led to the development of cost accounting systems which provide valuable information about production and distribution costs. A discussion of the ways in which costs vary and the analysis of costs is covered in the chapters on Production and Control. An important responsibility of the marketing department is to provide top management with information regarding probable consumer reaction to different price schedules which can be used with production and distribution cost data in determining price quotations.

Stage of the product life cycle

A range of pricing strategies may be used in the business enterprise depending upon the pricing considerations discussed above and the stage of the product's life cycle. Skimming the cream and market penetration represent two extremes in pricing strategy.

Skimming the cream pricing. A policy of *skimming the cream* results in setting a price at the high end of the possible range of prices for a product. Such a policy is likely to be most effective with a distinctive product in the introduction stage of its life cycle or for products where nonprice competition is important. Early in the product's life the demand for it will probably be less elastic with respect to price and competition not as intensive as later. High prices at the introduction stage may generate greater profits which can be used to cover development costs and provide a reserve for a later stage when expanding the market may necessitate lowering the price. Also, if a mistake is made in initial pricing of a new product it is much easier to lower the price than to raise it once the product is on the market. As the product moves through its life cycle, the cream skimming strategy can be used in a series of planned price reductions to broaden the market thereby increasing sales and meeting price competition.

Market penetration pricing. In *market penetration pricing* the initial price is set relatively low in order to achieve mass market acceptance quickly. This strategy can be successful if demand for the product is highly sensitive to price and if the business enterprise is likely to face considerable competition as soon as the product is introduced. Also, in some cases lower costs per unit of production can be achieved when a large volume of goods is produced. This is especially true of products which have high fixed costs that can be spread over volume production. An enterprise which has a large investment in plant and equipment or which has spent large sums in product development might profit from mass marketing early in the product life cycle. Also, a low price initially may give the product's developer a degree of acceptance in the market which will help him meet competition better in the future.

Government controls

In some instances prices charged by a business enterprise are directly controlled by a governmental body. This is especially true with public utilities where rates to be charged for service within a state are established by state regulatory commissions. Interstate utility services are governed by federal government agencies. Governments also directly affect prices when they buy goods from business enterprises. In many instances contracts for government purchases are let on the basis of competitive bidding, or profits may be limited by some form of cost plus a fixed fee or percentage of the contract.

For goods and services purchased by individual and business consumers there is a body of legislation, which has evolved since before the turn of the century, setting the ground rules to which business practices must conform. This legislation includes the Clayton Act and the Robinson-Patman Act, which were discussed in Chapter 2. Generally price fixing by enterprises in an industry is illegal as is the division of markets, bid rigging, and other forms of activity which seek to restrain competition. It is unlawful to practice price discrimination among different purchasers of products in interstate markets of similar grade and quality where the result may tend to injure competition. Differences in price must be based on cost differences or because of competition. Some governmental attempts have been made to prevent large enterprises from setting prices too low so as to drive out smaller competitors. The fear here is that once competition has been reduced or eliminated prices will be increased by big business perhaps even higher than those which prevailed before the predatory price cutting.

Place

Place is an important dimension of the marketing mix since it includes the factors which relate to providing time and place utility to satisfy customers. Place decisions have to be made regarding channels of distribution for a product and the transportation and storage systems needed for goods to reach consumers. Services as well as goods have place considerations.

Channels of distribution

Channels of distribution determine the route which a product takes from the producer to the ultimate consumer or industrial user. Thus, channels of distribution include those enterprises and individuals which are active in the transactions associated with the movement of goods or the provision of services. Channels include the producer and the final customer along with any middlemen who are involved in the transfer of title to the goods. Although enterprises such as railroads, trucklines, airlines, banks, and insurance companies render services in moving goods from producers to consumers they are not included as institutions in the channels of distribution for a product unless they have a significant direct role in the transactions between buyer and seller.

Channels for industrial users. Channels of distribution vary depending partially upon the nature of the customer. Frequently goods for industrial users will be marketed directly by the producer to the user. In some instances a middleman may take title to industrial goods and in turn sell them to industrial users. Figure 12–5 illustrates typical channels for products of industrial users.

FIGURE 12–5
Channels of distribution for industrial products

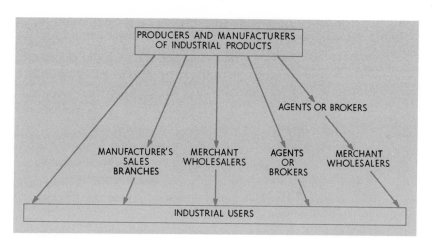

Channels for ultimate consumers. Channels of distribution for goods to ultimate consumers vary considerably in their complexity. The most simple channel is from the manufacturer of goods directly to the consumer. More complicated channels of distribution include one or more middlemen between the producer and the consumer. Figure 12–6 illustrates the range of channels for consumer products.

Institutions of distribution—wholesalers

Wholesalers are middlemen who normally sell to industrial users or to retailers. There are three principal types of middlemen which are used by manufacturers to distribute their products to retailers or indus-

FIGURE 12–6
Channels of distribution for consumer products

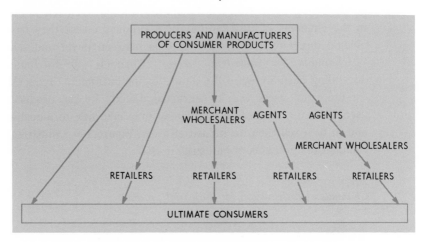

trial users. These are the merchant wholesaler, manufacturer's sales branch, and the agent or broker. In making the decision as to which system is best for distribution of his products the manufacturer must analyze the alternatives in view of the nature of his product, the services he will provide, and the customers he wishes to reach.

The *merchant wholesaler* performs several important functions for the manufacturer. He purchases merchandise from manufacturers and thereby takes title to the goods and assumes the risks associated with selling them. The merchant wholesaler stores the product, delivers it to retail or industrial customers, handles the collection of accounts, and may provide service facilities and sales promotions for the product line.

The importance of the merchant wholesaler's activites varies with the product and the customer serviced. For example, a manufacturer may find a merchant wholesaler desirable if his product is bulky and requires regular deliveries and extensive servicing or repair. Also, if the retail or industrial customers are small, numerous, and need extensive credit arranged, the services provided by the wholesaler would be useful.

Jobbers, drop shippers, and cash-and-carry wholesalers are other types of wholesalers which normally take title to goods as they move through the channel of distribution but usually do not provide all the services performed by the merchant wholesaler.

If the product is complicated and requires considerable technical knowledge or is not widely known, a merchant wholesaler which sells a broad product line from many manufacturers may not be a wise choice. Under these circumstances a *manufacturer's sales branch* or office may be more desirable for the producer. These sales branches are owned and operated by manufacturers separate from their factories and may or may not carry inventories from which orders are shipped directly. If no inventories are carried at the sales offices then they are merely places out of which the manufacturer's salesmen and service personnel may operate. This means of distributing a product at the wholesale level enables the manufacturer to control the selection of retail or industrial customers and permits the manufacturer to maintain close contact with his dealers. When sales branches are established by manufacturers, the producer performs the functions of storage, shipping, credit financing, and servicing.

Agents and *brokers* constitute the third class of wholesale middlemen. The distinguishing characteristic of agents and brokers is that they customarily do not take title to goods but negotiate the purchase or sale of merchandise. For this service they are paid on a fee or commission basis. In many instances they represent specialized product lines such as is the case with processed foods brokers, livestock commission men, or building supplies manufacturers' agents. The agent does not normally perform many of the risk-taking functions of either the merchant wholesaler or the sales branch. However, customarily the agent or broker is in close communication with potential customers and is able to provide good information on the state of the market for the goods at any time. This also permits the manufacturer to avoid the expense of developing a sales force and enables a large area to be covered through the selection of a network of independent sales agents in various parts of the country.

Institutions of distribution—retailers

Retailers are enterprises which sell goods and services to the ultimate consumer. This puts the retailer in a key position to test consumer acceptance of the product, its price, and to provide necessary service to the customer to assist him in making his purchase.

No longer can retailers be easily classified as department stores, mail-order stores, specialty shops, grocery stores, or by some other title depending upon the merchandise offered for sale and the services provided to customers. Retailing classification systems have been blurred with the development of discount houses and with supermarkets and drugstores diversifying their lines of merchandise so as to appear as small department stores. Today retailing ranges from highly impersonal vending machine selling to small, specialty shops dealing in luxury merchandise with much personal service. Some manufacturers such as Firestone, Pittsburgh Plate Glass, Singer, Rexall, and Van Heusen are moving into the retail field with their own stores designed to serve the consumer directly.

What kind of retailing will prevail in the future American economy? Obviously no one has the final answers. As new products are brought onto the market and as consumer wants and shopping habits change, the retailer must meet the challenge. In the past 20 years retailing methods have changed dramatically beginning with the advent of discount houses, then shopping centers, and now the enclosed shopping malls. The retailer who is capable of sensing new ways to fulfill consumer wants will be the one who will prosper. Those retail institutions where no imagination or creative marketing is used will likely fade from the American scene or at best linger in the shadows of retailers who are able to meet aggressively the problems posed in today's markets.

Functions performed in channels

In recent years there has been a tendency in some markets to reduce the number of middlemen between the producer and ultimate consumer.

However, there are certain marketing functions which must be performed in moving goods from producers to consumers. If one institution in the channel of distribution does not perform or bear the cost of a particular function then someone else must do so. Wholesalers perform the economic function of storage, imparting time and place utility to goods. The wholesaler usually buys and sells in larger quantities than does the retailer. For example, a food wholesaler purchases canned goods by the carload and sells to the grocery stores in case lots with the retailer selling to the housewife in quantities as small as a single can of food. Other marketing functions to be performed include transporting, grading or sorting, financing, and risk taking by holding title to the goods. When some middleman is bypassed or eliminated from the channel of distribution, either the manufacturer, remaining middlemen (if any), or consumer must perform or share the cost of these functions.

Marketing functions can be shifted forward or backward in the channel of distribution or shared but not eliminated. In deciding which channels to use the choice should be treated as a system of action to reduce costs and improve service for the benefit of consumers as well as business.

Physical distribution

Physical distribution in marketing consists of moving and handling goods through channels of distribution. For goods to have possession utility they must be moved to a location where they are available to the consumer at the proper time. The physical distribution system includes the transportation of goods and their storage.

The transportation of goods is critical in our interdependent society. The importance of transportation to business and consumers is highlighted during a major truck or railroad strike. Transportation systems are so important to our society that some economists have traced the economic development of the United States by analyzing the growth of new means of transportation over the years. In selecting a form of transportation for his product, today's manager can choose among railroads, trucks, waterways, pipelines, and airlines.

Railroads. As Figure 12–7 indicates, railroads carry more intercity freight than any other single means of transportation in the United States. Railroads are well suited for long hauls of products which are bulky and have a low value relative to their weight. Coal, steel, and building materials are examples of products which railroads can haul economically and efficiently.

Railroads have faced stiff competition from other forms of transportation in recent years in the movement of less bulky, more costly freight which has been considered more profitable to carry. To meet this competition, mainly from trucks, railroads have provided a number of services and special features to serve the needs of specific types of shippers. For example, when faced with the loss of the shipping of new cars from auto assembly plants to dealers the railroads designed a triple-deck car carrier which won back a considerable amount of this business from truck transport operators. With the new subcompact American automobiles coming onto the scene the railroads devised a carrier which would stack these minicars vertically so more can be carried per freight car than by the traditional horizontal stacking method.

Another innovation in recent years by railroads is "piggyback" service, where loaded truck trailers are carried on railroad flatcars. The transported goods can be packed at the shipper's site and not handled again until they are unloaded at the buyer's freight dock. This provides additional flexibility for the railroads since the loaded truck trailers can be driven directly to the buyer's location even if he is not on a rail siding. Also, with less handling the goods are not exposed to as much

FIGURE 12–7

Freight traffic by mode of transportation, 1969

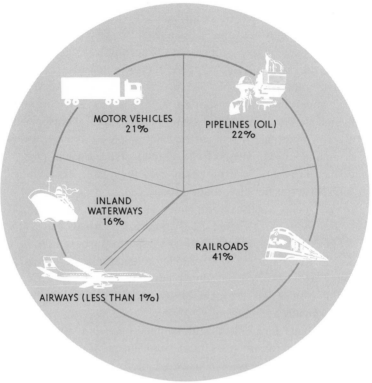

Source: Interstate Commerce Commission, *1970 Annual Report.*

risk of damage or theft. For long hauls across the country the cost of this piggyback service may be less than sending the goods by highway freight.

Trucks. Truck transportation has more than doubled its proportionate share of freight carried over the past 30 years. Based on distance and weight of goods carried, over 20 percent of intercity freight is now carried by trucks. This growth has been achieved because of the flexibility of trucking operations, the improvement in the nation's highway system, and truck freight rates that are competitive with railroads. The trucker can pick up goods at the shipper's dock and deliver them directly to the buyer's location. The railroads can do this only if both parties are on railroad sidings unless piggyback service is used.

Waterways. The coastal and inland waterways in the United States are used by ship and barge traffic to haul a considerable amount of bulky, nonperishable products such as mineral ore, sand, coal, cement, and petroleum products. Water transportation is the cheapest method of moving goods but also is the slowest, and some waterways are closed by ice in the winter.

Improvements have been made in recent years in water transport with the development of containerization with ships designed to take standard-size containers directly from freight cars or trucks without repackaging. "Fishyback" service using truck trailers similar to rail piggyback service has been developed to increase the flexibility of water transportation.

Pipelines. Pipelines are used primarily to carry products such as crude oil and natural gas. While water transportation is less costly for refined petroleum products, pipelines are used extensively for natural gas and to carry oil from the fields to refineries.

Airlines. Airlines are the newest, fastest, and most expensive means of transportation. Although air freight rates are lower now than just a few years ago, the fact that they are still considerably higher than rail or truck rates has caused the airlines and their shippers to analyze the total cost of physical distribution in justifying this type of transportation.

The speed of air transportation has resulted in opening up new markets for products which are fragile or perishable. Orchids and other tropical flowers can be shipped from Hawaii to the mainland, electronics parts can be less expensively packaged, and inventories can be reduced as the result of speedy availability through use of the air transport medium. Although the volume of air freight is now small in relation to the total amount of goods moved in this country, this means of transportation should be considered by managements interested in improving their physical distribution system.

Storage. The storage function is the holding of goods from the time they are produced until their final use. For the business enterprise this involves a system of warehousing, materials handling, and order processing.

Warehousing. Warehousing, or physical storage of goods, may be done by the manufacturer, wholesaler, or retailer. While most of these business enterprises have some type of storage space, the ownership of warehouse space is an added cost of doing business. Unless there is a continuing need for permanent warehouse space, the business enterprise may find it desirable to rent space in a public warehouse.

Public warehouses are located rather widely across the country and overseas. Their function is to provide storage space along with numerous services associated with storage to public customers. These warehouses generally are prepared to receive goods in large quantities and can repackage goods into smaller quantities for subsequent shipment to customers. A public warehouse may assist in the financing of inventories held by them by issuing a warehouse receipt that can be used as security for a loan from a bank. The public warehouse company assumes responsibility for damage or loss of goods placed under its custody. Storage facilities for perishables and agricultural commodities are maintained by some public warehouses.

Materials handling. The efficient movement of goods into warehouse facilities, their placement, storage, and subsequent removal from the warehouse provide a challenge for materials handlers. The handling of materials is a major part of storage cost.

As a generalization, the movement of goods in a vertical plane is more expensive than horizontal movement. Therefore, the older warehouses consisting of several floors connected by slow-moving freight elevators are being replaced with new one-story warehouses.

All kinds of mechanization are being applied to materials handling including forklift trucks, conveyor belts, and hydraulic ramps to make unloading and loading easier. The use of pallets, wooden racks which can hold a number of boxes or items for easy storage or movement as a unit, is widespread in warehousing today. Some grocery and drug warehouse operators are moving forward with automated order-filling and radio-controlled equipment for greater efficiency. Enterprises are beginning to use containerized packaging of standard sizes which can be more easily handled, stored, and transported.

Order processing. Once an order from a customer has been received it must be processed. Processing includes the flow of paperwork covering the transaction and the physical shipment of goods. Order processing should be done as accurately and expeditiously as possible to maintain customer goodwill. Mistakes in order handling or delayed shipments can undo the favorable image of the enterprise and its product which has been created by earlier steps in the marketing mix.

Organization of the marketing department

When an enterprise adopts the marketing concept of business it emphasizes the profitable fulfillment of consumer wants. This means much more than just changing the organization structure of the sales force. Perhaps the most important aspect of applying the marketing concept is in orienting the thinking of all personnel to improved customer service. Once top management has accepted the marketing concept of business there are certain functions that should be performed in the marketing system.

The top marketing executive should report directly to the chief operating officer of the enterprise, which usually means either the president or executive vice president. Figure 12–8 shows a partial organization

FIGURE 12–8
Partial organization chart of a marketing department

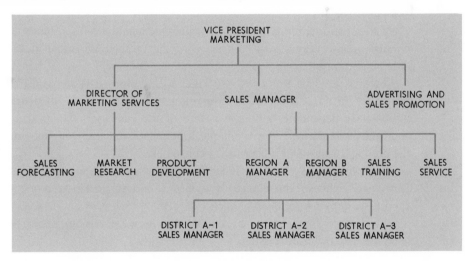

chart of a marketing department. Each manager will have responsibility for certain functions and subordinates depending upon the size and needs of the enterprise.

Pricing and arrangements for transportation services may be carried out within the marketing system. Frequently pricing decisions are made by top management in consultation with marketing personnel.

Summary

The marketing program of a business enterprise can be thought of as being composed of four variables which constitute the marketing mix. These variables are Product, Promotion, Price, and Place. They all focus on the consumer, which is consistent with the marketing concept of business.

New products are the lifeblood of many business enterprises since the typical product life cycle reaches a peak after which profitability and then sales begin to decline.

Consumer products may be classified as convenience goods, shopping goods, and specialty goods. Consumer buying habits for each group of these products differ.

Promotion consists of personal selling, advertising, and sales promotion. Advertising is the process by which the enterprise's marketing message is communicated to potential consumers through a visual or oral medium. Sales promotion acts as a link between personal selling and advertising.

Pricing considerations include consumer demand, the importance of nonprice competition, costs, the stage of the product life cycle at the time, and government controls.

Channels of distribution, transportation, and storage systems all relate to the factor of place in the marketing mix. The channels of distribution vary depending upon the nature of the customer, the product, and who is to perform the economic functions associated with moving the product from the producer to the consumer.

Transportation systems include railroads, trucks, waterways, pipelines, and airlines. The choice of a means of transportation requires careful study by marketing managers.

The storage function includes a system of warehousing, materials handling, and order processing.

The marketing department is an important part of the business system and functions to fulfill consumer wants resulting in a profit for the enterprise.

Terms for review

marketing mix	sales promotion
product life cycle	nonprice competition
convenience goods	skimming the cream pricing
shopping goods	market penetration pricing
speciality goods	channels of distribution
personal selling	wholesaler
advertising	retailer

Questions

1. Interview a retail store manager in your area to determine what products his store now sells that were not on the market five years ago. How would you classify these new products based on consumers' buying habits?

2. *a*) Based on Figure 12–2 what are the implications for the enterprise which does not market new products?

   b) How does the nature of the product line influence the need for new products?

   c) Give examples of products which have different length product life cycles.

3. Evaluate the relative importance of the 4 *P*'s for small specialty shops and large department stores as they compete in the same enclosed shopping mall.

4. What long-term changes may occur in the consumers' shopping habits as the result of the development of the enclosed shopping mall? What are the implications for the older, established retailers in downtown locations?

5. Select examples of product and institutional advertising which you found appealing. What made these ads effective for you? Give an example of how your buying behavior for a particular item was influenced by advertising.

6. By examining the nature of the promotion program for a product, try to determine the general nature of the pricing strategy being followed by the retailer or manufacturer. To what extent is nonprice competition a factor in selling the product you selected for study?

7. Comment on the following quotation by a manager of a discount store in a suburban location: "We have eliminated the wholesale middleman and buy direct from the manufacturer. Since we do our own warehousing and servicing we are able to pass these savings on to the consumer." How would you test the manager's statement?

8. After a study of materials available in the library, write a 300-word paper either supporting or opposing the statement that advertising simply adds to the cost of goods without adding to the value received by consumers.

BUSINESS BRIEFS

"Avon calling"

Since World War II American retailing has changed from emphasis on downtown department store selling to the discount house, to the suburban shopping center, to the enclosed shopping mall. Now there is an increased interest by business enterprises in direct selling in the customer's home.

Door-to-door selling has long been a part of the American retail scene. Fuller brushes and Electrolux vacuum cleaners (both now owned by Consolidated Foods) are familiar products to many housewives. Avon Products is the world's largest manufacturer of cosmetics and toiletries. Avon has added costume jewelry which is sold directly in the customer's home to its product line. Avon sales more than doubled from 1965 to 1970 and so did profits. Encyclopedias and other books and magazines are widely sold on an in-home basis. Tupperware (part of Dart Industries) effectively utilizes neighborhood gatherings of housewives, called Tupperware parties, to sell its kitchenware and other products. Other retailers are also using the idea of neighborhood hostesses where company representatives display and demonstrate a variety of products.

1. How do you account for the continued success and growth of in-home selling?

2. Why will consumers permit strangers to come into their homes to extol the virtues of products ranging from cosmetics to vacuum cleaners?

3. What types of goods are particularly suited for direct sale in the customer's home?

Baskin-Robbins ice cream

While many merchants are finding consumers to be price conscious, one ice cream shop chain is thriving on a premium-priced product. Baskin-Robbins ice cream stores, a franchise chain with home offices in California, has more than 900 shops across the United States. In 1970 sales were $52 million, up 30 percent over 1969. This chain now sells more "hard" ice cream than any other chain-shop operation—including Howard Johnson's.

Baskin-Robbins shops carry at least 31 flavors of ice cream and sherbet with such exotic names as Blueberry Marshmallow Ribbon, Berry Berry Good, and Mango Sherbet. Flavors are changed frequently with several new ones being introduced monthly throughout the year. Although many new ice cream flavors are concocted each year in the company's research laboratory, only a handful are deemed appealing enough to be marketed across the country.

Unlike other ice cream chains which also sell coffee, sandwiches, and other snack items, Baskin-Robbins stores sell only ice cream. Their ice cream is of high quality, with some flavors containing twice as much butterfat as the minimum federal standard. All Baskin-Robbins ice creams are made with fresh cream.

Prices for Baskin-Robbins ice cream range from 15 cents a scoop up (depending on the store's location) to 65 cents a hand-packed pint. In contrast some supermarkets sell ice cream for as little as 69 cents per half gallon.

1. How do you account for the success of Baskin-Robbins despite the relatively high price of their product?
2. How important do you think that location would be for a Baskin-Robbins ice cream store in a community?
3. What advantages would a Baskin-Robbins retail franchise have over a local ice cream shop selling a similar quality product?

CASES

The Sure-Cover Company

Jack Holby, marketing manager of the Sure-Cover Company, listened as members of the company's marketing committee discussed a new type of wallpaper which was being considered for marketing.

Jack realized that there was a temptation to grab at this new product as a possible solution to the company's declining sales. Sure-Cover, a major producer of wallpaper, had been able to maintain its share of that market in recent years. However, the total industry sales had been steadily declining, despite rising construction of new homes and additions. The reason for this was the increasing use of paint as a substitute for wallpaper. Economy was apparently the chief consideration. The cost of having a professional apply wallpaper was not much greater than the cost of having a room painted. However, with the cost of professional application of both paint and paper rising, more home owners were turning to do-it-yourself projects. In almost every case, the do-it-yourself customers were using paint because of the mess associated with hanging wallpaper.

The new product now being considered consisted of the standard Sure-Cover line of paper with a pressure sensitive adhesive applied to the back. The paper was to be called "Ready-Stick."

"With this paper," Jerry Forbes of the product development department stated, "any amateur can do a professional job of paper hanging with little trouble or mess." Forbes also pointed out that, based on his conversations with personnel in production and purchasing, it was clear that production costs would run at least 50 percent higher than the cost of producing standard paper.

As Forbes concluded his remarks, Jack Holby reflected on some of the views which his subordinates, members of the marketing committee, had previously expressed concerning the new product. Although he was their superior, Holby realized that each of these men, because of his own experience and individual perspective, could contribute a great deal toward the effective solution of this top management problem.

Jack had discussed this problem with Tom Monroe, director of market research, a few days earlier. Tom's biggest concern was the reaction of customers to the price of Ready-Stick. If normal retail margins were allowed, the paper would have to be sold at $5 a roll compared to the $3 price on the standard roll. Past experience had shown that consumers are very responsive to changes in the price of wallpaper, partly because there is little preference for one brand over another. (Most consumers cannot even name a brand of wallpaper.) Furthermore, the price of Ready-Stick would seem even further out of line when compared with paint. The cost of standard wallpaper per square yard was already in excess of the cost of paint necessary to cover the same area. At a higher price, Ready-Stick would be more than double the cost of a comparable amount of paint.

Jack Holby shared Tom Monroe's concern over the high price of Ready-Stick and agreed that the consumer's reaction to this price would be an important determining factor in the product's success. He was not certain, however, that it was helpful to compare the price of Ready-Stick with the price of either standard paper or paint; he wondered whether either of these was a comparable substitute for Ready-Stick. Were there not features about Ready-Stick that would justify its higher price in the consumer's mind?

Tom Monroe went on to say that if the product were introduced, he believed it should be marketed through different retail outlets than those now being used. "Sure-Cover presently distributes their paper only through 5,000 stores which specialize in wallpaper. This provides for a rather limited exposure, especially as compared with paint which is sold through about 40,000 hardware stores as well as in most wallpaper stores. Since this is a new product it is important that it receive maximum exposure to the consumer."

Monroe recommended that the new product be sold through supermarkets. This, he explained, would provide the necessary exposure to the consumer. The high markup on wallpaper should be especially attractive to supermarkets. Furthermore, he thought the product would not seem "out of place," considering the increasing trend toward "scrambled merchandising" in supermarkets. Many supermarkets now carry nonfood lines ranging from cosmetics to lawn-mowers. Holby was intrigued by this idea; as he turned the idea over in his mind he tried to imagine how the purchase decision was normally made for this kind of product and whether the consumer would accept a supermarket as the place to buy it.

Holby had also talked recently with Bill Mason, director of advertising. Bill was enthusiastic about the product but said that it might require an entirely different promotion program than that being used for the standard line of paper. Bill pointed out that since brand preference among consumers was not significant, only a small proportion of the promotion budget had formerly been designated for consumer advertising. The average consumer tended to select the store and then select the paper from among those which were shown. For this reason, Sure-Cover had found that promotion efforts directed at the dealer had better results than those directed at the consumer. The dealer could be influenced to (1) stock the paper and (2) "push" the Sure-Cover brand, if he was convinced of the quality of the paper. Accordingly, more than 80 percent of the promotion budget was expended for trade journal advertising, mailers, catalogs, and samples, with the remainder being devoted to consumer advertising. Mason felt that this strategy would have to be revised considerably for Ready-Stick.

Paul Fiedler, the sales manager, saw possible problems in distributing the new product. If the Ready-Stick were marketed through the present dealers, he felt that they would not actively support it. "These dealers derive much of their income from the application of wallpaper," he explained. "They are not likely to be enthusiastic about a paper which does not require professional application." If alternative outlets were chosen, Fiedler also anticipated difficulties. "Almost all of our present sales are of paper which is applied professionally. If our present dealers feel that we are taking away from their sales by selling Ready-Stick through other outlets, there could be serious repercussions." He went on to emphasize that dealer support was essential to the sale of the firm's standard wallpaper. Even though Sure-Cover was a leader in the industry, this position depended upon the continued support of the dealers. Since brand recognition was lacking, a dealer would feel no necessity to retain the line if he felt that he was being treated unfairly.

Jack Holby turned his attention back to the discussion now taking place among the members of the marketing committee. Although he had had prior conversations with each man on this problem, this was the first opportunity for them to discuss it as a group. Jack realized that he would have to make a recommendation to the company president within the next few days as to whether the product should be produced. Furthermore, if the decision was made to introduce the Ready-Stick paper, he and his subordinates would have to develop a detailed plan for marketing the new product.

1. Would you recommend that Sure-Cover proceed with the production of Ready-Stick? Justify your recommendation.

2. If a decision were made to proceed with this product, recommend a program of promotion and distribution.

Mansfield National Bank

In October, 1970, Mr. Kenneth Wilcox, vice president of marketing and business development for Mansfield National Bank, was faced with the responsibility for developing a program to secure new individual accounts for the bank. He was also interested in analyzing the factors which had contributed to the bank's growth during the early months of its existence.

Mansfield National Bank was chartered on January 2, 1970, and shortly thereafter opened for business in temporary quarters just one block from where their permanent building was to be constructed. Mansfield National was located on the northwest edge of Mansfield in order to take advantage of the growing business and residential development in that part of the city of 150,000. Their new building was to be located directly across the street from a new multimillion dollar enclosed shopping mall.

As the result of an aggressive program which actually started before the bank opened, a number of commercial accounts were obtained from existing business enterprises in the area. An extensive program was initiated to secure the accounts of the major firms which had announced plans to locate in the new Parkwood Mall.

A special approach was used with the prospective mall accounts. Each company was researched, regardless of size, and a suitable format for approaching the management was outlined. In some cases the bank's executive vice president flew to the home office of the firm. In all cases telephone calls were made until the decision maker within the prospective customer's organization was reached. Follow-up letters were always written, giving additional information about the bank, the community, and making sincere offers to assist the firm or its employees as they encountered the difficulties involved in moving to a new community. In several instances managers were assisted in finding rental housing or in obtaining financing for homes.

Ninety percent of the 70 enterprises in the new mall opened accounts with Mansfield National. In most cases those firms on the mall which did not select Mansfield National Bank were those which had prior banking connections in the city through their other retail stores.

Arrangements were made with an out-of-town advertising agency to handle media advertising for the bank. The budget for all advertising, materials, and promotional items was set at $40,000 for the first 12 months of operations with $15,000 of this designated for grand opening expenses.

To develop individual accounts, both checking and savings accounts, the bank held a much publicized ribbon cutting and open house. The special emphasis in all promotion and advertising was the "Millionaire for a Day" contest, a weekly registration for four weeks giving away the interest on $1 million ($167.00) four different times. Over 3,000 persons registered in the bank's lobby during the promotion period. Some new accounts were generated, but the bank's management felt the real value of this promotion was the appeal through the media with a gimmick which was a very good attention-getter and a conversation starter.

As an adjunct to the opening of the Parkwood Mall the bank sponsored a special advance premier showing of the movie "Patton" at the new Parkwood Theatre on the mall. Letters were sent to all depositors and selected prospective customers offering free tickets on a first-come, first-served basis and the response was tremendous.

There were no service charges made by Mansfield National Bank on individual checking accounts provided a minimum balance of $200 was maintained monthly. A monthly service charge of $1 per account was made when the account fell below $200 but remained at least $100. The maximum service charge was $2 per month when the account fell below $100 any time during the month.

With the opening of general business operations on Parkwood Mall in late July, the bank's advertising program turned to more general messages with an emphasis on dynamic growth, loan funds, advantages of home-owned banking, and a national bank in northwest Mansfield. Advertising throughout late summer and early fall tended to be concentrated on radio because of its lower cost, although television and newspaper advertising were also employed.

As he sat at his desk, Mr. Wilcox reviewed some of the possibilities for the remainder of the bank's first year for acquiring new individual accounts. Mr. Wilcox knew that the new bank was the most convenient to several of the newest and most affluent residential areas in the city. Having made progress in developing commercial accounts, the bank's management was interested in building up a strong base of individual accounts. A summary of the bank's expenditures for promotion (Exhibit 1) to date indicated that $33,500 had already been spent of the original year's budget of $40,000. However, the bank's directors had authorized an increase in this amount so that up to $8,000 could be spent in the last two months of 1970.

EXHIBIT 1

Marketing expenditures, January–October, 1970

Advertising agency*	$ 5,000
Printing	2,000
Give-away items	3,500
Complementary advertising	2,000
Newspaper advertising	5,000
Television advertising	6,500
Radio advertising	7,500
Miscellaneous	2,000
Total	$33,500

* Includes advertising production costs and artwork.

The vice president jotted down the following notes as he contemplated the possible use of direct-mail promotion, radio-television-newspaper advertising, and use of premiums:

Direct mail—useful to zero in on particular persons or areas. Estimated cost per letter delivered is 45 cents for computer typed, individually addressed letter. Costs would be lower for less personalized approach. What pitch should be made to potential customers? What group of people should be concentrated on?

· · · · ·

Radio–Television–Newspaper advertising—would be more of a shotgun approach to promotion. What criteria should be used to evaluate effectiveness and relative costs? What balance between various types of media? What theme to use in ad program?

Radio time cost averages about $2.50 for each 30-second spot.

Television time cost averages about $30 for each 20-second spot, higher for prime time, lower during the day.

Newspaper ad space costs about $4 per column inch for combined evening and morning issues plus extra charge if ad runs in color.

· · · · ·

Premiums—reported in banking journal as a hot item for increasing bank business. Wide variety of premiums available. Typical cost estimates of various items:

Wigs	$9.00
Walnut bowls	3.50
Blankets	3.00
Ponchos	2.50
Holiday candles	1.50

Premium cost is usually held to about $3 unless for large savings accounts of several thousand dollars or unless the premium program extends over a period of time and subsequent premium items are also sold so as to cover part of the promotion's cost.

If we decide to use premiums should they be given for checking or savings accounts or both? What would the cost be per customer including media promotion expense? What would be the reaction of other bankers in the city? Should we use premiums for new or old customers or both? What would be the effect on the bank's image?

· · · · ·

New bank building—construction hopefully will begin before Christmas, slightly behind schedule. How important is the new building for increasing business? How can we obtain maximum public relations benefits from the entire construction cycle from ground breaking to ribbon cutting of the new building?

Mr. Wilcox knew that the bank's growth in total deposits to date had exceeded the directors' original expectations. However, he felt that there was a real need for increasing the number of individual accounts and for building up the proportion of the bank's time and savings deposits in relation to demand or checking deposits. Many banks have half of their deposits in time and savings deposits. Data relating to the bank's deposits are provided in Exhibits 2 and 3.

EXHIBIT 2

Number of deposit accounts
(as of dates indicated)

	Total accounts	Commercial accounts	Individual accounts
March 31, 1970	702	172	530
June 30, 1970	1,450	290	1,160
Sept. 30, 1970	1,980	360	1,620

EXHIBIT 3

Time, savings, and demand deposits
(as of dates indicated)

	Total deposits	Time and savings deposits	Demand (checking) deposits
March 31, 1970	$1,260,000	$ 410,000	$ 850,000
June 30, 1970	3,338,000	730,000	2,608,000
Sept. 30, 1970	4,550,000	1,110,000	3,440,000

1. Given $8,000 to spend in November and December on promotion, how would you allocate this amount among the different options available to the bank? Indicate the reasons for your recommendation and what objective could be achieved by your promotional choice.

2. Before a final decision is made on the promotion expenditures for the next two months what other information would be useful? How would you attempt to obtain this information?

3. How do you account for the bank's growth in the first nine months of its existence?

*The production of
consumer electronic
goods requires extensive
inspection and
calibration.*

13

Production

A person who wants a sports car is not interested in sheets of steel, glass plates, synthetic fabrics, and unprocessed rubber. Unless these materials are combined with others in the proper way into a completely assembled automobile they will have little value for the typical consumer who wants a car. Production consists of providing goods with form utility by turning raw materials and semifinished products into finished goods for either consumer or industrial use.

Great strides have been made in the production process in the United States during the past 50 years. Without the increased productivity of American industry the present standard of living we enjoy could not have been achieved. The ability to mass produce goods at prices which make the goods available to millions of people is one of the outstanding accomplishments of the private enterprise system. The increased productive capacity of our economy in part stems from more women entering the work force, from the improved productivity of workers made possible by better general education and training methods, from increased investment in capital equipment, and from the application of improved production techniques and management methods. The demand by consumers for more and better goods and services has also stimulated the increased flow of products from American factories and shops.

For a better understanding of the production function the following questions need to be answered.

How does management determine the location of new production facilities?

What factors must management consider in setting up the production system?

Why is production control and scheduling so important?
What is the role of purchasing in the production process?
How does automation relate to production?
How may the production department be organized?

The location of production facilities

The importance of factory location

The selection of a factory site is a decision of major importance for any business enterprise which has a significant amount of processing as part of its operations. The location of production facilities is normally a long-term commitment as it is usually not easy to dispose of large amounts of machinery and buildings if management decides a mistake has been made in the factory's location. The initial location of a plant or a proposed change in factory location involves careful consideration of the following factors.

Nearness to raw materials. When raw materials used in the manufacturing process are bulky and expensive to transport it is wise to consider locating the factory near the source of these commodities. Iron and steel plants are frequently located near sources of iron ore or coal because of the bulkiness of these raw materials. When many different types of components go into the manufacture of a product, it is not possible to locate the factory near all raw materials. Management must decide whether the advantage of being close to some of its raw materials sources outweighs other factors which influence factory location.

Nearness to markets for finished products. To achieve economies of distributing its products a manufacturer may select a plant location close to significant markets for the goods produced. This involves an analysis of future expected markets as well as present distribution patterns. With nationwide and international distribution of many manufacturers' product lines this may mean having multiple-plant operations situated to serve geographical areas where the enterprise's products are sold.

Quality and cost of labor available. An important question asked by management in determining factory location is whether there is an adequate supply of workers available to man the new factory. There is more to be considered here than whether there are a given number of unemployed individuals in a community or whether enough persons could be recruited to work in the new factory. Management must determine what kinds of skills are required for the new plant and whether the area can supply the workers in a satisfactory cost-quality relationship. If the necessary number of skilled workers are not already available, are there persons in the community who are capable of being trained for the new jobs? Are wage rates in the area in line with what management will encounter in other areas and with what its competitors are paying? Realistic managements do not expect to obtain skilled tool and die makers or machinists for the wages they might expect to pay for unskilled laborers in another area of the country. On the other hand, if prevailing wages in the area are higher than elsewhere in the industry, especially without increased skills or productivity, then management may find itself at a competitive disadvantage in its cost of production.

Sometimes enterprises relocate manufacturing facilities in an attempt to avoid unionization of the work force. Examples of this type of move are seen by the location of manufacturing facilities in areas of the country where traditional attitudes toward unions have been less positive than in heavily industrialized areas. However, with today's nationwide unions and the protection given union members and organizers by national legislation, managements cannot depend upon plant location to prevent union membership.

Access to transportation facilities. Because of the importance of time in delivering manufactured products to customers, access to good transportation facilities is a factor in deciding factory location. The type of transportation facilities used depends upon the nature of the product as to bulk and the importance of speed in transportation. An example of locating a factory with regard to access to transportation can be seen where a plant manufacturing electronic components is located adjacent to an airport because of the use made of air transportation for both company products and personnel.

Today many railroads are willing to provide railroad spurs alongside new factories in order to give better service to manufacturers and encourage greater use of rail freight. Some railroads are developing industrial parks strategically located near important rail junction points with long-term lease or purchase plans which are attractive to industry. When these individual parks are developed the railroad will receive significant freight revenues from shipments into and out of the plants.

Availability of utilities. An enterprise's management interested in a new factory site wants to know whether a community has sufficient electrical power, gas, and water available at economical rates for manufacturing needs. This need becomes especially important when the manufacturing process includes consumption of large quantities of electricity, gas, or water.

Satisfactory tax situation. There are several state and local taxes which business enterprises must pay. One of the most important is the real estate and property tax imposed by local and state governmental units on factories, equipment, and inventories based on assessed valuation, which is less than full market value. This tax usually varies between 3 and 6 percent of the assessed value of the business property. Frequently, states and communities will impose sales taxes and income taxes on enterprises as well as individuals doing business in the locality. The impact of these state and local taxes has to be weighed by the manager in deciding upon a new factory location.

The cost of municipal services in the form of taxes is a minor portion of an enterprise's manufacturing costs and is therefore generally not given top consideration unless all other factors involved in a choice between several factory locations are virtually equal. Probably a more important consideration than the amount of taxes is whether the community is providing a level of services commensurate with the tax dollars collected.

Miscellaneous factors. A variety of other factors influence factory location, including the quality of the community as measured by its schools, colleges, cultural programs, and churches, along with the attitude of its inhabitants toward new enterprise. The availability of land for factory sites, adequate zoning, and up-to-date building codes are all necessary to encourage new industrial development.

From the wide range of elements influencing factory location it is obviously impossible for management to take each factor equally into account. Management's problem is to determine those elements for its particular situation which are most important and then seek a balance to get the best location under the existing conditions. Information regarding possible plant locations along with the merits of each are available from local chambers of commerce, state industrial development commissions, industry trade associations, and such facilitating enterprises as railroad and utility companies. Management can use much of this information but should recognize that each locality is certain to picture itself in the most favorable light and gloss over possible problem areas. Ultimately the decision for factory location must be made by management from its own analysis of available information in light of the enterprise's own unique requirements.

The production system

The production system of a modern business enterprise operates as a smoothly functioning unit when it is at its best. Throughout the production process every step should be designed so as to operate in harmony with the other elements. Through the design of efficient production systems we have achieved mass production of goods that can be priced within the reach of millions of consumers. One example of improved production processes which have lowered costs is the development of color television. When color television was a new product a set would cost about $1,000. Technology and improved production have reduced costs, and now the price of color television is down by half or more of its initial price. The elements of the production system discussed here include research and product design, process design, production control, purchasing, and automation.

Research and product design

Research and product design are undertaken by production, engineering, and marketing departments and are sometimes organized under separate research departments. Regardless of the organizational aspects of research and product design the ultimate product to be manufactured should be the result of close cooperation between production and marketing personnel.

Research in most manufacturing enterprises is directed primarily toward *applied research,* which involves practical application of scientific knowledge to deal with definite problems or needs. Applied research is wide ranging in scope. It might be directed toward the development of new products or perhaps toward discovering ways of reducing costs of long-established product lines. *Pure research* is carried on to extend man's frontiers of knowledge without regard to the immediate utility of its findings.

In many industries as much as 10 percent of annual expenditures is directed toward research and development. Corporations like Du Pont, Merck, and IBM are noted for both pure and applied research in the fields of chemistry, pharmaceuticals, and computers. Governmental agencies also conduct research both alone and in cooperation with universities and private enterprises. Both pure and applied research are important in today's economy.

The objective in *product design* is to develop a product that will perform properly, appeal to consumers, and be sold at a price that will be profitable for the producer. Performance relates to how the product works, its reliability, its good mechanical design, and its ease of repair. Consumer appeal relates to the form and appearance of the product. Automobile designers have to take both performance and appearance into account to come up with a model which will be successful. A particular model lacking consumer appeal may not sell well, but by redesigning its appearance it may be quite successful even though there is relatively little change in the performance qualities of the car. But good styling alone is not enough for a product to be successful. Because of certain mechanical or performance difficulties a given auto model may be labeled as a "lemon" and sales may suffer even though the styling is considered to be good. Successful product design results in the development of a product which rates high both in performance and appearance.

Process design

Whereas product design has to do with the product's characteristics, *process design* is the development of the means of producing the good. One of the objectives of good production management is to have the most efficient method for manufacturing a given product. Essential elements to be considered in process design include the way in which the factory is laid out, the type of machinery to be used, and the development of prototypes.

Factory layout. The way in which machines and production lines are arranged in a factory makes a great deal of difference when the cost of production is calculated. A good factory layout is one in which materials move through the manufacturing steps in the quickest and most direct manner. In a good factor layout, transportation, handling, and clerical expenses are held to a minimum. The good factory layout is one which makes the most efficient use of available machines and manpower.

There are two basic types of factory layout. The factory may be laid out according to either product or process. *Product layout* is the arrangement of machinery and assembly lines by chronological steps in the manufacture of the product. As the product moves along through a plant organized on a product layout basis there is a gradual buildup of the product from raw materials or small parts to the finished product.

Product layout is especially economical when the articles being produced are of standard specifications and required in large volume. In the product layout the use of automatic equipment, continuous production lines, conveyors, and routine jobs results in low costs per unit produced even though the total investment in the layout is large. The product layout results in moving materials through the factory rapidly with a minimum of handling and transportation.

The advantages of product layout also provide the foundation for its weaknesses. As nearly as possible all machines must be kept operating with a minimum of idle time. When something goes wrong along the product layout it is frequently necessary to shut down an entire assembly line until the trouble is remedied. The product layout therefore requires numerous persons including maintenance men, setup men, materials suppliers, and engineers to back up the workers tending the machines. Careful attention must be given to balancing production facilities so that backlogs of materials in the process of production do not pile up at any one point along the layout. Once the product layout is set up it probably will be costly to change.

Process layout occurs when different types of machines or functions are located together in a factory without regard to where the particular process comes in the production of any one product. In the process layout the same kind of machines are grouped together. This means that all grinding is done in one location, all polishing in another, all drilling in another, and so on throughout the various steps in the manufacturing cycle. Process layout provides a great deal of flexibility. Products which require specialized manufacturing operations can be scheduled into the different areas and machinery can be fully occupied if this scheduling is well done.

A breakdown of one machine is not as critical with process layout as with product layout, since if a machine breaks down its work can be transferred to another similar type machine in the area. With no continuous production line as in product layout the balancing of the production time for machinery is not as important in the process layout. Process layout is especially appropriate when a variety of products are produced with the same machines and with job-lot orders in small quantities.

However, process layout also presents some problems for production managers. Transportation and materials-handling costs are usually high because the conveyors and mechanized handling used with product layouts are not present. Goods in process of manufacturing move more slowly, resulting in higher inventories and greater financial costs. The scheduling routine of materials and the accounting for costs of production are different for every order in contrast to the more standardized procedures in product layout.

The process layout and product layout both have their advantages and disadvantages. In practice most manufacturing enterprises make some use of the elements of both types of factory layouts depending upon the nature of the product, the variety of goods produced, the length of production runs, and the importance of being flexible to meet changing conditions.

Machinery selection. The machines used in production are considered either general-purpose or special-purpose machinery. *General-purpose machines* are those which can be used for a variety of different jobs requiring the same kind of work. A drill press is an example of a general-purpose machine. A drill press can be used to drill one or many holes, of different sizes, to different depths, and into different types of materials by simply changing the drill bit. General-purpose machinery is fairly well standardized and available from a number of different machinery manufacturers.

The general-purpose machines which may be found in many factories include shapers, lathes, drills, presses, grinders, polishers, boring machines, and milling machines. While each of these machines performs a different function, in general their purpose is to change the form of raw materials or semiprocessed goods by removing material, cutting holes, smoothing, bending, or shaping. Because of standardization the general-purpose machine is likely to be less expensive than the special-purpose machine which may require special design and production attention by machinery manufacturers.

General-purpose machines are usually slower than special-purpose machines and may require skilled operators if the parts are hand-fed into the machine. Goods produced on general-purpose machines may require more inspection as there is no guarantee that every part will be the same with hand-fed machinery. However, general-purpose machines can be fitted with special automated controls to insure greater uniformity, or highly skilled operators may be used to assure greater conformation to quality standards.

General-purpose machines are especially useful when the work in the factory is varied and the volume for any particular product is small. Skilled machinists are able to operate more than one type of general-purpose machine, and this provides flexibility which is necessary for the job-lot shop but also results in somewhat higher unit costs than when longer production runs and standardized products permit the economical use of special-purpose machines.

Special-purpose machines are designed for a particular job and have the right tools and adjustments built in. Through automatic control devices it is possible to reset the special-purpose machine's cutting edges when they begin to get out of adjustment. Because of its design and the degree of automation which may be built into it, once the special-purpose machine is calibrated and set in operation a semiskilled worker can be used to tend the machine. In some instances all that will be required will be for a worker to supply raw materials to the machine, remove the parts which the machine has produced, and make an occasional check to see that the machine is producing to the standards which have been established. Special-purpose machines are appropriate when long production runs of a given part justify the investment of large sums in a machine for that one job.

Prototypes. Frequently before production starts on a new piece of goods or before a new factory is built, a prototype of both the product and the production process is constructed. A *prototype* is merely a model or pattern which will be used as the basis for subsequent production. A good example of a product prototype is the clay model which is made of an automobile during the design process to give an idea of its styling and appearance in three dimensions. Later hand-tooled automobile models will be put together, complete with mechanical work. These models will be extensively tested before the final production line car will be decided upon.

A prototype of the production process usually consists of a scale model of the complete factory or the production line and is called a *pilot plant.* Engineers carefully check out every detail of the pilot plant trying to anticipate and eliminate as many of the problem areas as possible before the factory is built and machinery purchased. The construction and testing of a pilot plant may involve a cost of thousands of dollars, but this money is spent to reduce the risks involved in the investment of millions of dollars in buildings and machinery designed for full production of the new product.

Once the product and process designs have been settled management must place orders for the tooling which is necessary to get production started. *Tooling* consists of such items as cutting and grinding attachments for machine tools, clamps, gauges, loading devices, and other fixtures. Tooling is designed to adapt machinery and assembly lines to the production of a particular product and may cost from a few hundred dollars to several million dollars depending upon the complexity of the product and the amount of new tooling required. The automobile industry spends millions of dollars each year for new model tooling. Tooling is only part of the expense of getting geared up for a new product since new machinery may be required or even a new factory building may be constructed to house the new production facilities.

The final step before full-scale production begins is to put the new production facility through a series of test runs. Here production personnel and engineers will work to iron out difficulties and eliminate "bugs" which may appear despite all the advance precautions that have been taken. During this time the personnel department will have recruited and trained any additional workers necessary for the production department. Prior to this time the marketing department will have completed its analysis of the expected market for this product. Pricing and distribution decisions will have been made, and top management will be coordinating the efforts of the various departments to effect a smooth introduction of the new product to the consumer.

Production control and scheduling

The heart of the modern factory system is production control. *Production control* consists of a wide variety of activities, including authorization of orders, scheduling, routing, checking on the progress of orders, and correction of difficulties in achieving production schedules. While the particular responsibilities of production control personnel may vary somewhat from one manufacturing enterprise to another, the job of coordinating and controlling the production process to meet delivery schedules is basic to production control. For a smooth operation in the factory, production control must maintain excellent communications with the marketing department as well as with production superintendents and foremen.

A master schedule of anticipated production is normally prepared in order to provide a general basis for control. This master schedule is based on an overall forecast of the demand for the enterprise's goods during the coming year. Such a forecast is determined by top management after considering estimates from the company's sales force, statistical measurements of trends for the enterprise's sales based on past records, data from industry sources, and forecasts from government economists of overall economic activity. The factory's capacity as well as the anticipated demand for the enterprise's goods is taken into account in making the master schedule. Forecasting is a continuous process for the business enterprise and is not confined to once a year.

Orders and authorization of production

Orders for specific customers are placed by the marketing department with production control, which has the responsibility for scheduling these orders in such a manner that delivery dates can be met. The sales organization has a responsibility for coordinating its efforts with production control so that unrealistic delivery dates will not be promised customers when their orders are placed. In some instances the sales department is not permitted to give a firm delivery date until it has been cleared with production control. This type of coordination illustrates the importance of both marketing and production departments working together and recognizing the problems which confront each area.

The specific orders coming from the sales department constitute the authority to the factory to produce the goods. Once an order has been placed the authorization to produce the goods is prepared by the scheduling section of production control. The specific scheduling assignment takes into account the status of other orders already in the production process, the present utilization of factory capacity, whether the continuous nature of the production process requires holding the order back for a period of time, and the promised delivery date. A master schedule is used as an overall control device to summarize units produced to a given date, orders on the books, and the state of available productive capacity for a given time in the future.

Production scheduling

Production scheduling is concerned with the sequence and timing of orders from the time orders are received from the sales department until finished goods are shipped to customers or to the enterprise's warehouse for future shipment. The objectives of good production scheduling are to assure that delivery schedules are met, that the most efficient utilization of production capacity is achieved, and that proper coordination is maintained with the purchasing, sales, and production departments.

Before setting up production schedules an important factor to be considered is *lead time,* which is the time necessary for all arrangements before production can begin. This includes the work of the purchasing department, engineering, tooling, and personnel if additional hiring will be necessary to complete an order. In the case of simple or repeat production orders the lead time may be measured in days whereas with model changes in automobiles, appliances, and other complex goods the lead time will be measured in months. Several years of lead time will be required with such items as new aircraft or aerospace products where new technology must be developed.

Scheduling and the follow-up represents a valuable control device in the modern factory. A complex system of production scheduling is required in large manufacturing enterprises today because of the thousands of parts which go into many of the products which we take for granted. The complexity of scheduling systems can be illustrated by the manufacture of a portable typewriter which has more than 1,750 parts. Each part must be available at the right place, in the proper quantity and quality, and at the time when it is required in the assembly of the portable typewriter. This scheduling is further complicated when more than one model of typewriter is manufactured in the factory in several different colors with different type faces and other varying features. Maintaining scheduling systems becomes even more difficult when you consider the problems involved in the production of aerospace products of significantly greater complexity, having much more exacting standards, and requiring coordination with other manufacturing plants and operations facilities in different parts of the country.

Routing. An important part of production control and scheduling is *routing,* which includes detailed instructions as to how a particular order will move from department to department, which machines will be used at each point along the line, and when inspections will be made. The routing sheet provides the foreman in each department with specific information regarding the order, how it is to be processed, and where the materials go after his department has completed its particular operations.

In the most simple cases the written instructions on the routing slip will only call out the flow of work from one department to another with a general notation of the work to be performed in each area. This may be the case when the product has been manufactured before by the firm and where the process is relatively simple. With new or complex products the routing sheet may include detailed procedures containing methods for most efficient production as determined by industrial engineers, or these methods may be further spelled out on separate sheets which accompany the routing sheet.

Maintaining production schedules. There are a number of means available for following up to see that production is on schedule. A variety of charts are used to plot visually the comparison between the scheduled and the actual progress of an order through the factory. These charts show the detailed operations required for an order, when they should occur in the production process, and what the state of actual production is. Visual control boards are available to measure the status of orders. Obviously all these devices require constant revision to keep check on production and to reflect changes in schedules. These charts and boards must be kept up to date or they may be misleading for management.

In many instances the electronic computer has replaced these charts and control boards. The ability of computer systems to provide information instantaneously on the status of orders, machine time and utilization, and future most efficient scheduling has been of great benefit to production managers. Frequently, computers are used on a continuous basis to receive information from the factory machinery for constant control of the production process. This means that machinery or reporting stations in the factory are connected electrically to the computer so that information on jobs completed is fed immediately into the computer for analysis and reporting. The development of better production control systems and the application of computers to production problems has lessened the need for expediters, whose function is to unsnarl orders which get out of schedule, to find lost orders, to push rush or emergency orders through the factory, and in general to help straighten out problems which occur in the production process.

Purchasing industrial goods

The purchasing of industrial goods is important in most business enterprises. In many manufacturing enterprises the value of materials that are purchased makes up 50 percent or more of the cost of the final product. In most manufacturing operations the materials that are purchased represent the largest single expense incurred in the manufacturing process. Even in service enterprises, where purchasing is limited to supplies and equipment rather than raw materials or components, the purchasing function merits the careful attention of management.

Purchasing is defined as the procurement of industrial materials and supplies for use or for further processing, not for immediate resale. This excludes buying merchandise for sale to the consumer without changing its form, as is done by retail and wholesale merchants.

Steps in the purchasing process

The essential steps in the purchasing process are outlined below. Since the purpose is to provide a broad understanding of purchasing, no attention is given to the details of forms and records. The steps in the purchase of industrial goods are as follows:

1. It is determined that there is a need for specific industrial goods. For maximum efficiency purchasing schedules should be planned carefully in advance. However, at times emergencies, such as sudden design changes caused by unexpected shifts in market conditions or breakdowns which cause parts shortages, may necessitate rush orders.

2. An accurate description of the goods desired is drawn up on a purchase requisition form.

3. Once the requisition has been drawn up and filed with the purchasing department, the negotiations with possible sources of supply are undertaken.

4. After negotiations and analysis of the different vendors, the purchasing department selects a particular vendor and places an order for the goods. The purchase order contains such data as precise merchandise description, quantity, price, delivery date, and the signature of the purchasing officer.

5. Prior to the anticipated delivery date, a follow-up on the order is carried out by the purchasing department to confirm that the promised delivery date will be met.

6. Upon receipt of the vendor's invoice, which is an itemized statement of merchandise shipped by the seller, the purchasing department checks that the goods shipped match the description on the purchase order.

7. When the industrial goods arrive they are inspected for quantity and quality and to see whether damage has occurred in transit. After the merchandise has been received and inspected the invoice is approved for payment and the record on the transaction is closed with the information on the goods being routed to the departments concerned.

Price and quality considerations

There is no doubt that price is a major consideration in any purchase transaction. Even so, price is frequently overrated in its importance in the total purchasing function. Naturally management expects its purchasing agents to negotiate and to buy at the most favorable prices obtainable. However, price is just one of the many important terms and conditions of the purchase agreement. Price is rarely considered alone but rather in connection with other factors to achieve the objectives of economical and efficient enterprise operations.

The complete cost of acquisition of materials can be determined only after all relevant considerations are taken into account. For example, invoice price is one element of cost, but not the only one. Delivery costs must also be considered. A low price paid to a supplier a great distance away may result in such high packing and transportation charges that the delivered cost of a low-priced item is actually higher. At times, a lower invoice price may be obtained through quantity purchasing. However, the expense of handling and storage may outweigh this price differential by the time the materials have been issued and put to use. These examples illustrate the point that low unit prices on invoices do not always mean the lowest ultimate cost to the manufacturer.

Most purchasing agents are unwilling to discuss price considerations without taking into account quality of materials. Quality is a relative term. *Quality* can be defined as the possession of the necessary criteria which fit a product to a given use. Taken out of the context of the specific use for a particular material, quality has no real meaning. Thus selection of the quality of an item requires careful definition depending upon the purpose for which the goods are being ordered. For an enterprise to purchase materials that are either better than necessary or not good enough represents potential waste. There is no reason to spend money to purchase a good or higher quality than is necessary to accomplish a particular mission.

There are two steps which are vital in the determination of the right quality. First, the purchasing enterprise must define the minimum standards of quality suitable for the intended purpose beyond which superior qualities may be desirable but not essential. Second, this defined quality must be balanced with other factors such as price, durability, convenience, and sales appeal, in order to make the most favorable purchase which must have at least the minimum quality standards.

Selecting sources of supply

In the process of selecting the sources of supply for the enterprise, the purchasing department normally goes through four successive stages before it determines a particular vendor with whom to place a purchase order. These stages include:

1. The information or survey stage, where possible sources for a product are considered.
2. The inquiry stage, where the relative qualifications and merits of potential suppliers are determined.
3. The analysis and selection stage, where the inital order is placed.
4. The administration or experience stage, where the vendor-customer relationship is established or where the selection process is repeated to search for a more satisfactory source of supply.

Make or buy decision

There are times when the question arises as to whether it is better to manufacture a particular item in one's own plant or to buy from an outside vendor. This kind of a decision is one which requires careful consideration by top management of the production, engineering, financial, and personnel departments. All these points of view must be taken into account since a decision to "make or buy" is not as simple as merely deciding to change from one vendor to another. To help top management with the make or buy decision, comparisons should be made in the areas of costs, quantity desired, and necessary quality.

The *cost of purchased goods* may be determined rather easily. The complete cost up to the time of use is the figure which should be used. This cost includes the price of the goods plus transportation charges and costs of handling and storage. Against this purchased cost must be balanced the total estimated cost of producing the goods in the enterprise's own shops. This cost calculation should include not merely the cost of materials and labor, but the investment and carrying charges including depreciation on necessary equipment, overhead charges such as utilities and supervision costs, and normal waste and spoilage. Only when a full inclusion of all costs of production are included is a fair comparison possible.

The *quantity of goods* required is an important consideration because this may determine whether the potential cost savings are sufficient to justify undertaking special manufacturing processes. Also, quantity has an important bearing on actual costs through the economies of mass manufacturing and spreading the fixed costs of starting up the operation over many units of production.

Quality control of a produced product may tend to assure that the desired quality will be strictly maintained. In general, the greater the need for strict quality control and the more exacting the requirements the more important this consideration becomes. The production of the good in one's own plant makes close coordination simpler and may place responsibility for quality manufacture in a spot where it is easier to guarantee all components of the process. On the other hand, if quality standards are significantly different for a new product than personnel have been accustomed to dealing with, then quality may be improved by purchasing the component from a manufacturer who is used to dealing with such high standards.

There are other problems associated with the self-manufacture of a component part. Once the enterprise is committed to such a policy, especially where special equipment is necessary, an element of inflexibility is introduced into the procurement process. Freedom of selection is sacrificed, despite subsequent cost savings available through outside purchase. Also, shifting demands for the component may be beyond the control of the manufacturer, and the enterprise will be subject to all the risks which are a part of the industry which presently manufactures the component. Problems in the personnel area may crop up with the manufacture of a new product. Efficiency is not merely a matter of equipment, but of production experience, skilled workmen, and effective supervisors. The new staff must be fitted into the rest of the organization. Frequently, the decision to manufacture a component rather than to purchase from an outside vendor is made without taking into account some of these intangible, but vital, considerations.

Inventory control

Inventories typically represent a substantial part of a manufacturing enterprise's assets. Inventory control is important to three different departments in the business enterprise. The production department must be assured of an adequate supply of materials on hand when needed. The marketing department must be able to fill sales orders and meet customers' delivery dates. The finance department is concerned with the need to minimize the amount of funds invested in inventory at any given time; to reduce handling and storage costs, insurance and interest expenses; and to reduce the risk of losses from obsolete merchandise or falling prices.

Policies on inventory control deal with questions of which items will be carried in inventory, what quantity of goods will be stored, and how the physical inventories and records will be maintained. The basic decisions as to which items will be carried in inventory are determined by the enterprise's actual requirements based on production and sales estimates. This requires coordination between marketing and production personnel. The quantity of inventory should be considered both in terms of total dollars invested in inventories and on individual classes of goods. Inventory requirements usually are adjusted from time to time because of such factors as changing demand, production schedules, and the enterprise's financial condition.

Manufacturing inventories are classified as raw materials, goods in process, or finished goods. *Raw materials* include the unprocessed commodities which go into the manufacture of a given product and any component parts purchased from another manufacturer to be assembled into the finished product. Once the inventories have been placed in the production cycle they become *work in process*. Here their form is changed or other parts are added to them to increase their value and to move the materials along nearer to product completion. Once the goods have completed the manufacturing process and have been placed in storage to await distribution to consumers they are referred to as *finished goods*. Finished goods inventories represent the buffer between immediate sales needs and the ability of the factory to produce goods. All these various classes of inventories are carried on the accounting records of the enterprise at the cost of the materials plus the calculated additional costs added to their value during the manufacturing process.

The administration of inventories includes the receipt of goods, their storage and maintenance, and the issuance of materials to production departments or shipment of finished goods to customers upon proper authorization. The system of records which provides for accountability of goods, information on turnover of individual inventory items, and notification when reorder points have been reached is as important as the physical handling of inventories. The analysis of inventory turnover is discussed in Chapter 14. Today inventory control is frequently facilitated by computer systems and mathematical models which improve the inventory management that has become more complex over the years.

Purchase of major equipment

The purchase of major equipment, or capital equipment, such as machinery, transportation equipment, or office equipment requires a different type of analysis than the purchase of supplies or materials which themselves go into the manufacture of a product. Such major equipment is called *capital equipment* because it lasts longer than a year, is used to manufacture other goods, and does not itself enter into the product that is being manufactured. New capital equipment is purchased because it makes the production of some goods more efficient or more economical. Capital equipment may result in greater speed of output, less variation in the product, lower costs, or greater dependability, just to suggest a few of the ways in which this type of purchase is justified.

There are special problems which arise in the purchase of capital equipment because of its particular characteristics:

1. Capital equipment usually requires the outlay of substantial sums of money which may necessitate some special form of financing. The purchase of capital equipment is generally a decision of major financial consequence for the enterprise.

2. In view of the long life of most capital equipment items, the purchase of major equipment is an infrequent occurrence. Although the enterprise's annual budget may provide for capital expenditures for equipment or land and buildings, the type of capital equipment purchased will likely vary from year to year. This makes the purchase of this equipment difficult to routinize.

3. The total costs of capital equipment are more difficult to determine with a high degree of preciseness than with raw materials. The initial cost of the equipment is only part of its total cost. Other important elements in the total cost pattern are the effects of obsolescence of equipment, amount of idle time when the equipment is not being utilized, frequency of maintenance and repair, and operating efficiency.

4. The characteristics of capital equipment produced by different manufacturers are seldom identical. A machinery manufacturer normally has different features and options for his particular line of equipment than those of his competitors. Therefore, direct comparison of machines and prices is difficult.

5. Because of the long-term nature of the capital equipment purchase, management may commit itself to a series of other decisions of a comparatively permanent nature, such as the type of product to be manufactured, the method of production, and the costs of operation. It is much easier to move in and out of a situation involving the purchase of raw materials than one involving the purchase of major equipment.

Because of these special problems associated with the selection of capital equipment, not only the price must be analyzed but also' such elements as plant layout, type of machines used for other purposes, and services to be provided by the supplier of the equipment. The proposed capital addition must be viewed as a part of the established production process and its purchase must be coordinated with existing facilities even though sometimes extensive changes may be required to improve operating efficiency.

Other elements of the production system

Other important elements of the production system include motion and time analysis, quality control, and maintenance.

Motion and time analysis

Motion and time analysis refers to the work done by industrial engineers to provide a basis for production standards on factory jobs. Actually the establishment of standards is a twofold process. First comes the motion analysis to determine the best way of accomplishing a particular job by reducing waste effort to a minimum. The methods engineer studies the job and breaks it down into its essential elements, eliminating the unnecessary movements, and establishing a pattern for efficient production.

Once the motion analysis has been completed, the worker is trained in this method. Then the industrial engineer conducts a time study analysis, using a stopwatch, to determine how much time is necessary to carry out the job under actual factory conditions. A number of observations will be required to determine fairly the amount of time necessary for a particular job since variations in the employee's work pattern caused by chance or unusual circumstances might make one or a very few observations result in an unrealistic work expectation with either too little or too much time being allowed for the job. This time study will be the basis for setting the work standard after allowances are made for worker fatigue, production delays, and necessary personal time for employees. These factors are added to the average observed time in computing work standards.

Time study is based on the assumptions that the skilled industrial engineer can determine when the best method for performing a job has been developed and can judge what a normal pace for doing that particular job is. These assumptions are sometimes questioned by labor unions, and work standards are often the subject of bargaining between management and organized labor.

With experience the worker is often able to reduce the time required for the job from what was originally set forth as he becomes more skilled and as he discovers little shortcuts and improves upon the original method which was developed for the job. These improvements are referred to as "creeping methods changes." The result of this improvement in job performance is that the worker is able to earn a somewhat higher rate per hour if he is paid by the number of units he produces, or that he is able to have more leisure time if he is paid on an hourly basis and expected to produce only so many units per hour. When management notes this it will often restudy a job and tighten up the work standard by reducing the allowable time for a given job. Workers generally object to this.

In establishing work standards a desirable psychological practice is to set an expected rate of production which the average worker can exceed by 10 to 15 percent by exerting just a bit more than normal effort. The establishment of piece rates or hourly production standards is a tedious job as management seeks to strike a balance between fairness to the workers and at the same time hold down production costs so that the enterprise can be competitive and earn a profit. When the labor agreement contains a statement regarding motion and time analysis and work standards, management should be meticulous in observing the procedure set forth in order to minimize the number of disputes between the union and management over work standards.

Quality control

An important element in the production system is the maintenance of the desired quality in manufactured products. Once the standards of quality have been established a means of inspection must be devised. A good quality control system not only includes adequate inspection to determine which goods should be accepted or rejected, but also includes means for preventing the continued production of unsatisfactory goods.

Inspection can occur as goods move along the production lines or at central inspection facilities which are located away from the production process. When inspection is done while goods are on the production lines there is a good chance that it will prevent the buildup of an excessive accumulation of defective work. Inspection during the manufacturing process permits the immediate location of points where problems are arising which cause quality to fall below acceptable standards. Also, there are many parts which must be inspected before the product is completed in order to avoid a defective part being covered by a coat of paint or hidden by another component.

Central inspection facilities may act as receiving stations for products or materials from all over a factory. This might be a laboratory where detailed inspections under carefully controlled conditions are made. Here the inspection can be made more objectively since the inspector is not standing by a production worker who may be responsible for the unsatisfactory work. Central inspection facilities may make the work of the inspector more efficient than if he has to wait for goods to come through the production process. However, central inspection does require more handling and perhaps more storage expense than process inspection. The nature of the product and the type of inspection required will dictate what type of inspection is best for a given product.

The different types of inspections carried out on manufactured goods include examination by use of the human senses of sight, smell, taste, hearing, or touch; measurements with various instruments; laboratory tests requiring chemical or physical analysis; and performance tests. A highly skilled chef might taste and smell a vat of soup before it is pronounced fit for canning. An inspector on an assembly line using a gauge might check the measurements of a metal part. A metallurgist might analyze the properties of a metal alloy and test its hardness. And a test driver might put a new automobile just off the assembly line through a series of driving tests before it is shipped to a dealer. All of these are examples of the different types of inspections which might be carried out in a factory.

Sometimes every product in a factory will have to be inspected. A completely automated production line usually includes every piece being inspected during the production process. However, more often every part in the product will not be inspected either because this would be too time consuming, too expensive, or a complete test might destroy the product. Thus some form of partial inspection called sampling is necessary. A wide variety of statistical measurements are available to determine what test sample should be used under different circumstances depending upon how much expense is involved in the inspection of the product and how important it is to maintain rigid quality standards.

Maintenance

The work of the *maintenance* force is to keep the factory in efficient operating order. This includes a wide variety of activities ranging from keeping plumbing and wiring in good condition, lubricating moving parts, repairing or overhauling machinery to fixing a leaky roof. All the physical facilities in a factory are in the process of wearing out from the day they are installed. Therefore, a sound maintenance program must be instituted if production is to continue uninterrupted by breakdowns.

Hiring skilled maintenance men, providing them with proper tools, and keeping an inventory of spare parts is costly. However, a breakdown which stops the production line causing men and machinery to be idle and fall behind schedule is even more costly. This means that *preventive maintenance* should be part of the maintenance program in a factory. Frequently, it is less expensive to do routine preventive maintenance than it is to wait until a machine breaks down and requires a complete overhaul. A good preventive maintenance program can help keep the factory running smoothly.

A dilemma exists for the factory manager who is anxious to keep his plant running smoothly, avoiding costly breakdowns, but who at the same time feels that having a large maintenance staff may involve too great an expense. If the maintenance staff is large enough with a wide variety of skilled workmen to handle all breakdowns promptly to prevent a major work stoppage, then there is bound to be a considerable period of time when some of these well-paid skilled workmen are engaged in more routine tasks which do not require such a high degree of ability and training. On the other hand, if the number of skilled workers is reduced to an absolute minimum, they may not be able to handle the situation if they are needed in a number of critical places at the same time. If they are working on one job and an additional breakdown occurs in another department an assembly line may be down until the first problem is cleared up. This means that spending a small amount for maintenance forces can result in a large amount of expensive downtime for production personnel and machinery.

There is no easy, inexpensive solution to the problems involved in maintenance. It is possible to overmaintain with excessive amounts spent on preventive maintenance. However, the other extreme is to spend too little on maintenance, risking substantial costs associated with serious and frequent breakdowns. Most factory managements adopt a middle course of action with a staff of skilled maintenance personnel who can be moved from routine, preventive maintenance to critical breakdown points when the occasion arises even though this results in some inefficiencies part of the time in the use of skilled personnel.

In recent years there has been a move toward the use of machines and tooling which are designed to last only for a model run. These machines are sold at a price which makes substantial overhauls uneconomical. This tends to reduce the cost of maintenance, not only by cutting down on the number of maintenance men employed but also by reducing the spare parts inventory. Additional advantages include more rapid depreciation allowances for tax purposes plus less risk involved in commitment to expensive machinery which might soon become obsolete. However, careful analysis is required by management to determine if the total costs of production are lower by adopting such a policy since this will necessitate an increase in annual expenditures for new equipment.

Automation

Automation is a term which has been used much in the past two decades and means something different to different people, depending upon their frame of reference. To planners it may mean the promise of a fantastic world of factories producing huge quantities of goods requiring very little human physical effort. Workers may look upon automation as a threat to employment and a cause of industrial strife as labor unions seek to protect the job security of their members. Owners may view automation as a means of lowering the cost of production, thereby increasing profits, while idealists may see automation as a means for better answering the basic economic questions of our society through greatly increased production. Actually automation contains all of these dimensions but requires a more precise definition for the business manager.

Automation today represents an extension of mechanization which began in the latter half of the 18th century with the invention of the steam engine by James Watt. *Mechanization* is the application of power-driven tools in factory production and results in a saving of both human energy and time. The textile industry was the first to be mechanized as the result of inventions by James Hargreaves, Richard Arkwright, Edmund Cartwright, and Eli Whitney. Mechanization represents the first phase in the process of automation.

The second phase in automation is the use of the *continuous process assembly line* where goods are moved from one stage of the production process to another by use of automatic conveyors. The continuous production process can be seen today in such industries as steel, glass, and nonferrous metals.

The third phase in automation, or what sometimes is called the *fully automated process,* consists of the feedback of information from the machine as it inspects its own output and actuates controls to correct deviations from previously established standards. This type of automation is already in use in the metalworking industries, in oil refining, and in hydroelectricity production. Automatic feedback and control systems in modern factories are made possible through electronic data processing equipment and controls. The result of the use of electronic computers and the increased automation is the elimination of many of the routine production and clerical jobs in industry. Workers with increased technical knowledge are required to program, check, and maintain these automated processes. With the application of electronic data processing equipment management is finding that information is available today more rapidly, in greater quantities, and in wider variety than ever before. Because of the importance of computers today, Chapter 17 is devoted to a discussion of this subject.

Organization of the production department

In a manufacturing enterprise the production department is a line department since it contributes directly to the main function of the enterprise. The complexity of the organization of the production department depends upon the size of the enterprise and the nature of goods produced. The organization for the production function in a typical manufacturing enterprise is illustrated in Figure 13–1.

Manufacturing management

The executive in overall charge of manufacturing has a title such as vice president for manufacturing. The line organization directly responsible for production goes down through the production manager to the division superintendents and then to the foremen and assistant foremen. The maintenance department headed by a master mechanic or superintendent of maintenance reports to the production manager, as does the inventory or stores superintendent.

FIGURE 13–1
Partial organization chart of a typical production department

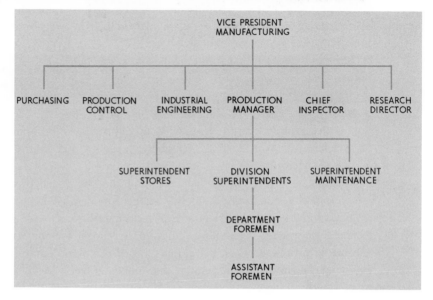

A number of production staff departments assist line managers by performing functions which support manufacturing operations. These manufacturing staff departments typically include production control, industrial engineering, inspection, purchasing, and research. Other departments, particularly personnel and accounting, play an important staff role in the production function by providing advice and assistance, services, and control. The legal department may also assist by assuring that manufacturing processes and products are properly protected by patents and that the enterprise is not infringing upon previously granted patents to other firms by making proper licensing arrangements.

The factory foreman

The role of the foreman is extremely important in manufacturing operations despite the increased use of automation and the need for more skilled staff personnel in the modern factory. The foreman represents the point at which management comes into direct contact with the workers. The typical factory worker views the foreman as being the management, and the impressions created by the foreman will determine in large measure the work force's attitude toward the business enterprise. The foreman must be trained in the technical requirements of his department. While he need not necessarily be more highly skilled technically than any of the workers under his direction, he should have some degree of technical skill and a deep understanding and appreciation of the problems associated with the work of his department.

As important as technical skill is for the foreman, he should also have a keen awareness of the importance of good personal relationships in dealing with subordinates. This usually requires some explicit training in human relations and a thorough understanding of the enterprise's policies and operating rules. He must interpret and administer enterprise policies as they affect employees. It is the foreman's responsibility to communicate the enterprise's position on questions which may be raised by employees. How well the foreman does in these areas will greatly influence employees' attitudes toward their work situation.

The foreman must understand how the work done in his department relates to the total operation of the factory and should be fully informed of the role of production control, industrial engineering, and other departments which will influence the production work. The foreman must be given training and supported by higher management if he is to perform his function effectively as the supervisor of production employees.

Summary

Production consists of providing goods with form utility by turning raw materials and semifinished products into finished goods for either consumer or industrial use.

The location of production facilities involves consideration of such factors as proximity to raw materials and markets for finished goods, access to transportation, availability of labor and utility services, and a satisfactory tax structure.

The first steps in the production system are research and product design and process design, which entails factory layout, machinery selection, and building of prototypes. Production control and scheduling, purchasing, and inventory control are also important elements in production. Other significant elements in the production system are motion and time analysis, quality control, and maintenance. The purchase of capital equipment involves recognition of a number of special problems.

Automation progresses from mechanization to the continuous process assembly line to the fully automated process which has a control system to correct deviations from established standards.

The vice president of manufacturing customarily is in charge of the production system. In large factories an extensive organization is necessary to support the foreman, which is the point at which management is in direct contact with the work force.

Terms for review

production	finished-goods inventories
product design	capital equipment
factory layout	motion and time analysis
production control	quality control
production scheduling	maintenance force
purchasing	automation
raw materials	foreman
work in process	

Questions

1. *a)* What advantages does your area have for the location of manufacturing enterprises? Talk with Chamber of Commerce personnel, public utilities managers, and realtors to develop this information.
   b) What type of manufacturing activities would be particularly desirable for your community?
   c) What negative as well as positive implications are there for a community as the result of a new factory?
2. Examine current publications and find specific examples of research which has resulted in new industrial or consumer products.
3. If possible, arrange with the personnel or public relations department to tour a factory in your area. Observe the type of factory layout and the machinery which is used.
4. What are some various examples of the application of "quality" to a product? Why would quality specifications be quite different for a product depending upon its intended use?
5. If a manufacturer is able to produce a component part for less than its purchase price would you advise the enterprise to go ahead and produce the part? Explain your answer.

6. Why is the purchase of capital equipment an important decision in most enterprises?

7. What factors make the position of factory foreman an important and difficult one? What does this imply for the top management of a manufacturing enterprise?

8. After a study of materials in the library, write a 300-word summary either supporting or opposing the statement that automation results in the elimination of jobs and causes higher levels of unemployment.

BUSINESS BRIEFS

Motorola, Inc.

Motorola, Inc., is the largest domestic producer of mobile and portable two-way radios, integrated circuits, and transistors. Consumer products include radios and television sets. The company has 36,000 employees.

In 1971, with the introduction of a new model receiver for a paging communication system, the management initiated a dramatic change in the production process. The plant which was to make the new paging receiver eliminated the conventional assembly line. Each employee working on the product will assemble and test the entire unit himself. The worker then sends along an individually signed note with each unit: "I built this receiver in its entirety, and I'm proud of it."

1. What do you think will be the effect on employee morale of this change in production methods at this Motorola plant?

2. What possible effects could this change have on the production cost for the paging receiver? Explain your answer.

3. Discuss the potential feasibility of extending this approach to other manufactured products. What limitations might there be to the kinds of products for which this approach would be effective?

Northwestern Steel & Wire Company

In an industry of giant-size producers, relatively small Northwestern Steel & Wire Company ($159 million sales in 1970) is a model of production efficiency. In the five years ending with 1970 the company averaged after tax profits of 11 percent on sales and 17 percent on stockholders' equity.

Northwestern's technology is at the heart of its efficiency. The enterprise operates electric steel furnaces utilizing scrap steel instead of iron ore. The key to this enterprise's productivity is the use of ultrahigh power which permits higher temperatures and provides faster melting and more economical steel production. The company has pioneered in the development of electric steel furnaces, and its new 400-ton electric furnace is the largest in the world.

Elements of Northwestern's technology are closely kept secrets which have so far eluded competitors in the industry. This technology provides a cost advantage to Northwestern in fuel savings and capital costs compared with its competitors. For example, the new 400-ton furnace reportedly cost less than one third as much as conventional steel producing facilities with the same production capacity.

The management of Northwestern has emphasized development of its own technology rather than depending upon some other company. Because of the wide fluctuation in the price of scrap steel, this management is presently working on the problem of utilizing iron ore in its production process. However, this will require additional steps in production since iron ore cannot be used in an electric furnace without first reducing it to pure iron. One processor of iron ore into iron pellets suitable for electric furnaces reportedly offered a stable supply to Northwestern at a price fully competitive with scrap steel. However, Northwestern's management refused the offer, preferring instead to develop its own cost-saving technology to reduce iron ore to pure iron rather than depending on some other enterprise.

Two thirds of Northwestern's common stock is closely held by one family. The company's chairman of the board is a son of the enterprise's founder with a grandson and great-grandson having key management positions.

1. Compare Northwestern's profitability with the steel industry figures given in Figures 4–1 and 4–2.
2. What factors do you think might contribute to the greater productive efficiency Northwestern has achieved over some of its larger competitors?
3. What problems might Northwestern face in the future in connection with its production process?
4. What would have been an alternative approach Northwestern could have taken in research and improved technology as a small steel producer?

The Drivewell Corporation

The Drivewell Corporation, which has been in business for one year, is engaged in the design and manufacture of devices and component parts for manufacturers in the trucking industry. The founder of Drivewell, Jim Schollenbach, had been a successful engineer in the industry for a number of years. He had considerable experience in the invention of new products and had supervised the establishment of a new manufacturing plant for a former employer. Schollenbach organized his company after he became dissatisfied with the management of the firm where he had been associated. He had long dreamed of going into business so he could be his own boss. He felt his products were simpler, more efficient, and could be sold profitably for the same or slightly lower prices than competing products.

During the early months of the Drivewell Corporation most of Schollenbach's time was spent in handling the many varied details necessary to starting a new enterprise. Finances had been a limiting factor although he had been able to negotiate a major borrowing arrangement with a local bank to go along with limited equity funds. A draftsman, sales manager, and a few general machinists were hired along with a part-time clerical girl who kept the company's books with the assistance of a local certified public accounting firm.

Manufacturing operations and office work were carried out in a small plant which was rented on a monthly basis. Emphasis was placed upon developing pilot models which could be used for samples to be tried out by prospective customers. These pilot models met with a good response in the industry and within a few months some limited orders were being produced and shipped.

However, Schollenbach was disappointed that things were not moving along as rapidly as he had hoped.

He was discussing his problems with Herb Johnston, a friend who had been helpful in organizing the enterprise.

"Even though we planned for a period of time in getting operations started," began Schollenbach, "I never dreamed it would take so much of my time in dealing with details. Also, we have encountered numerous delays in obtaining parts. For example, one of our main products requires a particular type of rubber bushing which is not standard in the industry at present. As is the customary practice we paid for a special mold which we put in the hands of a large rubber manufacturer when we placed our initial order. As it turned out, we had to contend with a strike in the rubber industry. Then when production started again our order must have been pushed back down the line because we were delayed over seven weeks in getting the bushings beyond the date I had been promised for delivery. As we get into volume production we can afford to make large quantity orders on these bushings, but we really were delayed on getting out pilot models and on an initial small order from a customer because of the failure to get the first batch of bushings."

"How about other raw materials," asked Johnston, "do you have this problem with other suppliers?"

"Partially," answered Schollenbach, "since we are a small purchaser we aren't able to command much respect by the big companies in getting any special treatment for our orders. We have been able to buy steel from a local distributor. Much of our steel fabrication has been done in our shop for the pilot models. Later on we will place special tooling in the hands of a particular steel manufacturer which will cut down on our fabricating costs. However, this tooling will cost several thousand dollars and we aren't ready for that now either in terms of volume of production or finances.

"Another problem we have had is getting delivery on the proper kind of springs. One of the spring manufacturers we have been dealing with shipped us an order of the wrong spring. We were able to adapt our models to this spring because of the necessity of getting our orders out, but this has been time consuming and somewhat more costly than we had anticipated.

"The most encouraging part of our business so far has been the excellent reception that our pilot models have received when they have been placed in operation in the field. The reports have been good from the first and enough pilot models are now in use that we can begin to expect some substantial orders in the near future. Morale is high among our employees because we all believe in the product, but it will be good to get some profitable contracts under our belts."

1. What are the major problems facing Jim Schollenbach in expanding the Drivewell Corporation's operations?

2. What, if anything, can Schollenbach do to deal with these problems?

3. From the point of view of a purchasing agent for a large manufacturer, at the present time what would be the strengths of selecting the Drivewell Corporation for an order of component parts? What weaknesses would the Drivewell Corporation present from the point of view of a large manufacturer who might like to use their parts?

The Sunflower Dairy

The purchasing agent for the Sunflower Dairy was reviewing the sales proposals of manufacturers of metal tanks which were needed to equip an expansion of Sunflower's milk-processing facilities. The purchasing agent recalled the conversation he had with the salesman from the Walter Monroe Container Company. Although it was the purchasing agent's impression that the product line of the Monroe Company was more expensive than top management of Sunflower Dairy initially had in mind, he had consented to visit the Monroe manufacturing plant along with the chief engineer of Sunflower Dairy who was responsible for the expansion project.

Upon arriving at Monroe's plant the purchasing agent and the chief engineer were greeted by Monroe's sales manager, Tom Huntington, who quickly got down to business. "Gentlemen," he said, "we have invited you here to show you first hand what our capabilities are for producing stainless steel tanks that will meet your needs for a quality product."

The sales manager and the two visitors toured the company's manufacturing facilities. Sunflower's chief engineer was impressed with the cleanliness of the manufacturing plant which fabricated metal products and the apparent industry of the workmen as they went about their production duties. When he asked the sales manager about this general attitude of productivity on the part of the work force the sales manager replied, "We have had seven expansions of our plant in the past ten years. Our work force is well paid by local labor market standards, and management emphasizes high quality on all work. This attitude goes right down to the first-line supervisors and to the men who are doing the work on the floor. The success we have enjoyed with our products by emphasizing quality workmanship and being willing to pay for it has justified the higher prices we have had to charge."

Using a medium-size container the sales manager pointed out the attention given to finishing the outside of the tanks with final grinding and polishing by hand. He stated that the purpose of this extra work was to give a pleasing appearance to the product and that special attention was given in the design phase of such equipment to provide more safety features than were customarily required. "We realize," the sales manager indicated, "that many of the purchasers of our products have plant tours by their customers and the general public. We think that an attractive, well-designed piece of machinery is important from a public relations viewpoint as well as from the point of view of the production manager."

The sales manager of Monroe Company also showed them how the fillets[1] on the inside of the tanks were carefully filled in and finished to eliminate the possibility of residue building up in the close corners of the tanks. This feature not only represented a health and safety feature, but made it easier for the tanks to be cleaned and reduced maintenance costs for the user.

After the plant tour the sales manager outlined the product which the Monroe Company hoped to sell to the Sunflower Dairy for their expanded facility. He pointed out how some of the specifications of the Monroe product exceeded those called for in the initial request for price quotations on the part of Sunflower and why his company felt these changes were desirable. Monroe engineers had made some design changes which they believed improved the product and made it easier to service. The sales manager frankly stated that Monroe's price was as low as was possible in view of the product and quality. In spite of this, the purchasing agent for Sunflower Dairy knew that this price was some 10 percent higher than competing products which would lack some of the quality features but which would probably provide satisfactory service.

Upon their return to the home office, as the two Sunflower executives discussed their trip, the chief engineer concluded by saying, "I am very impressed with the Monroe operation and they have given me some good ideas on equipment design. However, their price is higher and you know what the president said at the last management meeting about costs on the new expansion."

1. What issues face the purchasing agent at this point?
2. How should he proceed to deal with these issues?
3. Appraise the production and marketing philosophy of the Walter Monroe Container Company in the light of a competitive market for their products.

---

[1] A fillet is a concave junction formed when two surfaces come together. In this case two metal pieces come together to form the edge of a tank creating a concave surface inside the tank.

Accounting and finance

Accounting systems must be devised for the efficient recording and analysis of business transactions.

14

Understanding accounting statements

Accounting consists of the recording, analysis, and reporting of enterprise transactions in monetary terms. Accounting has been called the language of business because it provides the basis for financial reporting of profits or losses and for presentation of the economic picture of the enterprise. Every manager should understand the basic accounting statements regardless of his particular role in the organization. Because an understanding of accounting is so important to management, the following issues are discussed.

How are accounting data used by management?
Why are financial statements important for groups other than management?
What are the basic accounting statements?
How are these statements analyzed?

The use of accounting data

The information provided by the enterprise's accounting system is of vital interest to groups both inside and outside the business enterprise. Within the enterprise the effective management of operations would be impossible without some type of financial progress reports made on a periodic basis. Groups outside the company which make use of financial statements include stockholders, bankers, and governmental agencies.

Management uses of accounting

An essential use of an enterprise's accounting system is in the determination of operating results. Accounting provides the basis for determining profits or losses over a given period of time. The measurement of income and the statement of an enterprise's financial position at a given point in time are an essential part of the management process, especially with regard to control.

For control purposes accounting provides a basis for establishing quantitative standards, a means for measuring performance, and suggests ways of analyzing variations from expectations. Accounting reports are helpful for communicating plans throughout the organization. Standards set in financial terms are easily disseminated and provide a good basis for evaluating subsequent performance. These evaluations may result in promotion of personnel, commendations, or salary increases, as well as corrective action, demotions, or possible dismissals. While evaluation of personnel should not depend solely upon the quantitative data provided by the accounting system, much valuable information for control purposes is available through this medium. Financial reports and budgets give management personnel a specific set of criteria so that they know what is expected of them.

Outsiders' use of accounting information

Information derived from the enterprise's accounting system is useful to individuals and organizations outside the enterprise. Outsiders who make use of accounting data include stockholders, governmental agencies, banks, and creditors of the enterprise.

Stockholders' use. In the small business enterprise organized as a proprietorship or a partnership where the owners are directly involved in the management there is no need to publicize the financial results of operations for the benefit of the owners. The owners are already aware of the enterprise's profitability and financial condition. However, in today's large corporations there is a separation of ownership and management. The thousands of stockholders who are the owners of the corporation have no direct voice in the management of the enterprise and no knowledge of results unless published financial reports are made available to them. The managements of widely owned corporations have a responsibility to provide this information to their shareholders through regularly published financial statements. This information is made available to the general public since it is of interest not only to present stockholders of the corporation but also is necessary for analysis by those who may be considering the purchase of stock in the corporation. Thus both present and prospective shareholders are vitally interested in the financial statements of large corporations.

Governmental use. The reporting of financial information is required by numerous governmental agencies. Tax authorities require detailed financial reports from business enterprises to accompany the payment of a wide variety of local, state, and federal taxes. Customarily, tax returns are considered confidential by governmental agencies except that in recent years there has been a move toward greater cooperation between state and federal income tax authorities to assure better conformation with tax regulations of both. Public disclosure of the financial standing of widely held corporations is required by the Securities and Exchange Commission, an agency of the federal government established in 1934. The SEC requires that corporations provide adequate information to investors about new stock and bond issues, reveal dealings in their own stock by enterprise executives, and in general protects the interests of the public with respect to misinformation and actions taken by management. Stock exchanges and investment advisors are also subject to SEC regulations to protect stockholders.

Banks' and creditors' use. Accounting information about enterprise operations is required by banks and other financial institutions before they lend money to the enterprise. The business manager should be prepared to provide complete information, not only about past results of the enterprise but also a financial projection of future plans, when he appears before a banker to borrow funds. This financial planning should include some evidence that the management has considered its needs carefully and has estimated when the loan can be repaid if it is granted.

The business enterprise is also required to provide accounting statements to its trade creditors, especially when trade credit is being established for the first time. The *trade creditor* is an individual or enterprise which supplies merchandise or services to the firm and is willing to ship such merchandise without requiring cash payment upon delivery. Before a trade creditor will ship merchandise to a firm for the first time, it is customary to analyze the financial statements of the customer to determine that the chances are good that the merchandise will be paid for according to the terms of the credit. The terms of trade credit vary with the industry and local circumstances. Customarily, trade credit is granted for periods of 30 to 60 days with cash discounts of 1 or 2 percent of the billed price being given for prompt payment, such as within ten days from the date on the invoice. Whatever the credit terms, the purchasing enterprise should observe them faithfully to maintain good relations with its suppliers and to retain its good credit standing in the community.

The basic accounting statements

The balance sheet and the income statement are the two most widely used accounting statements. They provide much information about the enterprise's financial condition and operations. An understanding of these two statements is essential for financial analysis and control.

The balance sheet

The *balance sheet* is a financial picture of the enterprise at a given point in time, usually at the end of a fiscal period. It is a statement of the assets which the enterprise owns and the claims against those assets. The claims against the enterprise's assets are either claims by outsiders, called liabilities, or claims by the owners, called owners' equity or net worth. It is this balancing of the assets of the business enterprise against the claims to the assets that gives the balance sheet its name. Therefore, the equation which represents the balance sheet is:

$$\text{Assets} = \text{Liabilities} + \text{Net Worth}$$

Most accounting systems are set up using what is known as *double-entry* record keeping. Whenever an asset is acquired there is an entry to account for both the asset and any change in liabilities or other accounts of the balance sheet which would have occurred as the result of the transaction. Transactions involving changes in liabilities or net worth accounts also require another accounting entry to keep the accounts in balance.

Assume that a new enterprise is started by a person who set aside $5,000 of his own money to initiate the business. The balance sheet of his new business enterprise after this initial act would be:

Cash $5,000 (assets) = Owner's equity $5,000 (claims)

Next the owner-manager went to a bank and borrowed $3,000 to provide sufficient funds to begin business operations. After this transaction the balance sheet of the enterprise would be:

Cash	$8,000	Owed to bank		$3,000
		Owner's equity		5,000
		Total liabilities and		
Total assets	$8,000	net worth		$8,000

The balance sheet will continue to reflect changes in the accounts of the business enterprise as more assets are acquired, sales are made, and in general the enterprise becomes a functioning system. The balance sheet lists only those assets which are owned by the business enterprise on a specified date; leased or rented assets do not appear on the balance sheet.

The balance sheet in Figure 14–1 illustrates the year-end statement of assets, liabilities, and net worth for a typical manufacturing corporation in simplified form. A discussion of each item on the balance sheet is on the following pages.

FIGURE 14–1
Stewart Manufacturing Corporation balance sheet as of December 31, 1970
(thousands of dollars)

Assets		Liabilities	
Current assets		Current liabilities	
Cash	$ 8,000	Accounts payable	$ 5,000
Accounts receivable	13,000	Notes payable (current)	2,000
Inventories	35,000	Wages payable	1,500
Total current assets	$56,000	Accrued taxes payable	1,000
Fixed assets		Miscellaneous payables	500
Property, plant and		Total current liabilities	$10,000
equipment	$43,000	Long-term liabilities	
Less: Accumulated		Bonds due 1980	$15,000
depreciation	16,000	Bank loans, due 1977	7,000
Net fixed assets	$27,000	Total long-term liabilities	$22,000
Other assets		Total liabilities	$32,000
Patents and trademarks	$ 1,000	Net worth	
Deferred charges	1,500	Common stock	$ 4,000
Miscellaneous assets	500	Capital paid in excess of	
Total other assets	$ 3,000	stated value	23,000
		Retained earnings	27,000
		Total owners' equity	$54,000
		Total liabilities and	
Total assets	$86,000	net worth	$86,000

Assets. *Current assets* are those assets which are cash, realizable in cash, or expected to be sold or consumed during one accounting period and are customarily listed on the balance sheet in order of liquidity.

Cash is listed first since it is easiest to transfer into other assets or to use in paying off the current obligations of the enterprise. Normally cash is held in bank accounts, although sometimes small amounts may be kept in the enterprise's cash drawer for small expenditures or for making change in retail transactions.

Accounts receivable represents the amount of money owed the enterprise by customers to whom credit has been extended. Normally accounts receivable are considered to be relatively liquid since they should be turned into cash during the collection period.

Inventories are made up of the stock of goods the enterprise has available for sale to customers either in its present state or after further processing. Inventories are customarily carried on the books of the enterprise at their cost. The varied nature of inventories is discussed in Chapter 13 on production.

Prepaid expenses are current assets which have been paid for and which will be used up within one year. A typical example is a fire insurance policy purchased to protect the enterprise next year as well as in the current year.

Fixed assets, sometimes called capital assets, represent long-term assets such as buildings, land, and equipment which will not normally be turned into cash but which are necessary for the generation of income for the enterprise. The gross amount of the fixed asset account represents the acquisition cost of such assets. *Accumulated depreciation* represents the amount of the cost of capital assets which has been charged off during the years as the annual cost of using those assets by an enterprise. The depreciation accounts are subtracted from the appropriate fixed asset accounts to arrive at the net value of fixed assets as of the date of the balance sheet.

Other assets is a "catchall" category that includes all assets not listed either as current or fixed. Other assets are sometimes intangible in nature, such as patents and trademarks. *Patents* are exclusive rights to a product or process conferred by government authority to the holder, while *trademarks* are words or symbols which identify a particular brand of merchandise. Registered trademarks are protected by legal restrictions against their use by unauthorized persons or enterprises.

Deferred charges are classified as other assets. Deferred charges are longer term expenses which have been paid in advance and which will be charged against revenue in the future. The cost of organizing the enterprise is sometimes handled in this way.

Liabilities. Liabilities are claims against the business enterprise other than ownership claims. *Current liabilities* are those obligations which will fall due within a short period of time, customarily within the coming year.

Accounts payable are amounts owed to suppliers for purchases of inventory goods. If appropriate written acknowledgment of the debt is made by the enterprise the account payable becomes a *note payable.* Sometimes notes are signed to recognize formally the financial obligations to banks, to other financial institutions which supply money, or to vendors which supply merchandise.

Wages payable represents amounts owed to employees for their services performed. This obligation is paid each payday, and the amount which accrues will depend upon both the level of wages paid and the frequency of their payment, such as weekly or monthly.

Accrued taxes payable is the size of the enterprise's current tax liability to various governmental bodies. Customarily, a large proportion of this figure is to cover income tax liabilities which build up with profitable operations and which must be paid according to the tax schedules set up by federal and state authorities. Sometimes the taxes payable account on the balance sheet will be broken down into the types of taxes payable, such as income taxes, social security taxes, and property taxes to mention a few.

Miscellaneous payables is another "catchall" account for any outsiders' recognized financial claims against the enterprise which have not been listed elsewhere. The *total current liabilities* is the amount of funds which the management expects to have to pay out in the near future.

Long-term liabilities are those financial obligations which will not have to be paid off during the coming year. These may stem from a variety of borrowing arrangements. In the Stewart Manufacturing balance sheet illustration there are two long-term liabilities, bonds and bank loans. The bond is a debt contract which is discussed along with other aspects of long-term financing in Chapter 16 on financial management.

Net worth. The *net worth,* or owners' equity, section of the balance sheet gives the amount of the claims by owners to the assets of the enterprise. Although the net worth section of a corporation is divided into various accounts such as preferred stock, common stock, capital surplus, and retained earnings, these divisions are for legal or accounting purposes and do not have much financial significance except for preferred stockholders who constitute a different class of owners.

Preferred stock, of which there is none in Stewart Manufacturing, is the class of ownership shares in a corporation which has preference over common stock as to a stated amount of cash dividends each year and also priority as to assets in event that the corporation should be liquidated. If the corporation's assets were liquidated and the enterprise disbanded, the preferred stockholders would have a claim to a stated amount of funds after all liabilities to outsiders had been settled. Then, after the preferred stockholders' interests were satisfied, the common stockholders would divide up the remainder of the corporation's assets proportionate to the number of shares of common stock each one held.

When a corporation's common stock is sold, a stated amount of the proceeds is recorded in the *common stock* account. The sample balance sheet shows $4 million for common stock. Any amount paid for the common stock in excess of the stated value is recorded in an account titled *capital paid in excess of stated value.* Both accounts reflect the amount of funds received by the corporation for the common stock which has been issued. A detailed balance sheet will normally indicate the number of shares of common stock held by the corporation's owners. In the case of Stewart Manufacturing the number of shares of common stock outstanding is approximately 1,600,000.

An important part of the net worth section of the balance sheet is the *retained earnings* account, sometimes called *earned surplus,* which shows the amount of profits earned by the enterprise over the years and kept in the business to strengthen and expand operations. The amount of retained earnings varies each year, depending upon annual profits or losses and the amount of dividends authorized by the corporation's board of directors to be paid on a per share basis of stock outstanding. Profits earned would increase the amount of the retained earnings while losses would decrease the amount as would any dividends paid to shareholders since these payments would remove capital funds from the control of the business enterprise.

The balance sheets for corporations, partnerships, and proprietorships are similar in the listing of assets and liabilities, although there are some distinctions in accounting for ownership interests among these different forms of business organization. Even though the net worth sections have the accounts designated differently, each type of enterprise has a net worth section which shows the owners' claims to the assets of the enterprise. In all instances the owners' claims are satisfied after the claims of others. For this reason the net worth, or owners' equity, is called a residual claim to the enterprise's assets.

The analysis of the balance sheet is discussed after a description of the income statement, which is also essential for the financial analysis of business operations.

The income statement

In contrast to the balance sheet which portrays assets and liabilities as of a certain date, the income statement summarizes what has occurred in the business system's operations between two different points of time. Thus the income statement is drawn up to cover a period such as a year or some other period of time over which management wants to measure its operations. The income statement is sometimes called the profit and loss statement or the operating statement and can be expressed in the following simple equation:

$$\text{Revenue} - \text{Expenses} = \text{Net Income}$$

or stated using different terminology,

$$\text{Sales} - \text{Costs} = \text{Profit}$$

The accrual concept of accounting. The basic calculation of profit for any given period of time consists of matching the revenues of that period against the expenses which were necessary to generate the revenue. In the *accrual concept* of accounting, income is recognized in the period when it is earned and expenses in the period when they are incurred regardless of whether there is an actual exchange of cash during that period. This distinction between receipt and disbursement of cash and the accrual of revenues and expenses is a very important aspect of accounting. Following are two examples to clarify the distinction between changes in cash balances versus income and expense determination.

First, consider the income resulting from sales of merchandise ordered by a customer in December, shipped during that month, and charged to his account. When an income statement is prepared for the year ending December 31, this sale of merchandise will be considered as revenue for the year even though on the books of the enterprise which made the sale the customer still owes for the goods. The selling enterprise has increased its accounts receivable in recognition of the trade debt of one of its customers. The expenses of the sale, including the cost of the merchandise and the other expenses associated with the sale, were also charged to December's operations.

It is assumed that the customer's credit is good and that the account will be paid when it is due or shortly thereafter, since the customer's credit standing would have been investigated before merchandise was shipped to him on open account. If a question had arisen as to the credit-worthiness of the prospective customer, the selling enterprise would have either sold merchandise for cash only or have required a written note in acknowledgment of the credit extended or have refused the order. When the customer pays his account the selling enterprise's accounting system will show an increase in cash and a coincident decrease in accounts receivable. However, the income and expenses were charged to December's operations and not to when the cash was actually received for a credit sale. Should the customer have failed to pay his account the bad debt would have been recorded during a subsequent year's operations to reflect a failure in the collection process.

A second example of the accrual concept has already been shown by the illustration of prepayment of fire insurance discussed as a balance sheet item. Let us assume that in early January the enterprise buys a fire insurance policy which runs for three years and has a total premium of $3,000. The company's treasurer signs a check for $3,000 when the policy is taken out, but only $1,000 is charged as an expense for the current year. To charge the entire $3,000 insurance premium against the current year's operations just because the cash was paid out then would place an unfair burden against that year's income since the fire insurance policy has a three-year life and will be of value over this entire period. Thus the cost of this insurance coverage is prorated over the three years of the policy's useful life without regard to when the premium was actually paid.

In summary, in the accrual concept of accounting, the recognition of revenues and expenses is made independently of when cash is actually received or paid out by the business enterprise. Revenues are usually considered to be realized when goods are shipped and not when cash is received for their payment. Expenses are matched against revenues as being those costs necessary to generate the revenues. Those costs incurred today which affect current operations are charged as expenses against current revenues in the determination of profits during the current accounting period. When a cash expenditure is made today to pay for some future anticipated expense this cost is capitalized (placed on the enterprise's accounting records as an asset) and is charged off in a future period when it is realized as an expense.

Example of a corporation's profit and loss statement. Figure 14–2 is an illustration of a simplified profit and loss statement, or income statement, of the Stewart Manufacturing Corporation for the year's operations ending on December 31, 1970. Each item on the statement will be explained as an example of the income statement of a typical manufacturing corporation.

FIGURE 14–2

Income statement of Stewart Manufacturing Corporation for the year ended December 31, 1970

Net sales (after deducting returns and cash discounts)	$100,000,000
Less: Cost of goods sold*	70,000,000
Gross income	$ 30,000,000
Less: Selling, general, and administrative expenses	18,000,000
Operating income	$ 12,000,000
Less: Interest expense	1,000,000
Profit before income taxes	$ 11,000,000
Federal income taxes	5,500,000
Net Profit for the Year	$ 5,500,000

* Depreciation of plant and equipment is included in "Cost of goods sold" in the amount of $4 million.

Net sales means that all cash discounts given for prompt payment of goods and credits for returned merchandise have been deducted from the gross sales billings.

Cost of goods sold is the value of merchandise sold calculated at its costs rather than the price for which it is sold. For an enterprise such as a retailer or wholesaler which does not change the form of the goods it sells, the calculation of cost of goods sold is relatively simple. The cost of all purchases made by the retail enterprise is added to the value of its inventory at the beginning of the year. This gives the cost of goods available for sale. Then the value of the inventory at the end of the year is subtracted to give the cost of the goods sold during the accounting period.

In a manufacturing enterprise such as Stewart Manufacturing the cost of goods sold includes the costs added during the manufacturing process. Thus a calculation of cost of goods manufactured is made by adding up the costs of raw materials used during the year, direct labor, factory expenses such as utilities and supplies, insurance, and depreciation on plant and equipment. The costs of goods manufactured is added to the beginning inventory. This sum represents the total amount of manufacturing costs. From this total subtract the value of the inventories at the end of the accounting period, and the difference is the cost of goods sold. Although in actual practice the determination of cost of goods sold is somewhat more complicated than this because of different types of inventories and problems of allocating various costs, this is the essence of the process.

Gross income is found by subtracting the cost of goods sold from net sales and shows the amount from which all other expenses must be deducted.

Selling, general, and *administrative* expenses are deducted from gross income to give operating income.

Operating income is the profit generated from the mainstream of the enterprise's activities. The amount of operating income is a measure of how effective the management is in manufacturing and selling its products. Operating income does not take into account how the enterprise's assets are financed; that is, no deduction has been made for interest expense. Also, no other income items have been added which might arise from investments in land or securities which are considered an ancillary part of an enterprise's operations. And no federal income taxes have been deducted. The reason these items are not considered in determining operating income is that they are either beyond the control of the management of the enterprise or have no direct bearing on operating efficiency. Operating income as a percentage of sales is a good comparative measure of one enterprise with another within an industry in determining relative managerial performance.

Interest expense is the cost of borrowed money and is deducted from operating profits in Figure 14–2. If the enterprise had other income such as interest received or rental income it would be included before interest expense is deducted. The next step in the income statement is showing *profit before taxes* on which amount *federal income taxes* are calculated. The effective rate for corporation income taxes is approximately 50 percent of taxable income.

The bottom figure on the operating statement represents the *net profit* for the period which the statement covers. If this figure is negative the enterprise has suffered a loss during the accounting period and the owners' equity shown on the balance sheet is decreased by that amount. If profits have been earned the owners' equity is increased.

Supporting records. Each of the accounts shown in the balance sheet and income statement is a summary of detailed accounting records which are designed to reflect changes in the totals and to provide specific information about the account. For example, on the balance sheet of Stewart Manufacturing the *accounts receivable* total of $13 million is substantiated by an accounts receivable ledger showing each business enterprise to which Stewart has extended credit. These individual accounts show the value of merchandise shipped, the date of the invoice, and the amount and date of payments received from the customer along with other identifying information that could be used to check the details of transactions with this customer.

The manager has more accounting information available to him other than just the balance sheet and the income statement to use in analyzing enterprise operations. However, these two basic statements provide a summary of the enterprise's situation and may be used as a point of departure for further analysis.

The financial analysis of accounting statements

Once the balance sheet and income statement have been compiled from information provided by the enterprise's accounting system, the analyst must interpret these statements according to his needs. The absolute figures contained in these financial statements are more useful for analytical purposes when they are used to compute ratios which relate different parts of the statements or which can be compared with previous years' situations or with other enterprises in similar industries. Ratios which measure an enterprise's liquidity, profitability, and solvency are helpful tools of financial analysis. The statements shown in Figures 14–1 and 14–2 are used as the basis for illustrations of various financial measurements.

Measures of liquidity

Liquidity is the ability of the enterprise to meet its current financial obligations when they become due. Measures of enterprise liquidity are widely used in analyzing short-term financial strength and operating efficiency.

Current ratio. The current ratio is the relationship of current assets to current liabilities. The current ratio for Stewart Manufacturing is

$$\frac{\text{Current assets}}{\text{Current liabilities}} = \frac{\$56,000,000}{\$10,000,000} = 5.6 \text{ times or 5.6 to 1}$$

This means that current assets are 5.6 times the amount of current liabilities.

This is one of the most widely used balance sheet ratios. It is a measure of the enterprise's short-term liquidity since the ratio gauges the company's ability to pay financial claims which must be met in the near future. The current ratio provides management with a means of determining the margin of safety available for meeting short-term obligations since inflows of funds cannot be timed perfectly in the operation of the business.

Acid test ratio. The acid test ratio is the measure of *quick assets* to current liabilities. Quick assets consist of cash, short-term investments which are held instead of cash, and accounts (or notes) receivable. For Stewart Manufacturing the acid test ratio is:

$$\frac{\text{Quick assets}}{\text{Current liabilities}} = \frac{\$21,000,000}{\$10,000,000} = 2.1 \text{ times or 2.1 to 1}$$

Essentially the acid test ratio is a measure of short-term liquidity like the current ratio except that inventories and prepaid expenses are excluded from the assets which may be turned into cash. This makes the acid test ratio a more severe test of enterprise liquidity. With the current ratio, before the value of inventory could be turned into cash, additional sales of inventory would have to be made and the accounts collected. There would necessarily be a time lag before inventory could be liquidated. By use of the acid test ratio the measure of immediately available liquid resources is determined, assuming that the accounts and notes receivable from customers can be collected.

The stronger the short-term financial position of the enterprise the higher will be the current and acid test ratios. The quality of the items contained in the ratios is important to consider since inventory may not be worth the value at which it is carried on the books if it is obsolete or in poor condition. Likewise, if the accounts receivable are of low quality, with customers being slow to pay their accounts or refusing to pay, then a high ratio may delude the analyst. An enterprise's management will have access to such information, but the outside analyst customarily must rely on further analysis of the accounting statements.

Average collection period. A calculation which may be used to reflect the quality of the enterprise's accounts receivable is the *average collection period*. This ratio is sometimes called *days' sales outstanding in receivables*. It consists of the ratio of trade accounts receivable plus notes receivable to average daily credit sales. Average daily credit sales are calculated by dividing total credit sales for the year by 365 days.

Most published statements do not give a breakdown between credit and cash sales. In this event the analyst should use the annual net sales figure. In retailing establishments a knowledge of the relation between credit and cash sales would be helpful. However, in most manufacturing enterprises nearly all sales are made on some type of short-term credit arrangement. So annual net sales is virtually the same as annual net credit sales. For Stewart Manufacturing the average collection period is calculated in two steps:

$$(1) \quad \frac{\text{Annual net sales}}{365 \text{ days}} = \left(\begin{array}{c} \text{Use credit sales} \\ \text{if available} \end{array} \right) = \frac{\$100,000,000}{365 \text{ days}}$$
$$= \$274,000 \text{ average daily credit sales}$$

$$(2) \quad \frac{\text{Accounts receivable} + \text{Notes receivable (if any)}}{\text{Average daily credit sales}} = \frac{\$13,000,000}{\$274,000}$$
$$= 47 \text{ days' sales outstanding in accounts receivable}$$

Sometimes an average of accounts receivable at the beginning of the accounting period and at the end of the period is taken to give a better approximation of the average amount of receivables over the entire period for which sales are calculated.

The number of days of receivables outstanding should be compared with the credit terms of sale given by the enterprise to customers. While it is usual to expect that the collection period may be somewhat longer than the stated credit terms, the analyst should compare collection period figures with previous years' experience and with other enterprises in the same industry if these statistics are available. If the collection period is lengthening management should take steps to improve its credit granting and collection practices or face an increasing financial burden caused by the larger amount of credit outstanding.

Inventory turnover. The *inventory turnover* ratio gives an indication of the number of times that merchandise moves through the enterprise during the period under study. Inventory turnover is computed by dividing the cost of goods sold by the average inventory. Average inventory is commonly determined by adding the beginning and ending inventories for the accounting period and dividing this sum by 2. The inventory for Stewart Manufacturing on January 1, 1970, was $31 million and on December 31, 1970, was $35 million. Therefore, the average inventory over 1970 for Stewart was $33 million

[($31 + $35)/2]. The annual average inventory turnover was:

$$\frac{\text{Cost of goods sold}}{\text{Average inventory}} = \frac{\$70,000,000}{\$33,000,000} = 2.1 \text{ times,}$$

or the inventory turned over once in 174 days.

The inventory turnover ratio is a fairly accurate measure for a retail or wholesale enterprise where the cost of goods sold consists essentially of its purchases during the year. In a manufacturing operation the additional costs of labor and factory expenses are added to materials purchased in calculating cost of goods sold. Therefore, when this ratio is computed for a manufacturing enterprise the analyst should realize it is not a true measure of merchandise turnover. However, when used in comparison with earlier periods or with similar type enterprises the turnover figure is useful for comparison purposes. If the beginning inventory figure is not known, then the ending inventory may be used to calculate inventory turnover.

An increase in the turnover ratio may reflect higher absolute sales of merchandise or a reduction in the amount of inventory in relation to sales. Too large an inventory turnover ratio may mean that sales are being missed because inventory is too small in relation to sales potential. On the other hand, a decrease in inventory turnover may mean an accumulation of inventory because sales have fallen or that some inventory is no longer attractive to customers or that management is anticipating even greater sales and is building inventory to meet this expectation. Under any circumstances, management should carefully investigate changes in inventory turnover to determine the reasons for the change.

Measures of profitability

Overall measures of profitability may be derived from the income statement and the balance sheet. The ratios of net profit to sales, total assets, and net worth are discussed along with a vertical analysis of the income statement.

Vertical analysis of income statement. The vertical analysis of the income statement consists of a percentage relationship of all items in the income statement to sales. This reflects the proportion of the various expenses and the resulting profitability. Vertical analysis is useful when comparing the enterprise's current operations with past periods or with industry statistics. However, sometimes an enterprise's financial statements will have to be rearranged if they are compared with industry statistics if different items are included in one heading or another. The percentage breakdown of Stewart Manufacturing's income statement derived from Figure 14–2 is:

Vertical analysis, income statement for the year ended December 31, 1965

Sales	100.0%
Less: Cost of goods sold	70.0
Gross income	30.0%
Less: Selling, general, and administrative expenses	18.0
Operating income	12.0%
Less: Interest expense	1.0
Profit before income taxes	11.0%
Less: Federal income taxes	5.5
Net Profit	5.5%

From the income statement percentage breakdown the relative importance of the different expenses is apparent, and management can go to work in analyzing those of greatest importance which show the most need of attention. By comparing changes in the different income statement percentage breakdowns from one year to another, the reasons for changes in net profits can be more easily pinpointed than if only the dollar amounts are studied. The vertical analysis provides an important overall measure of profitability: *net profit* (net income) *to sales.* In the case of Stewart this ratio was:

$$\frac{\text{Net profit}}{\text{Net sales}} = \frac{\$\ 5{,}500{,}000}{\$100{,}000{,}000} = 5.5\%$$

Net profit to total assets. To measure the overall rate of return management is earning on all the assets of the enterprise, the ratio of *net profit to total assets* is used. For Stewart this is:

$$\frac{\text{Net profit}}{\text{Total assets}} = \frac{\$\ 5{,}500{,}000}{\$86{,}000{,}000} = 6.4\%$$

Net profit to net worth (owners' equity). Since the profits earned by an enterprise represent the return on the owners' investment, a good measure of profitability is that of *net profit to net worth.* Since part of the assets are financed through the use of outsiders' funds, creating the liabilities portion of the balance sheet, the percentage of net profit to owners' equity will be higher than the measure of net profit to total assets. For Stewart this ratio is:

$$\frac{\text{Net profit}}{\text{Net worth}} = \frac{\$\ 5,500,000}{\$54,000,000} = 10.2\%$$

The use of debt to increase the rate of return on owners' equity is discussed in Chapter 16 on financial management.

Measures of solvency

Liquidity, which was discussed earlier, refers to the ability of the enterprise to meet its cash needs for current business operations. *Solvency* refers to the enterprise's ability to pay the principal on long-term financial obligations when it falls due as well as to meet the interest payments on outstanding indebtedness. With the creation of more indebtedness the owners of the enterprise assume more risk since these debts will have to be repaid at some time in the future. Measures of solvency include the ratio of owners' equity to total debt, long-term debt to total assets, the capital structure, and the number of times interest is earned.

Owners' equity to total debt. The ratio of *owners' equity to total debt* measures the amount of the net worth of owners compared with the amount of claims against the enterprise by outsiders. This is an important measure of how much protection creditors have against shrinkage of the value of the assets of the enterprise. For Stewart the ratio is:

$$\frac{\text{Owners' equity}}{\text{Total debt}} = \frac{\$54,000,000}{\$32,000,000} = 1.7 \text{ times or } 1.7 \text{ to } 1$$

This means that for each $1 of liabilities outstanding on December 31, 1970, there was $1.70 of net worth. The larger this ratio the greater the protection for creditors and the less risk that the business enterprise will be faced with insolvency.

Long-term debt to total assets. While the previous ratio took into account all the liabilities of the enterprise, the ratio of long-term debt to total assets only measures the proportion of indebtedness which falls due more than a year in the future in relation to the total assets of the enterprise. For Stewart this ratio is:

$$\frac{\text{Long-term debt}}{\text{Total assets}} = \frac{\$22,000,000}{\$86,000,000} = 25.6\%$$

This ratio shows what proportion of the enterprise's assets are being financed by long-term debt. Both interest and principal repayments must be made according to a schedule agreed upon at the time long-term funds are borrowed. Since future business conditions cannot be forecast with extreme accuracy, the prudent management is unwilling to finance too great a proportion of total assets by use of long-term debt. To do so might jeopardize the enterprise's solvency at some time in the future as the result of circumstances which arise subsequent to the borrowing. Management should analyze the nature of its anticipated cash inflows over future years before undertaking long-term borrowing. The advantages of borrowing for such business needs are discussed in Chapter 16 on financial management. Each management must establish its own policies regarding long-term debt after examining its industry patterns and its own enterprise's specific circumstances and opportunities.

Capital structure. The capital structure is the composition of the long-term funds, both debt and net worth, that are committed to management's direction. The determination of the proportion of debt and equity funds is such an important issue that the alternatives for management are discussed in Chapter 16.

Times interest earned. The *number of times interest is earned* is a measure of the enterprise's ability to meet current interest charges on borrowed funds. For Stewart Manufacturing this ratio is:

$$\frac{\text{Operating income}}{\text{Interest}} = \frac{\$12,000,000}{\$\ 1,000,000} = 12.0 \text{ times}$$

In this instance the annual interest charge is covered 12 times by operating income. Since interest is a tax-deductible expense, any interest charges are deducted before income taxes are computed. Thus the operating profit plus other income, if any, is used as a measure of the enterprise's ability to pay this expense rather than net profit, which is an after-tax figure. The more times interest charges are covered by operating income the safer the situation from the viewpoint of both lender and borrower.

The basis of accounting data

Information drawn from accounting statements is useful for a wide variety of purposes and by a number of different groups. The calculation of profits is essential for businesses in the private enterprise system. Accounting statements provide outsiders with information which is useful for their decisions regarding their relationship to the enterprise.

Management uses the accounting system to provide a basis for planning and control. The analysis of accounting statements may lead a business enterprise to improve its future business practices.

The foundation of the accounting system which provides the basis for this information and analysis is the completed business transaction. Accounting consists of the recording, analysis, and reporting of the monetary transactions of the business enterprise. The accounting system is geared to provide data which will be consistent from one accounting period to the next. This facilitates comparison of results with previous periods, with plans and standards, and provides management with a yardstick for measuring its financial stewardship of the owners' investment in the business enterprise.

Summary

Accounting is the recording, analysis, and reporting of enterprise transactions in monetary terms. Management uses accounting data for the determination of operating results and for control purposes. Accounting statements are also used by present and potential owners of business enterprises, by governmental agencies, and by present and potential creditors.

The balance sheet presents a financial picture of the business enterprise's assets, liabilities, and owners' equity at a given point in time. Typical current assets include cash, accounts receivable, and inventories. Fixed assets are represented by land, buildings, and equipment. Other assets include patents, trademarks, and deferred expenses.

Current liabilities usually include accounts payable, wages payable, accrued taxes, and miscellaneous payables. Long-term liabilities may be items such as bonds and bank loans which do not fall due during the next year.

Owners' equity, or net worth, shows the amount of the claims of owners to the assets of the enterprise.

In contrast to the balance sheet which portrays assets and claims against those assets as of a certain date, the income statement summarizes what has occurred in enterprise transactions between two different points of time. The income statement, or the profit and loss statement, shows the revenues during a given period and the expenses associated with their generation. The difference between revenues and expenses is income for the period.

In the accrual concept of accounting, income is recognized in the period when it is earned and expenses in the period when they are incurred, regardless of whether there is an actual cash flow during that period.

In financial analysis, measures of liquidity analyze the ability of the enterprise to meet its current financial obligations when they become due. The current ratio and the acid test ratio are common measures of liquidity. The collection period for accounts receivable and the inventory turnover ratio are measures calculated to analyze current operations.

Measures of overall profitability include the ratios of net profit to sales, net profit to total assets, and net profit to net worth.

Solvency measures the enterprise's ability to pay the principal as well as to meet the required schedule of interest payments on long-term financial obligations such as bonds. Measures of solvency include the ratio of owners' equity to total debt, the ratio of long-term debt to total assets, the composition of the capital structure, and the number of times that interest charges on borrowed funds are earned.

Terms for review

accounting
balance sheet
owners' equity (net worth)
double-entry record keeping
current assets
fixed assets
current liabilities

long-term liabilities
income statement (profit and loss
   statement)
accrual concept of accounting
liquidity
solvency

Questions

1. In addition to managers and owners, why are outside groups interested in accounting statements of corporations?
2. Explain the accounting equation.
3. Indicate how changes in assets, liabilities, or net worth sections are reflected in the balance sheet.
4. What information does the income statement provide?

5. Explain the accrual concept of accounting.

6. Examine either *Moody's Industrial Manual* or *Standard & Poor's Corporation Records* in the library for examples of balance sheets and income statements. In what ways do these vary from the examples in Figures 14–1 and 14–2?

7. Select a balance sheet and income statement of a corporation and suggest changes which would make it more meaningful to the average stockholder.

8. What is the purpose of ratio analysis? Explain the usefulness of the specific ratios relating to liquidity, profitability, and solvency to (*a*) management and (*b*) a potential investor.

BUSINESS BRIEF

Interpreting accounting statements

Penn Central railroad in 1971 was the largest railroad in the United States, operating some 21,000 miles of line from the East Coast to the Midwest. In mid-1970 Penn Central's deteriorating financial condition brought on the initiation of reorganization under bankruptcy proceedings. The question was then raised as to whether some stockholders had benefited from inside information about the railroad's worsening financial condition enabling them to sell Penn Central common stock before it had declined in market price all the way from a 1970 high of more than $30 per share to less than $6 per share by December 1970.

The accused stockholders, several large financial institutions, denied any improper actions. These institutions claimed that their decisions to sell Penn Central common stock had been based on information that was publicly available to any investor. To support this argument, they pointed out that the public accounting statements of Penn Central at the end of 1968 had shown $161 million more current liabilities than current assets although the company earned $90 million in profits that year. One year later, at the end of 1969 the excess of current liabilities over current assets was $206 million and profits had declined to $4 million. At the end of 1970 the railroad was in bankruptcy proceedings, and losses from operations amounted to some $330 million.

At present certified public accountants are required only to certify that a company's accounting statements are accurate and fairly presented. There is no law or accounting requirement for the CPA to present an analysis of the corporation's financial condition and past performance. Financial institutions and large investors have the knowledge (or financial analysts) to analyze the published accounting statements of publicly held corporations. Some authorities point out that the typical individual investor does not have such knowledge and therefore is at a disadvantage.

1. Should there be a change in present practice to require the CPA to point up problems and interpret past accounting transactions to stockholders instead of simply certifying that the published statements (such as the balance sheet and income statement) conform to "generally accepted accounting principles applied on a consistent basis" with previous years' statements?

2. If such a change were made in the work of the outside auditor (CPA), who would determine what constituted a problem area or transaction important enough to be brought to the public's attention through analysis and interpretation?

3. How could the outside auditor's analysis and interpretation be useful to the internal management of a business enterprise?

4. What problems might arise for the outside auditor making an accounting analysis and interpretation of a publicly held corporation's operations?

CASES

The Chocolate Heart Candy Store, Inc.

The Chocolate Heart Candy Store was opened in the new Parkwood Mall, an enclosed regional shopping center, in the summer of 1970 and soon became very popular. In addition to prepackaged assortments the store carried quality candy which was boxed to the individual customer's specification.

In January, 1972, the owners of the shop, Mr. and Mrs. Gerald Ford, were reviewing the first full year's operations. Up to that point the only formal accounting statements which they had used had been the balance sheets and income tax returns which were prepared by a tax accounting service. The Fords felt that the candy store was a success, but they

EXHIBIT 1

Chocolate Heart Candy Store, Inc.
(balance sheet—December 31, 1970)

Assets			Liabilities		
Current assets			Current liabilities		
Cash	$	900	Wages payable	$	300
Merchandise inventory		4,100	Accounts payable		2,600
Supplies		300	Income taxes payable		250
		$ 5,300			$ 3,150
Fixed assets			Long-term liabilities		
Fixtures	$8,000		Bank loan, due 1977		3,000
Less: accumulated depreciation	400	7,600	Total liabilities		$ 6,150
			Net Worth		
			Common stock $6,000		
			Retained earnings 750		6,750
			Total liabilities and		
Total assets		$12,900	net worth		$12,900

EXHIBIT 2

Taken from the cash records of Chocolate Heart Candy Store, Inc. for 1971

Cash receipts		Cash disbursements	
Cash sales	$48,250	Wages paid	$11,000
		Rent	5,000
		Advertising	2,500
		Utilities	1,060
		Insurance	200
		Interest	240
		Income taxes, 1970	250
		Miscellaneous cash	
		expenses	350
		Paid on accounts payable	
		for merchandise and	
		supplies during 1971	24,100
		Total expenditures	$44,700
		Cash balance,	
Cash balance, Dec. 31, 1970	900	Dec. 31, 1971	4,450
	$49,150		$49,150

EXHIBIT 3

As of Dec. 31, 1971

Inventory on hand	$3,700
Supplies on hand	300
Accounts payable	2,200
Wages payable	300

Annual depreciation rate on fixed assets is 10 percent of original cost.
Income tax rate is estimated to be 25 percent of taxable income.

believed that some additional analysis would help them make a better judgment in the matter.

In addition to the balance sheet for the year ended December 31, 1970, the records of the Chocolate Heart Candy Store included a record of all checks paid during 1971 and a file of unpaid invoices which were owed to suppliers. All candy sales were for cash.

1. From the information given in Exhibits 1, 2, and 3 determine:
    a) sales for 1971
    b) cost of merchandise sold
    c) total expenses for 1971.
2. Prepare an income statement for 1971 and a balance sheet as of December 31, 1971.
3. How can these statements be useful to the Fords? What measures could they use to determine how successful they were in their first full year of operation?

Stewart Manufacturing Corporation

Richard Knight was a loan officer at a Boston bank. For several years he had been interested in Stewart Manufacturing Corporation. Stewart

EXHIBIT 1

Stewart Manufacturing Corporation balance sheet as of December 31, 1971 (millions of dollars)

Assets		Liabilities	
Current assets		Current liabilities	
Cash	$ 5	Accounts payable	$ 16
Accounts receivable	15	Wages payable	1
Inventories	54	Accrued taxes payable	2
Total current assets	$ 74	Miscellaneous payables	1
Fixed assets		Total current liabilities	$ 20
Property, plant and equipment	$ 45	Long-term liabilities	
Less: Accumulated depreciation	21	Bonds due 1980	$ 15
Net fixed assets	$ 24	Bank loans due 1977	7
Other assets		Total long-term liabilities	$ 22
Patents and trademarks	$ 1	Total liabilities	$ 42
Miscellaneous assets	1		
Total other assets	$ 2	Net worth	
		Common stock	$ 4
		Capital paid in excess of stated value	23
		Retained earnings	31
		Total owners' equity	$ 58
Total assets	$100	Total liabilities and net worth	$100

Manufacturing produced a variety of industrial products and had experienced some growth over recent years.

Knight was one of several hundred stockholders of Stewart Manufacturing Corporation's common stock. In February, 1972, he received the company's annual report for 1971 which was mailed to all stockholders along with a notice of the annual stockholders' meeting which would be held in approximately two weeks. Although Mr. Knight did not plan to attend the stockholders' meeting, he wanted to analyze the company's financial records to see what progress had been made over the year and to compare the results with 1970.

Exhibits 1 and 2 are summaries of information taken from the annual report which Mr. Knight used in his analysis.

EXHIBIT 2

Stewart Manufacturing Corporation income statement for
the year ended December 31, 1971
(millions of dollars)

Net sales (after returns and cash discounts)	$120
Less: Cost of goods sold*	85
Gross income	$ 35
Less: Selling, general, and administrative expenses	19
Operating income	$ 16
Less: Interest expense	2
Profit before income taxes	$ 14
Income taxes	7
Net Profit	$ 7

* Depreciation of plant and equipment is included in cost of goods sold in the amount of $5 million.
Note: Dividends on common stock were paid from retained earnings during 1971 in the amount of $3 million.

1. Compare sales, profits, and total assets shown in the 1971 Stewart statements with those given in Chapter 14 for 1970.

2. Prepare a financial analysis for 1971 using the measures of liquidity, profitability, and solvency developed in Chapter 14. Compare 1971 ratios with those given for 1970.

3. What significant changes occurred in the company's financial picture during 1971?

4. As a stockholder what additional financial information would make your analysis more meaningful?

*Financial institutions
serve individuals
as well as business
enterprises.*

15

Financial institutions

The influence of financial institutions upon the functioning of business in the United States and abroad is profound. Without an effective means in the economy for regulating the money supply and for providing necessary debt and equity funds, business would not be able to operate. The financial institutions of this country act to make money available for business, consumers, and government and to direct savings into avenues for investment. Either directly or indirectly every business enterprise's success depends upon the money and capital markets. This chapter deals with the following issues.

What is the nature of our system of financial institutions?
What is the role of the U.S. Treasury and the Federal Reserve System in influencing the financial markets?
How are financial markets classified?
What are the different financial institutions and how do they serve the private enterprise system?
What are the services performed by investment bankers?

Our system of financial institutions

Financial institutions are those establishments which regulate the money supply and which serve as channels for savers' funds to those business enterprises, individuals, and governmental bodies which need them to carry out economic activity. Although business can expand by reinvesting its profits generated by producing and marketing goods and services, frequently additional money from outside the enterprise is required. The external funds are obtained through various financial institutions either in the form of debt incurred through borrowing or as equity funds through the sale of additional shares of stock in the corporation. When the business enterprise needs either short-term or long-term loans or equity capital, financial institutions exist to provide the particular type of funds which are required.

Besides providing funds for business enterprise, financial institutions loan money to various governmental units and to individual consumers. The federal government, states, counties, cities, and school districts borrow money through the issuance of bonds on which different financial institutions bid. Then these governmental units spend the funds obtained from the sale of these bonds for goods and services which in most cases are provided by private business enterprises. Other financial institutions specialize in providing individual consumers with funds which they may use for the acquisition of goods and services from business. Thus business is influenced both directly and indirectly by the activities of financial institutions which act as intermediaries between those in the economy who have savings to be invested and those who want to spend the funds for goods or services.

There is a wide range of financial institutions which act to influence the money supply and which tie together the sources and the uses of the money and capital funds markets. The U.S. Treasury and the Federal Reserve System are active in determining the money supply, while investment bankers act as intermediaries for channeling both debt and equity funds to business enterprises. Commercial banks, life insurance companies, savings and loan associations, mutual savings banks, pension funds, and a number of other specialized financial institutions exist to fulfill particular financial needs. The role of each of these financial institutions needs to be understood by the student of business.

Role of the U.S. Treasury

The U.S. Treasury is included in a discussion of financial institutions because of its functions in providing part of the money supply and in managing the debt of the federal government. The money supply in the United States consists of two chief components: currency and demand deposits. Currency is the token coin and paper money in circulation. Demand deposits held in commercial banks in the form of checking accounts represent the bulk of the public's money supply. As of June 30, 1971, the money supply consisted of $51 billion of currency and $174 billion of demand deposits.

The U.S. Treasury is also an important borrower of funds and provides an opportunity for investors who are interested in a high degree of safety for their principal. The gross direct debt of the U.S. government amounted to $398 billion at the end of June, 1971. This debt was held by lenders ranging from federal agencies, banks, and corporations to individuals holding U.S. saving bonds. The ownership of direct U.S. Treasury debt which is fully guaranteed by the federal government is shown in Table 15–1.

TABLE 15–1
Ownership of direct and fully guaranteed securities of the
U.S. federal government as of June 30, 1971
(billions of dollars)

Held by:

U.S. government agencies and trust funds	$103
Individuals	78
Federal Reserve banks	65
Commercial banks	61
Foreign and international	33
State and local governments	21
Other miscellaneous investors	17
Corporations	10
Insurance companies	7
Mutual savings banks	3
Total	$398

Source: *Federal Reserve Bulletin,* August, 1971.

This U.S. Treasury debt arises out of an excess of expenditures over receipts on the part of the federal government over the years. A large portion of the federal debt was incurred during World War II when huge sums were expended in defending the nation against the Axis powers. In December, 1941, the debt was $64 billion; and at the end of 1945, after four years of war, it had risen to $279 billion. When government expenditures exceed tax collections the government is said to be engaged in deficit financing. When revenues exceed expenditures in a given period the government has a surplus of funds which may be used to reduce the level of indebtedness.

The Federal Reserve System

The basic purpose of the Federal Reserve System is to provide for a flow of money and credit that will foster orderly economic growth and stable prices. The system was established in 1913 although its powers and functions have continued to evolve over the years. The United States is divided into 12 districts with a Federal Reserve bank located in each district to meet regional needs. Figure 15–1 shows the boundaries of the Federal Reserve districts in the continental United States.

FIGURE 15–1
The Federal Reserve System: Geographic boundaries

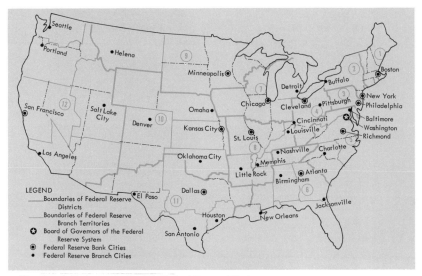

Hawaii and Alaska are in the 12th Federal Reserve District.
Source: *Federal Reserve Bulletin,* April, 1971.

The Federal Reserve System is controlled by the Board of Governors located in Washington, D.C., which consists of seven members appointed by the president of the United States and confirmed by the Senate. The Board of Governors is the most powerful body in the System and is highly influential in determining the level of bank reserves, credit conditions, and rules affecting commercial banks which are members of the Federal Reserve System. Figure 15–2 shows details of the organization of the Federal Reserve System.

All nationally chartered commercial banks are required to belong to the Federal Reserve, and state chartered banks may belong. About 80 percent of deposits in the commercial banking system in this country are in banks which are members of the Federal Reserve System. The stock in the 12 regional Federal Reserve banks is owned by commercial

FIGURE 15-2

The Federal Reserve System: Organization

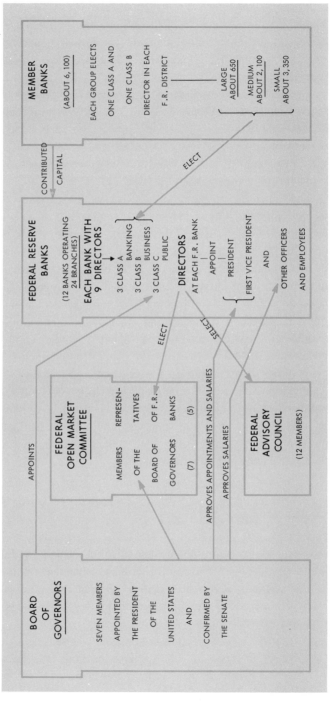

Source: Board of Governors of the Federal Reserve System, *The Federal Reserve System: Purposes and Functions.*

banks which are members of the system. In essence the Federal Reserve System is the U.S. central banker and acts as a banker's bank where member commercial banks which deal with the public can maintain reserve balances, borrow when necessary, and receive advice and direction concerning the economy's movement. However, unlike commercial banks which are private financial enterprises interested in making a profit along with serving their customers, the 12 Federal Reserve banks are not profit-oriented. Any excess of income of Federal Reserve banks after providing for reserves and a fixed percentage return on the bank's stock is turned over to the U.S. Treasury.

The functions of the Federal Reserve System may be summarized as regulating the flow of money and credit and providing certain services for the member banks of the Federal Reserve, the U.S. government, and the public. Services for member banks consist mainly of handling member bank reserve accounts, furnishing currency for circulation and making currency shipments, acting as a central agency for clearing and collection of checks, and lending to member banks under current regulations. For the U.S. Treasury and other governmental agencies, the Federal Reserve System acts as fiscal agent, custodian, and depository for government funds. Services for the general public include collecting and interpreting data bearing on the economic and credit conditions in the country, working with business and academic economists, and undertaking research on monetary and general economic problems. The Federal Reserve also examines and supervises the member banks for good banking practices and cooperates with other bank supervisory agencies of the federal and state governments.

Types of financial markets

Financial markets may be classified according to the users of the funds, the length of time until the debt instrument matures, or whether the transactions represent transfers of debt and equity claims among investors instead of providing new funds for business enterprises, governments, or individuals.

Markets: Users of funds

Individuals, business enterprises, governmental units, and foreign enterprises are four different groups which make use of financial resources provided by savers and made available by financial institutions. Individuals, farmers, and small business enterprises all make use of bank credit of varying maturities along with mortgage credit on real estate extended by banks, savings and loan associations, and insurance companies. Individuals also utilize the services of consumer finance companies and various installment plans of businesses which extend credit to their customers. Business as a user of funds depends upon the financial system for short-, intermediate-, and long-term debt funds as well as the issuance of common stock for equity money from time to time.

The market created by governments' needs for funds include short-term, medium-term, and long-term borrowing by the U.S. Treasury plus state, county, and local governmental units. Despite the increased amount of municipal government obligations outstanding in recent years, the federal government obligations are still highly significant in affecting the availability of credit because of the impact of the federal budget on the economy and the interaction of Treasury operations with the Federal Reserve.

Although the use of American funds by foreign business enterprises and governments has been limited in the past, there has been an increasing investment by American financial institutions in foreign bonds and stocks since World War II. Indeed, the flow of American private investment funds abroad in recent years has been one of the important factors contributing to the net outflow of dollars in America's international balance of payments.

This wide variety of users in the financial markets illustrates the complexity of these markets. Demands by one sector of the users' market can influence the availability of money to other groups. Classification of financial markets based on the type of user of funds provides one useful means of studying the financial markets.

Markets: Length of debt maturities

Financial institutions provide substantial amounts of debt funds for business. These loans include debt contracts which have some form of property as specific collateral and debt which is based on the business enterprise's general credit rating without any specific assets backing up the loan. Many financial institutions deal almost exclusively in the debt markets.

Different financial markets can be distinguished by the length of time for which debt funds are loaned. The *short-term* or "money" market consists of those debt instruments which have maturities of one year or less. The "capital" market constitutes the remainder of the maturity ranges. Usually the capital market is divided into *intermediate-term* and *long-term* sectors. Intermediate-term credit runs from over one year in maturity up to about ten years, with long-term debt capital being those loans which mature in more than ten years.

Markets: Primary or secondary

The *primary securities market* is that which channels funds directly to corporations or governmental bodies in exchange for their securities. In the primary market the issuance and sale of stock or bonds increase the financial resources of the particular enterprise which is issuing the securities. *Secondary markets* are those where the debt or equity instruments which are already outstanding are bought and sold among investors. In secondary markets none of the funds go to the enterprises or governments upon which the debt contracts or equity claims are drawn since they received the funds when the securities were originally issued and sold.

A substantial proportion of transactions in the capital markets consists of transfers of existing securities among investors instead of raising new funds for users. The organized trading markets for corporate bonds and stocks, including the New York and American stock exchanges, are excellent examples of these secondary markets. An active secondary market also exists for various governmental debt issues as well as a secondary market for outstanding real estate mortgage obligations.

Although the secondary markets do not channel any additional funds directly into the business enterprises, an active secondary market for corporate obligations is important since it provides liquidity for commitments made in the primary markets. This degree of liquidity makes investors more willing to participate in the primary securities markets as they feel they can dispose of their securities to other investors should circumstances make this desirable or necessary. Most of the financial institutions discussed in the remainder of this chapter are active in both the primary and secondary markets.

Specific financial institutions

Four types of financial institutions have a very significant influence upon the functioning of the entire economy through their actions in the money and capital markets. These institutions are commercial banks, life insurance companies, savings and loan associations, and mutual savings banks. Their relative size is shown in Table 15–2 which gives the total assets by class of financial institution as of June 30, 1971.

TABLE 15–2
Total assets of selected financial institutions as of June 30, 1971
(*billions of dollars*)

Commercial banks	$599
Life insurance companies	214
Savings and loan associations	193
Mutual savings banks	86

Source: *Federal Reserve Bulletin,* September, 1971.

In addition, there are several other financial institutions of a more specialized nature which are also discussed in this section.

Commercial banks

The commercial banking system is the keystone of the American monetary and financial system. The 13,700 commercial banks in this country are the only financial institutions which accept demand deposits, commonly known as checking accounts, from the public where the customer can request currency from his account or direct that it be paid to someone else at any time. Also, the commercial banking system as a whole is capable of creating money through loans stemming from its presently held checking accounts. This is possible because the commercial banking system is a *fractional reserve system* which means that each bank is required to keep only a portion of its deposits in reserve form and may lend out those funds which are in excess of the required deposit reserves.

The multiple effect of fractional bank reserves. The following illustration demonstrates how the fractional reserve concept may be used to expand the money supply for the commercial banking system as a whole. Suppose that a commercial bank receives $10,000 in currency from a customer to establish a checking account and that the bank is required to maintain 20 percent in reserve against these accounts either in the form of deposits with the Federal Reserve or in cash in the bank's vaults. This means that a given commercial bank must have 20 percent of its demand deposits in reserves but may create additional demand deposits, and hence increase the money supply either by lending out the remaining 80 percent or by purchasing such assets as government bonds. Also assume that the checks drawn on all additional demand deposits created by commercial banks are immediately deposited back into some bank in the system. As the result of all these transactions a total of $50,000 of demand deposits will be created including the initial $10,000 deposit of currency which started the cycle. How this expansion occurs is demonstrated by Table 15–3.

Table 15–3 shows a total of $50,000 of demand deposits including the required $10,000 in reserves plus a total of $40,000 excess reserves which were used to create the additional deposits. The multiple effect

TABLE 15-3
The multiplying effect of new deposits in a fractional reserve banking system

Transactions	Amount deposited in checking accounts	20 percent required reserves	Excess reserves loaned out
Initial currency deposit in checking account	$10,000	$ 2,000	$ 8,000
2nd transaction (deposit of amount just loaned)	8,000	1,600	6,400
3rd transaction	6,400	1,280	5,120
4th transaction	5,120	1,024	4,096
5th transaction	4,096	819	3,277
6th transaction	3,277	655	2,622
7th transaction	2,622	524	2,098
8th transaction	2,098	420	1,678
9th transaction	1,678	336	1,342
10th transaction	1,342	268	1,074
11th transaction	1,074	215	859
12th transaction	859	172	687
13th transaction	687	137	550
14th transaction	550	110	440
15th transaction	440	88	352
Plus all additional transactions necessary to complete the cycle	1,757	352	1,405
Total for all transactions	$50,000	$10,000	$40,000

of increases in bank deposits caused by the power of fractional bank reserves illustrated in Table 15–3 assumes that each bank in the system will increase its deposits to the maximum extent permitted by its reserve position. Furthermore, it is assumed that all deposits are left in the banking system by the public with none being withdrawn in exchange for currency or for transfer outside the United States.

No single bank can lend out more than its excess reserves at any one time. Therefore, each bank depends upon additional deposits for the funds to create additional loans. However, the fractional reserve requirement does permit the entire banking system to achieve the multiple expansion effect of the money supply as what is loaned to a person by one bank becomes a demand deposit in that bank or other banks, thereby permitting the latter additional reserves for further loans.

Federal Reserve influence upon bank reserves. The availability of money and credit is a significant determinant of economic conditions. When the economy is expanding and the demand for goods and services is great the money supply must expand to facilitate the economic growth. On the other hand, if too much money and credit is made available the excessive demand will drive up prices and the result will be inflation. When the economy is in a recession, providing a sufficient supply of money and credit with lower interest rates will tend to stimulate the economy toward recovery. The Federal Reserve through its influence on commercial banks has the important and delicate function of carrying out a constructive monetary policy for the country.

The Federal Reserve influences the money supply and the amount of credit in the economy by regulating the reserves of commercial banks in three ways:

1. Setting the reserve requirements for commercial banks.
2. Determining the discount rate.
3. Carrying out open-market operations.

Required reserves. The Federal Reserve's Board of Governors has the power to set the specific reserve requirements which commercial banks must maintain to back up their deposits. With higher reserve requirements, more funds have to be held in reserve by commercial banks against deposits and less funds are available to be loaned out. As reserve requirements are lowered, this frees some bank reserves and permits bankers to expand their loans to business enterprises and individuals. In 1971 the required reserve ratio for demand deposits in city commercial banks was 17.5 percent.

Discount rate. The Federal Reserve has the authority to change the *discount rate,* which is the interest rate that member commercial banks pay to obtain funds from the Federal Reserve bank in their district. These funds are obtained from the Federal Reserve to strengthen a commercial bank's reserve ratio in relation to deposits. The higher the discount rate the less encouraging it is for commercial banks to obtain reserve funds from the Federal Reserve. When the discount rate is lowered it is more attractive for commercial banks to utilize Federal Reserve funds to improve their reserve positions, which enables the banks to expand credit to their customers.

Open-market operations. The third method used by the Federal Reserve in influencing commercial bank reserves is *open-market operations,* which is the purchase or sale of federal government securities.

When the Federal Reserve buys government securities in the bond market the result is an increase in the commercial banks' reserves which tends to increase the money supply and has an expansionary effect on the economy. When the Federal Reserve sells government securities, commercial banks' reserves are decreased and the money supply is reduced. This has a deflationary effect on the economy which is desirable when inflationary pressure is present. Through open-market operations it is possible for the Federal Reserve to make more gradual changes in bank reserves than is the case with a change in the reserve requirements for commercial banks or a change in the discount rate.

Activities of commercial banks. The commercial banking system is unique among those financial institutions which deal directly with business and consumers in its ability to create money through the fractional reserve system. All other financial institutions must use funds which they receive from deposits, premium payments, the selling of equity shares in the particular financial institutions, borrowing, or retained profits. More than 90 percent of the typical bank's sources of funds are provided by either demand or time deposits. Capital accounts for commercial banks consist of only about 9 percent of the total liabilities and net worth of the bank's balance sheet. Since equity funds provide a relatively small proportion of the typical bank's funds and since a large proportion of the bank's funds must be available for payment "on demand," the banker must walk a narrow tightrope in putting his assets to work profitably and at the same time with safety.

Commercial banks are the largest single class of financial institutions according to the amount of total assets. They are the principal source of short-term credit for business enterprises. It has been estimated that over 90 percent of all short-term business loans in this country are made by commercial banks. Commercial banks are also important sources of funds for mortgage and consumer loans, such as for the purchase of a home or an automobile. Commercial banks hold the major proportion of federal, state, and local government debt issues.

Commercial banks also provide such services as acceptance of time and savings deposits, safety deposit boxes and vaults, and correspondent relationships with other institutions for national and international financial transactions. Nearly all commercial bank depositors' accounts are protected by insurance provided by the Federal Deposit Insurance Corporation, a governmental agency which insures accounts up to $20,000 each. Commercial banks provide loan funds to other financial institutions such as finance companies and investment bankers as well as to business enterprises and individual consumers. The commercial bank has been called the institution prepared to provide a "full range" of financial services. Indeed, in recent years commercial bankers have expanded their services to provide an institution where businesses and individuals can invest excess funds or obtain loans to meet the legitimate needs for bank credit which are necessary for an expanding economy.

Life insurance companies

Life insurance companies constitute the second largest class of financial institutions, being second only to commercial banks in total assets. Many people think of the life insurance company only as an institution which sells insurance protection and savings programs to individuals, who in turn pay premiums for this coverage which pays a specified amount to the policyholder when he reaches a certain age, or is disabled, or to his beneficiary if the policyholder should die. This underwriting of insurance risks certainly does represent an important aspect of life insurance companies' operations since policy premiums constitute their major source of funds.

However, there is another important side to the life insurance business besides the selling of insurance and savings protection. The premiums which are received are invested, and the earnings from these investments are used to meet future payments to policyholders and beneficiaries, to generate income for operating expenses, to increase reserves, and to pay taxes and dividends.

Life insurance companies have at their disposal a tremendous portfolio of investments to manage. Whereas commercial banks provide funds mostly to the short-term or money markets, life insurance companies are active in several sectors of the capital markets because of the difference in the nature of the demands upon their investment portfolio. Life insurance companies are able to program rather accurately the expected payments to their policyholders through statistical analysis of accident and death rates. These actuarial studies enable the management of life insurance companies to determine premium rates, forecast policy benefit payments, and provide for reserve additions in such a manner as to permit investment of funds in the long-term or capital markets.

The major investments of life insurance companies at the end of 1970 fell into the following categories:

Bonds of business enterprises	35%
Real estate mortgages	36
Governmental bonds: federal, state, and local	6
Stocks	7
Policy loans	8
Miscellaneous investments	8
Total investments	100%

These investments indicate the importance of life insurance companies as a source of funds to business enterprises of all kinds, including industrial corporations, public utilities, and railroads, as well as the significant role of providing mortgage funds for all types of construction.

Savings and loan associations

Savings and loan associations constitute the third largest class of financial institutions. They act as financial intermediaries between individual and business savers and borrowers, most of whom use the credit for financing real estate construction.

Approximately 85 percent of assets in savings and loan associations are mortgages on real estate with most of these funds committed to the financing of one-to-four family homes. Savings and loan associations hold 45 percent of the mortgage loans outstanding on these family units, demonstrating their great importance as local institutions which stand ready to finance home construction.

Those savers who place their funds with savings and loan associations technically become shareholders in the savings and loan rather than depositors and therefore actually receive dividends on their savings rather than interest. However, this distinction has not been of practical importance in recent years since associations have customarily been willing to cash in a saver's account on demand, although legally the saver could be required to wait up to 30 days or more depending upon the financial condition of the savings and loan association at the time of the request.

The vast majority of savings and loan associations are members of the Federal Savings and Loan Insurance Corporation, a governmental agency which insures each saver's account up to $20,000.

Mutual savings banks

Mutual savings banks are financial institutions which encourage individual savers to establish deposit accounts and are the oldest class of strictly savings institutions in the United States. All but a few are located in New England and the Middle Atlantic states.

A mutual savings bank has no shareholders; all depositors have a "mutual" interest in the enterprise's operations. Thus payments for savings accounts are dividends in the strict sense of the word and not interest payments. Mutual savings banks are governed by boards of trustees which appoint their own successors. Many wealthy individuals serve as trustees for little or no remuneration and consider it an honor to be asked to be a trustee. This concept goes back to the founding of mutual savings banks when they were viewed as a place where the common man was provided with a place and the encouragement to save money in good times to provide for himself when times were hard.

Over 70 percent of the assets of mutual savings banks are invested in mortgages. Unlike the lending practices of savings and loan associations which concentrate their lending activities on residences, mutual savings banks lend large amounts on apartment buildings and commercial real estate developments. In this respect, the mutual savings bank deals in mortgage markets similar to the life insurance company, although insurance companies also make some residential loans. The balance of mutual savings bank assets is concentrated in U.S. government securities along with corporation bonds.

Other financial institutions

Besides the four previously discussed financial institutions there are a number of others which are active in particular markets. These financial institutions include various types of finance companies and credit unions which provide important sources of funds to businesses and individuals. Institutions with dealings chiefly in the secondary financial markets include personal trust departments, pension funds, fire and casualty insurance companies, and investment companies. Following a brief description of each of these institutions, the role of the investment banker and the stock market is discussed.

Finance companies

There are a variety of different types of enterprises which fall under the general category of finance companies. These firms all lend money but are not classified as banks or more traditional financial institutions such as life insurance companies or savings and loan associations. Generally *finance companies* have a significant amount of their financing provided by equity capital with the balance being borrowed in relatively large amounts from commercial banks, through selling short-term promissory notes called commercial paper, and by issuing various types of long-term debt. Loans are made to business enterprises and individuals at higher rates than the interest paid by finance companies for borrowing. This differential in interest provides funds for operating expenses with enough left over for profits for the owners.

Finance companies which specialize in direct loans to individuals are called *consumer finance* or *personal finance companies*. Consumer finance companies make installment loans directly to individuals for the purchase of automobiles, consumer hard goods such as major appliances, television and stereo sets, and personal loans. Consumer finance companies provide a significant amount of installment credit.

Sales finance companies also specialize in installment loans. However, instead of making loans directly to individuals or business enterprises, they purchase installment receivables from retailers who sell such products as autos, appliances, industrial equipment, farm equipment, and other durable goods. Sales finance companies also loan money to retailers and wholesalers to finance their inventories. Usually installment loans and inventory loans are secured by the merchandise on which the loans are made. These financial institutions provide substantial amounts of credit without which business enterprises would have to finance themselves or seek other sources of credit.

Commercial finance companies provide loans to business enterprises, many of which would have difficulty obtaining credit from commercial banks because of the size of the enterprise or the risk involved in the lending arrangements. Most of the loans by commercial finance companies are secured by accounts receivable of the borrowers, although loans based on equipment and inventories are also made. Interest rates are generally higher than those made by commercial banks because of the additional risks involved and the increased costs of handling such loans. At the end of June, 1971, installment credit outstanding from all types of finance companies was $31 billion.

Another highly specialized type of business financing is called factoring. *Factoring* is the purchase of a business enterprise's accounts receivable by a finance company, which then assumes the responsibility for collecting the accounts. Factoring is used widely in the textile industry and is considered a relatively expensive form of short-term financing. However, the factor (which the financial institution is called) provides a variety of services when it purchases the receivables of a business enterprise. These services include credit investigation and collection as well as taking the risk of any bad debts which result from failure to collect the accounts.

Credit unions

Credit unions are cooperatives which promote saving on the part of their members and also provide sources of personal loans for members at relatively low interest rates. Credit unions are organized and sponsored by fraternal groups or labor unions for their members, or by individual business enterprises for the benefit of their employees. Therefore, membership in a particular credit union is limited to those individuals who are part of the sponsoring group. Because of their cooperative nature, credit unions are normally managed by their members who serve on a part-time basis with little or no compensation, although some credit unions have paid secretary-treasurers or receive clerical support from the sponsoring organization. This type of financial institution is important in the consumer credit market with $13 billion in installment credit outstanding at the end of June, 1971.

Personal trust departments

Personal trust departments of commercial banks and trust companies take legal possession of personal assets and manage them for the benefit of the person creating the trust or for some other designated person. The trust department of a commercial bank (called the trustee) would take possession of funds provided by a businessman (the trustor) and provide investment management of the money. The income from this trust fund would be paid to whomever the trustor designates; perhaps to the businessman during his lifetime and then to his widow upon his death. Personal trust departments also act as executors and administrators of estates, receivers in bankruptcy, and trustees of private pension funds.

Personal trust departments control vast sums of wealth with the funds invested primarily in corporation stocks, state and local government bonds, and corporation bonds. Their investments are made essentially in the secondary capital markets of stocks and bonds which have already been issued by corporations and governmental bodies. As a class of financial institutions they have developed a reputation for responsible financial stewardship of the funds placed under their control.

Pension funds

Pension funds have become very important sources of investment in all sectors of the capital markets since World War II. Pension funds basically are accumulated out of the contributions of employers and employees and are invested in stocks, bonds, and other types of investments, such as mortgages. These funds are administered so as to provide retirement income for the individual beneficiaries and their families in their old age.

There are two general types of pension funds which are important for investment purposes. These are private and government plans. Private pension plans provide retirement benefits for employees of business enterprises, union members, and employees of nonprofit organizations such as educational, religious, and welfare organizations. Private pension funds invest heavily in common stocks of corporations and corporation bonds with smaller holdings of U.S. government securities, mortgages, and other assets. They represent important buyers of securities in the secondary capital markets.

Government retirement plans also provide significant sources of funds for the capital markets. State and local government retirement monies represent significant sources of funds for U.S. government bonds, state and local government securities, corporate bonds, and mortgages. Many states prohibit the investment of these funds in common stocks of corporations. However, a number of states now permit investment in high-grade common stocks. The rate of growth of state and local government retirement funds since World War II has been exceeded only by the increases in private pension funds and savings and loan associations.

A second class of government retirement plans is that of the federal government. The U.S. Treasury acts as the fiscal agent for a number of governmental retirement funds. These include the Old Age and Survivors Insurance Trust Fund, National Service Life Insurance Fund, Unemployment Trust Fund, and Railroad Retirement Fund. The investment monies for these trust funds are obtained from taxes such as social security payments by employees and employers, premiums, and contributions to specific fund accounts. After benefits are paid out to recipients, the balance in these funds is invested in U.S. government securities. These funds, along with other governmental agencies, represent an important source of financing for government bonds since at the end of June, 1971, they held approximately 25 percent of the direct debt of the federal government.

Fire and casualty insurance companies

Fire and casualty companies sell insurance service to their clients to cover destruction of property by fire or other hazards. Some also provide personal liability insurance and other types of insurance protection. Whereas the life insurance company guarantees a fixed dollar return for its policyholders, the fire and casualty insurance company assumes contingent liability and pays its policyholder only if a loss actually occurs. The fire and/or casualty policy has a limited amount of dollar protection depending upon the terms of the policy. Payments to policyholders may be no higher than the amount of the loss.

The fire and casualty insurance company's funds come mainly from premium income from policyholders and from investments made by the company. These funds are invested in a manner which will provide reserves to underwrite the risks assumed by the company in the policies which it has issued. Normally most companies are able to meet expenses and losses on policies from new premium income. This provides some flexibility for the insurance company's investment policies. However, in order to be able to meet calamitous losses from natural and man-caused disasters the insurance company must provide a cushion of readily marketable securities in its investment portfolio. This need is met by quantities of U.S. government securities. Fire and casualty insurance companies also hold substantial quantities of corporations' common stocks and state and local government securities. Their dealings are mainly in the secondary securities markets. Unlike the life insurance companies, the fire and casualty insurance companies do not invest heavily in the mortgage and corporate bond markets.

Investment companies

An important purchaser of corporate securities, especially of common stocks, is the class of financial institutions called investment companies. *Investment companies* obtain funds by selling shares in their operation and using the proceeds to purchase securities of other corporations. Although there are a variety of different types of investment companies, two important types are the *closed-end* and *open-end* investment companies. Closed-end companies have a fixed amount of capital outstanding and buy and sell securities to improve their income and capital gains profit picture.

Open-end companies, commonly known as *mutual funds,* do not have a fixed number of shares outstanding, but issue more shares whenever an investor desires to purchase shares in the fund. Shares are purchased at the net asset value which is computed twice daily based on the market value of the securities in their portfolio plus a "loading charge" to cover the sales commission and other expenses of the sale. When the individual investor desires to sell his shares in the mutual fund they are sold back to the fund at the then current asset value, and on some funds minus a small redemption charge.

Some mutual funds, known as "no-load" funds, are sold to the public at net asset value without a loading charge. In these mutual funds there are no salesmen. Therefore, the individual investor saves the cost of the sales commission (loading charge). However, in order to purchase the fund the investor must contact the fund's management directly, usually by responding to an advertisement in a financial newspaper or magazine.

Investment companies, especially the open-end funds, constitute an important medium of investment in a diversified portfolio of corporate securities for the small investor. While this type of financial institution provides little capital directly to corporations, it does actively operate in the secondary securities market and broadens the interest of small investors in the stock and bonds of American corporations.

Functions of the investment banker

The investment banker performs a valuable service as a middleman between corporations and investors in the capital funds markets. Investment banking includes the following functions:

1. Underwriting new issues of bonds and stocks for corporations.
2. Selling new securities issues without underwriting participation.
3. Acting as a broker in buying and selling securities for clients in the secondary securities markets both in organized exchanges and in the over-the-counter market.
4. Buying and selling securities for the investment banking firm's own account.
5. Providing advice to corporation managements in the timing and details of obtaining long-term funds in the capital markets.

Underwriting

Investment bankers are important in the primary securities markets since they provide a needed link between business enterprises which require external capital and savers who wish to invest their capital in corporations. Most business enterprises undertake the public sale of stocks or bonds only infrequently, and the assistance of an investment banking house to company officials is invaluable. Matters of financial market timing, terms of competing securities in the market, and other market conditions are appraised by the investment banker to provide expert advice to the enterprise's management.

As underwriters, investment bankers assume the responsibility for the sale of a corporation's stock or bonds and guarantee a specified amount of money for the securities to be sold. This puts the investment banker in the position of being a merchandiser of corporations' securities.

Since underwriting security issues involves financial risk on the part of the investment banker because of rapidly changing conditions of supply and demand in the capital markets, frequently a group of investment bankers will cooperate in the underwriting and subsequent sale of security issues. This grouping of investment bankers is known as a *syndicate* and is formed only for marketing a particular security issue. After the issue has been sold, the syndicate is dissolved.

When the investment banker underwrites an issue he is paid a fee to cover certain of his expenses and then sells the securities for a small markup over what the issuing corporation receives from the banker. This is the banker's *spread,* which represents the gross margin of profit between what he pays for the issue and what he receives for its sale. The delicate job of the investment banker is setting an offering price so that the issue will be well received by the investing public and at the same time bring as much for the issuing corporation as possible.

At the same time, the investment banker must receive a sufficient margin to compensate him for his services and the risk he bears in the transaction. An unexpected downturn in the stock or bond market immediately after the issue comes to market may result in the securities being left on the investment banker's shelves, which leaves the choice of selling the issue at what it will bring (with a probable loss for the banker) or holding the issue in the hope that market conditions will improve so that it can be sold satisfactorily.

Private placements

In addition to their function as underwriters of securities to be sold to the public, investment bankers may assist enterprises in the sale of their securities through private placements. A *private placement* is the sale of an entire issue of securities to a single or limited number of investors who buy the issue for investment purposes rather than for resale in the near future. A number of corporate debt issues in recent years have been through private placement to such institutions as life insurance companies and private pension funds. The investment banker's role in the private placement is to represent and advise the business enterprise during the negotiation process with the financial institution and to handle various details associated with the issuance of the debt instruments.

Best-efforts offering

The investment banker may also sell securities for corporations without underwriting the issue. This is known as a *best-efforts* offering, where the investment banker assists with the planning and details connected with the issue and uses his marketing organization to sell the stock or bonds, but does not assume the risk for their sale. Under these circumstances the business enterprise itself takes the risk of the sale of its securities, and the investment banker is compensated with a fee for his services.

Brokerage function

The brokerage function of the investment banker is the one which is probably best known to the public. Brokerage operations are carried on by the marketing organization of the investment banking house. As a broker the investment banker buys and sells securities, acting as an agent for his customers. For this agency service the broker receives a commission on each transaction. Commissions for most sales or purchases on the stock exchanges or the over-the-counter market vary from about 6 percent on small transactions down to less than 1 percent on amounts of several thousand dollars. The role of the broker in security transactions is illustrated in the discussion of the stock market.

The investment banking firm also may buy and sell securities for its own portfolio or for those of its partners or officers. The transactions of investment bankers are policed by industry groups and also by the Securities and Exchange Commission with the objectives of preventing manipulation of the securities markets and protecting the interests of the investing public.

Investment banking houses are financed by equity capital provided by the individuals who own the firms. The traditional form of business organization for the investment banking house has been the partnership, but in recent years a number of investment bankers have incorporated their operations. In 1971 the largest investment banking house, Merrill Lynch, Pierce, Fenner & Smith, Inc., sold a portion of its common stock to the public to increase its capital and broaden its ownership.

In addition to equity capital, debt funds are provided by commercial banks, usually in the form of short-term loans to finance the securities inventory which the investment banking house must carry from time to time.

The stock market

Organization of stock markets

A great deal of the trading of corporate securities in the secondary market takes place on organized exchanges such as the New York Stock Exchange and the American Stock Exchange. Indeed, when people talk about "the stock market" they normally are referring to the New York Stock Exchange (NYSE), or the Big Board as it is informally called, which accounts for about 70 percent of the trading volume on organized exchanges.

A corporation's management must apply to have its securities listed for trading in the New York Stock Exchange. In order to qualify for trading the exchange has set certain minimum requirements as to demonstrated earning power, value of corporation assets, number of shares of stock outstanding, and the number of shareholders. The purpose of these requirements is to provide a marketplace for securities which are sufficiently well established and with enough shares and shareholders to provide a potentially active market for the stock. At the end of 1970 there were 1,297 U.S. corporations and 33 foreign corporations which had a total of 15.5 billion shares of common stock listed on the New York Stock Exchange. The market value of these common stock shares was $612 billion. Also, there were 510 preferred stock issues and 1,729 bond issues listed for trading.

Trading on the floor of the organized exchanges is carried out by individuals and brokerage firms which hold membership in the particular exchange. On the NYSE there are about 1,400 memberships or "seats" which are held by about 570 organizations and individuals. A membership permits a single individual to buy and sell securities on the floor of the exchange. Many investment banking firms hold more than one membership on a given exchange and are members of not only the two big exchanges in New York City, but also of regional exchanges located in Chicago, San Francisco, and elsewhere in the country. These memberships may be sold to other qualified individuals or firms with the approval of exchange officials. The price of seats on the NYSE ranged from $130,000 to $320,000 in 1970.

About one fourth of the members of the NYSE are specialists who perform the function of "making a market" for one or more stocks. This means that they carry an inventory of shares in the particular issues in which they specialize and are willing to deal with other exchange members who are trading for their own account or who represent their customers, who are members of the public.

Buying and selling stock through an organized exchange

If you wished to purchase 100 shares of General Motors common stock on the New York Stock Exchange you would relay that order to your broker. If the broker is associated with a NYSE member firm he would send the order by wire to his New York office where it would be relayed to the trading member of the firm who is on the floor of the exchange. If your brokerage firm is not a NYSE member then it would likely have a correspondent relationship with a NYSE firm which would carry out the transaction on the exchange. The member on the NYSE floor would take the order to the place, called a trading post, where the specialist dealing in General Motors stock is located and would carry out the transaction. The purchase and sale of stocks on the Big Board is accomplished through the specialist who conducts a continuous two-way auction-type operation where he quotes prices at which he is willing to buy or sell stock of a given corporation. The "bid" price is the price at which the specialist is willing to buy stock, and the "ask" price is what he is willing to sell for. The difference between these is called the "spread," which is his margin.

A variety of different types of orders for securities may be placed with brokers by members of the public. Usually orders to buy or sell securities are placed either at a particular price or "at the market," which means the transaction will be executed immediately for the best price your broker can obtain. Each broker who acts for a customer is charged with the responsibility of obtaining the best price for his customer, and he receives a commission for his services set on a sliding scale of a fixed fee plus a certain percentage of the total dollar amount of the transaction. As was noted earlier, brokerage fees range downward from 6 percent depending upon the amount of the transaction.

After the broker on the floor completes the transaction both he and the specialist make a written notation of the deal. This information is sent back to the New York brokerage offices and then wired out to the branch office from whence the order came. At the same time, a report of the transaction is relayed to the exchange reporting service where it is sent out across the country on a wire service and reported on the visual tape, called a broad tape, which virtually every brokerage office has in continuous operation during the hours which the market is open for trading. This public report gives the symbol which represents the name of the corporation's stock, the number of shares in the transaction, and the price per share of stock. Likewise, brokerage officers may use their wire services or other reporting devices to obtain quotations of the bid and ask prices for their customers direct from the trading floor of the exchange in a very short time. It is possible for a customer to receive a quotation, place an order, have it executed on the floor of the stock exchange, and receive the report back in the broker's office in a period of less than ten minutes.

The prices of individual securities are determined by the relative supply and demand for them as received by the specialist. While the specialist is charged with maintaining an orderly market for the stocks in which he deals, the willingness to buy or sell on the part of those institutions and individuals interested in securities will ultimately determine the price at which transactions are completed.

FIGURE 15–3
How to read stock market reports

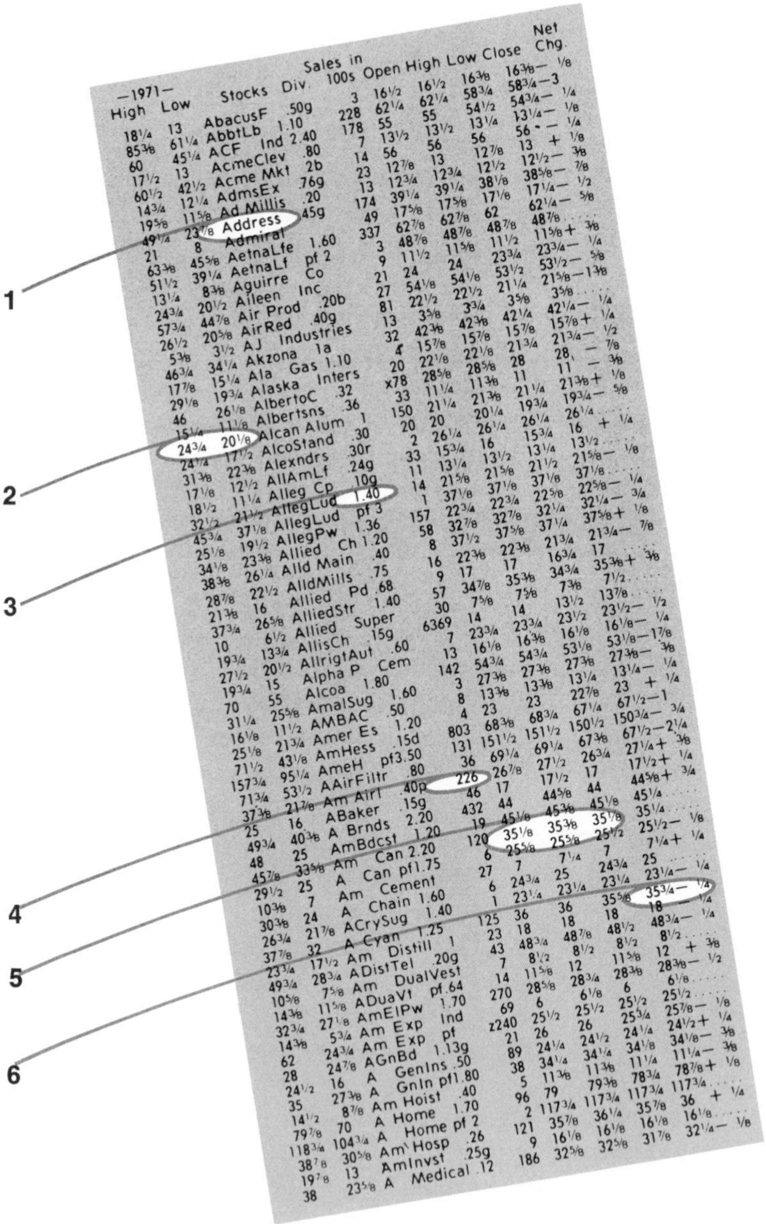

1971 High	1971 Low	Stocks Div.	Sales in 100s	Open	High	Low	Close	Net Chg.
18¼	13	AbacusF .50g	3	16½	16½	16⅜	16⅜	−⅛
85⅜	61¼	AbbtLb 1.10	228	62¼	62¼	58¾	58¾	−3
60	45¼	ACF Ind 2.40	178	55	55	54½	54¾	−¼
17½	13	AcmeClev .80	7	13½	13½	13¼	13¼	−⅛
60½	42½	Acme Mkt 2b	14	56	56	56	56	−¼
14¾	12¼	AdmsEx .76g	23	12⅞	13	12⅞	13	+⅛
19⅝	11⅝	Ad Millis .20	13	12¾	12¾	12½	12½	−⅜
49¼	23⅞	Address .45g	174	39¼	39¼	38⅛	38⅝	−⅞
21	8	Admiral	49	17⅝	17⅝	17⅛	17¼	−½
63⅜	45⅝	AetnaLfe 1.60	337	62⅞	62⅞	62	62¼	−⅝
51½	39¼	AetnaLf pf 2	3	48⅞	48⅞	48⅞	48⅞	....
13¼	8⅜	Aguirre Co	9	11½	11⅝	11½	11⅝	+⅜
24¾	20½	Aileen Inc	21	24	24	23¾	23¾	−¼
57¾	44⅞	Air Prod .20b	27	54⅛	54⅛	53½	53½	−⅝
26½	20⅝	AirRed .40g	81	22½	22½	21¼	21⅝	−1⅜
5⅜	3½	AJ Industries	13	3⅝	3¾	3⅝	3⅝	....
46¾	34¼	Akzona 1a	32	42⅜	42⅜	42¼	42¼	−¼
17⅞	15¼	Ala Gas 1.10	4	15⅞	15⅞	15⅞	15⅞	+¼
29⅛	19¾	Alaska Inters	20	22⅛	22⅛	21¾	21¾	−½
46	26⅛	AlbertoC .32	x78	28⅝	28⅝	28	28	−⅞
15¼	11⅛	Albertsns .36	33	11¼	11⅜	11	11	−⅜
24¾	20⅛	Alcan Alum 1	150	21¼	21⅜	21¼	21⅜	+⅛
24¼	17½	AlcoStand .30	20	20	20¼	19¾	19¾	−⅝
31⅜	22⅜	Alexndrs .30r	2	26¼	26¼	26¼	26¼	....
17⅛	12½	AllAmLf .24g	33	15¾	16	15¾	16	+¼
18½	11¼	Alleg Cp .10g	11	13¼	13½	13¼	13½	....
32½	21½	AllegLud 1.40	14	21⅝	21⅝	21½	21⅝	−⅛
45¾	37⅛	AllegLud pf 3	1	37⅛	37⅛	37⅛	37⅛	....
25⅛	19½	AllegPw 1.36	157	22¾	22¾	22⅝	22⅝	−¼
34⅛	23⅜	Allied Ch 1.20	58	32⅞	32⅞	32¼	32¼	−¾
38⅜	26¼	Alld Main .40	8	37½	37⅝	37¼	37⅝	+⅛
28⅞	22½	AlldMills .75	16	22⅜	22⅜	21¾	21¾	−⅞
21⅜	16	Allied Pd .68	9	17	17	16¾	17	....
37¾	26⅝	AlliedStr 1.40	57	34⅞	35⅜	34¾	35⅜	+⅜
10	6½	Allied Super	30	7⅝	7⅝	7⅜	7½	....
19¾	13¾	AllisCh .15g	6369	14	14	13½	13⅞	....
27½	20½	AllrigtAut .60	7	23¾	23¾	23½	23½	−½
19¾	15	Alpha P Cem	13	16⅛	16⅜	16⅛	16⅛	−¼
70	55	Alcoa 1.80	142	54¾	54¾	53⅛	53⅛	−1⅞
31¼	25⅝	AmalSug 1.60	3	27⅜	27⅜	27⅜	27⅜	−⅜
16⅛	11½	AMBAC .50	8	13⅜	13⅜	13¼	13¼	−¼
25⅛	21¾	Amer Es 1.20	4	23	23	22⅞	23	+¼
71½	43⅛	AmHess .15d	803	68⅜	68¾	67¼	67½	−1
157¾	95¼	AmeH pf3.50	131	151½	151½	150½	150¾	−¾
71¾	53½	AAirFiltr .80	36	69¼	69¼	67⅜	67½	−2¼
37⅜	21⅞	Am Airl .40p	226	26⅞	27½	26¾	27¼	+⅜
25	16	ABaker .15g	46	17	17½	17	17½	+¼
49¾	40⅜	A Brnds 2.20	432	44	44⅝	44	44⅝	+¾
48	25	AmBdcst 1.20	19	45⅛	45⅜	45⅛	45¼	....
45⅞	33⅝	Am Can 2.20	120	35⅛	35⅜	35⅛	35¼	....
29½	25	A Can pf1.75	6	25⅝	25⅝	25½	25½	−⅛
10⅜	7	Am Cement	27	7	7¼	7	7¼	+¼
30⅜	24	A Chain 1.60	6	24¾	25	24¾	25	....
26¾	21⅞	ACrySug 1.40	1	23¼	23¼	23¼	23¼	−¼
37⅞	32	A Cyan 1.25	125	36	36	35⅝	35¾	−¼
23¾	17½	Am Distill 1	23	18	18	18	18	−¼
49¾	28¾	ADistTel .20g	43	48¾	48⅞	48½	48¾	−¼
10⅝	7⅝	Am DualVest	7	8½	8½	8½	8½	....
14⅜	11⅝	ADuaVt pf.64	14	11⅝	12	11⅝	12	+⅜
32¾	27⅛	AmElPw 1.70	270	28⅝	28¾	28⅜	28⅜	−½
14⅜	5¾	Am Exp Ind	69	6	6⅛	6	6⅛	....
62	24¾	Am Exp pf	z240	25½	25½	25½	25½	....
28	24⅞	AGnBd 1.13g	21	26	26	25¾	25⅞	−⅛
24½	16	A GenIns .50	89	24¼	24½	24¼	24½	+¼
35	27⅜	A GnIn pf1.80	38	34¼	34¼	34⅛	34⅛	−⅜
14½	8⅞	Am Hoist .40	5	11⅜	11⅜	11¼	11¼	−⅜
79⅞	70	A Home 1.70	96	79	79⅜	78¾	78⅞	+⅛
118¾	104¾	A Home pf 2	2	117¾	117¾	117¾	117¾	....
38⅞	30⅝	Am Hosp .26	121	35⅞	36¼	35⅞	36	+¼
19⅞	13	AmInvst .25g	9	16⅛	16⅛	16⅛	16⅛	....
38	23⅝	A Medical .12	186	32⅝	32⅝	31⅞	32¼	−⅛

Many newspapers carry stock market reports similar to this sample taken from New York Stock Exchange transactions which occurred on July 23, 1971.

1   *The abbreviated name of the company issuing the stock. In this case it is Addressograph-Multigraph Corp. The stock is common stock unless the company name is followed by "pf," which indicates that the issue is a preferred stock.*

2   *These columns show the highest and lowest prices paid for a given stock on the exchange during the year. In this case it is $24.75 and $20.12½ per share.*

3   *Figures following company names indicate the annual dividend rate estimated on the basis of the latest quarterly or semiannual payment. Here the annual rate is $1.40 per share. Letters following the dividend numbers indicate other data regarding dividends. For example, "b" indicates that, in addition to the cash dividend that is shown, a stock dividend is issued. Other symbols are explained in a footnote on the market reports page.*

4   *This column shows the number of shares traded for the day, expressed in hundreds. In this instance 22,600 shares of American Airlines stock changed hands during this day on the New York Stock Exchange. A "z" indicates the actual number of shares traded.*

5   *These three columns show the stock's price on the first transaction of the day, the highest price of the day, and the lowest price that day at which the stock traded. In this case the stock opened at $35.12½ per share, hit a high of $35.37½, and a low of $35.12½.*

6   *These final two columns show the closing price of the day and the change from the previous day's closing price. For American Cyanamid the closing price was $35.75 per share or a decrease of $0.25 per share (¼) from the previous day's close.*

In addition to transactions in round lots which normally consist of 100 share units, a quantity of odd lots of stock are traded in the secondary securities market. On the NYSE an odd lot in most stock issues consists of from 1 to 99 shares. Many individual investors purchase and sell odd-lot quantities of stock through brokerage offices across the country.

Over-the-counter markets

In addition to the securities trading which takes place on organized exchanges, there is the *over-the-counter* market (OTC), where security dealers buy and sell stock through informal dealings, usually by telephone, rather than in a central place such as an organized exchange. Many security dealers maintain inventories of the stocks which trade over the counter and their quotations for bid and ask prices are circulated in the investment community. When a member of the public places an order with his investment banker's brokerage office, the customer's representative will buy the stock where he can purchase for the best price, usually after contacting two or three dealers. Sometimes the broker will sell stock from his own firm's inventory but will first check to see that the price is not higher than that which could be obtained from a competing investment dealer who also makes a market in the same security issue.

Those security issues which are traded in the OTC market include the stocks and bonds of business enterprises, which are typically small or medium sized, where there is a relatively small number of shares of stock outstanding and trading is relatively inactive. Although there are exceptions to this, generally the firms whose securities are traded over the counter are not as large or as well known as those listed on the New York Stock Exchange. Also, the common stocks of nearly all commercial banks are traded in the OTC market along with many insurance company stocks.

While there are some U.S. government bonds listed on the New York Stock Exchange, most federal government securities are traded in the OTC market; and municipal securities are traded exclusively over the counter. *Municipals* include the bonds of states, municipalities, school districts, and other local governmental units. Most corporate bond trading occurs over the counter, although some corporation bonds are listed on the stock exchanges.

Investing in securities

Investment objectives

Investors in stocks and bonds, whether institutions or individuals, should establish their investment objectives and determine the type of securities to achieve these objectives before they select the specific securities to be included in their investment portfolios.

While the general objective of investing is to provide a monetary return on capital, there are several specific factors to be considered in judging· the suitability of a particular investment. An investor needs to determine the relative importance of current income, growth of the investment, and the degree of risk he is willing to assume. Current income can be provided from bond interest or dividends on corporate preferred or common stocks. Capital growth results from an appreciation in the market value of securities. Safety of principal is also an important factor in establishing investment objectives since some investments carry a much greater risk than others. Table 15–4 summarizes the general char-

TABLE 15–4
Securities characteristics and investment objectives

Objectives	Bonds	Preferred stocks	Common stocks
Current income	highest	medium	lowest
Capital growth (appreciation)	lowest	medium	highest
Safety of principal	highest	medium	lowest

acteristics of bonds, preferred stocks, and common stocks in relation to these three objectives.

Despite the generalizations outlined in Table 15–4, there are exceptions to this classification. For example, some low-quality bonds have less safety of principal than high-quality preferred or common stocks. This emphasizes the importance of the final selection of specific stocks and bonds.

Selection of common stocks

In attempting to judge the future market-price performance of the common stock of a given corporation a number of measures are used by investment analysts. These include a corporation's earnings and earnings growth, cash dividends, market price of the common stock, the price/earnings ratio, and the quality of management.

Earnings and earnings growth. Net profit is divided by the number of shares of common stock outstanding to determine earnings per share. If the corporation has preferred stock in its capital structure, the cash dividends paid on preferred stock are subtracted from net profit before the earnings per share for common stockholders are calculated. The earnings per share and their rate of growth in past years are important determinants of common stock prices, especially as this may reflect the likely continued growth in earnings in the future. Most analysts feel that earnings for at least the past five years should be studied.

Cash dividends. The amount of cash dividends per share paid to stockholders and the trend of cash dividend payments are also factors in evaluating a common stock. The trend of cash dividend payments over recent years should be considered along with the proportion of earnings paid out in dividends. However, the fact that a corporation may pay only a small cash dividend or even none at all does not necessarily indicate the common stock should not be purchased. In some cases the rate of growth of a corporation's sales, profits, and cash needs makes it desirable from the stockholders' point of view as well as management's to retain all earnings during the period of growth and development. For example, Polaroid Corporation pays out only about 15 percent of its profits in cash dividends to stockholders, yet an investment of $2,000 in Polaroid common stock in 1964 would have a market value of $11,000 in 1971!

Market price of the common stock. The present market price per share of common stock and the price trend over the years enables the analyst to determine whether there has been an increase in the value of corporate shares in the past. Generally an upward trend of market-price action is viewed more positively by analysts than a downward trend unless there is some valid reason for believing that the price of the stock is about to reverse its market action.

Price/earnings ratio. An important measurement which takes two key factors into account is the price/earnings ratio. The current market price per share of stock is divided by the past 12 months' earnings per share. This measure can be compared with the stock's P/E ratio in previous years and with other corporations' stocks in the same industry. Price/earnings ratios vary widely among different common stocks as they reflect investors' expectations of future corporate earnings. For example, in 1971 Occidental Petroleum common shares were selling for

FIGURE 15-4

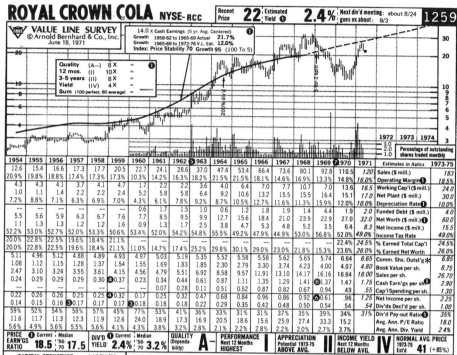

ROYAL CROWN COLA NYSE-RCC

VALUE LINE SURVEY © Arnold Bernhard & Co., Inc. June 18, 1971

Recent Price **22** | Estimated Yield **2.4%** | Next div'd meeting: about 8/24 goes ex about: 9/3 | **1259**

14.0 X Cash Earnings (5 yr. Avg. Centered)
Growth 1958-62 to 1965-69 Actual 21.7%
Growth 1965-69 to 1972-76 V.L. Est. 12.0%
Index: Price Stability 70 Growth 95 (100 To 5)

Quality	(A–)	8 X	=
12 mos.	(I)	10X	=
3-5 years	(II)	8 X	=
Yield	(IV)	4 X	=
Sum	(100 perfect, 60 average)	=

	1954	1955	1956	1957	1958	1959	1960	1961	1962	1963	1964	1965	1966	1967	1968	1969	1970	1971		1973-75
	12.6	15.4	16.6	17.3	17.7	20.5	22.7	24.1	28.6	37.0	47.4	53.4	66.4	73.6	80.1	92.8	110.5	120	Sales ($ mill.)	183
	20.9%	19.8%	18.8%	17.4%	17.3%	17.3%	10.3%	14.2%	16.3%	18.2%	21.5%	21.5%	18.1%	14.6%	16.9%	13.3%	14.8%	16.0%	Operating Margin	18.5%
	4.3	4.3	4.1	3.7	4.1	4.7	1.7	2.2	2.2	3.6	4.0	6.4	7.0	7.7	10.7	7.0	13.6	16.5	Working Cap'l ($ mill.)	24.0
	1.0	1.1	1.4	2.2	2.2	2.4	5.2	5.8	5.8	6.4	9.2	10.6	13.2	15.5	15.5	16.4	15.1	17.0	Net Plant ($ mill.)	30.0
	7.2%	8.8%	7.1%	6.3%	6.9%	7.0%	4.3%	6.1%	7.8%	9.2%	8.7%	10.5%	12.7%	11.6%	11.3%	15.9%	12.0%	10.0%	Depreciation Rate	10.0%
	--	--	--	--	--	--	0.6	1.7	1.5	1.0	0.6	1.2	1.8	1.9	1.4	4.4	1.9	2.0	Funded Debt ($ mill.)	4.0
	5.5	5.6	5.9	6.3	6.7	7.6	7.7	8.5	9.5	9.9	12.7	15.6	18.4	21.0	23.9	22.9	27.0	32.0	Net Worth ($ mill.)	60.0
	1.1	1.3	1.3	1.2	1.2	1.6	0.9	1.3	1.7	2.5	3.8	4.7	5.3	4.8	5.2	3.5	6.4	8.3	Net Income ($ mill.)	15.5
	52.2%	53.0%	52.7%	52.0%	53.3%	50.6%	53.4%	52.0%	54.2%	54.8%	55.5%	49.2%	47.9%	44.9%	53.0%	56.8%	52.0%	49.0%	Income Tax Rate	49.0%
	20.0%	22.8%	22.5%	19.6%	18.4%	21.1%	--	--	--	--	--	--	--	--	--	--	22.4%	24.5%	% Earned Total Cap'l	24.5%
	20.0%	22.8%	22.5%	19.6%	18.4%	21.1%	11.0%	14.7%	11.4%	25.2%	29.8%	30.1%	29.0%	23.0%	21.8%	15.3%	23.6%	26.0%	% Earned Net Worth	26.0%
	5.11	4.96	5.12	4.88	4.89	4.93	4.97	5.03	5.19	5.35	5.52	5.58	5.62	5.65	5.74	6.64	6.65		Comm. Shs. Outst'g	6.85
	1.08	1.12	1.15	1.28	1.37	1.54	1.55	1.69	1.83	1.85	2.30	2.79	3.30	3.74	4.23	4.00	4.07	4.80	Book Value per sh.	8.75
	2.47	3.10	3.24	3.55	3.61	4.15	4.56	4.79	5.51	6.92	8.58	9.57	11.91	13.10	14.17	16.16	16.64	18.00	Sales per sh.	26.70
	0.24	0.29	0.29	0.29	0.30	0.37	0.23	0.34	0.44	0.61	0.87	1.11	1.35	1.29	1.41	1.37	1.47	1.75	Cash Earn'gs per sh.	2.90
	--	--	--	--	--	--	0.07	0.28	0.31	0.51	0.52	0.87	0.82	0.67	0.94	.49	.55		Cap'l Spending per sh.	1.30
	0.22	0.26	0.26	0.25	0.25	0.32	0.17	0.25	0.32	0.47	0.68	0.84	0.96	0.86	0.92	0.61	.96	1.25	Net Income per sh.	2.25
	0.14	0.15	0.16	0.17	0.17	0.17	0.18	0.18	0.18	0.22	0.29	0.35	0.42	0.48	0.50	0.54	.54	.54	Div'ds Decl'd per sh.	1.00
	59%	52%	54%	58%	57%	45%	77%	53%	41%	36%	33%	31%	31%	37%	35%	39%	34%	31%	Div'd Pay-out Ratio	35%
	11.6	11.7	11.3	12.3	11.9	12.6	24.0	18.9	17.3	16.9	20.5	18.6	15.6	25.9	27.4	33.3	15.2		Avg. Ann. P/E Ratio	18.0
	5.6%	4.9%	5.6%	5.5%	5.6%	4.1%	4.3%	3.8%	3.2%	2.8%	2.1%	2.2%	2.8%	2.2%	2.0%	2.7%	3.7%		Avg. Ann. Div. Yield	2.4%

PRICE EARN'GS RATIO	❶ Current **18.5**	Median '56-'70 **17.5**	DIV'D YIELD	❶ Current **2.4%**	Median '56-'70 **3.2%**	QUALITY (Dependability) **A–**	PERFORMANCE Next 12 Months **HIGHEST**	APPRECIATION Potential 1973-75 **ABOVE AVG.**	INCOME YIELD Next 12 Months **BELOW AVG.**	NORMAL AVG. PRICE 1973-75 Est'd **41** (+85%)

CAPITAL STRUCTURE as of 12/31/70
Debt. $1.9 mill. Interest $0.1 mill.

Pfd Stock None Div'd None

Common Stock 6,636,684 shares

Cal-endar	SEMI-ANN. SALES ($ mill.)		Full
	June 30	Dec. 31	Year
1967	36.8	36.8	73.6
1968	38.7	41.4	80.1
1969	44.7	48.0	92.7
1970	45.9	64.6	110.5
1971	56.0	64.0	120

Cal-endar	QUARTERLY EARNINGS (per sh.)				Full
	Mar. 31	June 30	Sept. 30	Dec. 31	Year
1967	.21	.33	.21	.12	.87
1968	.22	.29	.25	.17	.93
1969	.18	.28	.27	.12	.61
1970	.16	.28	.28	.24	.96
1971	.23	.37	.30		1.25

Cal-endar	QUARTERLY DIVIDENDS PAID				Full
	Mar. 31	June 30	Sept. 30	Dec. 31	Year
1967	.12	.12	.12	.12	.48
1968	.12	.12	.12	.12	.48
1969	.135	.135	.135	.135	.54
1970	.135	.135	.135	.135	.54
1971	.135	.135			

Royal Crown shares merit the attention of investors with capital gain objectives. These high quality shares are expected to perform relatively well over the next 12 months. They offer superior appreciation potential to the 1973-75 period.

Share earnings rose 44% in the March quarter. On a restated basis, including Texsun, share results climbed 15%, from a restated 20¢ to 23¢. During the last half of 1970 Royal Crown acquired Texsun and two smaller home decor companies for about 900,000 shares of Royal Crown common. Texsun processes and markets citrus juices, both in single-strength and concentrated forms. Its sales were $13.3 million and profits $1.2 million in the year ended June 30, 1970. Since the consummation of the merger last year (a pooling of interests accounting treatment was used) Texsun's sales and profits have climbed significantly. Moreover, Texsun and the other acquisitions, Structural Industries and Hoyne Industries, help to level seasonal fluctuations.

Diet Rite continues to enlarge its position as the most popular soft drink among those who watch their calories. It now ranks number one by better than a 15% margin. Sales of Royal Crown Cola are also showing gains. The rate of expansion of Gatorade distribution has been disappointing, but sales will increase when more bottlers take on the product.

Three new products are being test marketed. Sugar Free RC Cola, a cola with one calorie in 16 ounces, is being tested in Scranton (Pa.), Grand Rapids (Mich.) and Rockford (Ill.) with excellent results. It will probably be introduced nationally before year-end. Flair, a new citrus flavored soft drink with one calorie per six ounce serving, was introduced in a number of markets, including New York this spring. Results have been fair. Gatorade Orange, a new flavor, is being introduced as a companion product to Gatorade Citrus. R.J.D.

GROWTH RATES – ANNUALLY COMPOUNDED					
Per Share	15 Yrs.	10 Yrs.	5 Yrs.	3 Yrs.	1970
Sales	11.8%	13.8%	11.7%	8.3%	3.0%
Cash Ern'gs	11.4%	20.4%	5.8%	4.5%	7.3%
Net Income	9.1%	18.9%	2.7%	3.7%	57.4%

BUSINESS: Royal Crown Cola is the nation's third largest soft drink company. Major brands: Royal Crown Cola, Diet Rite Cola, Nehi and Gatorade. Has a domestic network of 365 franchised bottlers plus 14 company-owned bottlers. Serves foreign market through 88 plants in 25 countries. Produces concentrate at facilities in Columbus, Ga., Granite City, Ill. and Toronto, Canada. Texsun markets fruit juices and citrus concentrates. Has about 2,000 employees, 10,000 shareholders. Directors control about 12% of the outstanding stock. Chrmn.: W.T. Young. Pres.: Wm. C. Durkee. Inc.: Del. Address: Tenth St. and 9th Ave., Columbus, Ga. 31900.

❶-See Explanation of Terms on p. 1297. ❷-Div'd payment dates: Jan. 2, Apr. 1, July 1, Oct. 1. ❸-Plus stock: 5%, '57, '60. ❹-Excl. 3¢ non-recur. income. ❺-Incl. all operations not previously consolidated. ❻-Excl. non-recur. charge of 30¢. ❼-Incl. Texsun. *-In millions at year-end, adjusted for all stock div'ds and splits.

only about six times the past 12 months' earnings partly because of investor concern over rumors of expropriation of this corporation's large oil holdings in Libya. On the other hand, Syntex, a drug company producing birth-control pills and other pharmaceutical products, was selling for 30 times the latest 12 months' earnings, stimulated in part by investor anticipation that a new asthma drug to be marketed by Syntex would further increase earnings.

Quality of management. One of the most important judgments, and perhaps the most difficult for the analyst to make, is an evaluation of the quality of the management of a corporation. The effectiveness of management in developing, producing, and marketing new products should be judged. Also, an evaluation is made of the enterprise's accounting statements with tests similar to those discussed in Chapter 14.

There are available a number of investment advisory services which provide a summary analysis of stocks and bonds. Some of the widely known services include *Moody's Stock Survey, Standard & Poor's Outlook,* and the *Value Line Investment Survey.* Investor use of such advisory material plus studies of the prospects of different corporate stocks made by stock brokerage firms provide a wealth of reference material for the potential investor. Figure 15–4 from the *Value Line Investment Survey* illustrates the kind of information that advisory services provide for investors.

The fact that investment services as well as investors come to different conclusions about the desirability of a corporation's common stock at a given time is what makes an active market for publicly held securities. Considerable study and analysis should precede the investment decision if the investor wishes to manage his capital prudently. Although the long-run trend in common stock prices has been upward, significant price declines have occurred from time to time. Also, the price movement of an individual corporation's stock may not follow the general market trend.

Summary

Financial institutions regulate the money supply and channel savers' funds to the business enterprises, individuals, and governmental units which desire to utilize these funds.

The U.S. Treasury provides the currency component of the money supply and also is responsible for the management of the federal debt.

The Federal Reserve System is made up of 12 regional Federal Reserve banks and is controlled by a seven-member Board of Governors. The Federal Reserve System is influential in determining the money supply, the level of interest rates, and the banking system's ability to provide credit to its customers.

Financial markets can be classified according to the users of funds, which include individuals, businesses, governmental units, and foreign enterprises. Debt contracts for business loans classified by the length of time for which funds are borrowed may be either short term, intermediate term, or long term.

The primary securities market channels funds directly to users in exchange for the securities of the users. In the secondary markets, debt or equity instruments which are already outstanding are bought and sold among investors.

Commercial banks, the largest class of financial institutions, accept demand deposits and have the ability to create money through the use of a fractional reserve system.

The level of commercial bank reserves is regulated by the Federal Reserve through its purchase and sale of government securities, changes in the percentage of deposit reserves required of member banks, and changes in the discount rate for member banks in their dealings with the Federal Reserve.

Life insurance companies constitute the second largest class of financial institutions. The premium payments which they receive for underwriting insurance risks are invested primarily in the long-term capital markets.

Savings and loan associations, the third largest class of financial institutions, receive savings mostly from individuals and in turn make loans for the financing of real estate, mainly one-to-four family homes.

Consumer finance companies, sales finance companies, and commercial finance companies are all financial institutions which serve particular segments of the borrowing market.

Personal trust departments of commercial banks and trust companies take legal possession of personal assets and manage them for the benefit of the trustor or designated beneficiaries.

Pension funds are accumulated out of the contributions of employers and employees and are invested to provide retirement incomes for the beneficiary individuals.

Fire and casualty insurance companies sell insurance coverage for fire and other hazards. They invest in U.S. government securities, corporate common stocks, and state and local government securities.

Investment companies obtain funds by selling shares in their operation and use the proceeds to purchase securities of other corporations. Open-end investment companies, commonly known as mutual funds, constitute an important medium of investment for the small investor who wishes a diversified portfolio of corporate securities.

The investment banker performs such services as underwriting new issues of stocks and bonds for corporations, acting as a broker in buying and selling securities for clients in the secondary securities markets, and providing advice to business enterprises in the timing and details for long-term financing.

Much of the trading of corporate securities in the secondary markets occurs on organized exchanges such as the New York Stock Exchange and the American Stock Exchange. Stocks not listed on organized exchanges are traded in the over-the-counter market.

Before investing in stocks or bonds an investor needs to determine the relative importance of current income, capital appreciation, and the degree of risk which he is willing to assume.

Useful measures to judge a common stock's future market-price potential include the corporation's earnings and earnings growth, cash dividends, historic market price, price/earnings ratio, and the quality of corporate management.

Terms for review

financial institutions	Federal Reserve discount rate
Federal Reserve System	open-market operations
money market	mutual fund (open-end invest-
capital market	ment company)
primary securities market	investment banker
secondary securities market	over-the-counter market (OTC)
commercial banks	cash dividends
fractional reserve banking system	price/earnings ratio
reserve requirements	

Questions

1. What functions do financial institutions perform in the economy?
2. Outline the role of the Federal Reserve System.

3. Explain how the Federal Reserve regulates the public's supply of money and credit.

4. Outline the services performed by commercial banks which justify calling them "the keystone of the American monetary and financial system."

5. *a*) Given an initial bank demand deposit of $10,000, what would be the maximum amount the commercial banking system could expand demand deposits if the required reserve ratio were 16⅔ percent?

   b) What conditions would have to prevail for such a maximum expansion to occur?

6. List the major types of investments made by each of the following financial institutions:
   a) Life insurance companies
   b) Savings and loan associations
   c) Mutual savings banks
   d) Consumer finance companies
   e) Sales finance companies
   f) Commercial finance companies
   g) Credit unions
   h) Personal trust departments
   i) Pension funds
   j) Fire and casualty insurance companies
   k) Investment companies

7. What specific functions does the investment banker perform?

8. Assume you have $2,000 of your own money to invest in the stock market. Select a corporation's common stock from *Moody's Industrial Manual, Standard & Poor's Corporation Reports,* or some other source. Plot the common stock's market fluctuations reported in the daily newspaper over a one-month period. How do you account for the changes in the stock's market price? What seemed to be happening in the stock market as a whole over this same period of time?

9. What are some of the important elements in a person's overall financial position that he should examine before deciding to invest money in the stock market?

10. Assuming each of the following had considered their overall financial situation and determined that they could invest $10,000 in corporate securities, recommend a specific investment portfolio of stocks and/or bonds for each:
    a) A couple in their middle thirties who are concerned about providing for their two sons who will be entering college within the next ten years.
    b) A retired couple whose primary source of income is social security benefits and a small company pension.
    Justify your recommendations for each investment portfolio.

Mutual funds and social responsibility

Some investors today are showing increasing interest in the actions taken by corporate managements on such social issues as pollution control, minority employment, and consumer protection. For years some mutual fund managers have expressed this concern by refusing to purchase the common stocks of corporations which the managers believed were not operating in the public interest. For example, the huge ($1.5 billion in assets) College Retirement Equities Fund, which invests the retirement monies of professors across the country, refuses to invest in liquor and cigarette stocks.

On the other hand, many investors and mutual fund managers take the attitude that a dollar is a dollar, regardless of how it is earned as long as the corporation's activities are within the letter of the law.

The newer approach to socially concerned mutual fund investing is typified by several new funds. One such mutual fund is marketed by the long-established Dreyfus organization. The prospectus for this fund, Third Century Fund, states that "private investment can be a positive force to enhance and encourage further social progress in America." This fund's management believes that enterprises which are concerned with America's social as well as economic problems will also be profitable in the future.

However, there are questions to be resolved with this approach to investing. Some mutual fund managers wonder whether they may be sued by fund shareholders who might charge that the fund management is failing to exercise proper financial stewardship over their investments by becoming too concerned over social issues. Also, how would the investment analysis of a corporation's common stock be made if, for example, the enterprise's management provided leadership in improving ghetto housing in this country but also sold products in South Africa?

1. Discuss the point of view: "A dollar is a dollar when it is invested in the stock market, regardless of the corporation's activities."
2. How could a mutual fund management resolve the dilemma of whether to invest in a socially responsible company that was not so profitable or invest in a less socially responsible corporation which was highly profitable?

3.   What kinds of tests should be applied to a corporation management's
varied activities to determine whether or not they are socially responsible?

The credit crisis of 1970

In May, 1970, almost 600 U.S. industrial, transportation, and finance
corporations had $32 billion in commercial paper outstanding. Commer-
cial paper (short-term promissory notes) is issued by large corporations
as a means of. obtaining short-term financing on an unsecured basis.
Major purchasers of commercial paper include mutual funds, pension
funds, insurance companies, and other corporations. When commercial
paper falls due, it is not unusual for the issuing corporation to pay off
the short-term promissory notes by selling more commercial paper.
When this occurs the commercial paper is said to be "rolled over" or
refinanced.

In June, 1970, the Penn Central Transportation Company had $82
million of commercial paper outstanding when it went bankrupt. (See
Interpreting Accounting Statements on p. 444.) In the days that followed a number of corporations which had commercial paper outstanding found it impossible to "roll over" their commercial paper and had
insufficient cash on hand to pay off the maturing obligations. In a period
of less than a month after the Penn Central collapse the volume of commercial paper outstanding declined by $3 billion, a drop of 10 percent.
Well-known financial subsidiaries of major corporations, such as Chrysler Financial, along with industrial corporations such as SCM and Evans
Products were squeezed for cash.

Corporate financial officers, who found it impossible to sell their commercial paper to their usual buyers, turned to commercial banks for
credit. However, the lines of credit usually established by corporations
with banks as backup for commercial-paper financing generally were
not large enough to cover the amount of money needed. Also, banks
were short of the reserves necessary to create additional credit. Without
additional reserves many banks could provide only token help for large
corporations with which they had formerly done business.

With a financial crisis approaching nationwide proportions because
of the Penn Central, the Federal Reserve System took a number of actions to make additional reserves available to the commercial banks to
enable them to provide financing for the corporations caught in the commercial-paper squeeze. The Federal Reserve System encouraged com-

mercial banks to use the "discount window," i.e., to borrow from the Federal Reserve to increase bank reserves. Also, the Federal Reserve permitted some increases in interest rates to attract more private savings to banks to increase their reserve positions. In addition, the Federal Reserve established a standby plan for making direct loans to corporations should the lack of bank credit at the time threaten the nation's economy. However, the crisis eased without this standby plan being put into effect.

1. Why did the credit crisis of 1970 develop?
2. Why were the nation's commercial banks unable to solve the problem immediately?
3. What steps did the Federal Reserve take to create an environment for dealing with this situation?
4. What benefits did the individual citizen incur as the result of the Federal Reserve's actions?

CASE

Family financial planning

Tom McCormick graduated two years ago from a well-known university with a degree in electrical engineering. While in college he took no courses in business administration or economics. He was married during his senior year and employed upon graduation by a large corporation which made about 30 percent of its sales to various federal government agencies.

During a vacation trip to his home town he raised the following question with his uncle who was a stock broker. "Uncle Max," Tom began, "Jane and I have saved $5,000 over the past two years since we've both been working. We were wondering if you could give us some tips on investing this in the stock market? I'm afraid we're not too sophisticated about money matters, but we seem to be living pretty well and still saving some money."

The uncle replied, "Well, Tom, each person or family should develop an overall financial program for savings. Two elements of this plan, insurance and an insured savings account, should be considered before investments in stocks are made.

"Insurance is a separate subject in itself. However, we can make a few pertinent observations here. Especially if you and Jane plan to start a family soon, you will want to make sure you have sufficient life insurance to provide for family financial security in case of early death of one or both parents. You probably already have a certain amount of life insurance. I would guess it would be *whole life* insurance, which provides both insurance coverage and cash surrender values for the policy owner built up from payment of premiums which are invested by the insurance company. Many young families also buy relatively low-cost *term* insurance to have added insurance protection in the child-rearing years. Term insurance provides insurance coverage for a specified period of time but has no cash surrender value. Your family should also be protected with health and disability insurance."

Tom commented, "Right now we have whole life insurance but no term insurance. However, we haven't really analyzed whether our coverage is sufficient. I have health insurance which is provided by my employer as a fringe benefit at a very reasonable rate. However, this group insurance is available only while I'm employed by the company."

Uncle Max went on, "Of course, you also have government social security insurance which would provide benefit payments to you if you became disabled or to your widow or children under specified conditions in addition to providing retirement benefits. However, social security payments are considered by most persons as supplementary minimum amounts and should not be considered sufficient to provide for all of a family's insurance or retirement needs.

"The second element in a person's savings program is the establishment of a savings account in a bank or savings and loan association. This account can provide money to meet unexpected needs which arise on short notice. A recommended amount in such a savings account would cover three to six months' living expenses. Such accounts should be placed only in financial institutions which are insured up to $20,000 for each account by the FDIC or FSLIC.

"Once these two financial keystones to a personal financial program are established, then other investment media may be considered. For many families the purchase of a house on monthly payments is an important part of their investment program as well as providing for living quarters. Before the purchase of a house is undertaken, factors to be considered include the family's preference for home ownership versus renting a house or an apartment; location of the house under consideration; the total costs of home ownership, including taxes, insurance, and maintenance; and the length of time the family expects to live in the area. Only after some of these factors have been considered would I recommend that you begin to invest in common stocks.

"I don't mean to make this a long lecture, Tom, but if you'll indicate how you stand on these factors, then we can talk about your investment objectives, and I'll make some suggestions for your study."

1. Make a list of the important questions Tom and his wife need to consider as they plan their family financial program.

2. Assume that Tom has adequate insurance and insured savings so that he could consider investing through the stock market. What investment objectives would you recommend to him and his wife at this time? What kind of securities would you suggest to achieve these objectives?

Courtesy Continental Illinois National Bank and Trust Company of Chicago

Financial markets
facilitate the
provision of funds to
finance enterprise
operations.

16

Financial management

The finance function is vital to the profitable management of every business enterprise. The impact of financial decisions is felt throughout the enterprise. Whenever a new product line is added, a new factory built, labor contracts negotiated, or dividend payments considered, questions relating to finance must be resolved. Are the funds available to undertake the proposed course of action? Will the project make good use of resources? How should the undertaking be financed? This chapter analyzes the following questions relating to the financial management of the business enterprise.

What is the finance function?
What are the responsibilities of the finance department for the profitable management of the enterprise?
What is the specific role of top management in the finance area?
How is the finance department organized?

The finance function

Although there are special responsibilities and problems which are specifically assigned to the finance department, the financial aspects of management should be viewed as an integrated part of the total management of the enterprise rather than as a narrow, specialized activity concerned mainly with writing checks and collecting accounts. Certainly it is a responsibility of the finance department to disburse funds for financial obligations which are incurred and to supervise the granting of credit and the collection of accounts receivable which represent amounts owed the enterprise by customers, but this is not the heart of the finance function. The basic elements of the finance function are the profitable utilization of the funds which management has at its disposal and the selection among alternative sources of funds in order to finance activities of the enterprise at the most economical cost.

Financial managers have a responsibility to analyze and review the proposals by production and marketing managers to ascertain potential overall effectiveness in promoting the profit objective of the enterprise. The finance department must be sure that funds will be available to undertake the specific projects selected by management. This does not mean that the finance department makes all the critical decisions as to which investments will be undertaken by the enterprise. The proposals for production and marketing programs still originate in their respective departments, as production and marketing executives should be the ones who have the necessary expert knowledge to decide which equipment is best for a particular job or what product is likely to sell best in a given market territory. However, the finance department must perform the task of review and control when major decisions are made as to whether the enterprise should commit funds to new or continuing projects.

Responsibilities of the finance department

In its role of decision making in both the use of funds and the acquisition of funds, the finance department in each enterprise should develop certain guidelines:

1. To determine the optimum size of the enterprise.
2. To select the best balance among different types of assets.
3. To provide the funds necessary to finance these assets.
4. To deal with the dilemma of profitability versus liquidity.

Size of the business enterprise

The size of a particular enterprise depends upon the nature of the industry of which the enterprise is a part, the legal form of enterprise organization, and the policies which are adopted regarding specific practices.

In some industries there is not much choice as to size of the enterprise. The management of a steel mill has no alternative except to provide substantial amounts of capital for the elaborate plant and equipment necessary to produce steel. Even the smallest steel enterprise requires an investment of many millions of dollars. On the other hand, there are industries in which a greater variation of size and financing is required. The retail grocery industry is an example of this. While there are some enterprises seeking the economies associated with large multistore supermarket operations, other food retailers operate a single store on a minimum investment with a reasonable expectation of profitable results by such methods as buying contacts through voluntary chain organizations and providing special consumer services.

The size of the enterprise is also dependent upon the legal form of organization which is chosen as this determines the amount of financial resources which can be obtained. The corporate form of organization lends itself to the accumulation of large amounts of capital which may be used for initiating or carrying on a business operation. Many sources of funds are available to the corporation, including numerous types of long-term debt, to which the partnership or proprietorship normally does not have access.

After considering the nature of the industry in which the enterprise will operate and the limitations of its particular legal form of organization, the management of a given enterprise has considerable flexibility in its use of financial resources depending upon the policies it adopts in such areas as expansion or new business operations, credit and inventory policies, and plant financing arrangements.

Specific asset management

Once the general size of the enterprise has been established and the broad limits defined which require financing, specific policies must be selected to determine the proper balance among the different classes of assets necessary for business operations. Policies relating to the following classes of assets contain key elements of financial management:

1. The size of cash and near-cash balances.
2. Credit policies—shall the enterprise extend credit to its customers, and, if so, what should be the terms of credit?
3. What shall be the size and composition of inventories?
4. Which fixed assets shall be acquired?

Size of cash and near-cash balances. One of the important operating responsibilities of financial management is the maintenance of cash and near-cash balances which are sufficient to pay the bills of the enterprise as they fall due. The cash account itself usually consists of money on deposit in commercial banks, although some amount of funds may be held in a small *petty cash fund* for minor disbursements in cash rather than by check. In the case of retail enterprises, working balances of currency and coin are kept on hand to make change for customers. *Near-cash* is any asset which is immediately transferable into money without risk of loss of value in the process. The customary form of near-cash for many financial managers is the 91-day U.S. Treasury bill which has a ready market. Although the interest rate on Treasury bills is relatively low, this type of investment does provide some interest on funds which are in excess of immediate cash needs, and at the same time the funds so invested can be turned into cash on short notice. The determination of the proper level of cash and near-cash balances may be a complicated and difficult procedure. Such factors as the fluctuation in the enterprise's scale of operations, the ability of management to predict cash receipts and disbursement patterns, the degree to which changes in the level of operations may be unexpected, and the ability of the enterprise to depend upon other sources of funds such as bank credit in case of cash shortage should all be taken into account before setting the desired level of cash balances.

Credit policies. The decision as to what proportion of the enterprise's assets is to be invested in accounts receivable depends upon the extent to which credit sales are an important part of the marketing department's sales effort and the way in which this credit is managed. Management may decide that sales will be made on a cash-only basis and thus avoid the problems associated with extending credit and making collections. This policy will avoid tying up funds in receivables from customers and will eliminate the possibility of bad debt losses. However, a no-credit policy may result in a much lower level of sales with a resulting decline in profits than if the enterprise pursued a policy of granting credit after a judicious evaluation of the credit worthiness of its customers. When credit is extended, terms are usually quoted in an abbreviated form such as "2/10, n/30" which means that a 2 percent cash discount is allowed the customer who pays his account within 10 days from the date on the merchandise invoice statement or else he is expected to pay the full amount of the bill with no discount within 11 to 30 days.

Although each enterprise's management is theoretically able to set its own credit terms, credit practices are strongly influenced by those which prevail in the industry of which the enterprise is a part. Such policies as the terms of the credit and the volume of credit sales will likely be similar to those which exist throughout the industry. However, management does have considerable freedom in determining the credit worthiness of customers and in pressing collection policies to see that customers pay promptly. Whether an enterprise adopts a conservative or liberal policy regarding credit extension should be determined after consideration has been given to the anticipated additional profits which likely will result from a proposed policy and the amount of energy management is willing to devote to credit administration.

Size and composition of inventories. The determination of the optimum size and composition of inventories is of key importance in both manufacturing and marketing enterprises. For the manufacturing enterprise there are three types of inventories which are necessary—raw materials, work in process, and finished goods. Beginning with the raw materials, value is added throughout the production process until the goods are completed and ready to be shipped to customers. Purchasing and production departments have primary responsibility for determining the specific levels of manufacturing inventories. However, the inventory policies which are followed influence the financial needs of the business enterprise. Hence, the finance department has a responsibility for anticipating requirements for funds which will arise from increasing inventories and should be alert for good investment opportunities to utilize funds that are released when inventory levels fall. Furthermore, the finance department should be concerned with the efficient use of inventories. In this respect, finance department suggestions are appropriate for the improvement of inventory turnover which will result in lower inventories and a reduction in the amount of funds required to finance them.

Acquisition of fixed assets. The specific industry and the scale of business operations will generally determine the need for fixed assets in a particular enterprise. Fixed assets, sometimes called capital assets, include land, buildings, equipment, machinery, tools, furniture, and fixtures. The commitment of funds to fixed assets is of considerable importance to the finance department because fixed assets usually involve an investment of substantial proportion. Before making a major investment in fixed assets, there should be a careful appraisal of the need for the specific assets and the prospects for profits stemming from their acquisition. Once funds have been committed to fixed assets the enterprise is tied up perhaps for many years. If borrowing is undertaken to acquire the funds the lender must be repaid regardless of how well the investment works out. If stockholders put up the money through the purchase of more stock they expect profitable use made of their funds. If the investment in fixed assets does not work out well it may be quite difficult, if not impossible, to dispose of the assets at what the enterprise paid for them or what the remaining value is on the records of the enterprise. For these reasons the finance department should confer with other departments to assure itself that all reasonable steps have been taken to analyze the desirability of investment of funds in a particular fixed asset.

Financing of assets

In addition to acting as an advisor to other departments on the acquisition of fixed assets, the finance department has the clear-cut responsibility of determining the best means of providing the funds for these assets. Enterprise assets may be financed by debt, by the use of leases, or by owners.

The specific source of funds to finance a given project will depend upon the length of time for which the funds are needed, the way in which other funds have been acquired in the past, the attitude of management toward assuming the risks associated with debt, and conditions which prevail at the time in the money and capital markets outside the enterprise.

Financing by use of debt. Funds provided by outsiders through short-term, intermediate-term, and long-term debt are important sources of business enterprise financing. Although the classification of debt on the basis of length of time until maturity varies, short-term debt is that debt which falls due within a year. Intermediate debt usually represents funds obtained for periods of time running from over a year until about 10 years; long-term debt customarily has a maturity more than 10 years in the future. Each of these types of debt is obtained from special sources in financial markets, and each type of debt is undertaken for somewhat different purposes.

Generally it is advisable to use the form of credit which has a maturity as long as the money will be needed. Thus one should not finance a seasonal buildup in inventory to meet holiday merchandise demands with a long-term loan from a life insurance company. More importantly, one should not finance a factory building that is expected to last for at least 20 years with a six-month bank loan. In the latter case the possibility exists that the loan might not be renewed by the bank after six months. This could result in severe financial difficulties for the business enterprise if funds were not available to repay the loan. This problem can be avoided if money is borrowed for the length of time it will be needed.

Short-term sources of funds include bank loans, credit extended by suppliers in the form of accounts payable by the enterprise, and other types of increases in short-term liabilities, such as notes to suppliers for merchandise and liabilities owed the government for taxes which are payable some time in the future. Short-term bank loans are an excellent means whereby the enterprise may finance inventory buildups to meet seasonal or unexpected needs for merchandise. After the merchandise has been sold and the enterprise has collected its accounts receivable, the bank loan is paid off with the money generated by the assets obtained through the loan. Likewise, suppliers frequently extend trade credit to their customers to finance merchandise or equipment purchases. The willingness of suppliers to grant trade credit depends upon both the industry practice and individual enterprise circumstances which were outlined earlier. In this country formal notes recognizing liability for accounts payable have not been widely used and normally merchandise is shipped on open-trade account. However, in cases where the enterprise is not known to the supplier or where the enterprise has been slow in paying its trade accounts, the supplier may ask that a note be signed to acknowledge formally the indebtedness. Since income tax liabilities are built up by enterprises as the result of profitable operations throughout the year but taxes are not paid until some time after the tax liability is recognized, this also represents a source of funds which may be used to finance short-term needs.

Intermediate credit may be obtained through banks, insurance companies, or finance companies which specialize in equipment loans for a period of years. The *term loan*, as intermediate credit is customarily called, is characterized by a loan running for more than 1 year and less than 10. Periodic repayments are normally made to reduce the principal amount of the loan outstanding so that upon maturity only a small amount of the original loan will fall due. The conditions of the term loan will be agreed upon by borrower and lender on an individual basis so there is room for considerable flexibility in the lending arrangements and provisions for repayment. Since there is only one party which makes the loan, it is relatively easy to modify the terms of the loan agreement if this becomes necessary over the years, a condition which is extremely difficult if not impossible with publicly issued debt, such as a bond issue which is held by many persons.

Long-term debt funds may be obtained through direct loans from insurance companies or through the sale of bonds to groups such as investment trusts, corporation pension funds, insurance companies, other business enterprises, or the general public. A *bond* is a debt contract whereby the borrower agrees to repay a certain sum of money at some specified time in the future in exchange for a given sum of money today. A wide variety of conditions may make up the *bond indenture* which is the legal contract giving the details of the arrangement between the issuing company (the borrower) and the bondholders (the lenders). If the borrower fails to live up to the conditions set forth in the bond indenture, there will be provision for some penalty which bondholders may invoke. The penalty might be a restriction upon the dividends paid to owners of the enterprise, having the bondholders take over certain assets of the enterprise to satisfy the amount of the bonds that are outstanding, or even taking some hand in the management of the enterprise. As has been implied, the borrowing of long-term funds is a momentous occasion for the enterprise. Especially in long-term borrowing, large amounts of funds are involved and the projects to be undertaken are substantial in their expected impact on future enterprise operations. Careful analysis of both the desirability of projects requiring long-term funds and the means of their financing is necessary for management. It is the responsibility of the finance department to provide the leadership and technical knowledge necessary for this analysis.

Financing by leasing. Because of its increased importance in recent years, leasing should be included in a discussion of long-term outside funds sources for the business enterprise. The *lease* is a form of long-term renting contract which an enterprise may sign to obtain the use of assets without owning them. The lease arrangement does not appear on the accounting records of the enterprise as a long-term liability, but it does result in a formal obligation for the payment of money over a period of time in the future which creates a contingent liability upon future operations. Business enterprises have made extensive use of leases on both buildings and equipment.

One popular arrangement is the *sale-and-leaseback* agreement where the enterprise constructs a building to its specifications, then sells it to a financial institution such as an insurance company, and simultaneously leases the building back for a long period of time. The result is that the enterprise has the use of the building without immediately tying up its funds. The enterprise then may use its funds for some other purpose, such as increasing inventories, improving product lines, or opening up new marketing areas. The advantages of this type of arrangement for the business enterprise are apparent. However, the mandatory long-term rental payments required by the lease and the questions that arise as to tax liabilities and ultimate ownership of the property make the lease arrangement one which should be carefully investigated before it is undertaken.

Financing provided by owners. In addition to the funds provided by outsiders, the owners of the enterprise provide funds through money generated by business operations and from the additional capital obtained through the sale of stock in the corporation (or of additional partnership or proprietorship funds being added when these legal forms of organization are used).

The amount of profits which an enterprise retains to finance future needs depends upon the investment opportunities that are available to management and the amount of earnings that top management decides to pay out to owners in the form of cash dividends. The determination of the enterprise's dividend policy is one of the important responsibilities of top management and is discussed in the next section of this chapter.

Because of the relative infrequency of the sale of stock by the corporation to its old stockholders or to the public at large, when top management decides upon this course of outside financing the finance department is well advised to obtain the services of an investment banker who has both the close touch with financial markets for the company's stock and also the organization which can sell the stock efficiently. Such difficult and technical questions as setting the price of the stock, timing its sale, achieving a wide distribution of the shares if the stock is not being sold to present stockholders, and handling the legal requirements of the Securities and Exchange Commission make the investment banker a valuable advisor to the enterprise's finance department when the sale of stock is being actively considered as a financing alternative.

The dilemma of liquidity versus profitability

One way of summarizing the finance function in the business enterprise is to say that the objective of financial management is to assure that funds are available to pay bills as they are due and to promote the long-run profit objectives of the enterprise. In a very real sense these two objectives are in conflict. In order to avoid being short of cash to meet financial obligations the finance department might carry huge cash balances on hand at all times. The major portion of the assets of the enterprise might be tied up in a bank checking account or invested in short-term government securities which could be instantly turned into cash. In this case, liquidity would be extremely high for the enterprise. All bills would be promptly paid and large cash balances would be available to meet any contingency, however remote. By achieving in the extreme this objective of liquidity, the finance department is ignoring its other vital responsibility of promoting the profitability of the enterprise.

To maximize profitability the finance department would attempt to calculate the needs for cash so that cash inflow exactly matched cash outflow with no excess of cash on hand at any time. In this case all funds would be invested in working assets such as accounts receivable, inventories, or plant and equipment. These working assets would be the basis for operations which would result in large profit potential for the enterprise. There would be no idle cash in the bank account and no funds invested in low-interest-yielding government securities. This mode of financial management would promote profitability but would subject the enterprise to considerable danger that liquidity would be impaired and, as a result, bills could not be paid on time.

The solution of the dilemma posed for the finance department by the cases of liquidity and profitability is that neither extreme case represents the best answer. Some funds must be invested in cash and near-cash assets to provide the liquidity to take up the slack in the bank balance which results from variations in cash inflows and demands for cash. The credit rating of the enterprise must be maintained in good economic times so that when the need for credit is pressing, creditors will be willing to provide funds. At the same time, most of the enterprise's funds should be invested in some form of assets which will be more profitable than cash and near-cash. The balance that financial managers strike between liquidity and profitability will come only after considerable calculating, deliberation, and discussion. Ultimately the decision will depend upon whether top management as representatives of owners prefers to "eat well" through greater expected profitability or "sleep well" by having greater liquidity and reducing the risks associated with small cash balances.

Financial responsibilities of top management

The top management of a business enterprise includes the men who head the main divisions of the enterprise, such as the vice presidents of marketing, manufacturing, finance, and personnel; the chief operating officer who usually has the title of president; and the group of individuals representing the owners of the enterprise. In the corporation the board of directors is the group elected by the stockholders to represent their interests and to determine the policies for enterprise operation. The partners in the partnership fulfill the function of the board of directors, and in the proprietorship the sole owner determines top policies.

The members of top management have responsibilities for financial decisions in the following areas:

1. Financial planning and organizing for profits.
2. Allocation of profits through dividend policy.
3. Determination of the capital structure of the enterprise.
4. Deciding special issues, such as consolidation and merger proposals.

Planning for profits

In the area of financial planning for profits, the top management has the overall responsibility for the effective utilization of enterprise funds. Investment proposals which are presented to top management should be scrutinized for the anticipated profitability of the project and the long-run benefits which are expected to accrue to the owners of the enterprise. The interests of the owners of the enterprise are important when top management is confronted by financial issues. If the financial affairs of the enterprise are not well managed, the owners stand to lose their investment. In the corporation it is the stockholders who possess the legal right to control the management and to change it if financial results are poor. This is true even though in the large corporation there are thousands of stockholders who do not exercise their right to vote on directors who will determine vital policies.

There are specific legal responsibilities which the board of directors has in a corporation. These include the restrictions imposed by the corporation's charter, the state laws of incorporation, and the general prohibition against *ultra vires* acts (those actions beyond the powers granted to directors). The board is required to act as faithful steward of the enterprise's assets.

As an important part of profit planning the board of directors must select the enterprise's chief operating officer and approve the selection of the financial officer from among the most competent men available.

Directors may render the corporation another very important service. They often act as an alter ego for the operating management in dealing with proposals which are vital to the enterprise's success. In the board of directors the management has an interested, informed group which usually is able to view more objectively the proposed plans of vital importance to the corporation. The board is capable of providing a perspective that is difficult to achieve for executives involved in the daily conduct of the business. An important function of directors is asking discerning questions of management regarding the problems and programs facing the enterprise.

Top management has the further responsibility of seeing that the finance department is organized so as to deal effectively with the financial issues which arise in both the day-to-day operations and the special financial problems which occur less frequently. The top management has one of its best tools for the evaluation and control of financial operations through the examination and approval of budgets. The use of budgets for planning, executing, and controlling the financial progress of the enterprise is very important, as is pointed out in Chapter 6.

Determination of dividend policy

The determination and execution of dividend policy for the business enterprise is the second area of financial responsibility for top management. In the corporation the board of directors sets dividend policy. In the partnership the partners decide how much of the profits will be withdrawn, and in the proprietorship the owner decides how much money will be taken from operations for his private use. The basic question of profits distribution is the same for all legal forms of organization—what policy will best allocate the profits of the enterprise to satisfy the needs of the owners for income and at the same time meet the needs of the enterprise for funds for profitable growth and development. Here the discussion centers on the determinants of dividend policy for the corporation, but the principles are generally applicable to the other legal forms of business organization.

There are several factors which top management must take into account when setting a corporation's dividend policy and should review each time a cash dividend declaration is made. These include the level of earnings now and anticipated for the future, the present level of dividends in the case of the established corporation, the projected profits on new investments which might be made, the size of the corporation's cash account, the needs of shareholders, and the prevailing dividend practice throughout the industry. For a particular corporation the various factors will be combined by directors according to the priority system which seems most relevant to them. However, all of these factors should receive top management consideration before a decision is reached on dividend policy.

Since dividends represent a distribution of the profits to the owners of the corporation, the amount of earnings is an important determinant of the level of dividends paid. Usually top management decides to distribute some proportion of earnings as cash dividends and retain the balance of profits for reinvestment in the enterprise. Although there is wide variation in dividend payout percentages, many corporations pay out between 40 and 60 percent of profits in dividends. Frequently, small or no cash dividends will be paid shareholders in the early stages of an enterprise's development when the need for funds is greatest, but with the maturation of the enterprise dividend payments are usually initiated or increased.

In the established enterprise where a cash dividend policy is already in effect, the management is influenced in its dividend decisions by the level of cash dividends which was paid the last time directors considered the question. In general, managements are prone at least to maintain the dividend rate which was paid in a previous period. Since most cash dividends are paid quarterly throughout the year, this means that directors are reluctant to increase the cash dividend rate per share of stock from a previous quarter's payment unless they are fairly sure that the higher rate can be continued in the future. Likewise, directors are hesitant to reduce cash dividend rates even in the face of lower earnings if they anticipate that the drop in profits may be temporary. The logic behind this attitude is that directors are reluctant to incur the displeasure of stockholders stemming from both the immediate loss of part of their expected cash dividend plus the decline in the market price for the corporation's stock which generally accompanies a reduction in cash dividends.

In deciding upon the level of cash dividends paid to shareholders, top management also takes into account the opportunities which exist for investment of profits in new projects. If the demands for internal investment in enterprise projects are great, with prospects for high rates of return on these investments, then management may be reluctant to pay out as large a proportion of cash dividends as it would if reinvestment prospects were not so bright. A reasoned approach to reinvestment of profits inside the corporation is that profits should be reinvested whenever the anticipated return would be greater than the return which stockholders would obtain from the profits by having them distributed as cash dividends. However, putting such a policy into operational form has severe complications in view of the different investment opportunities and needs of the many stockholders who compose the ownership of today's large corporations. The fact that the cash dividends paid shareholders are taxed as ordinary income by federal and state governments is another relevant factor as top management considers the desirability to reinvest profits inside the enterprise, along with the need to give shareholders a fair return on their investment. The last word on how best to meet both these needs has yet to be written.

One way to meet stockholders' needs for cash and the corporation's need for funds when profit prospects are good for new enterprise investments is to recognize that the higher future profits from good projects presumably will be reflected in a higher market price for the corporation's stock. This would mean that stockholders who needed current income from their personal investment in the corporation's stock could sell some of their shares and still have a dollar investment in the corporation's stock which would be as large as before the market price increase stemming from the profitable reinvestment. However, since the stock market does not always reflect the higher profits or profit prospects in higher market prices and there are other determinants of stock market prices than simply current earnings reports, this solution will not always work out.

One proposal to solve the dilemma faced by management in trying to meet the needs for reinvestment funds in the enterprise plus the legitimate request of stockholders for dividend income is to have a dividend policy which is clearly stated by top management to stockholders. Then at least stockholders will be aware of the guidelines under which management will operate in dividend matters, and stockholders may tailor their individual investment portfolios to include the stock of those corporations which have a dividend policy that suits their needs.

The type of dividend policy which prevails throughout an enterprise's industry is another consideration for directors. Although the fact that a competitor has a particular dividend policy is not a sufficient reason for management's taking the same action, if management does deviate significantly from the dividend practice throughout the industry there should be a reason for this variance. Otherwise, stockholders may be penalized by a lower market price being offered for the corporation's stock merely because it is "out of step" with established industry practice.

As directors consider dividend declarations, the ability of the corporation to have the cash on hand to meet this declaration is a mechanical factor which must be taken into account. This means that the finance department must manage the cash flows of the enterprise so as to have the money on hand to meet the cash dividend payments which directors authorize.

In addition to profit distributions through cash dividends, from time to time management may declare other types of dividends. Occasionally in the past, small corporations have declared *dividends in kind* by distributing some of the enterprise's product to shareholders instead of making a cash dividend distribution. More generally dividends have been issued through *stock dividends* which means that instead of cash dividend payments, or increases in cash dividend rates, the management issues more shares of stock to shareholders. The immediate effect of these stock dividends is an increase in the number of shares in the hands of owners. However, assuming management maintains or increases its present cash dividend rate, the long-run effect is to increase the amount of cash dividends paid out because cash dividend rates are paid on an increased number of shares. Individual stockholders have given a generally favorable reception to the distribution of stock dividends, although they have shown a preference for cash dividends when given a choice between the two.

Determining capital structure

One of the important responsibilities of the board of directors is the determination of the capital structure of the corporation. The *capital structure* is defined as all the long-term funds which are committed to the enterprise's operations. These long-term funds are supplied from two primary sources—owners' investment, both through the purchases of stock and the reinvestment of profits, and long-term debt. The determination of the balance between long-term debt and owners' funds to finance the assets of the corporation is a tedious issue for corporate managers. At one extreme, where there is no long-term debt and the entire capital structure consists of owners' funds there is no risk involved that the enterprise will ever be embarrassed by not being able to meet interest costs and principal repayments on debt. This type of capital structure would provide a maximum of safety for the investment of owners since in case of enterprise failure creditors have a prior claim against assets. However, the sole use of ownership funds in the capital structure ignores the profit possibilities which may result from the careful use of debt to improve the profitability with which owners' funds are employed. Consider the following example of two corporations both with the same total long-term funds, but with differing capital structures:

	Corporation A	Corporation B
Long-term debt—5% bonds	0	$10,000,000
Owners' equity: common stock and retained earnings	$20,000,000	10,000,000
Total long-term capital	$20,000,000	$20,000,000

One hundred percent of Corporation A's capital structure is made up of owners' equity, while only 50 percent of Corporation B's capital structure is owners' equity and the remaining 50 percent is supplied by an issue of bonds which will not fall due for 25 years. The interest rate on the bonds is 5 percent, which means that the interest cost on the $10 million in bonds outstanding is $500,000. Notice the simplified profit and loss statements of both corporations. These statements show that each management did equally well in selling products and in controlling operating expenses.

Profit and loss statement for year ending December 31, 1971

	Corporation A	Corporation B
Sales	$80,000,000	$80,000,000
Less: Operation costs	70,000,000	70,000,000
Operating income	$10,000,000	$10,000,000
Interest on bonds	–0–	500,000
Income before taxes	$10,000,000	$ 9,500,000
Federal income taxes at 50 percent	5,000,000	4,750,000
Net Profit	$ 5,000,000	$ 4,750,000

Notice that the operating income for both enterprises is the same— $10 million. However, after the deduction of interest cost on the bonds of Corporation B and federal income taxes for both corporations, the net profit for Corporation A is $5 million and for Corporation B $4.75 million. The profit for Corporation B is $250,000 lower than for Corporation A. However, when this profit figure is compared with the amount of funds provided by owners, the return on owners' equity is 25 percent for Corporation A and 47.5 percent for Corporation B. The substantially higher return on the owners' investment in the latter case is because of the use of borrowed funds of $10 million instead of having owners supply all the long-term funds as was the case in Corporation A.

Thus, with only half as large an investment, the owners of Corporation B reaped a return almost twice as great as the percentage earned on Corporation A's common stockholders' equity. This higher percentage return on owners' equity through the use of debt in Corporation B is the result of trading on the equity. In financial terms *trading on the equity* is the rate of return on the existing owners' equity in relation to the rate of return on the total long-term capital assuming that the entire capital structure is made up of owners' equity. In the case of Corporation B, trading on the equity results in a ratio of 47.5 percent/25 percent or 1.9. This means that the rate of return on the owners' equity is 1.9 times the return which would have existed had the bond issue not been used to provide part of the long-term funds.

Does this advantage of a higher rate of return on shareholders' investment mean that top management should continue to add more and more debt to the capital structure to improve the trading on the equity ratio? By no means! The assumption of debt brings with it the obligation to pay interest on the borrowed money whether or not the enterprise operates profitably. Furthermore, at some time in the future the debt itself must be repaid. Thus the advantage of an increased rate of profitability on owners' funds through trading on the equity must be tempered by the risks associated with undertaking the debt. Determining a proper balance between long-term debt and equity funds is one of the responsibilities of the board of directors, and a final answer can be reached only after weighing the conflicting aspects of profitability and the risks associated with indebtedness.

Consolidation and merger proposals

The last area for discussion of the responsibilities of the top management is that of special issues which arise from time to time during the operation of the business enterprise. These special issues include consolidation and merger proposals. A *consolidation* is the joining of two or more independent business enterprises into a new enterprise under a single management. A *merger* occurs when a smaller enterprise is taken over by a larger business enterprise. Frequently in the case of a merger the acquired enterprise will become a division of the larger organization. In either of these situations, top management must determine the value of its enterprise in relation to the other enterprise which is a party to the merger or consolidation. The two basic techniques which management may use to determine the value of the enterprise are the valuation of enterprise assets or the valuation of the expected stream of profits of the enterprise.

In using the technique of valuation of enterprise assets, the assets may be valued on the basis of their *book value,* which is their worth based on original cost as shown in the accounting records; on *reproduction value,* which is what it would cost to replace the assets with others of like characteristics; or on the basis of *liquidation value,* which would be the value of the assets if they were dispersed to different purchasers who presumably would be able to put them to some economic use. When the enterprise is valued on the basis of its stream of profits, the management must estimate future earnings and then determine the value of the business based on the yield resulting from those earnings.

No matter what valuation techniques are used the final determination of a satisfactory merger agreement will come about only as the result of bargaining by both sides after considering all factors, financial and others. Each board of directors has the responsibility to protect the interests of its own shareholders and to secure the best terms possible under the existing circumstances.

Organization of the finance department

The broad financial policies determined by the board of directors set the boundaries for the finance department in the performance of its duties although generally there is considerable latitude for further decision making in matters of financial management. In a particular corporation the degree of responsibility and authority exercised by the financial officer over finance matters and the responsibility of his department will vary depending upon such factors as his education and experience, personality, and the confidence in which he is held by the president and the board of directors.

In the large corporation there will usually be several executives who are concerned directly with financial management. Although there is a wide variation in the organization of finance departments and the titles used from one enterprise to another, a typical finance department (see

Figure 16–1) includes the following positions. The top finance officer who may be titled *vice president for finance* directs the overall activities of the finance department. There is a good possibility that he will be a member of the corporation's board of directors. Most of his time is spent in long-range financial planning and preparation of long-term budgets as well as supervising the activities of his direct subordinates. Besides the chief financial officer there will be a *treasurer* who is responsible for custody of cash funds, securities, insurance policies, and other valuable papers. He is responsible for receiving all incoming cash and for approving all cash disbursements as well as handling technical details of preparing financial data for directors, stockholders, and public presentation, and in dealing with bank borrowing, along with a variety

FIGURE 16–1
Partial organization chart of a finance department

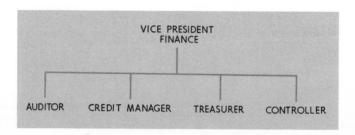

of other financial duties. The *controller* is responsible for the accounting function in the enterprise in both record keeping and in preparing financial statements and analysis based on these records. The controller, as the chief accounting officer, checks on budget preparation and follows up to see how well the budget is adhered to by the various departments of the enterprise. Although the treasurer will be responsible for all paychecks, the controller's office may prepare the payroll for the treasurer's approval. The *credit manager* may report to either the treasurer or the controller. As head of the credit department the credit manager is responsible for deciding which customers shall be granted credit and the extent of that credit. The credit manager presses collection of delinquent accounts and assists other financial executives in the determination of overall credit policies. The *auditor* and his staff check on the functioning of the accounting and control systems in the business enterprise. Company auditors not only verify the reported performance of the various divisions but also may act as staff advisors to make recommendations to management for the more effective operation of the enterprise.

Thus financial executives perform a wide variety of functions. The assignment of these functions may vary with the particular enterprise and the man filling the particular role, but the functions exist in all enterprises. Generally in large corporations the further up in the organization structure of the finance department an executive is, the more he works with long-range planning; outside sources of funds such as commercial banks, insurance companies, and investment bankers; and the president and board of directors of the enterprise. Despite his specific duties, the finance executive should be trained in accounting and have an overall understanding of the function of finance. In this respect, the chief financial executive and his subordinates have the great responsibility to work effectively with other departments in the business enterprise to facilitate the production and sale of goods and services in the framework of the profit-making system.

Summary

The finance function is not only the disbursement of funds, granting of credit, and collection of receivables, but in a more basic sense includes responsibility for the profitable utilization of funds available to management and the securing of funds at their most economical cost. The finance department in each enterprise should develop guidelines:

To determine the optimum size of the enterprise.
To select the best balance among different types of assets.
To provide the funds necessary to finance these assets.
To deal with the dilemma of profitability versus liquidity.

The dilemma of liquidity and profitability refers to the need of the finance department to have sufficient cash on hand to pay bills as they fall due and yet to maximize profitability by investing funds in such assets as inventories or plant and equipment.

Members of top management have responsibilities for financial decisions in the following areas:

Financial planning and organizing for profits.
Allocation of profits through dividend policy.

Determination of the capital structure of the enterprise.

Deciding on special matters, such as consolidation and merger proposals.

Dividend policy determination should take into account the level of earnings now and anticipated for the future, the present level of dividend payments, the projected profits on new investments which might be made, the size of the corporation's cash account, needs of shareholders, and the prevailing dividend policy throughout the industry.

When determining the enterprise's capital structure, management must consider the desired balance between owners' investment and debt. Since creditors have a prior claim against assets, little or no long-term debt gives a maximum of safety for the owners but may result in a lower level of profitability on the equity funds. Borrowed funds which are profitably employed will increase the rate of return on owners' equity.

A consolidation occurs when two or more independent business enterprises are joined into a new enterprise under a single management. A merger occurs when a smaller enterprise is taken over by a larger company. In a merger or consolidation, the two basic techniques which may be used to determine the value of the enterprises are the valuation of the assets involved or the valuation of the expected stream of profits of the enterprises.

The top officer of the finance department is usually the vice president for finance who directs the overall activities of the department and who reports to the chief operating executive of the enterprise. Subordinates of the financial officer include the treasurer, controller, credit manager, and the auditor.

Terms for review

finance function	stock dividend
term loan	capital structure
bond indenture	trading on the equity
lease	consolidation
cash dividend	merger

Questions

1. What are the major responsibilities of the finance department?
2. In what ways does an enterprise have control over extension of credit to its potential customers? How is the enterprise limited in its control over credit terms extended to customers?
3. List the sources of funds available to the large corporation. Discuss the different factors that management needs to consider in deciding on a specific source of funds for a particular project.
4. Explain the financial dilemma of liquidity versus profitability.
5. What factors should be taken into account in determining the amount of cash dividends to be paid to common stockholders?
6. *a)* How can the use of debt by the corporation increase the rate of return on the common stockholders' equity?
   b) How can the use of debt be detrimental to the common stockholders?
7. When a merger or consolidation is contemplated, what are the methods which may be used to determine the value of the enterprise under consideration?

BUSINESS BRIEFS

Ford Motor Company's increased dividend

After having paid 60 cents quarterly per share of common stock since 1965, in July, 1971, the Ford Motor Company increased its quarterly cash dividend to 65 cents. Over a full year this would raise cash dividend payments from $2.40 to $2.60 per share.

Ford spokesmen gave no explanation for the board of directors' action. However, financial analysts speculated that increased earnings in the first part of 1971 and anticipated higher profits for the full year would explain the dividend raise.

One brokerage firm analyst was quoted as saying the increase was "no surprise" and indicated that it was nothing more than a "token gesture" to stockholders. He said, "This increase doesn't make me want to buy or sell their stock."

However, an analyst for a different investment banking firm termed the dividend increase an "unexpected development which indicates pretty good optimism at Ford." The increase surprised this analyst because Ford had heavy tooling expenses connected with the year's model changeover and a high capital spending budget for the year.

A third investment banker indicated he thought that the change would have been made at the end of the year and at the rate of 70 cents instead of 65 cents.

The comment was made that Ford may have made the dividend increase at mid-year to beat General Motors, which some analysts anticipated would declare an extra cash dividend later in 1971.

1. Why would analysts have such varied reactions to the dividend increase?

2. Calculate the percentage of earnings paid out in cash dividends in 1969, 1970, and 1971 by Ford Motor Company. Obtain these figures for profits and dividends from Moody's or Standard & Poor's reports or from some other source of corporation information in the library. After making these calculations, what conclusions do you draw about Ford's actions?

Corporate debt increases

In the decade from 1960 to 1970 the proportion of debt in the capital structure of the 500 largest U.S. industrial corporations increased significantly. For example, in 1960 there were 83 of the largest 500 corporations which had no long-term debt. By 1970 there were only 19 of the largest corporations which had no long-term debt. In 1960 only 24 had more than 40 percent debt in their capital structure. However, by 1970, 106 of the largest corporations had more than 40 percent long-term debt. In addition, there was an increase in the amount of short-term debt owed by corporations.

This increase in debt obligations caused many corporate financial officers to have troubled times in 1970, especially during the commercial-paper crisis that was coupled with a recession in business activity (see The Credit Crisis of 1970 on p. 487). Later, corporate managements began moving back toward the use of more equity funds in an attempt to reduce their debt ratios. For example, in 1971 Trans World Airlines sold 1.5 million shares of common stock for over $37 million. Joy Manufacturing Company sold 400,000 shares of common stock for $22 million. In a number of similar instances the stated purpose of the equity financing was to reduce the amount of short-term debt outstanding.

Commercial banks are putting more pressure on corporations by increasing the standards they apply when granting short-term credit. Larger compensating balances (minimum deposits left with the bank by the borrowing company), a greater margin of current assets over current liabilities (working capital), and limitations on cash dividend payments are all restrictions which banks are enforcing more strongly now than in the past. Furthermore, commercial and investment bankers are urging corporate financial officers to be more careful in working out borrowing arrangements for the proper length of time over which money will be needed.

Some corporations have discovered that the cost of borrowed money is exceeding the return which they can obtain on the investment of borrowed funds. In 1970 approximately 200 of the 500 largest industrial corporations did not earn 9 percent on their assets before interest payments and taxes. However, in 1970 even many big-name corporations were required to pay more than 9 percent on borrowed money. For example, in 1970 Boise Cascade issued $75 million in bonds with a 10 percent interest rate. Ryder System borrowed long-term money at 11½ percent the same year. In 1971 American Airlines paid 10 percent to finance new equipment.

1. What reasons can you give for the increased use of debt by large corporations from 1960 to 1970?
2. Why are some financial institutions and corporate financial officers now taking a second look at the use of debt?

CASES

Pine Tree Wood Products Company

The Pine Tree Wood Products Company, Inc. had been in Atlanta for several years. Its principal products were wooden and metal fences which had become quite popular with home owners and which were also used by industrial firms for security purposes. Other products included flooring and unfinished furniture. The company had a reputation for quality products and workmanship.

Jim Curtis, owner of Pine Tree Wood Products Company, was 58 years old and had a son, 35, who was also engaged in the business.

The company employed 8 or 9 employees on a full-time basis with seasonal employment in the summer rising to about 40 as more sales personnel and laborers were required to meet the demand for fence installations.

Early in 1969, Jim Curtis approached Ned Ollis, loan officer of the First State Bank of Atlanta, for a loan of $70,000 for the purpose of acquiring a small company which produced materials to treat and preserve wood posts and lumber. The First State Bank had done business with Jim Curtis since 1965, when he became acquainted with Mr. Ollis as the two worked on a Community Chest fund drive committee together. Shortly thereafter Mr. Curtis talked with Mr. Ollis about moving his banking business to the First State Bank from a smaller bank which had been reluctant to meet his increasing needs for loans as his business interests expanded.

Beginning in 1965 the First State Bank had provided the Pine Tree Wood Products Company with an unsecured line of credit of $50,000 to finance seasonal inventory increases and accounts receivable during the peak periods of business. Although the unsecured line of credit was to the Pine Tree Wood Products Company it was personally guaranteed by both Mr. and Mrs. Jim Curtis. Provisions of the loan agreement included a 30-day cleanup period during which the loan would be completely paid off, with the added requirement that funds for this cleanup were not to come from borrowings at other banks.

This line of credit was handled to the bank's satisfaction during 1965 and 1966. Borrowings were made in amounts of roughly $10,000 beginning in the early spring and reaching a peak in the late summer. Then the loan was reduced in amounts of $10,000 until it was off the books for about two months during the winter period. In 1967 Mr. Curtis requested that the credit line be increased to $60,000 and this was approved by the bank's loan committee upon Mr. Ollis' recommendation. Summary financial information on the Pine Tree Wood Products Company and on Mr. Curtis' personal liabilities and net worth is provided in Exhibits 1 and 2.

In addition to the Pine Tree Wood Products Company, the Curtis family owned a 400-acre farm outside of Atlanta which was stocked with beef cattle. In early 1969 the bank had a loan of approximately $25,000 outstanding to Mr. and Mrs. Curtis to finance the herd of feeder cattle. This was in addition to the $60,000 line of credit for the company of which $20,000 was outstanding on December 31, 1968. Other personal liabilities, made up chiefly of real estate mortgages held by a savings and loan association, amounted to about $60,000 at the end of 1968.

It was in the autumn of 1968 that Mr. Curtis had first become aware of the possibility of purchasing a company located 150 miles from Atlanta which produced wood products, mainly fence posts, beams, and other lumber items treated with creosote and other wood preservatives. The company was owned by a man 67 years old who had expressed an interest in selling the business and retiring. Six or seven employees worked in the business. Timber products were purchased for cash directly from farmers and wood-lot operators in the area. Annual sales had varied between $75,000 and $125,000 per year with a few lumber dealers buying approximately 80 percent of the plant's output. Farmers and small business enterprises in the area constituted the remaining customers of the business and paid for their purchases in cash.

Mr. Curtis drove to the wood-treating plant and discussed the possible purchase of the business with its elderly owner. At the end of their discussions the owner verbally offered to sell the business for $70,000. Assets consisted mostly of machinery, used but apparently in good working order, and the inventory of wood products, some of which were treated, along with a supply of chemicals and petroleum products necessary for the treating process. Although formal records were scanty, on his initial visit Mr. Curtis estimated that profits had ranged between $8,000 and $20,000 in recent years. After the owner's offer to sell, Mr. Curtis left with the promise to return in the near future with his accountant to go over the company's records more closely.

Upon his return to Atlanta he discussed the proposed purchase with the First State Bank loan officer and sounded him out on the possibility of financing which might be available for adding this wood-treating operation to his Atlanta business. Mr. Curtis felt that the wood treating would be an ideal complement to his present business since the plant could supply many of the wood products which he currently was buying from outside sources. Also, he visualized markets for the wood-treated posts and lumber throughout the Atlanta area. Mr. Curtis pointed out to Mr. Ollis that he had space available behind his Atlanta shop for storage of a large inventory of wood-treated products so that expansion of his present facilities would not be necessary. Furthermore, he had an employee who had experience in wood treating and could manage the new operation, which would be 150 miles away.

Approximately two weeks after his visit to the wood-treating plant, Mr. Curtis and his accountant returned. An examination of the records indicated that the best information about the business had to be taken from the owner's individual income tax returns. While detailed financial information on the company's operations was not complete it appeared that actual profits had been somewhat higher than Mr. Curtis had originally estimated and had varied between $12,000 and $25,000 per year.

Two days later Mr. Curtis offered $70,000 for the business which was accepted by the owner. Since the offer was contingent upon satisfactory financing being arranged, Mr. Curtis immediately contacted the loan officer at the First State Bank to see if a $70,000 loan could be obtained and, if so, on what terms. He presented Mr. Ollis with preliminary statements on his 1968 sales and net income for the Pine Tree Wood Products Company along with the net worth of the corporation as of December 31, 1968.

EXHIBIT 1
Pine Tree Wood Products Company, Inc.

	(Thousands of $)			
	1968	*1967*	*1966*	*1965*
Sales	$440	$410	$420	$395
Net income	31	24	25	19
Net worth of corporation	120	100	76	80

EXHIBIT 2
Personal financial data, Mr. and Mrs. Curtis

	(Thousands of $)			
	1968	*1967*	*1966*	*1965*
Personal net worth (including ownership of Pine Tree Wood Products)	$220	$210	$180	$140
Personal liabilities (not including liabilities of Pine Tree Wood Products)	90	85	65	58

1.   What has been the extent of the bank's relationship up to this point with Mr. Curtis? How has this relationship worked out for both parties?

2.   What consideration should be taken into account by the bank's loan officer in deciding whether or not to grant the $70,000 loan request?

3. From the information given, how would you decide this request if you were the loan officer? If you would make the loan, what conditions would you require? If you would not make the loan, what are your reasons? If you would not make the $70,000 loan, what advice or assistance might you provide Mr. Curtis?

Zero Duplicator Corporation

Because of increasing demand for its products and good profit prospects, the Zero Duplicator Corporation's management decided to build a new factory located in the southwestern part of the United States where company manufacturing operations had not been previously located. The company's home office and manufacturing facilities were located on the outskirts of a large eastern city and would continue to serve the company's eastern customers.

Engineering estimates are that $5 million will be required for the new facility. Of this amount $1 million can be provided by reducing the corporation's cash and near-cash accounts, and $1 million will be generated within the coming year by retaining a large portion of expected profits in order to build this new plant. After consultation with investment bankers, management concluded the remaining $3 million might be raised in one of the following ways:

1. Sale of 30,000 shares of 7.5 percent preferred stock $100 par value.
2. Sale of $3 million of 8.5 percent bonds with a sinking fund to retire the issue over ten equal annual payments beginning the sixth year after the issue is sold.
3. Sale of 150,000 shares of common stock at $20 per share. The current market price of the corporation's stock is $25 per share. Investment bankers estimate that the new shares of stock could be sold at a price to net $20 per share to the corporation.

For the year just ended Zero Duplicator's balance sheet is summarized as follows:

Current assets (including			Current liabilities	$ 8,000,000
cash and near-cash)	$12,000,000		Common stock (2 million	
Net fixed assets	5,000,000		shares authorized, 1	
Other assets including			million shares out-	
patents	1,000,000		standing)	1,000,000
			Retained earnings and	
			other capital accounts	9,000,000
			Total liabilities and	
Total assets	$18,000,000		net worth	$18,000,000

Earnings before interest and taxes were approximately $1.7 million in the year just ended, or $0.85 per share of common stock after taxes. Management expected earnings to increase by at least 15 percent in the current year without the new plant facility. For planning purposes it is expected that income taxes will continue at about 50 percent of taxable income. Management feels that prospects for future growth are excellent. Three years ago the company successfully defended itself against a patent infringement suit by a large competitor. Although the duplicating equipment field is highly competitive, Zero's management believes they hold some key technological patents. However, at the present time the company's share of the market is small.

No cash dividends have been paid to common stockholders since the corporation was organized a few years ago. The corporation's stock is rather closely held among members of management and a few wealthy investors but some shares are held by the public. The stock is inactively traded in the over-the-counter market. No one person holds controlling interest in the corporation's stock.

1. What key financial issues are involved in dealing with the immediate problem presented in this case?

2. Evaluate the pros and cons of each proposed method of financing.

3. What broad management policies should be considered in this case in addition to the financing of a new factory?

Business in a changing world

Computers have revolutionized the processing of data for management decision making.

17

Computers

The development of the electronic computer has brought about a true revolution in the past 20 years. The computer has the ability to store and retrieve vast amounts of information, to make instantaneous calculations, and to provide opportunities for controlling many different operations. Major users of computers include governmental bodies, educational institutions, the legal and medical professions, and business enterprises. The production and distribution of computers has created an industry which was unknown prior to the early 1950s. In all likelihood the development of computers will be placed along with the development of nuclear energy and automation in importance when the history of the mid-20th century is written.

The computer has three features which distinguish it from the mechanical desk calculator. These three features are high speed, memory, and the ability to store programs, which are detailed sets of instructions necessary to solve problems or to perform operations on data.

Speed is achieved through the use of electronic circuitry. Mechanical calculators are limited in the speed at which they operate by the speed required to start, move, and stop their mechanical devices. Electronic circuits operate at the speed of light, which is the speed at which electricity is transmitted. Computers can hold data and instructions in an internal memory unit which greatly speeds processing of data. The ability of computers to store programs provides not only an automatic manipulation of data through a sequence of calculations which may be long and complicated, but also provides tests to determine which path or alternative set of instructions should be followed depending upon the nature of the problem.

This introduction to electronic computers for the business enterprise includes a discussion of the following questions.

How may computers be used by business enterprises?
What are the elements of computer centers and programming?
How does one communicate with computers?
What should be considered regarding the installation of a computer?

Uses of computers in business

Computers can be helpful in the management of a business enterprise in a variety of ways. A listing of just a few of their uses would include the speedup of routine record keeping necessary for the internal management of the business system; better control over major system functions, such as purchasing and inventory management; the design of more efficient production schedules, sales projections, and marketing decision making; and management decisions in such areas as major financial planning, plant expansion and location, and new product development.

Record keeping

The area of business record keeping is one which has been readily computerized. The flood of paper work, reports, and records from such departments as personnel and sales has made record keeping an important area for improved enterprise efficiency. It is estimated that more computer time is spent in record-keeping applications than in any other single function. The wide variety of records which are handled effectively by computers include payrolls, inventories and purchasing, customer records, and production scheduling.

Payrolls. When an enterprise has a large number of employees the preparation of payroll records becomes a considerable clerical task. Each employee's record customarily includes gross pay; deductions, such as income taxes withheld, social security payments, union dues, hospitalization premiums, and perhaps Community Chest contributions; net pay; and totals for the current year to date. Payroll checks along with reports for the various deductions listed above have to be made frequently, in some cases on a weekly or twice-monthly basis. Also, reports are usually prepared which allocate a particular employee's pay to a specific department or cost center. When the business enterprise has several hundred employees with varying deduction patterns the use of electronic means for reducing payroll processing costs is important.

Inventories and purchasing. To account for changes in inventories a record is kept of each item showing the number of units on hand and the cost of these units. Each time an item goes into or out of the inventory it is necessary to update the item record. Even inventories in small enterprises may include thousands of different items while large firms will have many more than this. Today computer programs cannot only show changes in inventories but also are designed to provide calculations on optimal quantities to order, reorder points, detection of slow-moving items, and forecasts of future requirements for a particular part based on past sales. Such information is an invaluable aid to purchasing.

Customer records. Department stores, banks, insurance companies, manufacturers, and many other types of business enterprises have lengthy lists of customer records which must be maintained on a current and accurate basis. These records include statements of amounts owed by customers and payments received from them. Department stores use computers to keep accurate records of charge accounts and banks to show current balances in individual accounts. Insurance companies not only use computers in the billing of customers but also feed information regarding a client's personal circumstances into a computer programmed to provide recommendations for possible changes in policy needs. Manufacturers use computers to keep sales accounts up to date. Computers have greatly facilitated the handling of such individual customer records both by increased speed, accuracy, and the ability to handle vast quantities of data.

An account is maintained by the Internal Revenue Service for each individual and business taxpayer which reconciles individual tax returns with the wages reported by business enterprises, interest and dividend reports, and other sources of individual income. The comparison of these millions of reports is feasible only through use of a computer system which is now nationwide.

Production scheduling. The complexity of coordinating personnel, raw materials, purchased parts, machine capacities, and orders for finished goods makes production scheduling a natural application for the computer. As was discussed in Chapter 13, a computer program can be designed to determine the schedule which minimizes cost and most efficiently utilizes production resources. Without computers, production scheduling is not only more time consuming but is likely to result in a less efficient use of scarce resources which make up the production process.

Information retrieval

Because of the advances in technical knowledge in recent years, it is more and more difficult for an individual to keep informed of developments even within a relatively narrow field. Business, scientific, legal, and medical data are now being stored in computer systems and can be called upon by the analyst or researcher when needed. Codes are available for drawing out information on various subjects which provide a printout of an abstract of the information desired along with references as to where detailed information may be obtained. Further significant advances are being made in the field of information retrieval which will make research more productive, less time consuming, and will result in greater amounts of information quickly available for decision making.

Computer systems

Computers have capabilities far greater than merely the processing of data for routine record keeping or for information retrieval. Today information systems are in use which provide new dimensions of efficient data handling. Such systems might include the complete handling of information relating to a business transaction once the data is placed into the computer. This could include the processing of an order from a customer; checking on the customer's credit rating; fitting the order into the production schedule; drawing out the necessary inventory items; costing out the item in terms of raw materials, labor, and overhead; providing shipping instructions; preparing the customer's statement; and notifying the customer of shipment!

Real-time systems. When the computer controls a particular environment by receiving and processing data with resulting action to affect the functioning of the environment *at that time* the computer system is called a *real-time system.*

There are different types of real-time computer systems. Continuous process manufacturing industries, such as chemical producers and oil refiners, use real-time systems for measuring and regulating the production process. Computers are programmed to control production from start to finish with automatic feedback of corrections needed for proper control of the processing of these products. The response time required for the system to make changes in the production process may be as little as five minutes or less.

Airline reservation systems are another type of real-time system. In this case a central computer maintains a record of all scheduled flights for a period of time into the future. Each reservation agent is able to communicate with the computer through a terminal to determine if space is available on a customer-desired flight. When the customer makes a reservation the computer records this in a memory unit and automatically reduces the number of vacant seats subsequently available on the flight. The entire process requires a response time of only a few seconds.

Further advances are being made in the development of computerized systems which indicate an expanded use of real-time systems with greater sophistication in the future.

Time-sharing systems. An important development in computer systems is the concept of *time-sharing,* which provides a number of users with access to a single computer at the same time from different locations for the simultaneous solutions of different problems. This simultaneous, remote access to the computer is possible because the computer switches from one user to another in a matter of milliseconds, which appears to the individual to be instantaneously. The use of time sharing makes possible the utilization of one centralized, expensive computer installation by many at a reasonable charge to individual users. Thus the small business enterprise which would find it difficult to justify the expense of having its own private computer may gain the use of a computer through time sharing.

Systems are now available which make time sharing possible for over 100 simultaneous users. Each user has a terminal through which electronic communication is made with the computer. These terminals have keyboards much like typewriters which give individual users access to the computer which may be located in any other part of the country. The computer keeps track of the time which each user makes of the system, makes corrections, and is capable of providing helpful hints to unskilled users. The system is controlled by a complex set of instructions called the executive which is stored permanently in the high-speed memory portion of the computer. Such time-sharing systems need large memories and some additional equipment, but the usefulness of these systems is being proven to both business and educational users, large and small.

Complex computation and business simulation

Computers can perform complex calculations which would require years of time to do by hand or by mechanical calculators. Because of the ability of computers to store programs for repetitive use it is possible to use computers to reduce both the time and cost required for problem solutions. Scientific and engineering problems are now possible to solve in a matter of minutes which previously were not feasible either because of the time required or the cost involved. It has been estimated that computers can accomplish calculations for a cost of less than $50 which would require a trained operator at a desk calculator a year to do.

Various mathematical models which simulate the real world become operational for better managerial decision making when these models utilize computers to handle the necessary calculations. Through linear programming a mathematical model can be developed to achieve the optimum allocation of resources of a business enterprise. Linear programming is used for a variety of business problems ranging from the development of efficient shipping schedules to determining the most profitable combination of products for a multiple-product company. Linear programming applications may require thousands of repetitive calculations, and without the computer these routine solutions would be impractical.

An interesting application of computers is in the field of business systems simulation. A model of the enterprise and its environment is developed and programmed into the computer so that decisions regarding the management of the enterprise can be fed into the computer. Decisions are then placed into the computer for such factors as product price, production levels, research and development expenditures, sales promotion and advertising budgets, and plant and equipment expenditures. The computer prints out the results of these decisions in terms of profits, market share, inventories, and financial position. Although such a program is only a model of the real world it can provide valuable information on possible consequences of decisions and can be a useful tool in business management.

Heuristic computer programming

The computer applications described up to this point have involved problems or computations which require the computer to perform every possible calculation in arriving at a solution by carrying out a step-by-step prescribed program. There are two types of problems which are not adaptable to this approach. One type is the problem which can be reduced to numbers and equations that can be accommodated by the computer but which requires too many calculations even for a computer to perform efficiently. An example of this type of overly complex computation would be the scheduling of work in a large shop producing metal parts which at a given time has hundreds of machines operating and thousands of orders in production or waiting to be put into production. Scheduling these jobs to minimize idle machine time, reduce lead time on orders, and keep deliveries to customers on time is not feasible with conventional computer programming because of the vast amount of computation necessary to work out every possible combination of alternatives in searching for a solution which optimizes all factors.

A second type of problem which has limited application on conventional computer programming is that which is not structured so it can be expressed in mathematical terms. Examples of such business problems include investing in the stock market, selecting executives for promotion, and selection of new products for development and marketing. In these problems judgment, creativity, intuition, and learning are important factors in arriving at a good solution. These factors are qualitative in nature rather than numerical.

Some of these two types of problems can be solved with computer programming which uses heuristics. A *heuristic* is an aid which can reduce the effort in arriving at a solution. Thus, a heuristic could also be defined as a rule of thumb which is helpful in solving problems even though it does not take into account all possible factors or all possible solutions. A computer program using heuristics could be written to direct the computer to bypass or ignore certain alternatives to the metal shop scheduling problem outlined above. The effect of this would be to reduce the number of calculations to a point where the computer could reach a solution to the scheduling problem which would be better than management could devise without the computer but which would not take all alternatives into account. Such heuristic computer programs using selective calculations have been useful in solving problems where previously it was not practical to make use of computers.

The application of heuristics to the solution of the second type of problems outlined above, involving ill-structured or nonquantitative issues, has not yet been as successful. In some instances where management decision rules can be clearly identified and formalized a heuristic computer program can be devised to aid in problem solving, but generalized programs for the solution of such nonquantitative problems are not now available. Heuristic computer programs have been available for some time for such applications as chess playing. However, these special-purpose applications have not proved to be as effective as human beings in decision making. Research and experimentation are continuing in heuristic applications of computer programs, and their more general application to business problems may occur in the future.

Elements of computer centers

Because of the variety of purposes for which computers are used and the number of equipment manufacturers in the field, generalizations are difficult regarding the specific types of equipment composing a computer center. However, the equipment necessary to utilize computer capacities must provide for the functions of input of data, data storage, data processing and control, and output of information.

Input of data

Data may be fed into computers in a variety of ways. The principal means of data input include card readers, paper-tape readers, magnetic-tape readers, magnetic-ink readers, optical-character readers, and console typewriters. Whatever the means of transmitting data into the computer it is translated into a language which the computer can assimilate and electronically place in its data storage unit for processing. More and more sophisticated means of translating data into computer acceptable language are being developed.

Data storage

Data may be stored within the computer in a memory unit which has the capacity to accommodate a substantial volume of data along with the program. However, for larger systems magnetic tape or random access files are used in order to provide for mass storage of data which will be available when needed. When magnetic tape is used the data are stored and retrieved sequentially. Random files, which take several forms including discs, magnetic drums, and coated plastic strips, permit information to be retrieved in random order. Punched-card files are also sometimes used for data storage outside the computer, and their data are then fed into the computer when needed.

Data processing and control

The data processing and control unit is the heart of the computer system. This is the unit which controls the operation of other equipment, performs computations on data, and receives directions from the program of instructions to accomplish the mission for a particular problem. Customarily the processing unit contains a control panel or console which is used by the computer operator.

Output of information

The computer system also includes some means for the output of information. A common means of receiving information from the computer is through a printer system. High-speed printers which print up to 3,000 lines per minute consisting of at least 132 characters per line are now in general use. Information may also be communicated by the computer through punched-card systems, console typewriters, or visual display devices such as graph plotters, cathode ray tubes, or microfilm. Voice reply systems are also available to answer inquiries to the computer.

Programming

Programming consists of providing the computer with a set of instructions necessary for solving a problem or carrying out a series of operations on data. In the process of programming, however, careful steps are necessary to assure a set of instructions which are usable by the computer. Customarily the programming process first includes an analysis of the structure of the data processing system itself. This means it is necessary to understand the capabilities of the system and whether the computer will be able to handle the assigned problem.

The second step in programming is to outline the necessary computer procedures in a logical fashion. At this step a program flowchart is constructed. Every specific instruction in the proper sequence is necessary at this point since the computer will process the data exactly as the program directs. The third step in programming is to translate the program flowchart into a set of detailed coded instructions for the computer.

The final step is the testing of the program to eliminate errors which may be present at any stage in the process. This debugging process is necessary to check the programmer's work since the output of information will be no better than the data which is put into the computer or the program which is used to process the data.

Flowcharting is a means of graphically presenting solutions to information handling problems. Flowcharting techniques have been adapted to computer applications of information handling. In 1970 the American National Standards Institute (ANSI) developed a revised list of flowcharting symbols. Some of these ANSI standard symbols are illustrated below.

Examples of ANSI flowcharting symbols:

 Processing—a single operation such as an arithmetic manipulation or a defined set of operations.

 Input or Output—a general symbol used to indicate the input or output of data.

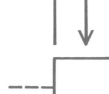 Flowlines—with directional arrows indicate the continuity of operations in the data processing sequence.

 Annotation—this outline provides a means of supplying explanatory or descriptive information. Dashed line indicates the outline to which this explanation applies.

 Decision—a point from which one or more alternate pathways may be followed; a switching point.

 Connector—when used with a number at the end of a flowline indicates that flowline is to be continued where the number appears elsewhere on the flowchart.

 Terminal—this indicates the start, the end, or a delay in the flow.

Some of these symbols are shown in the following simple flowchart depicting the processing of an individual payroll item.

Flowchart Sample of
Individual Payroll:

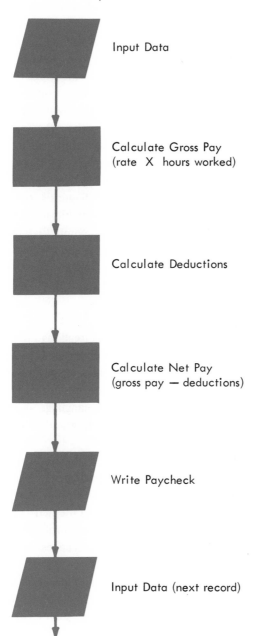

Input Data

Calculate Gross Pay
(rate X hours worked)

Calculate Deductions

Calculate Net Pay
(gross pay — deductions)

Write Paycheck

Input Data (next record)

As this illustration indicates, computer programs must provide detailed, specific instructions for every step of the way through the data processing sequence. A program must tell the computer what to do under all possible conditions. When different circumstances may be encountered in dealing with data the program must specify what is to be done under every alternative set of circumstances.

With more applications for computer problem solving and wider use of these applications, a number of packaged programs have been developed which are now available to users. These standardized programs are useful for operations that are the same from one business enterprise to another. In some instances these programs can be modified to fit individual circumstances in a particular situation without having to write an entirely new program. Numerous subroutine computer instructions are available which reduce the work of the programmer. These subroutines can be used for such applications as loading of programs, relocation of programs, assembly of data, accounting, diagnosis, or compiling data in particular ways. Subroutines are also available for a variety of scientific and mathematical operations such as computing the square root of a number, the logarithm of a number, or the sine or cosine of an angle.

Communicating with computers

The computer itself functions on the basis of directions given through electronic circuits which perform specific operations. It is necessary to translate the language which is understandable to a programmer into a language form which can be accepted by the computer. This operation is called compiling a program. Several compiler language systems have been developed to simplify the job of programming and to standardize computer operations.

The two dominant compiler languages are FORTRAN (FORmula TRANslator), which is an algebraic compiler particularly useful for research problems requiring the solution of mathematical or statistical formulations, and COBOL (COmmon Business Oriented Language), which is a commercial compiler useful for business problems involving file processing and record keeping. In all these languages certain words and symbols have specific meanings.

COBOL makes available a standard method of programming business data processing problems. Generally these applications have large files which require periodic or continuous updating. Such business transactions frequently involve large volumes of input and output data but may not require elaborate processing. FORTRAN provides a means of programming scientific data and business models which usually require relatively limited input and output but have extensive processing.

A number of other computer languages are used depending upon the purposes to be served and the particular manufacturer's computer which is available. Two of these are BASIC and PL/1. BASIC (*B*eginner's *A*ll-Purpose *S*ymbolic *I*nstruction *C*ode) is a language for solving numerical problems. It is sometimes used as a first step for students before they learn one of the more complex languages such as FORTRAN. BASIC is also useful in developing models to simulate business operations.

PL/1 (*Programming Language, Version 1*) is a language suitable for problems involving both business data processing and numerical scientific computations. It combines concepts from other computer languages and was developed because of weaknesses in some of the other languages. PL/1 was developed in the mid-1960s and has wide application in fields which had previously used FORTRAN or COBOL.

Despite the advantages to programmers of having standardized languages to prepare programs, it is not necessary for the user of computers to have detailed knowledge of the technical aspects of computers or their programming to make valuable use of their capacities. Today individuals can be trained in a short time to use computers for problem solving. In these instances the computer will have already been programmed for the type of questions which will be asked. By placing a simple code into the computer through use of a terminal much like a typewriter the individual user can have the answer to a variety of conditions ranging from airlines schedules, inventory positions, a customer's account or bank balance, to solutions to problems in mathematics, statistics, or financial analysis. While additional training and knowledge is required before one becomes thoroughly acquainted with computer operations, a minimum amount of training is sufficient to enable the business manager or the student to make the computer a valuable tool for his own use.

Considerations when installing a computer

Before a computer system is installed management must come to grips with a number of problems. There are two benefits which may come from the installation of electronic computer systems. First, information is available faster and in better form than is possible without the computer. Not only are former data processing chores accomplished more expeditiously, but a variety of additional information is available for management use. As the computer system is developed in an enterprise there will be many applications which will come to light not originally envisioned when the computer was first installed. Volumes of data can be processed with computers which would be impossible in the time available without such assistance. The second benefit normally expected out of a computer installation is a reduction in the number of employees required for data processing, though the workers who will be required for computers normally will be higher paid and more skilled than the clerical employees whom the computer displaces since different kinds of skills are required in computer centers than are typically required in many routine clerical positions.

One of the most critical factors determining the success or failure of a new computer installation is the attitude of employees toward the new development. If a computer is installed it is important that managerial employees as well as clerical and blue-collar workers be oriented to the purposes and advantages of the computer. Despite the effect on employee morale while the installation of a computer is being considered, as is indicated in Chapter 7 dealing with human relations, a great deal can be done with proper planning to reduce employee dislocation and disruption of morale. If attitudes toward the new computer installation are not properly shaped, it may result in a reluctance on the part of employees to provide accurate information for input into the computer system or foot dragging on the part of managerial employees to utilize new information provided. This would negate the advantage of installing a computer in the first place.

The decision regarding computer installation should be made after a careful study by management as to the advantages and problems which likely will result from moving to a computer operation. This will require the time of management personnel in those areas of the enterprise which will be affected by the computer, and this will take time away from their other managerial responsibilities. Therefore, sufficient staff should be made available to handle routine business operations for those executives who are involved in the investigation of the installation and use of a computer system.

Once it is determined that a computer should be acquired, the question arises as to what specific computer system is best for the business enterprise's own needs. Cost estimates should be prepared for equipment produced by different manufacturers, and these should be considered along with the capabilities of the equipment to meet the enterprise's present and anticipated future needs. The ability of the computer manufacturer to provide a good service organization is also an important consideration in the selection of a computer system. The systems engineers, maintenance staff, and other highly trained personnel provided by the computer manufacturer will make a significant difference in determining how effectively a particular piece of computer hardware is utilized.

The question of whether to purchase or lease the computer is an important issue. While leasing may prove costly, the advantages of not having a huge initial outlay for computer hardware and the development of computer technology which tends to obsolete computers rather rapidly makes leasing a possibility which should be seriously considered.

A variety of other problems will face those managements which have new computer systems. These range from the physical location of the computer to determining organizational relationships for computer personnel and budgetary considerations for cost allocation of computer expenses.

Many managements will want to consider the time-sharing computer services discussed earlier before committing themselves to the purchase or lease of a computer installation. The availability of terminals connected to a large computer center which can be miles away serving many users may provide the economy and flexibility necessary for the small or medium-size business to use this important management tool. Another possibility for the small business enterprise is acquiring one of the new small computer systems which has many packaged subroutines available and is adaptable to a variety of applications.

In deciding on an initial commitment to a computer, management should also analyze the possibility of acquiring the use of an older computer which may meet the enterprise's needs effectively even though the computer is not the latest model. Where a computer system is already in use, management should make an independent analysis before acquiring a new computer which may have a greater capability than is necessary for the problems to be handled in the particular enterprise.

Summary

The development of the computer has made it possible to store and retrieve vast amounts of information, to make instantaneous calculations, and to control many different operations. Computers are used in business for such functions as record keeping, payrolls, inventories and purchasing, customer records, production scheduling, and information retrieval.

In a real-time system the computer receives and processes data so that action is taken immediately to control the environment. Under a time-sharing system a number of users have access to a single computer at the same time from different locations for the simultaneous solution of different problems.

Computer applications are available for complex calculations and for simulation of the business enterprise's operations to test possible management decisions.

Heuristic computer programming solves problems by selective calculations rather than by analyzing all possible combinations of input data. This has resulted in the application of computer data processing to some specific problems which previously had not been practical for computer application.

Computer centers have equipment to provide for the input of data, data storage, data processing and control, and output of information. Data is put into a computer by representing it in a language which the computer can assimilate and electronically place in its data storage unit for processing.

Computers use programs, which are a series of machine instructions to accomplish the mission for a particular problem-solving task or to carry out a series of operations on data. Standard symbols are used in programming, and special languages have been developed to simplify the job of programming. The two dominant computer languages are FORTRAN and COBOL.

When a computer is to be installed it is important to orient employees to the purposes and advantages of a computer since positive employee attitudes will facilitate the success of a new computer operation.

In selecting a computer system management needs to consider not only cost but also the ability of a computer manufacturer to provide the needed service. Leasing, rather than the purchase of a computer, has the advantage of not requiring a large cash outlay for computer hardware and also minimizes the risk of equipment being outmoded by new developments in future years. Time-sharing or leasing time on an existing computer installation can provide the small or medium-size enterprise a flexible and relatively economical way of obtaining the services of a computer.

Terms for review

electronic computer

real-time system

time-sharing system

heuristic computer programming

input of data

data storage

data processing and control unit

output of information

programming

program flowchart

FORTRAN

COBOL

BASIC

PL/1

Questions

1. Discuss the different ways computers can be useful to business enterprises.

2. What is a real-time computer system? In addition to the examples given in the chapter, what other possible applications for real-time computer systems can you suggest?

3. What are the advantages of a time-sharing computer system?

4. What types of problems may be solved by heuristic computer programming?

5. *a*) In what ways may data be fed into a computer?
   b) What means are available for the output of information from computers?

6. Why is attention to detail so important in computer programming?

7. If there is a computer center at your school, request a tour of the facilities. Determine the kinds of applications handled by the computer and the compiler language used.

8. Based on your study of this chapter and of current library materials, write a 300-word summary of the issues which should be considered by management in the process of installing a new computer system.

BUSINESS BRIEF

Overseas data processing

One important step in utilizing computers is the process of translating raw data into a form that can be placed into the computer. A primary means for this is the punched card. Now, in an attempt to reduce processing costs some business enterprises are having raw data processed thousands of miles from their offices.

Computer service companies have been established which will take an enterprise's raw data, fly it overseas, keypunch the data on computer cards, and put the information on two magnetic tapes. One tape is kept as a backup and the other is flown back to the business enterprise. This work is done in such locations as Korea, Thailand, Taiwan, and Ireland, where labor costs are substantially lower than in the United States. The cost of such service is less than $50 per 1,000 cards or about half the cost of the same service in the United States. However, more time is required in view of the distance involved. Completed work is normally returned within a week to ten days.

1. What advantages for a business enterprise are there to having raw data processed overseas for computer analysis?
2. What potential problems are there for an enterprise which utilizes such overseas service?
3. Under what circumstances might such overseas keypunch service be especially attractive to a business enterprise?
4. What future do you see for the companies which provide this overseas data processing?

CASES

Middletown National Bank

The Middletown National Bank was located in a medium-sized city of approximately 150,000 in the Midwest. The bank was the largest bank in the community and had assets in excess of $200 million. In recent years the bank's traditional territory had become more prosperous as additional light industry and service business enterprises moved into the area. At the same time additional banks were chartered in the community which competed with other long-established banks in addition to Middletown National.

Early in 1965, several members of the top management of Middletown National Bank were gathered to discuss the growth of the bank in recent years and the need for improved means of handling this growth. Conversation soon turned to a subject which had been discussed before, whether or not to install a computer to provide for improved data processing.

As soon as the subject of computers was raised, Jim Jordon, personnel manager, voiced fears as to what changeover from traditional accounting and data processing methods might mean for the employees of the Middletown National Bank. "I have already heard discussion of computers among our employees," Jordon reported. "My secretary told me the other day that a number of our people are quite concerned that we may computerize our accounting operations and they don't know what this would mean for them. I don't think that most of our people could become computer technicians. How many of our employees would we have to let go with the installation of a computer?"

At this point Paul Bowlin, an officer who had come from a large bank in Los Angeles, entered the conversation. "Jim, I believe you are magnifying this personnel problem out of proportion. I don't think we will have a major personnel problem in making this changeover. As you know the bank's board of directors has already authorized studies for a new drive-in banking facility in an area of the city where we need to develop more business. If we can coordinate the development of this drive-in banking operation with the installation of a new computer, we can easily find jobs for any of our present clerical personnel whose jobs might be eliminated by a computer. I think that we should push right ahead and make a decision to install a computer. As soon as this decision is made we can test all employees for aptitude in dealing with the symbols and quantitative data required in a computer center. This ought to include testing of supervisory personnel as well since new jobs will be created and different types of skills required for these new positions."

"Hold on, Paul," interrupted the personnel manager. "Such a testing program might represent a threat to some of our employees. Some of our supervisory people who are giving quite satisfactory service to the bank may be very disturbed by this. We have supervisors with years of service to Middletown National. These men and women understand our problems like no computer will ever be able to do."

"I don't mean to say there won't be some problems," replied Bowlin. "We experienced this sort of thing in Los Angeles. However, it mainly necessitates teaching employees how to communicate with the computer. Don't sell our employees short. Once they learn the 'language' I'll bet many will be even more effective in fulfilling their jobs than they are now."

"Nobody's selling our employees short," said Jordon. "However, there is such a lack of trained computer people. How would we ever get the necessary staff? Who would train them, and wouldn't an extensive training program be costly to the bank? Furthermore, if we put money into sending some of our employees through a training program, how do we know they'll stay with us? This is a tight labor market."

One of the junior officers of the bank suggested, "We could always raise their salaries to become more competitive with other firms requiring computer personnel."

The personnel manager's response was, "Yes, and that would drive up the cost of the computer center even more. Also, it would tend to disrupt our whole wage and salary schedule. How could we justify paying technicians more than long-term bank employees who really understand the whole banking process?"

At this point the executive vice president, Martin Jones, broke into the conversation. "Gentlemen, I think we are getting bogged down on some side issues which can be dealt with later. As I view the bank's operations and growth in recent years there are some very crucial reasons why we need to consider seriously installing a computer center in the near future. I have asked Tom Murray, our auditor, to outline some of these considerations for our discussion. Tom, why don't you tell us in general terms what your study indicates without going into all of the detailed figures at this time?"

"Thank you, Mr. Jones. First, we need to deal more efficiently with the growth in the number of accounts we have and the number of items we handle. We are at the point where further specialization in handling paper work isn't reducing our costs. Costs are rising in proportion to the rise in items handled. Part of this is because of the higher volume of transactions, which means more machinery and employees are needed for record keeping.

"Our figures indicate that there is more activity in each checking account when we measure it in terms of activity per thousand dollars in deposits. There is no question but that the increased cost of servicing our checking account customers is a matter of concern. We hope that the installation of a computer will stabilize these costs.

"Also there are space problems associated with our present accounting services. The machinery for bookkeeping, posting, and so on has put us into a serious cramp with respect to space. Frankly, I don't know where we can locate any more conventional equipment in our present facilities.

"In summary I think it is fair to say that we are facing higher costs accompanied by servicing more accounts. Don't forget that we are dealing with a number of commercial customers as well as individuals. Also, we must provide high-quality services for some 60 smaller banks throughout the area which depend upon us for correspondent services. As the bank's auditor I feel that a computer installation is the only answer to these problems."

"Thank you, Tom," said Mr. Jones. "Furthermore, we must realize that we face increased competition in the banking business. Computer installations are beginning to be installed in banks similar in size to ours in other parts of the country. Right now no other bank in Middletown has a computer. With our ever-increasing costs, more active relationships with correspondent banks, local competition, and the possibility that other banks in our own community will go to computer operations, it will ultimately make it necessary for us to look seriously at computers anyway. Since we are the biggest bank in the city I feel we should be first with a computer. If we are, this may give us a marketing advantage and some further prestige. If we don't have a computer and other local banks do, won't our customers wonder if we are the 'complete service banking institution' we claim to be in our advertising program?"

"Well, you men have some powerful ammunition," responded Jim Jordon, the personnel manager. "It may well be that we'll have to install a computer center, but if we do I think we should make some decisions in the near future to cut down on employee rumors. It's going to be hard enough to make this decision and perhaps a changeover without disrupting all the bank's operations."

1. Analyze the bank officers' discussion. Discuss the merits of the various points of view expressed.
2. What should be the bank management's next step?
3. If the decision is made to install a computer center what further issues will need to be considered?

A computer decision reviewed

"Hello, Bob," greeted Martin Jones, executive vice president of Middletown National Bank, as he shook hands with Robert Johnson, an officer of Castle County State Bank, which was located some 300 miles from Middletown. "We're glad to have you visit us to talk about our computer installation. We hope your trip will be worthwhile in helping your bank make the decision we went through a couple of years ago in installing a computer center here at Middletown."

After initial greetings, Mr. Johnson was taken to the bank conference room where the key bank officers of Middletown National Bank who had participated in the decision to install a computer center were gathered. (See Middletown National Bank case for preliminary discussion of this installation.) Besides the executive vice president and Mr. Johnson, there was Jim Jordon, Middletown's personnel manager; Paul Bowlin, who was in charge of the computer center; and Tom Murray, Middletown National's auditor.

After introductions were made, Mr. Jones explained, "As you will recall from my memo, Bob Johnson is here today to learn something about our experience in converting to a computer operation on our data processing system. After this conference he will visit the computer center and talk with people individually before his plane leaves this afternoon. I have asked each of you gentlemen to prepare something for this conference on how we dealt with a particular phase of our computer center conversion. Let's start with you first, Jim, on the personnel side of the issue."

The personnel manager replied, "As soon as the decision was made to install a computer at the bank, all employees were invited to a meeting which was held to announce the decision. The announcement included a statement that no jobs would be lost as a result of the change-over. However, we did point out that there would be some changing of job assignments and some upgrading of positions in the bank. This meeting was held to minimize employees' fears about their job future that may have stemmed from rumors if we had said nothing officially about our plans to begin taking the steps necessary to install a computer.

"We had hoped to tie in the installation of the computer with the opening of a new drive-in facility which would stabilize employment. In practice, it actually didn't work out because the computer change-over came after the drive-in was opened up. However, we found that more people were required in the computer center than we had originally anticipated, so this factor coupled with normal resignations and moves meant that we were able to avoid any layoffs that might have been caused by the computer installation.

"The programming staff of the computer center was made up essentially of the bank's own personnel. Whenever possible, existing bank employees were trained and given computer jobs. We utilized a testing program for all personnel to determine which employees had the best aptitude for computer work. This aptitude test was given by the computer manufacturer. Then our people were trained by the manufacturer's representatives, and some key personnel were sent to take special courses. A considerable amount of time and money was spent on training people for the programming and operation of the computer center. Also, the ability of bank personnel outside the computer center to talk with programmers on a more or less equal basis is important in our long-run training program, and we expect that more of our officers will get experience in dealing with the computer.

"With the advent of the computer some interesting things occurred within our work force. New people emerged on the computer jobs as leaders. Some people who had not been supervisors became very exceptional employees in the computer center and now have supervisory positions. On the other hand, some of the individuals who had been quite satisfactory in their old supervisory positions were not effective in working in the computer center. They couldn't cope with the new job either intellectually or emotionally. This illustrates the different kinds of skills required when you move into a computer operation. The work is much faster, many more items are covered in a short period of time. There were symbols to be learned, a different kind of language, a different kind of system.

"A few of these supervisors who had been satisfactory in the past but were unable to adjust very well to the computer operation quit and found other jobs in the community.

"I think we can say in summary of the personnel phase of the computer that many new positions were created which required more ability and different kinds of skills. These jobs were generally more demanding and more sensitive than those which they had replaced. Sometimes different people became leaders, and we have faced some interesting human relations problems in making these adjustments over a period of time. On the whole though, I am pleased with how our people have come through with this challenge."

"Thank you, Jim," the executive vice president said. "I think I should say that Jim was one of those who warned us about some of the personnel problems we might face with such a move, but his department has done a good job of minimizing the difficulties in this personnel area. Tom, why don't you discuss financial aspects of the computer decision next."

"Because of the rapid evolution of computer hardware it was decided that the bank would lease rather than buy the computer from the manufacturer," began the auditor. "We found that there are a number of different ways to lease a computer. For example, there are leasing companies which buy computers from manufacturers and lease them to business enterprises, such as the bank, at a rate of one half or one third of the manufacturer's lease rental charges. However, these lease firms require five-year leases in contrast to the manufacturer of our equipment which requires only a 30-day notice if we want the computer taken out. With the leasing firms we would have had to pay the lease amount for the entire five-year period even though new equipment which would be better for our needs might become available.

"We feel that for us the choice to lease directly from the manufacturer, even with the higher rental charge, proved to be a wise decision because just two years after our original computer installation there was developed a new generation of computers which is now on the market. This new computer system is compatible with our existing computer programs and we are now in the process of moving to the new, improved system.

"When we started the computer center we found that the cost of the computer hardware itself was relatively inexpensive when you compare the other costs which are required in terms of personnel time. Our best estimates are that the cost of converting our conventional data processing equipment to an electronic computer system was about 4/7 for equipment and 3/7 for the other costs of transition, such as training programs and other essentially one-time costs. This means if the hardware cost $200,000, roughly $150,000 would be required for these other costs. I might add that the bank really had no expectation of breaking even over a five-year period while these conversion costs were being absorbed. So you see that we really had to look at this matter from the long-run point of view.

"We have pretty effectively converted the processing of our accounts along with some commercial jobs, such as payroll and inventory data handling for outside customers, to the computer operation. Also, we are effectively using the computer to handle our many correspondent bank items.

"I might add that we have been successful in selling computer services to some of our commercial customers on such items as handling their payrolls and inventory control. However, off the record, we may face the time in the future when competition from local banks with computers may force us to reduce these charges or perhaps provide some of these services free to particularly good customers."

The auditor concluded his remarks and the conference broke up for luncheon. After lunch Mr. Johnson was taken on a tour of the computer center where he discussed technical aspects of the computer with center personnel. As he was flying back home later that afternoon, Mr. Johnson turned over in his mind his visit to Middletown National Bank and began to block out his report to the president of Castle County State Bank.

1. Appraise the apparent effectiveness of the Middletown National Bank management in dealing with the personnel problems attendant to a transition to computer operations.

2. Based on information in these two cases, how did the expectations of the Middletown National Bank officers coincide with what actually happened in moving to a computer installation?

3. From your knowledge of computers gained through the Middletown National Bank case, this case, and Chapter 17, prepare a brief written report for the top management of Castle County State Bank on some of the problems to be anticipated in installing a computer.

*International business
operations by American
enterprises extend to
such areas as the
British Crown Colony of
Hong Kong.*

18

International business

A study of American business enterprise would not be complete without giving consideration to the importance of business operations beyond the geographic borders of the United States. In today's world where virtually instantaneous voice and sight communications exist between one side of the globe and the other and where transoceanic travel can take place within a few hours instead of days or weeks required in earlier generations, the American business manager cannot avoid the impact of economic activity in other countries.

Many U.S. businessmen have viewed foreign countries as being potential markets for their products, and with today's rising standard of expectations among foreign peoples this view has considerable merit. However, many foreign businessmen also aggressively view the United States as a great market for their products, as well as expressing a considerable interest in the expanding markets of underdeveloped countries. Foreign businessmen have been effective in international trade because of their long experience in dealing in many markets, the geographic closeness of the countries such as in Europe, and the encouragement by their governments in the form of subsidies and a permissive attitude toward practices which would be considered a violation of antitrust laws in this country. The result has been increased foreign competition to American manufacturers in such domestic markets as steel, automobiles, typewriters, sewing machines, textiles, television sets, transistor radios, cameras, and optical products. To meet these challenges American business has both improved its own management practices at home and moved into operations abroad by establishing sales and manufacturing branches in foreign countries.

To provide an introduction to the field of business abroad the following issues are discussed.

What is the importance of foreign trade to the U.S. economy?

What are the problems of doing business abroad?

What kind of training is useful for managers who deal in international business?

How does the manager build an effective work team abroad?

The importance of foreign trade to the United States

In 1970 United States business enterprises exported $43 billion worth of goods and imported $40 billion in merchandise from foreign countries. This international trade is important because of its amount and the nature of goods which we buy and sell abroad.

Table 18–1 shows the amount of U.S. imports and exports for certain years along with a comparison of our gross national product, which is the sum total of all goods and services produced in the economy. Although exports of merchandise compose only about 4 percent of annual

TABLE 18–1
Merchandise exports and imports for the United States and gross national product, selected years 1940–1970
(billions of dollars)

Year	U.S. exports*	U.S. imports	U.S. GNP
1940	$ 3.9	$ 2.6	$100
1945	9.6	4.2	212
1950	9.9	8.9	285
1955	14.2	11.5	398
1960	19.4	15.0	504
1965	26.2	21.5	685
1970	42.7	40.0	977

* Excludes military grant-aid beginning with 1950.
Source: U.S. Department of Commerce, *Business Statistics, 1965;* and *Survey of Current Business*, March, 1971.

GNP, these transactions provide important markets for many American businesses and jobs for millions of workers which otherwise might not exist. Such domestic industries as agriculture, automobiles, chemicals, coal, and machinery rely heavily upon export business.

Regarding imports, the United States is almost entirely dependent upon other nations for such commodities as bananas, coffee, spices, diamonds, natural rubber, tin, and nickel. In the countries where these goods are produced the U.S. purchases are of key importance to those nations' economic health. Table 18–2 indicates the principal commodity exports and imports for the United States during 1970.

Table 18–3 summarizes U.S. foreign trade by areas of the world. Table 18–4 shows the main countries with which the United States

TABLE 18–2
Principal commodity exports and imports of the United States, 1970
(billions of dollars)

Exports	Amount	Imports	Amount
Agricultural products	$ 7.2	Coffee and cocoa	$ 1.4
Automobiles and parts	3.5	Meats and preparations	1.0
Chemicals	3.8	Sugar	.7
Coal and petroleum products ...	1.6	Other agricultural products	2.6
Construction machinery	1.4	Automobiles and parts	5.1
Electrical machinery	3.0	Chemicals	1.5
Iron and steel	1.3	Iron and steel	2.0
Nonferrous metals	.9	Machinery	5.3
Other machinery	6.9	Metal ores	1.1
Other transportation equipment ..	3.0	Nonferrous metals	1.7
Textiles	.6	Other manufactured goods	8.5
All other merchandise exports ..	9.5	Petroleum products	2.8
		Textiles	1.1
		All other merchandise imports ...	5.2
Total exports	$42.7	Total imports	$40.0

Source: U.S. Department of Commerce, *Survey of Current Business*, April, 1971.

TABLE 18–3
United States exports and imports to areas of the world, 1970*
(millions of dollars)

	U.S. exports	U.S. imports
North and South America	$15,618	$16,931
Western Europe	14,465	11,175
U.S.S.R. & Communist Europe	353	226
Asia	10,023	9,625
Australia and Oceania	1,188	871
Africa	1,579	1,111
Other		24
Total	$43,226	$39,963

* Includes Department of Defense Shipments.
Source: U.S. Bureau of the Census, *Highlights of U.S. Export and Import Trade, Report FT 990*, December, 1970.

trades. About two thirds of our total foreign trade in 1970 was with these 10 countries.

In addition to the goods which we buy and sell abroad, American businesses have invested substantial amounts in foreign business operations. Private American capital in direct investments in foreign business operations reached an estimated total of over $67 billion by the end of 1970. These direct investments in foreign business were in addition to $26 billion invested abroad by Americans in foreign corporations'

TABLE 18–4
Major trading countries with the United States, 1970
(millions of dollars)

	U.S. exports	U.S. imports
Canada	$9,084	$11,091
Japan	4,652	5,875
West Germany	2,740	3,130
United Kingdom	2,537	2,196
Mexico	1,704	1,222
Netherlands	1,651	528
France	1,484	942
Italy	1,353	1,316
Belgium and Luxembourg	1,195	696
Australia	985	611

Source: U.S. Bureau of the Census, *Highlights of U.S. Export and Import Trade, Report FT 990,* December, 1970.

stocks and bonds and other financial claims of a long-term nature. Private short-term financial claims (composed mostly of bank notes and accounts) totaled $15 billion. All of these private investments by Americans were in addition to some $40 billion worth of U.S. government credits and claims against foreign governments and currencies.

Private direct investment abroad comes from funds which are sent from the United States or from profits generated in American-owned foreign operations. The incentive for American investment abroad is the prospect for profit stemming from better market conditions, lower production costs, or lower taxes than might be encountered by the enterprise expanding its business in the United States. Also, American businessmen have invested abroad to avoid the external tariffs imposed by such multinational groups as the European Common Market and to meet the difficulty which sometimes occurs in the repatriation of funds to the United States from foreign operations.

Differences between management here and abroad

Despite the increasing volume of trade between American business and foreign enterprises and the increased investment of U.S. capital in other countries, there are certain problems of management associated with foreign operations. These managerial problems can be grouped into five categories: government regulations, monetary differences, language and cultural barriers, relations between the home office and foreign operations, and the selection and training of managers who go abroad.

Government regulation

Business enterprises operating within the United States are subject, of course, to all the relevant laws and requirements set up by municipal, state, and federal governments. The business manager is usually well acquainted with these domestic regulations including patents and trademarks, licenses, labor law, and tax reporting. Government regulation of a business which also operates abroad is compounded since the manager must conform to U.S. laws and also to the regulations of foreign governments.

The U.S. government regulates export and import of merchandise through licenses, duty on imports, health and sanitary laws, and restrictions on trade with certain countries for purposes of national security. Because of the outflow of U.S. dollars abroad in recent years the government has also instituted a program of voluntary self-restraint on the American banking and business system regarding the sending of capital abroad. These regulations are in addition to the usual ones imposed on business which is active only in the United States.

Similar restrictions exist in foreign countries where Americans do business. As a general rule, except for strategic defense materials, there are fewer limitations on exportation of goods than upon imported merchandise. The main reason for this is that imported goods result in the outflowing of currency reserves from the importing country. A country which has a continued outflow of monetary reserves resulting from its imports exceeding its exports will experience a shortage of foreign exchange currencies and its monetary system will be weakened.

Besides the restrictions that may be imposed on imports and exports, foreign governments affect American business through regulations on their manufacturing and marketing operations which are based abroad. Managers should realize that when they move into other countries with manufacturing and distribution facilities it is they who are considered foreigners, not the governments or peoples of the locale. Such business operations may be subject to regulations because of a desire on the part of foreign governments to generate foreign exchange through exporting more goods or avoiding the import of certain products through the building up of a new industry. While there is a concern that the local economy may become dominated by American business, foreign governments are also interested in building up their economies and having profits retained in their countries. Economic nationalism is an important consideration not only in such underdeveloped areas as Africa, Latin America, and the Middle East, but also in such long industrialized nations as Great Britain and France.

American capital when invested abroad is also exposed to the risk that it may be expropriated by foreign governments. In some instances where American business assets are taken over by a foreign government the owners are compensated for their losses; in other cases no compensation is given. In 1960 Fidel Castro's revolutionary government in Cuba expropriated without compensation all Cuban properties owned by American companies. In 1971 properties of some American corporations were expropriated by the government of Chile.

Despite such notable examples where American investments abroad have been liquidated by political upheaval, many American enterprises have long operated profitably in political and economic climates which are something less than stable. Excellent examples of this may be found in the international oil companies which manage to maintain oil fields and pipelines despite political intrigue and change of governments. Furthermore, under carefully specified conditions there are guarantees which are available through U.S. and foreign government agencies which provide for safety of invested capital abroad.

Monetary problems

International monetary differences. When dealing in international business the manager is faced with the problem of different monetary systems and restrictions on the flow of funds among countries. Virtually every sovereign nation has its own monetary system. The U.S. currency is based upon the dollar; Great Britain has the pound sterling; France has the franc; India has the rupee; and so on for all the nations. Something of the complexity of the problem facing the businessman may be visualized if every one of the 50 states in this country had a different monetary system with many having restrictions on the flow of funds in and out of the state.

From time to time in the process of trade a given country may find itself short of another country's funds. This gives rise to two types of international monetary problems, foreign exchange rates and exchange control.

Foreign exchange occurs when there is a purchase or sale of the currency of one nation with the currency of another. The units which one U.S. dollar will purchase in a foreign currency, such as Japanese yen, are expressed by the *foreign exchange rate,* which is the price of each currency in terms of the other. In dealing with foreign exchange markets the American business manager is well advised to consult his finance officer and local banker to take advantage of the ways of minimizing the risk of loss through fluctuating currency prices.

Exchange control is exercised by most governments over access to foreign currencies by their private citizens and business enterprises. Usually exchange control is carried out through the holding of foreign currencies in central government banks or by government monetary authorities. Foreign currencies are then made available to private interests to settle international financial transactions. When a nation has a persistent outflow of its currency, brought on by large import balances of goods, flow of capital abroad, and other spending outside the country, it may be necessary for the government to restrict private transactions during the period of shortage of foreign exchange currencies.

In practice today most international transactions are settled with U.S. dollars, which are considered the key currency for international finance. The British pound sterling, which once held such a key currency role, is still an important world currency in many areas along with the French franc and the West German deutsche mark. Many nations hold our currency both to facilitate trade and as monetary reserves. In view of this international role of the dollar other nations hold relatively large amounts of our currency, but we hold relatively small amounts of foreign currencies.

Means of financing imports. Although U.S. businessmen have typically exported a greater dollar volume of goods than they import from foreign countries, the importation of goods is an important dimension of international business. If Americans do not buy the products of foreign countries this will diminish the buying power of foreign business enterprises, governments, and individuals to purchase American goods and services. The means of financing international commercial transactions include cash payment, open account, bills of exchange, and letters of credit.

Cash payment in the form of bank checks or international money orders may be used. Cash as a means of payment upon shipment of merchandise is generally unattractive to an importer. Implicitly there is a question raised that his credit is not good enough for some other form of financial arrangement; the importer may be out of funds a considerable period of time before receipt of the goods; and when cash is paid with the order or before merchandise is shipped the buyer places himself in a highly dependent state upon the promptness and financial integrity of the exporter. Relatively little international trade is on this type of cash basis, although sometimes a deposit will be required by the exporter for special orders.

The *open account,* which is widely used in the United States as a means of providing financial arrangements for business transactions, is used relatively infrequently in international trade. The open account has no accompanying document calling for payment and no written acknowledgment is made by the purchaser of the liability. Because of legal differences among countries, fluctuating exchange rates over a period of time, and differing customs, the shipment of exports under open account is rarely done except from a manufacturer to its own branches overseas.

Bills of exchange, or *drafts* as they are sometimes called, constitute the most common method of payment in international commerce. A bill of exchange is drawn by the exporter of goods and calls upon the importer to accept the obligation for payment of a sum of money at a specified time. The bill of exchange becomes a *trade acceptance* when an acknowledgment of the obligation is written across the face of the document by the importer, thereby obligating him to pay the amount specified at the designated time.

The three parties to a draft transaction are:

1. The *drawer* who is the person executing the draft (the exporter or seller).
2. The *drawee* upon whom the draft is drawn and who is required to meet the terms of the document (the importer or buyer).
3. The *payee* who is the party to receive payment (the exporter or his bank).

There are various ways in which drafts can be used in business transactions. A *sight draft* calls for the drawee to pay the draft upon its presentation (on sight). A *time draft* calls for the payment on a specified date in the future. The acceptance of a time draft obligates the drawee to meet the terms of the draft when it falls due. When drafts are drawn upon a bank and are accepted by the bank instead of an importer they become *bank acceptances* instead of trade acceptances. Although there are numerous applications in the use of bank acceptances, their effect is to substitute the credit of the bank for the credit of the importer.

A *commercial letter of credit* is a document issued by a bank upon the application' of an importer of merchandise whereby the bank authorizes drafts to be drawn upon the bank by the beneficiary and agrees to honor the drafts if all requirements are met. The terms and requirements by which payment will be made to the exporter are set forth in the letter of credit. The business enterprise which is importing the merchandise works out arrangements to pay the bank for the drafts which the bank accepts. For this service the bank receives a commission from the business customer for the letter of credit and handling charges for the subsequent drafts. If the drafts are time drafts the customer may pay an interest charge. Figure 18–1 shows a specimen application for a commercial letter of credit. In addition to the data required in Figure 18–1 the back of the application form has detailed agreements to which the applicant assents. Figure 18–2 is a specimen commercial letter of credit.

The three necessary parties to a commercial letter of credit are:

1. The *importer,* or *opener,* who buys the merchandise and who opens the credit with the bank.
2. The *issuer,* or the bank, which issues the letter of credit for the importer.
3. The *beneficiary,* or the *accreditee,* who is the seller of merchandise in whose favor the credit is opened and who is the payee of the drafts.

In addition, the beneficiary or exporter may have a bank to advise him.

There are a variety of documents required for international transactions. The most important of these include the negotiable bill of lading, insurance certificate or policy, and the commercial invoice. The *negotiable bill of lading* when endorsed constitutes a receipt for the goods, a contract of transportation, and evidence of title to the property with the holder being the lawful owner. In addition to these three documents,

FIGURE 18–1

Specimen

F. X. D. 798

APPLICATION AND AGREEMENT FOR COMMERCIAL LETTER OF CREDIT

Commerce Trust Company
Kansas City, Mo.

June 10 _____ 19 --

Please issue an Irrevocable Letter of Credit in accordance with the following instructions and transmit by

☐ Cable
☒ Airmail
☐ Mail

Amount..............	$ 10,000.00 (ten thousand dollars)
In favor of...........	Wool Company of Great Britain, England
For account of.......	General Textiles Company, Kansas City, Missouri
Available by drafts at..	☒ Sight; (_____) days ☐ Sight ☐ Date_____
	Drawn at your option on you or your correspondent for___100___% of the invoice value.
Invoice covering......	150 bolts of assorted woolen cloth
Shipment from........	London
Shipment to..........	Kansas City _____ Partial shipments allowed?__no__
	Prepaid or Collect? prepaid
B/L issued to order of	Commerce Trust Company, Kansas City
	Notify___Applicant
Insurance	Effected by ☒ Buyers ☐ Sellers___Western Insurance Company
	(If by buyers give name of issuing company)
	Coverage & Amount___usual risks $10,000.00
Confirm?............	This credit is { to be transmitted { through_____
	to be confirmed } by_____
	NOT to be confirmed (Name and address of foreign bank)
Expiration date.......	Drafts to be negotiated not later than___August 15, 19--
	Drafts to be presented at_____
Documents required:	—Please indicate by mark X.

☒ Commercial Invoice in triplicate   ☒ Clean Order Railroad B/L

☒ Consular Invoice   ☐ Interior Rail and/or River B/L

☐ MARINE / WAR Insurance Certificate   ☐ Parcel Post Receipt

☒ Full Set Clean Negotiable on Board Ocean B/L   ☐ Airwaybill
☐ Other Documents_____

Special Instructions: _____
_____
_____

In consideration of your opening such credit, I/we hereby agree to sign the agreement for the credit on reverse side hereof, the provisions of which are agreed to as defining your rights and my/our obligations.

Very truly yours,

An Irrevocable Credit may be cancelled only with the consent of all parties concerned. This credit is to be irrevocable unless otherwise stated.

_____
(Please sign with AUTHORIZED SIGNATURE(s) registered with us)
(OVER) Treasurer, General Textiles Company

FIGURE 18–2
Specimen

F801

IRREVOCABLE COMMERCIAL LETTER OF CREDIT

Commerce Trust Company

KANSAS CITY, MISSOURI 64141

To

Wool Company of Great Britain
England

No. 1236

Dated   June 12   19 __

We hereby authorize you to draw on us

for account of General Textiles Company, Kansas City, Missouri, U.S.A. up to an aggregate
amount of $10,000.00 (ten thousand dollars)

available by your drafts at sight   to cover;—

150 bolts of assorted woolen cloth, C&F Kansas City, from London to
Kansas City.

Commercial Invoice in triplicate.

Consular Invoice.

Insurance effected by the Buyer.

Full Set Clean Negotiable on Board Ocean and Railroad Bills of Lading
made out to the order of Commerce Trust Company, Kansas City (L/C 1236)
marked "Notify General Textiles Company, Kansas City, Missouri, U.S.A."
and "Freight Prepaid".

Partial shipments are not permitted.

All drafts drawn under this Credit are to be endorsed hereon and shall bear the clause "Drawn under COMMERCE TRUST
COMPANY, LETTER OF CREDIT NO. 1236   dated Kansas City, Missouri, June 12, 19--.   "
We hereby agree with the drawers, endorsers and bona fide holders of drafts drawn in compliance with the terms of this Credit
that the same shall be duly honored on presentation at the office of the Drawee.

if drawn and negotiated not later than. August 15, 19--.
*This Credit is subject to the "Uniform Customs & Practice for Documentary Credits (1962 Revision), International Chamber of Commerce, Brochure No. 222."

Very truly yours,

_____   _____
Vice-President   Vice-President and Cashier

such papers as customs' documents, export licenses, inspection certificates, and packing lists will normally be required.

When the merchandise is shipped, the bill of lading, along with the other shipping papers, normally is sent by the exporter to his bank along with the draft. The exporter's bank forwards the draft and shipping documents to the importer's bank which notifies the importer that the documents have arrived. The draft is presented to the importer for his acceptance. Upon acceptance by the importer, the trade acceptance (draft) is then returned to his bank for transmission through banking channels to the exporter or the exporter's bank. When the maturity date on the trade acceptance approaches it is sent to the importer's bank, which presents it to the importer for payment.

When the draft is accepted by the importer, he is given the bill of lading by his bank which he presents to the freight agent as evidence of his ownership of the goods upon their arrival. Sometimes there will be an inspection of the goods required upon their arrival before the importer will accept the draft which obligates him for payment.

Had the importer in the above illustration used a commercial letter of credit from his bank, the process would be essentially the same except that the bank would have accepted the draft under the terms which had been agreed upon among the parties.

Figure 18–3 illustrates the financial transactions which would normally follow the application for and issuance of commercial letter of credit which is shown in Figures 18–1 and 18–2.

The numbered steps in Figure 18–3 are discussed briefly below:

1.   General Textiles Company desiring to import woolen goods from Wool Company of Great Britain works out arrangements for the purchase with the British firm and then prepares an application for a letter of credit after consultation with its banker, Commerce Trust Company of Kansas City.

2.   General Textiles forwards the application for the $10,000 letter of credit to Commerce Trust Company.

3.   The Commerce Trust, having determined that the financial arrangements are in order, promptly issues a $10,000 letter of credit and transmits it to Wool Company of Great Britain.

4.   Wool Company sends the letter of credit, a draft drawn on Commerce Trust for $10,000, and the shipping documents to its bank, London Bank, which is also a correspondent bank of Commerce Trust Company. At the same time the merchandise is prepared for shipment and begins its transit voyage.

FIGURE 18–3
Illustration of a U.S. sight letter of credit transaction covering an import

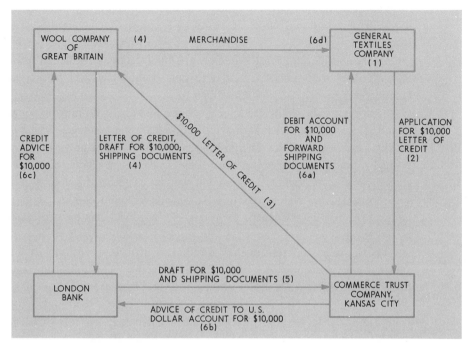

5. London Bank, acting for its customer, files the letter of credit and forwards the draft for $10,000 and shipping documents to Commerce Trust.

6. Commerce Trust, upon receipt of the documents, accepts the draft for $10,000 thereby making it a bank acceptance. Commerce Trust then (6a) debits General Textiles' bank account in payment for the merchandise and financial charges and sends the shipping documents to the importer so General Textiles may claim the merchandise from the freight agent (6d). At the same time Commerce Trust (6b) credits its correspondent, London Bank, with $10,000; and in turn (6c) London Bank credits the account of its customer, Wool Company of Great Britain, for $10,000 in terms of British pounds sterling for payment for the merchandise, thereby completing the transaction.

Language and cultural barriers

Language differences. It is important that the American manager overseas be able to communicate in the language of the country of his residence. Despite the fact that the English language is widely used throughout the world, the American businessman will find more doors open to him if he develops another language with some degree of facility. With concentrated effort, learning to speak and read another language fluently is not overly difficult. Therefore, this skill should not be too highly considered in making selections for foreign assignments, since an otherwise well-qualified candidate can probably master a second language.

A distinction should be made between the manager who may do some traveling abroad on occasion and the resident foreign manager. The occasional business traveler likely will not have an opportunity to learn several foreign languages in great depth. However, these managers should pick up enough of several different languages to be able to use some phrases and follow the trend of a conversation conducted in a language other than English. Considerable goodwill can be generated by doing this.

The manager who resides in a foreign country, however, cannot be satisfied with this minimal level of language facility. The ability to communicate with nationals, local authorities, and customers in their language is essential. The resident manager must be able to think in the language so as to be able to communicate effectively his ideas and to understand those with whom he has contact. Indeed, there is a mental attitude which accompanies the manager who is unwilling to communicate in any language other than English which may limit his effectiveness in a foreign assignment.

Cultural barriers. An obvious but extremely important consideration in any discussion of the differences in the management of domestic and foreign operations is the cultural setting in which the manager abroad operates. In many instances today, the physical office and plant facilities abroad will be quite similar to those in the United States down to the organization charts on the walls and the executive washroom. However, the cultural values relating to business, the individual, work, and social customs will be very different than those in the United States.

In the United States the role of the businessman is viewed generally with respect, and business leaders are accorded prestige and recognition both in business circles and by other sectors of society. In other countries the role of business is becoming more socially acceptable and receiving higher status. However, in the Orient this goes against a cultural background which for centuries has given the highest status in society to the scholars, politicians, and warriors. In the past the merchant held no such high social standing. This role has changed in considerable measure, especially in the past quarter century, and the international view of business is coming to be more that which prevails in the United States.

The American ethical concepts which are generally followed in this country are not necessarily followed abroad. Although bribery, illegal division of markets, rigged bids, and payoffs are not totally absent from our business scene, these practices are not advocated by business leaders here and are considered scandalous when discovered. The manager dealing in foreign business operations may find a different system of values and practices prevailing than those to which he has been accustomed in this country. This does not mean that he must accept such deviations from his standards as a new norm. Indeed, confidence in the word of American businessmen abroad is an advantage over the long run. However, managers should be aware of general business practices in their locale and know how to face competition which they may encounter. An understanding of what is considered honorable practice will enable Americans to learn when and where their confidence may be placed.

The individual and the way in which he views work may well be different abroad. In the United States we take a constructive attitude toward the work force and place a high value on labor and seek to stimulate its contribution to successful operations. An honest regard for the worth of workers and an understanding of the dignity of the individual has not been universally true in other countries. This is a positive aspect of the values which the American manager takes abroad but he should realize that initially the foreign worker is not likely to understand the evaluations and expectations of management to contribute to successful and profitable operations. This has implications for the kind of training programs that will be necessary in building a successful work force.

Social customs in every country abroad are different and time will be required before an understanding of their subtleties is gained. The formalities of Oriental politeness; the different value placed on time in the Middle East and the preliminaries to business discussion; the hours of work and dining; and a more reserved attitude toward strangers than Americans usually express are examples of the learning which will have to take place in the early days of the American's foreign assignment. A sincere attitude of interest in learning local customs combined with a friendly but not overly aggressive manner will stand the newcomer to international business in good stead.

Relations with the home office

The problems arising out of the relationship between the home office and foreign plants and sales branches are of the same type which exist between home offices and decentralized operations here in the United States. However, there are complications to these problems caused by the greater distances between home offices and foreign operations, relations with foreign governments, and the wide variations in the business and cultural environment abroad. The American manager of a foreign operation is faced with the problem that he must be able to deal with the home office where there may be a lack of understanding of problems faced in the field. At the same time he must deal effectively with foreign nationals and governments who have little understanding or interest in home office policies and problems.

Because of these complications, serious consideration should be given to providing the manager abroad with as much autonomy as possible to meet circumstances which would be considered quite unusual in this country. Management in the foreign office should be provided with guidelines or limits on its freedom of action, and then management in the home office should make every attempt to avoid interference as long as operations come under these guidelines and are proceeding according to overall forecasts. Another solution to this dual responsibility of foreign managers is to have at least one key person in the home office who has had sufficient foreign experience to appreciate the circumstances faced abroad.

Laws abroad and dealings with foreign governments will likely be different than those prevailing in this country. This means that managers who are on the scene should be permitted to cope with these problems with a minimum of interference from the home office. Often there are sound reasons for dealing with governments overseas differently than would be the case in this country because of local custom and the political systems prevailing abroad. In some instances the government will have a much greater influence upon managerial decisions than would be the case here. Especially in overseas operations the concept is valid that in today's complex world it is virtually impossible to separate economics and politics.

In view of the important cultural differences existing over the world, personnel in the home office should make every attempt to understand the nature of problems in overseas offices. Because it is impossible to truly understand the magnitude of these differences without having lived abroad, there is a particular responsibility on the part of both line and staff personnel in this country to avoid quick judgments regarding the conduct of foreign operations. The creation of profit centers in the various foreign fields of operation after providing them with sufficient resources and time to put enterprise plans into meaningful programs is frequently done. When this is the case, managers of these profit centers should be provided sufficient decision-making authority if they are to be held responsible for results.

Even though a substantial amount of local autonomy is desirable for foreign operations, these offices can benefit from the systems and procedures developed by the corporation's executives in this country, although they may require some modification before being placed in effect abroad. Usually a written policy statement outlining the nature of decisions which can be made by managers abroad and placing limits on decision-making powers, particularly regarding expenditures of funds is desirable. In some countries such a written definition of the authority of corporation managers is required by law. An overseas manager must usually get permission from his board of directors before making a major decision in such areas as changing the products and nature of the business, making large capital expenditures, borrowing funds in excess of certain amounts, and obligating the enterprise for contracts over a given figure.

The foreign manager has a particular responsibility to keep the home office informed of developments abroad and to explain the meaning and significance of events and circumstances which may not be understood at home. In this regard the importance of good communications which was stressed in Chapter 7 must be emphasized in the area of international business. Despite the improved communications and the jet airlines systems which make London, New York, and Tokyo only hours apart for the traveler, these areas are still great distances apart in many business practices and in cultural mores. Furthermore, foreign business operations are not only located in the big cities, many of which are truly international centers of language and culture, but may also be located in relatively isolated areas where communications and transportation may be inadequate when compared with major metropolitan areas.

A problem of communications between home office and foreign branches is further complicated because of the difference in time zones around the world. As the manager is closing his office in London at 4 p.m., the members of the home office staff in San Francisco are just finishing their morning coffee and rushing off to their offices at 8 a.m. that day, while in Tokyo the time is 1 a.m. the next day.

On occasion the foreign manager may feel that his superior in the home office is incompetent or does not fully understand the nature of the problems faced in the field. When this is the case the overseas manager should make every effort to keep his superior informed of developments of significance and attempt to educate him to the unique circumstances which the company faces in that area.

Importance of good management

Despite the emphasis placed upon the differences which exist in managing enterprise operations in this country and abroad, many of the same concepts and functions of management also apply to foreign management as in this country. The basic managerial function of directing the work efforts of other employees to achieve effective results is necessary throughout the world. The same importance is placed upon good planning, organization, staffing, and control. The generalizations regarding these elements of the managerial process hold true for foreign situations. It is the changed economic, political, and social environment which adds a new dimension to the manager's job. The manager who has demonstrated that he is effective with assignments in this country will find he can apply many of his skills to the foreign assignment. He will be successful provided he can also adapt to the differences which will be encountered abroad.

Training for overseas assignment

Before a domestic manager accepts a foreign assignment, he and his wife will want to know the duration and compensation of the assignment, something about the living conditions in the part of the country where he is to be placed, and the nature of the educational system if they have children. The manager who accepts a foreign assignment should have some special training before he and his family go abroad. For the manager this means preparation for his responsibilities in a new and different business climate from that which he is familiar with in this country. For his family it means preparation to accept new customs of living and orientation into the conditions and circumstances which will likely be encountered in the new location.

In the area of job preparation the manager may be given special training in such functional areas as marketing, production, or finance to update his knowledge in these fields and to tie this knowledge into the conditions which are anticipated abroad. Before the executive's departure he should be given a thorough briefing in the relationships which will exist with home office line-and-staff officials, other foreign-based personnel, and the degree of his decision-making latitude.

Because of the importance of language facility, special foreign language training should be undertaken in the United States if English is not the native tongue in the foreign location. A desirable policy is to include the executive's wife in language training as her good adjustment in the new location is important to the success of her husband.

To improve the Americans' effectiveness in dealing with peoples in other countries, representatives of American business should also have an understanding of the important social, political, and economic issues in the United States. Foreigners will be interested in the views of the new American manager and his family on these issues, and therefore the ability to discuss intelligently such subjects as American foreign policy, U.S. race relations, and the private enterprise system is vital. In many respects the American living abroad *is* the United States to those foreign nationals with whom he comes in contact.

Building the work team abroad

Once the manager arrives in his new location he will be faced with the responsibility of selecting, training, and directing the efforts of his management team. When the enterprise already has an established base of operations in the area this job is made easier since an organization already exists. However, even in these cases the new manager will have to review the situation carefully and may wish to initiate changes in personnel after he understands local circumstances. This is particularly true if the manager has been sent to correct a condition which the home office staff has reason to believe could be improved.

In many instances, however, it will be necessary for the executive to select and train his own personnel and to put together an organization to begin business operations. While he may have some experienced American specialists from headquarters to assist him, the proper selection, training, and treatment of local nationals is the key to successful future operations.

In building a new organization the manager's first step likely will be the selection of a national who thoroughly understands how to get things done in the country. A capable Man (or Girl) Friday can accomplish much that the new manager cannot and can act as a valuable advisor to him as he becomes acclimated to the new situation.

Despite the importance of language facility, this does not mean that any foreign national who is bilingual will be an effective key employee in the overseas operation. Foreign nationals will be likely to require extensive training regarding the enterprise, its products, and management in general before they are valuable in decision-making capacities.

Other key appointments will be persons to handle buying and marketing functions in the enterprise. These assignments should go to people who have experience in these fields in the country and who are fluent in the language and thoroughly aware of local customs. A competent legal advisor, called upon when needed, can make the morass of national and local regulations in the foreign country understandable and can offer advice to avoid legal problems in beginning operations.

If the enterprise is engaged in the production of goods then the selection of production executives will be important. Frequently, home office engineers and some production managers will be present to assist the enterprise in getting started. However, control of production should be transferred to local employees as soon as possible.

In the recruitment of local persons the American manager should acquaint himself with local wage rates and working conditions. While the enterprise may pay somewhat higher wages than those prevailing in the community it is generally not desirable to get too far out of line both from the point of view of controlling costs and in alienating local business against the enterprise.

In general it is desirable to develop a long-range plan to replace the enterprise's American managers with local personnel. This does not mean that some Americans may not be permanently stationed abroad. However, over the long run all key executive personnel positions should not be staffed with Americans. The new manager should establish early in his tenure employee training programs for improving the skills of workers and to provide a flow of technical and managerial persons into decision-making levels. Morale of employees will be increased if the opportunity is present for nationals to reach management positions. In summary, the success of U.S.-based enterprises abroad is largely dependent upon the success which the American executive has in putting together an effective organization of foreign nationals who understand the objectives and methods of good management.

Organization for foreign operations

The organization structure of enterprises involved in international business is similar in many instances to the organization chart for the enterprise operating only in the United States. When the enterprise has a functional type departmental organization the factory manager abroad might report directly to the vice president for production in the home office. Similarly, the sales manager for foreign products might report to the vice president for marketing or the general sales manager. However, there may be a vice president for foreign operations in the organization to whom foreign managers report. This development gives recognition to the increasing importance of international business in many enterprises today.

Some firms which have been successful in international business have created separate organizations with their own presidents and operational autonomy. This type of arrangement is especially beneficial when foreign operations have passed the initial stages of development, and the necessary staff personnel and organization required for independent operation can be economically justified. This separate arrangement has certain advantages of flexibility and operational mobility as well as providing some tax advantages. When an enterprise separate from its parent company is formed, control by the parent enterprise is maintained by financial means or through stock ownership. The use of patent and trademark license agreement arrangements also provides a means of control by U.S. enterprises over their relatively independent foreign operations.

When business abroad takes on a multinational character it may be desirable to decentralize these operations on a geographic basis. Just as lines of authority and responsibility must be well defined for businesses operating solely in the United States, the same is true with the enterprise having extensive foreign operations. Under these conditions management is faced with even greater challenges in view of the great diversity of circumstances that will be encountered. Management of the multinational business enterprise is complicated by the political, economic, and cultural differences inherent in international operations.

Summary

The American businessman cannot ignore the impact of economic activity around the world. While many businessmen have viewed foreign countries as potential markets for their products, many foreign business-men also aggressively view the United States as a great market for their products. To meet the challenge of foreign competition, American business has both improved its own management practices at home and moved into operations abroad by establishing sales and manufacturing branches in foreign countries.

Although exports of merchandise compose only about 4 percent of our annual gross national product, these transactions provide many American job opportunities.

The United States is almost entirely dependent upon other nations for certain commodities. In many countries the U.S. purchase of such goods is very important to the economy of the producing nation.

The incentive for American private direct investment abroad includes:

The prospect for profits stemming from better market conditions.

Lower production costs.

Lower taxes than exist in the United States.

Avoidance of external tariffs imposed by such multinational groups as the European Common Market.

Avoidance of the problems of repatriation of funds to the United States from foreign operations.

American businessmen engaged in international operations need to become familiar with the government regulations in the countries where they are doing business.

One of the risks faced in international investment is the possibility of having assets expropriated by foreign governments. Another risk faced is the possibility of currency devaluation of foreign monies.

Imports may be financed by cash payment, open account, bills of exchange, and letters of credit. Bills of exchange which may either become trade acceptances or bank acceptances are the most common method of payment in international commerce.

The American manager sent abroad needs a knowledge of the language and customs of the country where he will be residing. Also, the American manager overseas must be able to work with the home office where there may be a lack of understanding of the problems faced in the field. At the same time, the foreign manager must be able to deal effectively with foreign nationals and governments who have little understanding or interest in home office policies and procedures.

Many of the same managerial skills useful in this country will also apply to the foreign assignment. Nevertheless, before a domestic manager is sent abroad there should be special training for him and his wife on the new circumstances and problems which will be faced.

When building a work team abroad it is desirable to train local nationals to take the place of American personnel as soon as is possible.

The organization structure of the international operation is often similar to that of the enterprise operating solely in the United States. Sometimes, international operations are run as organizations separate from the parent company, with control being exercised through financial means, stock ownership, and patent or trademark license agreements.

Terms for review

exports	foreign exchange
imports	trade acceptance
tariffs	bank acceptance
repatriation of funds	commercial letter of credit
expropriation	negotiable bill of lading

Questions

1. Referring to Table 18–2, what American industries directly benefit most from foreign trade?
2. *a)* Using the most recent *Survey of Current Business,* determine the amount of exports and imports in the following industries:
   (1) automobiles and parts
   (2) iron and steel
   (3) textiles
   (4) chemicals
   (5) agricultural products
   b) By examining current periodicals establish what positions these domestic industrial groups have taken toward international trade questions such as U.S. import quotas and customs duties.
3. Which countries account for more than 60 percent of the U.S. exports and imports?
4. Why do U.S. business enterprises establish manufacturing or sales branches overseas?

5. What possible problems may be encountered by the business enterprise engaged in foreign trade or manufacturing operations overseas that would not normally be encountered in the United States?

6. Trace an international trade transaction as illustrated in part by Figures 18–1, 18–2, and 18–3.

7. In 1971 U.S. imports exceeded exports. It was the first time since 1893 that this country had a trade deficit. List some of the different actions that the United States could take to correct this imbalance of trade.

8. Based on your study of library materials and this chapter, prepare a 300-word summary analyzing the following statement: "More import controls and tariffs are needed to protect such American industries as textiles, steel, and automobiles against foreign competition."

9. What are the advantages to the U.S. economy and to consumers of reducing trade restrictions throughout the world? What disadvantages may result for some industries in the United States from freer world trade?

BUSINESS BRIEFS

Trade with Eastern Europe

As indicated in Table 18–3 U.S. exports and imports to the Soviet Union and Communist countries of Eastern Europe amounted to less than 1 percent of our foreign trade in 1970. However, business executives are beginning to look toward Eastern Europe as a potentially important market for American goods.

One reason for this interest in Eastern Europe is that the economies of such countries as Czechoslovakia, Hungary, and Poland as well as the Soviet Union are sufficiently developed so as to be able to utilize the industrial technology and products of American industry. This is in contrast to the underdeveloped countries in Africa, South America, and Asia, which are still years away from being able to absorb our advanced and laborsaving machinery.

American managers see growing opportunities for utilizing the excess capacity of domestic factories to produce industrial goods for Eastern Europe.

However, numerous problems confront the businessman who is interested in foreign trade with the Eastern European countries. Financing foreign deals can be difficult in the complex international money markets when the Communist governments are direct participants in any transactions. Also, Eastern European countries want reciprocal trade shipments to come to the United States or Western European countries in return for imports from the United States. Although the American businessman can work out a trade for an entire industry in some Eastern European countries by dealing with only a few socialist officials, these officials are notoriously tough bargainers.

Some American businessmen still are concerned about potentially negative reactions of their boards of directors, the federal government, or the public. Also, some businessmen have their own ideological reservations about trading with the Communists. The Ford Motor Company was approached by the Soviet Union to take an important role in Soviet truck production. After opposition was expressed by the U.S. Department of Defense officials, Ford backed away from the invitation. Later, other American truck producers, including Mack Trucks, expressed an interest in working with the Soviet Union.

Those who favor increased trade with Eastern Europe say that anything which the Communists can buy from the United States can be purchased elsewhere in the world. If American business does not become active in these markets, other countries will meet the needs of the Eastern European countries.

1. What are the merits of encouraging trade with the Eastern European countries by U.S. business?
2. What restrictions, if any, should be placed on such trade?
3. What problems will businessmen face as they attempt to do business in Communist countries?

Chile controls copper companies

In 1971, following the election of Marxist Salvador Allende as president of Chile, the properties of American copper corporations located in that Latin American country were expropriated.

Some of the richest copper deposits in the world are located in Chile, which is one of the four largest copper-exporting nations. Three, the Congo, Zambia, and now Chile, have nationalized copper properties and expropriated the assets of the producers. In 1971, Peru, the fourth nation, canceled foreign concessions on mining properties but did not expropriate the assets.

President Allende stated that Chile's basic copper resources were being returned to the people. Under a new law in Chile, compensation will be provided to the companies based on an evaluation of the book value of the properties by the Controller General. After this evaluation a determination will be made by the Marxist government of the "excess profits" made by the copper companies since 1955. These "excess profits" will be deducted from any compensation. Chilean law provides that the payment finally determined by the government will be made in no more than 30 years at no less than 3 percent interest.

Anaconda Company, Kennecott Copper, and Cerro Corporation all had extensive properties which were expropriated in Chile.

Reports indicated that the U.S. State Department was maintaining a "hands off" posture in the situation pending a determination of whether just and prompt payment is made for the properties.

1. What can American corporations do to minimize the economic effects of expropriation of foreign properties?

2. Why do American businessmen continue to invest abroad in view of such incidents?

3. What action, if any, should the U.S. government take in such cases?

Peoples Gas Co.

*A volunteer tutoring
corps provides help and
encouragement for
students with
learning difficulties.*

19

Business and society

As we approach the last quarter of the 20th century it is appropriate for students of business administration to consider the future of business in our economic system. It is the students of today who will be the decision makers in the decades to come not only in business but in the many other groups which make up society. This last chapter contains a discussion of business's responsibility to society and some of the problems which will be faced in the future.

The following issues are discussed.

What does society expect business ethics to be?
Does business have a responsibility to support philanthropic projects?
How can business enterprises help the public to understand better the role of business in America?
What are the responsibilities that business enterprises have in relating to the total society of which they are a part?
What are some of the problems which will be faced by business in the future?

Throughout this book the emphasis has been upon the important role of the business system in providing goods and services which can be sold profitably to consumers. The profit motive as a key dimension of the private enterprise system has been examined in a positive light, since in our economic system the goal of profit provides an incentive to business to supply goods and services. The private enterprise system, which has both the lure of profits and the possibility of losses, has provided the vast majority of the American people with the highest standard of living in the world.

However, to say that business managers are concerned only with profits would not be accurate. As was indicated in Chapter 4, the concept of maximizing profits is difficult to make operational and may well be detrimental in the short run. The conduct of economic activities requires consideration of other factors in addition to business profit. American business does not function in a social vacuum. To fulfill its role in a responsible manner, business must relate positively to the society of which it is a part.

Ethics in business

One element which society expects from businessmen is that they conduct their activities in an ethical manner. *Ethics* is a code of conduct and values that is accepted by society as being right and proper. In general, business managers support a concept of business ethics based on honesty, fairness, and adherence to the law. However, there is always a possibility of a divergence between what businessmen consider to be ethical and what they actually practice. From time to time when such incidents as expense account padding, rigging of bids, and price fixing come to light that contradict the concensus of what constitutes ethical business practices, the American public is generally shocked and disappointed.

There are several influences which shape the ethics which are practiced by persons in business. These include the individual's personal code, the behavior pattern of the individual's colleagues, the attitudes and actions expressed by superiors in the business enterprise, financial circumstances, the enterprise's policy on specific ethical questions, and the ethical practices of the particular industry of which the firm is a part. From this lengthy list it should be apparent that no single factor is going to determine completely the manager's actions when faced with making a decision which poses the possibility of taking a course of action that might not be considered completely ethical. However, out of all the factors listed as influencing the ethical decisions of a businessman, a case could be made that the individual's own personal code and that expressed by his superior are especially important in influencing his final decision. This places great responsibilities upon the superior in a business situation in setting the proper ethical climate. As was discussed in Chapter 7, the top management in a business has the responsibility for setting the basic tone of the enterprise.

In every industry there is a generally accepted way of doing business.

These industry practices also have an important influence upon the ethics which exist in a given enterprise. When industry practices leave something to be desired, the responsibility for improving these conditions clearly lies with top management within the industry. An industry which continues to ignore the basic codes of conduct that are considered to be right by the public can expect that eventually the public will demand changes. In the past these changes have come through government legislation and increased regulation of American business. Enlightened self-regulation is one of the best ways to prevent outside control from being placed upon business conduct.

Contributions to educational, health, and charitable institutions

There is a wide range of views regarding the practice of business philanthropy. At one extreme are those who maintain that the corporation should refrain completely from philanthropic giving, leaving the support of nonprofit institutions to individual shareholders and employees. The proponents of this negative attitude toward corporate giving indicate that the sole function of the business corporation is to provide goods and services which can be sold at a profit. Persons with this viewpoint suggest that corporate giving acts as a kind of indirect tax on shareholders, employees, and customers which results in shareholders receiving somewhat lower dividends, employees receiving somewhat lower wages, and customers paying somewhat more for goods and services.

At the other end of this range of views regarding corporate giving are those who call for a much greater share of corporate wealth to be devoted to socially desirable projects. Advocates of substantially higher contributions by business enterprises point to increasing profits which they say demonstrate the ability of private enterprise to support such gifts. These advocates suggest that private business and citizens need to be leaders in meeting recognized social needs which otherwise would go unmet, perhaps to the detriment of all, or would be handled by governmental programs which might not be as effective as if they were privately initiated and carried out.

Most business managements follow a practice somewhat between these extremes. Corporate contributions amounted to $900 million in 1970 according to the American Association of Fund-Raising Counsel.

Most managements attempt to be prudent in their corporate giving. They consider a wide variety of factors—ranging from a desire not to antagonize shareholders or employees by what might be considered excessive gifts, to the extent to which contributions can be counted as federal income tax deductions. Under present federal law, a corporation may deduct those qualifying charitable contributions which do not exceed 5 percent of the corporation's taxable income before calculating income taxes. Some small corporations exceed the 5 percent tax deductible limitation. However, for the nation as a whole, total corporate giving in the past years has amounted to about 1 percent of corporate income before income taxes.

Some business managers prefer to contribute to those programs which relate to the specific objectives of their enterprises. Under this criteria there would be benefits that would accrue to the corporation, as well as to those recipients of the contributions. Gifts to Community Chest programs, local educational institutions, and medical facilities or research programs are easy for the business enterprise to fit into this framework. Presumably gifts such as these will tend to provide a better community for the location of the enterprise, or they will provide better training opportunities or improved medical facilities for their employees. However, serious problems can arise as to how far one can carry this concept of contributing to those programs which will aid in the better attainment of corporate objectives. Does a corporation in New York further its objectives by contributing to a private college in Arkansas? If so, how is this benefit measured? If not, at what point between New York and Arkansas does the corporate benefit cease?

Some corporate managements view philanthropic giving as an investment in the needs of society without attempting to measure the direct benefits to the corporation. Such contributions, made within financial limits set by management, go to those institutions and projects which management believes will produce the greatest future returns to society. In many instances projects are supported because of the personal interests of executives. While pet projects of a few executives should not cause business to overlook the broad social programs which need support, the personal involvement of managers in philanthropic projects can provide great individual satisfaction and an increased awareness by the business community of the role it can play in meeting social needs.

While corporate giving is frequently thought of in strictly financial terms, the time and effort devoted by managers and other enterprise employees to philanthropic projects should not be overlooked. Civic projects, committees, and organizations occupy a considerable amount of time of many persons engaged in business. With the approval of top management, much of this time is given during office or factory hours. In a very real sense this represents corporate giving to a wide range of socially approved projects.

Public relations in business

At its best, public relations in American industry has provided a means of relating the business enterprise and its purposes and programs to the different groups constituting the public. Identifiable groups with which the enterprise needs to communicate effectively include shareholders, customers, employees, suppliers, and governmental agencies as well as the public in general. There are four basic ways in which the public relations department can aid in improving the relationship of the business enterprise to others in the society.

First, the public relations department or outside counsel can assist management in clearly defining the company's own broad economic and social objectives. Second, the public relations department can help translate these goals into imaginative programs which can be effectively achieved. Third, this department provides advice on the ways and means by which the total image of the socially responsible business enterprise may be effectively communicated to the various groups which have an interest in the firm's activities.

Fourth, the public relations department should be sensitive to determining what misunderstandings might exist between the enterprise and its public. After a diagnosis of these problems, recommendations should be made to management for their correction. In some instances the difficulties are due to an inaccurate and unjustified image in the public's mind stemming from ignorance, misinformation, or distortion. However, sometimes the problems can be traced to unsound actions on the part of the enterprise or to circumstances which indicate the need for a change in the way in which the firm is being operated. When this is the case, then part of the public relations function is to assist in improving the enterprise's policies and actions.

The broad definition of public relations given here makes its function much more than merely gaining publicity for the enterprise through the press, radio, or television; or resorting to manipulation and subterfuge to present a picture of the enterprise which is not wholly accurate. In the long run the public relations program of the business enterprise should focus attention on clarifying the needs of the society and should point to ways in which the enterprise can help meet those needs.

Business and the political process

A question exists in the minds of many as to what is a proper role for business in the political arena. Under federal law and legislation in the various states no business corporation may engage directly in political activity nor may a business corporation provide direct financial support to political candidates. The reasons for this restrictive legislation have roots in the earlier history of America when business interests frequently dominated political decisions.

However, the fact that the business corporation itself is prohibited from having an active political voice does not preclude business owners and managers from being active in the political process. As one of the important groups in our society, business's viewpoints are considered in deciding political issues which frequently have profound economic implications. The views of business groups on national political issues are expressed publicly by trade associations, business study groups, and statements by top officials of corporations. The counsel of businessmen is frequently called upon by politicians at all levels of government.

Each business manager should accept the responsibility of being active individually in the political process. For some this may mean a relatively modest role, such as voting in all elections after becoming informed on the candidates and issues, along with an occasional communication with elected officials regarding a particular public issue. For other businessmen political involvement may include actively supporting political parties and candidates or perhaps even running for office themselves. Notable examples of businessmen who have turned to politics can be called to mind at all levels of government.

Social responsibility of business

In the decades following the Civil War when the United States was being industrialized the concept of progress of business was synonymous with progress for society. The Carnegies, Hills, Cookes, Rockefellers, and others who were the businesses giants of that day were considered by many to be the men who were building America. However, by the latter part of the 19th century there was a reaction against the giant business enterprises of the day which resulted in the political and legislative changes discussed in Chapter 2.

Part of these regulations stemmed from the fact that the means of attaining profits, a key objective of business, did not always measure up to what today would be considered ethical business practices. Working conditions and management policies left much to be desired in many factories; financial manipulations resulted in the sale of stock in corporations which had little assets but the blue sky above; and trusts were formed which were able to control whole industries. With this background, serious questions were raised as to the role of profits and the responsibilities which business had to the public.

The prolonged depression of the 1930s resulted in widespread unemployment, financial disaster for many individuals and businesses, and raised serious questions in the minds of some as to whether the economic and political institutions of the United States could meet the terrific challenges of the times. However, the American economy did survive, although the role of government was increased to meet some social and economic problems which no single enterprise or industry could solve alone.

With government assuming a larger role in looking after the public interest in economic matters the question has arisen as to whether private enterprise has any responsibility to society beyond providing goods and services. Many businessmen answer this question in the affirmative. They maintain that the business manager has the responsibility for the production and distribution of goods and services at a price commensurate with their quality and purpose; these goods should be fairly advertised and merchandised; employees should have fair wages and satisfactory working conditions; and that enterprises and business managers should contribute a portion of their resources to improving the community of which they are a part.

In examining the social responsibility of business further, business managers should provide conditions which will permit each person to develop his particular capacities. Operationally this has implications for personnel policies in avoiding discrimination in hiring and promotion, in providing training programs for those who may lack immediate job skills, and in cooperating with other enterprises, unions, and government to help find a constructive way to deal with the complex problem of America's unemployed.

Business has a responsibility to work with other groups in society in dealing with such nationwide problems as air and water pollution. While no single enterprise can prevent air and water pollution for our country as a whole, the cooperation of those industries which contribute to this problem can bring about a more satisfactory solution. Some persons say that this role should be reserved for public agencies alone. However, one reply is that the ultimate burden on business and the economy will likely be greater without the expertise of industry in evolving workable solutions. With business doing its fair share the added resources should provide for satisfactory solutions in a shorter time and at less expense than if business waits for government to carry out the entire program.

The general nature of business's social responsibility just outlined is relatively easy to state. The difficulty comes in making the decisions regarding specific dilemmas. What constitutes a desirable mix of enterprise funds and executive time spent on community projects, and how far does the definition of the community go? When a labor union negotiates for higher wages and fringe benefits for its members, to what extent is management responsible for meeting labor's increased demands and to what extent should these demands be resisted to preserve profits for stockholders or to avoid higher prices for enterprise products? How does one draw the line between fair and misleading advertising? It is often difficult to answer such questions when they arise in a specific enterprise. However, the fact that questions are difficult does not mean that they do not have to be answered.

One might say that the social responsibility of the businessman is no more but no less than that of every American citizen. However, because of the concentration of economic power at the command of the business manager there is a great burden of responsibility placed on his shoulders for good stewardship of these resources. The words of Robert G. Menzies, former Prime Minister of Australia, which were applied to America as a nation are also appropriate for today's business leaders: "Great power can breed great selfishness unless it is wedded to great responsibility."[1]

Business and the future

Man, unlike other biological species, is capable of making great changes in both his physical and social environment. As one of the sig-

---

[1] From an address delivered at Drury College on October 15, 1966.

nificant groups in society, business can have an important role in determining the changes which will help mankind deal constructively with problems now and in the future. It is difficult to forecast the future for society in general and business in particular. However, from the character of our economic society today trends can be identified which can provide considerable insight into the near future.

One thing which can be said with a high degree of certainty regarding the future of America is that change will occur. Americans have been pragmatists in the evolution of our social system and have been willing to accept social changes when those changes seemed desirable and workable. The continuing evolution and change in our economic society over the past 200 years clearly indicates this. Problems of economic instability which were pressing during the depression years of the 1930s have been greatly reduced in magnitude. The economic transitions from World War II and the Korean conflict were accomplished. The inflation largely caused by the military operations in Southeast Asia is abating in the early 1970s. New relationships between business and other groups in society are evolving, one of the most notable being the business-government relationship which has changed substantially over the past 40 years.

One issue which is especially relevant to the immediate future for business in the United States may be summed up in the question of what is the proper role of private economic power in the last quarter of the 20th century. This basic question embraces such subordinate issues as the balance between the allocation of resources in the private and public sectors of our domestic economy; how private enterprise can help in the solution of some of the economic and social problems of massive urbanization and play its part in the development of human resources; and the role of American private enterprise in assisting other nations in their economic development. Other issues which will continue to be dominant in the American scene include inflation, unemployment, management-labor disputes, and automation. However, these latter problems are really part of the basic issue. What is the proper role of private economic power in the United States?

With billions of dollars being spent annually on national defense, space exploration, highways, and other types of governmental services, the question as to what should be the balance between the private and public sectors of the economy will be one which will influence business decisions. An increase in the allocation of resources in the public sector of the economy will result in higher government budgets financed either with increased taxes, government borrowing, or both. At the same time, the government represents an important customer of business enterprises. The balance between allocation of the national income between public and private sectors will continue to be a matter of interest to business and other groups in society.

Sociological problems identifiable today will be extended into the future as solutions are tried. The goal of eliminating poverty is a prime

FIGURE 19–1

Persons below the poverty level by sex and race of family head 1959 to 1969

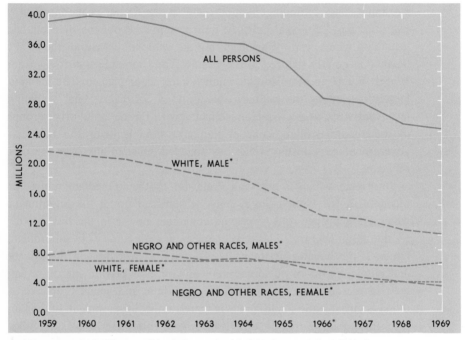

* For persons in families, sex of head; for unrelated individuals, sex of the individual.
Source: U.S. Bureau of the Census, *Current Population Report*, Series P-60, No. 76, 1970.

example of the complex social problems facing America. Poverty has been greatly reduced in the United States in recent years but by no means eradicated. Figure 19–1 shows the number of persons below the poverty level from 1959 through 1969.

The detailed definition of which families or individuals are considered to fall below the poverty line depends upon such factors as family size, sex of the family head, number of children under 18 years old, and farm or nonfarm residence. In general the poverty line was drawn by the federal government to include one-person families with less than

$1,800 annual income up to about $6,000 for families with seven or more members. Annual revisions are made of the poverty income cutoff points based on price changes of the cost of food.

Based on this definition, in 1970 about 13 percent of Americans were poor compared with about 22 percent in 1960. Although this represents a significant decline over the past ten years, there were still over 25 million Americans living in poverty in 1970. The number of poor was almost equally divided between those in metropolitan areas and those living in rural areas, although over the ten-year period the proportion of the poor living in cities increased.

Poor families headed by a man decreased by about one half over this decade, while there was no significant change in the number of poor families headed by a woman. Persons of Negro and races other than white constituted 32 percent of the poor in 1970, although they made up only about 12 percent of the total popoulation.

Business alone cannot solve the massive problems of poverty in American society. Based on government estimates it would have taken approximately $11 billion to raise the aggregate incomes of all poor families to the poverty cutoff level. To help the poor will require the concentrated effort of all groups in society, in many instances through the vehicle of government. However, businessmen can be influential in determining the priorities and the means chosen to effect solutions.

In the development of human resources a major share of the responsibility for training and retraining necessitated by continuing automation, changing product demand, and consequent new skills required will be with business. Although business and organized labor have made some progress in the past in meeting the challenges of changing job requirements, the point has not yet been reached where all individuals have an opportunity to be utilized in their most effective capacities.

An example of what business is doing to provide job training and opportunities for the hard-core unemployed is the National Alliance of Businessmen. This organization was formed after the Detroit riots of 1967 to expand employment opportunities, especially for persons who had been considered unemployable because of a lack of job skills. Many leading corporations are participating in this program along with thousands of smaller business enterprises which make up the voluntary alliance.

Some of these programs have had notable successes. Levi Strauss & Co., makers of the popular denim "Levis," has been one of the leaders in the NAB and has had a long experience of hiring employees from minority groups. In the early 1960s Strauss moved to integrate its plants in the South beyond the level of tokenism and before it was required to do so by law. This company has also opened its management ranks to qualified persons from minority groups in significant numbers. Western Electric Company, manufacturing and supply company for the Bell Telephone systems, has developed creative programs for hiring and training disadvantaged Americans. Both Western Electric and Strauss have encouraged the development of minority suppliers.

Despite the success stories, many problems have been encountered and not all cases have worked out satisfactorily. One major automobile corporation executive reporting on his company's experience said that many of the hard-core unemployed were unable to fill out a simple job application. Some of the applicants who signed up for job training failed to appear, others who did report were consistently late. Many had never been counted in a census, had no social security number, had never registered to vote, and had no community ties. Some employees had trouble getting to work because of the inability to read the route markings on the city buses. As the result of these problems many of the trainees have been given basic courses in reading, writing, and arithmetic.

In the decline in economic activity in 1970, problems arose in instances when it became necessary to lay off part of an enterprise's work force temporarily. Formerly hard-core unemployed persons who had been put to work customarily were at the bottom of the seniority list established by the union contract. In these cases management was faced with the dilemma of abiding with the union contract and letting these new employees go or protecting the newly trained persons and laying off more senior employees at the risk of a union grievance or strike and an injustice to employees who had been with the company longer.

The increased population and its concentration in metropolitan areas provides another indication of the problems of the future. Figure 19–2 shows the Standard Metropolitan Statistical Areas designated by the U.S. Bureau of the Census as urban areas having at least one city with a population of 50,000 or more. The 247 SMSA's contain about two thirds of the country's population. Major problems facing many of these cities include increased costs of government; high property taxes; traffic congestion; robberies, assaults, and other crime; need for improved housing and recreational areas; and racial tensions.

A fight or flight response has developed on the part of some businessmen to these urban problems. Some managements are relocating home

FIGURE 19–2
Standard metropolitan statistical areas

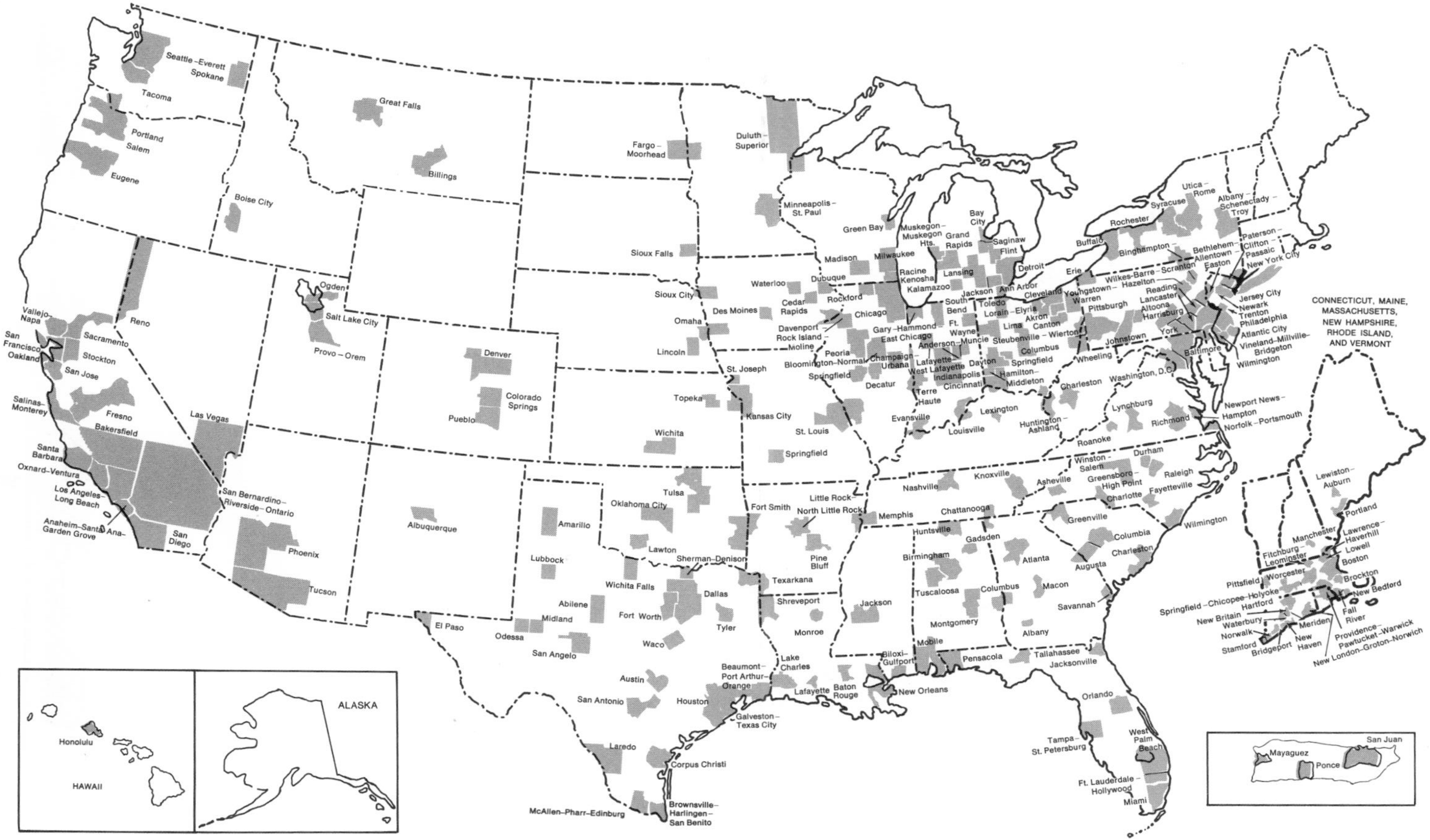

Source: U.S. Bureau of the Census.

offices and other facilities outside the heart of the central city metropolitan areas. Several major corporations have moved their headquarters from New York City to the suburbs or to other less populated areas of the country. Such moves by industry tend to aggravate the problems of the central cities by decreasing the property tax base and reducing the number of jobs available to inhabitants of the inner city.

Other business managements have chosen to stay in the cities and become more involved in community action. For example, in St. Louis, businessmen helped in developing and carrying out programs to clean up the Mississippi River waterfront. In Los Angeles and Chicago, businessmen joined in supporting improved law enforcement. In numerous cities other examples can be found where businessmen have helped with such problems as improving slum housing; providing municipal recreational areas and downtown parking; and supporting public education needs.

More than one economist has suggested that a sustained period of economic growth without the steady inflation which persisted during the latter 1960s and early 1970s would provide the best cure for many of the nation's economic problems. Such economic growth would have the effect of stimulating business investment, creating new jobs which would reduce unemployment, raising family incomes, providing tax revenues for public services, and improving the position of the U.S. dollar in international financial markets.

In summary, when we consider the proper role of private economic power it should be emphasized that economic power is not an end in itself. Indeed, even the goods and services produced by business in the hands of industrial and individual consumers are not the ultimate objectives of our economic society. The end purpose of the way in which we organize our economy is to provide a fuller measure of freedom for our citizens. The wealth of the American economy should be used in such a way as to further individual dignity and meaningful living. Only as the businessman, individually and as part of the institution of business, acts to serve these ends will he be meeting his responsibility to society and justifying his reason for existence.

Summary

Society expects business to fulfill its role in a responsible manner. This includes the expectation that businessmen will be ethical in the conduct of their activities.

Business contributes to a wide range of philanthropic projects both in terms of money and time of enterprise personnel.

The public relations department can help the business enterprise to relate its purposes and programs effectively to the different groups in society.

Business responsibility to society goes beyond providing goods and services. Business cannot solve all of society's ills. However, business can help by working with other groups to try to solve some of our major social problems associated with poverty, urbanization, and minority relationships.

Changes are occurring in our economic society. A key question for business is what is the proper role of private economic power in the last quarter of the 20th century?

The provision of goods and services by business is important. However, the end purpose in the way in which our economy is organized should be to provide a fuller measure of freedom for our citizens. The wealth and ingenuity of the private enterprise system should be used in such a way as to further individual dignity and meaningful living.

Terms for review

ethics	National Alliance of Business-
philanthropy	men
public relations	Standard Metropolitan Statistical
poverty level	Areas

Questions

1. What factors determine the ethics practiced by a business manager at a given time?

2. *a)* Develop an argument to support the following statement: "As a stockholder in American corporations, I resent their philanthropic gifts to charitable, educational, and community projects. I wish corporate boards of directors would declare higher cash dividends for the stockholders and let the individual stockholders give to the philanthropic projects of their choice."

   b) Develop an argument to refute the above statement.

3. *a*) What does a positive program of public relations do for an enterprise and its public?

b) Comment on the statement: "Public relations is simply a gimmick to whitewash the practices of business and to dodge the real issues."

4. Why is it so important that business managers have socially responsible attitudes and practices?

5. What can business enterprises do to help reduce poverty in the United States?

6. Through a study of current publications, select examples of practices or projects that businesses have undertaken which demonstrate an awareness of the critical economic, political, and social issues facing the country today. What can be learned from these examples that would be helpful to other business enterprises?

7. Based on your study in this course and your outside reading, write a 300-word summary of the most important issues that will be relevant for business enterprises in the next five years.

BUSINESS BRIEFS

Campbell Soup Company

In the 1950s the Campbell Soup Company management surveyed the many problems surrounding the location of its corporate headquarters and main plant in the decaying inner city of Camden, New Jersey. This management could have followed the example of many other corporations faced with a similar situation and fled to the suburbs. However, Campbell decided to stay. In addition to building a $12 million Campbell research center in the inner city, the company has worked to improve the total environment. Campbell has spent some $6 million on improvements ranging from the creation of new parks, summer job programs, and day-care centers to working with other businesses to turn a waterfront slum into a modern complex containing new apartments, a motel, offices, and shopping areas. Programs have been undertaken to purchase and remodel old homes and then sell them to low-income families in cooperation with a federal government subsidy program. Since 1968 some 250 families have been aided in buying their own homes.

1.   As a member of management how could you justify to your share-holders the spending of $6 million of company money on the types of projects outlined above?

2.   Shouldn't the federal government be the unit in society to sponsor such social welfare programs rather than private business? Why or why not?

Social benefits—social costs

In a corporation's recent annual report to its stockholders the chairman of the board said,

The greatest change in the last 20 years has been in employment costs. Since 1950 our average straight-time hourly rate has doubled—but this is not the whole story. The really spectacular change has been in the cost of fringe benefits. These are expenses for such things as vacations, holidays, pensions, and employee insurance for hospitalization, medical payments, accidents, death, or unemployment. These costs are incurred for employee benefits for which the company gets no production. In 1950 they cost the company about $440 for an average employee. In 1970 the cost was almost $2,900—an increase of 560 percent.

Similar changes in employment costs have occurred in all industries. The general public and all of us enjoying the benefits need to realize that the cost of providing them must come eventually from the prices we consumers pay for the things we buy.

Fringe benefits for this corporation took about 15 percent of each sales' dollar.

In addition to these costs, many corporations are now facing added costs of cleaning up the water and atmosphere in connection with their manufacturing processes or in adapting their products to reduce environmental pollution. Also, some corporations are spending money to train workers who need remedial education before they can be placed on the job. Generally such social costs of doing business are not reported separately to stockholders. Little or no information is made public of these costs.

1.   What do you think of the definition of social costs as those costs which do not contribute directly to the production and distribution of an enterprise's products?

2. Should stockholders (and the public) be informed on the extent to which social costs are included in a corporation's cost of doing business?

3. How would you react if you were informed that as much as $450 of the price of a $3,000 automobile could be attributed to social costs?

CASES

The image scrimmage

Bob Cramer closed his notebook and rose to his feet, "I believe I have all the background information I need at this point, Mr. Chase. We will conduct our investigation into those problem areas we have discussed and submit a report detailing our findings and recommendations."

As Cramer left the office he reflected on his conversation with Craig Chase, president of American Wood Products, Inc. This was his third meeting with the president, who had contacted the firm of Bayer, Bassick, and Botlich a week ago. Bayer, Bassick, and Botlich (B, B & B) was a medium-sized public relations agency; Chase was considering the possibility of contracting for their services as public relations consultants. Bob Cramer, a senior account executive with B, B & B, was chosen to develop the account.

In their first meeting Chase had told Cramer, "Public relations is something we have always taken for granted. Consequently, we do not have an adequate understanding of what is involved or of how the function should be managed within our organization. It is my hope that our experience with the problems we are now facing will generate a better understanding and appreciation for public relations so that we can eventually manage this function ourselves."

In his conversations with Bob, Chase had outlined those problem areas where he thought better public relations might be a help. First, American Wood was not in very good standing in the various communities in which it operated plants. The company had trouble securing the cooperation needed from many different groups. For example, some of American's timber holdings were not readily accessible from public roads. As a result, the forest management division depended heavily on the cooperation of farmers and landowners in leasing temporary access across their property so that timber crops could be harvested. These persons had been very reluctant to provide this cooperation. The resulting delays and the need to use indirect access routes had proved very costly for the division.

Another problem of increasing concern was the pressure in the state legislature and in Congress to set aside certain of American's timber holdings as parklands or as state-controlled conservation preserves. The pressure emanated from various interest groups concerned with wildlife conservation and the preservation of natural timberlands. Governmental agencies, such as the National Park Service and the state fish and game division, had provided little support for American's position in these matters. Even legislative representatives from the district in which American's home office is located had not taken a strong position in the company's behalf.

Still another major problem area was that of recruiting new personnel for the company. Personnel officers reported that, despite competitive wage scales, American was finding increasing difficulty in competing with other employers for top quality recruits.

Problems were also being experienced in the sale of the company's products. Most of their products were distributed through retail and wholesale lumber dealers who supplied a variety of contractors, decorators, and individual consumers. While sales in the industry had been rising, American was not maintaining its share of the market. In some cases dealers had dropped the American line altogether and the company had been unable to gain the support of another qualified dealer in that area.

In the weeks that followed, Bob Cramer and the other B, B & B personnel who helped him on the American account conducted numerous interviews, in person and by questionnaire, in an effort to shed more light on the problems which company president Craig Chase had outlined. In every case, the objective was to determine what image American had and how this image had been gained.

In conversations with landowners, state fish and game officials, and other persons interested in conservation, American was portrayed as an inconsiderate neighbor and an usurper of the area's natural resources without regard to the consequences for those whom their actions affected. Landowners who had denied access across their property felt that this privilege if it were granted would be abused by the company. They cited reports of previous incidents in which heavy logging equipment had torn up roads with no attempt by the company to restore these roads; in which gates had been carelessly left open; and in which logging crews had violated property lines. State conservation officials generally regarded the company as "either inconsiderate or ignorant" of the importance of managing timberlands with regard for the fish and game resources which can be affected. In some cases entire valleys had been denuded by logging crews; the resulting land erosion had made the area unfit for replanting, and the silting of the river had taken a substantial toll in the fish population.

In talking with local officials and community leaders, it was apparent that American was viewed as a "mediocre" or "apathetic" citizen of the various communities in which it operated. It did not become actively involved in community projects, either as an organization or through the participation of its management personnel as individuals. One official stated that "the company seldom does more than what is necessary in cooperating with community interests. In controlling their contamination of local streams, for example, American meets the standards imposed by current pollution control legislation; but that's as far as they go. There is no effort to go further than that just for the sake of being a good citizen."

Conversations with state employment security officials and the personnel officers of other companies provided some insight into American's recruiting problems. The company apparently had developed a bad image as an employer. Such problems as poor first-line supervision, an inadequate grievance procedure, and poorly devised promotion and layoff policies had contributed to rather serious incidents which gained a considerable amount of attention in the communities in which they occurred. In recent years the company had made considerable progress in dealing with these problems and the present situation was much improved. "But apparently this fact has not been communicated to the community and to potential recruits," noted one observer. "The negative image seems to have lingered on."

A survey of dealers and customers for wood products revealed something of the image American projected in the trade. Dealers did not consider the company to be reliable or cooperative as a supplier. They cited failure to meet delivery schedules, inadequate sales and service calls, and unwillingness to cooperate or make special arrangements when problems arose. Contractors and other users were familiar with the American brand, "Timberline," which was associated with paneling, wallboard, insulation, and other construction materials produced by the company. However, they did not associate either the brand or the company with the idea of a "progressive or innovative supplier, a front runner in new product development." In contrast, American's competitors seemed to have the connotation of being more progressive. This "nonprogressive" image was surprising since American, at least in recent years, had been more active in new product development and research than any of its competitors.

Customers also felt that American had an image of unreliable product quality. This was apparently a carry-over from the introduction three years earlier of a new type of wall paneling. The product had not been adequately developed before being placed on the market and a number of serious defects, including warping and discoloration, had occurred. The product was quickly withdrawn from the market but not before considerable damage had been done to the company's image.

In reporting his findings to the president of American, Bob Cramer realized that he would have to submit detailed recommendations as to the action which should be taken to remedy the various problems facing the company. These recommendations should define the various publics with whom American should be concerned and should suggest the kind of image which should be projected to each public. In each instance specific measures should be suggested as a means of developing the desired image.

1. Identify the various publics with which this company should be concerned.

2. What is the image of the company which each of these publics has?

3. What can American Wood Products management do to improve its public image?

Personal decisions in business

I

"See you in the morning, Norma."

"Good night, Mr. Keating."

Norma Spalding looked up from her typewriter and watched as her boss stopped at the supplies cabinet before leaving the office. It was a common practice for executives of the company to take note pads, pens, and other items for use at home. Although these were, in part, used for company work, they were often used for other purposes in the home. Norma had never before given much thought to this practice; it seemed to be accepted by employees and executives of the company. Now, however, as she turned back to her work, she wondered if it was "right" to take company supplies for one's personal use.

II

"It's silly to go out and buy this stuff," Sam said as he reached into a carton marked 'rejects.' "Here, take one of these." Tom reached out and caught the can of car polish which Sam had tossed to him.

Tom Farber was finishing the second week of his summer warehouse job. He had been assigned to work with Sam Bartels, lift truck operator and senior man on the warehouse crew. Sam was a good-natured, easy-going, middle-aged worker who knew his job well. Tom had already learned a good deal from Sam, not only about the warehouse, but about people. In his relationship with his peers and superiors Sam demonstrated an understanding of human nature which had quickly won Tom's confidence and admiration.

Turning the can of car polish in his hands, Tom found the reason it had been "rejected": a small dent in the side of the can. Although such rejects were not given to employees, it was not uncommon for warehouse personnel to "help themselves" when they had a need for some item. "After all," they reasoned, "these rejects are to be destroyed, so it's no loss to the company."

III

Larry Peters looked over his travel expense form. He had just returned from his first sales trip with the Sun-Ripe Food Company. During his training period, Larry had been associated with several of the other salesmen of his district. From his conversations with these men Larry understood that it was common practice for the salesmen to report travel expenses equal to the amount allowed by the company, whether they spent that amount or not. For example, if a salesman spent only $15 of the allotted $21 per day, he reported the full $21 and kept the difference. They justified this practice in the following manner: "If the company is willing to have one spend $4 on a steak dinner, but I would just as soon have a hamburger, why shouldn't I keep what I save?"

IV

Herb Schelling studied his shipping records carefully. There seemed to be no question about it—one of the tank cars which had been shipped that morning was contaminated.

Herb was the shipping coordinator for the Ace Chemical Corporation. Most of the company's products were shipped in railroad tank cars to a wide variety of industrial customers. Since a variety of products were shipped, a tank car had to be flushed out if its shipment was different from the chemical which it had previously carried. Herb's subordinates had told him that no cars had been flushed that morning because they had all previously contained the same chemical that was being shipped that morning. Herb's records, however, clearly showed that this had not been the case. One car had carried a different chemical and therefore should have been flushed.

Herb considered the possible consequences of letting this shipment continue. He knew that the contaminating chemical would not react with the shipment. Furthermore, there seemed to be little chance that the customer would encounter difficulties in processing the chemical. This, however, would depend upon the use to which the chemical was put. For some uses it is possible that the "batch" in which the chemical was used would be ruined. The customer in question was a small plant which ordered only about five cars each year from Ace. Schelling knew that he would risk losing this customer if they should encounter problems with the shipment. However, he felt confident that the chances of such problems were quite slim.

On the other hand, the cost of correcting the error would undoubtedly be very high. The shipment would have to be called back and another sent in its place. The contents of the shipment would have to be reprocessed, or possibly disposed of. Herb estimated that the cost of such an effort would be between five and ten thousand dollars. In addition, the customer had placed a "rush" on this order and would not appreciate a delay.

How to Analyze

a case

The case as it is used in the study of business administration is the presentation of a real business situation which contains an issue or problem. In some cases the actual names of the business enterprises and individuals are used, while in other cases they are disguised. The study and discussion of cases is useful in training students to think about problems faced in business and to analyze new situations. This approach may be frustrating at times since there is always more than one alternative in dealing with the issues, depending upon the interpretation of the facts of the cases and the values of the decision maker. This does not mean that all alternatives or solutions are equally good. The student's job is to determine and to be able to justify which course of action he feels is better than others under the circumstances.

Early in the course, perhaps throughout an introductory course, the instructor's emphasis may be upon problem identification and a definition of the possible alternative actions. Later, as the student's knowledge and experience are expanded, the emphasis in case analysis may turn to the recommendation and justification of specific courses of action. Then the student is required to analyze the case to determine alternative courses of action with the possible consequences of each alternative.

Generally every alternative in a particular case may be expected to result in both positive and negative consequences. When such a dilemma occurs, the decision maker must select the course of action which will result in the best probable consequences from his frame of reference.

Sometimes cases are used for the purpose of examining how a problem developed or of assessing the actions taken in a given situation. In such cases the student may find it useful to determine the key circumstances and decisions which led to the eventual outcome of the case.

At times the student will wish that more information had been provided in the case in order to improve the analysis. When this occurs the student may find it desirable to make certain assumptions about the facts of the case. These assumptions should be practical in light of the information provided and should be able to stand the test of questions from either the instructor or fellow students. The student should also remember that in the real life situation the business decision maker rarely has all of the information which might be desirable. Furthermore, there would be a cost to obtaining additional information even if it were available.

The following approach is suggested in analyzing a specific case for class discussion:

1. During the first reading of the case read rapidly. Do not become too involved in the details or figures. Try to understand the environment in which the case is set and the broad issue or issues involved.

2. Read the case a second time, making notes on key facts or information relating to the issues or problems. Examine the exhibits or figures. Evaluate the information given. Some of the facts provided in the case will be more relevant than others in outlining the problems and alternative solutions.

3. Read the case a third time, making a list of the significant problems or issues along with possible alternative solutions.

4. In the light of your analysis, outline a recommended course of action with the probable consequences. Check your recommendation against the facts of the case and the alternatives which you rejected.

When a written analysis or brief is assigned, the following approach is recommended:

1. Identify and state the problem or problems in the case.

2. List the alternative solutions to the problem.

3. State your recommended course of action.

4. Indicate the reasons for your decision. Why is your recommendation better than the other alternatives? State any key assumptions you may have made in arriving at your decision.

5. Do not spend your time in the brief simply restating the facts of the case. It may be desirable to state briefly a fact from the case to strengthen your analysis. However, your analysis and reasoning are more important in the brief since it normally may be assumed that the person reading your analysis has a clear understanding of the facts presented in the case.

glossary

Glossary

Accounting. The recording, analysis, and reporting of enterprise transactions in financial terms.

Accounts payable. Amounts owed to suppliers for purchases.

Accounts receivable. Amounts owed to the enterprise by customers to whom credit has been extended.

Accrual concept of accounting. An accounting method in which income is recognized in the period when it is earned and expenses in the period when they are incurred, regardless of whether there is an actual exchange of cash during that period.

Accrued taxes payable. The amount of tax liability owed to various governmental bodies.

Accumulated depreciation. The amount of the cost of capital assets that has been charged off during the years to recognize the declining value of the assets.

Achieved status. Status that comes when an individual works to fulfill the requirements for a particular position and attains it.

Acid test ratio. A test of an enterprise's short-term liquidity; it is the relationship of an enterprise's quick assets (cash, short-term investments, and accounts or notes receivable) to current liabilities.

Actuarial studies. Statistical analysis of accident and death rates for insurance purposes of calculating risks, premiums, and benefit payments.

Advertising. The visual or oral communication of a message to a group regarding a good, service, or idea.

Advertising media. The various means by which an advertising message can be transmitted to a potential consumer, including newspapers, television, direct mail, magazines, radio, or outdoor ads.

Agents. Wholesale middlemen who customarily do not take title to goods, but negotiate the purchase or sale of merchandise for which they are paid on a fee or commission basis.

Air pollution. The presence of one or more contaminants in the air in quantities great enough to be injurious to life or property.

Air Quality Act of 1967. This act extended federal authority in the field of air-quality control and provided for federal cooperation with state governments in developing air-quality control standards.

609

American National Standards Institute (ANSI). The national body which has worked out standard symbols for flowcharting for computer applications.

American Stock Exchange. A major organized trading market for corporate stocks and bonds; located in New York City.

Antimerger Act. A federal law, passed in 1950, that strengthened the Clayton Act. It provided that not only was the purchase of stock of a competing corporation a violation of the antitrust laws, but it was also illegal to acquire the assets of a competing firm.

Antitrust laws. Legislative acts designed to promote competition and to prevent large business enterprises from practices such as illegal price setting and division of markets.

Application blank. A form that a job candidate fills out, giving general information about himself plus answers to questions the business enterprise has found to correlate with job success.

Applied research. The practical application of scientific knowledge to deal with specific problems or needs.

Appraised value. The value of an asset determined by someone with expert knowledge for purposes of taxation, insurance, or other reasons.

Apprenticeship training. The employee works under supervision of trained employees and is required to meet rigid performance standards. It is used in jobs that require long periods of training and a high degree of skill.

Arbitration. A judicial process in which an impartial third party assumes the role of a judge and makes a binding decision in a dispute.

Ascribed status. Status assigned to a person on the basis of some inherited characteristic, such as sex, race, or the family he is born into.

Ask price. The price at which a stock market specialist is willing to sell securities.

Assessed value. The value placed on property for purposes of taxation.

Auditor. The financial officer who has the responsibility to check on the functioning of the accounting and control systems, including verifying reported assets and liabilities and making suggestions for overall management improvements.

Authoritarian leadership. Leadership based on centralized authority and autocratic decision making. Subordinates are given little or no discretion in carrying out work assignments.

Authority. The delegated power to make decisions.

Automation. In manufacturing, the process by which goods are produced, moved, or inspected by self-operating machinery or electronic controls.

Average collection period. A calculation that may be used as a means of evaluating the quality of the enterprise's accounts receivable. It is the ratio of trade accounts receivable plus notes receivable to average daily credit sales.

Balance sheet. A statement of the financial position of an enterprise at a given point in time, usually the end of a fiscal period, which shows the assets the enterprise owns and the claims against those assets.

Bank acceptance. A draft drawn on a bank and accepted by the bank instead of an importer or some other private party.

Bargaining unit. The definition in the union contract of the employees and the employers covered by the agreement.

BASIC. *B*eginner's *A*ll-Purpose *S*ymbolic *I*nstruction *C*ode is a computer language for use in solving numerical problems.

Beneficiary. A person named to receive the proceeds or benefits of an insurance policy, will, and so on.

Best-efforts offering. An agreement whereby an investment banker will sell securities for a corporation without underwriting the issue.

Bid price. The price at which a stock market specialist is willing to buy securities.

Bill of exchange. A document drawn by the exporter of goods which calls on the importer to accept the obligation for payment of a sum of money at a specified time. Drafts used in international business.

Blacklist. A list circulated by an employer which contains the names of former employees who have been discharged for union activities. This practice has been determined by the National Labor Relations Board to be an unfair labor practice.

Board of directors. A body elected by the stockholders of a corporation to exercise control of the corporation in the best long-run interests of the stockholders.

Bond indenture. The legal contract that gives the details of the arrangement between the issuing company (the borrower) and the bondholders (the lenders).

Bonds. Interest-bearing certificates of indebtedness issued by a governmental body or private enterprise which promise to pay the holder a specified sum on a given date in the future in exchange for a specific amount of money today.

Book value. The worth of enterprise assets based on original cost as shown on the accounting records of the firm.

Break-even chart. A projection of an enterprise's operations, assuming a particular pattern of variable and fixed costs in order to analyze the profit or loss resulting from different levels of sales volume or selling prices.

Break-even point. The point where revenues equal costs. At the break-even point, the equality of sales and costs means that there is neither a profit nor a loss.

Broker. An agent who receives a commission for acting as an intermediary between a buyer and seller.

Budget. A financial plan that serves as an estimate of and a control over the operations of the enterprise for a specified period of time.

Budgeting process. The gathering of data to translate the goals of the enterprise into quantitative terms and to set a basis for control.

Business cycles. The recurring expansion and contraction in the level of economic activity.

Business enterprise. A privately owned and operated organization that brings together the factors of production to provide goods and services sold with the expectation of earning a profit.

Business profit. The calculation of profit by subtracting from the total receipts for a product's sale the appropriate portion of fixed and variable costs.

Business systems simulation. Development of a model of the enterprise and its environment, which is programmed into a computer so that business decisions can be tested to evaluate their consequences.

Capital. In an economic sense, capital is wealth used to produce goods and services. In accounting terminology, capital is either the amount invested by owners in an enterprise or the total long-term funds committed to management's use.

Capital budget. A budget that details the investment plans for assets that will last longer than a year and the means for their financing.

Capital equipment. Machinery and facilities having a length of life over one year that are used to manufacture other goods.

Capital market. The coming together of those institutions and individuals who are users and sources of long-term funds.

Capital paid in excess of stated value. A balance sheet account, showing the amount paid by stockholders for the corporation's common stock in excess of par or stated value. It is also sometimes called capital surplus or paid-in surplus.

Capital structure. The composition of the long-term funds committed to management's use, including equity funds and long-term debt (if any).

Capitalism. An economic system in which the capital used in the production process is privately owned and invested with the expectation of earning a profit.

Cash. A legal medium of exchange. The most liquid of current assets.

Cash budget. An estimate of cash receipts and cash disbursements over a specified period of time and of cash on hand at the end of the period.

Cash disbursements. Any payment of cash by a business enterprise.

Cash dividends. The dollars paid to shareholders from earnings, usually stated on a per share basis.

Cash flow. The receipts and disbursements of an enterprise over a particular period of time.

Cash receipts. The cash received by a business enterprise over a specified period of time.

Chain of command. A detailing of authority-responsibility relationships, so that each employee knows who his immediate superior is and for what he is accountable.

Channels of distribution. The series of enterprises through which goods flow in moving from the producer to the ultimate consumer.

Charter. A charter is a document issued by a government which authorizes the formation of a corporation and grants it certain powers.

Check. A written order that directs a bank to pay a specified amount of money on demand.

Checkoff clause. A clause in the union contract that authorizes management to deduct union dues from the employee's pay and to turn this sum directly over to the union treasury.

Child Protection and Toy Safety Act. Legislation providing increased protection for children from toys which might have mechanical or electrical hazards.

Cigarette Labeling and Advertising Act. Legislation which requires warnings on cigarette packages regarding the health hazards of cigarette smoking and also regulates cigarette advertising.

Civil Rights Act of 1964. Federal legislation outlawing discrimination in voting, public accommodations, schools, federal assistance programs, and employment.

Clayton Act. A federal law, passed in 1914, directed against unfair competition. It outlawed price discrimination, exclusive and tying contracts, intercorporate stockholdings, and interlocking directorates.

Clean Air Act of 1963. Legislation with later amendments which authorized the federal government to take action in interstate air pollution matters and establishment of exhaust standards for new autos.

Clean Air Amendments of 1970. Federal legislation which set specific standards for auto emissions beginning with 1975 models along with other pollution controls, such as on new stationary sources of pollution.

Closed shop. An employment situation in which workers must be members of the union before they may be hired by an employer. The closed shop was made illegal by the Labor Management Relations Act of 1947.

Closed-end investment company. An investment company that has a fixed amount of capital stock outstanding, and buys and sells securities to improve its income and capital gains profit picture.

COBOL. *CO*mmon *B*usiness *O*riented *L*anguage. A compiler language for computers, useful in solving business problems such as file processing and record keeping.

Collateral. Property pledged as security on a debt.

Commercial banks. Financial institutions that accept demand deposits from the public and have the power to create money through a fractional reserve system.

Commercial letter of credit. A document issued by a bank on application of an importer of merchandise whereby the bank authorizes drafts to be drawn on the bank by the beneficiary and agrees to honor the drafts if all requirements are met.

Commercial paper. Short-term promissory notes sold by large business corporations to raise funds.

Common stock. Certificates which represent shares of ownership of a corporation.

Common stock account. A balance sheet account that contains a stated amount of the proceeds stemming from the sale of the corporation's common stock.

Communication. The transmission of understanding.

Comprehensive employment interview. An interview held to complete or correct the picture of the applicant that has been provided by the screening interview, application blank, testing program, and check of job references.

Computer terminal. A device with a keyboard that allows an individual to make use of a computer which may be located a great distance away.

Conceptual skill. The ability to diagnose the different facets of a problem in relation to its total environment and to activate creative solutions.

Conciliation. Action of a third party to bring together management and labor when a dispute exists between them.

Conglomerate merger. The joining together of enterprises that produce or distribute different product lines.

Consolidation. The joining of two or more independent business enterprises into a new enterprise under a single management.

Constant dollars. Dollar amounts which have been adjusted for changes in the purchasing power of the nation's currency to permit dollar comparisons from one time period with another in real terms.

Consumer durable goods. Products used by individuals and households that typically last over a period of years, including automobiles, television sets, refrigerators, and other appliances.

Consumer goods. Goods that satisfy individual needs directly rather than goods that are for use in the production process or for resale.

Consumerism. The movement by consumers to exert pressure on business and government to improve the quality of products sold and to protect the interests of ultimate consumers.

Continuous process assembly line. The movement of goods from one stage of the production process to another by use of automatic conveyors.

Contract. An agreement between two or more parties which can be enforced by law.

Control. A systematic measuring of the progress that the business enterprise is making toward its objectives, including the process of correcting deviations in performance.

Controller. The financial officer who is responsible for the accounting system and for developing the necessary financial controls to assure the security and the efficient use of funds.

Convenience goods. Products which are usually low priced and are purchased by consumers with a minimum of effort at the nearest available location.

Copyright. An exclusive right granted by law to the control of an artistic, literary, or musical work or a merchandising label for a period of 28 years with the option of one renewal for another 28 years.

Corporation. A legal entity, separate and distinct from its owners, who are called stockholders. A business corporation receives a charter from the state which outlines its powers to engage in business activity. It may have perpetual life, and the stockholders have limited liability.

Cost accounting. The branch of accounting that classifies, records, allocates, summarizes, and reports current and prospective costs.

Cost of goods sold. The value of merchandise sold, determined by adding together the cost of material, labor, overhead, and other expenses involved in the production of the goods, but not including selling costs or the general costs of management.

Council of Economic Advisors. Three professional economists appointed by the president to analyze and interpret economic developments and recommend national economic policy. The council was created by the Employment Act of 1946.

Council on Environmental Quality. The federal government agency which reports to the president and is responsible for studies and policy recommendations on the quality of the national environment.

Craft union. A union that organizes workers who perform a particular skilled type of work. Entrance into full status in the craft is usually preceeded by an extensive training and apprenticeship program.

Credit manager. The financial officer who has responsibility for the administration of trade credit, including determination of which customers will receive credit and the collection of accounts.

Credit rating. The estimate of an individual's or enterprise's ability and willingness to meet payments when they are due.

Credit unions. Cooperatives that promote saving on the part of their members and also make small loans to members at relatively low interest rates.

Creeping methods change. A reduction in the time required to do a job as the employee through experience improves on the original method developed for a job through motion and time analysis.

Currency. Token coin and paper money in circulation.

Current assets. Assets that are cash, realizable in cash, or sold or consumed during the current operating period, customarily thought of as one year.

Current liabilities. Obligations that will fall due within a short period of time, customarily within one year.

Current ratio. A test of an enterprise's short-term liquidity; it is the relationship of current assets to current liabilities. The current ratio is one of the most widely used balance sheet ratios.

Customs duty. A tax or tariff on goods imported from a foreign country.

Data processing and control unit. The part of the computer that directs the operation of other equipment, performs computations on data, and contains the program of instructions to accomplish the mission for a particular problem.

Data storage. The storage of information in a computer's memory unit.

Debt. Money owed to another by virtue of an agreement that gives rise to a legal obligation to pay.

Decentralization. The dispersion of decision making throughout an organization. Also, the location of facilities over a wider geographic area.

Deferred charges. Longer term expenses that have been paid for in advance and will be charged against revenues in future periods.

Deficit financing. The condition when expenditures exceed revenues; applied to government finances when spending exceeds tax collections.

Delegation of authority. The authorization of a subordinate to make certain decisions, thereby creating a new responsibility relationship from the subordinate to the superior.

Demand deposit. A deposit in a commercial bank that may be withdrawn on demand (without advance notice), commonly called a checking account.

Demographic changes. Changes in the size and composition of the population.

Departmentalization. The division of the business enterprise into units or subsystems to accomplish the objectives of the firm.

Depletion allowance. A charge made to account for the reduction of a natural resource such as oil or minerals over a period of time, which has the effect of reducing the amount of income taxes paid by enterprises in these industries.

Depreciation. The decline in value of an asset over a period of years.

Depression. A pronounced and prolonged recession in the business cycle.

Dilemma. A situation where there are two or more possible alternative courses of action, each of which may lead to some desirable and some undesirable consequences.

Direction. The process of aiding an enterprise's employees in carrying out their work activities.

Discretionary income. The income left after deducting the amount of income required for necessities.

Dividend. The amount of profits distributed to shareholders in proportion to their ownership of stock in a corporation.

Dividend payout percentage. The proportion of earnings an enterprise distributes to shareholders as cash dividends.

Double-entry record keeping. A method for transaction recording in which both changes in assets and claims against assets are shown.

Downgrading. Transfer of an employee to a job that requires less skill than the job previously performed.

Draft. An order directing the payment of money from one party to another.

Earnings. Profits generated by an enterprise. When applied to individual workers, usually stated in terms of dollars per hour or per week.

Earnings per share. The amount of a corporation's net income (profit) divided by the number of shares of common stock outstanding.

Economic indicator. A measurement of one part of the economy that can help in evaluating the entire economy and in forecasting its future course. Economic indicators are classified as leading, lagging, or coincident with the general level of economic activity.

Economic profit. The calculation of profit by subtracting opportunity costs from business profit; the difference is called economic profit.

Economic resources. All the scarce natural, man-made, and human factors that go into the production of goods and services.

Economics. The study of how scarce resources are allocated in a society of unlimited wants.

Effluent charges. Payments that would be made to the government by an industry based on the amount of pollutants is discharged. Such charges presumably would stimulate industry to install antipollution systems or would provide funds to combat pollution.

Elasticity of demand. The condition in which a small change in the price of a good results in substantial changes in demand for the good.

Electronic computer. A data processing device which is capable of the storage, processing, and retrieval of data through the use of electronic circuitry, memory elements, and programmed instructions.

Employee hiring. Hiring of nonmanagerial personnel into the enterprise.

Employee induction. A program of providing a new employee with useful and accurate information about the enterprise, the policies that will affect him, and the services that may be provided for his benefit.

Employee transfer. The movement of an employee from one job to another at about the same wages and on the same level in the organization.

Employment Act of 1946. Federal legislation that stated as a matter of national policy the responsibility of the federal government in assisting the private sector of the American economy to promote maximum employment, production, and purchasing power.

Entrepreneur. Originally a French word meaning enterpriser. The entrepreneur is a person who provides the managerial ability to bring together land, capital, and labor to produce goods and services; one who assumes the risk of doing business.

Environmental Protection Agency. The federal agency established to carry out the policies of the Council on Environmental Quality.

Equal Employment Opportunity Commission. This commission, established as a result of the Civil Rights Act of 1964, is charged with combatting employment discrimination based on such factors as race and sex.

Equity (net worth). A right or claim to assets by owners of the enterprise.

Equity funds. Ownership financing provided through the sale of stock in a corporation or by the retention of earnings.

Esteem. The recognition and regard resulting from how well a person performs the role associated with his status.

Ethics. A code of conduct and values that is accepted by society as being right and proper.

Exchange control. Government control over access to foreign currencies by private citizens and business enterprises.

Excise tax. A tax levied on goods or services inside a country at time of their manufacture, sale, or use.

Export-Import Bank. A federal administrative agency that aids in financing trade between the United States and other nations.

Exports. Goods sent out of a country to be sold in a foreign nation.

Expropriation. Action by a government of transferring ownership of private property to the state.

Facilitating enterprise. A business enterprise that performs auxiliary functions in such fields as finance, insurance, transportation, construction, and services.

Factoring. The purchase of a business enterprise's accounts receivable by a finance company, which then assumes the responsibility for collecting the accounts. Factoring is widely used in the textile industry.

Factors of production. The four ingredients necessary for the production of goods and services—natural resources, labor, capital, and management.

Factory layout. The arrangement of machines and production lines in a factory in order to move materials through the manufacturing process.

Fair Credit Reporting Act. Legislation designed to protect consumers in credit matters, including individual credit ratings and their use by merchants, insurance companies, or employers.

Fair employment practices (FEP). A type of legislation passed in the majority of the states which outlaws discrimination in hiring, promotion, and discharge of individuals.

Family income. The total money income received by family units over a specified period of time before deductions for personal taxes.

Featherbedding. A union practice that requires an employer to pay for services not performed. Declared an unfair labor practice by the Taft-Hartley Act.

Federal Deposit Insurance Corporation (FDIC). A governmental agency that insures depositors' accounts up to $20,000 each in commercial banks that are FDIC members.

Federal income taxes. Taxes which enterprises and individuals must pay to the federal government on annual profits or earnings.

Federal Reserve discount rate. The interest rate that member banks must pay to obtain funds from the Federal Reserve bank in their district.

Federal Reserve System. A system of 12 Federal Reserve banks, presided over by a seven-member Board of Governors in Washington, D.C., and charged with the responsibility of providing for a flow of money and credit that will foster orderly economic growth and stable prices.

Federal Savings and Loan Insurance Corporation (FSLIC). The governmental agency that insures each saver's account up to $20,000 in savings and loan associations that are members of FSLIC.

Federal Trade Commission (FTC). A quasi-judicial administrative agency of the federal government established to strengthen the observance and enforcement of the antitrust laws. The FTC also has responsibility for policing advertising and marketing practices for consumer protection.

Federal Trade Commission Act. A federal act, passed in 1914, that enumerated unfair methods of competition in commerce and declared them unlawful. The legislation also established the Federal Trade Commission to police the antitrust laws.

Feedback of information. The inspection by a machine in the production process of its own output and the activation of controls to correct deviations from previously established standards.

Finance companies. Financial institutions that make loans to business enterprises and individuals. Those that specialize in direct loans to individuals are called consumer finance or personal finance companies, and those that provide loans to business enterprises are called commercial finance companies.

Finance function. The activity involving the provision of funds from various sources for an enterprise's operations and the profitable utilization of those funds.

Financial institutions. Establishments that regulate the money supply and channel funds from savers to business enterprises, individuals, and governmental bodies who want to engage in economic activity.

Finished goods. Goods that have completed the manufacturing process and have been placed in storage to await distribution to consumers.

Fire and casualty insurance companies. Companies that sell insurance service to their clients to cover destruction of property by fire or other hazards. Some of these companies also provide other types of insurance protection, such as personal liability insurance.

First-line supervisor. The management person who is directly responsible for the work efforts of employees in producing goods or providing services.

Fiscal period. A span of time over which financial transactions are reported. For example, the federal government's fiscal year begins on July 1 and ends on June 30.

Fixed assets. Sometimes called capital assets, these are long-term tangible assets, such as buildings, land, and equipment, which will not normally be turned into cash but are necessary in the production of goods and services.

Fixed costs. Costs not directly affected by the number of units produced, such as rent, executive salaries, minimum utilities, property taxes, and interest on borrowed money.

Food and Drug Administration. The federal agency which has responsibility in such areas as the safety and effectiveness of drugs, cosmetics, and food products marketed in the United States.

Foreign exchange. The purchase or sale of the currency of one nation with the currency of another.

Foreign exchange rate. The price of the currency of one country in terms of the currency of another country.

Foreman. A supervisor who is the first level of management and who is in direct contact with workers engaged in the production process.

Form utility. Utility that stems from a good's possession of the physical characteristics necessary for its purpose.

Formal organization. A detailing of the status positions and lines of authority and responsibility from the board of directors and the president throughout the enterprise.

Formal training programs. Structured management training through such methods as lectures, special training courses, discussions, or provision for employees to attend an institution of higher learning for professional management training.

*FORTRAN. FOR*mula *TRAN*slator. An algebraic compiler language for a computer that is particularly useful for research problems requiring the solution of mathematical or statistical formulations.

Fractional reserve banking system. The system of financial reserves used by commercial banks, whereby each bank is required to keep only a portion of its deposits in reserve form and may lend out those funds in excess of the required deposit reserves.

Frame of reference. The perspective from which a person views his environment. An individual's frame of reference is influenced by his past experiences and his value system.

Franchise. The right to market a good or service in a particular area, sometimes on an exclusive basis.

Free-rein leadership. The work group is left to itself to define goals and provide solutions to problems so that the leadership emerges from within the group.

Fringe benefits. Items provided to employees that, in effect, increase real income but are not included in the basic wage. Fringe benefits include health insurance, disability benefits, sick leave, life insurance, pensions, and paid vacations.

Fully automated process. Manufacture of a good by a process that includes the automatic inspection of production which actuates controls to correct deviations from previously established standards.

Functional departmentalization. Organization of an enterprise by grouping together the activities of a similar nature, such as production, marketing, or finance.

General purpose machine. A machine that can perform a variety of different jobs requiring the same type of work, such as a drill press that can be used to drill different numbers of holes, in different sizes, different depths, and for different types of materials.

General Services Administration. The agency of the federal government which has responsibility for the maintenance and upkeep of federal buildings including the negotiation of purchasing contracts for supplies and services.

Geographical departmentalization. Organization of a business enterprise on a territorial basis.

Good. In economic terms, anything that is useful in satisfying a human want.

Grapevine. Informal communications that stem from informal work groups.

Grievance procedure. A specified succession of steps through which workers' complaints are to be processed from lower to higher echelons of management.

Grievances. Complaints expressed to management by employees relating to the work situation.

Gross income. Net sales less the cost of goods sold.

Gross National Product. The total retail market value of all the goods and services produced in a nation, usually stated in annual terms.

Gross profit. Another term for gross income which is net sales less the cost of goods sold.

Guaranteed loan. A loan which will be paid back by the government or some other institution or individual in the event that it is not repaid by the borrowing enterprise.

Guide. A recommendation for action, not necessarily mandatory.

Heuristic. An aid to problem solving that can reduce the effort in arriving at a solution.

Heuristic computer programming. The use of computer programs to solve problems by making selected calculations rather than computing all possible alternatives.

Horizontal merger. A joining together of two or more companies that manufacture or distribute the same product.

Housekeeping staff. Staff personnel who perform custodial and maintenance duties, record keeping, health services, and routine personnel functions.

Human relations. The interactions arising out of the association of two or more persons. Management's actions to provide a climate in the business enterprise that will both foster the employee's individual satisfactions and result in achievement of the broad economic objectives of the enterprise.

Human resource development programs. Any of the variety of programs sponsored by federal or state governments designed to improve the employability of jobless and underemployed Americans through education, job training, counseling, or other supportive services.

Human skill. The ability to work with people and to build effective work teams.

Human subsystem. That element of the work system which consists of the values, motivations, and interactions of persons in an enterprise.

Imports. Goods brought into a country that have been purchased in a foreign nation.

Income statement. A summary of the revenues and expenses of an enterprise's operations over a specified period, such as a year. The income statement is also called the profit and loss statement.

Income tax. An annual tax on the income of persons or corporations.

Industrial union. A union such as the United Auto Workers, which draws its members on an industry-wide basis, regardless of the kind of jobs performed.

Industrial user. Enterprises which buy products for use in producing other goods or services.

Industry. Those business enterprises that engage in the same type of economic activity.

Industry-wide bargaining. A situation in which a single series of collective bargaining negotiations result in an agreement or agreements covering substantially all the firms in an industry.

Inelasticity of demand. The condition in which changes in the price of a product bring about little or no change in the demand for it.

Inflation. An increase in the price of goods or services caused by an expansion of the supply of money or credit in the economy faster than the ability of the economy to produce more goods and services.

Informal organization. A self-grouping of employees in the work situation that depends on the personalities of individuals for its being rather than on formal organizational relationships.

Injunction. A court order that directs an individual or an organization to do or not to do some act. A violator of an injunction is subject to a contempt of court proceeding.

Input of data. The feeding of data into computers by such means as a card reader, paper-tape reader, magnetic-ink reader, optical-character reader, or console typewriter.

Installment plan. A credit system in which a purchased article is paid for by a series of payments to be made over a specified period of time.

Institutional advertising. An advertising message which seeks to develop goodwill for a business enterprise or an industry rather than directly selling a specific product.

Institutional discrimination. Differential treatment of persons stemming from the overall structure of society, such as stereotyped views of minority capabilities or segregated housing patterns.

Insurance premium. The amount paid periodically to an insurance company or its agent for coverage that will provide reimbursement in case of damage or loss.

Interest. The amount paid for the use of borrowed funds.

Interest income. In economic terms, the return to capital resources.

Intermediate-term credit. Debt instruments that have a maturity from over one year to approximately ten years.

Interstate Commerce Commission (ICC). A federal agency that regulates carriers engaged in interstate commerce.

Inventories. The stock of goods the enterprise has available for sale either in its present state or after further processing. As a balance sheet item, inventories include the total of finished goods, work in process, and raw materials.

Inventory turnover. A ratio that gives an indication of the number of times merchandise moves through the enterprise during the period under study. It is computed by dividing the cost of goods sold by the average inventory.

Investment banker. An institution or person who functions as a middleman between corporations and investors in the capital funds market by such activities as underwriting, or guaranteeing, the sale of securities from issuing corporations.

Investment company. A financial institution that sells shares in its operation and uses the proceeds to purchase securities of other corporations.

Investment portfolio. The list of stocks, bonds, and other investments owned by a financial institution or individual.

Invoice. An itemized statement of merchandise shipped by the vendor.

Job description. A description of the essential elements of a specific job including such factors as physical effort, skill, responsibility, mental effort, and working conditions.

Job evaluation. A measurement of the value of each job in the enterprise in relation to the other jobs in the enterprise.

Job references. Previous positions held by a job applicant, used to check on his past work record.

Job rotation. A planned approach to management training which involves the transfer of the trainee through a series of different types of positions.

Job specifications. A list of the requirements of a specific position in an enterprise.

Jurisdictional strike. A strike that grows out of controversies about which craft union has the right to perform particular jobs or which union should organize the workers in a particular industry.

Labor. All physical and mental talents that individuals expend in producing goods and services, with the exception of entrepreneurial talent, classified separately.

Labor contract. See Union contract.

Labor Management Relations Act of 1947 (Taft-Hartley Act). A series of amendments to the National Labor Relations Act of 1935 which added certain unfair labor practices for unions and which made certain procedural changes in the act.

Labor-Management Reporting and Disclosure Act of 1959 (Landrum-Griffin Act). Federal legislation that imposed certain limitations on unions in organizing workers and in the internal management of union affairs.

Labor relations. A situation in which management bargains over wages, hours, and working conditions with the employees as a group through union representatives.

Laissez-faire capitalism. Stemming from a French term that means "let us alone," laissez-faire capitalism in its most extreme form limited the government's participation in economic activity merely to providing essential services such as police and fire protection.

Land. In economics, all natural resources used in the production process, including timber, oil and mineral deposits, and water, as well as land itself.

Layoff. A reduction in the size of the work force frequently stemming from a drop in demand for the enterprise's products.

Lead time. The time required in development of the production process before goods can be produced.

Leadership. The element of direction that causes subordinates to follow and results in accomplishment of the goals of the enterprise.

Lease. A form of long-term renting contract through which an enterprise obtains the use of assets without owning them.

Liabilities. Claims against the enterprise's assets by outsiders.

Life insurance companies. Business enterprises which provide both insurance coverage on the lives of policyholders and a source of capital through investment of the insurance premiums they receive.

Limited liability. A legal concept whose application to a corporation is that if the enterprise fails, the stockholders' losses are limited to the amount of their investment in the enterprise.

Line function. Those activities that specifically and directly result in achievement of the goals of the business enterprise.

Linear programming. A systematic approach to the solution of problems, resulting in the best allocation of limited resources through the use of linear equations and relationships by analyzing a number of variables given certain constraints.

Liquidation value. The value of the enterprise's assets if they were dispersed to different purchasers who presumably would be able to put them to some economic use.

Liquidity. The degree of readiness of conversion of an asset into cash. Liquidity measures the ability of an enterprise to meet its current financial obligations when they become due.

Lockout. Management's refusal to permit workers to enter the enterprise's facilities because of a dispute.

Long-term debt. Loans that mature in more than 10 years.

Long-term liabilities. A balance sheet category made up of financial obligations that fall due more than one year in the future.

McGuire Act. A federal law, passed in 1952, that permitted states to include in their resale price maintenance laws the nonsigner clause, which provides that all retailers in a state are bound by resale price agreements as long as one retailer in the state signs such an agreement.

Macroeconomic analysis. The study of the functioning of the economy as a whole.

Maintenance force. Personnel whose work is to keep production facilities in efficient operating order.

Management. The achievement of results by directing the activities of other people. Also, the group of individuals in an enterprise responsible for the achievement of results.

Management succession. The process of providing for a continuing source of qualified management personnel either through training and promotion of present employees or by hiring executives from outside the enterprise.

Manufacturer's sales branch. An office operated by a manufacturer separate from his factories for use by sales and service personnel. It may or may not carry inventories from which orders are shipped directly.

Manufacturing enterprise. A business enterprise that fabricates consumer and producer goods out of raw materials and/or component parts.

Market. A group of consumers who are willing and able to buy the goods produced by a particular business enterprise.

Market penetration pricing. A policy of setting a relatively low initial price for a product to achieve mass market acceptance quickly.

Market system. The coming together of buyers and sellers with money as a medium of exchange for goods and services.

Marketing. The business activities that move goods and services from producers to consumers to satisfy needs. Marketing imparts place, time, and possession utility to goods.

Marketing concept of business. An approach to business that centers management thinking around the importance of the consumer by ascertaining a need and developing a product to satisfy this need.

Marketing enterprise. A business enterprise that distributes finished goods to consumers.

Marketing mix. The market program of a business enterprise consisting of the variables of product, promotion, price, and place.

Maslow's hierarchy of needs. A priority of human needs discussed by the psychologist, A. H. Maslow, including psychological, safety, love, esteem, and self-actualization needs.

Mass media advertising. The promotion of a product to many people simultaneously through newspapers, television, radio, magazines, and outdoor signs.

Maturity. The date on which a financial obligation comes due.

Mechanization. The application of power-driven tools in factory production, which results in a saving of both human energy and time.

Median. In a series of data, the midway point that divides the number of units in half.

Median family income. The midway point in the distribution of family income with half the families having incomes above this amount and half with incomes below.

Mediation. The process whereby a third party brings together the two sides involved in a dispute and actively participates in the discussions in order to bring about a compromise acceptable to both parties.

Merchant wholesaler. A middleman who purchases merchandise from manufacturers, and thereby takes title to the goods and assumes the risks associated with their sale.

Merger. A smaller enterprise is taken over by a larger business enterprise.

MESBIC. A *M*inority *E*nterprise *S*mall *B*usiness *I*nvestment *C*ompany which is formed to provide capital and management assistance to minority-owned business enterprises.

Microeconomic analysis. The study of the functioning of a specific unit of the economy, such as a given business enterprise.

Middlemen. Enterprises or individuals, such as wholesalers and retailers, who handle the goods as they move from the producer to the ultimate consumer.

Miller-Tydings Act. A federal law passed in 1937 as an amendment to the Sherman Act, it exempted resale price maintenance contracts from antitrust laws, provided they were permitted by state legislation.

Minority group. Part of the population distinguished from the dominant society by some characteristic such as race, nationality, language, or religion.

Miscellaneous payables. A catchall account for any outsiders' recognized financial claims against the enterprise not listed elsewhere in the balance sheet.

Money market. The coming together or lenders and borrowers of short-term funds, including both private and governmental financial groups.

Monopoly. Control over the supply of a good or service in a given market by a single producer.

Monopoly profit. The additional profit of a business enterprise resulting from higher prices because of the enterprise's sole control over the production or distribution of a product.

Mortgage. The pledging of property by a borrower to a lender as security for payment of the debt.

Motion analysis. A determination by industrial engineers of the most efficient method of accomplishing a particular job by reducing waste effort to a minimum.

Motion and time analysis. Work done by industrial engineers to provide a basis for production standards on factory jobs.

Mutual fund. An open-end investment company that does not have a fixed number of shares outstanding, but issues more shares whenever an investor wants to purchase shares in the fund, and stands willing to repurchase its shares from investors.

Mutual savings banks. The oldest class of savings institutions in the United States, a mutual savings bank has no shareholders, but all depositors have a mutual interest and receive dividends for their savings.

National Alliance of Businessmen. A voluntary organization of business-men formed in 1967 to expand employment opportunities, especially for persons who were considered unemployable because of a lack of job skills.

National Environmental Policy Act of 1969. Legislation which commits the federal government to a continuing policy of improving the environment for present and future generations. The act established the Council on Environmental Quality.

National income. The aggregate earnings of labor and property that arise in the current production of goods and services by the nation's economy. National income is the sum of compensation of employees, proprietors' income, rental income, net interest, and corporate profits.

National Industrial Recovery Act (NIRA). A federal law passed in 1933 as an attempt to stop some of the extreme business competition in the depression years by such means as stabilization of production, pricing, and marketing practices. The NIRA was declared unconstitutional by the Supreme Court in 1935.

National Labor Relations Act. Federal legislation, passed originally in 1935, that guarantees the right of the worker to form and join labor organizations and to select representatives of his own choosing; provides procedures to determine the appropriate bargaining unit and the union the employees want to represent them; defines certain unfair labor practices for both unions and employers.

National Labor Relations Board (NLRB). The five-member body that administers and enforces the National Labor Relations Act.

National Recovery Administration (NRA). The federal agency set up to carry out the provisions of the National Industrial Recovery Act.

National Traffic and Motor Vehicle Safety Act of 1966. Legislation which provides for the setting of standards for auto and highway safety and which requires auto manufacturers to notify first purchasers of cars of safety defects discovered subsequent to their sale.

Near-cash. Any asset immediately transferable into money form without risk of loss of value in the process, such as 91-day U.S. Treasury bills.

Need. A lack of something that is useful, required, or desirable to carry out a way of life.

Negotiable bill of lading. A document that when endorsed constitutes a receipt for the goods, a contract for transportation, and evidence of title to the property, and makes the holder the lawful owner.

Neighborhood Youth Corps (NYC). A program sponsored by the Department of Labor designed to aid young people in entering the job market through remedial education, skills training, summer jobs, and other assistance.

Net profit. The amount that remains after all relevant costs, including income taxes, have been deducted from revenue; the final figure shown on the income or profit and loss statement.

Net sales. Gross sales less all cash discounts given for prompt payment for goods and credits for returned merchandise.

Net worth. The amount of claims by the owners against the enterprise's assets; also called owners' equity.

New York Stock Exchange. The largest organized trading market for corporate stocks and bonds; located in New York City.

Nonprice competition. Factors other than the cost of a product that influence consumer demand, such as sales promotion efforts, quality and service competition, and fashion.

No-strike clause. A clause in the union contract that prohibits concerted work stoppages and interference by employees with production during the life of the contract.

Notes payable. A balance sheet item showing debts for which written acknowledgments have been made.

Objectives. Statements that embody the goals toward which the group activity of the business enterprise is directed.

Odd lot. Generally defined as the purchase or sale of stock in units of less than 100 shares.

Office of Federal Contract Compliance. The Department of Labor agency which coordinates the administration of executive orders to prevent discriminatory employment practices by government contractors.

Office of Minority Business Enterprise (OMBE). The Department of Commerce agency designed to assist minority persons in establishing and operating business enterprises.

Oligopoly. Control over the supply of a good or service in a given market by a few producers.

On-the-job training. The worker is placed in the shop at a machine or workplace where he will be trained by a supervisor, a special instructor, or an experienced employee.

Open account. Extension of credit to a customer without requiring specific collateral or a written acknowledgment of the financial obligation by the purchaser.

Open market operations. The purchase or sale of federal government securities by the Federal Reserve System to affect the level of commercial bank reserves.

Operating income. Income generated from the normal operations of the enterprise before interest payments or income taxes are deducted.

Operations budget. A budget that covers operating revenue and expenses it consists of a forecast of expected sales, along with an estimate of the costs necessary to achieve the sales goal. Operations budgets can be further subdivided into budgets for such areas as sales, sales promotion and advertising, production, purchases, maintenance, and overhead.

Opportunity cost. An economic concept that represents the cost assumed when a person or business enterprise forgoes the alternative of making some other use of economic resources.

Organizational subsystem. That element of the work system which consists of the way in which the technical and human subsystems are organized, directed, coordinated, and controlled by management to achieve the enterprise's objectives.

Other assets. A catchall category on the balance sheet that includes all assets not listed either as current or fixed, such as patents, trademarks or deferred charges.

Other income. Revenue that stems from other than the mainstream of an enterprise's activities.

Output of information. Any of the numerous means of showing the results of a computer's data processing, such as by printer systems or visual displays.

Overt discrimination. Differential treatment of persons on an open basis such as refusing to hire a person for a job because of race or nationality.

Over-the-counter market. The purchase and sale of securities through informal dealings, usually by telephone rather than on an organized exchange.

Participative leadership. Authority is decentralized among subordinates, suggestions are encouraged, and an emphasis is placed on communication between the leader and all members of the group.

Partnership. A form of legal organization of business enterprise made up of two or more individuals who share in the ownership of a business according to a contractual agreement. At least one partner must have unlimited liability.

Patent. Exclusive rights to a product or process for 17 years, conferred by government authority to the holder.

Peak. The high point in economic activity during a particular business cycle.

Pension funds. Funds accumulated out of the contributions of employers and employees, and invested in securities in order to provide retirement income for the individual beneficiaries and their families in their old age.

Performance rating. A formal rating of an employee, used to make merit increases in wage rates within job classifications and to guide management in making promotions.

Personal assistants. Staff persons who provide busy executives with information or recommendations, or who handle details that the manager may not have time for but does not want to delegate to a lower level in the organization.

Personal income. The total money income received by individuals before personal taxes are deducted.

Personal selling. A method of promotion that involves an individual presentation of a product to a customer.

Personnel management. The function in the enterprise of recruitment, selection, induction, and training of employees to build a well-motivated and effective work force.

Philanthropy. Services and gifts to help mankind.

Physical distribution. The process of moving and handling goods as they flow through the channels of distribution.

Pilot plant. A prototype of the production process, which usually consists of a scale model of the complete factory or the production line.

PL/1. Programming *L*anguage, Version *1*, is a computer language suitable for problems involving both business data processing and numerical scientific computations.

Place. The dimension of the marketing mix concerned with providing products with time and place utility to satisfy customers. Place decisions include determination of the channels of distribution and the transportation and storage of goods.

Place utility. Utility that stems from goods being where the consumer has access to them.

Planning. The process of rational decision making done sufficiently far in advance to promote the more effective operation of the business enterprise.

Poison Prevention Packaging Act. Legislation requiring manufacturers to distribute dangerous substances in containers with safety caps which are difficult for children to remove.

Policy. A statement of principles or purposes that provides a framework for decision making consistent with the objectives of the enterprise.

Pollution. An undesirable change in the environment which can harm the quality of life.

Portfolio. A list of securities owned.

Possession utility. Utility that stems from a person's being able to own or control a good.

Poverty level. The level of income designated by the federal government below which families or individuals are considered to be poor.

Pragmatist. One who takes a practical approach, testing the validity of a concept by its results.

Preferred stock. The class of ownership shares in a corporation that has preference over common stock on a stated amount of cash dividends each year and also priority on assets in event that the corporation is liquidated.

Prepaid expenses. A balance sheet item that represents a portion of an outlay for a benefit that will extend over more than one accounting period, such as for insurance or royalties.

Prestige. The recognition and regard that result from a person's status.

Price/earnings ratio. A frequently used measure for analyzing common stock prices which is calculated by dividing the stock's current market price by the past 12 months earnings per share.

Primary boycott. Employees' refusal to use the products of an employer with whom they have a dispute.

Primary securities market. The market that channels funds directly to corporations or governmental bodies in exchange for their securities.

Printer system. The means by which a computer communicates information to users through a card punch system, console typewriter, or visual display device, such as a graph plotter or cathode-ray tube.

Private enterprise system. The form that capitalism has taken in America, characterized by private property, the profit motive, the free market system and competition, and a particular relationship between business and government.

Private placement. The sale of an entire issue of securities to a single or limited number of investors.

Private property. Property owned by an individual and therefore the right to exercise substantial control over it.

Procedure. A specific method or a series of steps carried out in a particular sequence to implement a given policy.

Process design. The development of the means by which a good will be produced.

Process layout. The location of different types of machines or functions together, without regard to where the particular process comes in the production of any one product—i.e., all grinding would be done in one location, all drilling in another, and so on.

Processing enterprise. A business enterprise that transforms the natural resources from the mines, forests, farms, or oceans into the raw materials used to manufacture goods.

Producer goods. Tools, machines, and equipment used to make consumer goods or other producer goods; thus, they indirectly satisfy individual needs.

Product.   A good or service which satisfies customer needs.

Product advertising.   An advertising message which provides information and attempts to sell a specific good or service.

Product design.   The development of a product that will perform properly and have consumer appeal.

Product layout.   The arrangement in a factory of machinery and assembly lines by chronological steps so that as the product moves through the plant there is a gradual buildup from raw materials or component parts to the finished product.

Product life cycle.   The pattern of a product's sales and profit margins which first show an upward slope as the profit margin reaches a peak and begins to decline while the sales continue to rise for a period of time before peaking and declining.

Product line departmentalization.   Organization of a business enterprise according to the various types of products it manufactures and sells.

Production.   The provision of goods with form utility by turning raw materials and semifinished products into finished goods for either consumer or industrial use.

Production control.   The coordination and control of the production process to meet delivery schedules.

Production scheduling.   A detailing of the sequence and timing of orders from the time orders are received from the sales department until finished goods are shipped.

Production transfer.   Changing the employee's work assignments from one department to another because of a change in a department's job requirements.

Profit.   The residual left after all appropriate costs have been deducted from business revenues; the return to enterprises or individuals for risk bearing, innovation, or some degree of market control.

Profit before income taxes.   Operating income plus other income and minus other expenses, including interest, before income taxes are deducted.

Profit and loss statement.   See income statement.

Profit center.   A responsibility center in which revenues are generated which enables management to measure profitability as well as costs.

Profit motive.   The desire to engage in economic activity in order to earn profit; a central controlling mechanism in a capitalistic economy.

Program.   A mixture of policies and procedures that have been developed to achieve the outlined objectives of management.

Program flowchart.   Instructions given in the proper sequence for the computer to process the input data. The flowchart is translated into a set of detailed coded instructions for the computer.

Programming.   Providing a computer with a set of instructions necessary for solving a problem or carrying out a series of operations on data.

Promotion.   In personnel management, the advancement of an employee to a better job with more responsibility, increased skill, or higher status and an increased salary. When applied to marketing, the communication of information regarding a product to potential customers to persuade them to buy.

Property tax. A tax levied on the assessed value of tangible property such as land; business buildings, equipment, and inventories; and individuals' houses, automobiles, and home furnishings. Sometimes a tax is assessed on intangible property such as stocks and bonds.

Proprietorship. A legal form of business organization owned by a single individual. It is the oldest and most common form of business enterprise; it is generally small in size, and its owner also has unlimited liability.

Prototype. A model or pattern that will be used as the basis for subsequent production, such as a clay model of an automobile made up during the design process to give a three-dimensional view of its styling and appearance.

Proxy. The written authority given to some person or organization to act for the signer in some matter such as in voting at a corporation's meeting of stockholders.

Psychological needs. Needs that pertain to the individual's own self-image, including the need for love, self-respect, and a feeling of accomplishment.

Public relations. Those functions of an enterprise that are concerned with creating a favorable image of the business enterprise and with communicating its purposes and programs to the different groups who constitute the public.

Purchase contract. A purchase order that has been accepted by a vendor.

Purchase order. A document that authorizes a vendor to deliver described goods at a specified price.

Purchase requisition. A formal request for the purchase of a particular item.

Purchasing. The procurement of materials and supplies for use or for further processing, not for immediate resale.

Pure research. Research carried on to extend man's frontiers of knowledge without regard to the immediate utility of its findings.

Quality. Possession of the necessary characteristics that fit a product to a given use.

Quality control. A system of inspection to determine which goods should be accepted or rejected, and a means for preventing the continued production of unsatisfactory goods.

Ratio of profits to owners' equity. The profitability of a business enterprise or an industry measured by profits as a percentage of owners' equity.

Ratio of profits to sales. The profitability of a business enterprise or an industry measured by profits as a percentage of sales.

Raw materials. The unprocessed commodities that go into the manufacture of a given product, and any component parts purchased from another manufacturer to be assembled into the finished product.

Real income. The actual purchasing power of a person's or family's income after adjustment for price changes of goods and services.

Real-time system. A computer system in which the computer controls a particular environment by receiving and processing data with resulting action to affect the functioning of the environment at that time.

Recession (or contraction). A decline in economic activity in the business cycle.

Recognition clause. A union contract provision that defines the bargaining unit and recognizes a particular union as the bargaining agency for the employees.

Recovery (or expansion). The upturn in the business cycle characterized by greater demand for goods and services, higher production, and improved profits.

Recruitment. The process of seeking and hiring new employees for a business enterprise.

Remedial transfer. A transfer made because of some problem that has arisen with a particular employee on a job.

Rent. In an economic sense, rent is the return that accrues to land.

Repatriation of funds. Returning of monies from business operations in another country to the home country of the business enterprise.

Reproduction value. The amount it would cost to replace the assets of an enterprise with others of like characteristics.

Reserve requirements. The amount of reserve funds held by commerical banks to back up deposits, usually stated as a percentage of deposits.

Resource Recovery Act of 1970. Federal legislation which provided for research programs to encourage the development of innovative solid waste disposal systems.

Responsibility. Accountability to others by those who have authority.

Responsibility centers. A designated unit of a subsystem in which the manager can be held responsible for the control of costs.

Retailer. A merchant who sells goods or services directly to individual consumers.

Retained earnings. The amount of profits earned by an enterprise over the years and kept in the business to strengthen and expand operations; less frequently called earned surplus.

Right-to-work laws. State laws that make illegal union security provisions in labor contracts under which workers are required to join the union after a specified period of time.

Robinson-Patman Act. A federal law passed in 1936 as a revision of Section 2 of the Clayton Act, it sought to give increased protection to smaller retailers against unfair competition from large competitors.

Role. The expected behavior pattern associated with a status.

Round lot. Generally defined as a stock transaction unit of 100 shares.

Routing. The detailed instructions on how a particular order will move from department to department, which machines will be used at each point along the line, and when inspections will be made.

Rule. An established regulation that must be obeyed.

Rumor. Incomplete, unconfirmed information, which may be incorrect or malicious in its intent.

Sale-and-leaseback agreement. An arrangement in which an enterprise constructs a building to its specifications, then sells it to a financing agent, such as an insurance company, and simultaneously leases the building back from the financial institution for a long period of time.

Sales budget. A subdivision of an operating budget that translates the goals of the enterprise into quantitative terms not only for anticipated sales revenues but also for the expenditures necessary to generate those revenues.

Sales finance companies. Financial institutions that specialize in installment loans by purchasing installment receivables from retailers who sell durable goods, such as autos and appliances. Sales finance companies also loan money to retailers and wholesalers to finance their inventories.

Sales promotion. An attempt to bridge the gap between personal selling and mass media advertising through use of displays and other sales aids, material for training salesmen, and contests and premium programs for customers.

Sales tax. A tax levied on goods or services at the time they are sold to consumers.

Savings and loan association. A type of cooperative financial institution whose purpose is to promote thrift and home ownership where the savers who place their funds in it become shareholders and receive dividends on their savings.

Savings deposit. An account which draws interest in a commercial bank or other savings institution.

Scarce economic resources. All the natural, manmade, and human factors that go into the production of goods and services.

Screening interview. An interview usually conducted by a member of the personnel department to make a preliminary decision about an applicant's suitability for employment.

Seasonal changes. Fluctuations in economic activity due to the changing seasons of the year, holidays, or the calendar.

Secondary boycott. Action by workers against a company with whom they have a dispute by bringing pressure against a third party who is not directly involved in the dispute. The secondary boycott was declared illegal by the Labor Management Relations Act of 1947.

Secondary securities markets. Security markets where debt or equity instruments already outstanding are bought and sold among investors.

Securities and Exchange Commission (SEC). A federal government agency that regulates interstate corporation stock transactions. The SEC requires corporations to provide investors with adequate information about new stock and bond issues, and to reveal dealings in their own stock by enterprise executives, and in general protects the interests of the public.

Security. A general term that encompasses transferable certificates of ownership or debt. The term is sometimes used in connection with collateral for a loan.

Seniority. Priority or status attained by an employee based on his length of service in the enterprise.

Share. One of the equal parts into which a corporation's ownership interest is divided.

Sherman Antitrust Act. A federal law, passed in 1890, that made restraint of trade and monopolization federal offenses. The law is administered by the Justice Department.

Shift transfer. Transfer of an employee from one time shift to another.

Shop stewards. Workers elected or appointed by a union to represent employees in a department or area of a factory, particularly with regard to grievances.

Shopping goods. Products which are compared with competing products for price, quality, style, or service by the customer before the good is purchased.

Sight draft. A document that calls for the drawee to pay the draft on its presentation (on sight).

Single project type departmentalization. Organization of an enterprise to carry out by department one-time projects that will extend over a period of months or years, such as highway construction.

Skimming-the-cream pricing. A policy of setting a relatively high price for a product, usually in the introduction stage of the product's life cycle or when nonprice competition is important.

Small Business Administration (SBA). A federal agency concerned with the problems of small business management.

Social needs. All the needs that grow out of man's relation to other individuals and groups, including the need for recognition, acceptance, and group activity.

Socialism. An economic system in which the concept of private profit is lacking and the means of production and distribution of goods are owned by the state rather than by individuals.

Solid waste pollution. Pollution caused by the disposal of agricultural, mineral, industrial, and residential products or wastes.

Solvency. The enterprise's ability to pay the principal on long-term financial obligations when they fall due, as well as to meet the interest payments on outstanding indebtedness.

Span of control. The number of subordinates a manager can effectively supervise.

Special purpose machine. A machine specifically designed to produce a particular product or to do a given job.

Specialty goods. Products for which a customer has a strong brand preference or a desire for particular features which justify a special buying effort.

Speculative purchasing. A purchasing practice that seeks to profit from price changes in inventories rather than to generate profits through the usual processing and distribution of goods.

Spread. The gross margin or profit between what an investment banker or specialist pays for the securities he buys and what he hopes to sell them for.

Staff function. All activities that assist the line management in fulfilling the enterprise's objectives.

Staff personnel. Personnel necessary to support the line activities. These include technical advisers, personal assistants, housekeeping staff, and other specialists. They can advise but normally do not issue orders to line organizational units.

Staffing. The provision of qualified managerial personnel for the enterprise.

Standard. A predetermined performance level. These include monetary standards, physical standards, and intangible standards.

Standard Metropolitan Statistical Areas. Areas of the United States designated by the Bureau of the Census as urban areas having at least one city with a population of 50,000 or more.

Status. A particular position in the formal organization of the enterprise.

Status symbols. Visible evidence of a person's rank in the business enterprise or some other organization.

Stock dividend. Additional shares of the distributing corporation's own stock issued to shareholders.

Storage function. The holding of goods from the time they are produced until their final use, including warehousing, handling, and order processing.

Stream of profits. An approach to determining the value of an enterprise based on the yield of its estimated future earnings.

Strike. Concerted action taken by workers to cease work, which is usually followed by union members' picketing to prevent other personnel from entering the struck plant.

Subsidiary. A business enterprise which is owned or controlled by another company.

Subsidy. Government assistance to a private enterprise.

Subsystem. The elements within a system.

Supplementary unemployment benefit plan. A plan whereby employers make payments to a fund used to pay employees who have been laid off. This money supplements unemployment benefits paid under government programs.

Surtax. An extra tax in addition to the tax already levied. Sometimes used to increase the tax rate that must be paid if income exceeds a specified level.

Syndicate. A group of investment bankers organized for the purpose of marketing a particular security issue.

System. A set of elements which have a relationship to each other.

Tariffs. Taxes on commodities imported or exported. In the United States, tariffs are levied only on imports.

Technical advisors. Staff personnel, such as legal counselors, public relations men, and engineers, who provide information of a highly specialized nature.

Technical skill. A manager's ability in and knowledge of a particular process or technique.

Technical subsystem. That element of the work system which consists of the equipment, layout, and technology required to produce and distribute a particular product.

Technology. The accumulated fund of knowledge helpful in efficient organization for the production of goods and services.

Tennessee Valley Authority (TVA). The federal government agency which produces and distributes electricity, provides flood control, recreation areas, and other services in connection with the Tennessee River system.

Term loan. Customary name for intermediate credit; a loan running for more than one year and less than ten years.

Thermal pollution. The presence of excessive heat in a body of water as the result of some industrial process, such as the generation of electric power.

Time deposit. A type of bank deposit that bears interest. Formal notice must be given before withdrawal of funds.

Time draft. A draft that calls for payment on a specified date in the future.

Time-sharing system. A computer system that provides a number of users with access to a single computer at the same time from different locations for the simultaneous solutions of different problems.

Time study analysis. A determination by an industrial engineer of how much time is necessary to carry out a job under actual factory conditions.

Time utility. Utility that stems from the goods being available when they are wanted.

Tooling. The process of providing cutting and grinding attachments for machine tools, gauges, loading devices, and other fixtures in order to adapt machinery and assembly lines to the production of a particular product.

Trade acceptance. A bill of exchange that has had an acknowledgment of the obligation written across its face by the importer which obligates him to pay the amount specified at the designated time.

Trade credit. The credit extended to business enterprises by suppliers for merchandise or equipment purchases usually for stated periods of from 30 to 60 days.

Trade creditor. An individual or enterprise that extends credit to a business customer, and therefore is willing to ship merchandise without requiring cash payment on delivery.

Trade journal. A periodical that specializes in a specific field, such as a particular industry or business function.

Trademarks. Words or symbols that identify a particular brand of merchandise. Trademarks may be registered for 28 years and the registration renewed for another 28 years, which prevents their use by unauthorized persons or enterprises.

Trading on the equity. An increase in the return on the owners' investment by using borrowed funds profitably in the business enterprise.

Transfer payment. Income received by a person for which no service is currently rendered, such as social security payments or veterans' benefits.

Treasurer. The financial officer who has such duties as being responsible for the company's valuable papers, management of cash receipts and disbursements, and the development of banking relationships.

Trend. The underlying long-run tendency that persists despite short-term cyclical or seasonal fluctuations in economic activity.

Trough. The low in cyclical economic activity during a recession before recovery takes place.

Trust. A business combination created when the owners of the shares of stock in corporatons transfer control of their shares to a group of trustees in exchange for trust certificates that entitle them to a share in the profits of the combined corporations.

Trust company. A financial institution that takes legal possession of personal assets and manages them for the benefit of the person who created the trust or for some other designated person. A personal trust department of a commercial bank also performs this service.

Truth-in-Lending Act of 1968. Legislation requiring creditors to furnish individual borrowers with a statement of the amount of financing charges and the annual percentage rate of interest charged on the loan.

Type of customer served departmentalization. Organization of an enterprise so that each particular department will be geared to meet the requirements of a particular class of consumer.

Ultimate consumer. Individuals or households who use goods or services for the satisfaction of personal needs.

Ultra vires *acts.* Actions beyond the powers granted to a board of directors.

Underwriting. As applied to investment banking, the process of assuming the responsibility for the sale of a corporation's stock or bonds and guaranteeing the corporation a specified amount of money for these securities.

Undistributed profits. The amount of earnings retained by a business corporation rather than being paid out to owners as dividends. Also called retained earnings.

Unemployment insurance tax. Taxes paid by business enterprises to finance payments to workers who are out of work.

Union contract. The agreement negotiated by management and union representatives which spells out the terms agreed on with regard to wages, hours, and working conditions.

Union shop. A labor agreement provision that requires a worker to join the union after a specified period of employment, often within 30 days.

Utility. In economics, the power to satisfy human wants.

Value. A belief held by persons in a society as to the rightness or wrongness of an action, custom, or institution. In economic terms, the monetary worth of a good or service.

Variable costs. Costs directly influenced by the number of units produced, such as materials used in production and the wages of production workers.

Vendor. One who sells goods or services.

Vertical analysis of the income statement. A percentage breakdown of the income statement to show what proportion of sales the various expenses are and the profit margin.

Vertical merger. The joining together of enterprises involved in the successive stages of production and distribution of a product.

Vested interest in pension plans. A pension plan whereby after a specified period the employee is entitled as a matter of right to the amount contributed by the employer for the employee's pension, whether or not he is still employed by the enterprise at retirement age.

Vestibule training. Off-the-job training where workers are trained in an area of the plant physically separated from their ultimate work place, but with machinery and under conditions similar to the shop where they will work.

Vocational school training. An employee receives special training by taking courses outside the enterprise of practical application—i.e., a course in welding or blueprint reading.

Wages. The amount paid to labor.

Wages payable. An account that consists of compensation owed to employees for their services performed.

Wagner Act. The name sometimes used to refer to the original National Labor Relations Act passed in 1935.

Want. A recognized need.

Water pollution. The presence of one or more contaminants in bodies of water in quantities great enough to be injurious to life or property.

Water Quality Act of 1965. This act and other federal legislation provided for the establishment of water-quality standards and plans for their implementation.

Water Quality Improvement Act of 1970. Federal legislation which provided that cleanup costs of oil spills or other water pollution would be the liability of the persons or enterprises causing the pollution.

Wholesalers. Middlemen who perform the economic functions of storage, financing, and distributing a manufacturer's output to retailers.

Wholesome Meat Act of 1967. Legislation which updated and strengthened inspection standards for red meat animals at slaughterhouses and packing plants.

Wholesome Poultry Products Act of 1968. Legislation which extended federal inspection standards to poultry sold within a state as well as that which crossed state lines.

Work in process. Materials that have been placed into the production process and increase in value as they move through production.

Work system. A model of the business enterprise which includes technical, organizational, and human subsystems. Inputs to the work system are material and human resources. The outputs are goods and services and other satisfactions of human needs.

Working capital. The amount of current assets after the deduction of current liabilities.

Workmen's compensation tax. Insurance payments required of business to finance payments to workers who may suffer loss of income because of job-related accidents or injury.

Yellow-dog contract. An agreement signed by a worker stating that as a condition of employment he will not join a union. Such an agreement is unenforceable under federal and state anti-injunction acts, and is an unfair labor practice under the National Labor Relations Act.

index

Index

This book has been set in 10 point Times Roman, leaded 3 points, and 9 point Times Roman, leaded 2 points. Section titles are in 30 point Baskerville italic; chapter numbers are in 36 point Baskerville and chapter titles are in 24 point Baskerville. The size of the type page is 26 × 46½ picas.

American business activity, 1860–1913

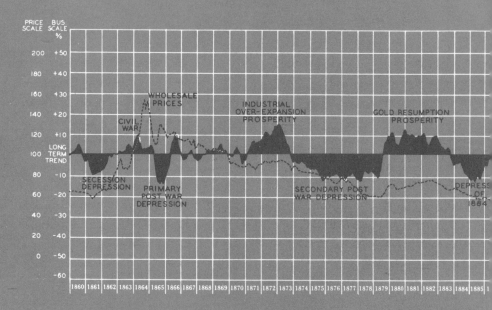